Theo

The Autobiography of

Theodore Bikel

To Phyllis & Mel

Theo

The Autobiography of
Theodore Bikel

The University of Wisconsin Press

The University of Wisconsin Press
1930 Monroe Street
Madison, Wisconsin 53711

www.wisc.edu/wisconsinpress/

3 Henrietta Street
London WC2E 8LU, England

5   4   3   2   1

Printed in the United States of America

Library of Congress Cataloging-in-Publication Data

Bikel, Theodore.
    Theo : the autobiography of Theodore Bikel
        pp.   cm.
    Originally published: New York : HarperCollins, 1994.
    Includes index.
    ISBN 0-299-18284-3 (alk. paper)
    1. Bikel, Theodore.   2. Actors—United States—Biography.   3. Singers—United States—Biogra-
phy.   4. Jewish actors—United States—Biography.   5. Singers, Jewish—United States—Biography.
I. Title.
PN2287.B4545 A3   2002
792'.028'092—dc21   2002020311

Grateful acknowledgment is made to:
Georges Moustaki for use of his lyrics "Je Chante Si Je Chante"

The Estate of Bertolt Brecht for use of an excerpt from "Gleichnis des Buddh vom Brennenden Haus,"
copyright © 1961 Suhrkamp Verlag

Contents

Preface   vii

1   Flashback   1
2   Hebrew Theatre   22
3   . . . Trippingly on the Tongue   37
4   The Kindness of Strangers   56
5   The Guitars of the Exile   73
6   East End, West End, and the Palace   93
7   How Much Does He Want?   113
8   America—Love at First Sight   134
9   Folk Lure   152
10   Peregrinations   184
11   The Hills Are Alive   204
12   Union Dues   219
13   Come, Let Us Reason Together   249
14   I Sing and I'll Keep Singing   267
15   Versatility   289
16   Tevye   321
17   From Jerusalem to Jerusalem   355
18   Entebbe, Vanessa, and Other Thoughts   366
19   Zorba   382
20   Toward the Millennium   406

Epilogue   429
Postscript 2002   431
Index   443

Photographs follow page 184.

Preface

WRITING ABOUT ONE'S OWN LIFE is surely one of the more dangerous undertakings. Remembrance has an infernal habit of slipping into misremembrance; actuality and dreams become entangled; and fiction often enough repeated turns into an assertion of fact. Theatre people are especially vulnerable to such temptations; most careers as told and retold to press and public are given a cosmetic layer—God forbid any warts should show. Sometimes even genuine attempts at honesty are thwarted by a lifelong habit of blowing one's own trumpet. A theatrical producer, so the story goes, had a terrible flop on his hands. He went to the theatre one evening, counted the house, and stood outside under the marquee, shaking his head dejectedly. Seven paying customers: a disaster! A friend walked by and inquired, "How's your show doing?" The producer, attempting an honest admission of failure, said, "Not good, not good. Small audience—eleven people." If my unconscious should play tricks of this kind that I am unable to detect or prevent, I hereby apologize in advance.

Plato quotes Socrates as saying: "The unexamined life is not worth living." I have, from time to time, been accused by my family of living an unexamined life. In truth, I have always felt, rightly or wrongly, that my life was worth living, whether examined or not. I have admittedly not been eager to subject myself to a self-examination, possibly for fear that the shortcomings I would find might overwhelm any sense of worth I have about myself. Now I suppose I must take that look and chance a possible endangerment to my inner equilibrium.

Most people lead two distinct lives—a private life and a public one. Others lead multiple lives; I am one of those. Professionally I can count three or four separate existences, politically three or four more. Add the personal aspects and altogether they add up to a cat's count of nine. Among them I play no favorites, and for the most part I've managed not to be overwhelmed by their number or by their demands for different kinds of attention and different aptitudes. I have dealt with them by compartmentalizing. Each of the lives, as I live it, I treat as though it were the only life I have. Yet in some way each in turn has served to inform other facets of me. In this book I have tried to open each one to see if they hang together. In the process I often abandon strict chronology, letting the themes be my guide rather than the calendar. Bear with me.

1

Flashback

*I*T IS A FINE DAY IN THE SPRING OF '92. I am arriving at the Pico gate of the 20th Century Fox studio, as I have done many times over the years. Normally the feeling of reporting for work on a new show is one of pleasant anticipation; today, not quite so. Of course, simply driving through the gate at 20th Century Fox is apt to trigger mind games, most often pleasant, occasionally strange, but rarely disturbing. Memories of a time when there was no Century City, when the lot was accessible from Santa Monica Boulevard through gates to the north, west, and south, and all the guards knew you by sight and by name. The memories usually take me back to interesting work with interesting people in feature films and, much later, TV shows.

But today my mind is on none of these. The show is *L.A. Law,* a prestigious job with people I have long admired; by rights the prospect of playing a guest-starring role on this program should bring me nothing but pleasure. It's the role itself that causes strange and disquieting thoughts, thoughts that can't be chased away with "It's just a job." I never take that attitude anyway. There is no such thing as "just a job," not if you have any sense of responsibility toward your craft. No, the reason for my discomfort is that this role cuts awfully close to home.

The set presents the usual picture of activity: a mixture of high organization and frantic confusion. Carpenters are hammering away, occasionally stilled by an assistant's call of "Hold it down," there's a to-and-fro of cables being pulled, a call for hairdressers and makeup people, and a cluster of actors, extras, and temporarily unbusy crew around the coffee urn and the tables of munchies. (The quality and quantity of the munchies is in direct ratio to the success and popularity of the show.) There are huddled conferences between the director, the producers, and various departments; there are wardrobe people making sure that the actors' clothes match the right scene numbers; prop people are dressing the set after opening up the usual canvas chairs for the cast; actors are complaining about script changes given to them only this morning—"How am I going to unlearn what I studied last night?" And in the middle of all this here am I, trying to concentrate on the acting task before me, and today on much more besides.

Kurt Rubin, the character I am playing, now a very wealthy man in Los Angeles, is a survivor of the Holocaust. His parents were taken to the camps while he was away in the woods climbing trees like any normal eleven-year-old. He came back to an empty house, waited for days in vain for their return, and then became one of the many child fugitives across Europe, hiding in barns and cellars, eventually being smuggled to Switzerland and freedom. Rubin never saw his parents again, and learned of their fate much later, from a fellow prisoner who watched the Nazis butcher them. He is called upon to retell all this on the witness stand, testifying as a plaintiff against a woman researcher who has received a grant from a foundation he administers, and who proposes to use "medical" data gathered by Nazi doctors at Auschwitz.

In an interesting twist of the story, Mackenzie Brackman, the resident firm on *L.A. Law*, does not represent the Holocaust survivor but rather the researcher who is being sued for the return of the grant. Specifically, it is the young black attorney Jonathan Rollins, played by Blair Underwood, who argues the case in her behalf. As Kurt Rubin and others give vivid testimony about the horrors of the camps, Rollins maintains his outward composure but becomes quite uncomfortable as the parallels between one persecution and another are brought home to him. Under cross-examination, Rubin shouts at Rollins, demanding whether he can be certain that the next time it will not be a black man at the receiving end of the murderers' wrath.

Kurt Rubin's anger on the witness stand triggered something in me. It also made me fear that as an artist I was in danger of allowing my own feelings to overpower me and drive the character out of my grasp. Of course it's true that an actor must look for feelings and mental associations within himself to approximate the required emotion of the moment. But that has to be left in the background, more an evocation of mind-set and mood than a full-blown expression. It certainly cannot intrude and take on a life of its own outside of the drama to be enacted. I was aware of the danger, and I was afraid.

As it turned out, I should have been less apprehensive of what might happen to the role and more of what was happening to me. Oh, I did what professionalism demanded; I sublimated my own emotion and gave the role all I could. But in between shots and setups it was another story. There was much less of the usual banter and joking on the set, and to the extent that I participated, I did so on autopilot. As I sat in my chair between takes, the ghosts of my childhood came to visit.

Vienna, March 1938

For weeks now there have been rumblings. For weeks, also, the handful of Jews in my class have been beset by intensified jeering and taunting from "them." It was always "them"—I do not recall friendships between Jewish and Gentile students, or even camaraderie. I guess that must be difficult for an American to understand; after so many years of living in the United States I can barely understand it myself. Having non-Jewish friends is nothing out of the ordinary for me now, and totally natural for my sons. That is how it should be. But that was not how it was when I was a boy. They hated us, and we feared and mistrusted them. Most of them grabbed any opportunity to inflict bodily harm—nothing serious, but enough to hurt. If some of the Jews excelled in class, that made it even worse: smartasses were singled out for the extra cuff and kick. The teachers were not much help; they looked away unless the attack was really blatant, and then the offenders were called on the carpet not for the injustice of the hurt they had inflicted but—Austrians can be awfully German—because "order must be maintained."

Newspaper and radio reports had made it clear that the political situation in Europe would worsen, and that little help could be expected from any quarter to avert a German takeover of Austria. There was much speculation among the Austrians about the Jews finally getting theirs, and some regret on the part of a few decent souls who remembered that Austria had fared best under a benign socialist system. Some people even experienced a little apprehension, not about what would happen to the Jews—no one, not even the most rabid Nazi, could have predicted that—but about what would happen to their own lives, their culture and their comfort, if the Jews were no longer part of the fabric of society. Germany's treatment of Jews for the preceding five years was common knowledge, and it was assumed that the fate of Austria's Jews would be no different. Jews barred from public office, from teaching posts, from journalism, possibly from all the arts—a fairly dismal prospect, given Jewish contributions in all these areas.

None of this was lost on the thirteen-year-old boy I was then. While I may not have been able to make political assessments, I was adult enough to perceive the scope of the threat. Some of my Jewish classmates, influenced by their parents' wishful thinking, argued with me. "It will blow over," they said. "Don't exaggerate." Alas, many Jews retained their ill-placed optimism a little too long, and perished as a consequence. One Jewish classmate of mine, Munk by name, argued that his father had been a decorated Austrian officer and that no one would dare touch him. Fat chance. Of course, my thinking was also influenced by my parents, chiefly by my father, who had always been an intensely political man. He was a socialist and a Zionist, passionately devoted to labor and to Jewish survival and culture.

My argument with my classmates was bolstered by a book I had read, Hugo Bettauer's *Stadt ohne Juden (City Without Jews)*, which posited the hypothetical case of a Vienna whose authorities decide to expel all the Jews. Part of the decree stipulates that the Jews are to take everything with them—all their possessions and also all they have created—so that the city may be totally *judenrein*. The mass exodus is described, a predictably moving tale. But what follows is the author's scenario of a city falling apart, unable to function even on the most elementary level of social and medical services, not to mention the arts and sciences. As a young Jewish boy, perhaps overly imbued with pride in the achievements of his people and their contributions to the world around him, I devoured Bettauer's book with glee. I was hoping his prophecy would somehow come true.

March 11, 1938, was a Friday. I remember it well; we were all glued to our radios listening to the Austrian chancellor, Kurt von Schuschnigg. Chancellor Schuschnigg had gone to see Hitler in Berchtesgaden in an effort to forestall a putsch. The trip was unsuccessful, and Schuschnigg returned with the idea that the Austrian people would decide by plebiscite whether they favored Austrian independence. But Hitler was not about to allow that, and forced the chancellor to cancel his plans and resign. It was late in the evening when Schuschnigg announced his resignation and spoke of Austria's inability to withstand the German pressure. Tears choked his voice as he finished with a prayer asking God to bless and preserve Austria. Then, before the station went off the air, a string quartet played the Austrian national anthem in a manner I had never heard before and have not heard since—a mournful dirge, slow, somber, and dark.

There is an irony here: the Austrian anthem has the same melody as the German anthem. But where the Austrians sing, *"Sei gesegnet ohne Ende, Heimaterde wunderhold"* (Eternal blessings upon thee, wondrous native soil), the Germans have other words: *"Deutschland, Deutschland über Alles, über Alles in der Welt."* (Need I translate? I don't think so.)

About thirty-six hours later the Germans marched in. Not only were they prepared, so also was their reception, and it was not something hastily put together. Thousands of seamstresses had not been pressed into service to sew hundreds of thousands of swastika armbands between Friday night and Saturday afternoon. The armbands and flags, not imported but of Austrian manufacture, had been there for some time, waiting for the moment. Most shockingly, the Nazi emblem adorned the arms of all the Austrian policemen along the route—"our" policemen, loyal until last night to the Austrian republic and its government. Did they become Nazis overnight, or had they all held swastika armbands and swastika minds in readiness for this day?

I remember the invaders' procession well. Its route led just past our windows in the Mariahilferstrasse, a main thoroughfare. No trams were running, and the familiar street that I had taken every day on my way to school looked both festive and frightening. The despised red flags with the *Hackenkreuz* (swastika) in the center were hanging from every lamppost. It was gray and overcast, I think, but I am not sure that this recollection is not a trick played by the sense of threat and evil foreboding that gripped me then. We peeked out from behind the curtains and watched with sinking hearts as column after marching column was hailed and *heil*ed by our own neighbors. Already afraid of discovery, we were careful not to show our faces. What if someone looked up and saw people who were not cheering in the street with everyone else and were not even waving from their window? Then, more horror. In the middle of a column of armored vehicles, standing up in an open limousine, a fat man—unmistakably Göring. A little farther on, the ogre himself, moustache and all. The crowd downstairs went wild. To the sounds of *Sieg Heil!* we huddled together, my mother and father and I. It suddenly seemed very cold.

And so the Anschluss came, unanticipated only by the most naïve, a grim surprise nonetheless.

The next few weeks were harrowing. There were immediate changes, even at the high school. Jews were singled out for renewed and harsher taunting. Far from interfering, the faculty stood by. Indeed, at a general assembly on the first day of school after the Anschluss, the principal made a speech welcoming the long-awaited reunification "with our German brothers." (My European history had taught me that Germany and Austria had never been unified as one country before, but no matter.) Then he said, almost offhandedly—and I have never forgotten his exact words—"If, in the first exuberance of joy, incidents involving students should occur, we will not be inclined to prevent them or interfere." No wonder Jews were considered fair game.

In a class of about forty-five students, ten of us were Jews. I do not remember a single Gentile name or face, but I recall my Jewish classmates well—not that we were a close-knit group ourselves. The most brilliant student among us was Alfred Eisenpreis, whom none of us liked much because he was a teacher's pet.

A few days after the assembly, some older Gentile boys walked into our classroom. Two or three grades ahead of us, they looked big and menacing. Their faces were flushed with anticipation of an officially sanctioned minipogrom; hateful faces they were. "Let us have your Jews," they commanded shrilly, drawing out the word "*Juden*" as if it were a curse. The ten of us in the class were easily pointed out. Our Gentile classmates surrounded us and pushed us into the hall. Resistance was out of the question; our tormentors outnumbered us and were physically much stronger than we were. The beating they gave us in the hall that day really hurt. The injuries themselves would have been enough, but the greater pain was our feeling of utter helplessness, and the sure knowledge that this incident would be repeated again and again.

I came home that day with visible bruises on my face and dried blood on my shirt from a nosebleed. My mother was hysterical. My father—well, he was not an unemotional man; from time to time I had seen a tear or two in his eyes when he recited a poem or read us a play, as he often did on Tuesday nights around the living-room table. But those were intellectual tears, evoked by literature that moved him. The day I came home after the beating, my father wept bitterly and openly, not only for the hurt inflicted on his son, but for the dark despair that threatened his beloved Jewish people.

What happened to our friends and acquaintances after the Anschluss was far more serious than being roughed up by some hooligans at school. For many, it was immediate dismissal from positions in firms they had built up and made prosperous. For others, it was harassment and worse. Store owners found charming slogans on their shop windows in smeared paint: "*Juda verrecke!*"—"*Judensau*"—"*Juden raus!*" (Die like a dog, Juda—Jew pig—Jews get out!) A lady we knew was roused from her apartment by brown-shirted storm troopers and ordered to accompany them. They asked her if she owned a fur coat ("All you people do") and told her to bring it along. If she thought they were afraid she might catch cold, she was quickly disabused of that notion when they forced her to get down on her knees on the sidewalk and spend several hours cleaning the dirt and grime off it with that coat. At least she was allowed to return home after this ordeal. Others were not so lucky; they were quickly shipped off to concentration camps. Those who had occupied important positions were taken first.

It must be categorically stated that the Nazis I speak of were Austrian. They were not poor victims of invading German hordes— something they like to claim to this day. Indeed, like all people who have found a new religion, they were far more zealous and therefore far more cruel than their German mentors. They took particular pleasure in rounding up Jews and eagerly organized transportation for the ones chosen for deportation.

The camps had existed in Germany for some time. The name of Dachau, a concentration camp near Munich, was already familiar to me. Even then, long before the camps became places where the Final Solution was played out, mere mention of them evoked consternation and fear among Jews. It was as if some collective and atavistic déjà vu was at work here. As a people we were no strangers to the sorrow and the pity. Or to the horror. The specter of hatred, of murder, rape, and pillage visited upon us by a hostile surrounding world had always been central to Jewish memory. The destruction of the Temple and the ensuing dispersion; the Crusades; the burnings at the stake in the Spanish Inquisition; the ghettoes and pogroms in the Ukraine and the Pale of Settlement—all are distinct group memories. Until modern-day Jewish life in America came along and changed the perception, the most salient fact Jewish children everywhere learned from an early age was that people hated us, enough to want to kill us. And that even those who had no taste for such a bloodthirsty quest would not speak out while the murders were being committed.

My parents and I lived under the Nazis for six months. We had always assumed that we would end up living in Palestine. The plan had been for me to go and study at the Hebrew University once I finished the Austrian equivalent of high school. Hitler's invasion only changed our timetable. Of course, we could not be certain that the doors of the Promised Land would be open to us; the British bureaucracy was very tight where visas for Jews were concerned. So we applied at various embassies with little hope of success, secretly wishing for only one destination: Palestine. In the meantime, we prepared for other eventualities. My father and I studied Spanish in case South America worked out, and my mother learned corset-making so she would have a marketable skill. In the end we were lucky; my father's active Zionism secured for us one of the few coveted visas the British allocated to the Jewish community of Vienna.

Taking leave of my alma mater in the Amerlinggasse was not terribly difficult. As the high school prepared to adjourn for the summer, the Jewish students knew that they were not coming back; a decree had been issued that Jews had to attend all-Jewish high schools in the future. Shortly before I left, my Greek professor, who also conducted the school choir in which I participated—Gruber was his name, I believe—called me into his office for a chat, in an attempted gesture of kindness. A known Nazi sympathizer before the Anschluss, he had been the first faculty member to sport a swastika on his lapel. The summons to his office was therefore all the more surprising. In a gruff voice he said, "I suppose you will be leaving the country; that would perhaps be best for you people. A word of advice, though. You are a good singer; if you want to keep it up, stay away from sports, especially football" (soccer in Europe). When I asked him why, he replied, "Playing fields are dusty places. You inhale a lot of the stuff and ruin your voice. All right, you can go." How much this warning had to do with my predilections later in life I do not know. The fact is that I have never been much interested in sports.

We left Austria by a circuitous route, via Germany, across the Rhine into France, and thence to Venice to board a ship for Tel Aviv. A direct trip from Vienna to Venice would have been much shorter, but there were rumors that this was not such a good idea. (We all lived on rumors in those days.) The Austrian border guards, we heard, were capricious when it came to Jews, liable to turn you back even if all your papers were in order, or to confiscate even the few things you were able to bring out with you. Presumably the German border guards did not like Jews any better, but they were more apt to follow routine. It turned out that there were no hitches. Lucky. I recall that when our train crossed the bridge over the Rhine and the conductor assured us that we were now traveling on French soil, I spat out the window toward the Germany and Austria we had left behind. Small satisfaction, perhaps, but it suited the feelings of a fourteen-year-old boy who had been appalled that the nation that gave birth to Mozart, Haydn, Schnitzler, and Strauss could show such barbarism.

The Bettauer scenario about expelling Jews with all their possessions was not fulfilled. In the first instance, far from expelling us, they made it quite difficult for us to leave. When we finally did leave, having satisfied endless bureaucratic whims, they did not order us to take everything with us, they forced us to leave practically everything behind. Our belongings, furniture and all, were put into storage containers, to await disposition by a newly created office headed by a high-ranking Nazi responsible for the "property of elements hostile to the Reich." How we finally managed to get our things after all is a wonderful story of courage and perseverance.

My maternal grandmother, Regina Riegler, stayed behind in Vienna. Our British visa covered only the immediate family Bikel—father, mother, and son. Immediately upon arrival in Palestine, then a territory held by the British under a mandate from the League of Nations, we took steps to apply for permission, on compassionate family grounds, for my grandmother to join us. It would take many months to accomplish, but in the meantime this old lady set out to liberate our possessions from the Nazis. Her system was simple. She would sit in the office of the Gauleiter (Nazi party district leader) every single day, from the time they opened the office until they closed the doors. She would sit and weep. Whenever the Gauleiter passed, she would stand up and try to speak to him about her children's effects. Each time she was brushed off. Undaunted, she continued to sit and cry. After weeks of this, the Gauleiter became so unnerved by the sight that he started to come in by a different door. My grandmother simply switched her seat. Whenever the Gauleiter entered or left, she was there. Finally, he told his staff in exasperation to get that old Jewish woman out of his sight at all costs. He would sign the necessary papers to release the damn furniture or whatever—anything to get rid of this nuisance. He signed, she left his sight forever and arranged for the things to be shipped to us by the slow sea route.

It took two more years, but we did manage to obtain a visa for my grandmother. She arrived in 1941, with the war already raging in Europe and North Africa. We were reunited only for a few months before she fell ill and died. Miraculously, of the ten Jewish boys in my class, seven of us eventually escaped. Four ended up in America; two in Palestine/Israel; and I, the seventh, everywhere. Spira, Slutzky, and the brilliant Eisenpreis made their homes in New York, while Walter Streng, who died of cancer in the 1980s, based himself in Dallas and became a traveling art dealer. The two who settled in Palestine and took the kibbutz route were Seinfeld and Braun. Otto Braun had been my closest friend in Vienna; his family was quite poor, and he and I spent a lot of time together at my home. He became the younger brother I never had.

Venice, September 1938

As a rule, a sea voyage from Northern Italy to Palestine would depart from Trieste on the Adriatic and arrive at the Mediterranean port of Haifa about five days later. Our schedule was somewhat different: We boarded the ship in Venice instead of Trieste. The reason for the change was Mussolini; we were told that the *Duce* was addressing a mass rally in Trieste that day and that all extraneous traffic had to be moved elsewhere. Frankly, I did not mind; the whole thing was an adventure anyway, and by now I could face it with a mind freed from the worry of ever having to deal with Nazi chicanery again. The voyage itself was uneventful. I spent a lot of time roaming around the decks and below with a kid my age whom I had known from Vienna and the Zionist youth movement, of which we had both been members. His name was Robert Starer; he went on to become a well-known and highly respected musician and composer both in Israel and in New York, where he now makes his home.

The ship did not dock at Haifa as planned, but unloaded us in Tel Aviv instead. Why the switch was made I never found out. It was the first day of Rosh Hashanah, the Jewish New Year, but that should have made little difference. Jewish laborers, despite their respect for the holiday, were hardly likely to stay away from the job—not to a man anyway—and Haifa would have made more sense on that account, as the majority of workers there were Arabs. Still, Tel Aviv it was, and with an all-Jewish work crew.

The irony of "Tel Aviv harbor" was immediately apparent; there really isn't any. There was a Hebrew song about building one, but frankly, the natural requisites for a seaport along that part of the shore can only be found a few miles to the south in Jaffa, then a completely Arab city and probably not too safe for a boatload of Jewish immigrants. So the captain dropped anchor offshore at Tel Aviv, and together with our baggage we were taken off the ship in a tender. The water was rough, and the brief trip aboard that small vessel took its toll even on those passengers who had come through the Mediterranean crossing unscathed; most of them landed with a greenish tint to their faces. If I was also on the point of getting seasick, I didn't notice; I was too excited. I was looking forward with such great anticipation to the moment when I would finally arrive in a Jewish harbor. And this was Tel Aviv, the first all-Jewish city since biblical times! It would be the adventure of my life. Though the harbor was only a small jetty, we were thrilled at setting foot on the soil of what had for so long been the land of our hopes. Hearing the dock workers speak to each other was a further thrill—Hebrew as an everyday language! And how fortunate I felt for having learned and practiced the language for years, while some of my compatriots and copassengers were faced with the monumental task of adjusting not only to a new country but to a new language in a different script that at best they had barely been able to decipher in their prayer books.

What we found was a country at once alien and strangely familiar. The faces, the gait, the attitudes, the lilt of speech—even when the languages were neither German, Hebrew, nor Yiddish, they were of a pattern we could easily recognize. Even Jews from Oriental lands such as Yemen, Iraq, or North Africa somehow conveyed an impression of cousinhood. As for Tel Aviv, here at last was a city where Jews could feel themselves to be in their own land. You took great comfort from the thought that here, in Tel Aviv, everyone was Jewish. The grocer, the bookseller, the clerk, the beggar, and the teacher—sure, those Jews you had met before. But the policeman, the fireman, and the mayor? I suppose the thought should have occurred to us in the midst of all this prideful boasting that as sure as night follows day, the burglar, the arsonist, and even the murderer might eventually turn out to be Jewish. No, no such thoughts were allowed to intrude. Years later these contradictions would surface quite sharply when the world Jewish community split over actual or putative wrongdoing by Israelis. In that argument, one segment hotly defended the notion that Israel should not be expected to be any better than anyone else, that it had striven to become *"am k'chol hagoyim"* (a people just like all others). The opposing viewpoint insisted that Israel was required to be *"am segulah"* (a people of distinction), and must therefore be better and nobler than anyone else, both by its own determination and by historical calling.

For the moment, however, all we felt was the euphoria of being home at last.

MINE IS NOT A very harrowing story of escape and survival. Yet the comparative ease of it has haunted me for many years—almost as much as the Holocaust has, the specter of which I carry with me always. When so many died by vapors of poison, by starvation, by the guns and knives of murdering Jew-haters, why was I saved? Years after the war I visited the concentration camp at Dachau, now a sort of grisly museum of Nazi atrocities. As I went from room to room and from site to site, the old feeling began to haunt me again: Why was I spared? When I got to the crematorium, I attempted to say the kaddish, the prayer for the dead, and I was unable to do it aloud before these ghosts. I had no right to a voice while theirs was stilled.

Why me? Since there must be a purpose, perhaps the answer was to be found here. I looked around me and saw many visitors, of many nationalities. As I watched them, it occurred to me that those who were here did not need to be reminded, and that those who did need it were not here. Maybe I was meant to use my voice as a warning that history must not repeat itself. I would sing the songs of my people right here in Germany, the very songs that were on their lips as they were led to the slaughter.

I did do that. I sang on television and in live appearances. I sang *"Zog nit keinmol az du geyst dem letsten veg"* (Never say that you're walking your last way) and *"Ani ma'amin"* (I believe with full faith in the coming of the Messiah, and even if he should tarry, I shall still believe). Even though I could not bear witness with as much right, authority, and eloquence as Elie Wiesel, I could demonstrate in the words of the song that "the beat of our steps will proclaim: We are still here!" And I would not be maudlin, would not even be somber and solemn, but would demonstrate that my people had mastered the art of survival even when death was staring them in the face. They knew how to laugh, to pray, to sing and dance, even when the very act of walking in the street meant mortal danger.

Some of my Jewish contemporaries refuse to travel to Germany; some refuse to buy German goods, specifically automobiles; some Jewish artists will not perform before German audiences. I have a different attitude. My quarrel with Germany's past is far deeper than can be expressed by a petulant refusal to drive a BMW. Israel's attitude toward German collective guilt has not been softened one iota by the fact that Israel's roads are filled with German cars. And if I stay away from Germany and Germans, how will they be reminded of their past and their shame? So I do perform in Germany from time to time, both live and on television. I do so with conditions attached to my appearance: Nothing I say or sing may be cut or edited, even for technical reasons, without my express approval. On past occasions when I performed there, I sang songs of the ghetto, concentration camp songs that were saved in milk cans and found after the liberation. I also sang German freedom songs, several hundred years old, and explained that I meant to remind them that once upon a time, before they succumbed to a bout of collective barbarism, Germans too had known songs of human dignity. The reaction was not much different from what I was told had happened after performances in Germany of *The Diary of Anne Frank:* stunned silence, no applause. It got to them.

All these memories were triggered by a role in a television show thousands of miles away on the West Coast of the United States. I was able to identify with my character's emotion rather than with his realities. On the face of it, the similarities between that man's life and mine were not very great. I did not lose my parents, and I did not have to endure the hunger and deprivation of a child on the run. But I understood so well what moved him that I had to work awfully hard to use my memories without allowing them to overshadow or intrude on the role. And in the end I was glad that all these thoughts knocked at the gates of my consciousness.

In a way, I too need to be reminded.

IN 1939 TEL AVIV, indeed the entire Jewish part of Palestine, was an easy place to get used to, with its insistence on informality of dress and address. Open-necked short-sleeved shirts were de rigueur, even at dinner or at the theatre. People called each other *chaver* (friend), and nobody locked doors. When you went to a movie, it was a levantine scene. Vendors hawking ice cream, chocolate, and the ubiquitous sunflower seeds that everyone cracked incessantly, spitting the shells on the floor. If the film was in French with English subtitles, you would also get Hebrew on one side of the screen and Arabic on the other, both reels operated by hand. These were not terribly well synchronized; sometimes, as a result, one line would get four different laughs. On the way home, you would get a freshly squeezed orange juice or some ice-cold cactus fruit, deftly split open by vendors who were not much older than me.

At last we had arrived in a place where Jews were free. Indeed, they wore their freedom on their sleeves openly, almost defiantly. It was something of a shock to confront old Palestine hands and especially native-born Palestinian Jews. Sabras, they were called, which is the local name for cactus fruit. The commonly offered explanation for this nickname is that these people are just like the prickly pear: the outside forbidding and stinging, the inside sweet and pleasant. Getting past that tough exterior could be a daunting prospect. At first blush, sabras seemed curiously un-Jewish to the young immigrant I was then. Frankly, I also envied them the one quality that was the obvious source of their brashness: They were fearless. In Europe we had never known Jews who were unafraid. Not that Europe's Jews were cowardly; but because their history was replete with pogroms, blood accusations, auto-da-fés, and all manner of persecution, they were cautious. Certainly, as a group we had never known the absence of fear. Sabras, a type new to me, were not only fearless Jews, they were also fighting Jews, as I was to find out very quickly.

Fighting Jews, to be sure, but hardly militaristic. Even later, when Israel became a state with a regular army, there remained an aura of informality in the conduct of the soldiery. To this day they are citizen-soldiers, rather than men and women who picked soldiering as a career. A joke used to be told about a private in the Israeli army who walks by a general without saluting. The general calls the soldier back and inquires, "What's the matter, you're angry with me?"

Many years before we left Austria, my father's studies at the university had been interrupted when he was drafted into the Austrian Imperial Army. Poverty forced him to abandon any further academic training after his discharge. He had to seek work to survive—as a clerk, as a commercial correspondent, and later as an insurance salesman. Outside the drudgery of earning a living, however, he remained an intellectual, a reader, an inveterate attender of lectures. He was also an amateur actor and a fountain of song from whom I learned much Jewish and Hebrew folklore. Our arrival in Palestine gave my father some hope that here, in the land of his dreams, his work might not only furnish a living for the family but also contribute to the *yishuv,* the Jewish settlement of Palestine.

When I was born, my father the Zionist decided I should be named after the father of modern Zionism, Theodor Herzl. I was named Meir after my maternal grandfather, but that was for synagogue use. Elsewhere, it was to be Theo. I would have been called Theodore had I been born on any date of the year, but by a curious coincidence I was born on May 2—Herzl's birthday. As a boy of nine or ten, with very little prompting from my father, I read Herzl's utopian novel *Alt-neuland (Old-New Land)*. I still recall the fantasies I indulged in after finishing it. They were dreams of orange groves and wheat fields tended by Jews and Arabs working side by side in harmony, of a free bicultural society with Jews applying skill and new knowledge to long-forgotten Middle Eastern climates and agriculture. I remember being taken to rousing speeches in some Viennese auditorium where emissaries from the kibbutz movement spoke in glowing terms of the land, of the work, and of the people. The speeches were in Yiddish, and the audiences were enraptured. There were also a couple of films on the subject that were shown in small movie houses—primitive versions of what today would be United Jewish Appeal fund-raisers. They uplifted and inspired us. I went to those movies twice, just so I could listen to the Hebrew songs. Once, Papa's Zionist activity brought us a little perk: a miniature produce crate sent from Palestine to a few selected workers in the "cause." In it were three pieces of fruit we had never seen before, much less tasted—grapefruit. Apart from bananas and oranges, subtropical fruit was not exactly available in abundance in Vienna, and even when available, it was not affordable for people of our modest means. And now here was this exotic taste, somewhat bitter, but who cared? It had come from a Jewish grove in Palestine! All this had whetted our appetite for the land and further fed our hopes of someday getting there.

Now it was all real and tangible. But work had to be found so that Papa could feed the family. I suspect that my father, imbued with Zionist fervor, would have liked to join a kibbutz and work the land, but he was enough of a realist to recognize his own limitations. A city intellectual to the core, he would not have lasted long among the livestock and grapevines. Ah, but there was his son. Surely I could mold myself into the *chalutz,* the pioneer he could not be. I was not averse to trying. Since I had to continue my general education as well, why not combine the two and go to an agricultural college? Mikve Israel was the logical choice, the oldest such learning institution in the country, established by the Alliance Israélite Universelle—a fraternal organization of French Jews who had maintained French as the teaching language of the college until the early part of the century, a requirement long since changed by the time I enrolled.

It was during my student days at Mikve Israel that I saw Jerusalem for the first time. My first trip there was a little unnerving. Since I had no fare money, I thumbed a ride in a truck carrying produce. The driver was an Arab, which gave me pause, considering the strained relations between the two segments of the population. But he was carrying vegetables. How dangerous could that be? Also, I was determined to get to Jerusalem. I should have worried less about the driver's possible nationalist inclinations and more about his sexual predilections. Sitting in the cab next to him, I suddenly felt his hand on my knee. Now, that was frightening. I jumped out when he stopped at the next intersection, and luckily found another ride in a vehicle whose driver was a sabra, and more important, was straight.

I loved Jerusalem from the first moment I set eyes on the city. The western wall (called the Wailing Wall) was what I longed to see, but Jews could not go there alone; one had to pass through the Arab quarter to reach it. I found some people who formed a group, and we went. The Wall was in a dark and narrow alleyway, with another high wall facing it. That wall has since been taken down to make room for a wide plaza. Though it was dark and somber then, my heart was in my throat as I saw and touched the Wall for the first time. In all the many times I have repeated the experience, that feeling has not gone away. Deep religiosity cannot explain it, because I am not deeply religious. Mysticism cannot explain it either, because I am not a mystic. It must be visceral, a sensation triggered by group memory.

This was wartime, and Jerusalem, unlike Tel Aviv, before the war had been a center where people of many nationalities and religious persuasions lived and worked. Some of these—chiefly the Germans and Italians—were now among the enemies of the Allies. After the outbreak of the war in 1939, German and Italian banks and other establishments were confiscated by the British government. The story went that some residents of Jerusalem who kept tabs on high finance had determined that a very rich Armenian had come to town and bought a lot of property. When asked what his name might be, they replied, "Koostodian"—a baffling answer until one looked at the locked and bolted German and Italian buildings, and saw the signs reading CUSTODIAN OF ENEMY PROPERTY or just plain CUSTODIAN. Clearly an Armenian name.

I spent the required two years at Mikve Israel attempting to learn the intricacies of agriculture. The language part was easy—that part is always the easiest for me. My years of studying Hebrew at home, and occasionally speaking it with my father, stood me in good stead. The theoretical courses at Mikve were also not too hard to bear, especially in the nonagricultural subjects. Upon graduation I was determined to go on to the kibbutz life, which my ideological streak still insisted was the right thing to pursue in a country so much in need of pioneers.

I joined a youth group in Masada, in the Jordan Valley, a hot place in a subtropical climate; later we were moved to Kfar Hamaccabi, near Haifa. The members of my group all hailed from either Austria or Germany, and most of them had been members of the Zionist youth movement. Ours was a work-study setup, with an emphasis on Hebrew, pragmatic socialism, and honest toil. In many ways, I loved kibbutz life. I probably should have guessed that my father's disinclination to till the soil had been transmitted to me, but in Masada I still labored under the illusion that the agricultural life was what I was destined to pursue and might even be fun. For example, I thought it would be nice to work the banana plants, since I liked to eat bananas. My job one day was to remove the occasional ripe banana from a green bunch (they get shipped green, and leaving the ripe ones spoils the rest). Throwing them on the compost, as I was asked to do, seemed such a waste, so I collected them and ate twenty-three bananas during a break! No wonder I couldn't look at a banana for months afterward. I must confess that I was a total failure at agriculture. All of it bored me to tears, some things more than others. Chickens, for example—horrible creatures, hateful smell, constant stooping. The fields were better, the orchards better still.

But I loved the social part of kibbutz life—the camaraderie, the seeking and finding of kindred spirits, the sense of fun at the end of the workday—indeed, the end of the day was by far the better part of it. Wishing the workday over so that one can enjoy free time is a normal frame of mind for most workers of the world, and therefore unremarkable. Looking back, however, I find it strange, since I have spent most of my years enjoying my work far more than any other part of living.

I especially loved the cultural life: the festivals, the pageants, the stage events, the singing until all hours of the night. There I was in my element, and could make a real contribution. The late evenings made working in the daytime a little harder, but I compensated. I often stood on heaps of manure, leaning on a pitchfork, singing Hebrew songs at the top of my voice—songs that extolled the beauty of callused hands and the nobility of work which I was not doing too well.

In my house is a painting I bought many years ago. The artist was nobody famous; it is a modest work. It was not the quality of the painting but the subject matter that caused me to purchase it: a young boy standing on a makeshift stage, arms spread out, singing. It reminded me of myself as a young child in Vienna. According to my mother, I sang before I could talk. I sang constantly around the house, alone or with my parents, both of whom had good voices. On Sundays when the weather was good, we would pack our rucksacks like any other family going for a weekend hike, but with a difference: the Vienna woods rang with the sounds of the Yiddish, Hebrew, or Ruthenian folk songs the three of us sang with abandon. When guests came to the apartment, I sang for them, too. My mother tells with amusement how, as a very small child, I would insist that she spread a newspaper on the floor, and I would stand on it before opening my mouth to sing. This was my stage; I have continued to sing on one stage or another ever since.

Everyone sang at the kibbutz, but very few played any instrument larger than a mouth organ. By chance I found an abandoned guitar in a luggage repository. It appeared that someone who had worked there briefly had departed under a cloud, leaving behind a suitcase and a guitar. It was not much of an instrument, but more than enough to learn on. I soon discovered that I was able to play a few chords by way of accompaniment. The instrument, I also discovered, was both deceptively easy and infuriatingly difficult. With three chords you could play fifteen songs; with four, another twenty. The guitar allowed you to "get by," something a violin, for example, does not. Play the violin badly and you get chased from the room; a badly played guitar raises few eyebrows and no ire. I was determined to do better than play badly, but I was hampered by the fact that no one else played. The resident pianist on the kibbutz was no help in mastering the intricacies of a fretted string instrument. I was left to my own devices, and so developed my own self-taught style. By the time I came into contact with others who played, I was used to doing it my way. While I did learn from them, it was by observing their fingers and listening to the sounds they made.

No matter how much we enjoyed ourselves, none of us on the kibbutz, myself included, forgot that it was wartime—at least not for long. The Jewish settlement in Palestine felt beleaguered on several counts. In the first instance, there was always the threat from Arab nationalists. Constant vigilance was essential, especially at night when attacks might come. We all took turns in the watchtowers and on foot patrol. I had grown familiar with the Lee-Enfield rifle while still at the agricultural college; there was some glamour attached to training with them and doing paramilitary exercises. We used British-style commands, albeit in Hebrew, including "Present arms!"—although to whom arms could be presented during such secret exercises was a mystery. The tours of duty watching over the kibbutz at night were a more serious business. Legally the kibbutz was permitted a number of weapons for the purpose of protecting the settlement and the fields from marauders. Marauders did exist, of course, and the fields did have to be watched, but our main purpose was to establish an armed presence that could be augmented at a moment's notice with undeclared weapons and personnel. These would vanish when an inspection by the British was threatened. Some of us, myself included, were legally entitled to bear rifles as part of the "Jewish Settlement Police." There was even some sort of a brownish uniform shirt and a hat with a badge affixed to the front. It looked good, especially when you were on horseback. I was glad, however, that I never had to fire a shot, except in training—my notion of glamour did not extend that far.

The British were our other problem. They had no desire to see us assume autonomous authority, except locally and in the most limited way. We, on the other hand, were intent on preparing for the day when self-rule would supplant British rule and self-defense would be a necessity. Consequently, there was continual underground activity that had to be hidden from prying eyes. Weapons and ammunition were often procured in ingenious and daring ways.

Sleeping in my tent one night, I was roused by a hand shaking me and an urgent whisper: "Come, you are needed!" "Wha—? Who? Why?" I managed to stammer. "No questions, get dressed, let's go." Still not understanding what was going on, I nevertheless obeyed and followed the veteran kibbutznik. He took me to a barn that looked deserted, and rapped on the door with some prearranged signal. The door opened a crack, and we entered to face a dark blanket used to black out any spill of light. Only when the door was firmly shut behind us was the curtain pulled aside. An astonishing sight met our eyes: A dozen or more men and women sat around a mountain of military hardware—rifles, machine guns, ammunition of all kinds. Everyone was busy oiling and cleaning parts before reassembling and wrapping the weapons for storage. I too was put to work, and we stayed at the task all night long and into part of the next day, until everything was cleaned and stowed away in a place known only to a few higher-ups in the Haganah, the Jewish self-defense organization, which later became the nucleus of the Israel Defense Forces.

Getting those weapons had taken some daring. Many Palestinian Jews, including members of our kibbutz, had joined the British army and were fighting in various theatres of operation. One of the kibbutz members was attached to a British supply unit stationed in Egypt. When he had a few days' leave coming, he commandeered an army truck (soldiers on leave were supposed to hitch rides) and managed, God knows how, to pretend that he was on official business and under orders to load a huge number of weapons into the truck. Unsuspecting British soldiers helped him fill up and wished him a good trip. He drove without stopping, all the way through the desert from Egypt into Palestine and to the kibbutz. He arrived totally exhausted, turned over the keys to the truck, and fell asleep practically before his head hit the pillow. Later he told us how he had gotten through: He had only a limited command of English, and he used that to his advantage as he "explained" his way through the checkpoints. Had his cargo been inspected, he would surely have had to face a court-martial. Perhaps it was his bad English that saved him; Englishmen are impatient with foreigners, even when they serve in the British army.

As it became more and more apparent to everyone that I was far better at the extracurricular activities that made up the artistic and cultural life of the kibbutz than I was at plowing, sowing, and feeding livestock, I became increasingly involved in those activities, both as participant and as organizer. The kibbutz was far more than an agricultural settlement. It presented a distinctly intellectual environment, which was surely the reason I stuck it out as long as I did. There were classical concerts, often on records, but listened to just as avidly as if they had been live; there were lectures, literary discussions, and pageants for the various festivals. And always, there was a genuine effort to create a sense of belonging. Despite the absence of any religious ceremony, on Friday night the tables in the dining hall were covered with white cloths, we were served white bread in approximation of challah, the rich, sweet bread made with eggs, instead of our everyday fare of coarse brown bread, and most of the men wore freshly laundered white shirts. *Shabbat shalom* was the universal greeting as the sabbath was acknowledged by everyone, even the atheists. It remains so throughout Israel even to this day.

One day, a letter arrived at the kibbutz secretariat announcing that the organization of kibbutzim was to hold a seminar in Tel Aviv where delegates would receive intensive instruction from playwrights, actors, musicians, makeup artists, and other experts in the various disciplines of the performing arts. The idea was that after these courses everyone would return to the kibbutzim better equipped to write, produce, and stage the pageants, festivals, and plays.

All kibbutz decisions were made democratically by the members at a general meeting. The kibbutz decided that I was the person to be sent from Kfar Hamaccabi to this seminar. As a junior nonvoting member, I did not attend the meeting. I gather that the decision was not unanimous. Some felt—not without justification—that I was not a productive asset to the kibbutz, and asked why, since I was not pulling my weight at the regular workload, I should be encouraged to do even less. Others argued that precisely because I was not pulling my weight, I should be put to work in an area where I would. As I was later told, the debate went back and forth. Kfar Hamaccabi, like many other kibbutzim, was a place where culture was held in high esteem. Many of its members had emigrated from Central Europe, chiefly Czechoslovakia and Hungary. It was the kind of place where if you called out "*Herr Doktor!*" in the communal dining hall, half the kibbutz would turn around. Everyone took pride in the extensive library and lecture series, and in the fact that one of the members, a noted concert pianist in Europe, worked only half-days so that he could practice the piano the rest of the time. In the end the decision was made that I should be sent.

This seminar was a turning point in my life, giving me a hint of the smell of greasepaint and some faint promise of the roar of the crowd. I spent three weeks there, attending lectures, analyses of plays, demonstrations of makeup techniques—one-on-one interchanges between theatre professionals and wide-eyed young amateurs like myself. It was a heady time, and it gave me the first inkling of what my life should be all about.

I returned to the kibbutz, but my days there were numbered. After a few weeks, with deep apologies to those who had supported my trip to the training seminar, I said good-bye and left. Having tasted professionalism at its available best, I knew that I would be unable to remain an amateur. And so began the journey that led me to the theatre and a lifelong devotion to an occupation that sane people undertake only at their peril. Human beings fashion their lives drawn or driven by images and dreams. In my case it was not stardom or riches—I was still enough of a *chalutz,* a pioneer, not to concern myself with these—but the burning urge to stand before an audience, to reach out, to make words come alive, hear the intake of breath in surprise or shock, hear the stillness of the imagination captured, or the laughter of release. To this day those are the most thrilling aspects of what I do.

2

Hebrew Theatre

I CANNOT SAY THAT MY PARENTS WERE overjoyed at my decision to leave the kibbutz and follow a career in which the chances of success were so slim. Still, to their credit, it must be said that they did not entirely close the door on my ambitions. The only condition my father attached to giving me permission—and money—was that I pass my university exams, "just in case things don't work out." On this point he was insistent. As it happened, this was a wise decision, not because I needed a degree to make a living, but because those studies gave me the underpinning for a full intellectual life.

Hebrew theatre in Palestine was a fairly closed-club affair. There were two major theatres in the country: Habimah, still the national theatre of Israel, and the Ohel, now defunct, whose basic support came from the Histadrut, the central labor organization. In addition, there was a satirical theatre, the *Matateh* ("Broom"), its name indicating a slant toward poking fun at political institutions, an aim not fully achieved in later years. In its earlier days, the "Broom" worked because the British were a handy target for its satire. As soon as the British were gone, Matateh became redundant because it was unable or unwilling to pick homegrown Israeli targets. In the first years of the new state, this same phenomenon affected all playwriting and proved to be a detriment, not to the theatre as an institution perhaps, but to the quality of original Israeli plays. Once I was able to define quality in scripts, it became apparent to me that plays dealing with Jewish or Israeli history had a basic flaw: The villain was invariably drawn from the outside—Jews oppressed by Germans, by Arabs, by the Spanish Inquisition, by Ukrainian persecutors. But it was only late in the game that I could give voice to my complaint: "Give me a credible Jewish villain and I will believe that the Israeli play has come of age."

For now, I was a young man filled with the wonder of a world that seemed to offer nothing but beauty, poetry, and magic. Not that entering that world was easy. Both major theatres were organized as permanent companies, with the veteran actors forming a kind of cooperative. The sole criterion for full membership in the Habimah was seniority. The nucleus of the troupe had come from Russia; they were disciples of Konstantin Sergeyevich Stanislavsky, the great actor-director who had created a school of thought and a technique of acting known as "the Method." In Russia the Habimah was viewed in theatrical circles as a curiosity for its insistence on performing in Hebrew, a language considered by many just as dead as Latin and ancient Greek. The noted directors Yevgeny Vakhtangov and Vsevelod Meyerhold, who worked under Stanislavsky, as well as the master himself, were probably intrigued by the troupe's desire to perform in the language of their ethnic heritage, and agreed to take them in hand. They did then what directors only in recent years have done: They worked with material in a language unknown to them. Even the very name of the troupe, Habimah, Hebrew for "stage," was unpronounceable for a Russian speaker. Russian has no "H" sound; they substitute "G" and pronounce it that way: Gitler instead of Hitler, Galifax for Halifax, and of course not Habimah but Gabimah.

In true European and especially Russian tradition, a theatre meant a permanent resident company whose actors played the repertoire, regardless of looks or age, until they dropped dead. It was not unusual for a sixty-year-old actress to play Juliet, a girl in her teens, or for an actor close to seventy to play Hamlet. The audience—which knew no other tradition and had not been "spoiled" by a naturalism of later vintage, dictated in part by the closeup in films—accepted the convention without demur. As a consequence, the theatre never looked for young blood, or *Nachwuchs* (new growth), as the Germans call it. This attitude was so pronounced at Habimah that the training of young actors was considered a no-no only a few years prior to my knocking at its doors. Tsvi Friedland, a director and one of Habimah's more daring members, decided to change that, but for quite some time he could not buck the trend. He did create a training place for young would-be professionals, but he had to do it underground, holding sessions in people's apartments and other borrowed premises. Only a short time before my arrival, the Studio, as his project became known, had come out of the closet and had reluctantly been accepted by the old guard, though less from principle than from expedience: Large-scale productions needed more bodies onstage than the company could muster, and the Studio furnished eager unpaid extras and bit players.

After rigorous scrutiny I was accepted by the Studio. Because of my father's edict I had to juggle times and commitments, shuttling back and forth between my studies and the Studio. In the evenings I was especially torn, but the desire to see theatre—even to watch the same play over and over so that I could observe performances and technique—usually won out. When I got home I would cram for the next day's load of lessons. Luckily, of the five subjects required I had picked two electives that gave me no trouble: German and modern Hebrew. History, modern English, and math were harder, but I was determined. I was also young and invincible, able to do with little or no sleep.

Since Palestine was British under the League of Nations mandate, the procedures in use throughout the Empire (there still was one) relating to studies, exams, and diplomas were followed. In places remote from London, the government permitted one to dispense with orals and take all-written exams. Such exams were administered periodically, under strict government supervision. My venue was a Catholic monastery, where I was locked up for five days of three-hour sessions, morning and afternoon. We faced no professors or teachers of any kind, only proctors positioned to watch for cheaters. The exams arrived from London in a sealed diplomatic pouch and were sent back by the same route. After a few months I was informed that I had passed.

With the exams behind me, I was able to devote myself to the theatre full-time. I studied the Method. I ate, drank, dreamed, and breathed the Method. I paid attention to its history, its development, and its application at the hands of the Habimah actors. Of course, since the Method was the only game in town, I had no way to compare it to any other concept or acting technique. I suspected that there were other avenues to the realization and interpretation of a role, but this I had to deduce from observing film acting and remembering theatre in Vienna, which I had attended as a child as often as finances would allow. Here in the Hebrew theatre, there was only one god and guru: Konstantin Sergeyevich Stanislavsky—a pseudonym, by the way, which he took to escape the disapproval of his wealthy family for choosing an unworthy profession.

Stanislavsky elaborated his theory of "theatrical truth" through a radically different approach to acting than had been employed theretofore. Actors were to consider their roles not primarily as exercises in art but as problems of psychology—a psychology that was also supposed to link their performance to equivalent elements in their personal lives. This required two kinds of analysis—of the role and of one's self—before the process of fusion could begin. A problem, of course. It is evident that no matter how good actors may be at divining the author's intent, very few of us are capable of competent self-analysis. Stanislavsky's method obviously worked for many, and most certainly for the actor Stanislavsky himself. But it is doubtful—now, in hindsight, more than it was then—whether extending the life on stage into the actor's personal life, and vice versa, works universally, as its adherents claim it should. What happened to me on the set of *L.A. Law* was an exceptional case of such a crossover from the dramatic role into the actor's psyche. This can be useful, but it can also be damned uncomfortable, if not downright perilous. As I said, I managed to escape the danger whole, but I was a little singed at the edges.

What the Method does do for actors is to instill in them a heightened sense of discovery, of observation of the world and the people around them. It also creates a sense of understanding and rapport within a company, because all the actors are employing the same tools. And at its most productive, the Method uncovers essences: of the play and its vision, and of the strengths and weaknesses demanded by each portrayal. The drawbacks are to be found not in the understanding of the Method but in its acceptance as gospel.

Much of what Stanislavsky taught related to his own experience as a working actor and was therefore intensely personal. When followers of the Master were tempted to accept for themselves not an intellectual notion but something that was at best anecdotal, the results were unfortunate and sometimes ridiculous. For example, Stanislavsky insisted that mental preparation was essential before each performance so that the transition from the everyday world to the sanctum of the stage would be a smooth process. In *The Actor Prepares,* he described some of his own techniques of achieving this. Standing by himself in the wings, he would empty his mind of everything except the task at hand and hum a little Russian folk tune until his concentration was complete. I myself can appreciate this, since Russian folk tunes would serve the same purpose for me, but during my stint at the Habimah I witnessed tone-deaf actors standing in the wings trying to hum tunes—Russian ones at that—in the fervent belief that they were doing the Method thing!

Aside from such ludicrous misapplications, actors at that time and in that place—myself included—had genuine faith in the Method. Like all disciples, we tended to question neither its utilitarian purpose in general nor its applicability to us as individuals. Later it became evident to me that cultivating the idea of theatre in all its manifestations was far more important than blind adherence to any method. Quite a bit later.

By joining the Studio I became not only a student of the theatre but, like the others, an unpaid performer of walk-ons and small roles. Most memorable, especially in view of my later career, was my first appearance on a professional stage. The play was Sholem Aleichem's *Tevye, the Milkman,* a straight drama with incidental music but no songs. I had two chores, one behind the scenes, where I was put to work playing my guitar—already handy—to simulate a mandolin "played" by Fyedka, Chava's suitor, when he comes courting. Onstage I played the Constable, who appears in only one scene where he announces the expulsion, reading from a district order on which the ink is not yet dry. He delivers his message, blots the ink by pressing the paper against the whitewashed wall, leaving a black mirror image of the writing, and then exits. My part had twenty-nine words; I counted them, twice.

Needless to say, the prospect of my first twenty-nine professional words was as emotionally wrenching as if I had faced doing Hamlet. "I mustn't mess up," I kept saying to myself, "I mustn't mess up"(the Hebrew equivalent of this mantra was silently delivered with the perfect diction I was so proud of—can't be sloppy even when talking to yourself). My nervousness was obvious to everyone backstage—actors, dressers, stagehands.

Some of the theatre staff were a bit eccentric; so were the actors, but you expected it from them. Caspi, the head wardrobe master, was a character if ever there was one. His mother tongue was Yiddish, but he spoke no language well. After observing me pacing up and down in the corridors and the green room, he got a chair, pushed it up to the wall, climbed up on it, and reached for the picture of Konstantin Sergeyevich Stanislavsky that was prominently displayed. He took it off its hook, hopped off the chair, and came up to me. He raised my right arm, thrust the picture into my armpit, made sure it was firmly lodged there, and then announced in Yiddish in a loud voice, "*Na! Efsher vet dus helfen!*" (There! Maybe this will help!)

There was another aspect to Hebrew theatre that everyone accepted as a given, actors and audiences alike. It was a matter of accent. The Hebrew spoken on stage may have been of a high literary and poetic quality, often of great beauty, but the accents were invariably Russian, heavy Russian. So heavy indeed that, if you merely listened to the lilt without paying regard to the words, it seemed that you were in a theatre in Moscow or Kiev. On the streets the accents were varied and manifold, as varied as the birthplaces of the Jewish population of this old-new land. There were German accents and Polish, Yemenite, North African, a smattering of English and American, French, Spanish—one could hear them all. But onstage it was pure Russian. Everyone affected the accent, including young people who not only had never been near Moscow or Kiev, but had not even been to Europe. I did the same; I have an aptitude for languages and accents anyway, so technically it was not difficult for me. We did it because this was the language of the Hebrew theatre and none of us dared contravene the convention or question it—even if it had occurred to us that we should.

Emulating the gait and accents of the veteran actors of the Habimah was part of the respect all of us paid, almost as a tribute, to the hierarchy that was so firmly established in the Hebrew theatre. The informality that characterized life in Jewish Palestine, and that continues to this day in modern Israel, was not part of the relationship between younger actors and the veterans. Some who dared contravene the formal conventions soon learned not to repeat a faux-pas. An amusing incident remains in my memory concerning a stagehand who managed to break the unwritten rule of obeisance to the Russian aristocracy. His name was Jamil, a Moroccan Jew, I believe, who had a direct way of addressing people, albeit with a pronounced stutter. After the final curtain one opening night, a cluster of fans surrounded the leading lady, the diva of the Hebrew theatre, Chana Rovina. Jamil barged through her circle of admirers, grasped the actress's hand in his, and said: "M-M-Madame R-R-Rovina, c-c-cong-g-gratulations, m-m-mazel t-t-tov!" Afterward people remonstrated with him: "How can you approach Miss Rovina like this?" Somewhat offended he replied: "Why n-n-not; she is also a h-h-human b-b-b-being!" The rest of us, lacking ingenuousness, simply did not permit ourselves such breaches of etiquette; we all observed the prescribed ritual of obeisance.

Yet in some ways I was far more impatient than some of my colleagues at the Habimah Studio. Some of them had preceded me by two years or more, and would remain in this indentured servitude for some years to come before either leaving or being accepted into the company as permanent members. But after about a year and a half as student/actor/walk-on, I took pen in hand and wrote a letter to the board of directors of the theatre, all veteran actors themselves. In it I questioned my position at the theatre with its undefined status of indeterminate length and I posed some questions. "There are only two possibilities," I wrote. "Either I have talent or I don't. If I don't, then why do you keep me hanging around to little purpose and no future? And if I do, then why don't you give me proper roles to play?" The letter, by all accounts, created quite a stir. It was considered impudent and an affront; *chutzpah* was the term most often used to describe it. Even biblical quotations were bandied about both to my face and behind my back in dressing rooms and corridors. Isaiah was quoted: "Sons have I raised and they have sinned against me!" Excessive, perhaps, and somewhat baffling for my parents, who were under the impression that they were the ones who had raised me, but I suppose the poetry of the prophet was too good not to be declaimed by actors who had probably been waiting for an opportunity to do so—with Jewish fervor and Russian accents.

My appeal was rebuffed. I was given to understand that I would just have to bide my time, "for years, if necessary," until an opportunity might come along, and maybe—it was stressed, maybe—there could be an advancement of some sort.

Maybes like that I was not prepared to wait for, and I left the Habimah. Leaving was not all that easy, though. I had formed some great friendships there, which in fact have lasted for decades; to this day one of my closest friends remains Ada Tal, then a fellow student and today still an actress with the Habimah. In later years, even those who had quoted Isaiah in bitter and accusatory tones welcomed me warmly whenever our paths crossed. It was mutual; when the Habimah toured the United States in the mid-1960s, I made sure as vice president of Actors Equity that they were properly and honorably welcomed. It felt a little like Joseph in the Bible who, after having risen to a position of prominence in Egypt, greeted his brothers, who much earlier had abandoned him in the desert and given him up for dead, "Is our father alive still?"

But at that point I was a not-yet-actor out in the cold without a job. There was no such thing then as a freelance performer: If you were not attached to a permanent theatre, you had nothing. The other major theatre, Ohel, was clearly not for me. Their setup was exactly the same as that of the Habimah, without the advantage of a training ground with proper acting teachers. So I tried the Matateh, the Broom, and they hired me for one show entitled *The King of Lampedusa,* a comedy about a British airman forced into an emergency landing on a mythical remote island. The populace, which had had no contact with outsiders, declare him king and submit to various crazy shenanigans he dreams up for them. Though the play was a little too topical to be of lasting value, it was an acting job, for money. Not much: I received some forty piasters per performance, less than two dollars by today's standards. My mother kept the money as a memento; after the currency changed a few years later, that is all it was—bits of sentiment to remember a beginning.

Another young actor had been temporarily engaged to participate in the production of *Lampedusa*. Josef Pacovsky was intense, witty, and irreverent. Pepo, as he was called by everyone, was Czech born and more European than any of the actors I had previously worked with; Western European, that is. He was determined to do theatre— bigger theatre, better theatre, the kind of theatre that derived its greatness from aspiring to the standards of great European plays and productions. We spent a good deal of time together and found that we thought alike in many ways. He was a little older than I, more experienced, and although our dreams were similar, his dreams had a clearer shape than mine. Both of us, however, knew that our dreams would not find their realization at the Matateh. Pepo had a plan to found a new company that would present chiefly European plays, in an attempt to broaden both our horizons and the audience's. I decided to throw my lot in with his and exchange a not-too-secure career in the established theatre for the much shakier prospect of doing the new and untried. I would become a *chalutz* again, but this time in a field that would bear fruit of a different—and to me more palatable—kind.

I was beginning to see what had disturbed me about the Hebrew theatre: it represented a style and culture neither created indigenously nor evolving by a natural process. The dominant cultural force in the Hebrew theatre was Russian. Good though it was—and at its best it was very good—it was imitative. The acting was imitative of Russian acting and the writing was imitative of Russian writing—Russian revolutionary-style writing at that, heavy and without the virtue of either self-criticism or humor. Whatever attempts there had been to create indigenous plays had failed; home-grown drama also seemed to lack self-criticism and objectivity. It was understandable, I suppose. A man who is trying to keep afloat in a raging stream is in no position to stand on the shores of the river and describe its awesomeness, its beauty, or his own struggle not to drown.

Of course, we too set out to be imitative of another kind of theatre, but one that had not been seen in Palestine. We were going to be innovators, and were proud of it. We could also expect more of an audience for what we wanted to present: The closed society we were living in began to open up as World War II neared its end and the Jews of Palestine looked forward to a new wave of immigrants. The wave turned out to be a trickle; the British government was as unmoved by the plight of Jews who had survived the German inferno as it had been while the carnage was going on. Legal immigrants were few in number, and entry permits were as hard to come by as ever. Illegal immigrants, after nearly perishing in voyages aboard unseaworthy ships, were hunted down, arrested, and often sent back to Mediterranean ports, only to be refused entry there as well. This had been going on during the latter part of the war and it continued after the war's end as the British sought to curry favor with the Arabs—an attitude not merely political and pragmatic in nature. (The most notorious and heartbreaking incident had occurred in 1942 when a ship named *Struma* was turned back because its passengers, almost eight hundred in number, were refused entry permits by the British. They all perished in the Black Sea. The entire *yishuv*, the Jewish settlement of Palestine, was outraged and devastated.) The British had a historic love affair with Arabs—the Lawrence of Arabia syndrome. The Jewish settlers responded with many heroic acts of rescue, tendering shiploads of refugees to shore in the dead of night and quickly distributing people to various kibbutzim before daybreak, under the very noses of British soldiers.

Meanwhile Pepo Pacovsky (who later adopted the Hebrew name of Millo) had assembled a small and eager company of actors who were willing to work for the glory of it and for little or no pay. Not all of us were youngsters, either. There was a veteran actress, Rosa Lichtenstein, a total eccentric with a strong German accent whose personal habits ran to putting face powder over every part of her body instead of washing. She was also in the habit of frying eggs atop her table radio, whose old-fashioned vacuum tubes radiated heat. But she was a terrific presence onstage. There was also Yemima Pacovsky, Pepo's wife, diminutive, a firebrand, and a spendthrift (especially with other people's money). When the rest of us walked or took buses, she yelled, "Taxi!" She was quite an organizer, too. She booked halls, yelled at printers, hired stagehands, read scripts, and acted onstage (fairly decently). She ran the company, she ran Pepo, and she drove us crazy. What drove us especially crazy was that you couldn't be mad at her; she was too lovable. Then there was Batya Lancet, Hungarian-born, tall, beautiful, a love goddess (and knew it), and also a super actress.

The star of our first ventures, without a doubt, was Avraham Ben-Yossef ("Bazik" to his friends.) He was urbane, very Western European even though he'd been born in Russia and spent years in Romania.

He was more French than anything else, as French as upper-class educated Russians and Romanians get, polite (positively un-Israeli!),
courtly with women, polyglot, and a major comedic talent. I had seen
him previously playing guest roles with the opera company, especially
Menelaus in Offenbach's *La Belle Hélène*, which I saw seven times for
his performance alone. He had a good career going and was able to
pick his roles. It was a major coup for Pepo to get Bazik to join our
fledgling theatre with its uncertain future, but join he did. Like the
rest of us, he was captivated by the prospect of getting closer to a
vision of world theatre.

Our first venture was an evening of four one-act plays, two of
them serious and two funny, by various European authors. We rented
a variety of halls, some with less than ideal backstage facilities, but no
matter. We hung out our shingle that announced AN EVENING OF
ONE-ACT PLAYS! for want of a better title. People came, and not just
family and friends—they actually bought tickets. Word got around
that there was something interesting happening, and that some young
renegade actors were making it happen. Why they came probably had
to do with a general dearth of live entertainment in those days. People
still felt the stresses of wartime and the need for release.

None of us was in great shape financially. Nobody had much, but
whenever anyone had any kind of windfall, he or she shared. Luckily,
I had parents; those were my resources, and they allowed me to share
them, too. My father was on a fixed salary as a health department official of the Histadrut, the federation of labor. My mother, resourceful
as always, managed to augment my father's income by putting to use
what she'd learned about corset making in Vienna. When it appeared
that the actors of the fledgling company needed a little boost, she fed
not only me but them also. My father, though always a little more
cautious than my mother, went along. Though they still voiced doubts
about my choice of a career, I think they began to believe, if not yet
in my talent, at least in my passion.

Our first venture was a modest success. Now we had to follow up
and do not just one-acters, but theatre for real. We still did not have a
name for the enterprise. After much discussion we decided upon
Teatron Cameri, "Chamber Theatre." We intended to be a small theatre of quality, and we reasoned that as chamber music was to sym-
phonic music, so chamber theatre would be to theatre. Our first real
play was Carlo Goldoni's *A Servant of Two Masters*, an eighteenth-
century commedia dell'arte piece, a grand piece of buffoonery with
mistaken identities and a sly and manipulative servant played by Ben-
Yossef. The beautiful Batya Lancet played one of the masters, I the

other. Pepo directed; he would direct all the productions at the Cameri that I participated in. He was, in fact, a much better director than actor. As an actor he had a habit of standing slightly outside the character, being amused by his own and other actors' performances. Most annoyingly, he had a habit of silently moving his lips along with the other actors' dialogue. One felt like reaching over and pinching his lips together to stop them from moving. He had a few personal quirks as a director, too: As he sat watching the performances he'd continually pick threads from the armpit area of his jacket. He went through a lot of them in short order. In America, he would have been able to deduct the purchase of jackets from his taxes as a professional expense.

By all standards, the Goldoni play was a big hit. It gave us the lift we needed to move up in the world. We rented the Mograbi Theatre, which up until then had been the home of Habimah. They had moved on to a brand-new building, one they occupy to this day. Being at the Mograbi gave us an added element of respectability in the eyes of the public, and we were now also able to print proper posters, placards, and programs. In general, we started to behave like a professional theatre company.

Working at the Mograbi was not always easy, however. The owner had no problem running the movie house upstairs, but we were live tenants, with requests and complaints that related to safe and sanitary conditions backstage. One time, three members of the company, myself included, formed a delegation to intercede with the owners, the Mograbi family, wealthy Jews originally from Iraq. One of the brothers, Avraham, managed the building, and we told him that in our opinion it was not nice to have only one toilet backstage. We asked that he build a second one so that the ladies in the company ("ladies" was an acceptable term in those days) would be able to use the new one; the men would continue to use the old facility. Mograbi heard our plea and then shrugged in a Middle Eastern gesture: "Gentlemen, I am not alone in this. I cannot make such decisions by myself. I have a brother Yaacov, a brother Shlomo, a brother Tewfik, and a sister Rakhel. I have to consult." A month later we had heard nothing. Once again we approached the man and announced: "Mr. Mograbi, we have come once more in the matter of the backstage toilet." He looked at us with sadness in his eyes and said in a plaintive voice: "My dear people, what can I do, my brother Tewfik does not understand art!"

We also toured a little. All theatre companies did, but they were locked into circuits to which our young theatre had no access. Still, despite organizational headaches, we managed to land some book-ings—and fulfill them. There were many danger zones in Palestine, especially at night when the van returning us home to Tel Aviv had to pass through areas that were unsafe because of Arab marauders and terrorists. Then there were British roadblocks. Capriciously, curfews were declared to be in force with no advance notice. They sometimes gave you a hard time at the roadblocks and tried to turn you back; no good for us, we could not afford to stay in hotels and needed to get home. It often took some fancy talking to be allowed to proceed. Yemima was good at that; her English was as fluent as mine. The others did not manage too well on their own. One time Rosa Lichtenstein was in a taxi on her way to a performance, having missed the van at the rendezvous in Tel Aviv. Apparently there had been an attack on British soldiers by the Irgun, the Jewish terrorist outfit that numbered Begin and Shamir among its members. The British put up roadblocks at once, and Rosa was stopped halfway to the town where, in just two hours, the performance was to begin. The British soldiers tried to turn her back, but she was frantic. Justly so: Without her we would have had to cancel the show. She tried to argue with the soldiers first in Hebrew, then in German, all without success. Finally, she wept real tears and shouted at the sergeant in command: "Shpektakle! T-e-a-t-e-r! *Um Gottes Willen*, I EM EIN EXTRESS!" They let her go.

There were also citywide curfews. Once all of Tel Aviv was under a dusk-to-dawn curfew, no movement was allowed on the streets whatsoever. My mother got stuck with me and two of my kibbutz buddies, plus two more friends from Jerusalem, all prevented from leaving town by the curfew and who thus had to stay at our house.

One of them was Klaus Glücksmann, a musician, who had become one of my closest friends. My relationship with Klaus, who later changed his name to Israel Gihon, endured through all the years, right up until his death in 1993, at the age of seventy-six. Despite long absences, our friendship became closer with the passage of time. Just as Otto Braun had been the younger brother I never had, Klaus became the older one.

Back then, being thrown together by the curfew was a lark, an adventure for us. The situation itself was serious enough: The British were doing house-to-house searches after the bombing of the King David Hotel in Jerusalem. All life in Tel Aviv stopped, and our problem was suddenly food and milk, since we were not prepared for all these guests. Sleeping was no problem—blankets on the floor, ornamental cushions for pillows—but food was another thing entirely. Klaus and I, over the objections of my mother, went in search of food and milk. This meant darting through backyards, over and under fences, feeling foolish and heroic at the same time. We got to a small grocery store, which was closed, of course. Luckily, the owner lived in an apartment on top; we begged, pleaded, and finally offered to sing. When this was declined, we offered money, which was accepted.

When we did not have to deal with political upheaval, we rehearsed during the day, gave performances in the evening, and had discussions far into the night about literature, acting, films, sex, theatre, politics, and any other subject that took our fancy. I recall conversations about the transitory nature of the art form we were pursuing, the notion that the memory of our work would recede and fade as soon as the curtain fell, about how audiences would forget details even of superb performances and spectacular achievements. Film did not yet enter into these discussions; we were altogether wrapped up in live and living theatre. These discussions about its pitfalls in no way discouraged us from pursuing it, just as a mountain climber, aware of the risks, would rather climb than desist.

I also continued playing and singing, sometimes to the annoyance of my colleagues, because they felt, quite rightly, that I was using them as guinea pigs to try out material and hone my skills as a pied piper. That habit stayed with me for many years; I have always preferred to rehearse before a live audience, and have been known to go to a party—and sometimes two—every single night, guitar in hand.

The repertoire we undertook to present, true to our promise, was culled from the literature of European theatre. *A Servant of Two Masters* was followed by Karel Čapek's *The Insect Play,* then Federico Garcia Lorca's *Blood Wedding,* and finally (for me, that is), Brandon Thomas's *Charley's Aunt.* In between we also managed to do an original children's play. Our company had grown: Tuvia (Herbert) Grünbaum had joined us, an excellent if also slightly crazy actor originally from Germany—are any of them ever sane and normal? Then there were Gerschon Klein and Chana Meron, both former child actors in German films. Chana later became one of Israel's leading ladies. Then there was Yossi Yadin, brother of the famous general and archaeologist Yigael Yadin. Chana and Yossi, then married to each other, had come from the army entertainment unit. Having spent a long time entertaining troops in the field, they were glad to perform before civilians in a proper theatre—and just as glad to shed their own uniforms. Years later, Chana Meron was in an airport bus in Germany about to return to Israel when terrorists bombed the bus. She lost part of a leg in the attack but was absolutely determined to return to the stage. With great courage and dogged persistence she managed not only to perform again but fill great and difficult roles with hardly a hint of a handicap.

Karl Guttman had arrived in the country while the war was still on. Born in Poland, he was educated in Vienna and started his career there. The war forced him to flee East with his young family. They settled in Galicia, Poland, in a Jewish area, far from the German threat, so they believed. To keep going as an actor, he switched from the High German of his training to Yiddish, and began a second career in that language. Then he was offered an engagement in Russia. He accepted, left his family in Lvov (the Austrian Lemberg), intending to send for them when he had made enough money in Russia, learned Russian, and began acting in yet a third language. In the midst of his engagement, he learned that Lvov had become a battleground, held, abandoned, and then reoccupied by the Russians. During one of the lulls in the battle, Karl rushed back to get his wife and child to safety, but the Nazis had taken them. He never saw them again.

With nothing to hold him and less than enchanted with Soviet society, Karl decided to make his way to Palestine, where his sister lived. Pepo and I first saw him on a rooftop where a few dozen people had been invited to a play-reading in German, Franz Werfel's *Jacobowsky and the Colonel*. Karl Guttman read the lead role, and we were captivated by both his charm and talent. Leading men as a genre were uncommon in the Hebrew theatre; everybody was a character actor. Karl, in contrast, was not only gifted but handsome as well. Pepo was determined to have Karl join the Cameri and take the lead role in our next play, Čapek's *The Insect Play*. The snag was that Karl knew no Hebrew, so another actor and I were put to work to get Karl up in the role. Since time was of the essence, he learned the entire part in Hebrew before he learned the language itself. He was damned good, too.

Karl's peregrinations continued after the war. He married a Dutch playwright, Luisa Treves, settled in Amsterdam, ran a theatre, directed plays, and served as dramaturge all in Dutch, his fifth working language in the theatre. Using his High German again, Karl served a guest director in several theatres in West Germany. In the early 1980s he directed a play in Houston, in English naturally, and the summer of 1992 found Karl directing in Bielsko-Biała, Poland—in Polish. And here I thought that I was the polyglot of the theatre and the true wandering Jew!

By the time the Cameri was halfway into its season, the war had ended. With it came a lot of anguish as the survivors revealed the true extent of the Holocaust. The Jewish settlement in Palestine mourned, but with that mourning came strengthened resolve to build a society, a self-governing one, of Jews in Palestine—forever to stand as a refuge and a home for Jews everywhere. Jews need wander no more.

This particular wandering Jew, however, realized that for some of us, the gates had opened both ways, and that the world was there to be explored. I had gotten some very decent reactions to my work at the Cameri, both in print and from audiences. But I was dissatisfied. How much of the positive reaction was due to the big-frog-in-a-small-pond syndrome? How good was I really? I needed to find out, to see if I could measure up to world standards. London beckoned. I had set my sights on the Royal Academy of Dramatic Art. My parents were willing to finance the trip, and the Cameri was willing to give me an indefinite leave of absence. I was on my way. It was November 1946.

3

...Trippingly on the Tongue

Royal Academy of Dramatic Art, 1946

My excitement about being in London was not marred by the fact that it is essentially a city of unrelieved gray—even on its brighter and sunnier days, few enough in number, it looks bleak. It does not feel bleak, however. The dead things are not really dead, the past is there as more than a memorial. London Bridge, Beefeaters, the Tower—you can drive on the bridge, talk to the beefeaters, smell the musty odor of the Tower, and be lectured by the guards. The Houses of Parliament are working institutions, Buckingham Palace is inhabited, and you can even tell whether or not the main inhabitant is at home—the flag flies when She's there. Actually, when I got to London it was a He, King George VI.

The Royal Academy of Dramatic Art (RADA)was also a venerable institution. The rehearsal rooms were somewhat musty and anti-quated. Some of them were quaint. Most of them were serviceable. The theatre, the central place where the students got to show their wares, ready or not, and where I was to have my trial at the audition, was well appointed. A decent production could be mounted with good sets and proper lights. The principal of RADA, Sir Kenneth Barnes, presided over the Academy in a sometimes bumbling, some-times autocratic fashion. He prided himself on the fact that his sister,

Dame Irene Vanbrugh, was a noted actress. The box where he held court was placed in our little theatre in the same strategic place where the royal box would be in a big theatre. At times his huge dog, Masha, would sit beside him in the box, and you had the impression that your success or failure depended on Masha's ear-wiggling. Sir Kenneth was obviously knowledgeable in the ways of the theatre, but old-fashioned and not too accommodating to experimentation. "What's he doing that for?" he might grumble audibly in the middle of a performance. Then one of the teachers would whisper an explanation. "Oh," he would say, just as loudly as before, "oh, it's mime. Well, I s'ppose that's all right. Still—he could have used a real broom—"

One of the pieces I was required to do at my audition for RADA was from Hamlet: "Speak the speech, I pray you, as I pronounced it to you, trippingly on the tongue. But if you mouth it, as many of your players do, I had as lief the town crier spoke my lines." I hoped that my interpretation would be looked upon for accuracy of pronunciation, passion of delivery, and the promise of a developing talent. What worried me was that they should fault me for not being a proper Hamlet. I knew that I was not exactly what I myself would have wanted in a Hamlet. I was sure that the etched profile, the posture, and the sense of style demanded for this foremost of classical roles were not attributes I possessed. I considered myself a character actor. I guess I still do. Little did I know, however, that such distinctions are at bottom meaningless and who said that Hamlet is not a character role? Labeling of this kind is somewhat demeaning. Talent is talent; in itself some talent may be limited in scope. But shove it into a pigeonhole and you confine and limit it even further.

Of course, while an etched profile is not something you can acquire, style and posture were some of the things I had hoped to learn by coming to the breeding ground of classical actors in the English language. It would have been defeating if they turned me down for not possessing what I was intent on acquiring. As it was, I did have quite a lot to show that other would-be entrants to RADA did not: a respectable amount of experience as a professional. Still, I trembled a little as I did my audition pieces. There were three of them and I have forgotten what the other two were, only that one of them was from a modern play, by Priestley or some such. I had paid my entrance fee and filled out all the necessary papers prior to leaving Palestine, but this was the important event.

At the audition, Sir Kenneth sat in his booth with a couple of faculty members and made notes. He did more than that; he had a habit of making comments and asking questions of those around him while you were trying to perform. In a regular theatre this would have caused the ushers to ask him to leave, but this was the Academy and he was the Principal and could be as eccentric and crotchety as he liked. Later, as a student, one got used to this disturbing habit but at the exam it was downright vexing.

I spoke the speech, trippingly on the tongue, and was accepted. Frankly, I would not have known what to do had I not been. My father had paid for my passage: Haifa to Marseilles by boat, a train to Paris, and—my first plane ride—Paris to London. I had no return ticket but enough money to get me settled in and start a modest student's life. In fact, I had more than I had counted on because RADA liked my audition enough to give me a tuition scholarship for the two-year course. It was good enough to rent a room at 66 Abbey Road, St. John's Wood, and buy some groceries.

I was excited to be in London. My God, London, the center of an empire one had read about, the seat of a government that, through the Balfour Declaration, had permitted Jews to establish the beginnings of a homeland and then damn near ruined the chance to make it a reality. It was also the London of pomp and style, a place where one could actually see a doorman open a limousine door and with a bow say, "Good morning, milord." Nobility, royalty even, traveled the streets. London was where a pound was called sterling because it had actually been silver, a place where doctors were not paid in pounds but in guineas—nonexistent in actual coinage but one shilling more than a pound, conferring a sort of higher status on the recipient. When I found out that actors' salaries, too, were listed in guineas, I thought to myself, "My kind of place."

My landlady at Abbey Road was ancient, a former hostess at a bridge club where she still helped out. Her name was Maudie Wright. She had red hair, not her own, and gleaming teeth, also not her own. She also promised to be tolerant of the ways of youth. "I know you young people and the company you keep. . . . ," she cackled, obviously delighted with her own liberal savoir faire. By and large she kept her promise, too—being far more concerned with the contents of her grocery shelf and the refrigerator than with the morals of her boarder. England was still in the throes of postwar hardships, chief among them food rationing. This was new to me. Of course, I had come from an area that had also known shortages due to the war, but we had what we had; what we did not have was not scarce, it was simply unavailable. Rationing in England was something else. You guarded your ration coupon book better than your money. There was one egg per week to be had and a small packet of butter. You could get two eggs if you gave up your tablet of chocolate, or took margarine instead of butter. If you had a lot of money you could get other things, too, but who in my circle had a lot of money? Grocers might wink at a lady shopper and ask in inimitable cockney whispers, "Would ya loike a bit of the uvver, luv?" "The other" was any commodity he kept under the counter and whose name was not to be mentioned aloud. It was not until I enjoyed the hospitality of some rich Jews who opened their houses to students from Palestine that I managed to partake of luxury items like smoked salmon, fancy cheeses, and corned beef that didn't come from a tin (the only way I had known it before, British army style).

Unlike my landlady, RADA insisted on enforcing rules, something that I felt too grown-up to accept. Miss Brown, the registrar, a tall, lanky English lady, singularly unattractive and with buckteeth, insisted that all students sign in upon arrival at a big board in the entrance hall by transferring their name cards from one column to the next. It was not too difficult to get around this one: You asked a friend who intended to be there on time to do his own name and then yours. In return you promised to do the same for him should the need arise. Not to get there every day at the appointed time was for me not just a student's laziness or sloth. The were some classes I simply did not need. Voice production, for example; mine has always been excellent. This was not something I ever needed to learn; in fact, I could have taught it. A waste of time for me. General assembly with Sir K. leading off with the Lord's Prayer I could also cheerfully miss. My classmates, among them John Neville and Dorothy Tutin, faithfully attended everything.

Some things I rushed to attend because I thought I might find them useful. Fencing, for example, would give me the skill for some Shakespearean fight scenes. I bought my fencing gear, as required, and dutifully attended the classes. No role I have ever had to play, then or since, called for me to engage in swordplay. Oh well. One subject, elocution classes, given by Mr. Clifford Turner, I felt would give me the polished delivery in the much coveted King's English. Indeed, Mr. Turner was engaged by the Crown to give the King himself lessons. In what, you may ask? His Majesty King George VI, it seems, had a speech impediment: He stuttered. Clifford Turner was hired to teach him not to, or at least to make the stammer a little less obvious.

Despite the fact that he was a funny bird and an archetypal Englishman, Mr. Turner taught good stuff, albeit at times with silly tongue-twisters or poems whose purpose was to get a melodic line of speech to rise and fall with the meter: "Lily O'Grady, silly and shady, longing to be a *lazy* lady." (The "lazy" was supposed to be about a fourth interval higher on the musical scale.) Edward Woodward, later the star of some very good films and of the TV series *The Equalizer,* was in my class at RADA. Mr. Turner called on him, far more often than on any other student, to recite pieces. Some of my classmates developed a bit of an inferiority feeling about this. It didn't bother me, though. I knew why Turner was doing it. Teddy Woodward was not any better at this than any of the rest of us. Clifford Turner, elocution freak that he was, simply liked to say Teddy's name and say it trippingly on the tongue just as Will the Bard had commanded: "Next, Edward Wood*ward*," with the *-ward* rising up a fourth on the musical scale.

Another rule was harder to circumvent. No one was permitted to direct until his or her last term. I was intent on directing long before that because ever since my stay in Paris en route to London *Antigone* had been burning in my mind.

During those few days I spent in Paris on the way to London I managed to see a few plays, among them *Ardèle* and *Antigone* by Jean Anouilh. I was captivated, especially by the latter play, for which I retain a fondness to this day. What especially intrigued me about this play was that although it represents the retelling of an ancient saga, it is essentially a modern play. It was written during the days of the German occupation of France and performed right under the noses of the Germans, who realized only too late that the work was perceived by the French public as an allegory of their own situation: the small but unshakable voice of the individual saying no to the might of the state. Although the playwright's intent was not primarily political in nature, the play was colored by events of Anouilh's time and reflected his vision of the emotional and political conflicts inherent in the ancient Greek tragedy.

I summoned whatever amount of chutzpah I could muster and looked up Jean Anouilh. I, a twenty-two-year-old actor and soon-again-to-be drama student, sent a calling card to the celebrated author, asking to meet him. The Tel Aviv printer who did our programs and posters had thrown in a bonus for three of us "directors"—free business cards with the Cameri Theatre logo on them. Mine had Hebrew on one side with "Meir" on it; the English side listed the "Theodore" I was to become again. The calling card was an ego trip that went nowhere in a country like Israel, where everybody knew you too well to be impressed, but it worked in France. Anouilh received me in his apartment very graciously, and we talked over coffee and cakes. I had told him I wanted to meet with him because the Cameri was seeking his permission to perform *Antigone* in Hebrew. He seemed pleased at the request, and even more pleased at my praise of the play (which was, in retrospect, overly gushing—but what the hell; if actors are stroked by lavish praise, why not authors?). The praise was genuine enough; so was the gushing, simply because I did not know any better. Anouilh rightly surmised that these performance rights were hardly likely to make him any money, and he gave me a handwritten note agreeing in principle to a Hebrew production. Having gained this coveted audience with a master dramatist, I dutifully sent the note to the Cameri.

By the time I had settled into my second trimester at RADA, I'd become determined to stage at least one act of *Antigone* myself. I asked the redoubtable Miss Brown. No dice. I pleaded, I even used a mixture of what I thought was personal magnetism with a dose of flattery. Nothing doing. What could you expect from a woman who had been overheard telling a young female student: "The trouble with you, my deah, is the same as 'tis with me—no sex." Through her buckteeth.

So I lapsed into a version of my signing-in trick. I had a senior sign his name for me as director of record for *Antigone*. The trouble was, the piece received a prize for direction, and my very embarrassed colleague did not want to accept it; false feathers, y'know. I pleaded with him, let him get the glory and let me not get into trouble. He thought it was stupid; people should not be penalized for doing good work, let alone excellent work. In the end, he took the damn prize, but let Sir Kenneth know that I had done the major portion of the work as his "assistant." They bought that; they had no rule about assistants. I thought of this incident years later, when some of my black-listed writer friends had to have their finest work produced under either a fictitious name or someone else's.

None of this mattered at the moment. The task at hand was to take note of the differences between my previous training as an actor and the British concept of stage performing. I cannot call it a school of acting because, in a sense, there was no discernible school of acting on the London stage. Nor could the training at RADA conceivably be defined as part of a system. RADA taught the various externals that characterize British acting: the honing and perfecting of the "instrument"—the actor's body, his movement, his voice, his speech, his ability to convey poetry or prose (and to know the difference between the two). The Method people had simply assumed that a serious actor would pay some attention to these elements. The emphasis there had been on the emotional and psychological demands of a role, and it was taken for granted that the actor's physical and verbal prowess would be called into action to serve those demands. The external would fall into place as long as the internal elements were right. The British, on the other hand, worked from the outside in. The assumption here was that the emotional nucleus of the role would come about because the actor looked right, dressed right, walked correctly, said the text with the correct emphases, and conveyed the author's meaning—with seemingly little reference to himself. At first that was startling, to say the least. The result, in most instances, was what is known as presentational acting. The more thorough teachers, especially those who directed plays and scenes, might analyze the play and encourage the actor to analyze his role, but none would ever suggest that the actor examine his own psyche on the road to giving a performance.

Clearly, there were flaws in this approach, just as there had been shortcomings in the Method I had been taught. As I had examined the Method at the Habimah and had found it wanting in some respects, so I was now obliged to examine the British approach. The conclusion was inescapable that in both instances it was not so much the approaches themselves that were to blame for the shortcomings I found there, but rather their abuse, based on half-understood terminology and their acceptance as fetishes, rather than as flexible tools of stagecraft. Stanislavsky himself was painfully aware of these pitfalls when he wrote: "The pupils at the Studio had accepted the system more or less on trust. They learned the terms and then used the terminology to cover their own perceptions which were at times creative but mostly merely theatrical. Most of these were the old artificial habits, filled with theatricality and theatrical stencils (stereotypes). Then they accepted this to be the newness of which the system talked. . . . Many learned to concentrate, but this only made them make all their old mistakes and display them more and more, perfecting those mistakes, so to say. In that way the actor feels himself comfortable on the stage and he accepts this incorrectness of theatrical mood for 'living his part.' Then the actors are convinced that they have understood all, that my system has brought them unusual help, and they touchingly thank me and praise me for the discovery of a new America. But—'I will find but ill health in that praise.'"[1] This was written in 1924, the year of my birth.

Similarly, many users of the British system made a fetish of externalization and gave their blessing to a sacrament that bore testimony to no faith at all. When pomp and ceremony become ends in themselves, when nobility is not to be found beneath the heavy damask robes,

1. Konstantin Sergeyevich Stanislavsky, *My Life in Art.*

then the exercise may, at first glance, be beautiful, but it is ultimately neither instructive nor uplifting. Where do you go after the first gasp of surprise at a display of splendor, when little else is forthcoming? You remain with empty gestures and posturing. Again, it is not the system that is at fault. Such acting was known and dismissed as flawed even in Shakespeare's time. He spoke of "players that I have seen play and heard others praise, and that highly, not to speak it profanely, that neither having the accent of Christian nor the gait of Christian, pagan, nor man, have so strutted and bellow'd, that I have thought some of nature's journeymen had made men, and not made them well, they imitated humanity so abominably." Through Hamlet's mouth, he attempted to give instructions for avoiding overacting such as "Do not saw the air with your hands, thus"—but even in less immoderate man-ifestations, such externalism created only a grammar of expression, as it were, and was as removed from real language as mere grammar is apt to be. This was no isolated phenomenon in the history of the theatre. We find the complaint echoed by the eighteenth-century dramatist Gotthold Ephraim Lessing, who declared mournfully: "We may have actors but no art of acting."

I was determined to use the best of both systems, in a fusion of presentational acting on the one hand and the Method on the other, and discard that which was ballast and therefore useless. To this day I use my own analytical faculties to arrive at the core of the characters I portray, and call upon technical and external skills as needed. I still resist dragging too much self-analysis into the process; I let Theo the actor borrow only sparingly from Theo the person. If my approach to the work gets bad marks from the proponents of either school of thought, so be it. I have to serve a playwright, not a theory of acting; my task is to convey his work to an audience and, to that end, choose my own tools.

Although I didn't find London bleak, living there so soon after the war's end was no picnic, either. It was not only the food rationing; the general atmosphere was still permeated by a spirit of austerity. The British are a remarkably disciplined people, and self-restraint was a virtue much in evidence. Everything was still fairly regimented, and queuing up seemed almost a hallowed activity at bus stops, ticket coun-ters, stores, and entrances to cafés. The Hungarian-born humorist George Mikes wrote in his book *How to Be an Alien*, "An Englishman, even when alone, forms an orderly queue of one." The nearly univer-sal reverence for the Royal Family was another trait that was baffling at first for any newcomer, but soon accepted as the way things had to be. "God Save the Queen" was played at theatres before the show and in cinemas after the last screening of the evening. I recall a time I tried to move toward the exit after a seeing a film, only to be stopped by a British colonel type who barred my way with a haughty "Sir, the Queen!" For a second I fantasized that she was actually present in the theatre; but of course he was only referring to the film on the screen, which showed a fluttering Union Jack with a soundtrack of "God Save the Queen." Feeling guilty, I stood dutifully at attention.

The respect for the Royals extended even to Hyde Park, where anything and everything by way of free expression seemed to be tolerated and even encouraged—with the exception of insulting references to the Royal Family.

Hyde Park Corner offered the most amazing—and amusing— array of eccentrics I've ever come across in one place. Firebrand political speakers of the entire spectrum, from the far left to the far right; religious fanatics and also gentle ascetics, poets, nationalists of all kinds, African, Irish, Welsh, Scottish, Pakistani, Indian—it was a feast of accents for a linguist and a delight for a collector of the well-turned phrase. I went as often as I could. One of my favorite speakers attracted big crowds, and justly so, for he was colorful and irreverent as all hell. When it came to distributing barbs, he spared no one, including the Royal Family, which got him arrested on misdemeanor charges and landed him in jail with some regularity. I remember him well: His name was Edward Ray. He had a rasping voice, hoarse from overuse and wrong placement; he might have benefited from lessons given by Clifford Turner. Both the content and the delivery of his discourses were often hilarious and always outrageous. I remember almost verbatim one tirade he delivered:

"Don't talk to me about the army. I was in the army. One fine day I get a letter with a picture of the chief inmate of Buckingham Palace on the front of it [that's how he put it, honest!], inside there's a postal order for ten shillings and a message: Welcome to the Army! Well, that's nice, ain't it? Bloody nice. Old George saying hello. And ten bob, too. Well, I was to find out that that ten bob was the first part of the great fraud called the British army. A lawyer told me. 'E was in the army, too; I met him when he was moppin' up the piss-house. Look out, he said, they'll get you. He was right. Next thing I know, I'm in the mess hall. All of a sudden, plates come flyin' through the air. Whatever was on them stuck to them fast. You know something? Last week when I was a guest of His Majesty's at Brixton Prison for failin' to address a meeting in this here park in a respectful manner, they *brought* the food to me—not so in the army. I asked the sergeant, 'Sarge,' I said pointing to the plate, 'what is it?' He said, 'Rissole.' And

I said: 'I know a little bit about the inner and outer anatomy of things and according to my hexpert knowledge this isn't called rissole, it's *arsehole!* It was no coincidence," he continued, "that on the day I, Edward Ray, joined the British army, Hitler's army started to retreat. Why? Göring told him. He said, 'Adolf,' he says, 'Adolf, beware. One intelligent man has joined the British army!'"

Equally interesting were the listeners, a mixture of regulars and tourists, the merely curious onlookers, and, more especially, the vocal hecklers. There was one tall man, usually accompanied by a little boy, presumably his son, who would go from group to group, from speaker to speaker, and wait until the orator had to pause for breath. Then he would utter in a loud voice: "Why?" He would not even wait for an answer before moving on to attack the next speaker. This man also had a nervous tick that made him blink furiously all the time and a knack of not looking at the speaker at all but sideways with his right ear toward the speaker. Once I was witness to this man lending his ear to an elderly, gentle missionary type, and when the speaker opened his arms and said, "Name one man who has done more for the world than Jesus Christ," the heckler shouted, blinking furiously, "Danny Kaye!" And left the group in search of another target. I took it all in; you never know when one of these characters might come in handy on stage.

Instead of the usual six trimesters, I only did four at RADA. They made me skip two of them—as a compliment to my talent and my ability to absorb what was being taught, so they said. They also might have been relieved to get rid of someone who broke so many rules.

Neither the teachers nor my classmates at RADA seemed to have any understanding of my background, either as an actor or as a human being. Nor any curiosity about them, either. I ascribed this to the English trait of remoteness and casualness where personal relationships were concerned. Though these are generalizations, and although over the years I have had close friendships with Englishmen who were as warm and involved as any human beings I have ever known, those first contacts in London were quite discouraging. I was wondering whether the cool attitudes had anything to do with my being a Jew—or a Jew hailing from Palestine, given the recent history of the British authorities toward the Jewish settlers—but that was possibly Jewish paranoia. None of that coolness bore the marks of classical Jew-hatred. None of the religious or racial prejudice I had experienced in my early youth seemed to be at work here. It soon became clear that I was not singled out for this treatment in the Academy: Foreign students from other countries and backgrounds were treated similarly. Though some Jewish contemporaries of mine in other schools claimed that they were experiencing anti-Semitism, I was convinced that it was xenophobia, pure and simple. The British were suspicious of *anything* that was un-English; and although in recent years television has made more foreign stuff familiar to the English, a lot of them still are. Later, when I decided to make my permanent home in the United States instead of Britain, it was partly due to a realization that carrying a British passport would make me British in the eyes of my neighbors and coworkers, but could never make me English. I had entered Britain on the sort of British passport carried by colonials. Its color was brown, in contrast to the regular passport, which is blue. After a couple of years I applied for full British citizenship, and received the blue passport. No matter: In the end, the eight years I spent in England made me no more than an articulate foreigner. By contrast, eight weeks in New York suffice to make you feel like a New Yorker, and a couple of years in the States like an American.

Graduating early from the Academy—I did barely a year and a half there—came as something of a relief to me, too. Even though I lived frugally, I could barely make ends meet. In order to augment what little funds I had, I gave a few Hebrew lessons, but they paid very little. There was one month, I recall, in which I ate dinner no more than thirteen times. Weekday lunches were okay.: The cafeteria at RADA, bad though the food was, furnished enough sustenance. But had it not been for British Jews who took Palestinian students under their wing, I would have been worse off still. I did play for my supper, to be sure, but I never minded that. One man in particular, Abraham Perlmut by name, was very kind to me. He and his family had extended a standing invitation to Friday-night dinners at their house. I needed that, not just for the food but for the warmth of friendship in a place and among people who made me feel comfortable and at home.

The year was 1947, and there were many comings and goings of Jewish leaders from Palestine who arrived in London in search of political support and money—both essential if an independent Jewish state were ever to become reality. Perlmut played host to any visiting dignitary from the *yishuv* in Palestine. And so it came about that I spent one entire Friday evening in the company of David Ben Gurion. He always wore an open-necked shirt, the uniform of the kibbutznik, and his tousled, leonine white hair seemed to have but a nodding acquaintance with a comb. At the same time, he exuded an aura of authority that was in marked contrast to his completely informal appearance. He was, in fact, more of a scholar than a farmer. If ideology had driven him to kibbutz life (as at an earlier time it had motivated me also), his foremost interest was the classics. The conversation was fascinating: Ben Gurion was interested in the Bible and the Talmud, naturally, but also in Greek history and literature, in which he was exceedingly well versed. B.G.—as everyone referred to him—was also a lover of the arts, including the theatre. He never went to the movies, however. He is supposed once to have said in reply to a question about his refusal to see films, "Why should I? What's the point? I have seen Sarah Bernhardt."

If B.G. was a unique kind of prime minister, shedding neither the informal dress of the kibbutz nor his Eastern European outlook on politics, his wife, Paula, seemed even less adaptable to the life top government officials were supposed to lead. With her, it was always business as usual, her business being the care and nurture of her husband. If he had a cold, she would think nothing of barging in while the Old Man (yes, that's capitalized) was conducting a high-level meeting and insisting on taking his temperature. All Tel Aviv knew about the time she called to the sentry at the front gate and ordered him to go to the corner for half a kilo of butter. When the guard protested, saying that he was not allowed to leave his post, she insisted, "Go to the store; you'll be back in five minutes, what's the big deal?" The soldier argued with a pained expression, "Mrs. Ben Gurion, I can't, I simply can't. I have to stay here and guard your husband." She said, "Nonsense. Run to the store, I'll look after your rifle."

The best apocryphal story about Paula went like this: In the middle of the night she prods her sleeping husband. "David, David—listen to me." B.G. comes half awake and says, "What is it? What time is it?" He looks at the bedside clock and says, "Three o'clock in the morning, has something happened?" "Nothing has happened," she says, "I just couldn't sleep and kept thinking. Tell me something. In all these years we've been married, did you ever think that one day you would be sleeping with a prime minister's wife?"

As we sat in the Perlmuts' living room that night in 1947, and I sang and played the guitar, the Old Man requested some songs. It is important to remember that Ben Gurion, who was born in Pinsk, a Polish town near the Russian border, was passionate about the propagation of the Hebrew language. He had often disdainfully dismissed Yiddish, his own mother tongue, as a diaspora language "rightfully doomed to extinction." But that night B.G. asked me to sing in Yiddish, in particular one song that had been the anthem of the Zionist labor movement in Eastern Europe. I obliged and sang, "*Mir hoybn di hent kegn mizrach un shvern, bay Tzion zayn folk un zayn heyliger erd . . .*" (We raise our hands toward the East in an oath to Zion, to our people and our holy soil . . .) As I sang I detected a tear in the Old Man's eye. Forty-five years later, in the summer of 1992, I helped lead a large group of delegates from all over the world celebrating the ninetieth anniversary of the Jewish National Fund. We visited Ben Gurion's grave in the Negev desert at Sdeh Boker. The organizers of the convention had asked me to say a few words at the gravesite. Instead, I sang, "*Mir hoybn di hent kegn mizrach un shvern . . .*" My thoughts went back to that evening so many years ago, to this man who had raised a nation from the ashes of history, and this time the tears were in my eyes.

As was the custom at the end of the school years at RADA, a few choice students were picked to perform the play that marked the closing ceremonies. This was a big deal. The ceremonies were held at a large West End theatre and the Academy's patron, Queen Mary the Queen Mother, was to be in attendance. I was one of the five performers chosen. The play for the class of 1948 was a historical piece by the Danish playwright Kai Munk (the title escapes me), set some two hundred years earlier. I played an archbishop, resplendent in robes, and the others portrayed courtiers of high rank. The play went well, although everyone was nervous because the Queen Mum was sitting in the royal box, and she had a reputation of missing nothing. As is the custom, during intermission the actors were ushered into the sitting-room portion of the royal box to be presented to Her Majesty. Naturally, we had been briefed on court behavior: deep bows for the men, deep curtsies for the ladies. One of the actresses dutifully performed the very low court curtsy, but she lost her balance somewhat and wobbled on the way down. The Queen Mother looked at her with a mixture of stern rebuke and kindly tolerance, and then told her to go back to the door, approach, and do it all over again. "Not because of me, my dear," she said, "but because of you. You are training to behave on stage as queens, duchesses, and ladies of the court, and you must be able to do it properly." A lesson to remember.

So now it is late summer in 1948. I am through with my studies at RADA, having finished with a diploma and honorable mention. So now what? Get work as an actor, naturally. A few problems: Is a "colonial" entitled to work freely in Britain; will both the government and British Actors' Equity agree; and who will give me a job? Strangely, the last of these problems was the easiest: Many producers and practically all the agents had attended the final RADA performance and were ready, pen in hand, to give those who showed the most promise a chance. But for cutting through the red tape, I needed champions and defenders in my corner. As it turned out I needed no more than one, because the one I had was Dame Sybil Thorndike, one of the most respected, indeed revered, actresses of the British stage. She had seen me perform when she judged a RADA competition, and had commended "the zest, vigor, and talent of this young actor from Palestine." When I needed a recommendation to the Home Office for a change from a student status to permanent residence, she repeated her comments, adding that what I had to offer would, in her opinion, make a welcome contribution to the British theatre. With such words coming from Dame Sybil, who was to argue otherwise? Certainly no layman bureaucrat, nor her colleagues at British Equity, either. With that the government granted my change of status, and I have held active membership in British Actors' Equity ever since.

One of the first theatrical engagements that came my way was actually no engagement at all. In today's American theatre it might be called a workshop production; in London it was more of a vanity undertaking than anything else. The play was called *Citizen of the World,* by C. E. Webber, and the director was Kenneth Tynan, the undisputed enfant terrible of London's theatre society. His reputation as a brilliant eccentric had followed him from his student days at Oxford. There he had been so outstanding a student that he was clearly in line to receive a First, the British equivalent of summa cum laude. But he was also iconoclastic, uncontrollable, and an inveterate breaker of rules. It was rumored that in his senior year at Oxford, the master of Ken's college had announced at a faculty meeting, "Gentlemen, we have a grave problem. How can we prevent Mr. Tynan from receiving a First?" They could not and did not.

Ken Tynan actually had no ambition to become a director at all but was pursuing his destiny as a major theatre critic. To that end, he was determined to try his hand at various facets of the professional theatre, including dramaturgy, acting, and directing. He did all of those with varying results. My friend Stella Richman had introduced me to Ken, and needless to say, I was as impressed as the rest of London by his sharp intellect. When he asked me to take part in his workshop presentation of the Webber play, I was flattered and I accepted. Both Stella and I had roles in the piece, as I recall. I was an industrialist involved in high finance and intrigue; Stella played my mistress. As a director, Ken was less of a guide than he should have been, less inclined to use the actors' known qualities or to uncover their hidden abilities. He was like a chess player, moving the actors around, physically and mentally, like so many chess pieces. He did not do this as an ego trip born of a desire to dominate; to him it was all a legitimate exercise of stagecraft. But it was less than satisfying for us. We did not get paid to do this work; we had all volunteered, but even if we had been paid, actors should never be treated as guinea pigs or lab animals. At the time, none of this seemed so terrible. It was only for a couple of performances—what the hell, no big deal. We still liked Ken despite it all.

Besides, he gave good parties. Not that attending Ken's parties was altogether safe. He had a mischievous streak in him, sometimes bordering on the malicious. One night there was a mammoth gathering at Ken's house, a triplex of two floors over a giant living room. A multitude of people was milling around, the drinks flowing freely, although there was hardly any food. I have often thought how strange it is that WASP hosts think mainly of the drinks part of entertaining; no self-respecting Jewish host would neglect the food part. Anyhow, at this party there was the usual pairing off of couples, some of whom would from time to time more or less discreetly disappear into the upstairs bedroom. They would reappear sometime later, a little red in the face but otherwise not much the worse for wear. What they did not know was that Ken had acquired one of the first of the newfangled devices called tape recorders and had installed the machine under his bed. A couple of hours later, with the party still in full swing, he brought the machine downstairs and played the tape for all the assembled—all the conversations, the grunts, squeals, and related sound effects—as the "performers" got redder and redder in the face. Some of them, I was told, seriously considered emigrating to Kenya.

Ken Tynan's attempt to try his hand at acting was to be remembered as a misadventure of no small proportions. The setting was anything but modest: He appeared at the Old Vic in a production of *Hamlet* starring Alec Guinness. I have vivid memories of the performance. In the first place, that splendid actor Alec Guinness was, alas, a very disappointing Hamlet. He was all cerebral, cold, sometimes vengeful but without the apparent anguish or inner torture that marks Hamlet's character. There alone the production fell apart. As for Ken Tynan, he portrayed the Player King as if he'd paid as little heed to his director as his character did to Hamlet's advice to the players. To those of us who knew Ken well, it was not only embarrassing but painful to watch; aware that Ken had a very bad stutter, we saw the effort he made to suppress it and we kept wondering why he had insisted on subjecting himself—and us—to the torture.

No one fresh out of RADA dared hope for the West End, the British equivalent of Broadway—if you were fortunate enough to obtain work, it was likely to be in weekly repertory in the "provinces," that is to say outside London. In my case, that meant a season in Buxton, Darbyshire, followed by a couple of engagements in a place called Chorlton-cum-Hardy. It was theatre all right, but weekly rep presented a pace of working which was totally outside of anything I had been used to before. We did ten plays—count them— in the space of eleven weeks. The very first week was fairly easy, it just meant rehearsing with evenings free. Even so, a week seemed awfully short to me, who had never been in a play that rehearsed for less than two months—but it was manageable. The weeks that followed, however, were unbelievable. You opened a play on Monday night, cele- brated with a couple of pints of mild-and-bitter and went to bed really early. (Mild-and-bitter is beer drawn from a tap. It is a far cry from American beer, being lukewarm and, in color and temperature, remi- niscent of vintage urine. No wonder the Brits coined "pissed" as a description of drunkenness.) On Tuesday morning, you started work on the following week's play, reading through it before lunch and starting the blocking, script in hand, in the afternoon. ("Blocking" means staging the moves of a play.) After a break of some two and a half hours, you reported to the theatre for the evening performance of the current play. Wednesday morning, the blocking for the next play was completed. There was no rehearsal in the afternoon because we played two performances on Wednesdays, matinee and evening. Through it all everybody learned lines and bounced them off each other during free moments because on Thursday you were no longer supposed to work with scripts in hand and were expected to know all the lines. If you got stuck, the stage manager or assistant stage man- ager, known as the ASM,[2] prompted you; essentially from then on we just worked on the play, running scenes, running acts, both Thursday and Friday.

The Saturday routine was the same as Wednesday, rehearsal only in the morning and two performances of the current play in the after- noon and evening. Basically the Saturday morning was a full run- through of the play, with all the props and costumes but without scenery, as the sets for the current play were still in place. We had to work around them. Saturday night was the closing performance of the current play; the crew worked into the wee hours to strike the sets

2. As in any field, professional lingo could head to amusing misunderstandings. After attending a play in the country, the Duchess of Kent visited backstage. As the cast and crew were presented to her, she asked a young woman, "And what do you do, my dear?" The girl replied, "I am ASM-ing, Your Royal Highness." The duchess looked puzzled, clearly wondering what "ay-ess-emm-ing" might mean, until the theatre manager explained: "ASM stands for assistant stage manager. People in the theatre have as little trouble with these terms as Buckingham Palace has with HRH."

and put up the new ones. Daytime work on Sunday was reserved for technical rehearsals so that we could get acquainted with the new walls and furniture and the new lights and sound. Sunday night was a run-through rehearsal, also mostly technical in nature, with some necessary stops and starts. It was not until Monday afternoon that we got the first and only clean, coherent dress rehearsal and that very night we opened. Before leaving the theatre we were handed the scripts for the next play, so that we could start the routine all over again next morning. If anything was apt to deglamorize the life and work of an actor, this was surely it. It is worth mentioning that the plays we did were not just of the light drawing-room summer variety; one of the first I did in weekly rep was Shaw's *Saint Joan*. We were proud professionals, presenting performances of quality, something to which the audience was surely entitled. Despite the hectic pace and the hardship, we loved our work.

Contact with home was limited to correspondence; who had money for phone calls? My parents did not even have a telephone in the apartment. Before the advent of the telex and the fax, the only rapid form of communication besides the telephone was the telegram, but nobody in his right mind would send one to a Jewish mother, who between receiving it and opening the envelope might have three heart attacks. Among Jews, telegrams were used solely to convey news of disaster. In any event, my parents had no cause to worry; they knew I was safe. Now that I was working, I was no longer a financial burden to them, either. I did worry about them, though. Nineteen forty-eight was a fateful year in the life of the *yishuv*, the Jewish community, in Palestine. It was the year the British were to give up their Mandate amid turmoil and threats by all the Arabs of the area against the Jews, and against any attempt to establish a Jewish state. When the British left and immediate hostilities broke out, most of the young Jewish students from Palestine packed their bags and returned home to join the newly formed defense units organized along the lines of the previous underground forces of the Haganah.

I was confronted with a weighty personal dilemma. The decision I ultimately made not to return was made lighter by the fact that I was not faced with a choice between acting and fighting, but rather between acting and acting. My colleagues in the theatre back home had urged me to return with the others, not to join any fighting unit but to bolster morale by keeping the theatres open and performing before civilian and army audiences. Indeed, all those who had been professional actors prior to the war were doing exactly that. To be frank, I was reluctant to return for the sole purpose of taking up the acting chores I had left behind two years earlier, even though times of national emergency had put a higher purpose on the enterprise. Selfishly, no doubt, I wanted to continue on the road I had embarked upon. It was not an easy decision I made then. A few of my contemporaries regarded what I did as a character flaw, if not a downright act of desertion. And there were some, even some who had been close friends and colleagues, who snubbed my parents for a long time in public and shunned them in private—visiting the sins of the sons on the fathers, as it were. That hurt.

More painful was the loss of Otto Braun, my friend and classmate from Vienna. He had been a member of the first kibbutz to be overrun by Jordanian troops and Palestinian Arabs. Although the kibbutz put up fierce resistance, in the end it was almost leveled and my friend was killed. Afterwards the kibbutz put together a book of remembrances, and I received a letter in London that asked me to write an obituary piece for Otto. It was some of the hardest writing I ever had to do.

All this has been over for a long time now. Nobody seems to be nursing bad feelings from those times anymore; in fact, I've been regarded as a favorite son and "persona grata" by the Israelis for years. But my recollection of all this has not been made easier by the passage of time. Otto Braun's death added to my feelings of guilt. To the good, perhaps: Just as the thought of having been spared during the Holocaust caused me to feel a lifelong commitment to the Jewish people as a whole, so did these memories intensify my lifelong commitment to the welfare and survival of Israel. If, over the many years, I have been moved to champion the cause of Israel with a greater intensity than many of my contemporaries, then a contributing factor may have been a half-conscious desire to atone. In me there remains a small, still voice that asks whether I can ever fully acquit myself in my own mind. But I would hate to think that the prime motivation in any human being's life is a feeling of guilt or inadequacy—a notion that can take hold after repeated exposure to facile analyses of the Jewish psyche by many American Jewish writers. Surely one can be moved to perform good deeds for other and better reasons as well; one hopes that the nobler instincts are a part of us just as much as is our reaction to our own failures. I have long believed that human beings act from dual motivations. As a teenager I wrote a poem about the nature of man, saying that man is apt to rise from a brothel bed to commit the finest, noblest deeds. Although I failed to fight in the War of Independence, I have fought for Israel much and often since then, and I have done it with weapons I know how to use much better than guns.

The octogenarian Pablo Casals said something in an interview that struck a very responsive chord in me, it so closely mirrored my own feelings. He said, "My cello is my weapon. I choose where I play, what I play, and before whom I play." My guitar and I do the same. I also choose what I say, and where, and before whom.

I remained in London, and continued to work at my craft.

4

The Kindness of Strangers

London, 1948

I'd been in England close to three years, and the ups and downs of a struggling actor's career had begun to take their toll. I was nowhere near defeat, but I had started to wonder whether all this would lead to any more than just the taste of world theatre. Perhaps the training at RADA and on the British stage was no more than preparation for an inevitable return to Palestine—now Israel—and to the Cameri, which—nominally at least—was holding my place open should the prodigal son decide to expiate his earlier sins and return. The year 1949 found me in London at the Embassy Theatre, Swiss Cottage, performing in George Kaufman and Moss Hart's *You Can't Take It with You*. My role was the madly eccentric Russian ballet master Kolenkov, whose most memorable line in the play was his reply to a question regarding his student's talent for dancing: "Confidentially, she stinks!" Michael Redgrave saw the performance, came backstage afterwards, and congratulated me on giving "a very funny and refreshing performance." Unbeknownst to me, he was having dinner with Sir Laurence Olivier the following night and apparently my name came up. Olivier was in the process of casting Tennessee Williams's *A Streetcar Named Desire* at the time, and soon I was called—summoned, I guess—to the theatre to meet with the great man.

Streetcar was my first chance to perform in the West End—and in a work that had won a Pulitzer Prize the year before its author was hailed as *the* major American playwright of his time. The part of Blanche, moreover, would be played by Vivien Leigh.

It was indeed an experience. At the interview I was ushered into a room that looked as though the furnishings had been supplied from various stage sets. You took an elevator upstairs to offices above the theatre. I was ushered in by someone, but at the interview itself it was just Sir Laurence and me. I tried to hide my nervousness, and can remember little about the great man himself or what precisely transpired. He conducted the interview, had me read some lines for him, realized that accents were no problem for me, and seemed to like me. Otherwise I suppose he simply trusted Redgrave's assessment of me. He cast me initially in the small role of one of the poker players in the regular game at Stanley Kowalski's apartment. He also gave me the understudy plum of the year: both Stanley and Mitch. If I had to play either one, the general understudy would cover my regular role. Covering both leading roles created a sort of schizophrenia; the two men are so different from each other, yet part of the same milieu. Somehow, Stanley was the easier of the two to get a handle on; he is more physical, rough, irate, driven from within rather than moved by those around him. Mitch—vulnerable, touched by men, women, things, and poetry—is rough only on the outside. He is fascinated by Blanche's Southern fragility, intrigued by her weakness, and is, at first, gullible. Frankly, I could not wait to play either of them.

This, then, was the beginning of the "big time." With Sir Laurence directing, it could hardly be any bigger. The experience was both unnerving and exhilarating, for the atmosphere at the top of Mount Olympus was rarefied and allowed for only shallow breathing. Despite its being an American play, the basic elements of this production were British, of course; but there were other participants who hailed from elsewhere. The producer, Irene Mayer Selznick, was an American, daughter of one movie mogul and wife of another. She, too, was formidable. While not a threatening presence, she had been around powerful men all her life and exuded power herself, in the natural way of power that is acquired by osmosis. The two original male leads, both of whom I understudied, were neither English nor American. Bonar Colleano, playing Stanley, was Australian, and Bernard Braden, playing Mitch, Canadian. Stella was played by Renee Asherson, a well-known British actress. Vivien Leigh was at her most beautiful, a fragile kind of porcelain beauty one feared could shatter at any moment. That quality of hers was ideal for the part of Blanche. There are few actresses who could have uttered the last line of the play with more heartbreaking poignancy: "Whoever you are, I have always depended upon the kindness of strangers." Vivien played the role exquisitely, if in a somewhat stylized manner. That, however, was Olivier's doing; he directed the play as a partly naturalistic, partly stylized allegory, in which Blanche was the most extreme exponent of the stylized element, and Stanley of the naturalistic one. People who had seen the Broadway production could discern a distinct difference in this approach; but since there had not been a film version as yet, at the time none of us could make any comparisons. Nor would it have mattered. Larry Olivier was our guru, and we faithfully executed his *Streetcar.*

Olivier as a director was both fascinating and intimidating. As a rule, directors are supposed to lead or goad you into the performance they want you to give. In that regard, actors are like children who need a mixture of admonition, coaxing, and, alternately, threats and stroking. What actors mostly do *not* want from a director are physical demonstrations of the role and line readings. That, however, is precisely what Olivier did. He did not tell you what to do, he showed you. Whether this was due to his impatience with the longer process of coaxing, or his natural and irrepressible inclination to perform, was not entirely clear. It certainly was a most disconcerting practice, for he was absolutely brilliant, and the actor so instructed could hardly expect to equal the director's demonstration, let alone improve upon it. Still, no one dared ask Olivier not to give performances of the various roles. I heard of only one instance when an actor stood up to Olivier's practice of acting out roles. That was the oh-so-British and imperturbable Wilfred Hyde-White. When Olivier, directing the Cleopatra cycle (Shaw's *Caesar and Cleopatra* and Shakespeare's *Antony and Cleopatra*), demonstrated to Wilfred how a scene should be played, the veteran actor clapped his hands in applause and said with genuine admiration, "Bravo, old boy, bravo!" But then he added, "I could never do it that way," and continued to do it his own way.

As the royal couple of the British theatre, the Oliviers might have been far more aloof and unapproachable, but at most times they were friendly, if not chummy. Olivier asked you to call him Larry quite early on. We did, but the practice was not always safe. You could very well slap him on the back, expecting to find Larry, and he might turn around Sir Laurence instead, making you feel small and foolish. So we became a bit watchful, and took our cues from him as to when he would choose to be Larry. Whether he was Larry or Sir Laurence was idiosyncratic, and had nothing to do with who you were or what position you occupied in the cast; there were no class distinctions. In fact, he always showed great respect for all talent, including smaller roles and understudies. Once, during the run of the Cleopatra cycle, Vivien Leigh had an attack of some virus and was unable to perform. In accordance with custom and the rules of the theatre, the stage manager announced that the understudy for Miss Leigh would be appearing in her place, and that anyone in the audience who preferred not to stay had a choice of either getting a refund or exchanging his ticket for another night. A number of people in the audience got up to leave, but Larry Olivier stepped in front of the curtain and addressed the audience: "As you have heard, Miss Leigh is indisposed. But in her place tonight a young actress will play the role of Cleopatra who might turn out to be tomorrow's Vivien Leigh. I counsel you to stay." Now that's respect.

Understudy rehearsals were held frequently, and were quite thorough. I did double duty at these rehearsals, sometimes running through the play twice, alternating the male leading roles. But in truth, there is little hope for an understudy in most productions. Stage actors are guided by an ethic according to which you have to be either deathly ill to miss a performance—or dead altogether. As a consequence, the mind-set of an understudy is closely akin to that of a vulture. In lucid moments of self-examination, you feel disgusted that you actually hope for some disaster to befall a colleague so that you might have a chance at bat. Worse yet, when you push these inevitable feelings aside, envy takes their place. In the theatre, envy becomes the norm.

Luckily, I escaped most of that. For one thing, both actors whose roles I covered were friendly. I spent a lot of time with them, mostly in Bonar's dressing room, where conversation—and whiskey—flowed freely. We also had a chess game going most of the time. I was part of the inner circle, so to speak, and participated in the games and the talk regularly, although I mostly left the whiskey alone.

I suspect Olivier originally cast Bernie Braden as Mitch because the Canadian Braden had a North American accent, and probably also because of name recognition. Bernie had made a career in radio in both Canada and the U.K.; in England, he was a bona fide radio star. He was basically a sitcom person, a fair actor but not outstanding. His background was not in the legitimate theatre, and he did not have the attitude of "the show must go on," come what may. It was only a few weeks into the run that Bernie came down with his first bout of the flu. Although it was not severe enough to have kept most of us off the stage, in fairness to Bernie, the decision that he should stay away from the theatre could have come at Vivien's insistence. Mitch kisses Blanche at one point in the play, and our star's constitution was less than robust. Her health was always a matter of concern, both to herself and to the theatre management.

So it was that one morning, I got "the phone call." "Get to the theatre, you're going on tonight." A quick, unscheduled rehearsal was held that included only me and the other understudies and assistant stage managers. I had not rehearsed with Vivien Leigh and never did before I actually faced her on stage. I went to her dressing room before the performance to inquire whether she wanted to run any scenes or had any requests to make—any do's or don't's to give me. But no; she just said: "Go and do it; you are a professional, and Larry gave you this job because he trusted you to do it well. Let's see if he was right." Not terribly encouraging, that, but this is the big world and it does not call for you to be coddled.

Afterwards she was gracious and said, "Well done," and that was enough for me. The next night Bernie was still out, and I was asked to go to Vivien's dressing room. My heart sank. *Am I going to get fired?* I wondered. But no; she just had a few technical notes, and we had a nice chat. I left to get ready, and on the way out I passed Vivien's dresser, who winked at me and said something to the effect of, "Last night she was a little nervous before the show. She's all right tonight, so you must have done well." She winked again, and with a flick of her wrist snapped a piece of the star's clothing at me—Vivien Leigh's bra, complete with pads and false nipples. *All right,* I thought, *now I wonder if Larry will come to see me do it.* He did, in fact, show up, and stayed for one of my good scenes. Afterwards, I asked the stage manager whether Olivier had given him any notes or comments about my performance. "Not a one," he said, "and that's a good sign. There would have been plenty if he had found fault. Don't push your luck."

Lady Olivier, one half of the most celebrated stage couple in the world, was by now a superstar in her own right. Born in India, Vivien was brought up as a nurtured flower in a world of British upper-crust colonials, and it showed. That, however, was only part of her, the part that was readily visible and the part she presented to the outside world. To her colleagues she was a hard-working actress, a stickler for professionalism and for rigidly maintaining the level of performance. There was another part to her as well, the "truck driver" part. At one of the performances when I played Mitch, the audience was not the best—fidgety and unresponsive to some elements of the show that usually worked especially well. Vivien was clearly displeased, although none of it showed in her performance. At the curtain call, I was on her left, holding her hand, as the actors playing the four leads took their bows. Vivien looked especially gracious, Lady Olivier to the tip of her toes. We all bowed together, and when her head was at its lowest, with only the crown of her hair seen by the applauding audience, she hissed, "Stupid cunts!" Then her head came back up and she smiled beatifically, Lady Olivier once again.

By now I had moved on from my digs at Abbey Road and into a narrow duplex at 68 Carlton Hill in St. John's Wood, which I shared with two other young men. First there was Freddie Granville, who tried his hand at all kinds of odd jobs, never sticking with any one of them terribly long and dreaming of becoming a super impresario (an ambition he never realized). Then there was Kurt Schmerler, who was the most serious among us three. He was a respected eye doctor who had put himself through medical school, having arrived in a children's transport from Germany, together with his younger sister. They were the only survivors of their family. Then Kurt's sister was killed in the street by British hooligans perpetrating some crime. The poor girl simply found herself in the wrong place at the wrong time. With this tragedy Kurt became something which to me epitomizes the word "survivor" to this day. Despite a disposition toward gregariousness, there was a constant element of loneliness about Kurt that time and success never diminished.

We were a strange threesome, Freddie, Kurt, and I, all of us hailing from German-speaking countries, all refugees in our own way, and all so different from one another in attitude, temperament, and outlook. Nevertheless the partnership, which lasted for quite a few years, was a good one. The apartment was a very lively place. There was a constant stream of visitors, friends, girlfriends, actors, musicians, Israelis, Americans, folksingers, folklorists, Jews, Gentiles, Russian émigré nobility, socialists, liberals. Rarely any conservatives, however: They felt as uncomfortable with us as we with them. Sundays became an institution. Theatres were dark on Sundays; it was my day off and it became known that there was an open house at Carlton Hill where, without any special invitation, anyone could descend on us in the afternoon and stay until the wee hours of Monday. A young Liverpool-born doctor, Arnold Kalina, who was just establishing his London practice, was crazy about music and showed up regularly. He spoke with the telltale adenoidal accent of all Liverpudlians, including the Beatles. What was great in his case, however, was that he also had the accent when he spoke Yiddish. I usually bought a dozen or two bottles of inexpensive wine and some nibbles. We also relied on some of our regulars to bring supplies; we rarely ran out of everything. The routine, if there was one, consisted of chess, discussion of theatre, political debate, jokes, long sessions of charades (known simply as "the game"), and a lot of music. Anybody who played and sang showed up; it was a veritable feast of music—folk mostly—by both London-based performers and visiting firemen from all over the world. Word got around that if a singer or guitarist came to London for work or pleasure, on Sundays 68 Carlton Hill was the place to be.

Of the nonsinging visiting Americans who came to my apartment, Shelley Winters was without a doubt one of the more peppery. She was quite slim and beautiful in those days. She was about to do a film that was shooting in London for several months, and she had just had a baby. When she went looking for an apartment in Mayfair, the real estate agent showed her a beautiful old house of several stories. She wanted to know where the central heating was, and the agent, somewhat miffed, said that the house was three hundred years old. Shelley shrieked, "Three hun—and you expect us to live here with a baby?!" She once came to my place with a whole group in tow, including her cousin, Ben Schrift, who was a film distributor. (Shelley's real name was Shirley Schrift.) At my party she met several artists like Larry Adler and the Israeli duo Hillel and Aviva. On this particular evening she decided to stage-manage the proceedings. She said, "Theo, you play; Hillel will play the flute; Aviva will play the drum; Larry will play that mouth thing; I'll recite something—" Then she looked at her cousin and said, "Ben—you'll release a picture."

Mine was the kind of active social life you might expect of a twenty-five-year-old healthy young man, but it revolved around music far more than anything else. Not that there was a lack of female companionship, but it, too, mostly grew out of the music. If a young woman reacted to your playing and singing, chances were that she might end up in your bed. But for me the music was never a means to entice women; it was an end in itself. If the poetry and the cadences wove a spell, fine and good, but I do not recall ever putting down the guitar in order to "chat up" a girl at a party. If she stuck it out to the end when, because of a host's outlandish desire to throw everyone out and go to bed at three or four in the morning, I finally packed it in, we might continue on to my place. Most times, however, I just played and sang. I was constantly invited to parties and I went, often every night of the week, knowing full well that my guitar was one of the chief reasons I was asked. I brought it along automatically; when I neglected to do so people offered to drive me home to fetch it. My roommate Freddie, who had learned to play the *darbukke,* an Arabian-style drum, often went along, and we did little else but play music until it was time to go home. We would get back to the apartment in the wee hours of the morning, make ourselves a cup of coffee, sit in the two armchairs facing each other, and say, "Well, we didn't eat, we didn't drink, we didn't get laid—main thing is, we played the damn instruments." If I was being exploited at those parties, I didn't care. Parties were my rehearsals for new material. And I enjoyed myself too much to think of complaining. Then, playing at parties was a way of honing my craft and of learning about an audience's reactions and attention span. Those parties were useful lessons in how to create an intimacy with an audience, no matter how large.

One night, as I sat on a bar stool eating a steak-and-kidney pie in a pub near the stage door—a pub was one of the few places in London where you could get a quick bite after a performance—an old fellow with a typical cockney face was seated at the bar, eyeing me across the empty spaces between us. He inched closer, shifting his behind from stool to stool, and when he was right next to me he said with a smirk, "'Ere, you're an actor, ain't-cha?" When I acknowledged—not without pride at having been recognized—that indeed I was, he continued with a leer, "Bit of all right, eh?" I asked, puzzled, "What do you mean?" "Bit of all right," he repeated with another suggestive wink, "bet after the curtain comes down of a night, you and them actresses—*at it likes knives!*" That's some image, I thought. They ring down the curtain and the next thing you know, the actors tear off their clothes in a frenzy of sexual abandonment.

Maybe what the man in the street believed about the loose ways of actors was not so wrong after all. One night Freddie was out with Maxine Audley and the Oliviers, dining and dancing at Les Ambassadeurs. Maxine was Vivien's close friend—and Freddie's fiancée. After that evening Freddie told me in confidence—but not without glee— that while Larry and Maxine continued to drink champagne at the table, Vivien had propositioned him on the dance floor. He swore that she had also grabbed his crotch. Well, you know how these actresses are.

Of course I did have girlfriends myself, some of them more or less steady, but the arrangement was usually fairly loose and allowed outside involvements. Clearly the staid British frowned on such practices, but it was also clear that people outside the theatre, like my friend at the bar, were secretly amused by the antics of theatre folk. At Carlton Hill an old lady of indeterminate age named Beattie Bullock cleaned house for us. In England, ladies in this time-honored position were known as charladies. Old Beattie Bullock went about her chores with incredible slowness, but was nonetheless fastidious and regular in her habits and time schedules. For example, she always entered my bed-room at ten o'clock, no doubt on the assumption that even an actor needed to get up at some decent hour. So it happened that one morn-ing she opened my bedroom door, as usual without knocking, chirp-ing—as usual—"Ten o'clock, time to get up!" Then, slowly, she made the long trek around my bed to the other side and lifted the edge of the blanket. Discovering a young woman there she said, "Oh, it's you. I thought it was the other lady." As ever, the soul of tact.

We had another charlady for a time who held down other jobs and gossiped about them, unlike Beattie Bullock, who worked for us exclusively. It seems the other lady worked as a cleaning woman in a house of ill repute run by a mafia family known as the Messina Broth-ers. Apparently they had their hand in all sorts of rackets, of which prostitution was the mildest. Our charlady told stories about the goings-on, to which we listened eagerly; this was such an alien world to us, a world glimpsed only in newspaper reports and embellished in our minds by crime fiction. Our charlady painted the human side of the picture. "Old Mrs. Messina, the mother, was a lovely lady," she would say, "the girls all adored her. They worshiped the ground she stepped on. Do you know, when she died all the girls went into mournin' and on the day of her funeral not a stroke of work was done!"

I was back playing my minor poker-player role when my parents made their first trip to England. They were eager to see their son in a major West End theatre—and in a play starring the legendary Vivien Leigh. *Streetcar* had been sold out for months in advance, but they had planned their trip well in advance and I had prudently secured seats for them early on—for a Saturday-night performance. That morning I was called by the stage manager, who informed me that Bonar Col-leano, our Stanley, had broken an ankle, and that I was to go on that night and for as long afterwards until Bonar's foot was mended. And so it came about that on the night my parents thought they'd find me in a small role, I appeared opposite Vivien Leigh as Stanley Kowalski himself—the role that Marlon Brando had made famous on Broadway. An incredible coincidence, but no more than a coincidence—I swear I had nothing to do with Bonar's broken ankle. The guy was reckless enough on his own accord, and everyone who knew him was con-vinced that he was an accident waiting to happen. And unfortunately the broken ankle was just a forecast of worse to come. Some time after the play closed, Bonar was killed in an automobile accident. He was still in his early forties.

It was Mitch that I played on more than one occasion, sometimes for two or three performances in a row. During the later part of the run, Bernie Braden went to Vancouver to attend his father's funeral and see to family business matters. In those pre-jet-engine days, that was a much longer trip, even by air, and Bernie stayed away for almost two weeks. That gave me a chance to solidify my performance as Mitch—and was doubtless a factor in my being offered the role on a permanent basis some months later, when the play was sent out on tour.

When Vivien Leigh went to America, the producers debated whether they should close the London production of *Streetcar*. But the play was *such* a huge success, and it had not been seen in the provinces. Reason—and greed—prevailed, and they decided to send the play out on tour, retaining most of the minor roles and only one of the original cast in a major role—me. The role of Stella was given to a Canadian, Frances Hyland, and Stanley to an American, Bill Sylvester, who was permitted to work in Britain having married a young English actress, Sheila Sweet. (Coincidentally, all three had been contemporaries of mine at RADA.) Blanche was Betty Davis, no connection and no relation to the American actress, Bette with an "e." To avoid confusion, she was billed as Betty Ann Davis. Olivier was either unavailable or unwilling to direct the play again. With a new director and three new principal players, management thought that the play deserved a new look, more in keeping with the American version, and brought in Danny Mann, at the time one of Broadway's and Hollywood's foremost directors. Working with Danny was an experience. He was fun to be with, full of life and of stories; he was also that breed of New York Jew whose energy was infectious. In terms of theatre, he was something I thought I had left behind when I quit the Habimah. This was the Method, American style. To be sure, it was different from the Russian version as practiced by the direct disciples of Stanislavsky and Vakhtangov. But it was the Method nonetheless, and it demanded that one delve into motivations and atmospheric circumstances far more deeply than the British theatre had. An added difficulty was that those of us who had been in Olivier's production had, either consciously or instinctively, done that kind of homework already and had to go through the process again, somewhat unwillingly. There was some grumbling. I did not mind too much; working with Danny Mann was worth it.

Streetcar toured for some eight months and gave me a chance to get better acquainted with Britain and Scotland; a week in each place lets you do that. Touring in Britain was not all that comfortable. Sometimes instead of hotels we stayed in "digs," an institution fraught with uncertain amenities and various degrees of discourtesy, not to speak of dubious culinary offerings. "Digs" meant rooming houses with breakfast and supper, landladies either fawning on show folk or more than occasionally disapprovingly dour. The breakfast was of an unvarying sameness: fried eggs, soggy bacon, equally soggy white-bread toast, and tea with milk and sugar. There was coffee, but you drank it at your peril; it was a chicory brew and one taste served only to remind you of better days in better places. Supper was worse; they kept it for you in the oven, for by the time you got back from the theatre, the landlady had long retired to her bed. As a consequence there was no way to demur or ask for something different and possibly edible. The sojourn in the oven had turned what was barely acceptable to begin with into a dried-out mass of something that stubbornly stuck to the plate. Most times it was roast beef and Yorkshire pudding, which since that time I have yet to order, even in good restaurants. But you ate the damn thing; what you got at the digs was the only available food in town. Even in the bigger places, everything closed up around about the time you started on the second act. Leeds or Hull had nothing to offer after 9:00 P.M. We often tried to remind ourselves, while swallowing our sumptious dinners, that the life of an actor was supposed to be one of excitement and glamour. Yes, sure. In this country of Shakespeare and Shaw, the actor seemed to be held in such low esteem that an ancient English law, only fairly recently repealed, that classified actors as "rogues and vagabonds" made perfect sense.

One often wondered: Did no one in the audience have a yen for a chat and a bite after the theatre with a couple of friends? Did they not want to discuss the play, the performances, what Gladys wore, or why the alderman had attended without his wife? They had been enthusiastic enough when the final curtain fell, and some hardy souls even waited at the stage door for an autograph. Then they vanished into the anonymity of their own homes, evidently embarrassed by their own break with British reticence.

Our play itself gave certain people in the Midlands and the North of England some problems. I overheard a couple's comments as they were studying the theatre posters in a hotel lobby: "*Streetcar Named Desire*—h-m-m, bit of a liberty-taking piece, I'm told." That meant "too much sex," obviously; in fact, any sex at all onstage would be too much for these folks. Then they continued, looking at the actors' billing, "Don't know any of the names, must be foreigners. Ah well, let's see, what's on at t'other theatre." Lovely, I thought, prudery and xenophobia in one package!

As the tour wound its way from the Midlands to the North, some places emerged as more memorable than others. Hull was especially drab and dreary, definitely the low point of the tour. Leeds and Manchester were pleasant, mostly because I had been there before for small appearances, and met with friendly Jews who had taken me under their wing. But Scotland, I thought, was a special place. The Scots may officially be part of Britain, but are they ever different! They tend to appear dour, crotchety, and forbidding at first, but that is a misimpression that soon vanishes. The Scottish burr is music to a linguist's ears, and the dry sense of self-deprecation a Scot exhibits from an early age would make any actor appreciate the lesson in repartee, both of the irate and the laconic kind. I experienced both at various times, much to my delight. Once, in London, as I was chaperoning some visitors around town, I attempted to demonstrate to them how the English go out of their way to be helpful with directions, even when they themselves do not have a clue. As I was stopping a passerby with an inquiry, I was hoping for the usual bumbling reply: "Yes, now wait a minute, oh yes, Warwick Avenue, you continue past three traffic lights, no wait, four lights, no, three, one of them is a stop sign, then after you pass where the church used to be, you turn sharp left, no wait, there is a fork but one of them is called Warwick Place, leave that one alone, then there is a chemist's and a shoe shop—no, that's moved now . . ." and so on and so on. But the man I stopped turned out to be a Scot and instead of the effusive helpfulness I expected, he snapped at me, "Every time I go out to post a letter, some damn fool stops me tae ask damn fool questions!" or the Scottish lady who, when I inadvertently bumped into her, reprimanded me with "Why d'ye no toot your horn when ye come roon' the corner like that!" When we played Edinburgh—a place I grew particularly fond of—something happened one night which made us laugh at the time, but which in fact was incredibly sad. As two of my colleagues and I walked back to our hotel after the performance, bundled up against the cold (summer or no, it does get cold at night), I saw a young girl, maybe fourteen or fifteen years old, huddled in a doorway and shivering. It was close to eleven o'clock at night and I said to the girl, "Good God, child, you should be home in bed!" She snapped back at me, "Ach no, I'm a wee whore!" We gave her some money and made her promise to go home. She made as if to walk away, but I know she returned to ply her trade just as soon as our backs were turned.

After the tour ended there was the usual pang of fear that assails every actor on closing nights, even before the final curtain. It is called "I'll never work again," and it never fails to manifest itself in varying degrees of cold-sweat paranoia. Most times this feeling evaporates as soon as the first chance for a new job comes up. In my case, that was fairly soon.

Radio drama was very popular in the forties and assiduously listened to. BBC radio offered some good acting jobs; the work was not difficult and it involved no memorizing—just a quick grasp of characterization and the imagination to paint an atmosphere and a situation. The work wasn't terribly lucrative, but it was steady and fun. Because I knew German, I was cast in a number of plays and playlets in the BBC's European division. The broadcasts were beamed into East Germany as a way of persuading the population there that our world had more to offer than theirs. This was not necessarily political theatre. Sometimes it was purely that, but most often it was just good theatre that even included German versions of English classics. This division of the BBC made use of an extraordinary array of talented German-speaking actors who had fled Germany and Austria. Most were Jews, but not all.

An interesting case: One of the non-Jews had been a most respected theatre director in Germany but fled because he simply could not stomach the Nazis. He was, in fact, a Prussian nobleman; his name was Friedrich von Wendhausen. The Nazis, especially propaganda and culture minister Goebbels, had wooed him assiduously, trying to convince him to serve the Third Reich in whatever exalted position he desired. They offered him theatres to run and plays to direct, and asked him to present himself to the Führer to receive some kind of accolade, an arts medal of some sort. But on the day before his appointment with Hitler, Wendhausen made "a quick business trip" to Switzerland, and upon his arrival there he took a plane to London. The very first thing he did was to send a telegram to Goebbels which tersely stated: "*Goetz von Berlichingen*, Act II, Scene 3. Friedrich von Wendhausen." Anyone familiar with German dramatic literature would be able to identify the scene in Goethe's play as the source of the quote that translates roughly as "You may tell the count that he may kiss my arse." Although his opportunities of earning a living in England were limited to directorial chores at the BBC's German Service and small acting roles that required a strong German accent—much less of a career than he would have had in Germany—Wendhausen never returned to his native land, despite repeated attempts to woo him back.

Some of the other German-speaking actors on whom the BBC was able to call had better luck. They made a fine career in England; some even achieved international reputations. I worked with expatriate actors whose names had top billing in London theatres but who occasionally returned to the BBC's German "repertory," both for fun and out of nostalgia: Frederick Valk, Martin Miller, Lilli Palmer, and Herbert Lom, to mention but a few. Many, of course, were not so fortunate; they eked out a living as actors as best they could, relying on the BBC to furnish more or less regular employment. In the age of radio, the pay was not much, but it was a fixed pay scale that was the same for everyone. The BBC took no advantage of the fact that these people were hungry for the work and would have done it for even less than they were offered. There was also some work in the movie studios. British films began to tell the stories of the war—mostly stories of military exploits. During those years there was never any mention of Jews or the Holocaust. As a consequence, the Jews among the refugee actors who looked foreign without looking too Jewish were cast in the roles of French or Greek partisans. They were also invariably cast as Nazis—in or out of uniform. An irony of sorts, repeated many times in British and American films.

One of the expatriates was a funny bird. His name was Felix Knüpfer, which he eventually changed to Felix Kent, because his surname was all but unpronounceable for the English. They balked at the hard "k" before the "n" and did not even try for the umlaut. Knüpfer was always looking for angles, and was a wizard at getting in free anywhere. He was annoyed with me at one point because he had tried to sell me a chess set that I refused to buy. It was a nice enough set, but I already owned three. Enough is enough. "This Bikel is outrageous," he said to a mutual acquaintance, "why shouldn't he buy my chess set? The man is a millionaire, a millionaire, I tell you; he has maybe two hundred English pounds in the bank!" Some definition of a millionaire, I thought when I heard this—especially the "maybe."

One thing Knüpfer raised to an art form was attending plays, dress rehearsals, openings, and opening-night parties without ever buying a ticket or producing an invitation. He did this by pretending to speak and understand even less English than he did; when challenged, he waved officials and ushers aside with an imperious claim of "I am a Czech actor!" Despite his Austrian birth and the fact he spoke no Czech at all, he made this claim because "Czech" sounded better than "German." Having spent a few seasons as an actor in a German-speaking theatre in Czechoslovakia, he felt he was entitled to switch origins. And what British usher or stage-door man would be able to tell a Czech from an Austrian anyway—or from a Pole or a Dutchman, for that matter? So he sailed through side doors and stage entrances, sometimes pretending to fulfill a supervisory role before dress rehearsals, pointing to stage lights, calling out "Number fourteen! Number sixty-three!" to legitimize his presence, and eventually strutting through the pass door into the auditorium to watch the play. Even Olivier did not get the best of him in this game. At a dress rehearsal that was closed to any visitors, Knüpfer managed somehow to get in and settled in one of the back rows to watch. Since his bald head shone in the dark, his presence did not escape Larry's attention. He sent an assistant to the back to find out who the mysterious person might be. The man returned and reported, more than somewhat embarrassed, "I can't make head or tail of him, Sir Laurence; he says he is a Czech actor." Olivier decided to investigate himself. He went to the back and said to Felix Knüpfer, "Are you all right?" Translated from polite English, this means, "Who the devil are you and if you have no business here, then get the hell out." Unfazed, Knüpfer said in a jolly tone (and a very thick accent), "Okay, carry on!" Cowed by such obvious authority, Olivier shrugged and went back to his directing chores.

Another time Felix got into a performance and found an empty seat, settled into it, and waited for the performance to begin. An usher spotted him, came over, and inquired, "Excuse me, sir, is this your seat?" Knüpfer said, "Yes, I am zitting here." The usher persisted, "What I mean, sir, is this your proper seat?" Felix, "A zeat, a zeat? Yes, this iss a zeat." The usher, with some exasperation, "No, no, what I mean is, where is your ticket?" Whereupon Felix rose out of his seat, fixed the hapless fellow with a withering glance, and said in an accusing loud voice, "YES, WHERE ISS MY TICKET?!" The usher, now totally bewildered as well as chastised, said, "I am sorry, sir, I don't know," and left a triumphant Felix Knüpfer zitting in his zeat.

A theatre company is as closely knit as any close family. You depend upon each other, emotionally, even physically—for missteps on the stage can lead to accidents. The time spent at the theatre is concentrated together time; the emotions are charged, and both likes and dislikes are magnified and sharpened. Then, when a play is at the end of its run, you promise each other that you will keep in touch, but you rarely do. In later years I had very little contact with Larry Olivier and Vivien Leigh, apart from the occasional backstage visit after seeing a performance. When the play is over, it's over, and you go on to your next "family." That is, if you are lucky enough to land a job. I don't think I know a single actor who, at the end of a run, is not absolutely convinced that he'll never work again. And that includes stars.

I had one occasion to spend a little time with the Oliviers during a brief visit to England after I had settled in the States. Larry and Vivien, still married at the time, were doing a repertory season of Shakespeare at Stratford-on-Avon. The plays included *Coriolanus, Twelfth Night,* and *Titus Andronicus.* I decided to take a trip up from London, stay a couple of days, and see at least two of the plays. Luckily, I managed to see *Titus* and *Twelfth Night.* For the contrast alone it was worth it. Larry's roles were always so different in looks from each other: He was a master of makeup. That was one of the aspects of stage acting that Larry adored. One could have serious reservations about his portrayal of *Othello,* for example—his affecting the vocal mannerisms of an American black man—but the makeup was always stunning. The Stratford season was no exception. As for Vivien, she was as beautiful as ever and possibly even more frail than I had remembered; it may have been a premonition of the ultimate breaking of the porcelain figure. For now, however, she was in good form, perhaps because she was furious as well. The reviews of her performance in *Titus* had not been kind, despite phenomenal direction by Peter Brook. The rarely performed play is particularly gruesome and gory: The woman's husband is murdered before her eyes, she is raped, her hands are cut off, and her tongue cut out. Ken Tynan's review contained the following sentence: "Miss Vivien Leigh receives the news that she is about to be raped on top of her dead husband's body with the air of one who would have preferred foam rubber." Little wonder that for years afterward Vivien refused to speak to Tynan. When I saw her, she was still smarting and sore as hell.

On the Friday night of my Stratford visit, the Oliviers took me to a party that went on till all hours. There was a lot of storytelling and anecdotes were traded as well as backstage gossip. I remember Vivien's comment about the director of *Twelfth Night,* who had been none other than the redoubtable Sir John Gielgud. Everyone agreed that he was a dear man but not a first-rate director. On the few occasions when I had met him, he had always struck me as painfully polite and shy, forever seeming to shy away from you—not in fear or embarrassment, but rearing back with a small whinny, as though he were a thoroughbred horse. Vivien said that, in rehearsal, Gielgud would extemporize, sometimes with embarrassing results. He would say, "Sebastian, you enter from the left—yes, oh dear me, no, you're not supposed to see her yet, are you?" After the opening, she had said to Sir John, "You know you are a terrible director, don't you?" He replied with a mournful face, "Yes, I know, I know. I don't suppose anyone will ever want to work with me again. Ever." Then, as an afterthought, referring to Dame Edith Evans: "Edith might—at a pinch . . . "

When the party finally broke up in the wee hours, Larry Olivier said with a sigh, "Oh dear. What time is it? Three o'clock. What's tomorrow? Ah, Saturday. . . . What nose is that?"

5

The Guitars of the Exile

THE EARLY 1950S WERE A GLORIOUS TIME for me in England. The theatre was home and family, the music at all times a source of incredible pleasure, and I began to be paid an actual living wage for what I enjoyed doing most! Beyond that, I went to parties practically every night, made friends, and made carefree love (one could make carefree love in those days—even careless love, for that matter), and I thought there was little that could mar our joy. Except that some of my visitors who became very close friends had a problem: They were fugitives. Not necessarily fugitives in the movie plot sense, with a posse at their heels, but transplanted souls nonetheless—robbed of home and culture. No matter how successful they might have become in the place of their refuge—and some of them became very successful indeed— there was about them a perpetual aura of displacement, of exile.

My apartment in London was a safe haven for many expatriates: refugees and survivors of displaced-person camps; Israelis who were studying or working after graduation; South African blacks who managed to escape the brutal regime and make their home in Britain; White Russian noblemen who had long since given up any hope of ever returning to their homeland; and any American artists, singers, musicians, or actors who had arrived in England either through choice or by necessity. It was certainly curious that at the very same time I welcomed under my roof victims of anti-Communist witch-hunts in the West, I also forged close friendships with White Russians, fugitives from a Communist regime in Eastern Europe. The irony was not lost on me.

My White Russian friends were nobility. They were accepted as such by the British aristocracy, were addressed by their titles of "prince" or "count," mentioned in the society pages, and considered quite suitable as dinner, dance, or marriage partners by the British upper class. Indeed, my closest Russian friends, George and Emmanuel Galitzine, sounded, looked, and behaved as British as could be. They had served as officers in the British armed forces, their older brother, Nicholas, in the Royal Navy, George in the Welsh Guards, and Emmanuel, the youngest, in the youngest of the services, the Royal Air Force. At any given party they behaved like quintessential Brits—that is, until the third vodka and the fourth song. Then all that British veneer vanished and they became Russian through and through. "Goddammit to hell," they would shout (the "hell" aspirated to sound like "khell"), "goddammit to hell, that's beautiful!" Then they would settle down for a long session of Russian music. Both George and Emmanuel played the guitar reasonably well, and each had a preference for a different type of Russian music. George liked the sentimental songs—"romances," as they were called—and Emmanuel the rousing Gypsy tunes that he played and sang with wild abandon.

The Galitzines had left when Russia was in the throes of revolution. That they managed to escape at all was amazing enough; that they salvaged part of their fortune was a feat of ingenuity. Taking anything of great value was all but impossible when you had to leave with but a few suitcases of personal effects, and you were subject to searches and scrutiny by unfriendly guards. They did, however, come away with a good portion of the family jewels. Nick, a little boy then, was clutching a large teddy bear, and sewn into the bear's belly was a cache of brooches and necklaces—a fortune in gems. One thing they managed to take out openly and unchallenged was a small gold vodka cup.

It was in the shape of an upside-down helmet of the Chevalier Guards, a crack household regiment of the czar, of which old Prince Galitzine had been commander in chief. Years later, shortly after the old gentleman died, George Galitzine and I took a trip to Spain by car. In the will, the cup had been left to an old Russian colonel, now living in France, who had been the regiment's second in command. George decided that we would deliver the cup in person. The problem was, we knew his name but had no address; we had heard that he might be living in a small village to the south of Paris, whose exact name we also did not know. There were several such villages where a number of White Russian emigrés were said to reside. We had no luck at the first village. Every person we saw in the second one looked and sounded so French that we almost skipped the search there altogether. However, we decided on at least one try. We asked a Frenchman with a beret who was passing on a bike where we might find the person we were looking for. He gave a Gallic shrug. Then I had an idea. I said: "*Izvinitye, gdye zhivyot polkovnik—*" (Excuse me, where might we find Colonel—) I got no further; his face lit up and he answered in a torrent of Russian, led us to a house, knocked, bowed, and left. The door opened and there stood the man we had been looking for. We introduced ourselves, George earned a deep, courtly bow, and we were invited in. The door, which was so low we both had to stoop to enter, was deceptive, for inside was a fairly large room with a high ceiling. We were met by a sight I have not forgotten. The interior was a veritable museum of imperial Russian memorabilia: maps, photographs, paintings, icons. Towering over it all was a larger-than-life-size painting of the last czar. How that was gotten out, God alone knows. The man clicked his heels before it and bowed, a ritual one had a feeling he repeated several times a day. When he received the cup, there were tears in his eyes. We were served tea in tall glasses that sat in ornate metal holders and were offered cakes and also fresh croissants (this was France, after all); we made polite, superficial conversation, and after a while we continued our trip.

It was an eerie, unreal scene, which gave one the feeling that time had stood still, or that at the very least these people were convinced that a return to the old czarist days was not only possible, but achievable in their lifetime. It seemed to have escaped their attention that the cavalry regiments they had so valiantly commanded would be of little use against Soviet tanks and planes, even if they could be reassembled. One got the distinct impression that all over Western Europe, in Italy, Germany, and especially in France, old Russians, former officers, were sitting every afternoon around a samovar, drinking innumerable glasses of tea, and plotting to reconquer Russia—if Washington would only lend them the horses.

This sense of unreality permeated the doings around the White Russian colony much of the time. The Galitzines, the Obolenskys, the Vassilchikovs, the Kleinmichels were people I spent time with, went to parties with, sang or played with. George Vassilchikov was one of the younger ones; later he would settle in New York and become one of the interpreters at the United Nations—English-Russian and Russian-English, either way. The strange thing was that he had a terrible stutter in real life. On the job, the stutter disappeared entirely. In the general scheme of things, these Russians were like anyone else—working at jobs, running into personal or financial troubles, marrying, divorcing, having affairs. But to the other Russians they occupied an exalted, if not revered, position.

I recall being taken by Emmanuel and George Galitzine to the Russian Orthodox church for Easter Mass. This was one of two rival churches in London, each presided over by an archbishop. The one recognized the authority of the church hierarchy as it still existed inside the USSR, while the other was entirely a church-in-exile. Needless to say, my friends took me to the second one. As in all Eastern Rite services, the congregation stood through the entire ceremony. During the solemn procession, as the archbishop advanced at the head of a column of robed priests carrying religious paraphernalia and flags, everyone bowed deeply. Yet when the procession reached our group, it was the archbishop who bowed to us—not to me, of course, but to the nobility I hobnobbed with. At the time I must admit that I was impressed. Not for too long, though. Shortly thereafter I took a trip to the Continent for a location job, and decided to drop George a line. I addressed the letter to "HT the Prince George Galitzine." When I returned to London, George thanked me for writing but asked, "What was HT supposed to stand for?" As if it were the most obvious answer, I replied, "His Transparency, of course." He laughed; one of his more endearing traits was his ability to enjoy pinpricks in the balloons of self-importance.

We had become friends, these White Russians and I, mainly because of the music. Without that, we might not have had much in common. After all, they and their forebears were the very people who had little regard for Jews. They had either tolerated my people's persecution or forced Jews to take up residence in designated areas known as the Pale, and had otherwise given little thought to the sorry fate of the Jews in Old Russia. On top of this, these expatriates now saw the

Jews as having been among the architects and ideologues of world Communism, the very doctrine that had brought down the Russian aristocracy. Indeed, in a moment of frank revelation, Emmanuel confided in me that anti-Semitism had been a given in his upbringing. They were no rabid Jew-haters; they just accepted anti-Jewish sentiments as natural. The friendship the Galitzines and others formed with me and my crowd were among the few contacts they had with Jews as equals—perhaps the only contacts. They concluded that many of my friends were very talented people, and Russians admire talent. In the end, there was not only admiration but also respect. As for me, I liked the Russians' zest and their joie de vivre; in no way did I ever feel threatened or intimidated by their company. We were all expatriates, both in the literal and cultural sense.

There was a different expatriate scene in Paris, where I had spent some time as a boy visiting relatives—my father's brother Davide and his sister Miriam. Both had moved to Paris in the early 1920s. Davide Bikel (Dudel we called him) had always been my favorite member of the family. As a boy I stayed alternately with Dudel and with my Aunt Miriam. She had married a man named Henri Meyer, who early on had changed his name to Meyet because he had decided it sounded more French. I quite liked him, although he was not exactly beloved by the family. My Aunt Miriam was warm and also brighter than her husband, who was cautious and somewhat remote, but she hid her qualities in order to defer to her husband. She even deferred when he made one decision that in our family was totally unthinkable: He decided to have his two sons baptized in the Catholic church. The news of this step, designed though it was to ward off the looming persecution of Jews in France, was received by the rest of us with incredulity and horror. We felt betrayed. Ties were not cut, but there was a definite estrangement. My aunt's two boys, Marc and Michel, both old enough to be aware of the switch and the reasons for it, never returned to Judaism, even when it was safe to do so after the defeat of the Nazis. After the war, when things were back to normal and the family was back in Paris after hiding out in the south, Marc announced that he was getting married and that the wedding would take place in a church. He invited his Uncle Dudel to the ceremony. Dudel sent him a note in which he said words to this effect: "I am happy for you and wish you all the best in your marriage. If there is a wedding reception in a hotel or elsewhere, I shall be happy to raise a glass to your health and that of your bride. But as to my attending your wedding in a church, you must know that I will not come. I have no objection to entering a church; if a Gentile friend or business associate were to invite me to such a wedding, I would not hesitate to accept. But I cannot bring myself to witness a ceremony where my own flesh and blood kneels as a congregant. So I shall stay away." Marc was a brilliant scholar and he is family; it is a matter of regret to me that we lost touch.

After the visits of my childhood I stopped to see my Uncle Dudel and my Aunt Miriam again in 1946, on my way from Haifa to London and RADA. On the boat I'd been befriended by some Jewish businessmen who were disembarking in Paris and who asked me to look them up during my stay. They invited me out to dinner and to nightclubs, and I accepted eagerly. On my own, I could not have afforded any of it. The nightclubs we went to, several of them, were Russian, with Russian music—specifically Russian Gypsy music. Right there began a lifelong love affair with this kind of singing and playing which I have kept going long beyond the time when love affairs can decently be carried on.

During my years in London I returned to Paris as often as I could to soak up Gypsy music. The roles seem to have reversed among the Russian emigrés there. Unlike my friends in London, quite a few of the former aristocracy who had fled to Paris had fallen on bad times and were doing menial jobs or driving taxis, while the Gypsies, who had barely scraped by in Russia, now owned and ran successful—and expensive—nightclubs. Here were aristocrats who drove taxicabs and saved up money during the week so that on Saturday night they could go to nightclubs to hear music that had been played for handouts—at most—by the same musicians in the old country. I myself could ill afford to frequent these clubs; my "successes" paid a living wage, but they had not yet translated themselves into real money. Nevertheless, I was so enamored of the music that I spent money I did not have, on champagne I did not want, in order to soak up what I could. I was not the only Londoner who frequented these places: Sometimes I would arrive at a club to discover the Galitzines there.

The clubs themselves had a certain faded splendor about them. There was a lot of deep, dark-red velvet. There were candles on the tables and ornate sconces on the walls. Carafes of vodka were brought to the table in buckets of solid ice—not ice cubes, but solid ice, so that you had to tip bucket and all to pour the vodka. Since the nightclub attracted White Russians as both staff and customers, there would be one point in the evening when the owner of the club would announce a "cossack table." A small table would be placed in the middle of the dance floor, and the singers and musicians would sit around the table in a circle, singing a medley of old Russian czarist songs.

I enjoyed those evenings as I had rarely enjoyed myself before. I was lucky to have benefactors in those days who invited me to the clubs when I couldn't afford to go on my own. Expatriate Americans like the director Lewis Milestone and his wife, Kendall, were especially kind to me. I had played in a film he directed in England for Sam Spiegel, entitled *Melba*. Milestone ("Millie," as his friends called him) was somewhat closed and generally not easily approachable. But somehow what I did and sang opened a door for me there, too. Beneath that dour exterior, Millie was a very warm and caring person. He was also a man who had been hurt by Hollywood, which may have accounted for his guardedness. This great director had been the target of totally unfounded allegations of being a "Communist sympathizer." Discounting the fact that Millie's common decency had prevented him from joining the chorus of Hollywood red-baiters, the sole ground for such an accusation seems to have been that he was born in Russia. That there was nothing else besides this to substantiate the accusation disturbed the accusers, notably Hedda Hopper, not at all. (Millie had in fact begun his film career directing training films for the U.S. Army's Signal Corps during World War I.) So this director, with a most distinguished list of credits that included two Oscars, was forced, like some others, to seek employment away from Hollywood. He was not hurting for money—both he and Kendall (a descendant of Robert E. Lee, no less) were quite wealthy—but he was clearly bruised. They had rented apartments in both London and Paris and they took me under their wing, introducing me to people and places I might not have encountered on my own—at least not for a long while. The only way I could show my gratitude was to give what I had to give: I played and sang for them and their friends.

Later there were other Americans, some permanently and some temporarily residing in Paris, whose company I enjoyed and with whom I kept contact over several decades and several continents. These included the Romanian-born film director Jean Negulesco and his wife, Dusty. Negulesco, a very convivial host, gave lavish dinner parties at his house in Beverly Hills, some of which I attended over the years. After dinner, the men would go into the billiard room and play. Here was the Romanian twist: Negulesco was a terrific player and often won back from his guests the entire price of the dinner. Others who befriended me in Paris were Charles Torem, an American lawyer, and Theo and Midge Bennahum. Theo—the only other Theo of my close acquaintance—spoke Hebrew, Yiddish, and French, as I did, and also perfect Russian; he later helped me with my first Russian recordings.

Clearly, the Russians in Paris were perennial expatriates like their counterparts in England. No matter that in their former existence as upper-crust society of Moscow and St. Petersburg they had been suffused with French culture, literature, and mores; no matter that many of them spoke accentless French, just as my friends in England spoke accentless English—they were exiles. To be sure, not all of them had been of the upper crust: There were many expatriate Russians who came from the lower strata and who for one reason or another had fled or been forced to flee the USSR. Some of these made a life for themselves in France; some others, like the plotters around the samovar, were treading water and hoping for a return to Russia with the overthrow of the revolution. Others yet treated their sojourns in France as a mere way station to the life they hoped to establish elsewhere. An old Russian, so the story went, had been waiting for an immigration visa to Canada for some twenty years. He worked at odd jobs and never learned how to speak French properly: For him everything was just temporary. All that time, he kept a smallish suitcase fully packed under his bed so he would be ready to leave just as soon as the visa came through. When he finally did receive permission to immigrate into Canada, he grabbed the valise, went out into the street, and stopped the first passerby with the following words in his heavily accented French: "*Toi! Gare du Nord—où est?*" Translation: "You! Railway station—where is?"

Most of the free time I managed to grab was spent in Paris. The train trip by second-class coach and ferry was affordable, if not altogether comfortable. My earlier stays in Paris had been at my Uncle Dudel's house in the suburbs, but I did not want to be tied to commuter trains. They stopped running at an hour that may have suited French businessmen, but was far too early for a young man who frequented places where the music did not even get into full swing before midnight. Also, there was the question of being free to keep company with young women; Dudel was no prude, but I could not see myself bringing anyone to my uncle's house to spend the night. I loved my uncle and liked spending time with him when I could, but lunches worked fine for that purpose. For the rest of the time I stayed in small, inexpensive hotels on the Left Bank (where else?) and tasted *la vie bohème*. I had made friends in Paris—artists, writers, actors, would-be actors, singers, and composers. Most of them were worse off than I, and lived from day to day. We hung out at the cafés in a bunch, and whoever had money at the time—either because he (or she) had received some from home or had sold a painting or a story— paid for the drinks and sometimes even a full dinner at one of the little bistros. The area around St.-Germain-des-Prés on the Left Bank had always been the place for young artists; in the late forties and early fifties it was even more of a mecca for them, especially all those who flirted with existentialism. Jean-Paul Sartre held court at the Café Flore and everyone hoped to benefit from his presence, if only by osmosis. I was no disciple myself; even then I had misgivings about people delivering themselves, body and soul, into the hands of a guru. Besides, many of the adherents had some difficulty in defining what existentialism was, and were content just to assert how much it meant to them to be followers of it. Often, a few of these hangers-on attempted to explain to me and anyone who would listen the basic tenets of existentialism, with little success. The most cogent explanation I got was from a young poet—Jean Radiguet, I believe, was his name—and his was a graphic demonstration. He drew the following picture:

He then explained that one could look at this picture in one of two ways. You either look at the dark part and see a French Croix de Guerre or you look at the white portions and see a fleur de lys. What you cannot do is look at the figure and see both at the same time. Voilà, existentialism in a nutshell.

During those sojourns in Paris I often sang for my supper in small clubs. Stéphane Golmann, a songwriter and performer, very French despite his Jewish name, had opened a club with himself as the main attraction. He had a respectable following and there was usually a lively crowd of regulars on hand. Whenever I was in town his club became a hangout for me and I provided a welcome respite for Stéphane, who enjoyed my work and was delighted to give his customers the chance to hear his *collègue distingué*. For me it was a place to try my material on a francophone audience. I knew that the songs themselves worked, but I wanted to experiment with the explanations I offered between the songs. Over the years, what I say has become as much a part of the performance as the music. I wanted to make sure that I could do it in more than one language, and in a way that was both informative and funny. Late at night, we would go to other places and listen to music, to Spanish musicians who played and sang flamenco and to South American trios who played guitars, harps, and flutes and who had come to Paris because the money was good. As the dawn came up, we might end up at Les Halles, the giant early morning produce, meat, and fish market, rubbing shoulders with the porters and truck drivers in the bistros where the most delicious *soupe à l'oignon* was being served.

I tried to listen to as much as I could of the local music, although Paris was perhaps not the right place for French folklore; unlike London or New York, the music of the countryside had not established itself in the big city, but there was the popular music of the day. Charles Trenet, Yves Montand, Edith Piaf, Georges Brassens, Juliette Greco—I listened to their music and soaked up its flavor. Not necessarily for the purpose of performing this material: As far as I was concerned, this was definitely the realm of pop songs, and I was convinced that pop was not my genre. At least not then; even later, when I did venture into this field, I did so only sparingly. But I learned valuable lessons in showmanship when I watched these performers on the big stages or in clubs.

Other lessons I learned from the French theatre of the day. The work of Jean-Louis Barrault, then one of France's foremost actors, was especially impressive. What gave him particular distinction was the fact that he was a superb mime, a disciple of Étienne Decroux. Barrault's production of *Les Enfants du Paradis* exhibited a mixture of styles, with mime a prominent component of the performance. Determined to come back for a second look, I returned a few weeks later to discover that the company was on tour with the production and was at that moment appearing in Brussels. So I decided to become a camp follower, and immediately booked a train for Belgium. After watching *Les Enfants* for the second time, I went backstage and managed a short chat with Barrault and his costar and wife, Madeleine Renaud. The best part of the trip turned out to be an introduction to a young actor in Barrault's company, whose talents as a mime were at least as impressive as the star's. His name was Marcel Marceau. We took an instant liking to each other and started talking. Marceau never says one word onstage; offstage he never shuts up. And he is a very interesting talker. He is also very funny. And Jewish, too. That night in Brussels we talked until daybreak, walking the streets, exchanging views, reminiscences, and jokes. What is more, we did it in four languages—French, English, Yiddish, and even in German—Marcel being a native of Alsace. That friendship continued over the years of my stay in England: Whenever Marcel appeared in London, we spent time together. To this day, he remains a marvel in body coordination; I am still filled with admiration for his facility. My own performing skills are mostly in the brain, the face, and the eyes; I have to force the other parts of my body to do their bit, so that the whole makes sense. That task is not always easy, and the Marceaus of this world fill me with envy.

Many of the exiled whom I befriended in London were of another kind than those who had been banished for so long from their homes in Eastern Europe. They were Americans, and their problem was of a more immediate and urgent nature: They were fugitives from an ugly American phenomenon known as McCarthyism. Hardly any one of these people could be defined as a Communist or proved to be a member of the Communist Party. Most were left-wing liberals, to be sure, but, with very few exceptions, no flaming reds. Such subtle distinctions were lost on Joe McCarthy and his henchmen, Roy Cohn and David Schine. (To my lasting embarrassment, both these bastards were Jews.) The performers they persecuted might have signed a petition or two supporting a workers' strike in Europe or attacking racism. They might have attended a meeting or a rally. Or they might have attended an anti-Nazi demonstration before the rest of America woke up to the threat. Even though the entire nation eventually took up arms against Nazism and fascism, these early protesters had been guilty of an anachronistic rectitude; they were labeled "prematurely antifascist." No matter that most of them were also quickly disillusioned by the soullessness of the far left and its attitude of "Yosip Vissarionovich Stalin can do no wrong"; they could not shake the stigma. The accusation of having been a sympathizer sufficed to bar them from the American public's grace and from any hope of further employment in film or TV. Theatre was much better; neither the employers nor Actors' Equity buckled under the pressure, but how many people who had previously worked in all the media could make a living in the theatre alone? So these exiles came to England, hoping to find work in a language they knew and in an atmosphere that showed respect for talent—a respect that took no account of any extraneous social or political considerations.

To this day I marvel at the shortsightedness and stupidity that permitted a country as great as America to have allowed itself to be hoodwinked by demagogues and political charlatans into believing that writers included subliminal images in their scripts to corrupt the nation with Communist propaganda otherwise undetectable by the naked eye and ear. That a society should have been so unsophisticated as to believe that actors were conveying these messages—in some cases, supposedly without even knowing it themselves. And that all artists were suspect unless they cleansed themselves in a public confessional. "I am not and never was" was not a satisfactory declaration unless accompanied by a denunciation of friends and colleagues in response to the question "Okay, if you weren't, then who do you know who was?" (I would have said "Whom do you know," but what the hell, I wasn't there and if I had been, I would have been on the wrong side of the table.) If, God forbid, someone had at one time flirted with Communism or socialism (the difference between the two was unimportant to the inquisitors), then the naming of names had to be part of the purging process. Writers and actors stood accused of having done their nefarious deeds by way of the written and spoken word. But I wonder if anyone asked himself how Paul Taylor managed to do it with his dancing feet, or how Larry Adler conveyed Communism to America by blowing notes on a harmonica?

Larry Adler, a superb musician, had no difficulty establishing himself in London. He would have been at home anywhere in the world and welcome anywhere in the world. How ironic that the only place where he was not welcome was in the land of his birth. We saw a lot of each other in London; he came to my Sunday-night gatherings, and I went to his house quite frequently. Now, it was one thing for me to take my guitar to parties and play, but he was an acknowledged virtuoso, world renowned—yet he invariably brought his harmonica and played at these informal gatherings. This taught me a lesson I never forgot. If you enjoy making music and you go to a friend's house where the atmosphere is convivial, no matter how much of a name you have, don't behave like a star. Play, if the spirit moves you. Tell stories, entertain, give. You have actually more freedom to experiment and flex your artistic muscles when you're not being paid than when you are.

Larry Adler, by the way, is not only a superb musician, he is also a fine storyteller and conversationalist. Here's one story he told about himself: When he was a kid of about fifteen or sixteen, he was already beginning to be known as a musician of great talent and was hired to do jobs in grown-up places like nightclubs. He was hired as the opening act at a club in Chicago one day, and after the opening there was a big champagne party to celebrate a successful beginning of the engagement. Larry declined the champagne and drank Coca-Cola instead. A man came up to him and said, "You're terrific when you play that thing. Where you from, kid?" Larry told him that his home was Baltimore. The man asked, "You a Jewish kid?" Larry nodded yes. The man continued: "You go to shul?" "Not very often," Larry replied. "You should go every week, kid, every week." Then he asked, "Is your mother alive?" Larry said, "Sure." "You write to her?" Larry admitted that he did not do that too often, either. "Every day, you should write to her every day, you hear me?" With that the man walked away. Puzzled, young Larry Adler asked a man who was standing next to him, "Who was that?" The man said, "You don't know? That was Al Capone."

With the end of the blacklist, Larry Adler and all the others were free to return to the States from their enforced or self-imposed exile. Many did, some did not. Although Larry does from time to time perform in the United States, he has never returned to live in America; he continues to make his home in England. The same held true for Sam Wanamaker, who was, while perhaps not a direct victim, another fugitive from the poisonous McCarthy climate. He, too, would work in the States from time to time but continued to live in London until his death in January 1994. In the early fifties, Sam established himself in England and became a sought-after stage actor, specializing in American roles: *The Shrike* and Clifford Odets's *The Big Knife* were some of his early London successes. I kept company with him, too. He and his then wife, Charlotte, had sublet a flat near Regent's Park from Glynis Johns, who was spending months abroad on various film jobs. I recall one extraordinary night when London wrapped itself in one of those legendary fogs people write and sing about. This one was a beauty; you literally could not see the hand in front of your face. I was driving past Regent's Park on my way home to St. John's Wood when the fog suddenly materialized. Under normal circumstances I might have been home ten minutes later. In this fog, it would take hours—if I made it home at all. People were forced to abandon their vehicles on both sides of the road to avoid accidents. I did likewise. When I realized that I was only a couple of blocks away from the Wanamakers', I groped along the walls of the houses, avoiding several pedestrians who were attempting the same blind routine in the opposite direction, and managed to get to Sam's place in one piece. I rang the doorbell. Luckily they were home and let me stay the night. Like all the other drivers, I would be able to go pick up my car in the morning when the fog lifted. The Wanamakers did not have a spare bedroom, though, and I had to sleep on the living room floor. I remember being very thankful for the fact that Glynis Johns was such a successful actress that she could afford thick, luxurious carpets.

Foremost in my memory among the refugees from Joe McCarthy was J. Edward Bromberg, who became a close friend and with whom I spent many hours eating, drinking, laughing, playing chess, and talking. Joe was a fine character actor who had had a wonderfully creative career both in the theatre and in films in America. One fine day (Why do they say that? It was a lousy day) his career in America stopped dead. He had been cited to appear before the House Committee on Un-American Activities (HUAC). He went, refused to name names, and was, from that second on, unemployable. He came to England not only to find work and feed his family back in the States, but to escape the whole atmosphere of persecution there that had made him a premature has-been. Joe Bromberg and I saw each other almost every day—more accurately, every night—after the show. I was doing a play called *The Love of Four Colonels* at the time, and Joe was starring in a very funny American play about an undertaker entitled *The Biggest Thief in Town*. As it happens, the playwright was Dalton Trumbo, one of the blacklisted screenwriters known as the Hollywood Ten. Joe and I would meet just as soon as our makeup was off, and I would drive us both to the apartment of mutual actor friends, Ronan O'Casey and his wife, Mary Laura Wood. Both were Canadians, and Mary Laura had been Vivien Leigh's understudy in *Streetcar*. We all had a lot in common, including a liberal political orientation. As a consequence, Joe felt very comfortable with us and with the informality of our nightly visits. Sometimes our hosts were not even there when we arrived; no matter, we knew where the keys were hidden, and let ourselves in. Whoever got there first set up the chess game and put on the coffee. The chess was terrific; so was the conversation, which flowed as freely as the coffee.

Joe had a wonderful sense of humor: Although he had every right to be morose and embittered, his relationships with the people around him were friendly, open, and compassionate. It was only when the subject of the national shame called the blacklist was the topic of conversation that Joe showed his anguish. While it was easy to feel for him and to be supportive as he agonized over what had happened to him, to his friends, and to his country, no one could really know how deep the wounds were. It was not until I got to America and witnessed the last gasps of the tragedy and its aftermath that I was able to take the measure of it in a more immediate sense. For now, we were an ocean away from it and unable to experience the indignity viscerally. But we saw how Joe hurt, and it was deeply disturbing. The English cast he worked with was very fond of him—although, like most Englishmen, they dealt with the surface in their insular fashion and were unable or unwilling to probe what lay underneath. His more intimate friends besides myself—Casey and Mary Laura—sensed the deep pain in him.

And a tragedy it turned out to be. One night we got together as usual at Casey's flat and did what we always did. We played chess, joked, talked, drank wine, and nibbled cheese. At little before 2:00 A.M. I drove Joe home to his digs, and went home to bed. The next day, December 6, 1951, was a matinee day. I was at my theatre about an hour before curtain time, as usual, and took my time putting on my makeup. Half hour was called by the stage manager; then, just before the fifteen-minute call, I was paged to the stage-door telephone. The stage manager of Joe's play was on the line and inquired in a bit of panic whether I had any idea where Joe might be, since he had not reported to the theatre as usual. This was very atypical of Joe: He had the professional's discipline. The theatre had called Joe's landlady, who reported that he seemed to be out since no one answered her knock at the door. I could not believe that Joe would have gone anywhere except to the theatre. At my urging, the landlady tried to gain access to Joe's room with her keys. The door was bolted from the inside. A locksmith was called who cut through the bolt. Joe was on his bed, dead from a heart attack. In another two weeks he would have been forty-seven years old.

Shocked as we all were, we knew arrangements had to be made quickly and it would be up to his family to make the decisions that needed to be made. The bizarre and horrible twist of the situation was that Joe's wife, Goldie, and his daughter, Marcia, were at that moment on a ship on the high seas, traveling from New York to join Joe in England and start a new life for themselves in exile. His son, Conrad, was still in New York. I argued with the play's producers that it would be cruel to contact the ship and confront the family with a situation in which they were powerless to do anything until they landed; it would only fill two people with despair and anguish over their own helplessness. But we wired Conrad, who arrived by air the next morning. He was a budding playwright in his twenties and, despite his distress, was quite capable of handling things. Possibly the hardest thing he had to do was to meet the ship on arrival, and give his mother and sister the dreadful news. But that was still some days away.

Conrad bunked out at my apartment for the first few days, and I tried to give as much support as I could without intruding on his private grief. The arrangements kept him busy during the day: the funeral, collecting his father's belongings, disposing of some, settling with the landlady, meeting with the play's producers—the show had closed; it could not really work without Joe—and receiving the last of Joe's salary. The evenings were more difficult; that was when support was most needed. I was not the only one who held Conrad's hand during those evenings. Everyone who had liked Joe, friends and members of his cast, came by and did their best to dispel the gloom. We talked, commiserated, called up memories of Joe, and also spoke of the blacklist, which had surely contributed to his death. Doctors may have called it cardiac arrest, a medical condition, but I was convinced that Joe died of a broken heart.

One of the strangest, yet most generous, gestures in honor of Joe's memory came from a young actress who had been the ingenue in the play. This young girl, at the beginning of her career, had a dewy and very English innocence about her. She wanted to give Conrad something because she had liked his father so much. But this had been only her first or second job, and she was poor, as young actors who are starting out are apt to be. Still, she wanted to do something, and so she went to bed with Conrad—upstairs in my bed, which was the largest in the apartment. It may have been sex, but it was not a libidinous gesture—rather one that was born of pure affection and a wish to hold this young man in her arms and give comfort and solace the best way she knew how. We had all tried to offer support, but hers was by far the most gentle and humane.

Some time ago I came across a biography of J. Edward Bromberg in a reference work. Under "Recreation" it listed only one: chess.

Among others who showed up at Carlton Hill at various times were Israeli actors, singers, and musicians, some seeking their fortunes in England, some on vacation, some on their way to the States. Through their visits I maintained my contacts with the Hebrew theatre and kept up with the current Hebrew songs. A black South African, Lionel Ngakane, who was cast in the film *Cry the Beloved Country,* had come to London for the filming of interior scenes. Lionel, who became a regular visitor to my house, taught me the one Zulu song I later recorded—"*Mangwani Mpulele.*" He was a splendid young man who never returned to his native land with its oppression of blacks, but remained in London teaching African dialects—having been rescued, improbably, by Sir Alexander Korda's film company.

Then there was Chin Yu, a lovely Chinese girl whose name translates as "Golden Jade." *South Pacific* was in its first run in London, and Chin Yu had a small role and a big understudy in the musical. While not exactly a fugitive, she had developed fairly strong left-wing views in America, and was possibly more radical politically than any of my other expatriate friends. Had she stayed in America, she would most certainly have gotten into big trouble. We got very friendly very fast. It was she who introduced me to some recordings from the States that I had not known before. I was most impressed with a musical cavalcade called *The Lonesome Train,* about Lincoln's funeral train as it wound its way through the countryside from Washington, D.C., to

Illinois. The recordings were on several 78 rpm disks (remember those?) that were beginning to get scratchy. It was possibly the most patriotic work in the folk idiom I had ever heard. Ironically, one of the blacklisted writers, Millard Lampell, had written the script. Pete Seeger played his banjo in his inimitable fashion, and Burl Ives was the musical narrator. But more than with the work I was impressed by Chin Yu's reaction to it. There were often tears in her eyes as we played the records. Talk about inscrutable Orientals.

The preeminent folklorist in America, Alan Lomax, was among those who came to St. John's Wood to talk, listen, and sing. John and Alan Lomax, *père et fils,* had published the most comprehensive collection of folklore of the Americas and, because of the respect I had for their work, I was very eager to meet Alan. What he expected to gain from meeting me I had no idea. It was partly curiosity, I suppose, something that attracted most first-time visitors. Also, there were singers and performers in my house whom he had not known before, notably Eastern Europeans and sometimes Russian Gypsies, whose music was, as always, a focal point of my gatherings. For whatever reason, he came back a number of times. Alan was a dynamic presence, and a fair singer and guitar player himself. I cannot say that we became fast friends; there was something in the way which neither of us managed to overcome, neither then nor many years later when our paths crossed. At the time there was some sort of jealousy at work due to the fact that we were both vying for the attention of the same women. Moreover, Alan never seemed comfortable with me as a folk performer, grudgingly accepting my Hebrew, Yiddish, or Russian songs, but little else among the twenty-one languages in which I perform, especially any Anglo-Saxon material. I recall an occasion in Washington, D.C., when I served as master of ceremonies at a government-sponsored folklife-award ceremony. When Alan saw that I had brought my guitar, he had a fit and voiced strong objections to my playing a single note in setting the scene for the ceremony or doing anything but making verbal introductions. I did not insist upon playing; he may even have been right in terms of the programming, but his reaction was excessive. One more example of the folk purist fearing contamination from "show biz." For my part, I was and am grateful for Alan Lomax's knowledge and expertise and continue to make common cause with him and with all those who are defending the folk process.

I shall always remember the time Lomax brought Margaret Barry to my apartment. She was an Irish Gypsy with swarthy, leathery skin and a mouth that seemed lopsided because quite a few of her teeth were missing. Her words were slurred either because of the teeth or because of the gin whose smell permeated the room when she entered. Then she sang. She played an old, beat-up banjo in a sort of flamenco style and I thought she was simply wonderful. I have never heard "She Moves Through the Fair" sung as hauntingly. It was Irish all right, but it was also wild and darkly Gypsy. "It will not be long, love, till our wedding day"—the words of the dead lover to the still living keep ringing in my ears.

But always there were the Russians. The clubs I frequented in Paris—Scheherezade, Rascasse, and especially Novy—were the places where I learned the songs and came back time after time to listen for every inflection and chord progression. Old 78 rpm records by artists like Sarah Gorby, Lida Goulesco, and Nastya Poliakova had given me some kind of introduction to the material, but hearing it live was an entirely different experience. There was Dima Oussoff, part Gypsy and part nobleman, the latter portion having given him courtly manners and a polyglot education, and the former the talent to play the seven-string guitar and sing beautiful Russian "romances." There was Sonia Dimitrievich, a dark-complexioned Gypsy woman who had obviously been quite beautiful once. Of the women singers Sonia was my favorite. Her delivery was exquisite and she never held back. Each time there was passion in her performance, and each time you were moved. Did it matter if the emotion was produced by the singer through some psychological trickery that called it up at will and on cue? Not to me; after all, what does a good actor do when he needs to produce emotion at 8:00 P.M. every evening? Her songs had a flavor all their own, including some lyrics that switched from straight Russian into Gypsy dialect, with added syllables in between that Emmanuel Galitzine was unable to identify as belonging to any language at all. I happen to like those "divvy-divvy-divey" syllables and I use them in the songs just as I learned them. Sonia was often backed by a trio—violin, piano, and guitar—but she performed equally well with the guitar alone, as played by George Ivanov, a gentle man who deferred to the fiery lady in everything, yet still held his own while playing. No one knew for certain if he was her husband, lover, POSSLQ, or what. (Actually, POSSLQ is officialese of more recent vintage, a term used by the Internal Revenue Service that stands for "Person of the Opposite Sex Sharing Living Quarters.")

Sonia had an Aunt Valya who was also an exquisite performer. Because of some sort of Gypsy feud, the two women had not been on speaking terms for years. But when, on occasion, they found themselves in the same room and someone began to play, they would sing together with great harmonies and total togetherness without a hint of rivalry. Then, when the music was over, the feud resumed. They still did not speak.

There were good male singers, too, but they were fewer in number than the females. My undisputed favorite among them was Volodya Polyakoff. He had a resonant bass voice with a ringing tremolo, and played the seven-string guitar in a unique manner. Where other players of stringed instruments produce a vibrato by vibrating the fingers as they hold down individual strings, Volodya would achieve a vibrato by playing a whole chord and shaking the entire instrument, in a fast trembling motion. His vocal and instrumental rendition of "Two Guitars" is still the best I have heard, the close second being a rare recording by the team of Yul and Alyosha. Not that Yul, surely? Yes, the very same. Before becoming an actor and a star, singing and playing Gypsy songs was how Yul Brynner made a living. I count that recording among the prize possessions in my music collection. Another such gem is a record album produced in France, entitled *Les Derniers Voix Tziganes* (The Last of the Gypsy Voices). It combines the talents of Valya Dimitrievich and Volodya Polyakoff, and was made possible because the French author Joseph Kessel was just as crazy about this music as I—and rich enough to finance the recording. I last heard Volodya sing in 1988; he was in his nineties, still performing almost nightly at the Russian nightclub at 1 bis, rue des Colonels Renard, near the Étoile. His guitar was somewhat off-key, since he had become hard of hearing; no matter, he still sounded good. Talking to him was a sad experience, however. He greeted me like a long-lost friend, but in reply to my questions about various other Gypsy musicians he had little to say except *"Umer"* (Dead), *"Umer tozhe"* (Also dead).

Almost all of them are gone now. The Russian clubs still exist in Paris, still run by Russian owners or managers, some quite old, who greet you at the door, conduct you to your seat, and announce from time to time to the patrons and the performers, *"Attraction, s'il vous plait"* (Showtime, please). Then the music begins. But the acts are young, most of them no longer Gypsy or capable of rendering the songs with the authentic Gypsy flavor. While the Soviet Union still had a grip on emigration, many of these young artists were not even Russian; often they were Poles who had an easier exit from their homeland, and who quickly learned the Russian songs so they could somehow pass muster in the clubs and make a living. Now there are authentic Russians performing in Paris once again, but these are culturally removed from the emigré society which, in its day, had created its own ambiance. Gone is the faded elegance, gone the polite old

Russian waiters who served the ice-chilled vodka, the champagne, the caviar, and the *zakuski* (herring), *kulibiaka,* and *shashlik karsky,* all served to the sounds of authentic Gypsy music. The guitars of the exiled are still being heard; but both the sounds and the players have changed. It is a different exile.

6

East End, West End, and the Palace

AT THE END OF THE DECADE, IN 1949, my career took another big step forward. I was cast in yet another long theatre engagement—the result of a party, which gives the lie to the often-repeated warning by veteran show folk that social occasions never lead to professional advancement. For the life of me, I cannot remember whose party it was, or why it was given. I do remember very well that this was where I met Peter Ustinov. To say that we hit it off immediately would be inadequate to describe our instant rapport. We both delighted in doing characters, accents, and languages; we both liked to perform, to improvise monologues, and test our mettle with a ready-made audience. At the party Peter and I indulged in an elaborate sort of repartee: two actors who were also linguists, trading characterizations and accents back and forth.

That night we went on almost till daybreak, doing German and French professors mostly, as well as bumbling politicians, Russian folklorists, blustering military men of various armies—a fast, exhilarating linguistic Ping-Pong game. What I found so appealing in Peter's drawing-room talent was that it represented something I myself had been striving for, with varying degrees of success—something that to this day I still practice on the concert stage between songs. It is a rapidly vanishing art form that few people practiced then, and even fewer do now. The closest English term to describe Peter is "monologuist," but this is less than accurate, for it fails to note that monologuists paint with a narrower brush than Peter employed when setting color and mood before launching into his witty and often cruel character sketches. The French terms *raconteur* or *diseur* more accurately describe this manner of performing. Ruth Draper and Cornelia Otis Skinner were noted practitioners of this art form, and sometimes used the terms when referring to their own performances. At one time this led to an unexpected result. Cornelia Otis Skinner was scheduled to do her one-woman show in Glasgow, Scotland, and was interviewed in her dressing room prior to her performance by the local press. When she was asked how she would describe herself, she said that she preferred the term "*diseuse.*" The next day the paper carried a review that began: "Last night Miss Cornelia Otis Skinner, the well-known American disease . . ."

Within forty-eight hours of meeting Peter at the party, I received a script by messenger, entitled *The Love of Four Colonels,* by Peter Ustinov. There was no question that I was absolutely right for the Russian colonel, nor was there any doubt Peter wanted me to play it. Typical of Ustinov's writing, this was an atypical play giving free rein to bouts of fantasy. The play was set in a remote hamlet of occupied German territory just after the war. The occupation forces of the four great powers, Britain, France, the USSR, and the United States, are jointly administering the region with periodic meetings of the four representatives, each having the rank of colonel. So much for its veneer of reality. The fantasy revolves around the fact that the castle on top of the hill harbors the Sleeping Beauty, still asleep after her many years of dormancy. Each of the four colonels is determined to wake her up, and each one attempts to do so in his own fashion and in the literary style typical of his nationality. The Englishman employs the style of Shakespeare, the Frenchman a foppish comic style, and the American makes his attempt in a takeoff of a Western movie the Russian, in a parody of Anton Chekhov. Each of these scenes becomes a battleground in which the Good Fairy is a supporter of the undertaking, and the Wicked Fairy the opponent.

Playing the Wicked Fairy gave Peter a chance to do brilliant and sometimes totally outrageous impersonations within the various styles. He also improvised a great deal. Successful improvisations were repeated on other nights. For example, in the pseudo-Chekhov piece, Peter played an Uncle Vanya–type character who enters the garden where Sleeping Beauty, now temporarily awakened by me as the Russian colonel, is playing croquet as I sit knitting on a swing. The improvisations in that scene alone lasted a full four minutes; by theatre measurements a very long time indeed. Peter might admire the foliage, comment on it, walk over to the Beauty, who wore a straw hat with a crown of artificial fruit, pick a cherry off it, eat it, and then shoot the pit at me. I would react sharply, look at him accusingly, rub my cheek as though it had been hit, and so it would go on and on. When Peter was out of commission for a couple of nights because of a severe attack of the flu, his understudy, a very capable actor, played the part exactly as written, got all the original laughs—and yet we ran a full fifteen minutes shorter on the clock!

Sometimes we were forced into improvising. When, at the intermission, a new stagehand pulled the lever he thought controlled the fire curtain but activated the sprinkler valve instead, we had drizzling rain on stage for the entire second act. Since it was an indoor set, the justifications we came up with were hilarious. Most of us loved the improvisations; however, a few members of the cast were not able to adjust to Peter's ways and were either suffering in silence, grumbling behind his back, or challenging him openly. The square-jawed actor playing the British colonel, Colin Gordon, was especially rattled by the unpredictability of it all, and blew his top one evening after a particularly lengthy bout of improvisation. I was sitting in Peter's dressing room during the intermission when Colin marched in, red-faced, and called Peter "a nincompoop and a young puppy who did not understand the play," forgetting that he was not just addressing a fellow actor but the very author of the play. The accusation, though ridiculous on the face of it, was understandable in one sense. There was a tug of war of sorts between the two Ustinovs. One of the critics wrote, "The difficulty is that as actor he steals the show from himself as playwright."

The license to improvise was not reserved for the author-star alone. The rest of us could and did make use of the implied permission that it was all right to embellish. However, some rules were understood; your improvisation had to stay within the character and period, and the thing had to be done not as an in-joke in order to amuse each other, but primarily for the enjoyment of the audience. One of my own favorite ad-libs also came during the Chekhov scene. As the scene starts and I am discovered on the swing, knitting, I am supposed to say with a sigh—after a long Chekhovian pause—"I must leave for Moscow tonight." She asks, "Tonight?" And I say, "Yes," with another sigh. One night the dialogue went, "I must leave for Moscow tonight." "Tonight?" "Yes. The eight o'clock train is bound to leave before midnight." Sigh. Peter thought that the line was so in character and in keeping with the scene that he ordered it inserted in the prompt script for future productions. The sock I was knitting, by the way, got longer and longer with each passing week. By the time we had completed one year, it was so unwieldy that the stage crew undid most of it for me to start over, much to my chagrin.

When we began work on *The Love of Four Colonels,* Peter was twenty-nine years old, three years older than I. But he already had an incredible body of work to show for his young years. He had written plays, articles, and his own literary pastiches as material for his one-man performances. He had also written film scripts and had appeared on stage and in films for a number of years. Some of it he did while he was serving in the British army. He obviously managed to circumvent army regulations to do exactly what he wanted. His main duties in the British army involved writing recruiting scripts and propaganda films for the department of army psychiatry. In fulfilling these duties, he mingled with high-ranking officers, generals, and the like, but Peter himself never rose higher than the rank of private and refused to undergo the ritual of an army haircut.

That Peter Ustinov served in the army at all was curious. Although born in London, Peter and the rest of his family did not become British citizens until 1938. Their nationality was German, and Peter's father had been a diplomat at the German embassy in London at the time of Peter's birth. Their origin was indeed Russian, but the grandfather, a Russian nobleman, had been in disfavor at the court of the czar. It appears he was opposed to encroachment upon individual freedoms, and he proceeded to free his serfs long before the rest of Russia followed suit. Worse yet, he became a Protestant. In the end he was stripped of his title and his holdings and forced to abandon Russia altogether. He emigrated to the Middle East, of all places. As I recall, Peter's father was born in Jaffa and received part of his education at the German schools in Palestine and Lebanon. He continued his studies in Germany proper and, when World War I broke out, volunteered to serve in the German army. So it came about that this son of a Russian nobleman helped the Germans in their fight against Russia. He obviously acquitted himself of the task so well that, in recognition of his services, the Germans restored the old Russian family title to him and made it German. So he became the Baron von Ustinov. He joined the diplomatic service and was posted to London as press attaché at the German Embassy. Peter was born in 1921, a German national with

diplomatic status. When the Nazis took over in 1933, old man Ustinov stuck it out for a while, but found himself unable to serve these
new masters and their ambassador, von Ribbentrop. He quit, and
asked to remain a resident of Britain. Peter's mother, Nadia Benois, an
artist and painter, was also of Russian origin; her father Alexandre
Benois was himself a noted painter living in Paris. Those were Peter's
antecedents, giving him a clearly intellectual and cultured heritage.
Although our backgrounds were different, there existed a similarity of
outlook and a shared attitude toward modes of performance. That did
not go unnoticed. Once I heard myself referred to as "the poor man's
Peter Ustinov." I was not insulted.

Like my friend Peter, I also led more than one life. Mine always
moved along in parallels. While the life and career of the actor was
taking its course, there was a Jewish life as well. Not exactly the kind
of Jewish life I had been used to, either in my early years in Vienna or
later in Palestine. I had been used to little orthodox prayer houses,
shtiblach, as they were called, with old Jews wearing well-worn prayer
shawls and holding old, yellowing prayer books that were kissed before
they were opened and threatened to fall apart altogether. When they
did, the books were actually buried in a grave as though they had been
living beings. The Jews prayed loudly, each with a rhythm and pitch of
his own, disdaining unison; although there was togetherness, the general impression was one of unruliness, if not downright chaos. Even
the larger synagogues of Central and Eastern Europe had that kind of
atmosphere. With the exception of a few replicas of the *shtibl,* which
you had to know about in order to find them, the synagogues in London were staid affairs.

Obviously, at bottom, London Jews were not really different: Jews
are the same all over. Yet there was a British veneer on top of it all,
including the customs and the ritual. In my vicinity, St. John's Wood
or West Hampstead, the rabbi and the dignitaries sitting on the *bimah*
(pulpit) and even some of the congregants in the front rows wore
black cutaway coats, gray vests, and top hats. The ritual itself was
mostly orthodox—there were not many reform congregations—but
the general conduct seemed far too orderly. I suppose the congregants
had picked up British notions of polite manners from their surroundings by a process of osmosis. The announcements from the pulpit were
made in English accents tinged with either East European or East End
cockney; rabbinical oratory carried intonations of upper-crust British
schooling from which the occasional quotes in Hebrew stuck out with
startling incongruity.

The bar mitzvahs to which I was invited exhibited similar characteristics, which made them quite unlike their counterparts in other corners of the world. There was a master of ceremonies in a red frock coat who carried a long staff, which he occasionally banged on the floor in slow rhythm to call for silence, so that announcements, speeches, and toasts to the honorees could be heard. "My lords, ladies, and gentlemen," he would intone, "Pray silence for the Bar Mitzvah boy!" There would follow a speech by the hapless youth, who either read or recited a speech from memory, using obscure biblical quotes in an attempt to show his newly acquired Jewish adulthood and ending with a string of thanks to teachers and family, delivered with dubious sincerity. Then the emcee would call on various men—always men—to offer a variety of toasts, to the parents, to the rabbi, and to the grandparents. "My lords, ladies, and gentlemen, pray silence for Mr. Levy Bakstansky, who will deliver the toast!" Mr. Levy Bakstansky would wax lyrical, reciting memories interspersed with poetry in accents that clearly recalled his Yiddish mother tongue. At the toast's conclusion, everyone was bidden to rise: "My lords, ladies, and gentlemen, pray be upstanding for the toast!" All would rise and then our red-coated friend would solemnly declaim, "The toast is—Bubbeh and Zaideh!" I had a hard time keeping a straight face through most of it.

Still, I am no slouch. I learned to use the ways of societal ceremony rather quickly, and had occasion to apply them from time to time. On occasion there would be an impressive array of dignitaries present at a dinner or other function, each with a title that needed to be remembered and used properly at the proper time. Once on such an evening, when my turn came to speak and perform, I began my address to the assemblage by running down the titles in order of their importance. In that order, aristocracy came first, to be followed by the judiciary, elected and appointed officials, and finally the clergy prior to the lowly "ladies and gentlemen." But I am a stickler for accuracy. There were two rabbis present, one of whom was a man of impressive intellect, while the other had but doubtful credentials as a writer and thinker. And so I began my remarks as follows: "Your Lordships, Your Honor, Your Excellency, Your Worship" (a mayor's title), then addressing the admired rabbi on my left, "Learned Clergy"—and then, turning to the right—"Clergy," and finally, "Ladies and Gentlemen!" Luckily, there were but a few giggles.

Working-class and lower-middle-class Jews in London had their own jargon. Jewish cockney was somehow drier than American Jewish speech, which derives its attitudes from East European Jewish speech patterns. But it was no less humorous. A trip on Sunday mornings to Petticoat Lane in the East End yielded plenty of laughs. This once-a-week marketplace continues in full swing until about 2:00 P.M. Then the hawkers and colorful Jewish vendors roll up the outdoor stalls and leave to think up other phrases and sales gimmicks to be used the following week. Many a stand-up performer has found material on Sunday morning at the Lane. "Lookin' for something, deah, shoes? Nice pair of hand-made platforms?" My friend Miriam Karlin, a fine actress and a terrific mimic, used to do this character. "Come inside, deah, nobody is *forcing you!*"—that last with a powerful yank on the customer's arm to get her inside the clothing store. Then she would go on: "This is a model, just in this mornin'." She would then blow the dust off the merchandise and say, "Would you believe me if I told you that Princess Margaret came in here the other day and bought just such a one?" Then, after a pause: "So all right, so she didn't." None of this was all that exaggerated. I myself witnessed a vendor who was selling very cheap and gaudy cotton print dresses that hung in a row on a long rack. Like most of the others, he attracted customers by calling out selling slogans in a loud voice. "Nice dresses, fit for a queen, well, a beauty queen, anyway; come on, ladies, don't be shy!" Little shopgirls would stop by to look at this very affordable merchandise. Then, all of a sudden, I heard him yell at the top of his lungs: "Shiksa dresses!"

Most British Jews lead a life consisting of two parts. Their dealings with their surroundings, to the extent to which these are outside the Jewish community, are conducted in a cordial atmosphere that, while not exactly strained, preserves a distance. As a group, Jews are not exactly prone to pop around the corner to the local pub for a pint of mild-and-bitter after business hours. I am not suggesting that there is no socializing between the Jews and Gentiles in Britain. But, at least during my time in England, Jewish life away from the workplace was conducted on a separate plane; it took place in homes, social halls, and certain restaurants, and was determined by a calendar of festivals and family events. This much is true of Jewish communities in most countries: Jews are a people whose lives, both secular and religious, are governed by the calendar.

Kosher food had its own aspects and ambience. There were small food shops, quite unlike an American deli, where steaming sandwiches were the main bill of fare. There was also matzo-ball soup, smoked or salted fish, and potato latkes; but the main attraction was brisket and, most important, salt beef. This was the British equivalent of corned beef but looked anemic; it lacked the red color of Jewish corned beef, American style. It was quite good, though, if you did not fasten your attention on its appearance. The very term "corned beef" meant something entirely different in England. We had met this delicacy in Palestine during the war. British soldiers carried tins of corned beef in their kit bags, and sometimes gave them away as gifts to the local populace. It was ground, fatty meat that we devoured as though it were a gourmet treat. In retrospect, it was quite dreadful. No wonder that when American Jews came to England and asked for corned beef in a Jewish sandwich shop, the owner made a face.

Despite the xenophobic attitude of the British, there were certain Jewish influences on English language and custom in evidence. One takes such cross-pollination for granted in America, which is, after all, a land of immigrants. But even in staid England the influence was, though not as pervasive, certainly discernible. Words of Hebrew origin were found in English literature, possibly because the translators of the Old Testament were unable to come up with Anglo-Saxon equivalents for such words as *leviathan, shibboleth, cherub, shekel,* or *gehenna.* But even words derived from Yiddish, as distinct from Hebrew, crept into the English language, probably toward the end of the nineteenth century with the influx of immigrants from Eastern Europe. Some of these were borrowed by the underworld; petty thieves would use terms like *gonif* for thief and *shekels* for money. Around the turn of the century, Israel Zangwill, the Anglo-Jewish writer, used words like *schnorrer* (beggar), *shammes* (synagogue beadle), and *kaddish.* The most use, however, was gotten out of *kosher* and *treyf,* the former meaning "ritually clean for eating" and the latter meaning "unclean." Those words, too, acquired additional meanings unrelated to ritual cleanliness. I recall sitting in a small restaurant in Soho that, though run by Jews, was not a kosher place. Right next door was Isows, a well-known, strictly kosher restaurant; I preferred the smaller one, where you could get a cup of coffee with milk after a dinner of meat and potatoes. Once I overheard a conversation between the owner and the meat supplier who had come in with a delivery. The owner informed the man that he would not require any delivery the following week because the restaurant would be closed for a week's hiatus. The man was upset: "What am I going to do with my meat?" he lamented. The owner suggested that one of the other places around might take the meat off the supplier's hands. "All right," said the man, "I'll take it to Isows next door." "That won't do," said the owner. "Why not?" "Because your meat isn't kosher," said the owner. Full of indignation, the supplier raised his voice: "Why not? *I didn't steal it!*"

The strangest way Jewish custom was observed in Britain was by the Royal Family itself. The sovereign is not only the head of state, he or she is also the head of the Church of England. Britain knows no separation of church and state, to the bafflement of visiting Americans. British army units are marched into churches on Sundays as an obligatory exercise, without demurrer from anybody. In America there would have been an outcry on the part of the ACLU, the American Jewish Congress, and even some Christian groups who were not adherents of the official church denomination. Not so in Britain, which views itself as a Christian nation, yet is far less coercive toward groups outside the mainstream than religiously neutral countries. It is all the more surprising, then, that in this Christian realm, the male offspring of the royal house undergoes a Jewish ritual circumcision, including the prayers and blessings. The explanation for this custom was intriguing: All kings, I was told, are presumed to be descendants of King David. Hence the insistence upon observing a ritually correct *bris*. I know this to be true; I used to be a frequent guest in the home of Dr. Emmanuel Snowman, a London surgeon who was also an accredited *mohel* and who, in fact, had circumcised Prince Charles. When Queen Elizabeth was crowned, relatively few people owned television sets; I was watching the coronation proceedings in the home of someone who had one. I was surprised to see that in the solemn coronation procession following the Queen's horse-drawn carriage a Torah was carried by a venerable-looking man wearing a yarmulke, whom I assumed to be the Chief Rabbi of Great Britain. I have no doubt that this custom, too, derives its origin from the belief in the royal descendancy from the House of David.

The Love of Four Colonels was a huge success and ran for a full two years at Wyndham's Theatre in London's West End. It is fair to say that just about everybody came to see it at one time or another, including theatre and film people from America. Many of us in the cast received offers for plays and films, no one more so than Peter himself. Of course, he had also just been nominated for an Academy Award for Best Supporting Actor for playing Nero in the film *Quo Vadis*, a role he almost did not get to play. After they had cast him in the part, he received a telegram one day to the effect that they were having second thoughts and were thinking of casting an older actor to play the role of the wily emperor. This was one of those silly notions that Hollywood brass so frequently indulges in; clearly, Peter was absolutely perfect for the role. Peter told me what he had wired to California in reply. It said something like "Nero was 29 when he died. Stop. I am 31. Stop. If you wait another year I shall be too old. Signed Ustinov." They reversed themselves pretty quickly, and Peter went on not only to play Nero, but to win the nomination as well.

As for me, I had started to do movies before the run of our play and continued even while the play was on. In London that is quite possible, although somewhat exhausting. British films acknowledged the symbiotic relationship between the two media, and the fact that the best talent was to be found among working stage performers. Consequently, the schedules of stage actors working in a film while concurrently performing in a play were accommodated: Their matinee days were respected, and they were given timely release in the afternoon so they could make it to the theatre for evening performances. American movie people have an entirely different attitude, and it is not just because of the impossible distance from Broadway to Hollywood. When they take note of the theatre, it is mainly as a pool of talent for future casting purposes. I have never heard of anyone hiring an actor to take part in a film while he was performing in a play at the same time, even if the play was in Los Angeles or the film was on location in New York. In England we did quite a lot of that. You would get up at the crack of dawn, drive to the studios at Pinewood or Elstree some twenty-five miles away, work until about five-thirty in the afternoon, and then rush to the theatre, put on makeup (or modify the film makeup that was still on your face to suit the stage role), and do your play. You got home well after 11:00 P.M., studied the script for the next day's shooting, and, if you were lucky, got a few hours' sleep.

My first American film role came in 1950, during the second year of *The Love of Four Colonels*. I had been sent by my agent to an interview that we assumed would be conducted by the casting director. But the film's director jealously guarded his right to determine every artistic aspect of his films, down to casting the smallest parts. There was staff at the audition, to be sure, including the casting director, but it was quite evident around whom this world revolved. Not that there was anything imperious about John Huston: On the contrary, he was full of jokes and intent on putting you at ease. But through all the kidding and banter, you could always sense John's eye scrutinizing you and weighing your worth and possible usefulness for the movie. He asked me if I could do a German accent; in keeping with the jocular mood of the interview, I almost said no. Of course I could. I demonstrated, and was hired to play the German first officer in *The African Queen*.

For a young actor to do his first film working with Humphrey Bogart and Katharine Hepburn was a most extraordinary opportunity. The role itself was not difficult: an officer on a German naval vessel, the *Louisa*, plowing the waters of Lake Victoria in Central Africa. This is the ship that Bogart and Hepburn plan to blow up as their own private contribution to the Allied war effort against the Germans. The World War I saga by C. S. Forester was well known, as was James Agee, who wrote the script. What made this retelling unique wasn't just the principals involved but also the way in which the film had been put together. This had to do with a flamboyant figure named Sam Spiegel.

In remembering Sam Spiegel it becomes hard to keep fact and legend apart. There are so many stories about Sam floating about that the true story, even when accurately recalled, has an improbable ring to it. On a personal level it was difficult to dislike the man; he had about him a charlatan's generosity and a most hospitable manner. He had spent some time in Palestine and knew of my background, and frequently engaged me in Jewish banter. But as a businessman and an employer, he could hardly have been less trustworthy. He was a con man and a notorious cutter of corners. His very arrival on the Hollywood scene has been described as a sleight-of-hand achievement worthy of a deft Gypsy's street-corner *bajour,* a cross between confidence tricking and magicianship. Apparently, when Sam first arrived in New York he let it be known that he had been involved in film production in Europe. That impressed people somewhat, even though they could not check the accuracy of the claim—who knew or cared much about European films with unpronounceable names of stars with no American recognition value? The claim had to be backed up by some lavish entertaining and a prestigious address. Lacking the funds for either, he hit upon a simple but effective scheme. He bought two very elegant leather suitcases on Fifth Avenue, directing that the bill be sent to him at the Madison Hotel, then an elegant pied-à-terre. Then he piled whatever clothes he had into the cases, weighted them down with some bricks for good measure, and checked into the hotel. He stayed for some time, entertained useful people for cocktails and dinner at the hotel, made long-distance calls to the Coast to create some contacts in Hollywood, and in general played the successful European producer. When the time was ripe for him to move on—and before the hotel got impatient for payment—he went and bought two airline tickets and had them charged to his hotel bill. Then he simply left the hotel "for an appointment" with a smallish case, cashed in one of the two tickets for expense money, took a taxi to the airport, and flew to California. The suite remained empty for a few days, except for the two suitcases—which had yet to be paid for—as evidence that the guest was still in residence. At what later time he settled his bill with the hotel has never been made clear.

Then he started to make more contacts and more "deals." These days the majority of film business in Hollywood seems less concerned with actual moviemaking than with pitching deals, most of which never come to fruition. In the late forties and early fifties this was less true than today, because of the major studios, which between them financed, produced, and distributed most of the product. As a consequence it was harder for people outside the studios, such as independent filmmakers and entrepreneurs, to get a toehold in the film business, and they were forever devising schemes and deals—no one more assiduously than Sam Spiegel. The way *The African Queen* came to be made is a case in point. In the course of socializing with the Hollywood crowd, Sam met John Huston, who at the time was "between projects." In film jargon that means "not working at the moment." Spiegel asked John whether he had any out-of-the-way film projects that he wanted to direct but that major studios might be reluctant to undertake. John mentioned C. S. Forester's *African Queen,* and Sam asked him about casting suggestions for the leading roles. He was not sure about the woman's role, John said, but Bogie—whom he had directed in *The Treasure of the Sierra Madre*—would be ideal for the man. He had mentioned the idea to some major studio executives and nobody seemed very much interested; unless the big boys were keen on it, he did not think that the project could fly. After this casual conversation, John Huston did not think any more about the matter—but Sam Spiegel certainly did.

Sam quickly found out that the rights to *The African Queen* were available and that they could be gotten from the author's estate for a pittance. He secured the rights for a few months, with renewable options, and then approached Humphrey Bogart, saying that he owned a project John Huston wanted to direct and that John had mentioned what an ideal choice Bogart would be for the male lead. Bogie said that he would be delighted to work with John again, but he wanted to read the book first. Sam just happened to have brought along a copy, which he left with Bogie. He asked if they could talk again in a couple of days. When they did, Bogart expressed great interest in doing the role. Then Sam asked him if he had any suggestions for a female costar. "Katharine Hepburn" was the immediate reply; Bogie had never worked with her before, and thought she would be splendid in the role of the prim spinster missionary. Sam left and went into action. He made an appointment to meet with Katharine Hepburn; she agreed to see him because he mentioned that Humphrey Bogart had suggested the meeting. He told Miss Hepburn that he was producing a film with Humphrey Bogart based on the classic *African Queen* and that John Huston would be directing it; would she agree to costar? When she did, Sam went back to John Huston and informed him that he now had the rights to the property John had mentioned he liked so much, and that he had secured the services of Bogart and Hepburn to star in it; would John direct it with Sam as producer? "Absolutely," said John. They made a handshake deal.

At this point, Sam Spiegel still had nothing at all except an option on the rights, which had cost him next to nothing. But he now had some illustrious names to bandy about, and more important, he had a lot of chutzpah. Since the major studios still were not interested, Sam figured he had a better shot in England, where great literature was revered even by film folk. The larger British studios were not where he was looking; even if interested, they would not allow him the control or the financial compensation he hoped for. A smaller, independent, but well-heeled outfit suited his purposes perfectly. Excited by the illustrious names of Hepburn, Bogart, and Huston, and by the prospect of having their company make a movie classic, the Woolf Brothers agreed to finance the film and produce it under their banner. Their company was named Romulus, evidently in a whimsical allusion to the founder of ancient Rome, who as an infant had been suckled by a she-wolf. The brothers Woolf agreed to bankroll Sam Spiegel's movie; it was reported that they underwrote 100 percent of the cost for about 80 percent of the profits. A typical Sam Spiegel deal.

Ironically, Sam would not have been able to keep too much of the money, perhaps even none of it at all, since he had creditors breathing down his neck on both sides of the Atlantic. To avoid such a fate, Sam hit upon an ingenious idea: When the film was released, the world noted that it had been produced by a total newcomer named S. P. Eagle. Even though a more affluent Spiegel reverted to his real name for his subsequent projects, *The African Queen* lists S. P. Eagle in its credits. When the film was completed, there remained the question of who would distribute it, something of vital importance to the success of a movie. Sam wanted one of the most powerful distributors to take on the job, and thought he would have little trouble, figuring that any distributor would jump at the chance because of the film's superior quality and the drawing power of its stars. He wrote to Darryl Zanuck, the head of 20th Century Fox, offering the picture for distribution and waxing lyrical about such a superb piece of work being in the hands of the finest distribution outfit in the world. He signed it with a flourish "your friend, S. P. Eagle." Darryl Zanuck replied, opening the letter with "Dear Sam" and declining the offer with regret, adding that 20th Century Fox had a firm policy of only distributing films produced by its own studio. He concluded by wishing Sam luck and saying he wished he could have been more helpful. He signed his letter "Sincerely, Z. A. Nuck."

A few years after I participated in the film, I met my parents on a brief vacation in Paris. I had arrived by automobile after crossing the English Channel on the car ferry. We decided it would be fun if we all went back to England by car, to see the French countryside and stop at small inns on the way. While driving on a long stretch of road, we were chatting about this and that. Suddenly, my mother said, "By the way, I meant to ask you something. In the province of Bukovina, in the village where I grew up, Unter Stanesti, a kid named Shmulikl used to come to your grandmother's house from time to time. Mother always gave him bread with homemade jam. This must have been around 1912 or so. Somebody told me that he has made a big career, something to do with films. Perhaps you know him?" I asked for his last name. She gave the name the German pronunciation: "It was Shpiegel." My God—Shmulikl, a diminutive of Shmuel or Samuel. Samuel Spiegel! I nearly drove off the road. After I recovered a bit, I asked my mother what Sam was like as a young boy. She said, "*Aufdringlich*" (Pushy). "What else?" "He always had a runny nose." How the lowly have risen, I thought.

During the runs of my plays and the film jobs, the open houses at Carlton Hill never stopped. One evening Ken Tynan brought Tennessee Williams to one of my Sunday-night gatherings. Williams had never made it to London during the run of *Streetcar*, at least not while I was playing either of the leading parts, nor, I believe, at any other time. The great American author, as reports had it, was reticent and shy around strangers. Consequently I asked my other guests not to crowd him and make him uncomfortable. When he and Ken arrived, I greeted them cordially, chatted a bit about having played his famous characters, and then proceeded to do my regular Sunday hosting. The other guests, true to my earlier directive, mostly left him alone. Some days later I learned from Ken that Tennessee felt offended because of being "ignored" at my party. I was mortified to have achieved the exact opposite of what I had intended. By then Tennessee Williams had left for New York. I wrote to him, explaining what I had done and apologizing for any offense I might inadvertently have given. I told him that I had assumed he would welcome the chance of not being made a fuss of for a change. He answered with a charming note in which he in turn apologized to me about having obviously misunderstood my motives and the behavior of the others at the party, adding, "I have periods that verge on paranoia and we happened to meet at one of these crises. Then, of course, I don't really hit it off with a room full of Limeys, especially the 'smart' ones. I always feel gauche among them, it's all so cool and contained. It seemed to me that everybody was sort of walking around me as if, if I were visible, the sight was not pleasant." He expressed the hope that if I got to New York we might get together so he could show me a better side of him. He signed the note "10." It took me a little time to figure out that this stood for "ten" or more accurately "Tenn." I never took him up on the invitation; I suppose I was somewhat intimidated by the experience.

MEANWHILE, MANY FINE musicians had become old regulars at Carlton Hill. Isla Cameron, a British folksinger, taught me much of what I know and perform in my repertoire that hails from the British Isles. She did not always approve of my renditions; she didn't question my ability to assume authentic accents, but rather my willingness to make a song accessible and palatable to an audience unfamiliar with the material, instead of keeping the aloof stance of a purist. This argument surfaced many times later in my life; in the folk music field it goes on constantly between "purists" and "popularizers."

Through Isla I became friendly with many other singers and musicians who regularly turned up at my apartment. Seamus Ennis was a musician and folklorist who worked for the BBC's folk library. His was a great instrument, one that is rarely seen or heard outside of Ireland: the Irish bagpipes, or Uilleann pipes, as they are called. Even the Brits cannot easily identify the sound. They are different from the more familiar Scottish pipes, which have four "drones," each sounding one steady note, and a "chanter" on which the melody is played. The Irish pipes have a chanter also, but its three drones are variable and can produce four different chords as the player activates some levers. The result is a somewhat mellower sound than the martial one of the Scottish bagpipe. It also calls for greater skill. Seamus was a master of the instrument.

Jean Ritchie, a folk performer and collector who hailed from the Kentucky mountains, became a visitor on Sundays. She was on a study trip in Britain to research the roots of American music. She accompanied her singing with a dulcimer, but her main instrument was her voice, which produced a haunting and pure sound. The fascinating thing about Jean's material was that much of it was culled from her church background—songs originally sung unaccompanied for fear of secular contamination by instruments that might also be used for such frowned-upon activities as dancing. To this day, whenever I think of Jean Ritchie, I hear in my head the strains of "Guide Me, Thou Great Jehovah" with trills and ululations unheard of in any other Anglo-Saxon idiom. The dulcimer she played in the traditional style, running a little stick back and forth over the frets with her left hand to create the melody and plucking the strings with a feather quill in her right. The instrument she played was a modified version of the original mountain dulcimer. Hers was handmade by her husband, George Pickow, a photographer by profession. He made a perfectly authentic version of the instrument but with acoustic improvements that gave it a fuller sound than its prototype. Love does strange things; this typical mountain instrument saw its rebirth at the hands of Pickow, a New York Jew whose upbringing was as removed from the Blue Ridge or bluegrass as can be.

Oscar Brand, a singer, folk collector, and folklorist who in very short order became a very good friend, was another visitor from America. Oscar was originally from Canada but had left Winnipeg many years earlier to make his home in New York. He was—and is—a veritable fountain of knowledge about many things, especially folk music. He was also a lot of fun to be with. In the recording field Oscar was somewhat of an enfant terrible, the first person to record bawdy songs. But it would be doing an injustice to the catholicity of his folk knowledge to mention only those: He recorded and performed an astonishing array of Anglo-Saxon material culled from many sources. What endeared him to me, however, was the fact that no matter how far afield Oscar might go in the selection of his material, he never played down his origins. This was a bright, intelligent, extremely knowledgeable Canadian Jew, capable of absorbing folklore from many sources and giving a better than creditable account of what he knew. A quality I myself was striving for.

One evening the Galitzines brought along a young man by the name of Alexander who enjoyed the music, enjoyed the company, talked to beautiful women, noted down telephone numbers, and generally had a terrific time—but he excused himself quite early in the evening, saying that he was flying at dawn. A pilot, obviously. Emmanuel Galitzine, a fellow pilot, said laughingly that he hoped Alexander would not have to crash-land anywhere near Belgrade. No fear, said the young man. "The company never gives me any route that goes anywhere near Yugoslav territory. If I have to make an unscheduled landing, I hope it will be in Portugal; my uncle might be pleased to see me." It turned out that this was Prince Alexander of Yugoslavia, another member of royalty in exile. King Peter of Yugoslavia, Alexander's uncle, spent his years of banishment on an estate in Portugal. Alexander worked as an airline pilot for BEA—later to merge with BOAC to become British Airways—which flew only European routes. The fear about landing on Yugoslav soil was not idle; the former royal family was forbidden by Tito's government to set foot in the country. BEA even took the precaution of giving Alexander papers with an innocuous and English-sounding surname, just in case, to protect his identity elsewhere in Eastern Europe. Other countries behind the Iron Curtain might have been tempted to trade a flyer who was a member of the Karageorgevic family.

Alexander returned to Carlton Hill a number of times; we also met at various other parties and established a good rapport. I met members of his family, including his sister Elizabeth. (Many years later I would work, briefly, with her daughter Catherine Oxenberg when I played in several segments of *Dynasty.*) It was because of Alexander that I received invitations to places very few performers of foreign background were privileged to get, unless they were superstars or concert virtuosi. The Duchess of Kent was Alexander's aunt; before her marriage she had been Princess Marina of Yugoslavia. Convinced that his aunt, who loved Eastern European culture and music, would enjoy my performing, he whispered into a social secretary's ear that I should be invited to the duchess's next soirée. A very proper English gentleman, Sir Somebody-or-other, arrived at my dressing room with a verbal invitation to an evening at the Duchess of Kent's estate in Iver, Buckinghamshire, two Sundays hence. He also gave me driving directions: "Take all the roundabouts at twelve o'clock"—British army directions for continuing in the same direction after traffic circles— "then take the fifth country road to the right for about nine miles. You can't miss it." Then he added, as an afterthought: "Well, you can actually; I sometimes miss it myself." Well now, this party was a little different from Sunday nights at Carlton Hill. When the time came for me to entertain, I started with a little trepidation. But that soon vanished when I looked at the duchess's face during the Slavic songs, and then glanced at the feet of Princess Margaret, who was sitting on a couch directly in front of me. She was tapping her foot in rhythm with the song. Good, I thought, they are all human. From then on in I had as good a time as my listeners.

The people at the theatre were impressed with my royal outing, and somewhat envious. Even Peter Ustinov, who had met the royals before, was curious to find out about their reaction to my drawing-room performance. One morning, some weeks later, the phone rang while I was still in bed. It was eight-thirty or so, early for a working actor. A voice said, "Mr. Bikel? Good morning. This is Group Captain Peter Townsend, speaking for Her Majesty, the Queen Mother." Peter Townsend? That name had been in the news; there were rumors of a romance between him and Princess Margaret. I was groggy from sleep and not quite alert. I asked, "Who did you say?" "Group Captain Peter Townsend, Mr. Bikel." Now I was sure that Peter Ustinov, following up on my royal outing, was doing a number on me. I said: "Why don't you go fuck yourself?" The voice said, "No, no. This really *is* Peter Townsend."

There was quite a pause. "I am so sorry," I said, "I am mortified." "It's quite all right; I do get that reaction from time to time," he said calmly. I was still terribly embarrassed, and ready to sign my firstborn over to him if he would only forget what had just happened. "Now, can we proceed to the business at hand? Her Majesty, the Queen Mother, and Her Royal Highness, Princess Margaret, have the pleasure of inviting you to entertain their guests at a soirée at Buckingham Palace. May we count on your presence?" May we count on it? That was as close to a command performance as can be, and a private one at that. There was only one possible answer. "I would be honored."

On the day, I put on my best suit and set off in my car for the Palace, taking care to be meticulously punctual. I got to the gates, which were as always spectacularly guarded by members of the household regiment, wearing their tall furry busby hats and carrying rifles with gleaming bayonets mounted on them. Now what? I thought. I was not sure whether they had neglected to give me a password without which I would be challenged and possibly held at riflepoint. I decided to live dangerously and drove nonchalantly through the gates. Nothing untoward happened; no "Halt, who goes there?," no display of martial might. I was a little disappointed; the swashbuckling scenario I had painted in my imagination—of the palace guard defending the gate—had had more panache. There were, however, ordinary London policemen on duty inside the palace courtyard. They took my name, checked their list, and announced that I was indeed expected. They also parked my car for me; it was a funny sight to see a London bobby behind the steering wheel of my car with his tall hat bumping up against the roof. A liveried person then took over and led me to the place where the soirée was to be held, down an endless corridor lined with paintings of past kings, queens, and other nobility, who seemed to stare down at us as we passed. I asked my guide whether it was customary to take first-time visitors by this long route so that they would lose every shred of courage by the time they came face to face with the Royal Family. He just smiled.

Some of the guests were already having drinks in the White Drawing Room, which was lit by some two hundred candles in ornate candelabra. No electricity was employed, giving the room an appearance of coziness despite its large dimensions. I recognized several of the faces and was introduced to some people who bore familiar names: Dame Edith Sitwell, Sir John Masefield, and some titled folk. The Queen Mother and the princess made sure that everyone was properly introduced and, in general, exhibited the charming demeanor that comes from years of cultivating gracious hospitality. Princess Margaret reminded me that we had met before at the Duchess of Kent's party—as though I needed reminding—and then confided in me that she was determined that the setting should be perfect for this evening's entertainment. It was she who had chosen this particular room. Then she said, "This morning, Mummy and I came down here and started hollering just to make sure that the acoustics were all right."

When the Queen Mother decided that the time had come for me to play, she made sure everyone was settled and was able to see and hear. She herself sat a little to my left, fairly close—half turned toward me but also in a position to observe the other guests' reactions. Princess Margaret sat to my right in a similar posture. I was a little bit reminded of the attitude of theatrical entrepreneurs; they are checking up on the performance *and* on the house, I thought.

I played a whole array of songs, carefully including a fair selection in French, which everyone understood, but not shying away from the less familiar, and certainly giving weight to Jewish and Eastern European material. The Queen Mum seemed to enjoy it, and the princess's face had a look of proprietary pride, since as far as the Palace was concerned, I had been her discovery. After forty minutes or so, the hosts indicated that an intermission was in order so that people could be served some more refreshments; the entertainment would resume later. During the break we were informed that the Queen herself, accompanied by Prince Philip, was expected to arrive and join the party. The Queen Mother said to me with a twinkle in her eye, "You know, I only stopped you before because I did not want my daughter to miss all the splendid music." Talk about compliments.

The Queen and Prince Philip arrived shortly thereafter with a number of people in their entourage. It appears they had been attending a dinner in the Queen's honor in the City of London, given by bankers and businessmen and hosted by the Lord Mayor. "What was the evening like, darling?" the Queen Mother asked (like any Jewish mother). "Oh, it was quite boring," the Queen said with a sigh. "There were too many toasts and a few of the older gentlemen got quite tiddly and had to be propped up 'cause I was there." The she added, "They showed me the big insurance book that Lloyd's keeps—and there, on the front page, they listed my horse, properly insured." Then, with obvious pleasure and with a racehorse owner's pride, "Winston's was there, too, but way down below on the page."

I was presented to the Queen and to Prince Philip, did the proper court bow just as I had been instructed at RADA, and then I continued my performance. I do not know whether there may have been other times when a modern Hebrew song was heard by the Queen of England at Buckingham Palace. I do know that when I performed it there, it was the first time.

7

How Much Does He Want?

London, 1950

Somehow I had entertained the notion that Katharine Hepburn and Humphrey Bogart would be prototypical American superstars. How wrong I was! Neither of them was remotely like the kings and queens of filmdom whom I met and worked with later in my career. Bogie had a rough exterior that some people found downright intimidating. He tended to be vocal in his opinions, but he carried on conversations rather than making pronouncements. He talked and he listened and gave weight and consideration to your opinions. It surprised me that he did not lock himself away for the purpose of concentrating on his lines in the scenes to be shot, as so many actors do. As far as I could see, he made little preparation for a scene; rather than learning his lines the night before, he looked at the script in the early-morning hours as we sat in the makeup trailer. Then, while the hair people put a small hairpiece on him, he repeated the lines to the script person a couple of times and then he was set for the rest of the day. The hair business of his makeup was the longest part of getting him ready to face the camera; his face could look ravaged and therefore needed little makeup for the role. Despite the little time he took to prepare for a scene, he was in no way sloppy or neglectful of the work. When the cameras were rolling, his was the consummate performance of a professional. I just could not see when it all came together.

As a consequence of his work pattern, there was time for talk and play between scenes. Bogie had an acerbic sense of humor, which delighted people like the Americans and Europeans on the set, and exasperated the Brits, who did not understand it. His quips were usually delivered with the tough-guy demeanor that fooled many into thinking that this was the real person. This fake persona took on the air of a grumpy, misanthropic, misogynistic, and bigoted boor. The loving and caring person underneath all that was simply not a face he cared to show. I recall one day when the conversation turned to anti-Semitism. "I'm anti-Semitic," he said with that strange semiwhistled "s" sound of his. When he said that, people were shocked and I, too, was not quite sure what to make of this. Bogie's wife, Lauren Bacall, was Jewish. She was often on the set but was not present at the time, and we all wondered how she would have reacted to the remark. "I'm anti-Semitic," he said and then, after a pause that would have done justice to Jack Benny, he continued, "not just Jews—Negroes—people." Even the Brits finally got it and laughed.

During the ten days or so that I worked on the film, Bogart and I played quite a few games of chess. He was a much better player than I, and sometimes even pointed out to me that I should take back a move that might lead to a certain and earlier mate. One night we were invited to a party at the home of some rich locals in Mayfair. The hosts were falling over themselves to introduce the great Humphrey Bogart to all the guests, who had obviously come to ogle. But after a nibble and a drink or two, there was little conversation that was stimulating or interesting. One could not leave early; that would have been rude. "This is a dull party," Bogie said to me sotto voce. "Let's play some chess." "Good idea," I said. We asked for a chess set and the embarrassed host said with regret that he did not have one. When he was out of earshot, Bogie said, "What did I tell ya? Fuckin' dull people." Then we decided to play without a set, dictating moves to each other and trying to keep a mental picture of the board. We got up to about eleven moves before we gave up.

The public is under the impression that Arte Johnson of *Laugh-In* was the first to utter the phrase *"Verrry interresting,"* in his exaggerated German accent. But I had the distinction of saying it first, in a voice laden with sarcasm and the requisite German lisp, in the court-martial scene in *The African Queen* after Bogart and Hepburn are caught and brought to trial.

Katharine Hepburn was a little more aloof than Bogart, but that came from a sense of privacy that born and bred New Englanders seem to get with their mother's milk. She was often seen riding around the studio lot on a bike, something I have never seen any other female superstar do in forty years of being around film studios. She did something else that many actresses of far lesser caliber would not do: She stayed at the studio during an exterior night scene, even though she was not needed until the following night. We were shooting on a man-made lake on the back lot, all of us chest-deep in water. English nights are often damp and unpleasant, and this night was no exception. We were doing the scene that takes place after the explosion, when the German crew is trying to gather their wits, not too successfully, and I ludicrously salute the captain in the water. It was not an easy scene from a technical point of view, and we spent hours on it. Suddenly, there was an apparition on the lake. There was Katharine Hepburn, rowing along by herself in a little boat, stopping first at one group and then another to give out tots of rum or brandy to all of us who were wet and weary from the long night.

Eighteen years after I filmed *The African Queen,* my wife and I bought a house in Greenwich Village and had it fixed up. Among other improvements, we had air conditioning put in top to bottom. The firm that did the job asked my permission to give my name out as a reference to other prospective customers. It seems that Miss Hepburn was shopping around to see who could best do a similar job on her house, and the air-conditioning firm gave her my name as a reference. One day I received a telephone call. An unmistakable voice said, "Mr. Bikel? This is Katharine Hepburn. I wonder if you remember me?"

By the early 1950s things had started to go quite well. Financially, that is. I had some prestigious jobs, I had an agent, I was able to live a little better and entertain a little more lavishly. That meant some better restaurants—not the best ones yet; I was still not up in that rarefied stratum—and better wines for the Sunday-night open house. I had gained recognition of my abilities as an actor by my peers in the theatrical profession and sometimes even recognition of my face in the street and in restaurants. The beginnings of success. But what of the artist in me? Was the love of theatre that I had carried with me from my beginnings on the Hebrew stage in danger of being diminished or diluted by the vagaries of commercialism? The approval of my contemporaries was not reassuring on that score, nor were the sometimes effusive comments from my agents. Indeed, the agents themselves contributed to my sense of unease about where I was going. With each successful negotiation about a job I feared a concomitant diminishing of the idealism that had brought me this far. From making £6 a week (then about $24) I had progressed to £30. The film jobs carried a rate that was higher still. So when a producer offered me a job one day and asked my agent, "How much does he want?" the agent replied, in what I later termed a "fit of recklessness," "Ninety-five pounds a week." Had I been present, I would have gladly settled for £45 or £50 and would have considered myself fortunate. Ninety-five pounds in those days was rather high for an actor at that stage of his career. Well, the producers actually agreed to pay what my agent had asked for, and the job lasted for a number of weeks—booting me into my highest income bracket yet and putting an end to some very promising suffering.

Luckily, none of this removed from me the notion that as an artist I needed to grow rather than just maintain myself on a plateau. You had to prove yourself to directors, fellow actors, producers, to an audience, and—most important—to yourself over and over again. I managed to work at my craft, perhaps not in as concentrated a fashion as one might achieve in a workshop situation, but enough to feel progress rather than stagnation. In between the big jobs I went back to smaller theatre. We did Sholem Aleichem's *It's Hard to Be a Jew* at the Embassy Theatre, Swiss Cottage, where I had been "discovered" by Michael Redgrave. This Jewish play held a particular place in my affections. In Vienna, when I was thirteen, I had been among a group of amateurs who had performed the play in Yiddish. I had played the Bar Mitzvah Boy, and my father the paterfamilias, Reb Dovid Shapiro. This time I played the father, and felt that things were beginning to come around full circle. When asked by some friends whether doing this play was a wise career move, seeing that it might be considered too Jewish, I answered, "Too Jewish for what? Too Jewish for whom? And why does everything have to be a career move?" This question has been put to me many times over the years, both by well-meaning friends and by critical kibitzers. Such an issue is raised mostly by the timid and the unsure. It is almost never asked by Gentiles, and the Jews who do so would not ask an Irishman whether he felt constrained to stay away from Irish plays for fear of wearing his ethnicity on his sleeve. Every now and again I do, say, or sing Jewish things. If that is a hindrance to my career, I do not believe the fault is mine. It lies in the narrow-mindedness of those who would practice bigotry—or accept it.

While *Four Colonels* was still running, John Huston came to the theatre a few times, came backstage to chat with Peter and me, and generally enjoyed himself. He was shooting the film *Moulin Rouge,* and one evening he looked at me with this impish half smile and asked:

"How would you like to play the King of Serbia in the picture? It's a nothing role, one scene—one line, in fact. But we can have some fun." Sure, why not? I reported to the set and was outfitted with elegant clothes for the scene where the king visits the art gallery and buys one of Toulouse-Lautrec's paintings. I had one line: "I'll take it; send it to my hotel." With that I hand them my calling card, which says MILAN IV OF SERBIA, and that is the whole scene. It could easily have been done in one morning, even with the milling around of extras and takes of Toulouse-Lautrec watching drunkenly from the sidelines. John Huston dragged it out for three days, as much for the company as anything else. We did have fun, too. Peter Ustinov came to visit, and Huston had given orders to the crew never to let him be comfortable in one place. Wherever Peter stood to watch, there were grips and carpenters saying, "Excuse me, would you move please?" and shoving him out of the way. John Huston's eyes twinkled as he looked over, and after a while Peter got the idea that it was all a setup.

I met Zsa Zsa Gabor for the first time on the set of *Moulin Rouge*. I was intrigued by her Hungarian accent, which she has never lost, even after all these years. Years later I was on the *Tonight* show with Zsa Zsa and said to Johnny Carson, "I don't know what they all want from her. As far as I am concerned, she speaks a perfect accent without a trace of English!" I was also amused by her self-absorption, which seemed to admit no intrusion by any social concerns or political events that did not directly touch her life. She showed little curiosity about any of those matters, either. This self-involvement could have been annoying but for the fact that in her guilelessness she was likable. The previous weekend Joe Ferrer had taken Zsa Zsa to Stratford-on-Avon to see the Bard's birthplace. When we talked about the trip, she said she had enjoyed it very much. But when I asked her whether they had visited Anne Hathaway's Cottage, she said, "Oh, no. Ve didn't visit anybody, ve didn't see anybody."

The Cold War furnished material for many films in the early fifties. Many had gotten over it, many others had not. In any event, writers had a field day. They invented plots and stories, even where reality had been much more poignant. I took part in a few films, produced in England by American companies, that had a background of war, both cold and hot. Among them were *Betrayed* and *Never Let Me Go*. As it happened, Clark Gable starred in both. Both were filmed on location and in the London studios. For *Betrayed* we went to Holland and shot in and around Arnhem. I nearly came to grief there. The director was Gottfried Reinhardt, son of the famous prewar German director, Max Reinhardt. Unfortunately for him, Gottfried never got out from under the shadow of his illustrious father. He asked me if I could ride a motorcycle. There are very few actors who, when asked whether they have a particular skill, ever say no. I knew how to drive a car, what could be so different? So I said yes. They let me practice on the motorbike they intended to use, which had a sidecar, another complication. I promptly drove it into a wall, though slowly enough not to do any damage to myself. The bike, however, had to be replaced, and I almost was as well. In the end, they hired a stunt man who drove in the long shots pretending to be me. Victor Mature, one of the two male leads in the film, was all brawn and muscle. Portraying complex characters was hardly his forte. On the second day of location shooting he asked me to have dinner with him because, he said, he needed me to tell him some things. What things, I wondered, acting hints? Did he know enough to know that he didn't know enough? Well, what he was after was something quite different and surprising. After we were seated and the waiter had brought menus, Mature said to me, once the waiter was out of earshot, "You got to tell me about wines. You Europeans know about wines; we Americans don't." I became an instant expert by dint of the fact that I certainly knew more than he and had observed people who had known how to order with confidence from the bewildering array of names on a wine list. Theo Bikel—oenological maven.

The other picture starring Gable was *Never Let Me Go,* a Cold War story about a Russian ballerina who falls in love with an American who proceeds to spirit her out of the country to freedom. My role was—what else?—a Soviet naval officer involved in the Soviet Union's attempt to recapture the defecting dancer. My dialogue consisted mainly of yelling "*Lyevo na bord*"—(left-hand rudder). That was the easy part; preventing myself from becoming seasick was the hard part. The exteriors I was involved in were shot off the coast of Cornwall, at the best of times not very tranquil waters. Evenings were more fun, however. Gable was very friendly and unassuming. You ceased to be self-conscious around him pretty quickly. If his conversation was not exactly scintillating, you did not mind too much; how often do you get to spend time with Rhett Butler, especially after having spent months onstage with Scarlett O'Hara? In contrast to Victor Mature, Clark Gable did not want to know about wines. His conversation all centered around automobiles—how to care for and repair them. I had little to contribute to that topic; what happens under the hoods of cars was a mystery to me then and the intervening years have done little to lessen my ignorance.

Some time later, when I was on a trip to Spain with my friend

George Galitzine, we were on the Costa Brava in a resort town called Sitges. As we were walking through the charming little streets, a band of urchins spotted us and started to follow us. After a while they started pointing and shouting something that sounded like "Funiculi, funicula," a well-known Italian song. Then the cries changed to "*¡No me abandones!*" I was puzzled and so was George. Neither of us had been here before; how could we have paternity suits hanging over us in this place? Then it dawned on me that I was the target of their attention. It was not "Funicula" they had been shouting, but "Película," which is the Spanish word for motion picture. And "No Me Abandones" was the Spanish title of a film that had recently been showing there. Directly translated: *Never Let Me Go.*

Some of the movies I worked in during those London days were made strictly for home consumption. Although it's unlikely they'll ever be seen outside the British Isles, they gave me valuable experience and are a continuing source of pleasurable and sometimes amusing memories. Take, for example, a film called *Chance Meeting.* Small-scale international intrigue, Iron Curtain spies active in Britain, Theo Bikel playing yet another generic Slav, a henchman of sorts. If the spies had behaved in real life the way they were depicted in movies, they would have been picked off the street in a flash and shipped back to Upper Montenegro. Producers, directors, writers—and I suspect audiences, too—insisted on Iron Curtain types with menacing faces representing out-and-out villainy. We had a lovely incident on a location day. The production had rented an empty mansion on Cadogan Place to double as an Iron Curtain embassy—but the crew was told Cadogan Square in error. When our carpenters, grips, and set dressers arrived early in the morning to get the house ready for the day's filming, they naturally went to the wrong address—which happened to be the honest-to-goodness Romanian embassy. They rang the doorbell, and after a long wait a sinister-looking guard in civilian clothes opened the door and asked, "Yes? Vat do you vant?" The crew said, "We've come for the shooting." That frightened him. "Shootink?" he said with a guilty look, convinced that these people had stumbled upon one of his embassy's carefully guarded secrets.

I worked in many films that called upon my linguistic ability to do accurate accents. Frankly, the producers often did not know or care about the difference between an accurate foreign accent and a phony one. It was personal and professional pride that impelled me toward an authenticity about which others in creative control were not insistent. British producers and presenters—and to a great extent American ones as well—are content to accept any accent as Polish, Greek, Jewish, Russian, or Scandinavian, as long as it sounds "foreign." Thus, many actors, even good ones, have fashioned for themselves an all-purpose foreign sound that bears little relationship to the real thing. Not only do the accents sound false in their mouths, but so does the lilt as well. How often have you heard someone tell a Jewish joke, for example, affecting a singsong that has no home in any Jewish mouth? The fundamental flaw in their technique of producing these sounds is that they water down their English and bend it into some nondescript "foreign" shape, spoiling their good English, as it were. The truth, however, is that foreigners do not set out to speak English badly; on the contrary, they attempt to speak it as well as they possibly can. The limitation their mother tongue imposes upon them hampers them in the effort. In order to take this into account, an actor must familiarize himself with the character's mother tongue, at least enough so as to know what sounds the person's own language contains that are identical to their English equivalents, and which ones simply do not exist on his home turf so that they must be approximated with sounds that do. Some simple examples: Many Europeans do not differentiate between the sound of "bed" and "bad"; they both come out as "bed." Or "men" and "man"; they are both pronounced "men." If one could transcribe how a Mexican says "I am very hungry" it would be somewhat like "I yeng berry-ongry." Israelis—unless their names are Abba Eban or Binyamin Netanyahu, both of whom speak excellent English—pronounce "back" as "beck." (Most automotive terms in Israel are taken from the English and mangled in the pronunciation. "Brakes" becomes "brecks" and a back axle is universally called "beckexl." I have even heard a front axle referred to as a "front beckexl.") You have to learn how to listen and analyze what you hear so that you can make use of it as an actor.

In *The Love Lottery* (1954), a film starring the elegant David Niven, I played a Greek member of an international cartel; in *The Divided Heart* (also 1954), a Slovenian executed by the Nazis; and in *The Colditz Story* (1955) I was a Dutch prisoner-of-war in a German camp. *Colditz* was a very good film; despite the presence of such stars as Eric Portman, John Mills, and Richard Attenborough, it had an ensemble feel to it. It was the true story of a successful British escape from a supposedly escape-proof camp. Schemes were hatched, trial escapes ended in failure, tunnels were dug, only to be discovered by the Germans. During one such attempt, a British tunnel collapses on top of a Dutch tunnel which my contingent has dug, unaware of the British attempt. I emerge from the wrecked dig, my hair and face covered in mud and earth, mad as hell and shouting, "*God verdamme, Jullie rot Engelse hebbe onze tunnel gesaboteert!"* (Goddammit, you stinking Englishmen have sabotaged our tunnel!) We had just done several takes of this, with yet a few more to be shot, when lunch was called. The hair department was in the charge of Gordon Bond—terrific at his job, as gay as could be, and very amusing about it. He said, "God, I can't let you go to lunch like this. I'm going to wash your hair. Come over here to the sink. Just bend over, it'll only take a minute and it won't hurt." Then he clapped his hand over his mouth in mock horror: "What am I saying?" Gordon Bond was a riot. When I asked him whether he was any relation to James Bond, he said with the "s" more sibilant than usual, "Absolutely. I'm his cousin—Double-O-Sixty-nine." Years later, in the sixties, I worked with Gordon again, this time in *The Sands of the Kalahari.* On this remote African location we were only six actors, five men and one woman. The English crew also included a wardrobe man named Brian who was every bit as gay as Gordon. When the producer's wife flew over to visit, she remarked how lonely a location this must be for all of us, but said to Gordon that he was probably all right, seeing that Brian was along. Gordon drew himself up in reproach and said, "Ellen, if I told you once I told you a hundred times. Bread and bread don't make a sandwich."

Melba, a film released in 1953, was based on the life of the legendary opera star Dame Nellie Melba, played in the film by a real opera diva, Patrice Munsel. I played the director of the Brussels opera house who had given Melba her major break. This was another production by Sam Spiegel, now no longer S. P. Eagle. He had engaged Lewis Milestone to direct, a felicitous choice. Millie had a great touch; if ever they create a Hall of Fame for directors, Lewis Milestone will surely occupy an honored place in it. Starting with an Oscar in the first-ever Academy Award ceremony of 1927–28, and including *All Quiet on the Western Front, The Front Page, Of Mice and Men,* and *A Walk in the Sun,* he gave Hollywood a body of work which can only be termed "class." *Melba,* however, proved to be tough going, even for a master like Milestone. Spiegel was quite difficult; he had by now achieved some reputation as a producer, and was even able to organize financing more easily than before. There was an inverse relationship, however, between his newly found affluence and his ability to be openhanded with money. The relationship between Sam and Millie became a constant tug-of-war, both on and off the set, which produced a growing frustration among all concerned, and impaired the quality of the film. In fact, Sam's attitude created physical hardships for the cast and crew. I remember in particular one wet and freezing night when we were shooting on location at a house in London. The amenities were minimal, and we had a very hard time keeping comfortable enough to give proper performances. It was harder still for the crew. Sam was cracking the whip, determined that we should wind up the night's work before midnight so he would not have to pay the crew double time and go into an extra day to boot. They were bravely carrying on, but there was also mutinous muttering in the ranks. The last scene of the night was between an actor named John Justin and me. Justin, a very decent fellow, was just as incensed as I over the treatment of the crew. So we both decided to do something that neither of us normally would ever have thought of doing, something akin, in acting, to a boxer throwing a fight. At 11:45 P.M., with but one shot left, we deliberately flubbed our lines. They had to go for another take, and it pushed the shoot beyond midnight. Under our contracts, the actors did not benefit in any way, but the crew got their extra day, and we were delighted that Sam got screwed, for once. I have never done anything like that since—it's a matter of pride that I take no more time on a set than is absolutely necessary—but Sam had it coming.

Millie never got to finish *Melba*. Toward the end we were shooting on location at the Royal Opera House, Covent Garden. It was another difficult shoot with tedious setups, given the logistics of filling the seats with extras, first in one section of the house and then the other, and moving stage paraphernalia about. The assistant director had just called for the cameras to roll, the sound man had called "Speed," and the man with the clapper board had called out, "Scene Sixty-three, Take Five," when Sam Spiegel's voice boomed from the back of the auditorium, where he had just entered: "And what was wrong with Takes One, Two, Three, and Four?" Millie was outraged; if he had not needed a fifth take, he would not have asked for one. He got up from the director's chair and faced Sam Spiegel across the entire audience section of the opera house with its rows of elegantly dressed extras. "Fuck you, Sam," he said. Then, with three days of shooting still to go, he walked out and never came back.

In between the film work the theatre engagements continued. The small theatre productions I took part in yielded a variety of roles, each one different from the other. I did modern plays, naturalistic ones, stylized ones, period plays, and histories. In one of them, *The Thistle and the Rose* by William Douglas Home, I played Will Dunbar, a minstrel at the Scottish Court who was called upon to serenade the teenage English princess Margaret Tudor, who had come to wed King James IV in 1503. For the first time I used my musical instrument in a dramatic role on the English stage. *Thistle* also gave me my first chance to do a Scottish accent, which I have done on many occasions since. As Will Dunbar I sang: "Welcome the Rose baith reid and white / Welcome the flow'r of my heart's delight / The spirit rejoiceth frae her spleene / Welcome tae Scotland tae be Queene."

During this period, a number of former colleagues from the Hebrew theatre visited London. With most of them it was a welcome opportunity to renew the bonds that had existed in Israel. They had no problem with my expatriate status, and some even expressed regret about not being so proficient in the English language that they might also hope for a career in England. Only one, Yossi Yadin, responded negatively. Yadin, who had joined the Cameri before I had gone to London, came to see my performance in one of the small theatres I played in. He never made his presence known and returned to Israel, voicing his disdain to anyone willing to listen. With righteous indignation he declared that I had abandoned my country and my theatre and for what? To play small roles in small out-of-the-way theatres? I was, of course, not available to argue my central career principle: That I would play anything, anywhere, small or large, in the pursuit of my craft. Friends who came from Israel with these reports told me not to take it to heart. Yossi Yadin, they said, had acquired a demeanor of grandeur and haughtiness out of proportion to his own standing in the community. It had to do not with his own reputation, but with that of his brother, the famous war hero and archaeologist Yigael Yadin. In contrast to his brother, Yossi, General Yadin was a quiet and unassuming man. Yossi Yadin was arrogant, they said, because he had this famous brother, the general. In turn, the general was humble because he had this brother, the actor. Once again, for a little while at least, the gossips in Israel who had earlier snubbed my parents had a bit of a field day. But it did not last; as soon as word got around that I was receiving some critical acclaim for my West End roles, all was forgiven again. Sic semper success.

Among my early films, one demonstrated clearly how very different films are from the stage and what fundamental adjustments are required of an actor who wants to acquit himself in both media. The movie was entitled *Desperate Moment,* and it starred the handsome and brooding Dirk Bogarde and the lovely Swedish actress Mai Zetterling. I remember referring to her as "Anouk of the North." I played a character who had been involved in some shady deals and was hunted down and killed at the picture's denouement. Unlike my role in *The African Queen,* where my work had been confined to two scenes at the end, in this film my character popped up in various parts of the story. The script had been sent to me from the J. Arthur Rank Studios. I studied the part, learned all my lines, and was as prepared as a proper actor should be at the start of rehearsals. Much to my shock, when I reported to the studio there were no rehearsals, and the very first scene to be shot was my death scene. I quickly learned several lessons. The first one was that film acting required an ability to visualize oneself in a continuity of action that would be evident only in the final product; film acting required concentration on bits and pieces of a jigsaw puzzle that were often shot totally out of sequence. The reasons for this method of working are entirely financial: You shoot all the scenes that take place in a particular locality back to back, rather than in their proper dramatic sequence.

There were other lessons. One had to do with the elements of size and style in the actor's craft. While I had anticipated the necessity of some kind of adjustment, making it turned out not to be all that easy. A stage actor is trained to project his voice so that even a whisper will be heard in the last row of the balcony. Such things become second nature, and even the most naturalistic stage acting is done with the volume knob turned up. In films, that level is invariably too high. There is a sensitive microphone just out of the view of the camera, but so very close to the actor that no projection is required at all unless the intensity of feeling calls for it. In adjusting to the vocal demands— or nondemands—of film work, I was somewhat helped by the technique I had acquired while working at BBC Radio. Since there, too, the microphone was close to your face, you got used to a lower level of projection. Movies also demanded physical acting that was very different from any stagecraft one had practiced. In the theatre, the raising of an arm in emphasis may be a perfectly normal gesture; on the screen it is often far too large. Conversely, the raising of an eyebrow on the screen can be a major gesture; on the stage it will not register beyond the third row of the orchestra. These adjustments cannot be achieved merely by scaling down from theatre to film. A switch has to be thrown inside your head to make acting an organic process in either medium. Most of my colleagues who work in both media have successfully managed this; others, less successfully. There are superb film actors who wisely never do stage work, because they know its demands and are not prepared to overcome what, for them, would be a major psychological hurdle. There are also stage actors who have the same problem but who work in films nonetheless, never quite making the switch successfully. The reason they do it anyway is the money. An established movie actor can more easily afford to stay away from the theatre than a stage actor can from films. I was lucky: I managed to make the necessary mental and physical adjustments fairly early on and was able to continue working in both media.

Some kinds of inexperience created more mundane problems. *A Day to Remember,* not a memorable movie at all, was about a bunch of British day-trippers on an outing over the English Channel to Boulogne, France. In that I played a Frenchman whose fiancée was wooed away for a one-day romance by a young Englishman in the group, played by Donald Sinden. (The French girl was portrayed by Odile Versois, a delightful young woman whose mother tongue was Russian and with whom I established great rapport.) One scene was set around the dining table as the French family shares a meal. They covered the scene from every possible angle. God knows why; these days they make up their minds beforehand and do only the essential shots. But for this film, limited in scope as it was, they did some thirteen different setups around the table. I was not yet skilled enough to know which were my essential angles and even had I known, I was too new in the film business to argue. I also did not know how much of me was going to be in the various takes. It is always necessary to match everything to the master shot, and the prop people kept setting the table anew for the beginning of each take. As a result, I ate nineteen omelets that day—thirteen in the morning and, in the afternoon, six more! Needless to say, my relationship with eggs at breakfast was strained for months afterward.

THERE WERE OTHER GOOD postwar films, of course. *The Divided Heart* was based on a true story from the war. It concerned a baby snatched from his Slovenian mother after his father was shot. The child, handed over by the authorities to German foster parents, was told it was an orphan. The foster parents, in turn, never knew the child's real origin, nor that his real mother was still alive. After the war ended, the Allies made a giant search effort in order to help unite families. They found the child, now fully German, with no memory of any other family. An international court had the painful duty to rule that the child had to be returned to his rightful mother, whose language he did not even speak. My role was short, for my character was executed by the Germans fairly close to the beginning of the story. But we shot the scenes near Ljubljana, in the Slovenian part of Yugoslavia (now in independent Slovenia), and it gave me a chance to soak up new sounds of folklore in the local inns. There absolutely beautiful songs were sung after church on Sunday by large groups of farmers and workmen who managed to produce perfect harmonies, despite imbibing great amounts of slivovitz, the traditional plum brandy of Yugoslavia. After I finished my part on location, I had about two weeks before having to report to the studio in London for interiors. I decided to take the opportunity to absorb more local sights and sounds. I took the twenty-six-hour boat trip from Rijeka down the Dalmatian coast to Dubrovnik. As I sat on deck enjoying the view of the coastline, I heard the local harmonies once again—this time from the officers of the ship who sang while doing their chores. It was such a perfect blend that you had the feeling they had advertised for a second mate who, in addition to his nautical qualifications, also had to be a high tenor.

From Dubrovnik I took a train journey through the mountains to Sarajevo. Both were exotic and beautiful places; what a tragedy that both are now all but obliterated by nationalism once again gone mad. There existed different tensions then; they were international in nature and a source of some worry for me. After all, this was a place then firmly in the Communist camp; I came from a capitalist country and was traveling by myself in an area not too often visited by outsiders. I was not at all sure how I would fare. My apprehensions seemed to materialize when soldiers boarded the train at Mostar and proceeded to scrutinize all the passengers, their papers, and their belongings. A sergeant wearing a red emblem on his cap entered the compartment, barely took notice of the two other people, who were obviously locals, and demanded to see my papers. He looked at my passport (British, in those days), frowned, and was about to take my luggage apart to see what nefarious designs he could deduce from its contents. Then he saw my guitar in the luggage rack. He motioned for me to take down the case and open it up. Then he took the instrument, sat down, and proceeded to play for me for the next two hours. He made me play for him, too, and offered me swigs from his flask of slivovitz. It was one of the finest demonstrations of folk music vanquishing suspicion and turning potential enemies into friends. When he had to leave, he smiled, showing a couple of gold teeth, and embraced me good-bye.

By 1953, WHEN I WORKED on *The Divided Heart,* I'd begun to acquire a reputation as a singer and raconteur in London. I'd done some one-nighters for various organizations, and was even engaged for several weeks at a posh nightclub called *Monseigneur* in the West End. The owner was a funny bird, a Romanian named Rico Dajou; God knows what his real name had been. He spoke a mangled English with a strongly flavored Romanian accent; in fact, he did not just speak it, he flaunted it. Practically everyone whom he greeted at the door was awarded the title of knight, baron, or earl. "Ah, velcome, Lord Byulyi," he would crow. That could be anybody from the Earl of Beulay to Lord Beaulieu or even Mr. Burleigh. "You had dinner already? Vere you hav dinner, the Ambassadors? It was full?" This last question about his competitor would be accompanied by a vigorous headshake from side to side as if to say, "It wasn't full, was it?" When Greek shipping millionaires arrived in a group, he outdid them in Greek-type revelry. Greeks have a habit of showing their appreciation for performers in strange ways. They shower them with money. They tuck it inside the bras or waistbands of women; male performers get a flurry of bills strewn over their heads. They did this to me a couple of times. The first time it happened, I was startled, to say the least. I was annoyed to have someone walking up to me in the middle of a song and letting a wad of money flutter over my head; it broke the flow of my performance. I was also insulted; an artist should be paid for what he does, but I have never taken kindly to the notion of an artist receiving tips, no matter how generous. It is bad enough that indigent street musicians have to take tips. Consequently, I never picked up the money, although Rico did. I would not have taken any of it afterward, either, if he had offered it to me. But no fear, he never did, being true to the legendary reputation of Romanians. Having visited relatives in Romania as a child, I knew enough about their traits not to be surprised. I have often explained to audiences that a Romanian can be defined as a person who enters a revolving door behind you and comes out ahead of you.

The other way Greek magnates showed appreciation for performers was by sending dozens of dinner plates crashing one after the other on the dance floor. Rico got into this game as well: For every plate the Greeks broke, he broke at least two. Where the guest threw plates one at a time, he would grab an entire stack, walk to the middle of the floor, and dump them in one heap. Then he'd clap his hands and laugh louder than anyone else in the place, and repair to the kitchen for more plates. The cost of all the plates would later appear on the checks of the Greek party, naturally.

Rico Dajou was married to a very statuesque blonde woman, a former English model, who was at least a head taller than he. He was obviously very proud of having such a beautiful spouse, and introduced her loudly to anyone whose ear he caught. Once he was standing on the sidelines of the dance floor while his wife was dancing with one of the guests. He suddenly called across to her, "How are you, Rosalie, better?" She waved off the question and continued to dance. Rico then said loudly and with pride, "Mine vife." And then, just as loudly, he added, "She's got the period."

What I liked best was the way he would introduce me to the audience, a chore he insisted on performing himself every night: "Ladiss un gentelmen. You vill now haf a great pleasure to hear a artist vot iss a gut singer and also talks mit gut English vot he learned it from me. He iss mine gut freint. You all remember him, he vass the Russian coroner from the 'Lof from the Four Coroners.' I vant you should giv him my big hand—Teodor Birkl!"

One of the finest British movies I participated in during those days was a film shot on location in Scotland and at Pinewood Studios. The story was actually set in Nova Scotia, but British-financed films rarely traveled that far for exteriors in those days. In any event, the terrain and the flora of Scotland resembled quite closely the bleak portions of Nova Scotia that we needed as background. The picture was called *The Kidnappers* (later retitled *The Little Kidnappers* for American distribution). It had a bittersweet poignancy about it and also great tenderness. The main protagonists of the story are two young boys in the care of their Scottish grandparents and spinster aunt; their father has gone to fight in the Boer War. There is enmity between the Scottish and Dutch settlers in Nova Scotia because of the war in Southern Africa. There is a tender budding love story between the spinster aunt and the Dutch doctor of the village. The doctor is not welcome in the Scottish household, even when attempting to furnish medical assistance. The situation is exacerbated when a small Dutch baby disappears in the woods while its babysitting sister has wandered off for a spell. In the meantime, the two young boys have "found" the baby. In all innocence, they hide it from everybody, feed it, clean it, and take care of it as their own special secret. In the end, they must confess, and the boys are put on trial and receive a Solomonic sentence, after which Boers and Scots forgive each other. Playing the Dutch doctor was my first—frankly, my only—opportunity to portray a male love interest in a film.

Kidnappers was a lovely movie, and wonderful to be working on. The director, Philip Leacock, was one of the gentlest and most patient men I ever remember at the helm of a film. The director's position has always been one of great and, at times, absolute power. Some handle power better than others: Some use it sparingly, some others revel in it to the point of abuse, and a very few, such as Philip Leacock, use it almost imperceptibly and with grace. He had a good company of actors to work with: the veteran Scottish actor Duncan MacRae; Jean Anderson; a lovely and fiery redheaded actress named Adrienne Corri, another contemporary of mine from RADA days; and two children, Jon Whiteley and Vincent Winter. Children in the theatre and on a movie set can be troublesome and disruptive unless handled carefully; Phil was terrific with them. He neither pandered nor bullied; there was a firm hand in evidence but there was also an avuncular attitude, which the children liked in him. We took our cue from Philip and also became uncles and aunts on the set. As a rule, grown-up actors fear the presence of children; they are either pests or adorable scene-stealers. The British actor Eric Portman once told me in his hoarse delivery: "There are three things an actor should never be asked to work with—children, dogs, and foreigners." I have, throughout my career, worked with all three, and in most cases children were more trouble than either foreigners *or* dogs.

Not so on the set of *Kidnappers.* These two boys were almost always ready to play; they were equally prepared to work. The repetitive nature of film work often saps the spontaneity of even seasoned actors. But these kids were as remarkably fresh and spontaneous on the seventh take as they had been on the first. If scenes had to be scrapped in the final editing, the fault lay not in the children but in technical or other problems. To this day I am sorry that one particular scene between the old grandfather and the smallest boy had to be cut. We had shot an outdoor church service on location, with horses tethered to posts on the sidelines. In the scene the boys are fooling around with the horses, thereby creating a disturbance for the worshipers. Upon their return home, the grandfather decides to mete out punishment. He is talking to the little boy, aged about five, towering over the child. The dialogue goes: "You disturbed the Divine Service, you know what that means?" Looking up into the old man's face, the boy says: "No, Granddaddy." "You were disobedient, you know what that means?" "No, Granddaddy." "It means that you do something which I tell you not to do, or you don't do something which I tell you to do. Do you understand that?" "No, Granddaddy." "But you know why you are being punished?" "Yes, Granddaddy." "Well, why?" Looking up at the tall man, the little boy says with his lip trembling and a small tear forming in his eye, "Because you don't like me." It really broke my heart that they cut this scene; they had to, they said, because the previous shot with the horses had not come off properly.

I loved being in Scotland. We were in a place called Drumnadrochit on the shores of Loch Ness. They put us up in a charming small hotel and we were driven each morning to the location site, spending most of the day waiting for the rain to stop or the light to show some constancy. I usually shared the car ride with the makeup man, a diminutive Scot with a good sense of humor and a rapid delivery. Without fail he would say to the driver as we started out in the morning, "Right, follow that car!" Evenings were spent in the hotel lounge; the whiskey and the beer still held no attraction for me but the company did, mostly because of the accents that I managed to perfect further. The young receptionist at the hotel greeted me one evening with a pout as we returned from another fruitless day of waiting out the weather: "Mr. Bikel, I am terrible vexed wi' ye." When I inquired why, she said, "You gave me a postcard yesterday tae mail off tae London for ye." "So?" "Y'see I could'na help reading what ye wrote." "So, you read my postcard. Why are you angry with me?" "Because ye wrote that the only thing wi' sex appeal roun' these parts is the Loch Ness monster!"

We had a fairly short schedule of location filming in Scotland, about one week or so. But Scottish weather being what it is, you are at its mercy. We stayed well over three weeks and my salary for the movie tripled. Because of this I was able to put a down payment on a house; I had not thought that I would be in a position to do anything of the kind for quite a while. I had been a guest in this particular house on several occasions. The owner had just bought a larger place, and 12 Jeymer Avenue, Willesden Green, was on the market. Prior to moving in, I had also acquired a butler (manservant, really—I would never be grand enough for a butler, but what the hell, when in Rome. . . .) Now I had the space for live-in help so that the house and I would be properly looked after. My guy was nothing like the usual English butler; he was an expatriate Pole. His name was Taddeusz Wilczek, but he insisted on being called John. He had served in the Polish air force and had been stationed in Scotland with a unit belonging to the Free Polish fighting forces under General Anders. When the war ended and Poland went Communist, many of these Poles chose to remain in the West, Taddeusz ("John") Wilczek among them. He came south to London in search of any kind of work, was recommended to me by some Polish friends, and I hired him. He had never done this kind of work before, but he was very conscientious.

He was also funny. Where a proper English butler would have answered the telephone in the evening by informing the caller that he was very sorry but Mr. Bikel was out at the moment and could he take a message, John would crow with indignation at the caller's ignorance, "No-o, he's at the teater!" (No "th" sounds for John's Polish palate.) When the caller was one of my titled Russian friends, John would react with proper deference and say into the telephone, "Prince Galitzine" and bow and click his heels. Although his English was very Polish indeed, he had learned it in Scotland and it was incongruously littered with Scottish idioms. He also had a stutter. He might say, "I am s-sorry, s-sirr, b-but I cannae dae it." Once, when I had some friends sleep over after a late night and informed John that there would be four people for breakfast, he said with reproach in his voice, "S-sir, dis house is t-turnink into a b-bordel house." I did not have the courage to ask him whether he meant a boarding house or a brothel. The best malapropism I heard from him was one day when the radio in the kitchen was playing a Viennese waltz. He said in a voice filled with admiration: "Dis m-music from Vienna is immoral—vill never d-die."

On one of my frequent trips to Paris I met an Israeli named Ofra Ichilov who had graduated from the Sorbonne with a degree in political science. When I met her she was working as a ground hostess for El Al, Israel's rapidly expanding airline. She was pretty and very bright; also somewhat arrogant and opinionated but I chose to ignore that for the moment. We began a romance which was an expensive undertaking since it necessitated even more numerous trips to Paris for me than before and a few visits to London for Ofra as well. According to all the signs, this was a more serious involvement than I had had in my other relationships.

The last West End play I did was *Dear Charles.* I took over the role from Charles Goldner, who was leaving to do a film. He had achieved a fine reputation as a character actor, notably in the picture *Captain's Paradise* where he played the First Mate, who is so full of admiration for the double life his captain—played by Alec Guinness—leads. Yvonne Arnaud was the star of *Dear Charles,* and she let you know right away that that was what she was. Undeniably, she had made a great name for herself in England, where she was held in much higher regard than in her native France. By now she had worked in English theatre and films for many years, but her French accent was still as pronounced as ever. Clearly it was her stock in trade. I cannot say that acting with Miss Arnaud—no one dared call her Yvonne, except perhaps Noel Coward—was easy or altogether pleasurable. She hated to give over, and changed the staging constantly so that the audience's eyes had to be drawn only to her—even when the action demanded otherwise. She would even give directions to other actors onstage under her breath—and in French. At one point, after I had played only a couple of performances, she said, while her back was temporarily—very temporarily—turned to the audience, *"Parlez plus vite"* (Speak faster). Need I stress how distracting that can be?

After a few performances I noticed that the audience was not paying much attention to me during one of my long speeches that was important to the plot. I became aware of the fact that, though she was supposed to be listening downstage right to what I was saying at center stage, she was jiggling her silver bracelets and drawing away focus.

At the next performance, I checked and there it was again. At the third performance I walked right over to her, took her arms, looked deep into her shocked eyes, and delivered the speech directly to her, keeping both of her arms firmly in my grasp for the duration. I went back to the original staging in the next performance, and she never did her trick again.

During the run of *Dear Charles,* my agent called to say that a play was to be done on Broadway entitled *Tonight in Samarkand* and that MCA's (Music Corporation of America) New York office had suggested me to the director, Herman Shumlin, for the role of the French policeman, Inspector Massoubre. The company had looked at American actors, but were not satisfied that they had found the actor who had what was needed for the part. The young producers deferred to Shumlin's judgment entirely, but he was too busy to fly over to London to look at my current performance—where, incidentally, I played a flamboyant Polish pianist, quite different from the deliberate and exacting quality of the French inspector. As it happened, a close friend of Shumlin's, in whose judgment he placed a lot of faith, was coming to England on business. Shumlin requested that he see me in the play and phone him with a report. The man, Eddie Cook, was only tangentially involved in theatre; he ran a company specializing in theatrical lighting fixtures. Cook came, saw, and evidently I conquered. The report was "Grab him; he'll do great in the role."

The offer was made and I eagerly accepted. I was excited by the prospect of my first trip to America and especially pleased to be going not as a visitor but with a contract in hand. There was still one other hurdle to overcome. I was an alien, an actor carrying a British passport, and American Actors' Equity was seldom inclined to admit foreign actors without good and sufficient proof that all avenues to cast an American had been exhausted. Herman Shumlin and the two producers, Bruce Becker and Robert Ellis Miller, had to appear before the Equity Council and plead their case—my case. In retrospect I cannot believe that, at the time, there was no American actor able and willing to do this part. The producers must have been extraordinarily persuasive, or else the Equity Council was in an unusually benign mood that week, for they allowed them to import me for the role. Little could they suspect that, in the bargain, they were getting themselves a future president of their union

Samarkand was going to be strictly a one-shot deal. With luck, it would have a decent run of a few months. I packed enough clothes, left some instructions for payments, and left the car in the garage and John in charge of the house on Jeymer Avenue. The deal for the play specified first-class air fare, including a Pan Am sleeper berth. It meant traveling in style, a Jew arriving in America not on a boat, not in steerage, and without having to go through the ordeal of Ellis Island. I enjoyed the luxury of being a pampered passenger on a first-class trip. In a way I was sorry that they put me to bed for the long stretch of the journey; while asleep I would not be able to savor the experience fully. Those were the pre-jet days of piston-engine planes, and the London–New York trip not only took some sixteen hours but also required a refueling stop at Keflavik, Iceland. I decided to decline the berth until after the Iceland stop, as I wanted to stretch my legs and also make contact with an Icelandic school chum. We were given the choice of staying on board or getting off the plane for an hour and a half, and I chose the latter.

I went to the desk, which was manned by a very pretty ground hostess, and asked whether she could help me look up the telephone number of my Icelandic school colleague who had returned to Rejkjavik after graduating. She asked in her charming Scandinavian lilt which school we had gone to and when I told her that it had been the Royal Academy of Dramatic Art, she said with absolute assurance: "That would be Aivar Kvaran; his number is 45-47-43." A small country, this Iceland, I thought. Maybe Aivar is known because he is an actor and an opera singer, but to know his telephone number by heart is quite another thing. She dialed the number, listened for a while, and hung up, saying, "Well, there is no answer at his flat. But he sometimes sleeps with a girl, let me see, her number is 66-75-42"—and there she found him. Well, I'll be damned, I thought. He seemed not at all surprised to have been found in this way and was pleased to hear from me. We chatted and he wished me luck on my new venture. I reboarded the plane, had another snack and a glass of wine, and finally went to bed.

I awoke to the sound of the captain's announcement that we were one hour away from landing at the New York airport of Idlewild. The vague feelings of apprehension I had about how I would cope with America became stronger and started to border on anxiety. But then, so did the feeling of excitement and adventure. After a while the excitement won out. Soon we were circling over the New York skyline, so very familiar to me from numerous movies. We set down smoothly on the runway, taxied to the terminal, and were allowed off the plane after a brief routine scrutiny by U.S. health inspectors. I passed immigration and customs and emerged into a clear, brisk New York winter morning. There it was; I had arrived in the United States, which would soon become my permanent home. The date was December 11, 1954.

8

America—
Love at First Sight

*I*F A LULLABY IS A SONG THAT PUTS YOU to sleep, then there is no such thing as a lullaby of Broadway. It was a small culture shock to arrive from the staid and stolid life of Britain and face New York's nervous energy. Right off the bat, it was clear that I would never think or behave like a tourist or permit myself to be treated as one. New York itself helps you do that: Even the unfamiliar in New York is instantly familiar, and not only because you've seen movies or read books. You make an immediate effort to understand the mentality of its inhabitants, something that can be done only by becoming a New Yorker yourself as quickly as possible. Even though there was not much time to acclimatize because rehearsals were to start in a couple of days, I managed to soak up as much local color and speech as possible. The agency had booked me into a hotel right in the center of Manhattan, at Fifty-eighth Street and Sixth Avenue. One could eat in any number of small restaurants in the area, walk everywhere, and make friends with New Yorkers who seemed slightly astonished that you might want to take the time to do it. I had to watch expenses, since my salary would not be paid for a week, so I ate breakfast in a coffee shop on the corner of Fifty-seventh Street, lunch at a deli on Broadway, and dinner at small Chinese or Italian places.

What particularly pleased me was that you could buy tomorrow's newspaper on the previous evening; it sort of gave you the idea that you could somehow get a jump on time and know earlier than the rest of the world what tomorrow had in store. English and European visitors shared this feeling of prescience engendered by the early editions of *The New York Times*. When my former roommate, Freddie Granville, came to visit some time later, he went out on a Monday and marveled at being able to buy Tuesday's newspaper. He repeated the routine every single weeknight. On Saturday night he went out as usual and asked at the newsstand for *The New York Times*. As the man handed him the Sunday *Times*, slightly built Freddie buckled a bit under its weight and said, "I just want *one* paper." When the vendor assured him that what he was holding was indeed only one paper, Freddie became worried about the state of the world. "What could have happened since yesterday?" he asked.

The first rehearsal of *Tonight in Samarkand* should have been routine, as indeed it seemed to be for my American colleagues. You say hello to people you have met before, exchange pleasantries with the ones you are meeting for the first time, and settle down for a reading around the table. The routine itself was not much different from what I had been used to in England, except that I knew nobody at all and could not shake the feeling that I was being scrutinized by the rest of the cast. They were trying to determine what could possibly have been so special about me to have warranted bringing me all the way from England for a supporting role. Herman Shumlin, the director, was courteous in an Old World way, but he, too, was sizing me up. I had been brought to America on his say-so, or rather that of his friend Eddie Cook, and he had to make sure that it had not been a mistake. I felt I had to prove myself and do it quickly. Long before you vie for acceptance by an audience you have to gain the approval of your peers. Along with high-wire acts in a circus, theatre is among the most collaborative of art forms, where much rides on being able to rely upon the skill of others. For this, mutual trust is an essential. How to establish that trust quickly is a real trick. In most other areas of work, the collegial relationship is usually allowed to develop gradually while the measure of personalities is taken and the do's and don'ts of the workplace become evident. The theatre, on the other hand, is too much of a pressure cooker to permit grace periods. Four measly weeks of rehearsal before the test of facing an audience do not give you much of a chance to do anything beyond the work itself. But you take the chances you get, and the little waiting periods before rehearsing the next scene become important moments for forging relationships.

The star of the play, the perennially youthful Louis Jourdan, was helpful. We exchanged jokes in French, went to lunch either by ourselves or with various other cast members, and established a good rapport in short order. Other colleagues also became friends very quickly, among them Alexander Scourby and Felicia Montealegre. Alex Scourby, a Greek-American, was elegant and articulate, better known to audiences for his voice than for his face. Although radio drama was on the decline, there still existed "stars of radio"—a phrase soon to be relegated to the history books of show business. Alex was one of them. He also had another huge following few other performers could boast of: Once we started out-of-town previews, there were crowds of blind people waiting for him at every stage door. Alex had done more recordings for the blind than anyone; simply put, he was their books, their novels, their classics, even their Bible, which he had recorded in its entirety. Felicia Montealegre played the leading part in *Samarkand*. To us in the cast she was no more than a colleague, a fellow performer, but she led a double life by being wife and hostess in another artistic circle: She was married to Leonard Bernstein.

Herman Shumlin, the director, was a strange man—at once courtly in an Old World fashion, yet pedantic and obstinate in his work. He was a holdover from a time when the director wielded absolute power in the theatre and would brook no interference from anyone. The fact that his artistic decisions had to be approved by two producers many years his junior irked him, especially when they were vetoed for budgetary reasons. For example, there was the matter of the tiger cub. The play takes place in and around a circus, and Felicia played a tiger tamer who makes one of her entrances with a tiger cub draped around her neck. Shumlin wanted the producers to arrange for two cubs to be shipped to New York from India. Bruce and Bob were horrified at the thought of such an expense. Moreover, there was need for only one cub, why import two? It turned out that Shumlin actually wanted to cast the better one of two applicants for the role! The producers finally put their foot down and said no. They also refused to send to France, Brittany to be exact, for a prop newspaper that I would be pretending to read on stage. A French newspaper could easily be picked up at the giant newsstand in Times Square, said the producers. Ah, replied Shumlin triumphantly, French maybe, but not from Brittany! He grudgingly settled for a copy of *France Soir*. On the tiger cub matter he ended up having to make further compromises: We finally rented an animal from an upstate New York zoo, and it wasn't quite a tiger. We were told that tigers were too wild, even when very young, and unpredictable. We got a lion cub instead, and dyed streaks on its pelt to make it look like a tiger. To my knowledge, this was the only time in theatrical history that a lion was called upon to play a character part. When I wrote to my father in Israel and told him that I would be sharing the stage with, of all things, a young lion, he was very apprehensive. I told him not to worry: I had been assured that lions were quite tame until the age of eighteen months. He wrote back: "I know that and you know that, but does the lion know that?"

About four days into rehearsal I got a funny feeling in my stomach—literally, not figuratively. Shumlin got very solicitous about my well-being and sent me to his personal physician, who examined me and delivered his diagnosis: I had a tapeworm rummaging around inside of me. Apart from the fact that this is one of the most unpleasant sensations, it was also embarrassing that among my newfound colleagues this immediately became an item of discussion. Bets were taken as to whether this was an American tapeworm, recently acquired, or whether it had been imported from England, a stowaway without a visa, so to speak. The doctor prescribed some pills and a diet of carrots, which tapeworms evidently despise, and I was assured that I would be rid of the parasite in short order. The morning after I started the treatment, my call was an hour later than the rest of the company's. When I reported for rehearsal, Herman was in the middle of giving some direction on another scene, but he interrupted himself, looked at me, and silently mouthed, "How are you?" Just as silently I waved off the question, "Okay, I'm okay." Herman went back to work and occasionally threw me a glance. One of the full company scenes was supposed to be rehearsed next. Herman suddenly announced that everybody should take a break for half an hour, unusual that early in the day. Everybody left and he motioned me over to him and asked me to sit as he wanted to discuss something with me—something to do with my role, I assumed. "Listen," he began, "last night I looked up tapeworms. Now, they have a life cycle that starts . . ." Regardless of the fact that we were on rehearsal time, he gave me half an hour's private lecture on the habits of tapeworms.

The play opened in Princeton, New Jersey, then still one of the tryout towns for Broadway, and from there continued to Philadelphia, Boston, and Washington. Princeton was my American debut, celebrated without fanfare or champagne. We were all sort of nervous and unsure, the others no less than I. When the curtain rose, I was onstage with another actor. I played a short expository scene and then exited to return later for the longer scenes. On opening night, as I went back to my dressing room after the opening bit, I passed another actor in the corridor. His name was Michael Gorrin and he had started his career on the Yiddish stage. Although his accent was very New York

Jewish, in *Samarkand* he played a French impresario, and years later in *The Sound of Music,* a Nazi admiral. I was always amused by the incongruities of his speech patterns—the way they failed to relate to the roles he played. As I passed him in the corridor, he said to me in Yiddish, "Nu, you made already the impression?" How fitting for my debut, I thought. I have to make "already the impression" if this American experiment is going to go anywhere.

I liked Herman Shumlin and I was sorry that we had a sort of falling-out in the end. He was fired by the producers in Washington during the out-of-town tryout and was replaced by Alan Schneider. The play had had some problems—not insurmountable ones in my opinion—but the producers were jittery and feared that their first Broadway venture would fail. Herman had been especially close to Louis Jourdan and me; when it appeared that the producers wanted to get rid of him, he counted on our support, and both of us failed to give it, each for different reasons. Louis was not likely to mount any barricades. He was not a fighter; his wife, Quique, was, but she had not been close to Herman and was only intent on Louis's coming off well in the play, regardless of who the director might be. As for me, I was too new to the American theatre to know what one could do in such a case, and was hesitant to take any step that could jeopardize my own opportunity to appear on Broadway for the first time. I discussed the problem with some of my colleagues in the cast, expressing annoyance that I should be put in a position either to go out on a limb for Herman or do nothing, and accept an onus of cowardice. My embarrassment caused me to joke about the dilemma. That was thoughtless; when Herman heard about it, he was offended that I had made light of the situation. I had not only failed to give him support but had also, as he put it, "mocked him."

Many months later I wrote to him in an effort to mend fences because I had been truly fond of him. I told him that, although I believed he had made mistakes in the direction of the play, he could well have mended those imperfections himself. If his had been mistakes, I said, what followed his dismissal were veritable crimes by comparison, due to the inexperience of the producers and the colossal effrontery of the confused young man who had professed to take over his job. I asked Herman to reply to my letter, if only to tell me to drop dead. True to his own character, that is precisely what he did. "Dear Bickel," he wrote, misspelling my name, "the word 'dear' ought to be used dearly; but it has achieved a purely grammatical meaning, and so I use it in this case, for I must tell you that I do not hold you dear." He went on to say: "I do not hate you. And I think you are a pretty good actor, and I might even offer you a job, if I thought you were right for it. As a matter of fact, I think that you have the capacity of being a really good actor, but that you earn your praise at small cost, being bright and quick to function in an effective but rather superficial way." He ended his letter by saying: "I left a company of actors who looked like honourable, meaningful professionals, but when I saw the play in New York you were all shabby and even shameful to observe. You did not know what you had in me, and accepted the work of my fumbling replacement with the same [obedient] attitude as I demanded of you. You are not qualified to know the difference."

I do not know whether that last sentence referred to the entire company or to me alone, but I certainly did know the difference. Alan Schneider was a disaster. He began by replacing cast members, which did little or nothing to improve the play. Felicia Montealegre was fired and replaced, as was Joe Campanella. Joe's replacement was Pernell Roberts, later of *Bonanza* and *Trapper John, M.D.* fame. Both Joe and Pernell were fine in the role of the Juggler; the only reason I could see for the change was that Schneider wanted his own choices in the roles. There was a lot of psychobabble going on about motivations and sub-texts, things I was only too familiar with and whose misuse during the rehearsal process had long been an annoyance to me. Although in later years he did creditable work, at that stage in his career Schneider employed everything that I disliked about mock-Method concepts in the theatre. He was also neurotic and inclined to make the work into a tug-of-war of personalities. There was treachery in him, too. When he and I had an artistic disagreement, he actually threatened to use the fact that I was on a temporary work permit to get me deported unless I buckled under to his whims. If he had had his way, he could have aborted my entire American career and set my life on a different course altogether. The producers put a stop to that, but the incident left a very bitter taste in my mouth. I had never before faced such personal acrimony in the workplace and, thankfully, have rarely experienced it since.

I am sure it grated on Alan's sensibilities that the reception of my work by the New York critics was far better than that which they accorded to the play or its director. The dean of American theatre critics, Brooks Atkinson, wrote in *The New York Times*: "Theodore Bikel is responsible for two of the best scenes. . . . He plays with a relaxed deliberation that introduces order to disorder." With its overall notices, the play would have been termed a moderate artistic success in England, a succès d'estime, and could have run for quite a time.

Not so in America, where you are either a hit or a flop. We held on for a few weeks, but that was it. In the process even the lion cub came to a bad end; he caught a cold and died.

The fact that a number of producers quickly expressed interest in me was largely the result of Atkinson's review. I seriously contemplated extending my stay in America to see whether the promise of work would develop into the real thing. Despite the disappointment of the closing, my hopes were up.

By rights I should have left, returned to England and to my career there, to my house in Willesden Green and the stuttering Polish butler with the Scottish idioms. But during the few weeks while *Samarkand* held onto its slim margin of success, I had fallen in love with New York.

Upon the recommendation of Edie van Cleve, my American agent at MCA, I went to see an immigration lawyer who applied to the Immigration and Naturalization Service (INS) for a change of my status to permanent resident. The usual procedure would have been to leave the country, not necessarily all the way back to England but maybe to Canada, and wait there for a proper immigration visa, which would permit me to return to the United States as a permanent resident entitled to a "green card." The attorney opted for a seldom-used procedure that would allow me to remain in the country while the mills of the INS were grinding. Moreover, he assured me that this would place me in a convenient state of legal limbo and that, pending a final decision, I could even seek and accept work. "Until and unless they explicitly tell you no you can assume a yes." All well and good, I thought; maybe the immigration authorities won't throw any obstacles in the way of my looking for work, but surely Actors' Equity won't be so accommodating. I thought I had better wait for the green card before looking for theatre jobs. In the meantime there was plenty to do and see.

It was not the naïve notion about America held by the early immigrants that moved me to embrace New York. I had no streets-paved-with-gold illusions, was not lured by the invitation extended to the tired, the hungry, and the poor by the stone lady in the harbor, nor even by proclamations of truths held self-evident that all men were created equal. In any event, those were fallacies by any standard of objective observation. Gold was not to be found even in them thar hills; immigration was made difficult for many and impossible for some; and, looking at race relations in the fifties, it was clear that the WASPs had been created more equal than anybody else. But America, as seen through the prism of New York life, was simply intoxicating.

There were all-night movies on Forty-second Street, double bills even, which one could go to without fear of being mugged. There were concerts galore; there were small clubs with folk performers and larger ones with pop singers and musicians. There was theatre and more theatre—somewhat more expensive than in London, but worth the expense. Mostly there were the parties, similar to the ones I had given in London, with some of the same people whom I had befriended when they visited there. Once again I was playing and singing—a lot.

Music was still a sideline, however; my main interest was the theatre, which, quite apart from its lure, held the greatest promise of continuing employment in America. I was lucky on two counts: first, that my green card came through before I had to dip into my savings; second, that a Broadway producer named Kermit Bloomgarden, who was known for quality productions of literary merit, announced as his next production a play by none other than Jean Anouilh. The play was *The Lark,* another version of the Joan of Arc saga, once again a story of a lone voice standing up to the might of the state, a theme with clear political overtones. (At one time I made a pun, referring to both *Antigone* and *The Lark* as "Anouilh way to pay old debts.") I was delighted when my agent arranged a meeting for me with the play's producer and director, and came in for a mild shock when I saw the third person present at the meeting: Lillian Hellman, a legend to me in more ways than one. The play's English adaptation had been done by her, and apparently she would be actively involved in every aspect of the production. Reshaping someone else's play is not something a playwright of her stature would normally have considered doing. But this was about a courageous female who almost recants under torture, then realizes that, if she refuses to submit, though her body might be burned at the stake her soul will remain intact and unsoiled. Lillian Hellman, the woman who had stood up to the might of the state in her own time by declaring, when called by HUAC to name names, "I cannot and will not cut my conscience to fit this year's fashion," would have wanted to be involved in telling the story of Joan.

Julie Harris, with her exquisite waiflike quality, was to play Joan. The large cast included Boris Karloff, Christopher Plummer, and Joe Wiseman. Leonard Bernstein, who through my earlier association with his wife, Felicia, had become a friend, wrote the incidental music. The director was Joe Anthony, a gentle and considerate man, perhaps too gentle for the buffeting that theatre politics can subject you to. It was also his first Broadway directorial job. Little wonder that the constant presence of Lillian Hellman found him under more pressure than he should have been. It was a tense atmosphere that none of us managed to escape. My earlier admiration for the formidable Miss Hellman soon gave way to exasperation as she insinuated herself into a process that by rights should be the sole province of actors and their director. Playwrights as a rule do not interfere in this process; if they have comments about the work, they are voiced outside of rehearsals during production conferences. And this was not even Hellman's own play! Still, she was there, often interrupting the rehearsal with criticisms that more often stifled rather than encouraged any creative processes.

I had a most unpleasant encounter with her during one of the rehearsals. I played Robert de Beaudricourt, the landowner who is baffled by Joan's self-assured attitude, and who despite himself gives in to her demand for help in starting her crusade. At the end of my long scene with Julie, as she leaves having achieved what she had come for, I grabbed the sides of my head in exasperation and let out my breath. Suddenly Lillian Hellman's smoky bass voice boomed from the auditorium: "What was this supposed to mean? Don't do that—I don't like gestures." I stopped dead in my tracks (even now, as I am telling it, I get furious). I said with as much calm as I could muster: "Miss Hellman, I cannot accept such a statement. If you do not like a particular gesture, then we might discuss it with the director and if we should all agree that it is wrong or inappropriate, then we might consider changing or eliminating it. But to have you say to me, categorically, that you do not like gestures—in the plural—directly attacks one of the principal things my profession is all about. Words are your department, Miss Hellman, gestures are mine. I wish you would realize that my work starts where yours ends."

I retired into the wings and sat down, trembling with rage—but also with fear. I fully expected to be fired over this incident, especially since it had happened in front of my colleagues. While they did not fire me, my life was made more than a little difficult for the next few days, with extra rehearsals called just for that scene. But as we opened in Boston for the play's tryout, my scene—including the gesture—received prolonged applause from the audience. Hellman, clearly miffed, never talked to me again, and while she seemed to have backed down, she never apologized, either. I have never been able to reconcile the image of Lillian Hellman, the playwright who had stood up to the McCarthyite bullies, with the petulant woman who had such little respect for other artists. Afterward, even her other writing somehow became tainted in my mind, unjustly perhaps. While I think that Mary McCarthy's statement about Hellman's writing—"Every word she utters is a lie, including 'the' and 'and'"—is overly harsh, I can't say that I am part of Lillian Hellman's cheering section, either.

The out-of-town opening of *The Lark,* in Boston, was of necessity somewhat stressful. Apart from the producers, who naturally worried about the show and the intrusive presence of Lillian Hellman, various Broadway kibitzers were in evidence. Leonard Bernstein, his wife, Felicia, and his sister, Shirley, were camping out at the Ritz-Carlton Hotel. Their friendship with Lillian put a strain on my relationship with them. Later, when Lenny collaborated with Hellman on *Candide,* he found out that working with the woman was a nightmare, and he told me then, belatedly, that he sympathized with my earlier predicament. It came as no surprise to me that when Lenny had his blowup with Miss H., the issue boiled down to "I'll cut so much dialogue if you'll cut so many bars of music."

I was not the only target of the lady's ire in our production, either, nor was it gestures alone she objected to. Apparently it was anything outside the scope of words. One night, as I was waiting for Chris Plummer to join me for dinner after the show, I saw Joe Anthony, the director, enter the dressing room that Chris shared with Joe Wiseman. Joe Anthony wore the hangdog expression I had seen on his face before, when he was obliged to carry out "suggestions" from Miss Hellman. Suddenly, through the door I heard Joe Wiseman's voice saying in measured anger: "Why? Why is everybody—allowed—to—make—pauses—except—me? Oh—shit!"

Where most of us were infuriated with Hellman, Bill Ross, the production stage manager, was mostly amused. Still, he realized the precarious position Joe Anthony was in, and managed to protect him from the lady as best he could. One night, in a bout of playfulness no doubt, Lillian asked Bill, "If I were an actor, what role do you think I should play in this play?" Without hesitation, Bill replied: "The Executioner." No wonder Bill and I became lifelong friends.

For now, I could not wait for the brass to disappear back to New York so that we could get back to normal and get the piece into shape for Broadway. Once they left, everyone breathed a sigh of relief and we even managed to have some fun. Boston was—and is—an enjoyable place, and we took advantage of it. Chris Plummer and his fiancée, Tammy Grimes, made contact with some of their local friends—including Prince Sadruddin Aga Khan, who was then a student at Harvard—and we had some very enjoyable after-the-show parties, with lots of music, naturally.

The play's Broadway opening on November 17, 1955, was, by any measure, a great success. The lion's share of the praise deservedly went to Julie Harris, who gave an extraordinary performance as Joan. But we all did well by the critics and, more important, by the audience. Even my brief but flamboyant role—still including the disputed gesture—was singled out for commendation. What the major critics wrote about it must have irked Miss Hellman—Walter Kerr calling it "Theodore Bikel's unforgettable five-minute vignette" and Richard Watts writing about "Theodore Bikel's brilliantly humorous scene." The play had a very respectable run of close to a year. Some of us had an easier time of it than those who played spear carriers and monks at Joan's trial, who had long stretches of stage time with little to do but to look intense and gravely concerned. But even among the spear carriers were those who later made names for themselves: Milton Katselas, who became a noted acting teacher in California, and Michael Conrad, later of *Hill Street Blues.*

There was chess backstage here, too, and other games—some played with unanticipated results for the stage performance. We would make up rhymes, poems, limericks, and play games that twisted the text of the play. I am afraid I was the culprit one evening when, fooling around backstage, I turned some of the inquisitors' phrases around. The scene in question occurs when one of the priest inquisitors grills Joan on whether she was aware of the ways the devil had of ensnaring souls. "When the devil wants a soul for his own, he appears in the shape of a beautiful girl with bare breasts." Whereupon the cardinal cautions, "Let us keep our own devils to ourselves." That night the inquisitor, played by Roger de Koven, thundered, "Do you know what the devil does when he wants a soul for his own? He appears in the shape of a beautiful *bear* with *girl* breasts!" Even Boris Karloff, usually so very solid and serious, was hard-pressed to keep a straight face as he admonished the priest to keep his own peculiar devil to himself.

During the run of *The Lark* I was also busy trying to put down roots in America. I'd gone back to London for a few weeks to wind up my affairs, selling my car and the house in Willesden Green. I also paid off the trusted Taddeusz "John" Wilczek. Parting from my friends in London was the hardest part of all this: Of course I promised that I would return frequently, but none of us knew what a prolonged absence might do to our friendships. Stella Richman and Arnold Kalina miraculously remained as close to me through the years as they had been in London; other relationships inevitably went by the board.

I'd also gotten married. I enticed Ofra to visit me in America and spend some time in New York while I was appearing on Broadway. From there it was a short step to a decision to tie the knot. The actual ceremony was not a very glamorous affair. New York's City Hall hardly inspires nostalgic memories. But we did it and even had a friend from my kibbutz days, Aharon Gelles, as a witness. We rented an apartment on Eighty-second Street near Madison Avenue and made an earnest effort to lead a normal life—as near to normal as an actor's life can be. Things worked fairly well throughout the run of *The Lark,* and I enjoyed our domesticity—or at least the trappings of it.

During those years a radio program called *Eternal Light,* sponsored by the Jewish Theological Seminary, was a regular radio broadcast. Most of the scripts were Mort Wishengrad's work. It was clear from his writing alone that here was a sensitive and erudite human being who agonized over his subject matter and was aware of nuances that had escaped many others before him who had tackled the same material. I listened to that program every week, and was extraordinarily pleased to meet him when we were introduced by mutual friends.

Mort had written a play entitled *The Rope Dancers,* a dark and brooding piece about an American-Irish family in New York before World War I, whose daughter is born with six fingers on one hand. The father is a sometime writer who moves about drinking and complaining that the "words won't come." The mother is guilt-ridden, convinced that the child's deformity is a punishment from God for the sins of the philandering husband. She hides the child, refuses to let the girl go to any school, runs afoul of the truant officers, and is finally released by the child's death.

The play was accepted for a Broadway production and the cast was extraordinary. The couple was played by Art Carney and Siobhán McKenna, the crown jewel of Ireland's theatre, Joan Blondell played a kindly neighbor, and I was the doctor who wearily climbs to the attic, unable to help or prevent the tragedy. Remarkable also was the fact that this was the directorial debut in America of Peter Hall, the English director, later the guiding light of the Royal Shakespeare Company. This was quality work, so good that the producers had real hopes for a long Broadway run.

Peter Hall was able to bring to the piece a special quality, a sensitivity of his own that complemented Mort's yet was different in texture, a little more robust. I believe that as an Englishman he was better suited to the task than an American director might have been; the temptation to wallow in the morbidity of the subject matter was firmly resisted by Peter Hall, which might not have been the case with another director. (Strange how many British directors of the fifties and sixties were named Peter: Brook, Ashmore, Glenville, Hall.) At the time of work on our production Hall was married to Leslie Caron, who came along for the ride and to give moral support. Joan Blondell was a pleasant surprise: down-to-earth, not caring that she was heavy, full of good humor, and a pal in every way. She was also a very doting mother; her son Norman and her daughter Ellen (both from her marriage to Dick Powell) spent some time with us, and I recall all of us sitting around telling bawdy jokes. She held her own with the raunchiest of them, not at all bothered by the presence of her children. "Once they're past eighteen, you can't treat them as kids anymore," she told me. "Anyway, they grew up in Hollywood, fruit ripens awful fast there. They practically start dating the minute they are potty-trained."

Mort and I became very close during the out-of-town tryout. We talked about everything, exchanged anecdotes about our respective families and their background, made plans to do more work together, and laughed a lot. I did, anyway. Mort was the kind of quiet type who hardly ever guffaws; his style was to have a twinkle in his eye and chortle, at most. Once, though, I did make him laugh out loud. We were playing New Haven prior to Broadway. One night, midweek, the house manager came backstage before the show and told us that he had seen William Inge, the playwright, sitting in the audience. Mort Wishengrad was flattered but also baffled: "Why would Bill Inge want to come up all the way from New York to see my play?" he asked. I said, "Pencil envy."

The play opened on November 20, 1957, and ran for a few respectable weeks. Once again I fared well at the hands of Brooks Atkinson and other critics, but the production didn't last long enough to be counted as anything but a financial loss. Despite some moments of humor, this was a very heavy piece, appealing to the discerning few and not attracting much walk-in business.

After the play closed, Mort and I stayed in touch. We saw each other fairly frequently, on both coasts. For several years running, he came to my midnight Seder—a practice I had instituted during my London days to accommodate Jewish actors who were working in plays.

Once we found ourselves in California, both staying at the Chateau Marmont, the preferred digs of New York artists while on the Coast. Mort was writing a television script and had to be available for consultation with the producers; I was working also and neither of us was able to go to New York for the High Holidays. We had not made any arrangements to attend services in Los Angeles, but Mort knew Max Helfman, who arranged liturgical music and conducted the choir at a temple for the Rosh Hashanah and Yom Kippur services.

Helfman said that we were welcome to sit up in the choir loft and participate in the services; we would hear everything and have a bird's-eye view of the proceedings below. It was interesting to do it this way; the choral music from up close was quite spectacular. True to my nature, I participated in the service as any congregant would, including the recitation of sins for the year past. Afterwards, Mort told some friends of ours of the experience. He said that it had been quite a sight: Theo Bikel beating his breast in the familiar gesture of contrition, but keeping an admiring eye on the sopranos at the same time.

Possibly the description of me that tickled me most also came from Mort Wishengrad. When asked to define me, he thought a bit and then replied, "Theo Bikel? Theo Bikel is a rabbi who says 'fuck.'"

I recall one seder when Mort arrived fresh from his first—as it turned out, his only—trip to Israel. When I asked him what his impressions had been, he said with some enthusiasm, "It's an absolutely astonishing and beautiful country." "What about the people?" I asked. "Well," he said with a sad shrug, "as I said it's a great country—but not for Jews."

I knew what he meant; the sabra mentality was totally out of his ken.

Mort was altogether a rare human being. He looked too fragile to last, and, indeed, he didn't. He died, far too young, on February 12, 1963. He was fifty years old.

Ironically, the first offer for a film job I got while in America turned out to be for a picture shot entirely in Europe. It was an MGM film entitled *The Vintage;* its stars were Michele Morgan, Mel Ferrer, Pier Angeli, and John Kerr. I was to play the leader of a group of Basque grape pickers, all cousins. The director was Jeff Hayden, Eva Marie Saint's husband. The location was in the South of France. St. Tropez was not a bad place to be—and we got paid for being there to boot. The perks started with the trip to Europe, in a first-class stateroom on the *Ile de France,* then the French luxury liner par excellence. Also enjoyable was the fact that in addition to the cast, where there is always some collegial bonding, there were spouses on this location. Eva Marie was there for a time, and so was Audrey Hepburn, then married to Mel Ferrer. Although we knew that our film did not have the makings of a masterpiece—it was scheduled as part of MGM's policy of producing a number of pictures intended as "lighter fare"—the work was pleasant, by and large. Mel Ferrer could have been friendlier instead of exhibiting the don't-come-too-close-after-all-I'm-a-star attitude, but Audrey made up for it by being as nice as could possibly be.

I mention the film for two reasons. I had some free time during

the shooting and took a short trip to Barcelona. When George Galitzine and I had driven to Spain a couple of years earlier, we had
known nobody when we arrived. By the time we left, we had formed
some very fine friendships. In Sitges, a coastal town south of Barcelona,
we would sit in outdoor cafés, drink sangria, and play guitar. That
attracted people—not just musicians, but painters and other civilians.
Music was the immediate bond. So it came about that I met Narciso
Yepes, one of the world's finest classical guitarists. I also got to know
about guitar makers in Barcelona through a woman who had grown
up in the Philippines, Yvonne Perez, who became a very good friend.
They included Mateu, from whom I bought an instrument on that
first trip, and Ignacio Fleta. Mateu, a retired cabinetmaker, had started
to make guitars late in life. When I asked him how much he wanted
for the instrument, he quoted three hundred dollars. I told him that I
was able to pay considerably more than that, but he refused to take it,
saying that it took him one month to make one guitar, and three hundred dollars was all he needed to live on for a month.

On this trip I decided to look up Fleta. He was a famous maker of
other stringed instruments and for years had experimented and discarded model after model until he came up with the perfect prototype
for a concert guitar. I was taken to meet him at his house, having been
warned not to bring up the subject of guitars unless he did. We sat,
drinking coffee and nibbling on cakes. We talked about the world,
about Spain, about flamenco dancing—but not about flamenco playing. After a time, he said that he had been told that I played. "Yes,
maestro," I said. He motioned me to follow him, and we went into an
elegant showroom where I saw a number of cellos, violas, and violins.
Hanging in a glass case were some six guitars. He contemplated them
for a few moments, then chose one—by what criterion I do not
know—and asked me to play. I warned him that I was not a guitar
soloist, that I played mainly in order to accompany myself singing.
"Why don't you do that, then?" he said. The instrument was quite
exquisite; I would have loved to own one like it, but I did not dare to
ask the price. I sat down and played three or four songs. He motioned
me to continue and sing some more. I thought to myself, *What am I
doing? I'm auditioning, aren't I?* After half an hour or so he said, "*Bueno.*
If you want me to, I will make you a guitar. It will be ready in one
year but I will not ship it. You must come and pick it up in person."
True to his word, I received a note from his son eleven months later to
say that I should pick up my guitar in one month. It was worth the
trip from New York.

It was also because of *The Vintage* that I made my first trip to California. Although the whole picture was shot in France, after my return to New York I received a call from the studio asking that I do a couple of days' looping at the studio in Culver City. (*Looping* means synchronizing your own voice to film already shot. The original soundtrack is often unusable when filming is done outdoors; planes, trucks, dogs barking, etc. necessitate replacing the original with "clean" voice tracks done in a recording studio.) MGM was paying for a first-class round-trip fare; who could refuse? Moreover, they were in no great hurry and gave me the choice of plane or train travel. I chose the train; I was looking forward to getting a leisurely look at the American landscape, if only from a train window. The trip lasted four nights and three days, including almost an entire day traveling through New Mexico, with an Indian chief in the glass-domed observation car explaining the pueblos and their people. Terrific. It so happened that the bedroom compartment next to mine was occupied by the head of MGM, Dore Schary, and his wife. We got very friendly on that trip, played a lot of Scrabble, and dined together. Trains were very comfortable then, and a godsend for anyone who did not want to be bothered by phone calls and appointments. That was not my prime motive for choosing the train, but I could understand Dore's reluctance to fly for ten hours, only to be plunged immediately into a series of meetings.

I arrived in Hollywood in style; instead of getting off downtown at Union Station, the Scharys made me get off with them at the Pasadena stop, where a limo was waiting to take them to Beverly Hills. They dropped me off at the Chateau Marmont. Tony Franciosa was working on a picture for Hal Roach at the time, and he had invited me to share his suite—"Cut down on expenses, you know. We New York actors should stick together." I was grateful for the invitation; for the first few days at least I would not have to sit in a hotel room by myself. As it turned out, there was no need for that anyway. I knew a number of people, both from my London days and from my recent work on Broadway, who were either living or temporarily working in California.

I was fascinated by Hollywood, but at the same time I did not know what to make of its preoccupation with itself and its blatant denial that anything existed beyond the movies. On one of my subsequent trips, this time by plane, I carried a *New York Times* that had a very large headline that read **H-BOMB TESTS TO BE RESUMED!** Upon arrival I picked up the same day's *Los Angeles Times* and saw a headline, just as large as the one in New York, which proclaimed **ELVIS AILING!** I shook my head in bewilderment at the insularity of it; I still find it baffling. Even now I continue to come across the same attitude. At a recent party I talked with a group of friends that included a very beautiful blonde starlet. When I said something about kidnappings in Lebanon, she asked, "Who's producing it?"

Party talk in Hollywood is confined to who, where, and what's happening in movieland; what restaurants would be the new "in" places; or the ritual of taking phone numbers. Oh, yes, and to the other stars, the ones of the zodiac. An intense-looking young woman with long, stringy hair at a Hollywood party in the late fifties kept staring at me through her steel-rimmed glasses. She inched closer and closer and when she had gotten real close I figured, why wait for the question? and I said, "Taurus." She answered, "Outta sight!" which I took to be an expression of approbation.

Because of the friends I found and the work contacts I managed to make on that first trip to Hollywood, I stayed much longer than my looping job required. Even before leaving New York, it had become clear that my marriage was not working out and that a divorce would be the best for both of us. We decided to do this cleanly and, with as little rancor as possible, divide up our joint possessions, and live apart until the legal divorce. There was not much to divide up as far as tangibles were concerned. The intangibles were harder. As usual in a divorce, you divide up not only books and records but also friends. Ofra had become a close friend of Shirley Bernstein, Lenny's sister. As a consequence of the split, the Bernsteins went to her, to my regret; afterward I was no longer part of the Bernstein circle, meeting them only at public functions.

On the rare occasions when I engaged in postmortems about such matters and asked myself why the marriage fell apart, the answers tended to be a little too simple. Certainly, there was a reluctance to work at the relationship, a lack of commitment. But this was an acknowledgment only of failure and not of the reasons for it. At the time the marriage ended I figured that the cause was just my nomadic nature; now I suspect that it was a basic rootlessness and immaturity.

The formal divorce was not altogether easy to arrange in New York State, because New York law at the time did not recognize "irreconcilable differences" as grounds for divorce; it recognized only adultery. We were both loath to go through a charade of adultery so as to fabricate grounds. Woody Allen once spoke about this when he was a standup comedian. He said: "In the Bible it says 'Thou shalt not commit adultery,' but Governor Rockefeller of New York says you have to." The answer to our dilemma was Juarez, in the state of Chihuahua, Mexico. We wouldn't both have to go, it would be painless and quick, and I would not have to lie. I flew to El Paso, spent the night at an Israeli friend's house, and crossed the bridge over into Mexico. Within two hours all the court formalities were concluded and I was a free man. Relatively, that is; for the next twenty-five years there were alimony payments. "Why are Jewish divorces so expensive?" a comic asked, and then answered himself: "Because they're worth it."

9

Folk Lure

Wo gute Menschen wohnen, dort lass ich mich nieder
Nur böse Menschen haben keine Lieder.

Where good men dwell is where my heart belongs
For evil men alone possess no songs.

—GOETHE

I N ENGLAND I HAD CULTIVATED AND CHERISHED my contact with
other folksingers. In America there was so much more folk
music—a veritable feast. When I arrived in December 1954, the
Weavers were still blacklisted, no new records of theirs were available,
and their public performances had dwindled in number. But individual concerts were sponsored by organizations that did not give a damn
about witch-hunts. During my very first week in New York, something I had hoped for and thought would not happen for a long time
actually materialized. What a joy it was one morning to open the
newspaper and find that, on that very evening, Pete Seeger was performing uptown at Columbia University. I took a taxi—which it
turned out I could not afford. Who knew that Manhattan, which
looked so narrow on the map, had such expensive cab rides in store
when going uptown? In the end I did not care about blowing a chunk

of my rehearsal salary. Pete's concert was well worth it, especially with Sonny Terry and Brownie McGhee thrown in as surprise guests. I went backstage afterward and introduced myself. Although we had mutual friends and acquaintances, my name rang no bell; I had not thought it would. It was my first contact with the dean of the folk scene in America, but it certainly would not be the last.

Just as I had gravitated in England to the places frequented by singers and guitar players, so it was only natural that soon after arriving in New York I should gravitate to Greenwich Village, the home of artists, writers, painters, musicians, and other free-living types. Most of the folksinging parties took place there, either in cramped apartments or in drafty lofts. In the wintertime the apartments were invariably too hot or too cold. The radiators did not work or, when they did, could not be turned off. As for the lofts, these were always too cold; although with lots of people at a party it was not too bad. Being close to each other helped keep everybody reasonably warm.

The Village could be a confusing place for outsiders. For one thing, the streets had names, not numbers, and the rectangular scheme of the rest of Manhattan was not much help here. Even some of the numbered streets did funny things. West Tenth, Eleventh, and Twelfth crossed West Fourth, unaccountably. Driving a car you might ask a local for directions and be told, "You can't get there from here." There was another part of the Village population which was at the opposite end of the social and political spectrum from the artists and the hippies. The old-time residents, mostly of Italian descent, were among the most conservative, clearly frowning upon the lifestyle of their bearded and sandaled neighbors. While my sympathies and allegiances were with the artists, I also liked to observe the straight and un-hip.

The Italian-American speech patterns alone delighted me. I saw a man in a T-shirt leaning out of a window and shouting to a man waiting in the street, "Wha Loo?" The answer was a staccato "Coo-cah." Obviously some island language or, at best, a regional dialect from Calabria. But no, it was English. Translated: "What happened to Louie?" Answer: "Couldn't come." What intrigued me was not only the dialect and accent, but also the choice of words and phrases, grammar be damned. A woman, watering a plant, spilled some water out of a top-floor window, which hit a passerby in the street below. He looked up and saw the woman still standing by her window and yelled irately, "You outta your mind? Who the hell do you think you are?" She yelled back, "Drop dead. That's who!"

I met with, partied with, and sang with many folksingers. Although we all came from vastly different backgrounds, we quickly developed strong bonds of camaraderie. I renewed friendships begun in England with Oscar Brand and Jean Ritchie. I met and sang with the Clancy Brothers and Tommy Makem, with Ed McCurdy, Jo Mapes, Gene and Francesca, Leon Bibb, Glenn Yarbrough, Ray Boguslav (who later accompanied me both in concert and on recordings), and Cynthia Gooding. There were many others as well, some who played ballads, some who played the blues. There were some who sang sacred songs, some who sang bawdy songs, and some who sang both.

Quite early on, I ran into a young man named Jac Holzman. Together with Leonard Ripley, a fellow folk enthusiast, Holzman had started a record company named Elektra. He was, for his years, one of the most confident and self-assured people I have ever known. It appears he had been thrown out of college for breaking rules of attendance and of study. He was a genius, but interested only in the things that interested him—namely folk music and electronics. High finance was later added to this short list. At that time he was looking to add recording artists to his label, and thought that I had potential. He was not quite sure, however, if what I did at parties could translate to audio recording. He told me quite frankly that he feared too much of my appeal was visual, and that the passion I transmitted was as much engendered by my physical presence as by my voice. To test that theory, he asked me to make a recording of a few songs in his fourth-floor walkup in Greenwich Village, which served as his office and headquarters at the time. He then played the recording for some friends who had not met me; they reacted so positively that Jac offered me a recording contract which eventually resulted in some nineteen albums for the Elektra label. It was the start of a brand-new additional career for me. I never meant for folk music to be more than something I dearly loved to do for myself and for friends. But in America they would not tolerate your doing anything well without forcing you to accept money for it.

The very first record we cut was in 1955. *Folksongs of Israel* was a ten-inch LP (later to be expanded with added material to twelve inches to accommodate the universal format). Next, it was decided that my polyglot inclinations and my knowledge of international folk material should be given a forum. The resulting record was *An Actor's Holiday,* released that same year, followed in short order by *A Young Man and a Maid* in collaboration with Cynthia Gooding, and an all-Yiddish album, *Theodore Bikel Sings Jewish Folk Songs.* The covers of my albums were designed by Bill Harvey. *Folksongs of Israel* showed an Israeli pioneer girl walking through the fields of the Jordan Valley. She was actually a New York model, and the fields were on Long Island. *A Young Man and a Maid* daringly showed a bare-breasted beauty artfully photographed behind frosted glass.

The cover of the first Jewish record was more on the mark; it showed me leaning on a guitar in front of a Lower East Side brick wall with a theatre poster on it, listing the songs in Yiddish, and speaking to a young yeshiva boy. The boy looked right, but was hardly likely ever to see the inside of a yeshiva; when I called him over to offer him a few dollars to pose with me, saying, "Come here, *yingele* [kid]," he asked, "*¿Qué quiere?*" (What do you want?) in pure Puerto Rican. One piece of mischief on this album cover left a legacy that can be seen to this day by anyone who still has the record. I figured that a brick wall was not complete without graffiti. So before we shot the photo that ultimately ended up on the cover, I took a crayon and wrote a word on the wall next to the Jewish poster. The word consisted of three Hebrew letters: pe, aleph, kof. Pronounced that comes out "fuck." It was an in-joke that very few people caught.

Oscar Brand continued to be a source of friendship as well as material. With the exception of Alan Lomax, I know no one in the field of folk music who has more knowledge of songs, their histories and origins, than Oscar. He is much more than a performer: historian, folklorist, organizer, emcee, and book reviewer. He also holds the longevity record as host of a folk program on radio. His weekly show on WNYC in New York has been on the air continuously since 1945.

Fixtures at most of the early folk get-togethers were the Clancy Brothers. At first there were just two of them, Paddy and Tom Clancy. Later they were joined by their younger brother Liam and by Tommy Makem, who added a more lyrical and artistic flavor to their more roughly hewn Irish country delivery. One of our favorite hangouts in the Village was a café-restaurant called the Limelight. People sat, talked, drank beer and wine, and sometimes sang when the spirit moved them. I remember getting to the Limelight one night quite late. The Clancy Brothers sat there with a number of empty beer glasses lined up in front of them and full ones in their hands. As they saw me walk in, they rose to their feet and sang at the top of their voice: "We love you Theo, oh yes we do. We love you Theo, though you're a Jew." Then they sat down and ordered me a beer.

One of the most important places at the time was Washington Square, preferably around the fountain in the center of the Square. Where else could young—or not so young—singers test their mettle in a public place? Sure, there were political rallies and sometimes a picket line or two. But those were few and they were, moreover, theme-oriented and did not lend themselves to languid folk ballads or rural country dances. Washington Square was an ideal location for folk music because there was a built-in audience of students. New York University owned most of the land around the Square, including the building I lived in for a number of years, a high-rise named Washington Square Village. On Sunday afternoons the Square would be teaming with singers, guitar and banjo pickers, and an adoring crowd, which would wander from one performer to another to sample the smorgasbord of folk.

From the time of my arrival in New York, I would regularly go to Washington Square and listen. Often one could hear some very good music and excellent playing. In addition to the guitars and banjos there were also crude, homemade washtub basses. There were calypso steel drums and there were bluegrass groups, citybillies as I called them. When the spirit moved me, I picked up an instrument and played along.

No one played in the Square for any reason except the satisfaction of playing and the honing of musical skills in front of an audience. There certainly was nothing to be gained in terms of career advancement; folksinging was hardly regarded as a career anyway. In some way a competition of sorts was going on between the musicians who were trying to impress the young women who had come to listen. After all, this was the birthplace of the age of sexual freedom and one had the feeling that whoever picked the banjo best would also get best pick among the hangers-on, the sycophants or, as I called them, "folksinger-phants." A memorable line overheard by me in Washington Square was, "Can I fall by your pad later? I got no place to sleep with tonight."

It was not all smooth sailing. The locals were not pleased with the musicians or with the crowds they attracted. They unearthed an old ordinance, issued by the late mayor Fiorello La Guardia, that prohibited unlicensed street musicians. Over the years that ordinance had been first ignored and then forgotten. Since the end of the war in 1945, there had been singing in the Square more or less regularly. But in 1961 the pressure by local residents and the police mounted. Citing the old La Guardia edict, the police forbade singing in Washington Square Park. At the time I was performing in *The Sound of Music*, but Sunday was my day off. I decided to help the singers make their stand. The cops were out in force, but so were we. There was a large turnout. Israel Young, the proprietor of the Folklore Center on Macdougal Street, had seen to that. At first the kids sat silently holding instruments, but then the police started pushing to get people to leave the park. One of those who was pushed shoved back. Then the melee started. Someone began to sing. Although playing an instrument was prohibited, singing, according to the ordinance, was not. When the instruments joined in, it became a mini-riot. I went up to a mounted police officer and gave him the classic argument that at that very moment burglaries and other crimes were being committed which deserved the attention of the police far more than a few dozen banjo pickers, but to no avail. Only when I pointed out that everything was being recorded by television cameras did they start to withdraw. Too late: All of America saw the event on the news, and many sent their protests straight to City Hall. Americans do not like encroachments on free speech, nor, as it appeared, on free song.

The following week word came down that the folksinging would be allowed on a side street rather than in the park, ostensibly so that the grass would not be trampled. This was puzzling, since the area where the singers had previously held court was paved. Still, a side street was better than nothing. And within a few weeks the authorities relented and allowed singing around the fountain once more.

No one was a star around the fountain in the park. Pete Seeger was there at times, as were the Tarriers, the New Lost City Ramblers, and Roger Sprung, playing his banjo with various musicians jamming along. Roger and his group had just recorded an album for Elektra. I had sat in the control room for part of the session, and was suitably impressed by their musicianship. They had mostly learned the stuff in the time-honored oral tradition; they played it as though they had been together for years. At one point the recording engineer asked them to do one section over. "Take it back six bars," he said. There was a long pause and then a voice said: "What's a bar?"

Often you'd find another citybilly named Jack Elliott playing his battered guitar at the fountain in the park. Like his idol, Woody Guthrie, whom he emulated in every way, Elliott sounded every inch the country boy. In reality he was from Brooklyn and had a Jewish dentist for a father. By the time I came to hang out in the park, Woody Guthrie himself was no longer well enough to come and play. He was in the advanced stages of a degenerative and incurable illness known as Huntington's chorea. (Since the disease causes uncontrollable spasms of the limbs, much like dance motions, it was named "chorea," after the Greek word for "dance." Deemed unscientific and possibly demeaning, the name was later changed to Huntington's Disease.) His former wife, Marjorie, did much to help him in his last years. She was a very dedicated woman and a great supporter of Yiddish literature among other causes; she helped launch a project to preserve Yiddish books. Her own mother, Aliza Greenblatt, was a published poet who wrote in Yiddish. I recorded one of her poems set to music named "*Der Fisher*" (The Fisherman). Because of the strange combination of his parents' backgrounds, Woody and Marjorie's son, Arlo, had a folk Bar Mitzvah with banjos and guitars. Years later, after he had become a performer in his own right, Arlo called me to ask for the recording and transliteration of his grandmother's song. He thought that he might want to learn it, as an heirloom of sorts.

Mike Settle was a talented performer and songwriter whose material drew on various sources, including his own American Indian background. He was the first Native American performer I met. One day Oscar Brand brought another to my attention: a young woman who, he said, showed promise and whom I might want to have as a guest on my radio program, *Theodore Bikel at Home*. Buffy Sainte-Marie was very striking, both in appearance and in her music. Here was one performer who did not just reminisce obliquely about her people; she sang of their plight and their pride with great conviction. Years later, after we had not seen each other for a long time, I was standing outside a folk club named the Ash Grove in Los Angeles when from the other side of the street I heard the unmistakable voice of Buffy Sainte-Marie. "Theo!" she called and I shouted across, "I'm totally in favor of Indian fishing rights in the state of Washington and I'll sign the petition!" I am always up on causes.

Another forum for folk music was the coffeehouse. A time-honored tradition in Europe, it took hold in America mostly in the ethnic neighborhoods of New York and San Francisco. At first the proprietors of these establishments permitted no singing or playing; these establishments were meant for coffee, conversation, chess or checkers, and the perusal of newspapers. But when it became clear that a clientele would be attracted to a coffeehouse that served up music as well, the practice flourished. There were even places where music took precedence over the other activities. In New York, those were Gerde's Folk City, the Village Gate, and the Bitter End. In San Francisco there were the Purple Onion and the Hungry i. Soon other such places followed in other cities: the Second Fret in Philadelphia, Club 47 in Cambridge, and in Chicago, the Gate of Horn.

I was occasionally teaming up with other singers—not in a permanent setup, but for the purpose of isolated concerts and, in the case of Cynthia Gooding and Geula Gill, for recordings. Both these ladies were able to do songs in several languages, something for which I had become known on the folk scene. Cynthia was a very tall, angular lady who had a voice with a low register, so low that I sometimes

took the high harmonies when we sang together. Her forte was Spanish and French, but she also acquitted herself in Turkish and Russian.
She and I formed a duo for *A Young Man and a Maid*. Geula Gill, an
Israeli, was adept at singing material in quite a few languages with a
fair degree of authenticity. The one language in which she had a pronounced accent was English. Our album was called *Folk Songs from Just
About Everywhere*. I enjoyed making records with the two women; it
was a change from my usual solo appearances. Geula was a member of
an Israeli trio called Oranim-Zabar. The other two were her then husband, Dov Seltzer (who later became a composer of note), on accordion, and Michael Kagan on the *darbukke,* an Arabian drum. I
performed with the group on a number of occasions, notably for a
sold-out week at a big performance tent in Highland Park, Illinois,
not far from Chicago. During that week we had a terrible storm that
knocked out all electricity in the area—including our performance
tent, where the audience was already seated. I decided that we should
perform as announced. Geula balked, arguing that without electricity
there would be no amplification. "How did people sing for thousands
of years before the advent of electricity?" I asked. The answer was
obvious: "Louder." As for the stage lighting, since this was a theatre-
in-the-round, I had the apprentices drive automobiles into each of the
aisles and shine the headlights on the stage. It worked just fine; no one
left and no one complained.

Some years later I teamed up with a group of seven women from
the New York area who were known as the Pennywhistlers. They had
been organized by Ethel Raim and specialized in Eastern European
choral or group songs, sung mostly a cappella. We did no live appearances but made a splendidly collaborative recording entitled *Songs of
the Earth*. These women were the closest to the real thing in authenticity in the United States, a tribute to good musicianship and a good
ear. Ethel Raim later went on to found the Balkan Arts Center
together with Martin Koenig (renamed in the eighties the Ethnic Folk
Arts Center). It is one of the few places in New York where folk
music and folk dancing in their most authentic forms are still cultivated.

Inevitably there were friendships that transcended music-making.
My relationship with Jo Mapes was one; the music slid into intimacy.
This was different from the London love affairs with admiring ladies
who liked the music; she was no camp follower. Here was a colleague
with whom I liked to perform; the relationship was based on mutual
respect. We also learned from each other. Jo was a complicated
woman, given to moods that ranged from sunny and light to somber

and embittered. She had a life she did not particularly like. I was very fond of her, but in the end, there was a tension between us that neither of us could really cope with.

Jo lived on Third Avenue in New York with a roommate who was barely out of her teens. Tall, blonde, and quite striking, Mary Travers loved folksingers and the music they made; she was a genuine fan. Occasionally she would sing along with some people at parties, and she was quite good. At one point she had a personal crisis during which I helped her a bit just by being a friend. This nonromantic friendship I struck up with a young girl barely seventeen has continued for these many years; it startles me to realize that she is a grandmother now.

As soon as my first folk records caught on, I began to give concerts in venues as varied as community centers, college auditoriums, synagogues, churches, high school gyms, and concert halls. My New York concerts were at Town Hall at first, and later were shifted to Carnegie Hall when Town Hall turned out to be too small; we sold out just as soon as the first ads appeared. Harold Leventhal, who promoted my concerts for years—and who later also became my manager—had a cute way of dealing with the situation. After having told the box office to turn away any new customers for lack of seats, he would come into my dressing room before the concert with a seemingly worried frown. "Believe me, I'm losing on this concert," he would say.

THE PRIME VENUE for folk music in the Midwest was the Gate of Horn in Chicago, owned by Albert Grossman. In 1956, as I was about to embark on my first journey to the West Coast to do the looping for *The Vintage,* I got a call from Al, who had been trying to persuade me to appear at his club. I was willing, but I wanted to know more about the layout of the club and about the other people who would be appearing at the same time. Al told me he had a wonderful black singer he wanted me to meet; he thought the two of us would make a well-balanced program. I had never even heard her sing, so Al arranged for us to meet in person, to see if our respective chemistries would jell. My train to L.A. had a six-hour layover in Chicago, where the sleeping cars were shunted to another station for an evening departure. Al would bring her to meet me there.

Audiences often choose to refer to their favorites by first name only: Frank, Barbra, or Liza. Other performers are by their own choice known by their first names only. In the folk field, Odetta is the one. I doubt whether many people ever knew her family name. No doubt government record-keepers needed to know that her full name is Odetta Felious, but for the rest of us this is no more than a bit of trivia. Odetta is Odetta. We sang for each other in my compartment—not an audition, exactly, but a mutual feeling out. We decided then and there that the two of us would share the bill at the Gate a few weeks later. Odetta was then and is now an imposing, regal figure with a tremendous vocal delivery, unique in timbre and instantly recognizable.

By 1957, I was spending more and more time in California working in movies and television. I bemoaned the fact that Los Angeles had no places where folksingers could hang out and sing or play when they felt like it. In London, New York, and San Francisco, this was possible in the coffeehouses, but in Los Angeles there was nothing. When talking to other folkies I made no secret of my disappointment. After a while, an idea took hold. I was talking to Herb Cohen, a transplanted New Yorker from the Bronx who hung around the folk scene a lot. We decided to rectify the situation, and open the first coffeehouse in Southern California as a folk joint. We rented a place on Sunset Boulevard that had previously been a bar, and remodeled it as a place to serve nonalcoholic drinks and coffees. I wondered what name we should give it to convey the thought that this was a first for the area. Herb and I decided to call it The Unicorn. When people asked us why, we answered, "Because there ain't no such thing." The place became an immediate success. It was extraordinary to see the diverse clientele who flocked to the place and sat sipping cappuccino or espresso.

On hooks on the wall there were a couple of guitars and a banjo. Anyone who had a mind to picked one up and played. Some brought their own instruments and sat, playing and singing for hours. The cops could not understand the success of the place. They kept coming in, first the uniformed cops and then the plainclothes men, to see what underhanded hippie-type business we were conducting that attracted such crowds.

"What are you selling here?" a cop asked. "It's right here on this mimeographed menu: sandwiches, cakes, coffee, cappuccino—" "What's that?" "It's coffee with whipped cream and brandy or rum flavoring." "Brandy?" said the cop sharply, convinced that he had found a violation. Patiently I explained that this was nonalcoholic flavoring and showed him the container. Still convinced that we were doing something illegal, he said, "So how come all these people are here? What else are you selling?" "Atmosphere," I said. "What's that?" he wanted to know. "That's also nonalcoholic," I explained.

They kept bothering us, however. At one point they gave us a ticket for having a line of people outside, waiting to come in. Of course, so did popular restaurants and movie houses, as well as the nightclub Ciro's down the street. I went to the hearing, the outcome of which would determine whether we could keep our license to do business. I first inquired why we had been given a citation and was told that the crowds we attracted were creating a police problem. Very contritely I said that I appreciated the problem and that I was quite prepared to lose my license, provided, however, that the license to do business would also be withdrawn on the same grounds from the May Company and from the Hollywood Bowl. I was certain that the huge crowds they attracted were also creating a police problem. If it was necessary for me to run an unsuccessful business so as to accommodate the police, then so be it. The case was thrown out.

In truth, I did not even want to run a business at all; I was in this for the sole purpose of creating a friendly niche for folksingers and their followers. Especially in Hollywood, where the social strata were so strictly held apart, I wanted to break down the demarcation lines. I had never seen anyone who made less than $50,000 a year as a guest in the house of someone who made $200,000 or more. As Herb and I had expected, folk music broke the barriers. On some nights you could see beards and sandals at the Unicorn sitting next to tuxedos and evening gowns.

Still, the authorities would not understand. We had been open for well over a year when we received another citation, this time for "having entertainment in a public eating place without a license." We did not want to spend the money for an attorney, so I went to court to plead our case myself. I told the judge that I was puzzled, because one year earlier we had applied for a beer and wine license and had been turned down on the grounds that we did not serve enough food to warrant a license for beer and wine to be served with meals. Now, I said, we get a ticket for having entertainment in a public eating place. "It seems to me, Your Honor, that the county can't have it both ways. Either we are an eating place or we are not. If we are, then I suppose this citation is valid and we shall have to pay the fine. But then we reserve our right to sue the liquor board for having withheld a beer and wine license from a 'public eating place' for the past year, and we shall seek damages." The judge was a little taken aback by this argument, saying that he wanted to take the matter under advisement and that we should come back the following week for a ruling. When we did, he said, "I've looked into this matter and I don't know what kind of a place you are, a coffee place, a sandwich place, whatever. Go away, play your damn banjos, I don't care." A Solomonic ruling.

It was at the Unicorn that Bud and Travis got together as a duo: Bud Dashiel, the straight-laced former Navy man (or Marine, I am not sure which) and Travis Edmondson, the wild, unbridled hedonist, forever in trouble. They were as different from each other as night and day, but together they made terrific music. The Unicorn was such a success that we decided to branch out and get a second place, this time on premises where regular club-type performances could be held. We found such a place behind the Ivar Theatre in Hollywood. We named it Cosmo Alley after the back alley in which it was located. Here I performed regularly to keep the customers coming, but we had a wonderful array of artists, not only folk performers but comedians as well. Lenny Bruce would come regularly to try out new material, and Maya Angelou read her poetry. But basically it was a folk club. It was here that another group was born.

Glenn Yarbrough was an old pal. Both of us had recorded for Jac Holzman on Elektra. He had an extraordinary clear high tenor voice. In the late fifties he was still a solo performer looking for his niche, sometimes teaming up with other singers. Round about 1958 he had been performing at a club in Aspen, Colorado, with another folksinging friend of mine, Alex Hassilev. Alex was a talented musician with a European background; he was born in Paris, although his parents' native language was Russian. He was able to perform in various languages, including French, Spanish, Russian, and Portuguese. My kind of guy. Glenn and Alex had just finished an engagement at the Aspen club called The Limelite. They arrived in Los Angeles without any immediate prospects. I put Alex up at my hotel, the Chateau Marmont, for the first few days. This was his first stay in California. Alex and Glenn came to the club and performed the material they had been doing in Aspen. Then I went onstage and, with three voices and instruments, we did songs we all knew. It sounded terrific, and everybody said that the three of us should form a group. I was not able to entertain such a notion; I was too busy as a solo performer in concert and I had a theatrical and film career as well. I could not be part of a trio and have the other two members tread water while I filled other engagements. But it so happened that a man I had come to know and like up in San Francisco was down in Los Angeles at the time, temporarily at loose ends. This was Lou Gottlieb, performer, musicologist, bass player, and wit extraordinaire. Here was an ideal match, and so a new folk group was born. They named it after the club Alex and Glenn had just left: The Limeliters. A midwifely act on my part.

The Unicorn and Cosmo Alley stayed open for some three years.

Then I decided to pull out; I had done what I had set out to do.

The end of the fifties and the beginning of the sixties were booming times for folk music. As proof one needed only to look at the attendance records at folk concerts in the early sixties, not to mention the phenomenal increase in the sale of folk records, of guitars, banjos, autoharps, fiddles, and even dulcimers. In 1961, for the first time in the economic history of any country, the sales of guitars, in dollar volume, exceeded those of pianos. A truly staggering increase, considering that ten good guitars have to be sold to make up the price of one piano.

Outside of Elektra there were only two other major record companies that specialized in folk music. One was mainly devoted to the preservation of traditional songs, although they included more contemporary material from time to time. This was Folkways, founded by Moses Asch, the son of the famous Yiddish writer Sholem Asch. The other was Elektra's competitor in the commercial market, Vanguard Records. Its founders and directors were the Solomon Brothers, Maynard and Seymour.

By the time I made my fourth album, Jac Holzman had moved out of his Village loft to larger quarters, and so had the whole Elektra operation, a move financed in large part by the success of my records. In fact, the first big office and studio they moved into was nicknamed "the house that Theo built."

Perhaps the most significant friendship I formed during this period was with Fred Hellerman, one of the Weavers, who later became music director, arranger, and orchestrator of my first albums for Elektra. Much of the success of my early recordings must be credited to Fred; he guided me through the material and he knew much more about recordings than I. He was also able to get a lot of music out of relatively few instruments, a great advantage for a record company on the way up.

The phenomenon known as the Weavers has been talked and written about many times. My own feeling is that without the group's existence, America's musical tastes might have been different and we all would surely have been poorer for it. These three men and one woman—Pete Seeger, Lee Hays, and Fred Hellerman, together with the extraordinary rich voice of Ronnie Gilbert—achieved something wondrous with their music. Theirs was a fusion of human concerns, of a political, people-oriented awareness, and of fine musicianship. The material they sang—also people-oriented—created a turning point, finding a new mass audience not only for the group itself but for the whole folk genre. The last thing they had in mind was to make show business history; but without intending it that is exactly what they did.

Contrary to the popular impression that Pete Seeger is a product of rural upbringing, he was born in New York and educated in public and private schools, including Harvard. I knew both his parents. His father, Charles Seeger, was a noted musicologist, teacher, author, and editor. His mother was also a teacher and violinist. Pete himself is not always easy to get close to. He is forever an issue-oriented person, accessible when it comes to anything to do with new or old songs or with a cause he believes in; but on a personal level I have seldom caught more than a glimpse of the private man. I have always had the feeling that you get to the private Pete Seeger only through his wife, Toshi. Through successful and lean years they have lived in Beacon, New York, in a house that Pete himself built. Harold Leventhal, Pete's and the Weavers' manager, used to tell me that Pete's main problem was success. When money was coming in—sometimes a lot of it— Pete would not permit it to be used for such capitalist undertakings as investments. The most he would allow was the purchase of cameras or audio equipment.

At one time I gave a concert in Miami Beach. Unbeknownst to me, Pete Seeger's mother was in the audience. Afterward she came backstage and we chatted. We talked about music and she complimented me on my program. Then, surprisingly, she said, "You know, I like your music better than Peter's." Maybe as a classical violinist she took more kindly to my repertoire and my renditions than she did to her son's. Still, it was a surprising remark since Pete—I have only heard him referred to as Peter this once—is obviously a much better musician than I am.

The fifties gave rise to a new format of folk performing; it was no longer individuals alone who sang and played: Now there were performing groups. There had been get-togethers in the past, of course, with many singers, guitar strummers, and banjo players taking part. But these had been jam sessions; no structured group survived beyond the convivial evening. The Weavers had been the pioneers here as well, as they had been in attitude and choice of material. It was still very much folk, but it had structure to it and no small measure of musical sophistication. Much of this was due to the unique blend of the group, each contributing a different element and expertise, making for a whole that was much superior to the individual parts. Inevitably, others followed in the Weavers' footsteps, groups who did not seek to imitate anything except the group format. One of the earlier groups of this kind were the Tarriers. One of its original members was Alan Arkin, a very talented musician who later left to pursue an acting career with great success. The Tarriers were four in number, three of whom both sang and played instruments. Among them were two whom I had known since their student days at the University of Wisconsin at Madison. There they had performed as a duo: Marshall Brickman (he later became a screenwriter and director) on guitar and Eric Weissberg on just about any plucked stringed instrument you cared to name. Clarence Cooper and, after Alan left, Bob Carey rounded out the quartet. They had great drive and a wonderful sound; they were also an integrated group, two blacks and two whites. The Tarriers had the distinction of being the first to sing the "Banana Boat Song," before Harry Belafonte made it a popular hit. I was very impressed by them and wrote the liner notes for one of their early albums.

Purists decried popular success. Consequently, little credit was given by the folk world to Harry Belafonte or the Kingston Trio, which named itself after Kingston, Jamaica, as a tribute to the calypso rage in the country—largely initiated by Belafonte. It is true that a good portion of the Kingston Trio's material could no longer be called folk music by any definition. But a lot of their material was indeed in the folk vein, and they received little recognition for it, nor for the fact that owing to their work folk music enjoyed an unprecedented popularity by a large public which was not overly concerned with subtle definitions of authenticity. Belafonte, too, had to endure much scorn and criticism for "taking liberties" with his material; yet the fact remains that he chose to perform folk material and eschewed pop songs, after a few first attempts that left him unsatisfied. What held the public spellbound was a dynamic personality and a very handsome and proud young man. But it was also the music: a new kind of voice but also an old kind of song. Banana boats and songs about fellows named John Henry or Tom Dooley got to be proper fare even for the jukebox. People started by liking Harry with his calypso songs and the Kingston Trio with their folk material and then proceeded to Pete Seeger and Joan Baez. The more enterprising would include in their affection Sonny Terry, Doc Watson, or the New Lost City Ramblers. The next step was inevitable; from listening to this music, many proceeded to play and sing it, or both.

Just what *is* folk music? It's not altogether easy to define. There are the short descriptions such as Pete Seeger's curt definition: "If folks sing them, then they're folk songs." That is not quite as permissive as might appear at first, because I suspect that Pete is fairly particular about whom he chooses to call "folks." Oscar Brand's definition, "If it has that folk sound, then it is a folk song," gives the nod to contemporary creations in the folk vein. It takes the newly written broadsides off the hook by not forcing them to have the patina of old age upon them before they can be considered genuine folk material. I maintain that both the sound and the content are determinants. If a song concerns itself with work, with the land, with going down to the sea in ships, with the nobility of labor, with the anguish of the oppressed—traditionally the stuff folk songs are fashioned from—then I accept it, no matter when it was created or who the author might be. Anonymity of authorship also makes no sense as a criterion for determining authenticity. There used to be a common belief that a folk song was a communal creation by and for "simple folk." That theory was explored and discarded by eminent scholars some time ago. In 1953 Dr. Duncan Emrich, curator of the Folk Song Archives of the Library of Congress, declared, "The theory of 'communal creation' of ballads has been thoroughly exploded. At its point of origin, each folk song is the creation of an individual" (quoted from a letter to *The Saturday Review)*. Clearly, "the people" do not compose music or write lyrics—individuals do. Yet to this day not everyone has relinquished the idea that a folk song has no author.

Another theory that has been difficult to dispel is that folk music is of vulgar origin. This ties in with the first theory of collective authorship—if each folk song is the product of a musical illiterate, it follows that the next illiterate would reproduce it with mistakes, as would the third and fourth illiterate. The result would be a compendium of imperfections and voilà: communal authorship, a total obscuring of the original creator, hence a folk song. However, this theory also comes to grief. There exist many folk songs whose original composers and/or lyricists were bank clerks, "serious" composers, teachers, poets, and even army officers. Surprisingly, after decades and even centuries, some of their names are still known.

The test of how a song is transmitted is a valid one. In my kibbutz days, I knew a man who worked with sheep, which inspired him to make up melodies. Sometimes he would make up words also, or take biblical texts to fit the melodies. He would sing a new song in the dining hall, and people would remember it. The kibbutz truck driver delivering milk would sing it to the gas station attendant while filling up the tank. That man in turn would sing it for various cab drivers and, in a matter of months, the entire country would be singing it. I defy anyone to tell me that this was not a folk process. Closer to home, many folk "classics" were composed by performers such as Pete Seeger, Woody Guthrie and Leadbelly.

A folk song does so many things: It tells a multitude of stories, legends, fables, and jokes. It admonishes, lulls to sleep, calls to battle, rings with hope for the prisoner, with threat for the jailer, with joy for lovers, and with bitterness for him who might have had but didn't. It heralds birth, boyhood, wedlock. It soothes the weary, the sick, and the aged, and it mourns the dead.

We sing of so many things that no longer exist; not many of us churn butter by hand or plow with mules anymore. The singer should not be required to live the life the songs describe, any more than the actor is required to be the character he portrays. We are neither leprechauns nor ghosts and we sing of both; nor are we condemned murderers or Gypsy tinkers abandoning lovelorn maidens. And we sing of those, also. To quote folk singer Ed McCurdy: "I have never been a motherless child, but I know what it is to be sad." It is only necessary to find analogies in your own life, similes and parallels, to allow you to sing convincingly about just about everything. I know urban performers who have never been within ten yards of a pitchfork who can do anything a rural folk musician can do—and with dazzling dexterity to boot. In the sixties, you might have asked Earl Scruggs or Frank Profitt, genuine rural musicians, whom they considered to be the best banjo player in America, and they would answer without hesitation: Eric Weissberg, a kid from New York who had never worked the land and likely never will.

What is oral tradition anyway, in these days of radio, television, videos, tapes, and CDs? I do welcome twentieth-century technology; it allows me to learn better and faster than I would otherwise. In Philadelphia, I once spent three very cold and wet days in the basement of Dr. Kenneth Goldstein, the folklorist at the University of Pennsylvania. I listened to tapes he had collected in Scotland and Ireland over many weeks, recording the voices of tinkers and farmers. I got material for an entire record out of it, and those three days saved me from having to spend weeks, much colder and damper ones, in the field myself. I defy anyone to tell me that what I learned in that basement was not gotten in the oral tradition. Of course, the reliance on electronic transmission can muddy the process also. I recall the time when Margaret Barry, the Irish Gypsy, sang in my living room in London. She sang many songs, quite wonderful and quite authentic, and her style of singing was so uniquely Irish that we all accepted anything that came from her mouth as traditional. But then she sang something that sounded vaguely familiar, and someone asked her whether this was another one of her grandmother's songs. "Oh no," she replied. "There is a radio shop at the corner in Dublin where I heard this tune. . . ." We had been treated to her version of an American pop song she had heard on the wireless.

ALTHOUGH THE BLACKLIST fever was on the wane by the time I got to America, in the folk music field and most especially with respect to the Weavers, the blacklist was still in force. Nobody forgot or forgave anything, it seems. Not that there was anything to forgive. Beliefs held, beliefs expressed, whether in word or in song, were supposed to enjoy absolute protection under the First Article of the Constitution. Yet the very people who were charged with being the framers and keepers of laws were the very perpetrators who violated this fundamental protection of free speech. Self-styled anti-Communist crusaders compiled lists of "Communist sympathizers"; committees of Congress then mounted charade hearings, demanding public confessions and the naming of names. This was piling official injustice on top of private calumny. Everyone cited by HUAC and the Senate Subcommittee on Internal Security was thereafter tainted; the accusation alone was enough. Pete Seeger was one of the prime folk targets, along with the other members of the Weavers. Pete was cited for contempt of Congress; when he offered to sing in front of the sentencing judge to demonstrate the "subversive" qualities of his music, he was refused.

Some folksingers succumbed to the pressure and cooperated with the inquisition. It was a futile gesture, for it made them no more acceptable to a public that had already labeled them "reds." At the same time it angered former friends and colleagues, who vowed not to forgive them for this act of betrayal. This drama was often repeated among artists in other media. Those whose names had been mentioned by actors or directors cooperating with the witch-hunt felt mortally offended, and in turn ostracized the namers of names. Zero Mostel almost refused to do *Fiddler on the Roof* because Jerome Robbins, the play's director, had caved in to HUAC. In the end, Zero declared in his inimitable and irascible style, "The son of a bitch— Okay, I'll work with him but I won't talk to him." The directors Elia Kazan and Edward Dmytryk experienced similar treatment at the hands of colleagues who bore the grudge long after the blacklist had ceased to operate.

The folk world was angered at Josh White, who had performed an act of personal expiation after giving in to the pressures of HUAC by recording a song entitled "The House I Live In" as a demonstration of his patriotism. White, a legendary performer whom I had previously met in England, had been one of America's foremost singer-guitarists, with a seemingly endless repertoire of folk-based material. For many years a concert and recording star in the field, in the sixties he was not only ostracized by his colleagues, he was also suffering from poor health. His left hand was giving him trouble, having been injured years before in an accident. Since Josh insisted on playing a steel-string guitar and using sliding notes up and down the frets, his condition kept getting worse as the strings cut through his skin almost to the bone. Before a performance Josh would inject novocaine into his hand to numb the pain. I was horrified to see him shake the blood and pus from his fingers during a performance. Despite later imitators, Josh's recording of "The House of the Rising Sun" remains the definitive one. He, too, was accused of being a popularizer because he sang not only in the traditional vein but also made up his own versions. His own comment on this was, "I was a folksinger long before I knew what it's called. Even when I was a boy I made up and sang songs of ordinary people, trying to convey their joys and sorrows, their grievances and their hopes."

Josh White died at a relatively early age, too soon for any peace overtures on anyone's part. But if the community of musicians was angry at him, they were even more incensed at Burl Ives, who had named many colleagues in front of HUAC. Ives, America's finest balladeer, continued to perform, but not in concert with others. I cannot recollect a time when his name was included in any festival program in which other folksingers of the fifties or sixties were participants. Thinking of Burl in isolation always made me sad. This was the man who had recorded *The Lonesome Train,* the stirring epic about Lincoln's funeral that had moved me so in London. Other participants in this wonderfully patriotic work had been Millard Lampell, Pete Seeger, Earl Robinson, and Lord knows how many others who were later accused of being "Com-symps."

Burl Ives had been around longer than all the other folk performers. He was born in 1909, and was already a roving minstrel by the time of the great stock market crash of 1929. The story goes that during the Depression he was arrested in Utah for singing a "dirty song," and put in jail for a day and a night. Then he was taken to the edge of town and told never to come back. The song which had given such offense was the very song that later made him famous, "The Foggy, Foggy Dew." When he was brought to my flat in London by the singer Isla Cameron, I had long known of him through his recordings. In person, this man weighing three hundred pounds had a zest for life that surpassed all expectations. He also had a variety of interests outside of music: He was a writer, sailor, collector, and actor. That last talent would eventually do me out of an Academy Award.

It was not until June 1993 that Burl Ives, now very old, very frail, and in a wheelchair, sang on the same stage with others of the bygone days of the folk revival. The nostalgic evening at the 92 Street Y in New York was billed as a retrospective, "Fifty Years of Folk Music at the Y." Pete Seeger was at first scheduled to appear; then we were told that he would not. Everyone wondered whether the old feelings about Burl Ives had caused the change of heart. In the end, Pete did appear and it was a memorable evening, both artistically and emotionally. Burl still had the voice, but his body was failing; Pete no longer had the voice but his spirit was as buoyant as ever. When the two men sang together I was not sure whether I was witnessing an act of forgiveness. I do know that it was an act of grace. All of us—Odetta, Oscar Brand, Josh White Jr., Tom Paxton, Chad Mitchell, Eric Weissberg, and I—finished the evening by singing Leadbelly's "Goodnight Irene," and we knew that this was the last time we would be together with Burl Ives—the pioneer performer of folk ballads.

HAD I BEEN living in America in the early fifties when the witchhunt was in full swing, I would most certainly have been among its victims. I do not know what I would have done under the pressure. It is easy to imagine courage in yourself as an act of hindsight, but a performer in the middle of a successful career often succumbs to the fear of losing the tenuous hold he has on a fickle profession. I hope that I would have withstood the temptation to take the safe way out for the sake of being able to keep working. I trust I would have found the words to equal the eloquence of my colleagues who demonstrated more fealty to American ideals in their acts of defiance than all the pompous inquisitors who sat in judgment over them. But I also know that the people who did give in to the red-baiters were not the villains of the piece; those who threatened their livelihood and their children's future were. Not everyone has the fortitude to hold up under torture. For torture it was. Those who gave in were weak perhaps, but not evil. The screenwriter Dalton Trumbo, one of the "Hollywood Ten" forced out of work and out of the country by the blacklist, would have had more cause than most to be bitter about those who bought their freedom to work by denouncing others. Yet he had this to say: "When you who are in your forties or younger look back with curiosity on that dark time, as I think occasionally you should, it will do no good to search for villains or heroes, or saints or devils, because there were none—there were only victims."

Incredibly, the blacklist continued to cast a pall over the media even after the decade of the fifties had ended, keeping groups as honored as the Weavers off radio and television.

It is almost axiomatic to state that folk songs express and folksingers have political leanings, and that the leanings are invariably to the left. Pete Seeger's banjo had a legend written around its rim: "This weapon surrounds hate and conquers it." A more peaceful statement would be hard to find. I myself would be hard-pressed to name any reactionary or right-wing folk songs. Many of the songs with political content are broadsides—singing newsletters, as it were—telling of the events of the day. Many others go beyond the telling and become calls to conscience. No wonder that the Joe McCarthy crowd was uptight about folksingers.

In the spring of 1961 I was the host of a network television program on ABC entitled *Directions '61,* a noncommercial Sunday-morning program sponsored by the Jewish Theological Seminary. It presented a variety of topics, some dealing with the history of Jews in America, others with the quest for justice and equality, and others still with various religious themes. The programs invariably included music. One show that dealt with American history clearly needed a folk presentation. I requested that the Weavers appear to sing one of their numbers, "Wasn't That a Time." A flap ensued. The networks all had watchdogs in place, archly called "Continuity Acceptance." I was informed in no uncertain terms that the Weavers were not cleared for appearance on television—something I knew only too well.

I submitted the lyrics of the Weavers' song to the network people and asked them to point out to me which portions were subversive and liable to lead an unsuspecting viewing audience toward seditious acts. They did not even understand the premise of such a question; the Weavers were unacceptable and that was that. My friend Milton Krents, who headed the Jewish Theological Seminary's radio and TV department, pronounced himself unable to change the network's mind. But I was not prepared to let the matter rest there. I went to see Dr. Louis Finkelstein, the chancellor of the seminary, under whose aegis the program was presented. Dr. Finkelstein was a noted rabbi and scholar, a man who commanded deep respect. Well aware of the custom of diaspora Jewry to accept most dicta of authority, I feared that the seminary would not be prepared to make the fight in this case. At first it indeed appeared that Dr. Finkelstein would have preferred not take on the network over the entire issue of blacklisting. I argued that it would be incompatible with the Jewish stance of morality, so often stressed in our own program, to accept a process where rumor was tantamount to accusation, and accusation to conviction. I pointed out that, among other ills, the witch-hunters had demonstrated both anti-Semitism and xenophobia. At an earlier symposium on civil liberties and the arts organized by the American Jewish Congress I had stated: "We, as artists, must protest any act that seeks to compel the performer to bargain for his livelihood with other values than his talent." Now I informed Dr. Finkelstein that I was prepared to quit the program over this issue. He pondered the dilemma for a very short time, then told me that the seminary would stand behind me and, if necessary, also bow out of its sponsorship of the program.

The network gave in and the Weavers appeared on the program. They sang "Wasn't That a Time" without any ensuing stampede by the viewing public to join the hordes of underground left-wing revolutionaries. Briefly, there had been a chink in a seemingly impenetrable wall. Unfortunately, it was not the end of blacklisting for the Weavers. After all, *Directions '61* was a sustaining program with no commercial sponsorship. No detergent company could be pressured into withdrawing advertising dollars from a program such as ours. Several months later, in January 1962, the Weavers were scheduled to appear on the forerunner of *The Tonight Show*, usually hosted by Jack Paar. That night the guest host was the noted social satirist Sam Levinson. On the afternoon of their appearance, the Weavers were asked to sign a loyalty oath. When they refused, they were bumped from the program.

Later, when Lee Hays was asked about the period when the Weavers had been prevented from working, he said, "Frankly, if it wasn't for the honor, I'd just as soon not have been blacklisted."

Big, burly Lee Hays was responsible for so much about the Weavers that bespoke not only their artistry but their humanity. His homespun humor was a main ingredient of the group's performances. Rightly, he assumed the role of interlocutor for the group, introducing songs with a patter that was as funny onstage as he was off. At one time his sister, Fran, in North Carolina wrote a song called "Seven Daffodils," which the Tarriers performed with some success. The song spoke of a longing to be taken to the flowering hills where nothing but love was needed for happiness. Lee introduced it by saying, "I've got this matron sister with a family back in North Carolina who keeps writing songs about some Gypsies that are going to take her away and give her nothing to eat."

Lee was not a well person; he was beset by many illnesses, some real and others imagined. He treated the imaginary ones with as much care as the real ones—a true hypochondriac. But he had a sense of humor about it, as he did about everything else. With pills and nose sprays in his pockets and boxes of tissues on either side of the stage, he would declare at the Weavers' annual concert at Carnegie Hall, "Well, it's been an interesting year—medically . . . " Lee also liked his creature comforts, and made no secret of it. He would enjoy staying at the hotels on tour and using the amenities. In contrast, Pete Seeger, ever identifying with the poor, would often refuse to stay at the hotels and seek more humble lodgings with friends or acquaintances. Sometimes, however, he would sneak into Lee's room at the hotel to take a bath.

It was not imaginary illnesses which eventually took Lee's life. He was a severe diabetic, and his condition worsened steadily. Finally, his feet had to be amputated. Still he continued to be in touch with friends by phone and letter, and even participated in a last concert that the Weavers gave at Carnegie Hall, which was videotaped. Lee performed in a wheelchair and still acted as spokesman for the group, even narrating the video. His opening line contains the ultimate in self-deprecating humor. This man with both feet amputated announced: "I am Lee Hays—more or less."

When my wife, Rita, and I decided to move from New York City in 1971, we settled on an area in Connecticut where we already had friends. We found a house not too far from Weston, where Harold Leventhal and Fred Hellerman lived. It was a splendid old place, built in 1710 and enlarged by various owners over the years. Raymond Massey had owned it and built the swimming pool. Before him there was Lawrence Tibbet, the famous opera singer, who had added a huge A-frame structure where he gave private recitals. Despite these elements of splendor, this was rural living, the first for me since my kibbutz days. Soon after we got settled in our new home with its twelve acres, I received a letter from Lee Hays in praise of rusticity. For some time Lee had been living in rural surroundings in Croton-on-Hudson, which he clearly enjoyed. His letter was eight pages long, seven of which were devoted to a recommendation and to detailed instructions on making a compost heap by using all the available organic material. This was no idle matter for Lee. He believed in it so much that in his will he ordered his ashes to be strewn upon his compost heap to be of one last fertile use. I believe that when he died, his wishes were carried out to the letter.

During the fifties and sixties I continued to meet other singers and musicians who became close friends. My predilections always ran to music-makers who did international material, such as Martha Schlamme and Alex Hassilev. Another early friendship I formed was with Gene and Francesca Raskin. Both of them were immensely likable people. Eugene Raskin was a witty and talented friend to be with, and they made music together. What set them apart from the other folkies was the fact that they did not seek to make a living from the music. Gene was an architecture professor at Columbia University, they lived well, and the music was something they did for the love of it. To be sure, they made a couple of records and gave some public appearances, but no thought was given to leaving any regular jobs for a life of minstrelsy or a life of leisure. Ironically, in the end that is precisely what did happen. Gene, always drawn to Russian Gypsy music, had written an English version of *"Darogoy dal'nuyu"* (The long road), a song I knew well and had also recorded, which they sang as "Those Were the Days." In 1968 the Beatles got hold of Gene's version and decided to have a young singer, Mary Hopkin, record the song on the Beatles' own Apple label. That changed the Raskins' lives permanently. The record was a million-plus seller. Gene resigned from the faculty of Columbia, the Raskins bought a house in Spain, and they continue to commute annually from New York to Mallorca.

My own affinity for Russian music was known throughout the folk world. Consequently, on the rare occasions when Russian performers visited New York, I was always invited. One night I received a telephone call from Art d'Lugoff, the owner of the Village Gate. The Beryozka Ballet, a folk troupe, was in town and he had invited them to the club as his guests. He asked me to come also and bring my guitar. I had seen the Beryozka on stage, but we were in the middle of the Cold War, and visiting artists from the Soviet Union were closely guarded and chaperoned. When Art called me, I jumped at the chance to meet this group. At the club, the Russians all sat together in one area; by all appearances they were not supposed to mix with the locals. But they had brought their accordion player, a burly older guy with twinkling eyes. He played and the girls sang; onstage they mostly danced, but here they sang and very beautifully. After a while, Art asked a couple of the Americans to go up onstage and sing. When my turn came, I sang Russian songs. Their faces were a study in astonishment. Whether they had expected an American country singer or not, what I gave them was the last thing they expected. They applauded with great enthusiasm.

I decided to go over to the group and pay my respects. I sat down at the table with the accordion player and told him in Russian that I had enjoyed his music very much. An English-speaking fellow rushed over and said he was their interpreter; from then on the conversation had to go through him. He was obviously more than an interpreter: His ever-watchful demeanor and constant frown were in sharp contrast to the miens of the rest of the group. The musician said to me in Russian: "*Vy ochen' talantnyi artist.*" The interpreter: "He says you are a very talented artist." Me: "I know that's what he said." The irony was lost on him and he continued to translate. The accordionist asked me how it was that I knew all these Russian songs and where I had learned them. Through the interpreter I said that I loved Russian music and especially the Gypsy kind. As to learning them, I said, "I am not a trained musician; vocally and instrumentally what I do comes to me naturally; it's all from God." Without translating that last remark, the interpreter asked me sharply, "You are a believer?" I told him, "In this context, what I meant was that I don't play and sing from a music sheet. I listen and what I hear goes straight from my ears to my strumming fingers and my mouth." He chose to translate that description for my fellow musician. When he finished, the Russian said with complete understanding: "*Aha, at Boga!*" (I see, it's from God!)

ABOUT FOUR YEARS after I became friends with Mary Travers, around 1961, I was invited to give a concert at Cornell University in upstate New York. As was often the case, the event was sponsored by the folk song society of the college. Sometimes the English department of a college would sponsor a folk concert, other times it would be the history or the sociology department—but never the music department. Their brows did not droop so low as to consider folk music to fall within their discipline.

I arrived at the Ithaca airport and was met by the president of the folk song society, an earnest young student. We got into his car, a dilapidated affair which had a gerry-rigged loudspeaker mounted on the roof. As we drove through the campus, the student made commercial announcements into a microphone: "Theodore Bikel is at Cornell—this evening we have Bikel at Cornell—come to hear Bikel at Cornell—Cornell and Bikel—Bikel and Cornell—come to hear Bikel at Cornell . . . " When he paused for breath I asked him what kind of music he played. He said, "I play all kinds of music, including your kind." That was said in a tone which left no doubt that it was meant as a compliment. "And your name?" I asked. "Peter," he said, "Peter Yarrow." Then he continued the Bikel-to-Cornell routine. It was not until quite some time later, when all three were living and working in Greenwich Village, that Peter Yarrow and Mary Travers linked up with Noel Stookey to form a singing group. It was Al Grossman, the manager and former owner of Chicago's Gate of Horn, who understood how to promote the trio, including changing Noel's name to Paul.

In all my previous countries of residence, communications—telephone, radio, and television—had been funded by the state and subject to governmental control and regulations. Neither radio nor TV had any commercial sponsors, and as a consequence relatively little money was allocated for production, writers, directors, and actors. The creative elements were given their allocations but were otherwise mostly left alone with little interference. America was different. You kept reassuring yourself that having one's performance interrupted by all too frequent commercials could be tolerated because of the money you earned. What was less reassuring was the thought that artistic—or, one feared, journalistic—content was subject to control by noncreative elements. Success was measured not by quality, but by numbers. "How many people saw it or heard it?" replaced "How good was it?" as a criterion when accountants determined the survival of presentations on the air. That became a stumbling block as my friends and I looked for decent ways to present folk music on the air. TV was out for reasons of political censorship and "acceptability" of certain performers. In radio one could not assure commercial stations that they'd attract big enough audiences, which meant that AM radio was out also.

Which left FM radio. *Theodore Bikel at Home* was carried on a number of FM stations around the country. With the advent of FM, some stations were still able to present good talk, sometimes controversial talk, and also folk music, which had never found a niche on AM radio. Some of these stations were run by private individuals who were financing the undertaking because they liked FM radio's ability to be bold. Others were run by foundations such as Pacifica on the West Coast; others yet, like WFMT in Chicago, were basically classical music stations that had broadened their programming and changed their audience. In New York, WBAI was owned by a millionaire named Lou Schweitzer who simply loved the medium and who gave the programmers a free hand in presenting anything they thought worthwhile.

Radio was not the only enterprise in the arts that Lou had a hand in. He had also bought a theatre in Westport, Connecticut, as a present for his wife, Lucille Lortel. That theatre, the White Barn, is still run by her as a labor of love, many years after Lou's death. He was somewhat of an eccentric. For example, he bought a New York cab and a cab license for a young driver on whose services Lou would have first call; when not needed by Lou, the driver could operate freely around the city. The wrinkle was that the cab was a Mercedes. No New York City cabs were other than the standard yellow jobs. Not Lou's; he somehow managed to get permission to run what I believe was the only Mercedes cab in the country. He also bought his own gondola in Venice. He must have bribed a lot of people in order to be able to do that; the city fathers permitted no privately owned gondolas. In the end, Lou Schweitzer owned one. He also wanted to give the gondola a name, to be displayed on the bow. Gondolas had no names, either, he was told; they had numbers. He got his way there, too. For several years one solitary gondola in Venice bore the name *Lucille.*

Theodore Bikel at Home was carried on WBAI in New York, on KPFA in Berkeley, first on KRHM and then on KPFK in Los Angeles. From time to time some other FM stations carried individual segments of the program also. The title was both accurate and a misnomer. Since I traveled so much in the course of my work, "at home" literally meant any place I happened to be at the time. Thus the show might emanate from Texas, from Israel, from Africa, or from a studio on either coast. When away from a studio, I mailed in tapes to one of the stations, which broadcast the show and then circulated the tape to the others. At the studio I often had guests: many folksingers, some politicians, comedians who chatted, sang, or improvised in a free-for-all fashion. When I did not have time to get guests, or when I needed to meet a deadline, I might go to the studio way after midnight all by myself, talk and spin albums of my choice, often out-of-the-way material that I liked and no one else presented on the air. During my travels I could not do the disc-jockey routine, but there were plenty of guests to be had and events to cover. Among my guests were well-known performers as well as new folksingers who had yet to make their debut. A very tired Harry Belafonte was my guest on a show emanating from London; he had just come back to the hotel after his concert, and I made him talk to me for close to an hour. I have always been sorry for having been so inconsiderate as to put him through it, but he was a friend and I did not think of it as the imposition it must have been. It is to his credit, not mine, that he stayed a friend. Other guests on my show included groups like the Weavers, the Tarriers, and the Kingston Trio. There were also performers with their careers on the rise: Judy Collins, Woody Allen, Bob Dylan.

Elektra Records was always on the lookout for new talent. It was also around 1961 that Jac Holzman told me that he had found an extraordinary young singer with a pure vocal delivery. Her name was

Judy Collins, and he had signed her up to record for the label. He also wanted me to help give her exposure. At that time my concerts were regular features on the New York scene; they were always sold out and Jac suggested that I bring Judy on as a surprise guest at my next concert. I agreed; Judy and I worked on a couple of tunes which we could sing together and I did as I had promised: During the second half of my concert, I introduced Judy to the audience, we did the tunes we had rehearsed, and then she did a few songs on her own. Predictably, the audience loved her.

When I did *Theodore Bikel at Home,* Fred Weintraub, the owner of the Bitter End in Greenwich Village, offered to have me do the taping at the club in front of an audience. I could have his performers on my show, the club would benefit from having my occasional guests perform, and the exposure would help all concerned. It was there that I managed to record some of the initial Peter, Paul & Mary appearances. I also presented the Tarriers, Judy Henske, John Lee Hooker, and Leon Bibb, among many others. Fred Weintraub, who had been hooked on folk music before, became even more of an aficionado and eventually branched out to produce, as a motion picture, the music extravaganza that took place at Woodstock.

I do not know exactly where I myself fit in the folk scene. I can speak about the folk field but can hardly claim to speak for it. Since I bore some responsibility for the folk revival in America, it has been said that I occupy an avuncular position vis-à-vis the folk scene. (In view of my advancing years, instead of "uncle" that should perhaps read "great-uncle.") I cannot even claim to be a folksinger in the traditional sense. A folksinger is one whose material is drawn from one idiom based on the roots of his own tribe, his own people, his own heritage. Although I sing in twenty-one languages, I can legitimately call myself a folksinger in just one idiom—the Jewish one. In all the others I suppose I am, for want of a better term, a folk-song singer.

It was something akin to a tightrope act, being a keeper of the Jewish tradition on the one hand and doing the multicultural thing on the other—always straddling what is considered to be an artificially drawn line between "purity" and "popularizing." The position I came to occupy in the folk field during the sixties is perhaps best understood in light of my role as a cofounder of the Newport Folk Festival.

For a brief period in the late fifties there had been an attempt to establish a commercial folk festival in Newport, Rhode Island, whose sponsors included a tobacco company. It ran for a couple of years and then the promoters let it drop; the returns did not justify the effort. Then, in 1960, George Wein, a concert promoter with a background in jazz performing, asked to meet with Pete Seeger and myself with a view to reviving the festival, this time on a noncommercial basis. That idea appealed to both of us. A few meetings were held in my apartment in Washington Square, the first ones attended only by Pete, his wife, Toshi, George Wein, my secretary, Alice Conklin, and me. During these first meetings we devised a rudimentary plan. Our rationale for putting the festival back on the map was that we owed a debt to the grass roots of the folk field, a debt that needed to be acknowledged and repaid. The sources for our performances were mostly to be found in the oral tradition. Even when the text and music had been transcribed on paper, no one profited by the performance of the material, as it was considered to be in the public domain. The irony of it was that minor changes were sometimes made to the material and the persons making the changes began to draw royalties, while the original performers who had nurtured and preserved the songs for years remained unrecompensed and in obscurity. We thought this to be most unfair and disrespectful of the very people who had carried the tunes in community after community. Most of them had been poor all their lives and would remain so, while others—like Joan Baez, Bob Dylan, Peter, Paul & Mary, and indeed Theodore Bikel—sang their songs in concert halls and earned better than respectable fees. Occasionally we might give credit along the lines of "I learned this from a blind blues singer in Mississippi," but we owed that singer more than just a mention from the stage.

That feeling was one of the reasons for our decision to put a nonprofit folk festival back in place at Newport. The other was the upsurge of interest in folk music on the urban scene. We wanted to stimulate regional activity and, by using the profits from Newport, make it possible for smaller folk festivals to take place. Fiddlers' contests, bluegrass festivals, revivals of black music from the islands off the shores of Georgia and the Carolinas—all this we had in mind also. In order to fulfill our mandate to repay the debt owed to the folk field, we planned to purchase instruments for itinerant and indigent musicians and to provide tape recorders for folklorists engaged in collecting material in the field.

In order to accomplish this, we created a nonprofit foundation with a board of ten unpaid directors. Among the first batch of directors were Jean Ritchie, Clarence Cooper, Peter Yarrow, Eric Darling, and Bill Clifton. Others joined the board later: Ralph Rinzler, a bluegrass performer (later in charge of the folk program at the Smithsonian Institution), the redoubtable Alan Lomax, Oscar Brand, and Ronnie Gilbert. The way the festivals were run was very democratic. None of the performers received any pay except fare, lodging, food, and $54 in cash. We did have considerable expenses in bringing some of them to Newport from such far-off places as New Zealand, Ireland, and even South Africa, but everyone, from Joan Baez on down, received $54 without exception. As a result, the festival generated a great deal of revenue, and the Newport Folk Foundation was in a position to give away respectable sums of money. We still did not feel that we had acquitted ourselves of the debt, but it was a beginning and it gave us a warm sense of satisfaction.

In one instance, Newport rescued an entire genre of regional music from falling into total obscurity and becoming extinct. Cajun music in Louisiana was at the point of dying out. This was an interesting musical form, played mostly on fiddle, bass, small accordion, and triangle, with lyrics in Cajun French. (The word "Cajun" takes its origin from "Arcadian." These are the French-speaking descendants of Huguenots who, having once fled from France to Canada, were once more forced to flee to Louisiana.) We brought Cajun groups to Newport and they enjoyed success not only at the festival itself but, as a result, also on their home turf. The festival gave them a new lease on life: They went on to hold their own regional music competitions and song-swapping meets. In general, Newport became a rallying point for folk performers as well as academicians in the field, a place to look for help and guidance—and money.

The festivals themselves were a joy for the thousands who attended each event, but for us, the board members, they were an organizational nightmare. We had to be greeters, assigners of lodgings, traffic cops, nursemaids, adjudicators of disputes, caterers—and all this in addition to being presenters at the various festival events. We were also under constant pressure vis-à-vis the town of Newport. Our festival permit was not issued with terribly good grace; it seemed that each spring we had to explain anew to the city fathers the nature of the festival, its artists, and its audiences. Closer to the start of the festival we had to explain all this again to the Newport police, who were needed to make sure that the access roads to the festival site were open and that no untoward incidents should mar the week. But just as we had to explain the folk kids to the cops, we also had to explain the presence of the cops to the kids.

After all, many of the folk kids were of the beat generation, others were student activists—neither of these groups harbored any positive feelings toward the police and vice versa. I remember a conversation with a police sergeant who made disparaging remarks about the appearance of the young people who had come for the festival. I argued with him that his men should ignore mode of dress, language, and behavior, unless there was any evidence of palpable wrongdoing. I also argued with the kids to avoid the sorts of confrontations with police that had become commonplace around the country. The presence of the cops at Newport was not a political statement; they were there not to suppress revolution but to control traffic. Forget "pigs."

What the festival achieved was important. Many thousands who came because their curiosity was piqued left with some respect for musical traditions and with melodies swirling inside their heads that their parents had long forgotten. The daytime events, sometimes as many as a dozen at a time under various trees and in the corners of the field, covered ballads, storytelling, contemporary songs, freedom songs, bluegrass, dulcimers, international music, and much more besides. This was a veritable smorgasbord where you could either wander around and sample many things or stick to one diet. We brought singers and musicians from Hawaii and Ireland, as well as from the mountains of Kentucky and the Georgia Sea Islands. One year we even managed to have four prisoners paroled in our care for the week of the festival. The Texas state prison authorities only demanded of us that we guarantee their return, and that they would not be permitted to drink alcohol while in our care. These fellows sang work gang songs while actually splitting logs on stage.

The folk crowd was on the whole not a drinking bunch. People at the jazz festivals were more prone to drink hard liquor; beer and wine was the style of the folk people. When the festivals were discontinued by the city of Newport after riots at the jazz festival, they did not take note of the difference between the two crowds and bumped us all. Only on rare occasions did we have a problem in the drinking department with any of our artists. When Seamus Ennis arrived with his Irish pipes, we assigned two staff members to him to make sure that he would be a good boy and stay away from the booze while at the festival. That worked fine, but keeping Seamus sober failed to prevent one little crisis. Before the evening's events we had to make sure that no one overstepped his allotted time, as we simply had too many artists on the program to chance that. So we organized a run-through rehearsal of everyone's performance. Seamus had been told that he had eleven minutes for his evening appearance. We suggested that he do three tunes and finish up with a fast jig. As we started this portion of the rehearsal, two buses arrived with a large singing group from the bluegrass mountains. They were all members of a church who sang a cappella as part of their worship. There was no steady conductor; any one of them might stand in the middle of the circle and give the beat. We wanted to be very careful not to give offense to these religious people, and so we had carefully removed all traces of any kind of drink from the shelves of the rehearsal shack. All empty bottles and cans had been removed when the group arrived. They stood against the wall as Seamus played, clearly enjoying themselves and nodding to the beat of the music. Seamus took exactly eleven minutes for his numbers as he had been requested. When he was through, he laid down his pipes and said, "Well, there you have it. I'm a fuckin' virtuoso." It took some persuading not to have the entire church group turn around as a man and go back home.

There were a great many favorites at the festivals. Depending on your musical preferences, you might enjoy Tom Paxton, the New Lost City Ramblers, Bob Gibson, Judy Collins, Carolyn Hester, or Arlo Guthrie. At the Sunday-afternoon events, which were billed as "New Folks" concerts, you could hear such new voices as James Taylor in the year of his emergence as a singer-songwriter. At one of these afternoons an incredible event occurred. Just as Richard Fariña and his wife, Mimi, had started to sing, a monumental downpour began to drench the audience. Normally this would cause everyone to run for shelter. Not this time, though; people stood, laughed, sang, and clapped, strangers embracing each other. This must have been the forerunner of the love-in at Woodstock.

I believe it was Alan Lomax who managed to bring out of obscurity an old blues singer who everyone thought was no longer alive. Mississippi John Hurt arrived with his battered old guitar and an equally battered old felt hat. He played and sang, somewhat toothless, but still quite wonderful and totally authentic. The crowds loved him. The folk press was also eager to talk to him. That opportunity presented itself at one of the symposia we had arranged during the festival week. The old man sat on a collapsible chair, smiling at the folk who were throwing around erudite comments about the folk process and who tried to outdo each other in folk-upmanship. Finally one of the journalists asked Mississippi John Hurt a question: "John, what do you think about this renaissance of folk music in America?" "The what?" John asked. "The revival, the comeback of folk music in the fifties and sixties?" The old fellow smiled and said with a toothless grin, "Daddy, it ain't never been away."

10

Peregrinations

*I*T WAS EVIDENT TO ME THAT AMERICAN AUDIENCES love talent, love performers, even make a fetish of some of them. There are no kings and no aristocrats in America; Americans find their royalty elsewhere—among the wealthy, the powerful, and the talented. Tycoons and others who walk the halls of power are essentially out of reach. Performers, on the other hand, are familiar faces on the stages and movie screens and especially in living rooms. Radio was immensely important to almost every American, and TV was rapidly becoming much more so.

I entered the world of television very soon after my first job in the American theatre had ended. There was a tension in television work that was not much different from the angst of working on the stage. No film, no tape. This was live TV, no retakes to correct mistakes, no editing to make the product look better or more coherent. If you fluffed your lines, too bad—whatever you did, mistakes and all, is what the audience of millions saw. And, unlike the theatre, there was no second night after the opening, no "Ah, well, it'll be better tomorrow." The rehearsal process itself was very much like theatre; you spent some three weeks to get a ninety-minute show on its feet, you rehearsed in a ballroom, and hit the studio floor only days before the telecast. The difference was that, even in the ballroom, toward the end of the rehearsal period a bunch of technicians followed you around, weaving in and out, coming closer and retreating as the cameras would eventually do. You had to get used to that; there was no "fourth wall,"

Me at age two—Vienna, 1926.

Reb Shimon Bikel, my sometimes irascible paternal grandfather, circa 1927.

Regina Riegler, my maternal grandmother.

Three generations: my grandmother, mother, and I.

Mother and I in Vienna, about 1929.

Maier Riegler, the Austrian prison warden: the grandfather who died before I was born.

One of my earliest professional roles, in Goldoni's *Servant of Two Masters,* Tel Aviv, 1944.

At the Royal Academy of Dramatic Art in 1947, as Mr. Hardcastle in *She Stoops to Conquer.*

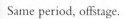

Same period, offstage.

Reb Dovid Shapiro in Shalom Aleichem's *It's Hard to Be a Jew*, Embassy Theatre Swiss Cottage, London, 1949.

In London's West End, as Colonel Ikonenko in Peter Ustinov's *The Love of Four Colonels,* one of my first major roles.

In what was to be the first of many supporting film roles, I played the first officer of a World War I German gunboat in *The African Queen*. Here, during a break in shooting, I am doing a bit of entertaining for John Huston, Humphrey Bogart (at right) and Katharine Hepburn (seated in the foreground with her back to the camera).

A famous scene from *The African Queen*, when Bogart and Hepburn are about to be executed by hanging. I am on the left, and Peter Bull, playing the ship's captain, is on the right.

In the J. Arthur Rank film *The Little Kidnappers,* I play the Dutch doctor, Willem Bloem.

Same film; I am opposite Adrienne Corri, one of the few times I was permitted to be the love interest in a film.

a scene from *Desperate Moment,* I hold a gun on Dirk Bogarde, an escaped convict.

With Clark Gable and Richard Hayden (far right), I hold a gun on myself in a game of Russian roulette in the MGM film *Never Let Me Go.*

A studio publicity shot from 1952.

1955. In my first U.S. stage role, I play
Inspector Massoubre in *Tonight in
Samarkand*, starring Louis Jourdan.

As Robert de Baudricourt opposite Julie
Harris's Joan of Arc in the Broadway play
The Lark in 1956.

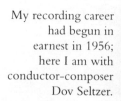

One of my earliest
television roles,
playing Julius Caesar
on the *Westinghouse
Summer Theater.*

My recording career
had begun in
earnest in 1956;
here I am with
conductor-composer
Dov Seltzer.

I am the strong yet benign Southern sheriff in *The Defiant Ones*. Unlikely casting, perhaps, but it got me an Academy Award nomination.

As Zoltan Karpathy, the "hairy hound from Budapest," in the film version of *My Fair Lady*.

As a stateless person stuck on a freighter and never permitted to leave the ship, in the U.N.-sponsored film *Who Has Seen the Wind* during the early sixties.

As Captain Von Trapp opposite Mary Martin in *The Sound of Music* on Broadway.

1960. On the campaign trail in New York's garment district with presidential candidate Senator John F. Kennedy and the celebrated New York labor leader David Potofsky (right).

With Vice President Hubert Humphrey during the early years of LBJ's administration; later things soured at the 1968 Democratic Convention in Chicago.

With senatorial candidate Bobby Kennedy during his New York campaign.

New York, 1963. Studying a page of Talmud with my father; my mother is proudly looking on.

In Athens, interviewing the exiled Archbishop Makarios of Cyprus for my radio program, *Theodore Bikel at Home.* At this time I was on location shooting *The Angry Hills.*

With schoolchildren at the Hollywood Bowl after a concert rehearsal: Bikel doing a "Pied Piper."

Campaigning for SANE in Nutley, New Jersey, in the mid-sixties. The best—and worst—was yet to come.

In the Namibian desert, playing opposite a nameless giant lizard during the filming of *Sands of the Kalahari*.

As the hapless and lost Russian submarine captain in *The Russians Are Coming, The Russians Are Coming*.

As a Scottish gravedigger in *I Bury the Living*, who must kill to bring order to his cemetery.

In a scene from Fox's *The Enemy Below.* Here we are singing a song with skipper Curt Jurgens and the other officers in order to bolster morale during a depth-charge attack by an American destroyer.

A still from *The Enemy Below.* I am the first officer of the German U-boat.

In Fox's *Fraulein* as a drunken, amorous Russian military officer wooing the beautiful Dana Wynter.

In the musical *Pousse Cafe*, based on *The Blue Angel*, one of two Broadway disasters with "cafe" in the title, I am the university professor besotted by the charms of a chanteuse. The singer is played by Lilo.

In Paramount's *My Side of the Mountain*, playing an itinerant folklorist.

In *Jacques Brel Is Alive and Well and Living in Paris,* its first production in the round. I am seen here with Chita Rivera (front), Gil Price, and Judy Gibson.

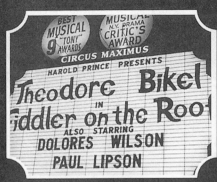

My first *Fiddler*, opening in, of all places, Las Vegas.

As Tevye, I would shlep this cart a thousand more times and "still going."

Backstage at *Fiddler* with my parents. Theo *and* Shalom Aleichem—for them it was a dream come true.

As the notorious "Mack the Knife," in Brecht and Weill's *Threepenny Opera* at the Guthrie Theater in Minneapolis, 1983.

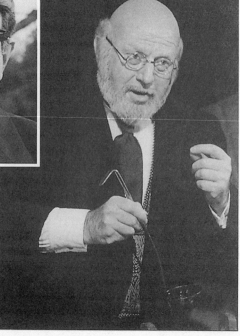

My Fair Lady again, this time live on stage and playing Eliza's father, Alfred P. Doolittle.

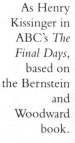

As Henry Kissinger in ABC's *The Final Days*, based on the Bernstein and Woodward book.

As one of the early Southern California pioneers in *Harris Newmark's Los Angeles.* My performance in this PBS program won me an Emmy in 1988.

With Gregory Peck, Julia Roberts, and SAG
board member Paul Hecht at a ceremony
honoring Audrey Hepburn, already too ill to
attend in person.

My mother, age 93,
Tel Aviv, 1991.

With American troops stationed in a Patriot
missile silo, under alert "somewhere in Israel," 1991.

Los Angeles, 1993. Renewing
an old friendship
with Harry Belafonte.

1993. Backstage with poet Yevgeny Yevtushenko
in New York. Before he read his poem "Babi Yar"
in Russian and I read it in English, his advice to
me was: "Don't be modest."

At the 1993 Madison Square Garden ceremony
commemorating the fiftieth anniversary
of the Warsaw Ghetto uprising;
here with Ben and Vladka Meed
and Vice President Al Gore.

the presumed line between stage performers and audience.

I liked the challenge. The immediacy of performing right there and then before the audience created a sense of excitement, even though you had to do it in a void, as it were, for an audience who did not laugh at your jokes, at least not so you could hear their laughter. Nor could you hear the collective intake of breath when they were moved. That aspect of it was possibly worse with movies: In live TV at least you knew the audience was there the night you did it. Make a film and you work for a laugh or a tear that may—or may not—come six months later. In the live TV days you still had the advantage of developing a play and your character in it because you started at the beginning and went through to the end. Later, after tape started to be used, it was not so much fun. You still had all the rehearsals to cope with, and you might get to tape an act at a time, but then they started to tape bits and pieces out of sequence, almost like film but under greater time pressure.

There was some interesting material for a performer on TV, some not so interesting, and some downright garbage. The trick was to avoid the garbage and go for the classy material; that is, if you could afford to do that and still eat and pay the rent. It was then that I discovered the ultimate usefulness of money: It allows you to say no. By and large I chose well in those "live" days. I did *The Bridge of San Luis Rey*, *The Dybbuk* (directed by Sidney Lumet), George Bernard Shaw's *Saint Joan* (with Maurice Evans, Raymond Massey, and Genevieve Bujold, directed by George Schaefer), and *Julius Caesar* (directed by Daniel Petrie). It was in *Caesar* that the pitfalls of doing live television were especially in evidence for me. It was the middle of summer, and we used a studio on Ninth Avenue that had no air conditioning. The crowd scenes were particularly uncomfortable; all these bodies emanating heat and sweat. I played Caesar. After being stabbed by all the daggers, I was lying dead on the ground while Brutus and Marc Antony delivered their orations. I had no way of knowing at what point the cameras would be on me, and I had to take care to pretend not to breathe at all. I was able to control that part better than my perspiration glands. A sweating corpse would surely tax the audience's suspension of disbelief. But I hoped we would get away with it. However, the crowd had been directed by Dan Petrie to react to Brutus favorably and to Marc Antony with scorn, at least until he managed to quiet them down. "Friends, Romans, countrymen," Alfred Ryder as Antony intoned, trying to be heard over the crowd's disdainful noise. They were supposed to quiet down only after his line "Lend me your ears!" On the live show it all went swimmingly until that moment.

"Lend me your ears!" Marc Anthony cried and the noise ebbed away as ordered. Except for one small determined high-pitched male voice who improvised into the silence: "Well, anybody could get up there and talk!" Actually very New York, it sounded like "toawk." There was a sweating and giggling corpse of Caesar lying on the floor, praying that the camera was nowhere near.

There Shall Be No Night was a TV movie set in Hungary. The prolific Mort Wishengrad had written the television script; the leading actors were Katherine Cornell and Charles Boyer. NBC's casting was enterprising; I played Boyer's uncle. He was, in real life, in his fifties, and I was thirty-seven. In the show he played forty and I played sixty. My makeup was worth the two hours in the makeup chair; it was a masterpiece—false skin over false jowls. (The makeup artist was Bob O'Bradovich. I asked him how he had come by that curious name. It appears that one of his forbears, an Irishman named O'Brady, had been conscripted into the British army to fight in the Crimean War. He deserted when the troops were on the march through Serbia, remained there, married a Serb woman, and added a Slavic ending to his Irish name.) We rehearsed the show in a large ballroom, Central Plaza on Second Avenue, three floors above Ratner's kosher dairy restaurant. This was a place where all the waiters were characters and knew it. When Sir Laurence Olivier rehearsed there for a TV show, the waiters insisted on calling him "Sir Label." One went to Ratner's for lunch every day as much for the arguments with the waiters as for the food. One day we had a tough rehearsal with some problems, and the director (George Schaefer again) kept me and Boyer for a conference during the lunch hour. Consequently, when we got downstairs, we only had about twenty-five minutes left for our lunch. I called the waiter to our table. He was old and bald, and he shuffled over with tired splayed feet. I told him that we had very little time for lunch, that the gentleman with me would like a fruit salad with cottage cheese, that I wanted a mushroom and barley soup, but that we needed to have everything fast. The old man looked from me to Boyer and back again, clapped his hands, and said, almost with pride: "I'm the slowest." And he was.

I was a new face on American TV screens and I was in demand. The producers and casting people were intrigued by the fact that I was able to master accents and languages, and that I did not shy away from work that sometimes made me fairly unrecognizable from role to role. I did not mind that; after all, I was a character actor and considered my craft to demand chameleon techniques. What distinguishes character acting from "personality acting" is this: Clark Gable or John

Wayne could be called Rhett Butler, Jim Higgins, or Joe Schwartz; they might wear different clothes and speak different lines—but they would not change their walk, their gait, or their speech patterns one iota from role to role. The American public actually likes that; they are comfortable with the familiar. I did not fit into any mold or pattern or pigeonhole; I still don't. As a consequence, people were baffled by the various faces and facets I kept presenting to them. "Do you know that there's a singer by the same name as yours?" someone asked me. Then he added, "But he pronounces it differently."

Even those who do know and acknowledge the variety of things I do professionally have a little difficulty with it. How often have I been asked which of the many things I do I enjoy most. The answer I tend to give to that question is: "Versatility in itself." It carries a big reward. I managed to act, to sing, to lecture, to write, to teach, and to stay active as a politically involved human being besides. As an actor on television I played a Greek peanut vendor, a blind Portuguese cobbler, a prison guard on Devil's Island, a mad bomber, a South African Boer. I portrayed Henry Kissinger, played a bald eighty-year-old Jewish-German California pioneer in the 1850s, even played a sinister Chinese underworld figure—and many more characters besides. This may have cut down on the recognition factor, but it prevented me from ever getting stale. The few times I was actually cast as a romantic lead were harder for me to come to grips with; there was no mask to hide behind. But I need to do everything well—professional pride alone demands that—and so I invented character envelopes of a sort even for those roles: a different voice, a different walk, or a different tempo of speech.

Still, in the late fifties I was basically a New York actor who made a few forays to Hollywood for the occasional film role. The TV work that emanated from New York consolidated a reputation which would assure me continued employment and a steady income. Sometimes they even paid you for not working. Once I was cast as the husband of a woman who is in a quandary: For medical reasons she needs an abortion without which she will have only a fifty-fifty chance of survival. With some anguish both wife and husband wrestle with the decision. It was a good script, and Gusti Huber, the expatriate Austrian actress who was to play my wife, and I were looking forward to doing the show. Two days before rehearsals were to start we received word that the network had developed cold feet over the subject matter—still a taboo in the fifties—and they had substituted another, less controversial, script in its time slot. We had a contract, of course, and like farmers who get paid not to grow certain crops, we got paid our fees for not airing the topic of abortion on television.

Another time we were doing a teleplay in an adventure series. The stars were Viveca Lindfors, George MacCready, and I. As in all live TV, we worked up to the last minute before showtime. After the dress rehearsal they gave us an hour's break for dinner so we could be back half an hour before the live telecast for makeup checks and last-minute adjustments. The director was in conference with the top brass in the control room when we returned. We would not get to see him again until after the show. We took our positions for the ten-second "teaser," with the announcer's voice booming over individual close-ups of the leading actors: "Presenting . . . George MacCready . . . Viveca Lindfors . . . and Theodore Bikel . . . in . . . *Appointment with Adventure.*" Then there was a thirty-second commercial break before the top of the show. I was standing in a garden set behind a hedge. Suddenly, I felt a tug at my pants. There was the director, crouched behind the hedge. He whispered urgently, "Cut the first six lines!" I wanted to ask, "Just mine or everybody's?" but there was no time to ask anything or get an answer before the live show began. Talk about thinking on your feet.

The more memorable roles in my early television career included a role as a killer-for-hire in a segment of *Naked City.* I played a devoted family man who does his ordinary fatherly chores on a Sunday morning (Keir Dullea was my son), then goes out in a little boat on the East River and machine-guns six people to death. Then there was a part in a show entitled "The Hands of Mr. Ottermole," a segment of *Alfred Hitchcock Presents,* and the role of Oliver Crangle in "Four O'Clock" on Rod Serling's *The Twilight Zone.* In the former I played a London bobby who turns out to be the murderer; the remarkable part was that I was permitted to play him as a Scot with a broad burr. My role in *The Twilight Zone* series was one of my favorites. Crangle is a total fanatic, not quite right in the head, who keeps volumes of records on everyone he considers an enemy—Communists, perverts, government officials, even housewives, just about everybody—and he is convinced that his scheme of uncovering each one of them will enable the FBI to pick them up off the street easily: At precisely four o'clock all the "evil" people will become two feet tall, because he'll will it. The FBI agent whom he calls is immediately convinced that here is a serious nut case. As he voices his doubts, Crangle is certain that the FBI, too, is part of the evil conspiracy. Then comes the eagerly awaited hour of four o'clock, and Oliver Crangle is the only one in the world who shrinks to two feet tall. Rod Serling spun a wonderful portrait of right-wing fanaticism with a classic comeuppance.

Serling was both a great innovator and a man of deep principles. Some time later, he defended me against a verbal assault made on a television talk show in which two veteran actors with very reactionary views, Adolphe Menjou and Corinne Griffiths, attacked me. They did so not for the views I espoused—that would have been all right by any civil libertarian standards—but they challenged my right to voice them at all, on the grounds that I was "a foreigner." Not just foreign-born, mind you, but a foreigner who had no right to open his mouth at all. I do not recall whether I was already a citizen or not at that point— but even resident aliens legally admitted to the United States are entitled to all rights and privileges except for the vote. A few days later, on the same program, Rod Serling said the following, in part:

"On this program an actor of considerable stature appeared by invitation. . . . His reputation as a gentleman and a human being is probably the most unsullied and exemplary of any man in this profession. He was subjected to a vicious and predatory attack by Miss Corinne Griffiths [because] . . . he was of foreign birth. . . . Anyone . . . who thinks that honor and patriotism can only be equated with those whose roots go deep into the third-deck planking of the Mayflower [should] . . . go over the roll call of the Congressional Medal of Honor winners. They read like a checklist from Ellis Island." He concluded by making a reference to his own background: "A democracy works because its basic tenet is simply the recognition of the dignity of its citizens. The kind of dignity that permits the son of Lithuanian immigrants to say . . . judge a human being by his works . . . by his compassion and his sincerity. Judge all of us not by our geography, but by our humanity."

Among my early television roles were two in which I was employed by Four Star, a studio co-owned by—what else?—four top stars. (At least, there were supposed to be four owners; in reality there were only three: David Niven, Dick Powell, and Charles Boyer. Ida Lupino was supposed to be the fourth, but apparently that did not materialize.) Dick Powell had created an anthology series, which was filmed at their studio. They blew a lot of money on the first show of the series, *The Price of Tomatoes,* with Peter Falk and a fairly large cast. As a result, the producer, Stan Kallis, had to do a modestly budgeted show for the second outing, and Richard Alan Simmons came up with a splendid script that used only two main characters until the last fifteen minutes of the program. The setting was a Devil's Island kind of prison with only two people on it, one prisoner and one guard. The prisoner is a former university professor exiled and jailed because of seditious writings. The guard is a disciplinarian who goes strictly by the book, locking up his lone prisoner at night in a cell, even though escape is a virtual impossibility with the nearest island hundreds of miles away. During the day he refuses to have any social contact with him, despite efforts by the professor to make friendly overtures. Only when the relief boat fails to arrive on the appointed day does the guard's world fall apart. He finally admits to having read the professor's books, relaxes the rules, plays chess with him, and even gets drunk with him on homemade wine. When the boat does arrive, it brings the professor's pardon. The guard, however, is court-martialed on board for dereliction of duty, and is himself sentenced to become a prisoner on the island for one year. The professor then begs the captain/judge to allow him to stay on the island as a guard. If he went back to France, he would only get into trouble immediately, so he argues. The ship leaves and the two men remain, alone once again, in reversed roles, but, at the professor's insistence, each in his old clothes and in his old quarters. They are, at last, friends.

The professor was played by Charles Boyer and I was the guard. It was, in every way, a most rewarding experience. Working with Boyer again, and in such close interaction, taught me a great deal about the man. He was not only a gentleman but also a professional in the best sense. One late afternoon when he had finished his close-ups in a scene we had together, they turned the camera around for my matching close-ups. Don Medford, the director, suggested that Charles take off his makeup and go home; we would be able to shoot my portions of the scene with the script girl reading Boyer's lines off-screen. Boyer said he wouldn't hear of it. This was a scene we had together, he said, and he would stand behind the camera and play the scene fully so I would have the benefit of his performance and his face to play to. Many others would have gone home. Not he; he wouldn't even take off his makeup. It occurred to me that he was also one of the studio's bosses, but it made absolutely no difference. Now that is a real star, I thought.

The other teleplay of the series in which I was a guest star was called *Pericles of 31st Street*. It concerned an old Greek hot dog vendor who teaches an entire street in a poor district of Chicago to stand up to the bullying of a slum landlord. I played the old Greek, and Carroll O'Connor the landlord. What made the show remarkable was that it was directed by Sam Peckinpah, then rapidly becoming the main contender for the title of Hollywood's premier enfant terrible. Some books have been written about him, about his volcanic nature, his sparring with executives, his iconoclastic attitude toward the work and the world. I found him extraordinary. His reputation was well deserved:

hard-working, hard-living, hard-drinking, in hard pursuit of women, and always insistent on having his own way. It was a gamble to hire him to direct television, where being fast is almost more important than being good. Indeed, by the end of the second day of shooting we were one day behind. The executives were worried; he wasn't. I knew we had something special, and suddenly realized that my agent had neglected to specify as part of the deal that I was to receive a filmed copy of the show. (Prior to the advent of tape, shows were preserved in celluloid format to be viewed by projection on a screen. The term was kinescope.) When I mentioned to Sam that I desperately wanted to own a copy both for artistic and sentimental reasons, he said, "I'll get you a copy, but it'll cost you." I said I was prepared to pay for it, but he said, "No, no. I don't mean money. It'll cost you an evening with me, two girls, and a guitar." We both kept our bargain.

My friend Mort Wishengrad wrote another script entitled *Hunted*, in which I played a Russian who has fled the USSR and ends up working as a janitor in New York. But for a broken-down former showgirl, played by Ann Sheridan, he knows no one; she befriends him because, at bottom, she is as lonely as he is. However, we are at the chilliest point of the Cold War. The Russians cannot abide the fact that anyone should have escaped their clutches. Even a lowly janitor is a threat to them, a witness to their tyranny. And so they send emissaries to alternately threaten him and lure him with promises. They bring a phonograph and a record of his old mother's voice begging him to return. He knows that the old woman had been forced to say those things, yet he is moved enough almost to give in. It is only his woman friend who gives him the courage to refuse the enticements. She offers to marry him so that, as the husband of an American, the Russians cannot touch him. He wants to refuse her generosity until he realizes that she needs him to dispel her loneliness just as much as he needs the shelter of her affection.

What made the script remarkable for me was the confrontation of my character with the Soviet commissar, played by Nehemiah Persoff. After a stormy session of alternately threatening and cajoling, he says to me in Russian, quietly and urgently out of earshot of the goon accompanying him, "*Za nami akhochetsya.*" Translated that means "They are after us." At first I was puzzled by this line and by the furtiveness with which it was to be delivered, but even without Mort's explanation its significance soon became clear to me. Nowhere in the story was there any indication that my character was anything but a refugee from Russian Communism. This subtly positioned line indicated that not only is my character Jewish, but the commissar as well.

"They are after us" means that he has to bring me back, or else his own fate will be on the line. Send a kike to fetch a kike, as Mort put it with bitter comment about the Soviets and their anti-Semitic proclivities. The script was written many years before American Jews started to be exercised about the fate of Soviet Jewry.

I am sure I could have had a much bigger career had I followed the advice of agents and friends: Stick to one aspect of what you do and stay in one place to do it—California for example. But it would have been a denial of who I am and what my professional life is all about. Horizons are not meant to be shrunk. You do as much as you can in as many fields as you know how to master. You do not have to spread yourself too thin to do it, either; the trick is to concentrate fully on what you are doing at the moment just as though it were the only thing in your life. This may not be a prescription for anybody else, but it worked for me, made me more fulfilled both as an artist and a human being. What does suffer in the process is the notion of "home." As one who has flown almost two million miles on just one airline in the last twelve years, I attest to that fact with some sadness. We have all heard of the Wandering Jew and the Flying Dutchman; I am the hybrid of those two, the Flying Jew. When recently a flight attendant asked me where my permanent home was, I pointed to the seat I had just left and said, "Four-B."

MY FIRST TRIP to Hollywood in 1956 was followed by a variety of juicy movie roles, small and large—the bulk of them calling on my language skills and ability to effect authentic accents. Stories and subjects drawn from World War II continued to provide grist for American moviemakers, just as they did for the British.

One that's become a minor classic was *The Enemy Below* (1957), which won an Oscar for special effects. It was directed by Dick Powell, who had made his name as a crooner but was by no means a lightweight where motion pictures were concerned. Although it co-starred Robert Mitchum and Curt Jurgens, I didn't ever actually work with Mitchum on this one; all his scenes were above the surface of the ocean on the U.S. destroyer, all mine were below in the German submarine. Curt Jurgens and I did become friends during our work on this picture; as the captain and the first officer of the German U-boat, we were thrown into a close relationship by the confines of the submarine and the beautifully crafted relationship in the film's script. Jurgens was a gentleman to the core, aristocratic in demeanor and as removed from the barbaric image of Nazi Germans as one could possibly get. The movie has become a classic of sorts; people remind me to this day of the line addressed to me by Jurgens: "We build them good in Germany, huh, Heini?" We spent many weeks wearing a stubble of beard which was always cut down to the same length to match the previous day's shooting, but never close enough to the face to look respectable. As a consequence, rather than dining out, Curt gave many dinner parties at the house he had rented in Bel Air. Many beautiful women were attracted to Jurgens; the fine food and the exquisite wines at his table were an added attraction. Once he suggested to the ladies a swim after dinner. When they protested that no one had thought to bring swimsuits, he shrugged and said that on such a dark night it would make no difference if no one wore anything at all. When they were in the pool, he smiled and turned on the floodlights to squeals that, after the first surprise, seemed to express no great displeasure.

It is no easy task to direct an action film at sea with vessels moving across the screen. The problem of who moves left-to-right and who moves the other way is a nightmare in itself. Dick Powell solved a major part of this problem in an ingenious way. The American destroyer moved on the surface in whichever way was indicated by the action and by the cinematographer. The movement of the German submarine, sometimes countering and sometimes evading its adversary, was almost impossible to plan in the filming stage, and would have to be determined during the editing. But how could it be shot so as to leave latitude for the editor? Fortunately, German submarines did not have names, they had numbers. Dick Powell gave our U-boat the number 181 and shot its movement going one way, left-to-right for example. If later they would need it to go the other way, the editor could reverse the negative and presto! the boat bearing the same number would travel right-to-left. We filmed much of the submarine's interior in the studio at 20th Century Fox; the set was put on a hydraulic platform that was rocked by the crew during the shooting to simulate the vessel's motion at sea. At first I did not think that it was possible to get seasick on a soundstage, but I was wrong. One can.

As usual, Hollywood was a little cavalier when it came to casting people with authentic accents. We had a cook in the U-boat galley whose accent came straight out of the Yiddish theatre on Second Avenue. We had a Czech navigator and a Serb radar officer. This role was played by Dan Tana, a soccer player from Yugoslavia who had earlier defected during the team's visit to the United States. Later Dan became a well-known restaurateur and sometime movie producer. Whenever we meet we still greet each other with our own secret password: one-four-zero. It was the course our submarine was set on.

I had rarely been able to form any close relationships with Germans, but Jurgens was an exception. Another exception was a German film director by the name of Helmut Käutner. There were too few opportunities for us to get to know each other really well, but I liked him very much indeed, as much for his talent as for his frankness. After we got to the point when tensions could relax, I asked him about his past during the Nazi period. He told me that he had managed quite successfully to stay away from any involvement with the Nazis. But then he added: "Look, I am a German who was already an adult during those times. Even if I had a letter in my breast pocket to the effect that I was one of the 'clean' ones, do you think I could produce it every time the conversation came around to this question?"

On one of my visits to Germany I met with Helmut Käutner and continued my probing about the aspects of the German character that led the Germans to commit such atrocities. How is it possible, I wanted to know, that a seemingly cultured people, a nation that gave birth to Beethoven, Goethe, Kant, and Schopenhauer, would follow a crass and barbaric house painter? Käutner said that he could not answer the question directly but would perhaps be able to demonstrate. He took me to a small suburban commuter station. The people waiting for the train consisted of a sprinkling of housewives, but there were also many men clutching briefcases, evidently businessmen or lawyers. I was puzzled, but he asked me to be patient. When the train pulled in, he suddenly shouted in a loud, commanding tone of voice: "*Die letzten Wagen sind hinten!*" (The last cars are at the back!) Without questioning the idiocy of this obvious statement, everyone ran to the back of the train. "You see," he said, "whoever and whatever they may be, Germans always follow shouted commands."

Greece was one of the most beautiful locations I spent time in. I had gone there in 1959 for *The Angry Hills,* a movie starring Robert Mitchum, and had fallen in love with Greek bouzouki music. The local musicians never really got started until about 11:00 P.M.; the music might go on until four or five in the morning, and I wanted to savor every minute of it. If I had a work call for the film, it was usually for 6:30 A.M. Who cared? I was young enough and energetic enough not to mind even a total lack of sleep. Besides, I could look like hell for the picture; my role called for me to look permanently rumpled in a no-longer-white suit. In contrast to some of the noble and courageous Greek characters, I was playing a slimy opportunist, a collaborator with the German occupiers. One of the Nazis, played by Stanley Baker, lusted after my beautiful half-sister; my character was only too eager to act as pimp and supplier. Jackie Collins played my sister; like her real-life sister, Joan, she had embarked on an acting career, but in her case it did not last too long. She became instead a highly successful writer of steamy novels.

Bob Mitchum, the star of the film, was somewhat of an enigma. At times I found him highly intelligent and amiable; but he insisted on hiding that part of his nature behind a facade of crassness and abrasiveness that was especially obnoxious when he drank. Occasionally he would cultivate my company and drag me to places I normally do not frequent. One time we went to a club that featured a female impersonator. Mitchum was quite taken with the creature and said to me, "God, she is gorgeous. I'm goin' after her." I said, "You can't." "Why not?" he said with a drunken pout. I said with the patience one reserves for dealing with drunks: "It's not a she, it's a he. It's an 'it.'" He was not to be deterred. "What the hell, she is beautiful. I don't care about the plumbing." He was joking, of course. Drunk or sober, Bob Mitchum almost always was.

During this stay in Greece, I mixed a great deal with locals, some of whom were of the rich-shipping-magnate set and some who were actors like a friend from my early Hollywood days, Irene Pappas. Through Hubert Humphrey and his sister Frances I also knew the family of the U.S. ambassador to Greece, James Riddleberger. The ambassador's daughter, Toni, and I had met in Baltimore and become friends. All this gave me a welcome opportunity to get away from the movie cast and crew, who always tend to form a clique on location shoots. In fact, the Riddlebergers invited me to stay at the ambassador's residence. I did move over there for a few weekends while keeping my hotel room at the Grande Bretagne. In the mornings we would all have breakfast on the terrace while the ambassador read the signals that had been sent from Washington during the night. He sometimes shared bits of information with us; in this manner I found out about the U.S. invasion of Lebanon ordered by President Eisenhower much earlier than the rest of the world.

To the envy of professional journalists, *The Angry Hills* gave me an opportunity to record a rare interview for my radio program, *Theodore Bikel at Home.* We had been put up at the Hotel Grande Bretagne, at the time one of the best in Athens. I continued to send my weekly radio program back to the States, including some terrific bouzouki music. The hotel's concierge proudly informed anyone who would listen that, apart from Robert Mitchum, their most illustrious guest was the famous churchman and Greek freedom fighter Archbishop Makarios. First off, I was intrigued by the fact that this man who had been exiled and jailed by the British would find himself staying at a hotel named Grande Bretagne. He was far more than a mere churchman; he was a political force and a rallying center for all Cypriot Greeks, engaged in two struggles: for independence from the British who ruled the island under a mandate, and against the Turkish inhabitants of Cyprus who had their own notions of independence. As a result the British considered the archbishop a danger to their rule and had exiled him to someplace in Arabia, placing him under house arrest. After a time they relented their decree and permitted Makarios to leave, but he was prevented from returning to Cyprus. For now he had taken up residence in Athens and continued to agitate against the British and the Turks. Eventually, when Cyprus gained its independence, Archbishop Makarios would become the new republic's first president.

The idea occurred to me that, if he were to agree to it, the archbishop might make a most unusual guest on my radio program. But he was staying in the penthouse, was rarely seen in public, and was giving no interviews. Taking a chance, I wrote a note to him and bribed a bellman to deliver it upstairs. In the note I introduced myself, explaining that I was not a journalist but a performer with a keen interest in people and their music and that, if he were to grant me an interview on tape, I would be respectful of his position and would observe any restrictions he cared to place on the subjects he was willing to discuss. One of his aides contacted me to say that the archbishop was amenable to grant my request, but would want to have my questions submitted to him in writing beforehand. That would remove much of the spontaneity, I thought, but if that was what he wanted, so be it. I made a list, sent it upstairs, and waited for an answer, which was not long in coming. The reverend gentleman would see me the next day and would answer my questions.

At the appointed hour I arrived at the penthouse with my trusted tape machine and also with the film unit's still photographer whom I had enlisted. It was too good an opportunity; I wanted a photo of us together as a memento. We set up the equipment in the living room of the suite and waited. Soon afterwards the archbishop arrived, dressed casually in slacks and a sweater. The minute he saw my photographer he said: "Ah, you will want me to put on my robe." Strong Greek accent but very good and fluent English. He disappeared back to his quarters and reemerged in full splendor, wearing the long black robe and the tall black cylindrical hat of the Greek Orthodox clergy. We sat down and, as we started to talk, we were served strong Greek coffee. It actually tastes exactly the same as Turkish coffee and is prepared the same way, but heaven forbid you should call it Turkish anywhere within the borders of Greece.

At first the interview was somewhat stilted, confined as it was to the screened questions. But he relaxed enough to permit me some extemporizing. One exchange at the end I remember with particular fondness. Somehow, the parallel between the British rule of Palestine and the British rule of Cyprus prompted me to formulate a question. I asked him whether, in the light of his history of turbulent relations with the English masters of Cyprus, he could find it in his heart to forgive the British for all they had done to him—or was it possible only to forgive "when they know not what they do?" He answered, somewhat wistfully, "I have no hate for the British—whether they know or know not what they do." He smiled at me, we finished our coffee, and the interview was over.

My film career took off in earnest after 1959. This was the year after the release of *The Defiant Ones,* the movie that earned me an Academy Award nomination as Best Supporting Actor. The noted director and producer Stanley Kramer had been familiar with my work for some time. He had used me, in fact, in a smallish role in one of his previous films, *The Pride and the Passion.* This film starred Sophia Loren, Frank Sinatra, and Cary Grant, but I did not get to work with any of these three stars, and met Sophia Loren only socially at Stanley Kramer's house. I played the French general who chases a rebel cannon through Spain until it becomes his downfall and the cause of his death. The film was mostly shot on Spanish locations, but my role was done on interior sets in the studio—with one exception: I stood on a set representing the ramparts of the town of Avila, which was on the back lot of Universal Studios. The cannon had fired its deadly salvo at the actual location in Spain; the shot found and killed me at Universal.

When Stanley Kramer was casting *The Defiant Ones,* he told me that he wanted me to play the southern sheriff. I was immensely flattered and pleased; the prospect of working with Stanley again, this time in a major supporting role with Sidney Poitier and Tony Curtis, would be an important step. Also, the film had an underlying theme that would subtly convey a message rarely promulgated in motion pictures. On the face of it this was a straight action film: two fugitives chained together and escaping from a penal colony, chased by a sheriff and a posse composed of police and quickly deputized rednecks. But one of the escaping convicts is white and the other black; they hate each other's guts and, as my character said, "would probably kill each other before they go five miles." The story very poignantly makes the point that these two men cannot get anywhere unless they run the same road at the same pace and together all the way. I later used this as an allegory during my civil rights activities. The two races, black and white, are chained together and can only make their way together; pulling at the chain each in a different direction will do nothing but give them chafed and bloody ankles. One of the two writers responsible for the script was blacklisted, but to Kramer's credit, he used him anyway. He wrote under the pseudonym of "Nathan Douglas"; his real name was Nedrick Young. He eventually received an Oscar for Best Screenplay for that movie, but had to accept it under his assumed name.

When Stanley Kramer talked to me about taking the role, I was surprised and told him so. After all, I was not a southerner, was not even a native-born American. There were dozens of actors around in whose mouths the role would sit naturally. Stanley said something to me that I have never forgotten: "A good actor is a good actor is a good actor." How seldom does such a thought surface these days when actors are supposed to *be* rather than *act*. Needless to say, I knocked myself out to give the best damn performance I was capable of. I talked incessantly to southerners to get the accent down, and worked myself into the role in other, more subtle ways. This sheriff is not an out-and-out villain; that role is reserved for the police chief. The sheriff is more complex: somewhat world-weary, doing his job without hatred or rancor toward the two prisoners. He knows he has to catch them and he will, but without the redneck histrionics.

The location shots in swamp and underbrush were not easy, especially when they had to be done at night. It got quite cold and there was a little rebellion going on until everyone was issued long johns. Some other imponderables hampered our progress. We also had to deal with nonhuman actors: One time I had to stand in a swamp for almost two days in mud that reached halfway up to my knees, waiting for two Dobermans to sniff right. They lured them with meat and liver during rehearsals; by the time the director rolled the cameras, the dogs would not play. Suddenly I felt ridiculous. Here I was, the product of classical dramatic training at the Royal Academy of Dramatic Art, in a situation that made me subservient to two dogs!

We all knew, however, that we were part of something out of the ordinary. Sidney Poitier already had the reputation of being a first-rate actor and everything he did was solid and exactly on the mark. But Tony Curtis was the surprise. Around Hollywood he was thought of as a lightweight, comedic talent at best. This was a serious and demanding role, and he did excellent work. So did everyone else, especially Stanley Kramer. Against the advice of quite a few associates who insisted that the film should utilize the newest color techniques, he decided to shoot the picture in black and white. It was a constant but subtle reminder that we were dealing with a story that revolved around the friction and agony of black-white relationships. Although this was a heavy topic compared to 1958's lighter fare of *Auntie Mame* and *Gigi,* when the film was released it received nine Academy Award nominations: Best Director, Best Picture, Best Actor for both Tony Curtis and Sidney Poitier, Best Supporting Actor for me, Best Supporting Actress for Cara Williams, Best Editing, Best Cinematography, and Best Screenplay.

Understandably, Oscar night at the Pantages Theatre was a time for butterflies. The other big picture up for awards was *Gigi,* also with nine nominations. Talk about apples and oranges; the two films represented such different styles and attitudes. It was anybody's guess how the Academy members would choose. As far as the Best Supporting Actor category was concerned, I did not think I stood as much of a chance as Gig Young, who had done such a splendid job in *Teacher's Pet.* What neither of us had reckoned with was an unforeseeable set of circumstances. Burl Ives, the troubadour-turned-actor, was up for Best Supporting Actor for a film entitled *The Big Country.* His performance was not thought to be in the same league as Gig Young's, or mine for that matter. But *Cat on a Hot Tin Roof,* in which Burl played Big Daddy, had just been released. It would not be eligible for any awards until the following year. Still, the film and the performances in it were fresh in everybody's memory as they voted for the current year's Oscars. Even though the voting rules mandate that acting awards be based solely on the nominated performance, no one was in any doubt that Big Daddy had put Burl Ives over the top. It was a disappointment; any nominee who says that the big prize does not matter is playing games with the truth.

The nomination alone, however, does matter where an actor's career is concerned. I was being offered more roles and the money was considerably better. For some reason I worked more often at 20th Century Fox than at the other studios. You can tell when all the guards at the gates know you and wave. *Fräulein* was one of the films I did at 20th; it was one of those postwar stories: Germany is still occupied by the Four Powers and the "fräuleins" are fair game for everyone. I played the Colonel, a high-ranking Russian officer smitten by the charms of a local lady, played by Dana Wynter. She reluctantly carries on the liaison, determined to make a break for the American Zone as soon as the opportunity arises. In the end the script had her making her escape and taking up with an American officer, played by

Mel Ferrer. Why anyone would want to leave me for him I could not for the life of me understand, but go quarrel with Hollywood. The studio also decided that I should sing and play the guitar. During the planning stages they asked me whether I knew any Russian songs. What a question! I smiled and said that I could lay my hands on several dozen. I sang them a couple and they said those were exactly what they wanted but that they couldn't use them. Why not, pray, I wanted to know. Because of possible copyright infringements, they said. I raised my voice a bit and said that these songs were at least a hundred years old and anyone likely to sue over them was dead. You never know, they said, maybe Shostakovich . . .

Well, I guess we'd better forget it then, I said. "No, no, it's a fine idea," they said, "here's what we'll do: We'll have a genuine Russian folk song composed for you." And that is precisely what they did. They asked a Russian-born composer who had written many film scores to come up with words and music that they would pay for and thus own all the rights to. The composer was Daniele Amfiteatrof—a beautiful name, if somewhat difficult to fit on a theatre marquee. The song he came up with was entitled "*Nichevo, Nichevo, Nichevo,*" which means "Nothing, nothing, nothing." I sang this song in a drunken stupor to Dana Wynter in an effort to penetrate the icy shell she displayed toward me. Henry Koster, the director, decided that at the end of the song I was to take the guitar and smash it against a pole. I was horrified; as I was using my own instrument, I would do no such thing. They quite understood and came up with a solution. An exact replica of my own Mateu guitar would be ordered, to look the same but to be made of balsa wood, material that breaks and splinters easily. That would be the one I would use in the take where the Colonel destroys the instrument. Ah, but what if we needed a retake? All right, we'll make two replicas. They made two; in the end I only smashed one of them. And each one of these nonplaying lookalike instruments cost more to make than my original.

Another film, again at 20th Century Fox, had me playing a leading role opposite Curt Jurgens. This was *The Blue Angel,* a remake of the German film classic by the same name. This time the Emil Jannings role was played by Curt Jurgens, and Lola, the role that had made Marlene Dietrich famous, by Mai Britt. Edward Dmytryk was the director. Eddie Dmytryk made no attempt to break new ground with this remake. Almost all of the shots were duplications of the original, except that this time we were in color. Jurgens, I thought, was very good in the role of the old professor who is besotted with the cabaret singer and allows her to ruin his life. I did well by the slimy and generally unsympathetic role of the nightclub owner. The big problem was Mai Britt, no Marlene Dietrich she. I suppose it was the studio's doing; Mai was under contract to them and they thought she could hack it, presumably because a Swede would make a believable German. The question in the end was not whether a Swede could be a German, but whether anybody could be Marlene. When the picture was released, everybody indulged in comparisons, with Jurgens not coming off too badly, and Mai Britt faring disastrously. I happened to run into Marlene Dietrich at a dinner later. "I saw the picture," she said to me. Not daring to ask what she thought of it, I waited. Then she said, "Well, it certainly didn't do *you* any harm."

I made two films with Susan Hayward, one memorable and one not. The less distinguished one was called *A Woman Obsessed,* and it co-starred Stephen Boyd, the Irish actor who had become famous after the chariot race against Charlton Heston in *Ben Hur.* From *A Woman Obsessed* I took away the memory of the director, Henry Hathaway, who could be an amiable old man or an ogre, and there was no predicting when he might be which. I played a Canadian country doctor in the picture. True to Hollywood custom, they tailored a tweed suit for me. The trouble was that I was supposed to have worn this suit for years, and it needed a beat-up look that no new garment could possibly have. I suggested that they let me have this suit a week before we were supposed to report to the location so that I could break it in. I took it, balled it up and put it under my mattress, slept on top of it for a week, and all but played football with it. When it came time to report to the California location up at Big Bear, the suit still did not have that lived-in look. I put it on to show to the director, and the wardrobe people shook their heads. He'll never buy this suit, they said. As we came closer we heard him yell as he was inspecting some other actors wearing their "country" clothes. "It's too new, take it off, it's too fuckin' new!" we heard him yell. "See, he'll never buy your suit," said the wardrobe guy. "He'll buy it, he'll buy it," I assured them. As I approached the director, I put on my spectacles, pushed them down toward the tip of my nose, and put out my hand. "Hi, Henry," I said in my kindly-country-doctor voice. He looked at my face, barely glanced at the suit, and said, "Yeah, this is great, fine, fine, splendid." I went back to the wardrobe people and said, "See? You have to know how to sell a suit."

The other Susan Hayward film was *I Want to Live!* This was based on the true story of Barbara Graham, a woman who had been the lookout for a couple of men who committed a robbery in the course of which the victim was killed. All three were tried on murder charges; the two who had committed the actual murder were somehow found guilty of a lesser charge. Barbara Graham, who was tried as an accomplice, was found guilty and sentenced to death. The case stirred a lot of controversy in California; many people had the memory still fresh in their minds and many were still angry. Robert Wise directed this picture with great sensitivity, especially the scenes in the actual women's prison and the execution scene—the latter shot in a replica of the gas chamber which had been built in the studio. This scene had every single one of us, including the stagehands, upset and rattled, just as though we had been put into a real gas chamber. It gave us the willies and we could not wait to finish the sequence and get out of there.

I played Carl Palmberg, the psychiatrist who was called in to evaluate the woman and testify as to whether she was capable of murder. I am supposed to put her at ease before administering various tests, including a Rorschach. Before we shot the scene, Susan confided in me that she did not know how to laugh out loud as she was supposed to in the scene. Could I help? I improvised a quick lesson on how to produce a laugh, pushing out all the air you have in your lungs and then pushing several bursts beyond it. This would produce a reasonable and convincing laugh. She practiced it, and it worked. My character in the film was interesting. The son of Swedish parents, he had been born in China where the couple was working as Christian missionaries. Carl Palmberg had been dead for some time when I played him, but there was plenty of material on hand, which enabled me to learn about him. As far as the Barbara Graham case was concerned, he had come to the conclusion that, while she was amoral and quite capable of forgery, treachery, or theft, she was incapable of murder. After the picture was released, I was accosted in restaurants and on Hollywood streets several times. "How dare you suggest that Barbara Graham was not guilty? She shacked up with those two guys and she was guilty as hell!" Even though I had only been playing a role, I felt compelled to defend the psychiatrist's position and point out that promiscuity was no proof of homicidal impulses; but I doubt if I managed to convince anyone. I did receive one letter that gave me a great deal of satisfaction. It was from Mrs. Palmberg, the widow of the man whom I had portrayed in the film. She wrote: "You do not look anything like my late husband and you do not sound like him; but he could not have had a better monument to his memory than your performance."

Over the years any number of agents have argued that I should have settled down in California and made film my primary pursuit. They argued that, had I done so, I would have reached greater heights as a film actor than I did. But I was a theatre person first and foremost, and when the chance for my first Broadway musical came along, I took it.

11

The Hills Are Alive

B Y 1959, MY FIFTH YEAR IN THE UNITED STATES, I had covered some distances—artistic, emotional, and geographical. I had done well in the theatre, in television, in movies, and I was considered one of the mainstays of the folk scene, the prime exponent of international folk songs. What next?

In the summer of '59 I went to Holland and Belgium to work on a film entitled *The Dog of Flanders,* a nice family type of picture—a genre preferred by its producer, Bob Radnitz. I played an artist, a painter, taking a young boy who shows promise as an artist under his wing. Apart from myself, the only recognizable names were those of Donald Crisp, a veteran of many films, and the youngster, David Ladd, who was not famous himself but had a well-known name long associated with films. We were well under way with the filming, there were some ten days left on the shooting schedule, when I received a telegram from my agents at MCA in New York to the effect that Rodgers and Hammerstein were casting a new musical based on a German book entitled *The Trapp Family Singers.* (MCA eventually ceased to be an agency and became the giant corporation known as Universal.) They had seen an Austrian film version of the same story and liked it. They had screened it for Mary Martin and suggested it as a vehicle for her next starring role. She, too, had been taken by the story of a young postulant nun who captures the heart of seven children and their stern nobleman father. This had transpired months earlier; by now the book, music, and lyrics were done and they were now at the point of casting the major roles. My agents thought I would be an ideal choice to play Captain von Trapp, and I thought so, too. I had seen the Austrian movie.

It goes without saying that almost every leading man in the New York theatre was dying to have a crack at the part, which forced my agents to work fast. They managed to do two things: They got me sprung from the movie set for forty-eight hours and they persuaded the play's producers that it was so important to see me that they should fly me in from Holland at their expense. They also arranged for me to work with someone on a couple of songs for the audition. I had never done a musical before. The music I was used to performing was of a different genre from Broadway tunes—not exactly audition material, they said. As it turned out, they were both right and wrong about that. Big question: When you audition for Rodgers and Hammerstein, do you do one of their own tunes and risk running afoul of their concept? Can your interpretation be different from what they have in their ear and in their memory? Even if you're brilliant, if you've shaped their music to your style, will it be seen as chutzpah or even hubris? Maybe you should pick someone else's stuff, in which the two Broadway legends would have absolutely no proprietary interest. I chose the latter route, and worked with the accompanist-coach on two Frank Loesser tunes from *Guys and Dolls,* "Luck Be a Lady" and "My Time of Day." I worked on the songs for much of the day before my appearance. Everything had to be done fast, since I was due back in the Netherlands forty-eight hours after leaving.

I did, however, take my guitar along to the audition. What the hell, I thought, that's what I do best; if they'll let me, I'll give them a folk tune. When I got there, I was introduced not only to Richard Rodgers and Oscar Hammerstein, but also to Leland Hayward, the producer, and to Mary Martin. "Introduced" is actually a euphemism; they were in a darkened auditorium and I was on a brightly lit stage. Their names rang out from down there, and I said, "Hello." For all I knew it wasn't Mary Martin at all but Zelda Schwartz. They chatted with me for a couple of minutes—to hear me talk, I guess, or to put me at ease. Somehow I did not need to be put at ease; to me this was just another play, music or no music. I had been through the process before and had no notion of the monumental difference between a straight play and a musical within Broadway psychology. "Fools rush in," and all that. Then they asked me to sing. I did the first of the Loesser tunes, and then I decided to slip in one of my folk songs. I finished up with "My Time of Day" and stood waiting while I dimly saw some heads bobbing in the dark auditorium. After a while they thanked me for having come in to do this, and said they would be in touch with my agents. Well, that's that, I thought. It won't come to anything, but the trip was worth it, anyway. I went to the airport and returned to the Dutch location. "How was it?" my colleagues wanted to know. I did not know what to tell them, beyond the fact that New York had been very humid.

A few days later I still had not heard anything, and I was more than ever convinced that if the answer had been positive, we would have heard right away. When the movie wrapped, I decided to go visit my parents in Israel, taking advantage of the fact that Amsterdam is much closer to Tel Aviv than New York is. After two or three days with family and friends, I started to wonder what exactly had transpired after my audition. I sent a wire to MCA, asking whether they had any news. The reply was unsatisfyingly short: "Negotiations in progress. Possible answer by Wednesday." It was then that I started to wonder whether this was really going to come off. Again a couple of days passed without any news. Now I was getting both curious and impatient. Yes, I did want to know. On Wednesday I decided to place a telephone call, not an easy task in those days. As a matter of fact, my parents did not even have a telephone in their apartment; my father had two of them in his office, and refused to have another one at home. So I decided to make the call from the house of my friend Ada Tal, the Habimah actress. It all had to go through operators and I asked very politely, in Hebrew, to be put through to the New York number. "It seems to me that there are no lines available," the operator said brusquely. (Brusque is normal in Israel.)

"What exactly do you mean by 'It seems to me'? Either there are lines or there aren't," said I. "Well, there aren't," she said, ready to hang up. Maybe speaking in Hebrew was the mistake, I thought. I might have gotten further as a foreigner. "Let me talk to your supervisor, please," I said, making a last attempt. After a while, the supervisor got on and did not even wait for me to make my case. "There are no lines. Try tomorrow," she snapped, no less abruptly than the other woman. I insisted, "But I must talk to New York today." "About what?" she asked. That floored me for a couple of seconds. "About things of vital importance to me and to the people in New York. Otherwise I might have attempted to walk there," I said, knowing as I said it that my brand of humor was not going to work with this lady. "Sorry," she said, not sounding sorry at all, and hung up.

I turned to Ada. "What do I do now?" I asked. She thought for a minute and then had a suggestion. As in most countries outside of the United States, the telephone service in Israel is run by the government as a subdivision of the postal service. "I have a girlfriend who some-times sleeps with the assistant postmaster general," said Ada. "Maybe she can help." Lo and behold, she did. We call it "pull"; the practice is called "*protektsia*" in Hebrew and known in most Mediterranean countries by various other names. I was put through to New York, talked to the agents, and found out that the role of Captain von Trapp was mine. Mary Martin later told me that after I had done my folk song at the audition, she leaned forward, tapped Dick Rodgers on the shoulder, and whispered, "We don't have to look any further, do we?" Now the contract had been negotiated, and rehearsals would begin in a matter of weeks. I was about to enter a new phase of my career: musical theatre.

While I was pleased at the prospect of a new role in a new medium, all my friends and colleagues were beside themselves with excitement. This was clearly a bigger deal than just another new role. It became evident from the start that no effort or money was going to be spared on the production. The costumes alone were worth a fortune; I dare-say even the nuns' habits were made of a fabric rarely worn in con-vents. Everything was custom-made, down to the shoes. Even my hair did not escape the attention of the designers. Since Mary Martin was a few years older than I, the producers decided to make her look younger and me look older. Distinguished but older. To that end they sent me to Mr. Kenneth, the most luxurious and expensive of all New York hairdressers. His charge was to dye a couple of gray streaks into my hair. There I sat, a lone male customer among a dozen or so ladies whose jewelry bespoke the affluence of their families, their husbands, or their lovers. I tried to make myself inconspicuous, and self-consciously tried to avoid overhearing their conversations, which were as frank and intimate as though they had been in a ladies' powder room. Of course, conversations backstage and in dressing rooms are every bit as intimate, but backstage itself is intimate: There is a bond among actors that does not exist between us and regular civilians. I had to repeat the process every few weeks, since the color of the streaks would grow out after a while. I always dreaded it.

Rehearsing *The Sound of Music* was not an easy chore. Not that learning the text and the music and putting it together were all that difficult. But getting used to the different attitudes toward the mate-rial, the psychological adjustments to a world removed not one but several steps from reality—that was hard. The play was set in Austria just before and during the Anschluss, a time and place I was all too familiar with. I had witnessed perfectly nice and ordinary people turn overnight into unfeeling brutes, sporting swastikas and threatening all who would not obey the party line. The second act of *The Sound of Music* is exactly about people and situations like that. One would have expected—at any rate, I expected—some adherence to accuracy, if not to history, then at least to the emotional wallop carried by those events. Surely the play demanded it. But no. This was musical theatre, where the edges had to be softened and the world viewed through tinted glasses. Our Nazis wore brown shirts all right, but of a paler shade of brown than the real ones. They wore swastika armbands only for the first dress rehearsal; they were ordered to take them off even before the first performance and were told not to wear them again, presumably because their shock value was deemed too great. They did not give the full "Heil Hitler!" Nazi salute, either, but merely a meek "Heil." Years later, during the era of *Cabaret* and thanks to Hal Prince, musicals got to be more biting about the portrayal of unpleasant historical memories. The trend continued with *Evita* and, later still, with such shows as *Les Misérables* and *Kiss of the Spider Woman;* no punches were pulled. But in 1959 there was a great deal of fudging with historical accuracy.

Ironically, almost all the actors who played Nazis or Nazi sympathizers were Jews: Kurt Kasznar, Michael Gorrin, John Randolph, and Stefan Gierasch. One night I was waiting in the wings for my entrance after the butler, played by John Randolph, was to bring Captain Von Trapp a telegram ordering him to report to the Nazi navy. John came across the stage and exited into the wings carrying the telegram on a silver tray. When he handed it to me he said, "Captain—*tsuris!*" That's Yiddish for "bad trouble." With Michael Gorrin I ad-libbed in Yiddish as well, and with Kurt Kasznar, who was as assimilated and Austrian as a Jew can get, in broad Viennese. Kurt stayed with the play after I left, and told me later that my replacement, an English actor, was thoroughly nonplussed when Kurt, from force of habit, said things to him under his breath in Viennese German. (Kasznar's mother, who was even more Viennese than he, became a naturalized citizen during the run of *The Sound of Music*. When the INS examiner, whose task it was to make sure that new citizens were sufficiently versed in American history, asked her for the name of the first president of the United States, she answered: "That's easy—George Washington Bridge!")

Where the producers looked for accuracy was in peripheral things. For example, technical advisers were brought in to check on the deportment and behavior of our stage nuns. (Luckily, offstage they were not made to conform to convent morality.) I, too, had a couple of technical advisers. In the first act, the Captain, being a Navy man, summons the staff and his children by blowing a bos'n's whistle.

(There was heavy reliance on the ignorance of an audience. Austria was, at the time of the Anschluss, and for years prior, a landlocked country without a seaport. But then Shakespeare set a scene for *A Winter's Tale* on "a coast of Bohemia," another landlocked country. Who cares?) The producers brought in a real live bos'n from the U.S. Navy and, for good measure, a marine sergeant. They attended a dress rehearsal to check on my whistling technique. Afterwards they came backstage and said to me: "Sir"—they called me "Sir," obviously accepting my stage rank—"Sir," they said, "you are holding it wrong and you are blowing it wrong—but you're making the right noises."

The show was so sweet I suspect diabetics in the audience had a little trouble with their insulin levels. Audiences adored it—children especially, and adults who did not mind exercising their suspension of disbelief. Nuns and priests came in droves, but so did entire theatre parties organized by Hadassah. The pull was the combination of Mary Martin and Rodgers and Hammerstein, whose collaboration in *South Pacific* was etched in the collective memory of theatregoers. But then, who could resist the other ingredients—seven adorable children, a chorus of glorious nun's voices, and a romance between a dashing widower and a young woman who had almost renounced any chance for a normal life? As we hoped, the reaction of the audiences during the out-of-town previews was very good, but no one in the theatre ever takes success for granted. Too often theatre people have allowed themselves to be lulled by the early approbation of audiences so grateful for the chance of seeing a new work that they refuse to be critical. We first played in New Haven for a number of weeks, then in Boston for an even longer run. During this time there was the usual flurry of chopping and changing scenes, a constant quest if not for perfection, then at least for the promise of it. Vincent Donahue, the director, and Joe Layton, the choreographer (his first Broadway chore), did the arranging and rearranging. But Dick Rodgers was also very much in evidence during the process of whipping the show into shape. Oscar Hammerstein was less so, although he bravely participated in as many of the rehearsals as he could and even wrote some additional lyrics. His health was clearly failing.

It was not all work, of course. We had a lot of fun on the road, and Dick Rodgers very much contributed to it. His was a contrary sort of humor; raunchy at times and impish at others, but he was funny. I recall one time in Boston when one of our performers, the dance captain Gloria Hamilton, complained that one tended to eat too much on tour. Pointing to her right buttock she said, "Look, this is New Haven," then, pointing to the left, "and this is Boston." Without a moment's hesitation, Richard Rodgers said, "Personally, I prefer Providence." On another occasion we went to dinner at a Chinese restaurant. It was a cheap sort of place, plastic place mats and Muzak playing in the background. The place was called Cathay House, its name, Dick said, derived from its owners', Irving Cathay and Sam House. Whenever the Muzak played a Richard Rodgers tune—which seemed to be just about every forty-five seconds—Dick got up, turned toward the rest of the diners in the place, and took a bow.

The second-floor lounge at Boston's Ritz-Carlton Hotel was the place where most of the principals in the shows stayed—not only those from our show, but some of the cast members from other Boston tryout theatres. A comedy starring Faye Emerson and John Newland was playing its pre-Broadway run in Boston at the same time we were. One night in the second-floor lounge, I saw them sitting at another table with their director and some of their supporting cast. I walked over to say hello and asked them how their play was going. They said, "Fine," and asked me how ours was doing. I said, "Fine," chatted a while, and then walked back to our table. My colleagues asked me what the people from the other play had to say, and I said, "They are having troubles, too."

We had been on the pre-Broadway tryout tour for quite a number of weeks and were finally getting ready to open on Broadway. The creative team was still making adjustments to the show, and probably would continue to do so for the remaining days prior to our return to New York. With eleven days to go, we thought that there could be no major additions or deletions. We were wrong. Rodgers and Hammerstein decided there was something lacking in the score, and it had to do with the character I portrayed. They argued that my "special talents" had not been fully used in the show, and that my folk background and my guitar playing could be used to better advantage. They retired to a special room with a piano that had been set aside for them at the Ritz-Carlton and proceeded to write a song for me. The song was "Edelweiss," and I sang and played it eight times a week for the next two years. This beautiful little tune sounded so authentic that one autograph-seeking fan at the stage door some months later said to me, "I love that 'Edelweiss'"—and then added with total confidence—"of course, I have known it for a long time, but only in German."

When Oscar Hammerstein died a few months later, we realized that the lyrics he had written for "Edelweiss" had been his last. And the very last word he had written as a creative artist was the word "forever." I have always been moved by the thought that human beings, in their urge to live beyond their physical existence, find ways to perpetuate themselves. When our time comes, we all want to be able to live just a little bit longer. And for "a little bit longer" read "forever."

We opened at the Lunt-Fontanne Theatre on November 16, 1959. Whatever the critics could say, our show was an assured success from the start. The advance sale of tickets was already so heavy that seats were sold out for months ahead. Nevertheless, there was incredible tension in the cast before the curtain rose on opening night. I shared in the excitement, but felt none of the fear that seemed to grip the other cast members—including the children and the chorus. Everyone had gotten flowers, telegrams, and presents. I received a solid gold whistle as a tribute to my bos'n's whistling onstage. Mary gave me a silver-framed photograph in which she wore the dress from our wedding scene. I gave gifts and went around the dressing rooms trying to calm everyone down, saying things like, "Remember that there are five hundred million Chinese in the world who couldn't care less." We opened, got standing ovations, and repaired to Sardi's in the time-honored tradition. There we waited for the reviews, all the while exhibiting a somewhat forced conviviality. The reviews were uneven—some gushing raves, some qualified raves, and some less than that. Walter Kerr in the *Herald Tribune*, for example, was not overly enthusiastic. That, I was told, had to do with the fact that he was a lapsed Catholic, that he had lots of children who might have gotten on his nerves that day, and such other silly excuses as only theatre people can dream up to soften the blows of unflattering notices. What did it matter? We were an unqualified success, and would run for years.

How do I remember Mary? In the first instance you have to understand that Mary Martin was first and foremost a professional with an awesome talent. She worked at her craft and she never let up, even after hundreds of performances. Working with her was a very rewarding experience. It was tough, perhaps, in one respect only. She was definitely overprotected, kept wrapped in cotton, as it were, surrounded by blow-softening material. She arrived very early at the theatre in a limousine, usually two and a half hours before the show, and was taken back to the penthouse in the limousine afterwards. The thought occurred to me more than once that she was portraying all these simple little people of humble background, and yet she had not been able to meet any such people for years. For that you need to walk about, ride on a bus, shop in little neighborhood stores. Of course she had known such people, but way back in Weatherford, Texas, and I suspect she relied on her memory a lot. One heck of a memory, I may add.

I suppose her husband, Richard Halliday, did the protecting. One evening I mentioned to her that I would be appearing on *The Tonight Show* with Jack Paar that night. She said, "Oh, good, I'll be able to watch that; Richard's out of town." I guess he dictated bedtimes as well. She once told me the following story. When they were still living on Central Park South (the Essex House, I think it was), on a day when Richard was also out of town, she decided to go out shopping alone. It was a beautiful day. She went down in the elevator and started walking. After a couple of minutes the thought occurred to her that in order to shop—something she had not done by herself recently—you probably needed some money, and she had not brought any from the apartment. So she returned to the building, went past the security desk, and got on the elevator. The elevator started up and, as luck would have it, there was a new man on elevator duty who asked Mary, "What floor, Miss?" After a long pause, Mary said, "Take me down again, I've got to ask."

One night when we had been playing *The Sound of Music* for well over a year there was a new twist to her performance. This little postulant nun who is supposed to face the Captain bravely at their first meeting was smiling all through the scene! In fact, she was smiling all through the first act, quite unaccountably. I could never get to talk to her during the act, as we were either onstage together, or she was on while I was off, or vice versa—in any event, we were never offstage at the same time. At the intermission I went to her dressing room and asked, "Is anything the matter? You are giving a different performance tonight." Mary said, "Why, what am I doing?" I said, "You are smiling. A lot." She said, "I am?" And then "Oh. Oh. I know why that is. This afternoon I went to the doctor and he gave me those things . . ." I said, "What things?" She said, "These things that you put in your eyes." "Contact lenses?" I asked. She said, "Yes, that's right. You know something? I could see what you were doing; that was so lovely . . ." She had never properly seen me before. Only a blur.

She was, as you must have gathered, not only wonderful, but also disarming. There was something perennially Peter Pan in her. Which is why Peter Pan will always be linked in our minds with Mary Martin, no matter how many other actresses give their own good performances in the role.

My relations with the management of the play were not always the best. I am sure I exasperated them because I did not conform to their idea of how a leading man in a top Broadway show should behave. I had too many outside interests; I sometimes went off at night after the show to play at small folk clubs and—horror of horrors—I was politically involved and outspoken about it. My political activism especially became a major point of contention between me and management in the summer of 1960. The country was embroiled in an intense presidential campaign, and I was intent on contributing to the effort of getting John F. Kennedy elected. I would speak at rallies, get up on soapboxes at street corners, and my name would, from time to time, appear in the papers—not as a star in a successful musical on Broadway, but in the unseemly role of an agitator—and a liberal one at that. I would get messages from the front office asking whether it was really necessary for me to engage in these activities, seeing that our audiences were made up of people of many political stripes. Could we afford to alienate the Republicans and other Nixon supporters in our audience (what other Nixon supporters?) by the spectacle of the play's leading man being so heavily involved in publicly supporting a Democrat? I argued back, saying that I considered myself no less entitled to a public expression of my opinion than the butcher at the corner of my street who had hung a picture of his preferred candidate in his shop window, taking a risk that some people of the opposite political persuasion would stop buying his meat for the duration of the campaign, and perhaps even thereafter. Management, I maintained, owned me and my talents as a performer for three hours every night and twice on Wednesdays and Saturdays; no less, but certainly no more. The rest of the time was my own; more important, my convictions were my own, as was my freedom to act upon them without encumbrance from any quarter.

They continued to grumble. One day, on a matinee day, I was due to speak at a rally in Queens between the shows. I had been informed by the Democratic campaign committee that a limousine would pick me up at the stage door after my first performance and would drive me and the other speaker to Queens. As it happened, Richard Halliday, Leland Hayward, and two staff members of the Rodgers and Hammerstein office were backstage at the end of the performance. I removed my makeup quickly and was soon informed by the stage-door man that the limo was waiting outside. Then I did something the memory of which causes me pleasure to this day. I asked Halliday, Hayward, and the two R and H staff members to come outside with me for a minute. Somewhat puzzled, they followed me outside; I opened the door of the limousine, and said to the gentlemen: "I would like you to meet Mrs. Eleanor Roosevelt." Their faces were something to behold. Thereafter I never heard another word from them about my political activity.

There were other moments of tension between me and the man-

agement. They refused to let me off for Yom Kippur, the most solemn
of all Jewish holidays, a day I had always observed from my early
youth. My agents had neglected to include a clause in the contract
that would have given me the day off. Not only was management
unbending, they made sure that I could do nothing about it by permitting my understudy to take his vacation that very week to go fishing somewhere. So I resigned myself to observe the fast while working. But to heap insult upon insult, when our stage manager needed
to contact the Rodgers and Hammerstein office on that day for something or other, *they* had closed in observance of Yom Kippur! For me,
that was the last straw, and I was determined to bring management to
its knees in some fashion. Naturally, Actors' Equity got involved in the
dispute, and it was Ben Irving, Equity's assistant executive secretary,
who came to find a solution.

Legally, under Equity rules, management had the right to do what
they did; I realized that I had no recourse through the grievance
mechanism of the union, as Ben gently informed me. But there
existed in New York State an outfit known as SCAD, the State Commission Against Discrimination, a forerunner of the Civil Rights
Commission. It was headed by Eleanor Holmes Norton. I asked Ben
to inform management that I would be filing an action against them
with the Commission on the grounds that they had violated my
rights. There followed a back-and-forth discussion, with poor Ben as
the go-between. Then management asked him to persuade me to
drop the action; why have unnecessary friction in the cast and all that?
He delivered the message but was clearly on my side, even though we
both knew that in this case there was only a fifty-fifty chance of success.

The fact that I decided not to proceed with the action had nothing to do with management's desire to have me drop the charges, but
was entirely due to my admiration for Ben Irving's caring attitude
about performers. This attitude was infectious. And so I made a
proposition that Ben enthusiastically endorsed. The producers had
given notice to a woman in the chorus, with the result that her
employment terminated one week before she was due vacation pay. A
cheap trick, especially in a show as successful as ours. I let the producers know that I would drop my action before the civil rights commission if they would rehire the chorus member and let her have her
vacation pay. I attached one condition to my demand: that if they
should agree to my plan, she was not to know why they had decided
to rehire her. They agreed, she was rehired, and she never knew. It felt
good to have done this; remembering back it still does. It was Ben

who had put me in a frame of mind that made the welfare of a colleague more important than the satisfaction of my own ego.

I loved Ben Irving and he was my friend. I admired him and learned from him and was in fact guided during the many years of my stewardship at Actors' Equity by much of what he had taught me. He was not just a spokesman for actors' rights, a representative of their union, a nine-to-five salaried executive; he championed the cause of those rights, gloried when battles were won, and agonized when they were not. He loved the theatre and knew the ins and outs of it intimately. Most important, he had an unerring sense of right and wrong, a rectitude both on a personal and political level that might have been the envy even of his detractors on the far right, had they not been so busy slinging barbs. Ben gave to the union far more than the union had a right to expect, let alone demand. He gave and he gave, ignoring any signs that the tension was becoming too great, and I am convinced that, in the end, it took his life. His heart gave out.

Today I treasure the memory of the friendship just as much as I treasured the friendship itself when Ben was alive. When Ben died, I was performing *Fiddler on the Roof* nightly in Las Vegas. The producer was Hal Prince. He knew how close Ben and I were, and he let me miss a performance so that I could fly to New York for a few hours and say a few words at the funeral. That was more than twenty-five years ago, in 1968, and since that time his memory has stayed alive for me, and his family has been close to mine.

Mary Martin and I left the show on the same day—two years and one month after we had started. I had wanted out earlier, or at least to be sprung for a film job with a promise to return to the show. No dice. For all our friendship, Mary insisted that I stay with the play. She hated change of any kind. In some cases, change could not be helped. For example, some of the children had to be let go because of the difference in their growth rates. The idea was that when standing in a line, they should look like organ pipes in an ascending or descending order. Some of the boys simply grew too fast, and two of the children suddenly were the same height. The faster-growing kid had to be replaced. But Mary was used not only to their height but also to the color of their hair. When she sang "Do-re-mi" she tapped the kids' heads for the different notes, some with dark hair and some, fair. Once they replaced a blond-haired child with a dark-haired one, and Mary insisted that they dye the new child's hair the exact color as the old one's so she wouldn't get mixed up. The only other change during our two-year run was that Brian Davies, the young boy who played Rolf and who sang "Sixteen Going on Seventeen," was replaced by

Jon Voight. As for me, when I received an offer of a six-week film job in Africa with Clark Gable and Ava Gardner and asked for a leave from the show, the answer was absolutely no. Just as well, I thought. If Mary had said yes, another actor might have had to dye *his* hair.

They did lose me for ten days, but that could not be helped. Eighteen months into the run of the play, the doctor put me in the hospital for ten days because my muscles had seized up. Bursitis was the diagnosis, but its cause was not physical but psychosomatic. I am convinced that long consecutive runs of plays are not healthy for a performer. Eight times a week for months on end is not something that is natural or that permits the artist an organic and creative growth. There can be no static existence anywhere, least of all in the theatre. You cannot, must not, give carbon copies of your own performance. Try to do it and you become a cropper very quickly. The laughs will not come, nor will any other reaction from the audience. Worse still, your own creative juices dry up. It is not the audience's fault that you have said the words before and sung the songs before. They are entitled to as fresh a performance as you can give, and you yourself must create the conditions in which such a performance can be given. The trouble is that after nine months, figuratively, the baby is born. There is little you can add by way of creativity other than resorting to gimmicks or "shtick." Some arrive at this point much earlier; very few get there later. Zero Mostel arrived at the shtick phase after a matter of only weeks. In the case of Theodore Bikel and *The Sound of Music*, it happened after eighteen months. I always felt a sense of responsibility to the audience, to the playwright, to the cast, and to my own craft that would not permit me to give a lax or sloppy performance. So when the juices gave out, I took what I needed from my nervous system. And then that gave out, too. A sign that it was not just physical was the fact that, in addition to the muscles seizing up, the hearing in my left ear did also. So I was put in the hospital for physical therapy.

During an enforced rest you do strange things. I read a lot, more than usual. I even read stuff in the newspaper that I had seen every day without ever taking note of what it said. The masthead of the *New York Post* had for years carried the legend "The New York Post is owned and published six days a week by the New York Post Corporation." I took pen in hand and wrote to Dorothy Schiff, the *Post's* publisher, saying that I had gleaned from this that on the seventh day the *Post* was neither published nor owned. That seemed to me to be carrying a concern for the sabbath too far. Miss Schiff dropped me a note to thank me and, on the following week, the masthead read: "The New York Post is published six days a week. It is owned by the New

York Post Corporation." When you're laid up in the hospital, even small triumphs are sweet.

Ken Harvey, my understudy, played my part while I was laid up. I knew he was all right in the role, but I got solicitous calls from Mary inquiring about my health—with the not-so-subtle subtext "When are you coming back?" Meantime the box office at the Lunt-Fontanne got held up and robbed of the day's take. I called Leland Hayward to tell him that no one ever had a better alibi than I.

Ten days later I was discharged, well again and ready to tackle the role afresh. I promised myself then that if I could afford it, I would never do a run as long as that again. In fact, although over the years I played *Fiddler* for many more performances than *The Sound of Music,* I never did a longer consecutive run than six months.

After two years, both Mary and I were quite prepared to say goodbye to a show that for us had run its course. But when the night came it was a surprisingly difficult thing for all of us to face. There were places in the performance that had us all choked up and almost unable to continue. The children singing "So Long, Farewell," which we had heard so often, suddenly took on a personal meaning and touched us not as the Captain and Maria, but as Mary and Theo. After the final curtain, Mary and I stood onstage amid grown-ups and children, all with tears in their eyes, and we did not want to leave. Finally, Mary's dresser pulled her away, I stayed and shook some hands, hugged stagehands, nuns, and children. Then I left to take off my makeup and clear out my dressing room, which would be occupied on Monday by a stranger. On the Sunday I was all right—that had been my day off all along—but on the Monday I was frantic, and could not bear to be in New York. I went to spend the day with some friends in Poughkeepsie, but even there, when seven-thirty rolled around, the time for the half-hour call, I was itching all over. This is what a junkie feels like, I thought, when he needs his fix.

By rights I should have repeated my stage role in the film version of *The Sound of Music,* which was released in 1965, but it was not in the cards. Mary Martin was not in the running for the film role; wonderful as she was, at the age of fifty she could not pass for a postulant nun in her twenties. Being ten years younger than Mary, I was the perfect age to play a widower with seven children. Later Robert Wise, who had become a friend, told me that the studio felt it impolitic to offer me the chance to repeat my stage role while bypassing Mary. Chris Plummer was chosen to play Captain von Trapp in the film. Apparently he did not particularly like the role, and was quoted to have said so in an interview, but I am sure he must have been grateful for the tremendous difference it made in his career. Bob Wise once said to me that he quite realized how my Hollywood career might also have been different if they had let me repeat my stage success in the film.

The Sound of Music kept me away from Hollywood for two years, and by the time I got back, the momentum engendered by my Oscar nomination for *The Defiant Ones* had dissipated. In later years I was asked again by people who had my interest at heart to return to California, stay put, and concentrate on films and TV. But there was a whole world out there that I belonged to and that I felt, rightly or wrongly, belonged to me.

12

Union Dues

Good my lord, will you see the players well bestowed?
Do you hear, let them be well used. . . .

——*HAMLET*, ACT II, SCENE 2

D URING THE FIRST YEAR OF *The Sound of Music*, 1960, the
Actors' Equity collective-bargaining agreement with the League
of New York Theatres ran out, and the negotiations for a new contract were not going well. Although at the time I was not involved
with any union matters, I was aware that the situation might impact
on all of us working under Broadway or touring contracts at the time.
By the end of May 1960, matters became critical. The issues which
led up to the strike were unusual for a negotiation involving actors.
The questions of wages and working conditions could be settled more
or less to the satisfaction of both sides—I say more or less because no
negotiation is ever totally satisfactory for all parties—but the sticking
point was pensions. Actors had never had that before; the producers
argued that with the sporadic pattern of employment in the theatre,
no system could be devised to achieve what the actors were after.
Complicating the issue was the fact that many of the actors did
not grasp the significance of the issue themselves. The younger ones,
especially, were clearly puzzled about being forced by the dictates of

labor solidarity to be out of work and pounding the pavement over pensions from which they would derive no personal benefit for many years to come, if ever. Consequently, we argued not only against the employers but also among ourselves. Nowadays an actor's contract without health and pension benefits is unthinkable—just as unthinkable as a contract was in 1960 *with* those provisions. Ominous messages from management were tacked up on the bulletin board backstage to the effect that everyone's job was being jeopardized by Equity's demands. Pressure was brought to bear on stars who were told that they were being victimized by minimum players, and chorus was told not to be idiots and go out on strike for pensions they would never qualify for anyway. On June 1, 1960, the Equity Council called a midnight membership meeting at the Edison Hotel, one half block from the Lunt-Fontanne Theatre, to inform the actors of the critical state of affairs. So many showed up that the streets outside were jammed with actors, creating a problem for police. Hurriedly, the meeting was moved to a larger space, the Grand Ballroom at the Astor Hotel a few blocks down. Pedestrians and motorists on Broadway were treated to quite a sight. Over two thousand Actors' Equity members marched down the street toward the Astor in orderly fashion, carrying an American flag, the Equity banner, and signs proclaiming the names of their Broadway shows. At the Astor, members made fiery speeches blaming the producers' intransigence for what was rapidly turning out to be a labor crisis of some magnitude. Only once before in the history of the American theatre, in 1919, had there been a similar upheaval, commonly known as the "Revolt of the Actors." It, more than anything else, had served to consolidate the collective resolve of the then fledgling actors' union not to be pushed around and made to kowtow to the whims of managements who exploited actors with impunity.

I attended the Astor meeting and all the ones that followed and was strangely moved. I had reached a stage in my life when I was comfortably off and had come a long way since my days as a worker on a communal farm. Yet, despite my position in the theatre, in music, and in films, I never allowed myself to forget what I had received in my genetic knapsack from my socialist father. That included the conviction that working people as individuals are helpless and powerless unless they band together to make common cause. The actors' strike of 1960 gave the impetus to what became a serious involvement on my part for over three decades in the affairs of actors' unions.

Once the strike was under way, I became an active participant in the meetings, spoke at some, and offered my services to the union in whatever capacity it deemed helpful. Some stars of the various shows were similarly involved, while others chose merely to obey the union's directives but otherwise to remain aloof. That was not my way. Before each scheduled performance, all actors were required by Equity to report to the stage door. Technically this was not a strike but a lockout; we had to demonstrate that we were ready and willing to work but that management refused to let us enter our workplace. Producers toured the theatre district in loudspeaker trucks announcing to patrons that "the inconvenience was caused by the Actors' Equity strike." The protesting actors cried in chorus, "Lockout! Lockout!" Every day thereafter we reported to our respective theatres at show time and found locked doors. It was quite a sight to see Mary Martin arrive at the stage door at the half-hour call in her usual limousine—and sometimes in a fur coat—to take part in what was basically a union exercise. Her husband, who was one of the show's producers, often accompanied her, but wisely chose to remain in the limo.

Some of the British actors working on Broadway at the time were supportive of the strike and attended the meetings. Vivien Leigh attended also but did not support Equity's position; she argued that actors had no business going out on strike. Hers was the only dissenting voice in a long line of speakers. Her remarks from the floor were received courteously, which was a credit to her colleagues. This was the last time I saw her before her death. She had been frail when we worked together in *Streetcar,* and was much more so in 1960, with her health quite obviously declining. But she was still working and striking, albeit unwillingly, with the rest of us. Individually, the strike was a hardship, mostly for those earning minimum or near minimum salaries. Equity furnished strike pay, which was barely at subsistence level—ten dollars for each missed performance. Some of us refused to take it so the strike funds could last longer for the rest of the members. While all this was going on, those representing management ran a public relations effort to get audiences mad at us. Although patrons had booked tickets for shows which were now dark, we wanted them to understand that we were the good guys and not guided by capricious motives. We distributed leaflets and went on radio and TV talk shows, sometimes debating our adversaries on the air.

During this time I had my first brushes with the producer David Merrick, later often to be repeated. Merrick was one of the League of New York Theatres' negotiators, perhaps the most combative among them. He had previously resigned from the League, but rejoined for the sole purpose of doing battle with the actors. He was then and has remained an ogre, to put it mildly. If he was not debating us on the air, he would call in and pretend that he was an ordinary member of the public who liked going to shows and that he was "disgusted with a union that deprived him of his theatregoing." He called us irresponsible rabble-rousers and other names. He was not a good enough actor, however, to be able to disguise his voice. I once answered him on the air and called him "David"; he said that wasn't his name and hung up. In later years, when I was one of the leaders of Equity's negotiating team and David Merrick was the chief negotiator for the League, he was an outrageous adversary. When an increase in salaries was our demand, he would actually say across the bargaining table, "What do you want more money for? For whom? Chorus? What is that?" When I replied, "They are human beings with families," he would snap back, "What families? They're faggots." I tried to reply as calmly as I could: "Even they have families." He would ignore that in his steamroller fashion and say, "Now, if you want more money for the girls, I'll give you more money. That damn pill is expensive."

At one point the two sides met in the Equity Council chamber (the venue alternated between their office and our office). Merrick got furious with us over some issue. He picked up our chairman's gavel, yelled, "You strike-happy sons of bitches," and hauled back as if to throw it at Ben Irving and me. At the last second the thought must have struck him that this would not be considered "bargaining in good faith" by the National Labor Relations Board, and he threw the gavel behind him, hitting one of his own team in the temple. It happened to be Herman Shumlin. Years later, after Merrick had a stroke, I ran into Garson Kanin and Marian Seldes. The conversation somehow got around to Merrick, and Gar Kanin said, "You know, God punished him where he sinned most—he can't talk."

At the time of the 1960 revolt of the actors, my involvement was still as a rank-and-file participant. Not for long, though. Since I am afflicted by a penchant for eloquence, I would not keep quiet. Equity's leadership started to take note of what I said in speeches from the floor. I had advocated involving government in some fashion in the process of settling the dispute, arguing inter alia that theatre was such an asset to the economics of New York that it would be in the interest of the city and state to make the theatre whole again. This was indeed what brought about a settlement in the end; the city earmarked a portion of the admissions taxes to help fund the pensions. After one of my speeches at a meeting of the striking actors, I received a note from a committee chairman, Eddie Weston, inquiring whether I would be willing to be appointed to the Legislative Committee of the union, which dealt with all government matters as they touched Actors' Equity and its members. I was flattered to receive the invitation, but had to inform Eddie that I was a resident alien and therefore, under the rules then in force, not permitted to serve in any official union capacity. They then appointed me an "observer," with all the rights of a committee member except the vote. That was of little concern to me; I was more interested in the process. Having a voice was more important than having a vote.

By February 1961, while still in *The Sound of Music,* I was heavily involved with Actors' Equity. The 1960 lockout and the Yom Kippur incident had urged me toward activism in union affairs. That February I became a citizen of the United States, and the very same week, the Actors' Equity Council appointed me to fill a seat that had become vacant. Three months later I was elected to the Council for a full four-year term. I did not serve out the term because in 1964, a year when Equity officers were up for election, I ran for vice president. Eddie Weston was nominated for president, and his opponent was Frederick O'Neal, a stage star and founder of the American Negro Theatre who had served for nine years as first VP under Ralph Bellamy's presidency. I was Eddie Weston's running mate on the "liberal" slate for the post of first vice president. My opponent was none other than the veteran actress Lillian Gish, already close to seventy years old at the time. Eddie lost to Fred O'Neal by some three hundred votes— 1964 was a civil rights year when few black candidates for any office were likely to lose—and I won over Miss Gish by a mere ninety. How different my life might have been had it turned out otherwise!

I tried to figure out what it was, beyond the legacy of my socialist father, that drove me to combine a passion for my chosen profession with a determination to better the lot of my colleagues as much as I was able. I looked back at the history of professional actors' guilds to find that the Hebrew Actors' Union preceded them all; it was not just America's but the world's oldest such professional guild. It was founded in 1888. "Hebrew" in its title is something of a misnomer, since it dealt exclusively with theatre in the Yiddish language until the 1940s, when Hebrew-language theatre was added to its jurisdiction. Actors' Equity was founded in 1913 by 112 actors. They were a courageous bunch, braving the ire not only of managers but of some colleagues who wanted nothing to do with such a radical endeavor as an actors' union. One of the foremost detractors was George M. Cohan, the actor-manager, who in 1919 was also the first strike-breaker. During the years of my presidency, I could see the statue of George M. Cohan from my office window over Times Square, still mocking the union he had spurned.

There was no doubt that up until 1920 the exploitation was real. Dressing rooms were often in cellars, without adequate heating and light, many of them without running water. Managers could schedule as many performances as they wished; sometimes there were as many as fourteen performances in a single week. When attendance at the theatres dropped, before Christmas or Holy Week, actors were arbitrarily given only half salary. Not only was there no pay for rehearsals, but the first two weeks of performances before a paying public were declared "public rehearsals," and for those the actors again received only half salaries. One of the more onerous devices was the so-called "satisfaction clause" managers made actors sign. Under it the actor was required to "play his role in a manner satisfactory to the manager." The manager was, of course, the sole judge, and there was no appeal and no arbitration. In case of any disputes, there were only the courts, which managers could afford and actors could not. An actors' union was long overdue.

The founders of Actors' Equity were a lonely little band. They bravely stood up to the moneymakers who had used and abused them and counted on their weakness. But many others who were in the same boat as they, sat it out and would not raise their voices or even contemplate walking with their feet. They waited for others to take the risks and only much later joined the union, riding piggyback on the courage of those few. Still, there were enough of them who got mad enough or hungry enough or who dreamed deeply enough to stand up to those who sought to make them less than dignified humans.

That wasn't easy; it never is. For actors it was harder still than for other workers. When workers on the assembly line took on the system, their alliances were forged not only by a common goal but by a shared fate that included facing the goons and the ginks and the company finks, the Pinkertons and police with clubs and bayonets who couldn't bear to see a picket line unless it was punctuated by a few bloodied heads. Those workers came by their solidarity quite naturally. But actors? Individualists to the core, with a caste system (or *cast* system) of their own, divided and subdivided into stars, featured players, bit players, older established performers, struggling neophytes—and all of them dreamers and spinners of tales. How were they going to perceive themselves as exploited, each as much as the next one, and equally powerless? How would the notion of equality—*equity*—sit with them?

Still, it happened as early as 1919. Perhaps because the enemy was in one place and easily recognized; perhaps because actors realized that they were not so different from other workers, after all. They finally and inexorably came to realize that their salvation would come, as for all other workers, when they understood that they had to fight for their rights and organize. They realized also that they could not do it each by himself, but had to band together as much for comfort as for strength. From the beginning their slogan was "All for one and one for all." Old-fashioned and outmoded as it might sound, it is a basic rule of unionism; on those occasions when we have failed to observe it, we have found that we ignore it at our own peril. For on his own, the weakest among us is dangerously vulnerable to all attack, and even the strongest is not nearly as strong as he believes himself to be.

Actors have always had a problem with their self-image and their attitude toward their life's work. To this day, many of them are not quite able to declare to the world that they consider themselves to be "workers" in the same way other workers do. Sometimes you might hear them say it but it often sounds insincere, as though they were saying a line written by a playwright who stretched their ability to dissemble just a little too much. Despite the fact that we work for hire, that we have wages, fixed working hours, discipline on the job, teamwork, and precision, there is a reluctance in many actors to consider themselves laborers. Perhaps this has to do with the fact that the raw material from which we fashion our product is made of gossamer, of ideas, of prose, of poetry, and of music. Perhaps it has to do also with the iconoclastic attitude of the artist who insists on his or her shell of individuality while reaching out, in a strange dichotomy, to masses of people at the same time.

Yet it is precisely because we, unlike sculptors or painters or writers, toil in a collaborative art form that we must close ranks. Certainly, the creative process of the actor is a lonely one—all individual creativity is—but his very safety on stage depends upon collective responsibility. In that we are not much different from other workers in other workplaces. The labor movement understood quite well when we joined its ranks that a heavy object falling on a stage is as much a hazard to those working upon that stage as any industrial risk of accident elsewhere. Yet the labor movement did not, still does not, grasp the whole picture.

The philosophical underpinnings of a trade unionist, to my mind, are rooted in a belief in abstract justice and a realization that this remains meaningless unless concrete ways are developed of achieving it. I saw the mission of the union as a two-pronged thrust: not just to protect the actor against exploitation, but to protect the actor against himself. For the theatre is a calling, not just a job, and a commitment to some kind of glorious folly. We who act as pied pipers to so many thousands are ourselves childlike followers of our own pied piper: the theatre. We follow its lure knowing full well it punishes and bruises just as surely as it delights and rewards. Most actors are so in love with what they do—perhaps besotted is a better word—that they would rather act than not, even if it pays next to nothing, even if their dignity is trampled upon. In that respect, we are indeed different from other laborers. No autoworker reveres the automobile, no steelworker worships the foundry. We, on the other hand, love the theatre beyond reason. If it were not for the unions and guilds, we would have nothing to protect us from our own folly or from those who seek to abuse our love for what we do.

Not that all employers are in the David Merrick mold. Some of them have a great passion for the theatre themselves. They might otherwise have chosen a different field of endeavor and would, with their business acumen, have made greater fortunes. But they must be reminded constantly that they cannot build their success at the expense of our dignity. I felt that once they acknowledged this, the relationship between us and the employers would progress to something better than a mere adversarial tug-of-war. The ritual of heavy breathing across the table every three years or so, when contracts are being renegotiated, is usually over in a matter of weeks. I was determined to see to it that during the mostly peaceful lull between negotiations, the theatre unions and the producers would be able to make common cause to benefit the theatre and those who toil in it.

Armed with these thoughts I entered my service in the two top leadership positions of Actors' Equity. I shall not attempt to retell the minutiae of my involvements; some issues and events I shall paint with a broader brush than my memory might prompt me to do. Suffice it to say that, as the Equity Council meetings were held on Tuesday of each week, for twenty-one years my Tuesdays were not my own. When in the New York area I chaired the meetings, more often than any other president before or since, except Fred O'Neal perhaps. When I was away working, I would send wires to the office or keep in touch by telephone. Once Eddie Weston and I happened to be in Europe at the same time; we cut short our respective stays and flew to New York on a Monday night in order to be present for a crucial vote on Tuesday. Having been elected vice president and later president of Actors' Equity was an honor, without a doubt, but it was also something I worked at very hard.

One of the more important undertakings was lobbying in Washington for the establishment of a National Council on the Arts and later the National Endowment for the Arts. I take pride in having performed a midwifely chore in the birth of these two bodies. Speaking for Actors' Equity, I was one of the first who testified in front of both the House and Senate committees in Washington, arguing for arts legislation and the creation of an official body that would advise the government on all questions relating to the arts. I began this effort almost immediately after my election. My ability to argue the case of the performing artist vis-à-vis the outside world had prompted the Equity members to put me in a position of leadership; these skills would have to be put to use and I was determined to be as eloquent as I could be.

It was not an easy chore to go to Washington hat in hand and plead for official recognition of the importance of the arts in the nation's life. Oh, everybody had been paying lip service to the importance of the arts in America. President Johnson himself had declared: "It is important to be aware that artistic activity can enrich the life of our people; which is the central object of government." And President Kennedy before him had said much the same thing, only more poetically: "If art is to nourish the roots of our culture, society must set the artist free to follow his vision wherever it takes him. I look forward to an America which will reward achievement in the arts as we reward achievement in business or statecraft." But to enact legislation, even on a minimal level of creating a governmental advisory body? Now, wait a minute. Should the government really get involved in the arts? Wouldn't that mean that they would exercise control over it? In trying to put my case I started at a disadvantage; I had to argue either the hen or the egg, only I didn't quite know which one came first.

The first fallacy to dispose of was that government support had to be synonymous with government control. In other walks of life that notion would have been easier to dispel than in the arts. Government subsidizes hospitals and roads, schools, and libraries. Yet woe betide any government official who would decree what kind of books are to be carried in a library, what curriculum is to be followed, what automobiles are to be driven on the roads, or how a surgeon should operate. I much doubted, as I said in my testimony, that bureaucrats administering a law would exercise the kind of control that the law itself expressly prohibited. Further, I refused to believe that the government of the United States would be less likely to be guided by wisdom and level-headedness than was the government of the United Kingdom, whose Arts Council had been operating since 1944. (In retrospect that might have been a foolishly naive assumption, seeing how in 1993 Senator

Jesse Helms and California Congressman Dana Rohrabacher were still straining at the leash to exercise just such controls.)

The other mental obstacle to overcome was the assumption that we were lobbying for arts legislation because we were the spokesmen for artists who sought personal benefits from such a move. I had to remind the legislators that, although the expansion of the national cultural life might increase employment for artists, we had a far greater aim in mind and a far greater stake to defend than a concern for our personal lives and careers. In whatever way the proposed law might benefit the arts and their practitioners, it must surely follow that the benefits would inure to the public we serve. I told the committee: "It is neither immodest nor inaccurate to say that what you do for us will be returned tenfold to the nation. What you sow in the nation's garden, for us to till, the country will reap."

Thankfully I was not the only one who argued for the passage of the legislation establishing the National Council in 1964 and later the National Endowment for the Arts (NEA), for whose operations the Council would be the advisory body. Fortunately Actors' Equity was not the only organization so visibly and audibly involved. If we had stood alone, there would have been little chance of success. We had some very eloquent allies, not only from the arts community but from the private sector as well; and we prevailed. The National Council on the Arts was created in 1964. JFK had supported the idea and the process had been set in motion during his administration. In anticipation of the legislation being approved, Kennedy had a list of names on his desk of potential appointees to the first Council on the Arts. According to Professor Arthur Schlesinger, one of President Kennedy's advisers, my name was on this list. When it came to appointing the first Council members, John F. Kennedy was no longer alive and LBJ had his own list. My appointment to the Council had to wait until 1978, when I was one of the first of Jimmy Carter's arts appointees.

I made the trek to Capitol Hill on many occasions, being forced to make the same arguments in support of the arts with stupefying regularity. It was as though the arts were perennially required to justify their existence within the framework of governmental concern. Each time there were voices prepared to dismiss us as frills and luxuries. Each time it was as though some of the legislators—not all, thank God—had forgotten that we had been there before and had made the case for the arts, had made it, moreover, with some eloquence. On the House side, it was thanks to such wonderful committee chairmen as Sid Yates, Robert Giaimo, John Brademas, and the late Frank Thompson that we were given the respect and the courtesy of a diligent and friendly audience. On the Senate side it was Hubert Humphrey, Jacob Javits, and Claiborne Pell. The latter had been chiefly responsible for the 1975 legislation establishing the National Endowment for the Arts. The person on Senator Pell's staff who drew up the language and chaperoned it through its passage was Livingston Biddle, later to become chairman of the NEA under President Carter. He also became one of my champions, arguing that I was ideally suited for a seat on the National Council; it was partly due to his urging that I received the appointment.

The pleadings before congressional committees were not without their humorous side. I testified before a committee chaired by Congressman Thompson of New Jersey, who knew me well. While serving in the Congress he had a distinguished career and was a great supporter of labor and the arts; it was all the more regrettable that he later got into trouble and fell into disgrace during the Abscam scandal. I liked the man and he did the labor movement a lot of good. He also had a wicked sense of humor. In the course of my testimony I made the point that the cultural muscle of the nation had to be exercised; otherwise, like any other muscle, it would atrophy and die. Knowing my nonathletic nature, Frank looked at me and interjected, "What do you know about exercise, Mr. Bikel?" I said, "Well, Mr. Chairman, I do a lot of jumping to conclusions." One of my better quips, I thought, and it tickled me that it ended up as part of the congressional hearing transcript. When Frank Thompson died, the AFL-CIO held a memorial for him in Washington. Lane Kirkland, Ted Kennedy, and the former Speaker of the House, Tip O'Neill, took part and eulogized Frank. So did I. I quoted Shakespeare: "The evil that men do lives after them, the good is oft interred with their bones." This man's good, which far outweighed his wrongdoing, needed to be remembered after his death.

My concern with union affairs extended to the other media as well. While I held no elected position in either the Screen Actors Guild (SAG) or the American Federation of Television and Radio Artists (AFTRA), I was a working actor in all the media and a member of all the unions that had jurisdiction in the various fields. Included in that list was the American Federation of Musicians (AFofM). Early on when I started performing with my guitar in earnest, I had to join this union as well. This was the only performers' guild where you had to prove that you knew how to perform before they let you join. In the others, all you needed was the offer of a job. Here they made you go through a kind of audition in front of a committee. I brought my guitar to this audition and was called in to face five people in shirtsleeves.

They asked me to play. Usually, of course, I would only play the instrument as an accompaniment to my voice, but this was not about singing. I took out my guitar and started to play the most intricate instrumental piece I knew, stuff I would never perform in concert. I had played for no more than forty-five seconds when the chairman interrupted, asking me to play an E7 chord. I was a little puzzled: E7 is one of the easiest chords to play. I did as they asked and the chairman asked, "What's that top note you're playing?" I said, "That's an E." "Okay, I guess you know what this instrument's all about. Raise your right hand and repeat after me . . ." I repeated the membership pledge and they asked me to go to window number one, give them my first dues check, and get the literature. Literature? I wondered. As it turned out, window number one had a sense of humor. After I had written out my check, the official handed me some seven or eight books, rules, regulations, membership lists, and the like. I said to him, "Gee, they told me I had to know how to play an instrument; nobody said I had to know how to read." The guy said in a stern voice, "You can't read?" I replied, "No, I'm a moron." And he said, "You've come to the right union."

In the middle of April 1967, the AFTRA actors were on strike against NBC. Pickets were up on both sides of the NBC Building, on Fiftieth and Fifty-first streets. During this time I was fairly busy professionally and also preoccupied with personal matters. I was getting married again. I had met my bride some years earlier when she was producing a live folk show taped for television in Washington. President Kennedy was in attendance; it was quite a big deal and many of my friends and colleagues participated. I had also been invited to appear, but Jac Holzman, then my manager, declined. I had done several shows recently for the Kennedys, and Jac thought we should let this one go. We pleaded unavailability. When the day of the show rolled around, it turned out that I was in Washington on some Equity business and I decided to go to the hootenanny as a guest. Somebody procured a ticket for me and I went. At the door was a redheaded lady, Rita Call, who was vouching for TV technicians for the benefit of the Secret Service agents. When she saw me, she said, "What the hell are you doing here, Mr. Bikel? You were supposed to be unavailable tonight." I made some lame excuse about plans having been changed and went in. Some time later we started dating.

Now it was April 14, 1967, and we were getting married. After the ceremony there was a big reception attended by friends, family, Equity people, and others, including Senator Javits, who proposed a toast that sounded suspiciously like a campaign speech. When the reception was over, Rita and I got into the limousine waiting to take us back to Washington Square. On the way downtown I asked the driver to go through Fiftieth Street and stop in front of the RCA Building, where NBC was being picketed. I asked Rita if she would mind waiting in the car for a little while and I got out, approached the AFTRA pickets, and asked one of them to lend me his picket sign. I started to walk alongside the other striking actors, holding aloft my borrowed sign. The man walking beside me eyed my attire suspiciously; in my Bar Mitzvah suit I looked too elegant for picketing duty. Then he motioned toward the limo and asked, "If you don't mind telling me, what's with the chick in the car?" I told him that I had just gotten married. He congratulated me, adding that he had to compliment me on having come to picket on this special day. I told him that it was something I felt I had to do. Then he asked, "What does your bride do?" I looked up at the building's facade behind which television production was at a standstill and said, "She is a television producer."

On our first anniversary Rita asked me whether I intended to look for a picket line to celebrate.

In 1967–68 we spent a whole six months in Las Vegas, my first run as Tevye in *Fiddler on the Roof*. Apart from the fact that Las Vegas taxes a person's endurance, I encountered some problems which the union man in me deeply resented. Within a couple of weeks, the management of Caesars Palace, where we were performing, put up a notice to the effect that the entire cast had to be fingerprinted and photographed at the sheriff's station so they could be issued casino employees' cards. There would be a fee of ten dollars per person. The reason, we were told, was that in Las Vegas all employees of places with gambling and/or liquor had to be so registered. I was horrified at the prospect. None of us was engaged in an occupation that had anything to do with liquor or gambling, nor were we employees of the hotel or the casino. Our employer was Hal Prince in New York, from whom Caesars Palace had purchased a packaged show. Even our individual paychecks came from New York. Being fingerprinted and photographed carried with it an imputation of potential criminality. Even if it did not, no Equity contract mandated that actors be subjected to any such practice as a condition of their employment. I informed the hotel's entertainment director that we could not comply with any such requirement.

Then followed phone calls, friendly at first. The hotel management told me that I, as the star of the show, would not be required to be fingerprinted but that all the others would have to be. I told them that they had failed to take my measure; if we were forced to do this, then I would not exempt myself from anything but would be the first one in line. But we were not going to do it; *no one* in my company would be reporting to the sheriff's office. Then they started to argue, saying that if it was a matter of the ten dollars, the hotel would be prepared to absorb the cost. No good, I said, I was not going to let the cast go through the humiliating experience of being fingerprinted. Then the threats started: They said I was jeopardizing my own standing, my career even, if I persisted in shielding these others. Who are you laying your reputation on the line for? Chorus people? In Las Vegas those were a dime a dozen. I told them that in my world chorus people were not bought by the dozen nor purchased with a dime; as far as I was concerned they were ladies and gentlemen of the theatre and I wanted them treated as such.

They called Hal Prince in New York and attempted to have him put the pressure on. To his credit, he never did; he told them that he was as bound as we were by the collective bargaining agreement with Actors' Equity. Meanwhile I had kept the Equity office informed of the goings-on, and they said that the union was prepared to make this a test case and fight it out in the courts if need be. Then the tactics changed. The hotel management told me that they would run a check on each member of the company and if they should find anyone with an arrest record for any offense, drugs, homosexual behavior, traffic offenses, anything at all, those persons would be put on a plane and summarily shipped out of the state as undesirables. I was not aware that Las Vegas casinos were such clean places that they could be contaminated by the presence of marijuana users, gays, or motorists going over 80 mph. I was also not aware that people could be summarily deprived of their right to be anywhere or work anywhere on the basis of a past arrest record. And I was intrigued by the notion that nobody cared if these undesirables remained in Las Vegas as long as they went to the sheriff to get a damned license. But I was not going to be a hero on the backs of people who might feel themselves to be vulnerable.

With Equity's permission I called a cast meeting that night after the show and explained the nature of the threat to the actors. I said that Actors' Equity was prepared to make the fight on the principle of "no fingerprinting," and that I personally wholeheartedly supported doing this. However, I also stressed that the fight need not necessarily be made when people were vulnerable. Therefore I proposed that we take a vote by secret ballot; not on the question of whether the fight should be undertaken, but whether it should be done now while *Fiddler* was playing. If there were just one "no" vote, then we would submit to the management's demand, it being understood that Equity would bring the case once our company was gone from Las Vegas. Sure enough, when the ballots were counted, there were a couple of "no" votes. I later learned that someone in the company had been arrested for marijuana use in Chicago. The reason for the other negative vote never became known. As I had promised, when we went to the sheriff's office the next day, I was the first one to be fingerprinted and photographed. Later, Actors' Equity did make the fight and won it; thereafter actors, singers, and dancers were no longer required to submit to the demeaning process I had so strenuously objected to.

During my tenure with Equity there seemed to be perpetual crises to be handled and I was in the midst of all of them. They came with regularity, spoiling festive occasions, family outings, and even planned Equity celebrations. I had just been reelected president when one such crisis arose and ate up all the time at the regular membership meeting that had been earmarked for me to deliver my presidential address outlining the direction the union would take in the following three years. At last I took the microphone and told the members that they were about to hear the shortest presidential address ever. I declared solemnly: "My presidential address is one-sixty-five West Forty-sixth Street." And I sat down.

One continuing crisis has been the horrendous unemployment rate in the acting profession. In any given year 70, 75, sometimes even 80 percent of all actors listed on the roster of the union were out of work! A horrendous picture. Granted, some chose to work elsewhere, some gave up pounding the pavement, others fell by the wayside because of having to make a steady living in other fields so as to feed their families—but all that still left an unemployment picture so grossly out of proportion to the national rate that we were jealously guarding all work opportunities. Like all other labor unions, Equity was concerned with conditions in the workplace; unlike other unions, we had to be equally concerned with the nonworking actors and their quest for a job. In the meantime our members had to undertake other work just to survive, and this created a problem for me when I had to plead their case. In Washington, as I was opening my briefcase and citing the unemployment figures for actors, I was practically called a liar. The Bureau of Labor Statistics had unemployment figures for actors also, and they were only half as high as mine. I soon realized why. When conducting their surveys, they would ask what a person's main source of income had been the previous year. An actor who earned a living as a waiter while auditioning for jobs in the theatre was carried on their books as "waiter." No wonder they had more hospital orderlies and gas station attendants than actors. To my deep regret, I presided for years over an association of people of whom most were full-time waiters and cab drivers, and only sometime actors.

The stage actor's ever-shrinking job market is not merely an economic phenomenon that the theatre has in common with the rest of society. It's difficult to tell how long it will take before the public and the press realize this. Their own lack of discernment has led to a diminished regard for the actor as a professional and contributed to the decline. News media blithely advertise plays and musicals employing nonprofessional actors with slogans such as "the Broadway hit" or "straight from Broadway." In truth, the only things in those productions that can be said to be straight from Broadway are the sets, the rented costumes, and the fact that the play itself has been performed there. I never had any objections to amateur productions being mounted in the traditional venues for such events: high school auditoriums, community centers, churches, synagogues, or gymnasiums. They clearly were what they were, they were mounted by the community for the community. If tickets were sold, they were modestly priced and the proceeds designed merely to defray the cost of renting sets, costumes, scripts, music, etc. Such productions were given for a limited number of performances, and always in one place. As far as quality is concerned, I am not denigrating the talent of some of the amateur performers for they are often quite good, and by definition love what they do (the word "amateur" comes from the Latin for "love"). What distinguishes even talented amateurs from professionals is that the latter are trained not only to be good at what they do, but to be good at it eight times a week, even when the muse does not rest on their brows. The problem with nonprofessional theatrical ventures is that among the amateurs you will find dilettantes; while some amateurs can be genuinely good, dilettantes invariably are not.

In recent years some promoters have begun to exploit the naïveté of an undiscerning public by the cost-cutting measure of using amateur casts in exactly the same venues and the same fashion as one would professional ones. They book their shows into regular theatres, they tour their plays, and, more grievously still, they charge full ticket prices, undercutting not only professional performers but also the producer down the street who must compete with them in the regular marketplace. The theatregoer who buys a ticket to a show with nonprofessional performers, a ticket carrying no warning label of "Buyer Beware," may be treated to Broadway lights and costumes but also to substandard performances.

In 1973 the Casa Mañana, a professional theatre in Fort Worth,

Texas, decided to go non-Equity and use nonprofessional casts in the future. Their advertising was silent regarding this fact, and the audiences were buying seats for shows that in the past had all been fully professional, without being told that things had changed. Actors' Equity decided to put up an informational picket line outside the theatre, especially for its first production. I flew to Fort Worth together with two other concerned colleagues, Rip Torn and Werner Klemperer, whose name value would help in the picketing effort. As the patrons filed in for the opening night, I engaged some of them in conversation. I asked a middle-aged man: "Excuse me, sir, may I ask you a question? If you had appendicitis, would you permit an amateur surgeon to take out your appendix?" The man said, somewhat puzzled, "No, of course not." "Then why do you entrust your soul to an amateur actor?" I asked. He went in anyway, why waste the ticket money? You can sometimes succeed in preventing people from entering a place which is being picketed, but only before they have spent their money. The picketing in this case was useful only because the media reported it and other audiences were dissuaded from buying seats. We also scored points with the people we talked to at the site by making them aware that they had been unwitting victims of unscrupulous advertising. It took a few seasons before the Casa Mañana saw the light and went back to fully professional productions.

When John F. Kennedy established the President's Advisory Council on the Arts, the forerunner of the National Council, he said the following: "I emphasize the importance of the professional artist because there is danger we may accept the rich range of amateur activities which abound in our country as a substitute for the professional. Without the professional performer and the creative artist, the amateur spirit declines and the vast audience is only partially served." That put the matter in its proper perspective. While showing due regard for amateur activity, the President stressed professionalism as the sine qua non of the arts. In the last analysis, it is the professional from whom the amateur takes his inspiration. There is not a single amateur violinist in the world who looks to another amateur violinist for his model; he looks to Isaac Stern or Itzhak Perlman. There is no amateur cellist who does not listen to the records of Pablo Casals in order to learn. Similarly, in the theatre, when amateurs are very good, chances are that, sooner or later, they will find their way into the ranks of professionals who do theatre not as a sometime thing but as their life's work.

It used to amuse me to hear the term "legitimate theatre." *Is there another kind?* I wondered. Of course there is; I have described it here.

While in England, I heard the story of an old Shakespearean actor who was walking down the street, wearing his cape and carrying his cane. A lady of the evening accosted him, inquiring whether he might be interested in spending the night with her. He looked at her for a long moment with sadness in his eyes, shook his head, and said with a voice full of grief, "Look at you and look at me. I—an actor, you—a prostitute. The two oldest and noblest professions in the world—both spoiled by amateurs!"

The unions themselves often have a psychological problem with the notion that all the members need to be represented, including the affluent ones. Featured actors and even stars can become victims of unscrupulous practices by management just as much as the rest of the rank-and-file, and the union is pledged to protect the contractual rights of every member. The tendency is to assume that successful actors have the means to protect themselves against abuse without the union's help. Accept that principle and you do violence to the notion of responsibility for all members in their relations with the employers. I sometimes had to argue with Council and staff about diligently following the mandate of protecting some of the better situated. In doing so I recalled a Chassidic story. (There is a Chassidic story for everything.)

A rich man and a poor man with a grievance against each other came before a rabbi. They started to argue their complaints, but the rabbi interrupted them and bade them be silent for a moment. He realized that he would tend to favor the poor man in rendering judgment, so he ordered them to leave and commanded the rich man to do one of two things: either come back dressed in rags or buy clothes for the poor man as fine as his own. "Because," he said, "even a rich man is entitled to justice."

How little understanding there is among civilians about the plight of the performer became evident again in the seventies, when a housing proposal for actors and others in the arts came to my attention. A couple of developers came to see me in my office at Actors' Equity. They had just completed a building project on the West Side of Manhattan, two high-rise buildings of forty-five stories each with some twenty units on each floor. Restaurants, shops, and a health club facility were planned as part of the development. The problem was that they had gotten cold feet because of the area. The block bounded by Forty-second and Forty-third streets and Ninth and Tenth avenues was in Hell's Kitchen, and the developers were having difficulty selling the units. They came to me inquiring whether something could not be done about making this into an actors' housing project; the buildings were right at the edge of the theatre district, and it would be an ideal place for such a venture. I almost laughed them out of my office. Actors could not possibly afford to live in places like the one they had built. Brownstone walk-ups and shared apartments were more the usual, I said. Queens, Brooklyn, Washington Heights, the ungentrified blocks in Hell's Kitchen, and maybe the Village, those were the places where they might be able to afford the rent. The two gentlemen said that they were aware of the situation; their thinking had been more along the lines of subsidized housing. That to me was an even more outlandish notion. I had never heard of anyone in any city government subsidizing individual actors' housing needs. I thanked them for having come but told them I did not think the idea could fly.

After they left, I got to thinking. Why was I dismissing this out of hand? I would have liked nothing better than to help actors live in decent surroundings with greater personal comfort and security. I talked it over with Don Grody, who was then Equity's Executive Secretary. He was enthusiastic and urged me to give this thing a try. It was in great measure due to his prompting that the idea went further. Both he and I made numerous attempts to get the city interested in a subsidized housing program for performers. No dice. We tried the state of New York, also without success. Then we made the trek to Washington. I recall conversations at the Department of Housing and Urban Development when the idea was presented. An assistant undersecretary quizzed me about the plan but warned me beforehand that HUD was only in the business of subsidizing housing for the poor. Actors, to him, did not seem to fall into this category. I asked him how he defined "poverty" and he said that the standard measure was $9,600 per person or family per year. Anything under that figure could be considered as being below the poverty line. I pulled out my figures and showed him that some 60 percent of the people I represented were making less than that sum. He seemed very surprised and frankly incredulous. I told him that it was a common misconception to think of actors as making considerable sums of money. That was due to the fact that the public, including government officials, it seemed, had only the image of Paul Newman or Barbra Streisand before their eyes when they thought about actors. The actors I spoke for were poor.

The official said all right, suppose this checks out and we institute this actors' housing project. We are concerned here with people who are poor *all* the time. What happens when one of the tenants who got in as a bona fide applicant happens to get a job and starts to make money and no longer qualifies under our guidelines? I said, "Why don't you charge negative rent?" The man said, "What is that? I never heard of that." Frankly, I had never heard of it, either, but it seemed to me to be a perfectly fine solution. I said: "When they are poor, subsidize them. If they get less poor, diminish the subsidy according to some formula to be worked out. And if they are no longer poor under any definition, stop the subsidy and charge them the going market rate." He said, "That's never been done before." I asked whether there was any rule or statute which said that it couldn't be done, and he admitted that to his knowledge there was none. I said: "Well, can we do business?" "Wait a minute," he said, "how do we know what they make?" "That's easy," I said. "Make them submit their tax returns and fix the rent according not to their present income but to last year's. Unless they are perjurers and tax cheats—in which case the IRS will catch them before you do—you will know their income." He scratched his head and said he wanted to consult with his people further. A good sign.

It took us at least eight trips to Washington to put the thing through. When Manhattan Plaza opened with a bit of fanfare, Joan Mondale, then the wife of the vice president and always a great supporter of artists, attended the ceremony. To this day the project works on the principle I outlined at the HUD offices. The poorer actors, musicians, and writers live at Manhattan Plaza under a Title VIII subsidy arrangement, the richer ones pay the full going rate. People who knew of my involvement with putting the project on the map would thank me when they ran into me in the elevator of the building. I was pleased by that, but the best thanks I got was the knowledge that for once the actor's lot had gotten a little better.

I continue to be concerned about the future of my profession, for a number of reasons: the devouring nature of the electronic media, the overwhelming unemployment, the pressure of never being allowed to fail. Add to this the newest plague, the scourge of AIDS. While it doesn't necessarily afflict actors in greater numbers than the rest of society, actors are more visible and more frequent topics of conversation. Suddenly, after coming out of the closet, people are not only frightened by this illness but shamed by the name it has acquired as a gay disease, a shame that follows them to the grave. There is enough of the unpleasant, the shoddy, and the cowardly in people, enough that can make them ashamed of their lives. At the end of their days, they should not have to be ashamed of their deaths.

As Vice President of Equity, I wholeheartedly embraced its move to join the FIA, International Federation of Actors, in 1969. Its initials stand for the organization's French name: Fédération Internationale des Acteurs. This body, in existence since 1952, was first established as a federation of European actors' unions, particularly from countries that had been devastated by the war, but it soon widened its scope to embrace actors' guilds from Latin America, Canada, and Australia. At the Tenth FIA Congress, held in Prague in 1967, both the USSR and Actors' Equity—the latter largely at Eddie Weston's urging—attended as observers. In 1969 the Cultural Workers' Union of the USSR joined FIA officially, and shortly thereafter so did American Actors' Equity and the Screen Actors Guild (SAG).

Practically until the demise of the Soviet Union as a Communist power, there were expressions of displeasure from the American labor movement about our being part of an international body that included representatives of organizations from behind the Iron Curtain. That these organizations called themselves trade unions was a particular bone of contention. The AFL-CIO strongly argued that no such thing existed in the Communist bloc, that these were all government-sponsored and government-controlled outfits that did not deserve the name "labor union." Although this characterization was not altogether inaccurate, we pointed out that these were fellow actors, colleagues of the theatre, of films, of dance, and of mime, and argued that this kinship was more important than the ideological differences between our respective political systems.

It was not our side alone that failed to grasp the concept of mutual understanding between ourselves and the Soviets. The Communist governments may have had political motives in permitting their unions to be part of FIA (resulting in some feeble attempts to proselytize for the Communist system during visits), but the Soviet press was puzzled by the new American and Soviet association with FIA. In 1977, during my first trip to the Soviet Union, the Cold War was still going on. At the conclusion of the executive meeting of FIA in Moscow that summer, I represented the U.S. delegation at the concluding press conference. A reporter from *Izvestia* asked me what the Americans and the Soviets could possibly have in common, seeing that we came from such disparate political and ideological backgrounds. I told him that my reply would probably not make much sense to him, but I was confident that the actors among our Soviet colleagues would understand it perfectly well. I said that the smell of greasepaint was stronger than he could imagine; actors the world over knew each other's lives intimately and had a visceral recognition of each other's problems. It would probably astonish the gentlemen from the Soviet press to learn that I considered myself to be much closer to an actor in another country—even if its government was hostile to mine—than I did to a nonactor in my own.

While our Soviet colleagues understood most of their fellow actors' problems very well and empathized with them, they had a different outlook on unemployment—a problem the rest of the acting world shared. Soviet citizens, including artists, were looked after from cradle to grave. It was artificial and not terribly well managed, but by and large, anyone who finished acting school was assured of a job—not necessarily in Moscow or Kiev, but they had a job. Our Soviet, East German, and Hungarian colleagues kept extolling the virtues of this situation until I begged them, in an address from the floor, not to paint so rosy a picture. After all, we were pleading with national governments as well as international bodies such as UNESCO, the International Labor Organization (ILO), and others for support, citing the deplorable tendency of most of the world to set the actor apart from the rest of society. It would undercut our argument if our own colleagues were to contradict our case. They understood and were more subdued thereafter.

In the rest of the world it was apparent that strong prejudices still existed which made it difficult for actors to function in any capacity other than as actors. In many parts of the world they were still thought of as little better than vagrants and traveling troubadours: to be amused by but not to be trusted. Even the most exalted members of the profession could not escape the stigma. In Britain less than a hundred years ago, the British Crown honored the great actor and entrepreneur Henry Irving with a knighthood, dubbing him Sir Henry Irving. He received this honor solely because of his work in the theatre. Because of an act of Parliament known as the Rogues and Vagabonds Act, however, Henry Irving was not knighted as an actor, God forbid, but as a "meritorious householder."

Even today, a century later, a similar prejudice persists. It is assumed that the actor's lifestyle will be wild and abandoned and will give a bad reputation to the neighborhood, that he cannot be trusted to pay rent on time, that he will vanish in the dead of night leaving behind him bad debts and pregnant ladies, that actresses will engage in immoral conduct—and all the other irrational nonsense that is the usual by-product of prejudice.

Let me count the ways.

"Bad credit risk." Actors' credit unions came into being because actors could not get loans elsewhere. I was among the first eight members of the Actors' Federal Credit Union, and its records reveal a better and more timely repayment rate and a smaller number of defaults than other credit unions.

"Bad auto insurance risk." Auto and homeowners' insurance is invariably higher for actors than for others. I pressed insurance companies for an explanation, and they muttered something about actors being emotionally unstable, drinking more, and being worse drivers than others. Statistically and actuarily not borne out by fact.

"Bad household insurance risk." Why? I asked. Ah, they said. Burglars know that actors are at the theatre at certain hours and their houses are more vulnerable. Presumably the informed burglar cannot find out that the actor's neighbor is away at his office or job just as regularly, and for longer hours at that. But go argue with prejudice.

Some of these were problems our colleagues from behind the Iron Curtain did not share. They listened attentively, but shook their heads in disbelief at a world they had barely glimpsed and clearly found bewildering. I sometimes think of those puzzled looks when I reflect on today's situation in the former Soviet bloc. Our colleagues now no longer have the luxury of total employment, and they have had to learn to adjust to a free market with its pitfalls. Worse yet, they have had to learn how to compete, something we in the West take to be our constant lot.

One other important point of divergence was the notion of the artist's responsibility toward society. The Soviets felt that the artist was obligated to serve the political or propagandistic needs of the state. Needless to say, to us this notion was anathema—misreading the very nature of art. At many of these international meetings I argued that in my world artists' responsibility is not to a political process or social status quo; our responsibility is to a world that might be—a world that should be. Plays, films, poems, or songs that are critical of society, and thus point the way to something better than what we have, are more central to the artist's task, as I see it. This presumes that the artist can be at odds with the society in which he lives, and can put his eloquence to use to further the dream of a better humankind. When I voiced such thoughts to my Soviet colleagues I imagined I detected a flicker of recognition in their otherwise unreceptive faces. After all, they had their Voznesenskys and Yevtushenkos.

For all of that, I had to stress that seeking to cure social ills is not the primary purpose of the artist's work, although it may be a by-product of it. Art carries its own demands and fashions its own imperatives. The actor is not intended to be the bearer of a message, and the theatre is not meant to do what a pamphlet would do better. Drama represents a distillation of ideas, not of ideologies. There may be comment inherent in the author's work and in the actor's interpretation, but such intentions are never more important than artistic excellence. If the audience is moved toward new thoughts as a result of our work, fine. But the art itself is central.

Nor do I believe the artists' function is limited to the lofty matters of "high art," as the Soviets argued. I maintained that we are neither educators nor preachers nor social workers. We are performers. We dance, we sing, we make grown-ups laugh and children clap their hands. While we sometimes draw the audience into a heightened awareness of their lives, we just as often make them forget the day and lighten their burdens. As an intellectual I was quite ready to engage in a lively colloquy regarding the actor's responsibility to society; as a union man I was far more interested in society's responsibility to the actor.

FIA furnished an opportunity to do something I had long hoped for. In a world where everyone jealously guarded his turf, there was mistrust and animosity in place of mutual understanding and collegiality. For years we had faced a situation where the sole communication between ourselves and our opposite numbers abroad was through unaccommodating voices on overseas telephone lines. In particular, there was constant and unrelieved tension between the American unions and British Equity. Many more Brits worked in the U.S. than Americans did in the U.K., much to the chagrin of the members of SAG, AFTRA, and American Actors' Equity. The reasons were twofold. Fewer Americans were prepared to work in England, where the salaries were much lower than in the U.S., while British performers were eager to come to America, rake in the money and the glory, and leave. The second reason was that in England there were established procedures under which the British government had to consult with the union before admitting an alien performer. As a rule, they went along with whatever British Equity was recommending, and only rarely was anyone admitted over its objections. The exact opposite was the case in America. Although they were required to, the Immigration and Naturalization Service often neglected to consult the unions and quite often overruled our objections even when they did. As a result, there was tension even when none was necessary. Stars of established reputation could come and go freely, but members on both sides of the Atlantic griped whenever an alien performer appeared in any role that could have gone to a native. Any good actor with a command of accents can play a British role in America or an American in England. If, for good reason or bad, an English actor was permitted to perform in New York, there was acrimony. The same in London; "The Yanks are coming!" was the cry. How many actors does it take to change a lightbulb? Answer: One hundred. One to change the lightbulb and ninety-nine to say, "I could have done that."

Frankly, I had always been uncomfortable with this "alien" stuff. For personal reasons alone I could not join the chorus of "keep them out at all costs." Whenever the question of putting up barriers arose, I heard a line from the Bible in my mind—"Remember, Thou wast a stranger in Egypt." Though I had to be watchful as president of a union whose members needed jobs, I knew there had to be a way of handling the situation so as to maintain a sane level of discussion and avoid the danger of strident jingoism. We owed our members every opportunity at employment. We had many members who themselves were former British subjects or permanent resident aliens in the U.S. They all had the same rights of full membership, and we needed to protect their positions in the U.S. as best we could. But we also had to avoid falling into the trap of opposing everything that came from Britain. For one thing, the public would have little patience with such an attitude. We could raise reasoned objections when persons below star status sought to come to New York just to work briefly and leave, but Americans are in love with British accents, and attempts at a blanket ban would have been fruitless. The INS's rulings reflected the commonly held view that British performers were much better than Americans—a notion that was as untrue as it was demeaning. Those who thought they were better had only seen the cream of their crop. There is neither more nor less mediocrity in the arts in England than there is in America. Once, in London, when I was a bit under the weather, I decided to stay in bed in my hotel room and watch TV for the entire broadcast day. I logged just as much crap there as I did when I repeated the experiment in Los Angeles.

In the end, it was due to regular contacts with our British colleagues at FIA meetings that we managed a reasonable solution and established a mechanism that would avoid the acrimonious exchanges of the past. Finally, we talked to human beings whom we got to know and like, and not to disembodied voices on the telephone. We instituted a one-for-one exchange between British and U.S. featured performers, which would even out the score over a period of time. There would also be regular meetings and other contacts designed to defuse potential conflicts before they arose.

Not only with British Equity did we establish a more cordial relationship, but with all the other unions as well, especially those in English-speaking countries: Canada, Ireland, New Zealand, and Australia. Years ago, when Canadian stage actors were in negotiations with producers who perceived them as weak, they looked south of the border for help. Having been asked to do so, Actors' Equity in the U.S. came in and took over jurisdiction. By the time I became president, there was a strong Canadian office in Toronto, with branches in Montreal, Winnipeg, and Vancouver. The Canadians had autonomy in negotiating contracts, they collected their own dues, and were basically on their own, but they were tied to U.S. Equity by an umbilical cord. Their decisions had to be ratified by the Council in New York; they were dependent where they should not have been. At the FIA Congress in 1973—my first—the Canadians had to sit under the American flag. It seemed silly to me that these people were able to represent their profession, but not their country. This set me on a course whose outline I submitted to the Canadian branch of Equity. They embraced it wholeheartedly.

I did not believe, nor did they, that Canadian stage actors should have to ask New York for permission each time they wanted to go to the bathroom. I argued for an amicable dissolution of the arrangement, and for the establishment of a separate, independent, and autonomous union to be named Canadian Actors' Equity. I wrote articles, spoke at meetings, and prepared the U.S. membership, who would have to approve the measure in a referendum. It took me well over a year of work, but the separation was approved in 1976, and it gave me a lot of pleasure to present a new independent union from Canada to a meeting of the FIA in Dublin in that same year.

What I enjoyed most about the work with FIA was the opportunity to travel to places I had not previously been, and to do it under the auspices of an organization of fellow professionals. The meeting in 1975 was in East Germany, then called the German Democratic Republic. It was something of a shock to travel from the lights and sounds of the very Western city of Berlin to its dark, austere, and forbidding Eastern counterpart. Although our hosts were doing their best to liven up our stay, it was a bit of a strain. On the first evening they invited us to a get-together in the artists' club Die Möwe (The Seagull). The chairman said: "Zis iss ze first evening togezer. Ve vill akvaint each ozzer viz each ozzer. It vill be informal, colleagues togezzer, *gemütlich*, very informal . . . " Very nice and reassuring to hear our hosts talk like this. But they were also German and so, after the *gemütlich* announcement, he pointed to each of us and continued in a more stentorian tone, "You vill sit here, you here, you here, you here . . . "

Language was apt to create a problem from time to time. Not for me, fortunately, as I was familiar enough with all four of the official languages of FIA (English, French, German, and Spanish) to follow all proceedings in the original. The other participants used earphones, which provided running translations by interpreters. I listened from time to time to enjoy the skill of the interpreters; the good ones have a phenomenal facility, which I envy. A translator is skillful also, but he or she can sit down and worry over the correct word or turn of the phrase before writing anything down. The simultaneous interpreter, especially one who works international conferences, has to do the job on the spot without any time to think. Sometimes things go awry. At the East German meeting the interpreters were good on language, but had a little trouble with technical terms relating to theatre or film. I happened to be listening to the translation when the general secretary, Gerald Croasdell, had just said in his modulated British tones, "In recent years we have had a problem with piracy of phonograph records." The interpreter rendered this into the following: "*In den letzten Jahren hatten wir ein Problem mit dem Diebstahl pornografischer Platten*"—"In recent years we've had a problem with the theft of pornographic records." I sent her a little note: "The word you are looking for is '*Schallplatten.*'"

The late Pierre Boucher of French Canada was president of FIA for three years. During the executive committee's visit to the Soviet Union he was called upon to make a speech or a toast (mostly the latter) in every place the group visited. At a *kolkhoz,* a collective farm, the chairman of the farmers' group welcomed the representatives of the actors of the world in a warm speech. Pierre Boucher started his reply by saying that we had much in common with the assembled farmers of the *kolkhoz.* The actors' group wondered silently what it could be that they had in common with settlers in remote Russia. Boucher continued by way of explanation: "*Nous sommes la culture; vous êtes la cultivation*" (We represent culture and you represent agriculture). An admirable turn of the phrase.

Having acknowledged the ideological differences between East and West, we managed to concentrate on the business at hand: devising the means to act as spokesmen for an international fraternity of actors. Specifically, the Russian and American delegations stressed the factors that united us as professionals and as artists rather than those that divided our two worlds. There were different arenas available for that debate, chiefly the United Nations (although its very name was an oxymoron more often than not). Only seldom did the political debate threaten to intrude on our deliberations, and then it was on account of others who did not regularly participate in the work of the Federation. A Cuban delegation arrived at the 1976 FIA Congress in Vienna. The delegates were a politicized bunch who took none of their text from Shakespeare, Shaw, Chekhov, or Gogol or even José Martí. It was pure Fidel. On the second day of the congress, having asked for the floor, their spokesmen delivered a blistering attack on American imperialism, sparing no epithets and giving vent to rhetoric never before heard among colleagues of the profession. They even lacked sufficient finesse to refer to actors and acting, to live or electronic performances, or anything else that might have served as a departure point from which to veer off on a political tangent. Most of us were outraged at this performance—and not just the Americans. Chester Migden of the Screen Actors Guild, then vice president of the FIA, sat on the dais, his face growing redder until I thought he would explode. When the day's session concluded, I told Chet that I would go and talk to the Russians and the Hungarians, with whom I had formed a good working relationship. I met with the Russian representative, Gennadi Pyatakov, and the Hungarian representatives, Imre Vass and Tibor Mészöly, and told them that what the Cubans had done could not go unanswered. Since the Cubans considered Iron Curtain delegates to be their ideological partners, they might be persuaded by them that a public apology was in order. Unless this was forthcoming, I gave notice that I intended to ask for the floor at tomorrow's session. My people and I considered what the Cubans had done an abuse of an international forum for purposes totally extraneous to the aims of the FIA and designed to disturb the equilibrium we had so carefully nurtured over the years. Gennadi and the Hungarians agreed that what had happened was disruptive. They would see what they could do, they said, but the Cubans were an unpredictable bunch and not easily influenced, even by their friends.

That evening our Austrian hosts invited all the delegates to Grinzing, the suburb of Vienna where the region's new wine is served in a time-honored tradition. There was to be a meal and the local musicians were going to play *Schrammelmusik,* also an Austrian folk tradition. We all went and had a terrific evening. At one point the musicians were told that among our group there was a well-known guitarist and singer from America. They came over, offered me their guitar, and asked me to perform. I took the instrument, sat down at the Cubans' table, and started to play and sing. I sang in various languages that included Spanish and South American songs. After a while they sang along with me, then sang to me, and poured drinks for me to encourage me to sing more. By the end of the evening, I had turned from an imperialist exploiter into a human being with a human voice. At the beginning of the following morning's plenary session the president of FIA, Mme France Delahalle, announced that the Cuban delegate had asked for the floor in order to offer a clarification. He rose and said, in effect, that his remarks of the previous day had been in the nature of a declaration of principle relating to his country's position in the world. As far as FIA was concerned, the Cuban actors' union had only one desire, namely to cooperate fully with all their colleagues, including those from the Western bloc. As he sat down to applause, Pyatakov came over to me and asked, "Do you still want me to talk to them?" I answered, "Nope. It will do." And I sent a message to the dais canceling my scheduled reply.

Most of us in the arts are committed to lively cultural exchange and the free movement of artists between countries. However, we are equally committed to a preservation of national identities, of artistic, cultural, and linguistic integrity within our respective communities. How to maintain the equilibrium between these two notions is surely one of our more important tasks. The hostilities between nations and ethnic or religious groups make it clear that nationalism is the plague and scourge of our time. Violent and ultranationalist movements most surely are. But the desire in most countries not to be overwhelmed by the cultures of stronger and richer nations is understandable. I am afraid that, knowingly or unwittingly, we in the United States have added to the Big Brother syndrome in the arts as well as elsewhere. The airwaves of Canada, Australia, and New Zealand are swamped with filmed shows from the United States. In other parts of the world and in other cultures this also occurs. There is more Swedish TV to be seen in Norway than the other way around; more British TV in Ireland and more Russian in Ukraine. Such situations must be confronted with sanity and wisdom—lest culture become a bone of contention rather than a valuable asset that all peoples may share.

WHEN CHET MIGDEN left his position at the Screen Actors Guild in 1981 and had to resign as vice president of the FIA, I was appointed by the Executive Committee to fill out his term and was elected to the post at the '82 Congress in Paris, reelected in 1985 in Athens, and again in 1988 at the Leningrad Congress. Much to my dismay, Actors' Equity decided in 1991 to disaffiliate from FIA, saying that it was a budgetary move. By then I was president emeritus of Equity and had served as a vice president of FIA for ten years. I passionately argued against this move. In the past I had had many occasions to offer advice and leadership to the Equity Council and the members. While no one could expect that such counsel would always be followed—reasonable human beings often do reasonably disagree—I recall no occasions when the Council so radically and grievously differed from my position. I regretted this ideological change in direction, which was only clumsily disguised as an economic move.

Actors' Equity had been an integral constituent of the International Federation of Actors for over twenty-one years. We had associated with FIA as a conscious commitment to the notion that, precisely because the world was a place of hostile camps and ideologies, actors the world over had more in common with each other's lives, hopes, and aspirations than most men and women in other walks of life had. We also harbored the hope that, in those situations where we found ourselves in disagreement with our colleagues abroad, only good could come from joining an alliance where such differences could be worked out. With supreme shortsightedness the union I had so diligently steered in a direction of global thinking chose to revert to an isolationism unworthy of its past liberal instincts.

I had held my position in FIA by virtue of being a delegate from Actors' Equity. Since I could no longer represent a union that did not wish to be part of the organization, I resigned as vice president of FIA, leaving tasks unfinished. Specifically, I had begun a mammoth survey of live theatre in the face of electronic encroachment. With the approach of a new century—indeed a new millennium—no look forward was valid without a careful look backward. I had always advised doing both. To me, FIA's importance lay in both what it symbolized and what it did, and the existence of FIA has become increasingly urgent with satellites whirring overhead, rapidly turning us into a global village. In the future, in a world rapidly becoming the sole province of technocrats, it is going to be even more important that an international body be in place to safeguard the actor's rights. In a world of chrome, steel, and computer chips, we cannot let ourselves be infected by the cold and impersonal ways that characterize much of the rest of our world. Enthusiasm and the human touch had always been the hallmark of FIA's work, and as long as working actors like myself were part of FIA's leadership, we were able to speak not only as artists, but for artists.

13

Come, Let us Reason Together

The answer to the question "Am I my brother's keeper?" must invariably be "No. I am my brother's brother."

—MARTIN LUTHER KING, JR.

*I*T SEEMS THAT I HAVE CONDUCTED MY LIFE on two different emotional planes: one lighthearted, gregarious, even frivolous; the other politically and socially involved and following a serious social and moral commitment. The activism based on this commitment was not limited to union work or even to the arts.

My involvement with politics in America started almost from the day of my arrival at the airport in New York, possibly even earlier than that. Many of my friends in England had been expatriate Americans who were victims of the mindless political witch-hunt of McCarthyism. I was determined, if I got the chance, to remind America of its own claim to liberalism, as expressed in Jefferson's ringing words, "I have sworn upon the altar of God eternal hostility to every form of tyranny over the mind of Man." This would have been presumptuous had I harbored feelings of superiority as a European, but Europe had too many sins of her own to answer for. Perhaps, like a freshman Congressman, one ought to shut up for a term or two before voicing an opinion. But I was a new American with a stake in the country's well-being. And I became a New Yorker very quickly. With that comes a certain combativeness: In short order you find yourself standing on soapboxes at street corners making campaign speeches without finding it at all strange.

Soon after my first marriage broke up, I rented a small apartment on Waverly Place in Greenwich Village, three doors away from Washington Square Park. My involvement with John F. Kennedy's presidential campaign had been star stuff—going to rallies and holding the crowd until the candidate arrived, making speeches, either short or long, depending on how late Kennedy's schedule ran. After JFK's election I became involved with local Democratic Party politics, specifically in the struggle to return decency to the way the Democratic Party in my district was run. This fight revolved around the attempts to oust an old-line Tammany Hall political machine run from smoke-filled back rooms by a sinister figure named Carmine DeSapio, who gave out patronage jobs all year round and Christmas presents in July to ensure a loyal following in the district. For years he had been unbeatable. But this was a new era, and a rival club of mostly young liberals known as the Village Independent Democrats (VID) decided to challenge DeSapio. The first few times the challenge was unsuccessful, although some other elective positions were wrested away from Carmine's crowd. Yet he himself was a harder nut to crack. By the time I got involved with the VID, they were gearing up for another round. This time DeSapio's opponent was a young lawyer by the name of Edward I. Koch. I was making street-corner speeches throughout the district, extolling the virtues of our candidate. Koch promised an open door and an open ear, in contrast to the back-room dealings of the man who always wore dark glasses indoors and who, instead of gaining your trust, bought it. Lo and behold, in 1963 we prevailed, and Ed Koch was elected district leader. From there he went on to be elected to Congress and eventually, in 1978, he became the flamboyant mayor of New York.

Years later, at a dinner we both attended, Ed Koch told the assembled guests the following story concerning our past association. "Theo Bikel campaigned for me in the Village when I was running my first race. We were on a street corner, Theo was making a speech, talking about my candidacy, citing virtues neither of us knew I had. I was quite enraptured by his eloquence, and so impressed that I was prepared to vote for this fellow Koch myself, any chance I'd get. A lady tapped me on the shoulder and asked, 'Do you like this speech?' I said, 'Yes, very much,' and the lady said with pride, pointing to the speaker, 'That's my son.' I said, 'Oh yeah? Well, that's my friend.'" Ed remembered this incident for years, it seems. In 1988, on my mother's ninetieth birthday, he issued a congratulatory mayoral citation and sent it to her in Israel.

There were other races in which I worked for VID-supported candidates. Bentley Kassal, now a judge, ran unsuccessfully for a seat in Congress. I traveled with him through his district, which cut across various ethnic lines. Part of the problem of promoting his candidacy was his name. "Bentley" sounded so white-bread, nondescript WASP, though *he* was not. I gave him different first names in different areas, calling him Ben-Zion on the Jewish Lower East Side and Benvenuto in the Italian South Village. We had some successes with this approach, although on at least one occasion I was disappointed. An old Jewish lady listened to our pitch and then shook Bentley's hand, saying, "I vish you luck." Then she added, "The other fella vat's running vas here yesterday, and he gave out doughnuts." I said I regretted that we had no doughnuts to give but asked what she thought of the "other fella." She said: "I took by him the doughnuts and vished him luck, too."

John Lindsay started his political life as a liberal Republican, which at one time I thought to be an oxymoron, but which certainly did exist if one takes note of the positions espoused from time to time by such politicians as Senator Jacob Javits of New York, Senator Lowell Weicker of Connecticut, or Senator William Cohen of Maine. I quite liked Lindsay even when he was a Republican for his support of the arts alone. When, in 1969, he switched parties and became a Democrat before his reelection campaign for mayor of New York he asked me to help him. There was absolutely no question—of course I would. With John Lindsay one could not play any name games; ethnics would have to be convinced that he was a good guy, not necessarily one of their own group, but that he deserved support anyway. I recall flying with him in a helicopter from Gracie Mansion to Long Island and landing in a meadow, where thousands of people were attending a Jewish festival. I made an introductory speech, all in Yiddish, and offered to translate the candidate's speech into Yiddish, which I did.

Despite his Brahmin appearance, Lindsay's appeal cut across ethnic and class divisions. I had chatted with the taxi driver who brought me up to Gracie Mansion before the flight, and asked him whom he supported for mayor. New York cabbies always gripe about the mayor.

This one did not. When I got to the mansion I told Lindsay that I had just talked to a taxi driver who actually supported him for reelection. He thought the driver must have been either a youngster with long hair or else black. I said he had been neither, but I was sure that he was going to attend a meeting of "cab drivers for Lindsay" at five o'clock at Grand Central Station, in the third telephone booth from the right.

I had lived in the Village continuously since 1957, first on Waverly Place, then at Washington Square Village, and after 1967 in the house Rita and I had bought on Bank Street. After our second son, Danny, was born in the spring of 1971, we decided to move away from New York City. What was attractive and exciting about it—mostly the theatre and the other cultural events—remained so. But it was also oppressive. You had to lock yourself in when you were in and out when you were out. When you took a baby for a stroll, you often came back with soot covering the baby carriage. It was time to move to cleaner air and safer surroundings. So we bought a house in Connecticut, and sold the Bank Street one. One of the newspapers reported that Theodore Bikel was moving. The next day I got a call from Mayor Lindsay: "Theo, is it true what I read? You are moving away from the city?" "True," I said. "Do you know what kind of an animal leaves a sinking ship?" he asked. "Yes, John," I said. "I'll grant you what kind of an animal it is if you'll grant me that it's a sinking ship." He laughed.

Even though I was no longer a New York resident, my involvement with the city and the state continued. After all, the theatre never moved out of New York City, nor did my desire to see that the city remained a place where the arts would flourish. If that meant continued involvement with politics, that was one of the necessities of the process. Labor and the arts had to form alliances with city and state government.

Earlier, in the late fifties and early sixties, I had become very active in the civil rights movement. Then it was a unified effort, in contrast to the polarized community of the post-seventies, when suspicion kept whites and blacks apart, even those who had previously been allies. "Black and white together" goes the second verse of "We Shall Overcome." We sang it and we meant it. We needed each other. Blacks realized that if the goal of racial equality could be attained at all, it would be reached far less quickly without white allies. Liberal whites needed the movement in order to reassure themselves that it was not just good talk, that they were taking concrete steps to bring nearer to attainment the goal of social justice. Some political commentators would scoff at the efforts of white liberals and accuse them of patronizing blacks. Gossip columnists would write up fund-raising parties given at the houses of rich white supporters such as Leonard Bernstein and call it "radical chic." Blacks themselves were not always sanguine about these efforts, for they were rightly suspicious of any hint of paternalism. In my case, there was no need to harbor such suspicions. I had never treated the civil rights movement as a fad. I did not consider it a mere abstraction. I truly believed in equality, and was intent on working for it to become a concrete reality.

With all of that there was the danger of misreading the thrust of the movement and making its activism a goal instead of the means to an end. There is a certain malady that afflicts many advocates of change. Freedom marchers turn into freedom fighters, often resorting to shortcuts that invariably involve violent means. The danger is that young people who resort to such means start by being in love with justice and end up in love with revolution—with the excitement of the fight. Not that I ever advocated gradualism; where the needs are pressing, the fight must be waged with all due urgency. But one cannot preach peace, hold the barrel of a gun, and declare a belief in non-violence all at the same time. In the beginning, the civil rights movement avoided the trap because its leading ideologue and spokesman had taken his inspiration from Mahatma Gandhi's movement in India, who waged a campaign for independence by strictly nonviolent means. Despite his espousal of nonviolence, Martin Luther King Jr. was a forceful leader, never cowed by the white power structure nor able to be co-opted by them. Others within the movement, however, believed in applying more force than Dr. King's prescription allowed. Although they paid homage to his position within the movement as they met with him in the loosely confederated circle of civil rights leaders, differences in attitude and style began to emerge. From the oldest of these organizations, the National Association for the Advancement of Colored People (NAACP), to Dr. King's own Southern Christian Leadership Conference (SCLC), to the Congress of Racial Equality (CORE), and the youngest such body, the Student Nonviolent Coordinating Committee (SNCC), differences in tone and substance could be discerned.

I was attracted to SNCC for several reasons. First, although they were younger than my generation, I felt close to them because of my involvement with folk music, which in the fifties and sixties seemed to be the province of the young and had played a role in progressive political movements. Second, SNCC activism revolved around voter registration drives in the South, a move toward empowerment of blacks, seeking to make them able to participate in the political process that had hitherto excluded them. The integration of public facilities—restaurants, drinking fountains, rest rooms, and beaches—was something all the organizations fought for; but the voter registration drive was one of SNCC's primary objectives, and that appealed to my view that the black community needed a tactical first step in order to be drawn into the political process. When I was approached by SNCC representatives with a request for help, I readily responded. In early 1963 I took part in meetings to establish a support group, Friends of SNCC. One such meeting took place in the office of Rabinowitz and Boudin on East Forty-second Street, and several others were held in my apartment in Washington Square Village. Even though some of the people attending these meetings had great political experience, we were mostly older—and white—and made no attempt to influence policy. We offered support and advice and helped raise funds. (The group included John Simon, a book publisher; Sarah Schoenkopf [later Sarah Kovner], closely associated with Reform Democratic clubs; Victor Rabinowitz, attorney; Teresa del Pozzo, Harlem Education Project; Michael Standard and William Mahoney, attorneys; and my secretary, Alice Conklin.)

I did a little more than that. Press conferences were held in my apartment with SNCC leaders in attendance. I felt that there was no substitute for hearing the story of discrimination and persecution first-hand from the mouths of those who had experienced them. Of the older black leaders present, there was Ella Baker of Atlanta, long an integral part of the movement; James Foreman, also of Atlanta, later to become chairman of SNCC; Chuck McDew, one of SNCC's first chairmen; Avon Rollins, Ruby Doris Smith, Robert Whitfield, and leaders from such other places as Knoxville, Tennessee, and Pine Bluff, Arkansas. Some of the students who appeared at the press conferences held at my place later achieved some prominence. Among them were John Lewis of Nashville, Tennessee, later to be a congressman from Georgia, and Marion Barry, who eventually achieved a considerable amount of notoriety as mayor of Washington, D.C.

When I made my first trip south on behalf of SNCC I was somewhat apprehensive. I would put myself in harm's way by doing something that, while absolutely logical and moral to me, when judged by local standards would open me to public attacks and likely even to prosecution: meeting with blacks as equals, eating with them, talking with them as one American to other Americans. At this point it was not even going to be a protest action but merely a get-together to discuss things. Nor was it being held in the deep Deep South; Atlanta was an urban center whose white inhabitants, one presumed, were not all members of the Ku Klux Klan. Still, it was a little scary, upon arrival at the airport, to be stared at by the locals solely because the people who met me at the gate were black. Even my travel companion, who had sat next to me and made pleasant chitchat all the way down from New York, looked at me askance as though he had suddenly discovered something sinister about me.

That we were in the South, urban sophistication or no, was evident from the fact that we met in the only hotel that in 1963 permitted both blacks and whites to rent rooms and to mingle socially. In the Peachtree Motel on—where else?—Peachtree Road, I was greeted by a number of black student leaders, some of whom looked harassed, tired, not too well fed, but determined to press on as the cause demanded. The youngest among them was Julian Bond; he looked no older than nineteen or twenty, although he was a few years older than that. Julian was SNCC's press secretary and public relations person. He looked somewhat out of place: too studious, too urbane, a little impatient with the slowness of the process, slowed even more by the ritual of having to woo allies like myself. It took me a little while and very little effort to make him realize that I did not need much wooing. Information was what I did need, and he was most capable in supplying it. Some five years later that same Julian Bond was actually nominated from the floor of the 1968 Democratic National Convention to run for vice president, which he had to decline because even then he had not yet reached the venerable age of thirty-five mandated by law for such a candidacy. But in 1963 he was still very much the college graduate, a black student activist, seeking to give America a new face.

At subsequent trips and at other meetings in New York, Chicago, and Los Angeles, I worked with older leaders and gave assistance to other segments of the civil rights movement. The Reverend Wyatt Tee Walker of Harlem influenced my thinking and broadened the scope of my awareness; he was the closest ally Dr. King had in the Northeast. The Reverend Andrew Young and I attended meetings and a three-day seminar in Atlanta concerned with freedom songs. Andy later became U.S. ambassador to the United Nations and, later still, mayor of Atlanta. And, of course, I was able to participate in mass meetings at churches and protest marches with Martin Luther King Jr. himself.

Birmingham, Alabama, was one of the worst places for civil rights activity. Its police chief, aptly named "Bull" Connor, made life miserable for blacks who dared ask for equal rights and equal access. He was even more incensed about "Northern nigger-lovers" who supported such demands and who made the trek to Birmingham to make common cause with the blacks. The fact that some of those whites were not from the North at all never stopped him from calling them so; he refused to admit that whites from the South were capable of such treasonous acts. It was in Birmingham that I spoke and sang at my first mass meeting in a black church. It was also in Birmingham that I was arrested with other civil rights marchers. At the church I did something which I know had never been done before and I am sure has not been done since. My presence there was as much due to my instincts as an American as it was a result of an almost atavistic memory of a Jew. The black choir had sung "Freedom!" and "Justice!" When I took the microphone I sang one of my father's Jewish socialist songs. I sang in the original Yiddish and my own English translation. I had no way of knowing whether the unfamiliar words and tune would—or could—evoke anything in this audience. But I did it and after it was over they rose to greet me as the brother I had hoped to demonstrate I was.

> Un Du akerst un Du zeyst, Un Du fiterst un Du Meyst,
> Un Du hamerst un Du shpinst, Zog mayn Folk vos Du fardinst.
> Brothers you that plow and sow, you that feed and you that mow,
> wield your hammer night and day, tell me if your sweat is worth the pay
> Cling-clong, cling-clong, listen to the hammer's song
> Cling-clong, cling-clong, we'll break the yoke, boys, it won't be long.

> Who prepares your evening meal, and who cares what grief you feel,
> When you die, will someone mourn; to what purpose, tell me, were you born?
> Now awake, the end's in sight, see your power, feel your might,
> Were it not for your strong hand, not a wheel could turn in all the land.

In the jail, they separated us, blacks in one section and whites in the other. Segregation even there. They were also cute about our treatment. They let the other white prisoners know that we were a bunch of "nigger-lovers"—and these thieves and rapists suddenly felt superior. They also surmised that no one would stop them if they roughed us up. Sure enough, they did just that. We got no help from the sheriff's people. In the first place, it would not have helped because we were set up for this kind of treatment by the cops themselves. They were the enemy and it would have been humiliating to call on them to rescue us from the yahoos. We did manage to help each other. We also managed to buoy our spirits by singing. The black freedom marchers were across the courtyard and we could hear each other as we sang. That helped.

When traveling in the Mississippi Delta we had an additional problem. The SNCC people were mostly black, and to be seen in a car that had blacks and whites traveling together was an open invitation for the cops to chase us, stop us, issue tickets, and even put people in jail for no reason at all. Consequently, when the blacks drove, we would lie down in the back seat or flat on the floor of the automobile. Then we would take turns driving and the blacks took our places on the floor. Accommodation at night was another problem that often had no solution. I found it ironic that in some Southern places where there was a Jewish community, I had to sleep on a bench in a church. Southern Jews had almost as little understanding of the moral precept underlying my commitment to civil rights as the others. Even where there might have been a little sympathy, it was overshadowed by fear. I remember seeking out the local rabbi in one such community and arguing with him, saying that in my opinion he had an obligation of moral leadership toward his congregation. I quoted to him the biblical commandment about safeguarding the strangers in your midst; I reminded him that Moses had taken a black wife. My efforts were unsuccessful. Although the rabbi was a Northerner and had studied at the Jewish Theological Seminary in New York, he asked me to understand his position. Unlike a Catholic priest, whose marching orders come from his superiors in the church, a rabbi is hired—and fired—by the congregation. It would do little good if he preached the courageous sermon as I had asked him to, only to find himself in the street looking for another position.

Traveling as a concert performer in the South rather than as a civil rights activist, I had a little better luck. For a number of years my regular accompanist was a black bass player named Bill Lee. He was a diminutive man, shorter than his instrument. He was married and had small children—among them a son, Spike, who would eventually become a famous film director. At one time Bill and I were scheduled to perform at an Orthodox synagogue in Savannah, Georgia, truly the Deep South. As in most Orthodox synagogues, the women's section was upstairs, separated from the men. The concert was to be held in the sanctuary, and I was to perform on the main pulpit or *bimah*. When word got around that Bikel would be appearing accompanied by a black man, many members of the congregation were up in arms and went to see the rabbi. "What can we do to prevent this black man from setting foot on our *bimah?*" they asked. To his credit, the rabbi answered, "The only circumstance under which I could prevent him from standing on the *bimah* would be if he's a woman." An answer that, although satisfactory at the time, would be upsetting to feminists.

But then, so would the entire system of separating men from women in Orthodox houses of worship.

Bill and I were performing at another time in North Carolina. Civil rights legislation had been passed nationally, but many places either had not heard about it or pretended not to have. After we had checked in at our hotel, I told Bill that I was hungry and that I thought we might have a bite in the coffeeshop downstairs. Bill looked a little startled. "Come on," he said "you want to start an incident? This is the South." "Do I want to start an incident? No," I said, "I want a hamburger and I think you should have one, too." He shrugged and we went downstairs. The hostess in the coffeeshop looked at me, then at Bill, her eyes full of apprehension. She was at least one head taller than Bill, but she looked as though she thought he was about to do her bodily harm. I told her that I had phoned from upstairs for a table, and after she had reluctantly seated us she asked me what I would like to have. I ordered a hamburger and coffee. Then she said to me: "Very well, sir, and what would *he* like to have?" This with a head motion toward Bill. "Well, let's ask him, shall we?" I said. "He does speak English, although he is an African diplomat." Bill looked almost as surprised and shocked as the hapless woman, but she did talk to him directly without me as an interpreter.

Some of my folksinging colleagues were as involved in the civil rights movement as I was. Some even more so: Pete Seeger and Guy Carawan, for example, who hit on the ingenious idea of copyrighting what became the anthem of the movement, "We Shall Overcome," for which they had written additional text. If the song, originally an old gospel tune, had remained in the public domain, no monies would have been collectable the thousands of times the tune was played on the air. As it was, the royalties were paid to Guy and Pete, who turned them all over to the coffers of the movement. In the early sixties there were hardly any singers who were not devoted to the cause, who did not sing of justice and freedom. Those who wrote songs in the folk vein drew heavily on the theme and got much of their inspiration from the reports of maltreatment and suffering emanating from the South. When I was invited to travel to a mass meeting organized by SNCC in Greenwood, Mississippi, in the middle of the Delta, I thought it might be a good idea to bring along some others who had not witnessed what I had seen with my own eyes. Since Bob Dylan had begun to emerge as a major songwriter with a liberal conscience, I mentioned to Al Grossman, Bob's manager, that Dylan would benefit greatly if he went with me to Mississippi. Al agreed, but since everyone had to pay for his own passage, he said he doubted that Bob could afford it. I thought it was important enough for Bobby to go, so I paid for his trip. We took a night flight down to Jackson, Mississippi; it would be easier for us to be picked up by the SNCC people and driven to Greenwood under cover of night. On the way down Bob scribbled furiously, writing lyrics on the backs of old envelopes. I suggested to him that he might want to wait; I was certain that different lyrics would flow from his mind and his pen on the return trip.

Much to my dismay, SNCC underwent a change after the first few years, when Stokely Carmichael took over the reins of the organization. I recall his first visit to my apartment in New York, and a trip to Larchmont to a meeting of Friends of SNCC at the house of Max Youngstein, then the head of United Artists. The conversation was friendly, but I felt an underlying tension. Stokely seemed to be worrying about something: either the usurpation of leadership by the white supporters—a totally groundless fear—or a resentment that there had to be an association with whites at all. It never occurred to me at the time that this was also the beginning of a new orientation that was directed against Jews. Most of the white Northern allies the movement had were Jewish liberals. It became evident after a while that this wing of the civil rights movement was espousing the theory of the Third World being pitted against the rest. The Middle East figured in this scenario: Israel represented an "imperialist power" and an oppressor, and so blacks had to side with Arabs against Israel. For a while I had hopes that this phase of spouting arrant political nonsense would give way to enlightened dialogue. But instead of getting better, it got worse. Finally, in 1967, SNCC engaged in openly violent actions in the ghettos, which most often hurt innocent blacks, and continued to commit excesses much against the advice of Dr. King and most other responsible leaders. The "Nonviolent" Coordinating Committee's new motto was "Burn, baby, burn." The last straw for me came when SNCC published a newsletter that contained a monstrous depiction of Jews, likening them to Nazis. I had had enough, and decided to sever my ties with SNCC. On August 16, 1967, I wrote an open letter that was carried in the press, including the black newspapers. It is a long letter, but it conveys what I and many others felt at the time, our anger and our frustration. Here are portions of it:

> You know me well. Or ought to. I am the fellow who, long before it was fashionable and safe, followed SNCC's call for help and advice. I am the man who helped organize money and bodies at the bidding of Jim Foreman, Robert Moses, Chuck McDew and John Lewis; who went to Alabama and Mississippi

because SNCC needed his presence; who slept in a different loft each night because he would not sleep or eat where his black[1] brother could not and because the sheriff resented his presence. I am the man who was called "kike nigger-lover" both to his face and in print.

You owe me nothing.

I did what I did as a commitment of conscience, a commitment that is as real to me now as it was then and one which will continue as long as I breathe.

But you owe yourselves an appraisal of recent actions and recent pronouncements. You who spoke of a "philosophical concept" behind your position on "Jewish oppressors" owe both friend and foe a clearer definition of such "philosophy." It appears from your statement that you have arrived at your position after exhaustive research which took you as far afield as the Arab embassies and the Atlanta Public Library. . . .

Let us briefly consider the "illegal" state of Israel. Palestine was, from 1922 until 1948, a British mandate which gave the Jewish people the *political right* to reestablish Palestine as a Jewish state. It was neither a gift of land to the Jews nor did it take land from the Arabs. Lands were purchased—at heavily excessive prices—from their holders. *Never in all history had Palestine been an Arab state.* Turkish yes, British yes, and certainly, from time immemorial, Jewish. . . .

You seriously assert that the destinies of Arabs and blacks are intertwined. You are, of course, perfectly correct. . . . Your own ancestors would hardly have arrived on these shores had it not been for the beneficence and diligence of Arab slave traders. . . .

I wonder if your researchers ever bothered to inquire from whence came the help and support for [emerging black African] countries in the days of their struggle? Whether it was Arabs or Israelis who trained engineers, craftsmen and builders, seamen and teachers? Ask who almost single-handedly built Ghana's merchant marine; ask whether emerging black Africa looked to Cairo or Tel Aviv for their "bond of friendship and brotherhood."

To top it all, you found yourselves actually capable of repeating the obscene comparison between Israelis and German Nazis replete with hideous caricatures worthy of the finest anti-Semitic

1. The letter referred to African Americans as Negroes, which was used in those days by the black community as the preferred descriptive word. In this text I have substituted the word "black."

pamphlet. I feel nothing but contempt for such irresponsible behavior. It insults the memory of the martyrs who perished in the mass slaughters; it also insults the dreams and hopes of their sons and heirs who built a home, a refuge, and resisted being "pushed into the sea." Their crime seems to have been that they resisted their annihilation successfully. Had the "holy war" called for by Nasser and accomplices succeeded, you might have joined the list of those offering condolences for yet another genocide— for the annihilation would have been total, make no mistake.

I am an American. I am a Jew. Thus I have a commitment, doubly reinforced by historical and moral commandments. I am determined to make equality and freedom a reality in this country, no matter what the setbacks. I am equally determined to honor the bonds of my ethnic and religious background. You have this day attempted to violate both my commitments. . . .

You may want to spit in my face for being "Whitey." But do not look to me for silence while you insult the memory of my people so recently martyred; you have no right to tamper with their graves. And think of Mickey Schwerner and Andy Goodman. You have no right to heap insult on their graves either; they died for a concept which you now cover with shame.[2]

That you have for some time past made a mockery of the word "nonviolent" in your name, both in word and in deed, was inadequately defended by the facile explanation of "violence begetting violence, chaos begetting chaos." . . . I supported Black Power as a political concept; as a tool of anarchy I find it reprehensible. Not that the concept of revolution is in itself frightening. . . .

What is frightening is a revolution without a blueprint. If it's a case of "Get-Whitey-first-and-worry-about-planning-later," then the tactic seems both stupid and dangerous. The assumption that, by definition, all whites are enemies and all blacks are friends is as simplistic as it is untrue.

What you have wrought in this latest of a long line of missteps will be with us for a long time to come. It will not deter those among us who are secure in the knowledge that the movement is bigger than your pronouncements and that it speaks responsibly and with reason. But many thousands not so secure will in bewilderment withdraw support from all civil rights

2. Three students, James Chaney, Michael Schwerner, and Andrew Goodman, were murdered while on a civil rights mission in 1963. Chaney was black, the other two were Jews.

causes because of your incontinence and folly. Thus once again you will have harmed no one but the cause of black equality itself.

With this letter I formally severed my ties with SNCC.

I hoped to convey two overriding messages in my letter. The first one was that no people can win the fight for its dignity while trampling on that of another. And second, it carried a strong suggestion that the student movement be guided by the motto "Seek justice, not revenge." My letter generated some heat in the civil rights community. The reaction from SNCC was expected. They suddenly denied that I had had much to do with them—some even went as far as to claim that there had been no connection at all. It is not possible to resign from an organization of which you had not been a member in the first place, so they said. Instead of addressing themselves to the issues I had raised, they concentrated on attacking the messenger. Of course, no one from Stokely on down had a membership card to show, but that did not bother those who rallied to the defense of SNCC. One of them was Julius Lester, a broadcaster on WBAI and a onetime ally of mine in organizing the folk field. His broadside was particularly saddening to me, as I had known him to be a scholarly and intellectual person. But what I had written obviously riled him, as it did other members of the Student—now not so—Nonviolent Coordinating Committee. Ironically, some years later, that same Julius Lester would undergo a profound change and become an orthodox Jew. Other black leaders such as Dr. King and Bayard Rustin reacted positively to my letter since they had themselves been critical of recent SNCC pronouncements and the organization's new policy. I offered my support to them and remained active in the movement as I had promised.

I had occasion to ponder the cause of black liberation in a different context when I was cast in the film *Sands of the Kalahari*, which was being shot in South-West Africa, then under South African rule (and much later to become independent as Namibia). Stanley Baker, the producer and star of the film, had arranged a location that to me was a source of fascination and of fear. South-West Africa, formerly German Southwest Africa, was a protectorate whose administration was given by the League of Nations to South Africa after the defeat of Germany in World War I. The main indigenous tribes were the Hereros, mostly cattle herders, who had suffered massacres at the hands of the Germans, and the Ovambos, mostly barely subsistent agricultural farmers. Some smaller tribes, Hottentots and Bushmen, inhabited the desert areas, neither of them Bantus but vaguely linked anthropologically to Australian aborigines. None of them fared well at the hands of the white South African government, whose apartheid rules were as rigidly enforced in this territory as they were in South Africa itself. The fact that they were merely caretakers did not bother the Boer-dominated authorities at all. On numerous occasions there had been attempts to intercede with the United Nations, the heir to the now defunct League of Nations and presumptive inheritor of the League's functions and authority. Although the UN had requested that South Africa relinquish its role in administering South-West Africa, the orders were ignored, and the indigenous blacks continued to be oppressed.

This continued to be the situation in the area when I was invited to take part in a project that would take me to South-West Africa. I did not go there uninformed. Some years earlier it had become evident that the government was blocking any attempt of the local Hereros and Ovambos to plead their case abroad by refusing any representative of theirs an exit permit. Allard K. Lowenstein, then on Senator Hubert Humphrey's staff, took a leave of absence and traveled to South West (as the locals called it) for the purpose of documenting the situation and bringing the voice of the area's unrepresented blacks to the United Nations. Lowenstein pretended to be a geologist on a scientific mission in this area rich in mineral deposits; under this guise he made clandestine contacts with black leaders and also with the few sympathetic whites in the territory. Luckily, no one questioned his credentials or knowledge of geology (which was all but nonexistent) and he managed to leave the country with extraordinary accounts of violations by the government of South Africa. Eventually he carried those to the U.N., together with an urgent plea for independence. Following his moving plea, a bust of the Herero chief, Hosea Kutako, was placed in the delegates' lounge of the world body. Al Lowenstein also wrote a book about his experiences which he titled *Brutal Mandate*. I took this to be required reading prior to my departure. I was determined to contact some of the tribespeople Al had met and of whom he had written in the book. However, I could not take the book with me for reference; it had been banned both in South Africa and South West just as soon as it was published. Still, I needed the names and also some of the meeting places he had described. I hit upon an idea: I made notes for myself, copying down everything I felt I needed in Hebrew script, which I was sure no apartheid supporter would be able to read.

I had a moment or two of fear when we arrived in Johannesburg, the point of entry prior to continuing to Windhoek, the capital of

South-West Africa. Of all the passengers on our chartered South African Airways plane, with only members of the cast and crew aboard, I was singled out and asked to follow a policemen to a back room, where I was confronted by two very blond and very dour-looking Afrikaners. "Mr. Bijkel," they said, pronouncing it in the Dutch-Afrikaans manner, "Mr. Bijkel, we've taken your passport." *Oh boy,* I thought, *here it comes.* I waited. There was a long pause, too long for comfort. "We've taken your passport," they repeated. As nonchalantly as I could I said, "Yes?" Another long pause while they stared. Then, unaccountably, the taller one said, "Well, here it is," and handed me the document. To this day I do not know what that was all about.

Windhoek presented another kind of surprise. Previously the capital of German Southwest Africa, it retained a lot of German in its character and even in the street names. I was shocked to discover that one of its main thoroughfares was named Göringstrasse. When I inquired of an older local resident whether it could be possible that the city had named a street by honoring that infamous Nazi pig, he quickly sought to reassure me, "No, no; the street was named after his uncle." Also incongruously, the mayor of Windhoek was Jewish, Levinson by name; his official residence was in a castlelike structure named Heinitzburg. I was invited to this house by dint of the fact that my name was not unknown to the Jewish community even in this remote part of Africa. Mrs. Olga Levinson, the mayor's wife, was an accommodating hostess who had a penchant for the arts and had had a book published. After I had spent a few weeks in the area, working on the film in the small coastal town of Swakopmund, I returned to Windhoek for a few days when the shooting schedule allowed me free time. It was then that I seized the opportunity to contact the black leaders whose names I had copied from Al Lowenstein's book. In this Mrs. Levinson became an unwitting accomplice.

Taking my cue from Lowenstein, I too resorted to a ruse in order to make contact. My pretext was more legitimate than Al's. I told Mrs. Levinson that as a folklorist I was very interested in recording indigenous black music, specifically of the Herero tribe. I had previously talked on the telephone with Clemens Kapuuo, the only Herero who had a telephone. He was the deputy leader of the tribe and was permitted to have a phone because he ran a small provision store and had pleaded for a telephone so that he could order merchandise from white suppliers. He, too, had been prominently referred to in *Brutal Mandate.* From him I learned that the tribe would be meeting on Sunday morning after church, and that much singing would be going on. He suggested that if I could manage to get to the native enclave at around that time, he could arrange for me to slip away and see Chief Kutako for a brief meeting.

Olga Levinson was prepared to drive me and my tape recorder to get to the native area, normally closed to whites and especially to foreigners. She herself was not keen to sit in on the singing session, and suggested that she remain in her car while I went about my business. That suited me just fine. We were admitted to the compound easily because Mrs. Levinson and her car were recognized by the guards; the requirement for an official pass was ignored. True to her word, she let me go in alone and remained waiting in the vehicle with a book she had brought along. I lugged my tape recorder—in those days a heavy and bulky affair—into the large meeting hut and was greeted by Clemens Kapuuo, my telephone contact, a very handsome and relatively young black man in casual Western attire. He was the tribal chief's lieutenant and also, I learned, his heir apparent. At first I did exactly what I claimed I had come to do: I recorded the singing, which was indeed lovely but, incongruously, more Christian than tribal. The missionaries had been at work in the area for many years. After a while, I was taken out by a back way and led through a maze of huts to a slightly larger hut than those we had passed on the way. Inside was Chief Hosea Kutako. He had been extremely eloquent in his pleas for United Nations help six years earlier, when Allard had met with him. Now he was some ninety-six years old and very frail. He sat on a mat on the ground surrounded by men almost as old as he; they were attended by old women who put before them cold drinks, fruit, small cakes, and what looked to be dried meat.

My guide, who acted as interpreter, said a few words to the chief by way of introduction. The old man nodded wearily. This was my cue; I said, "I wanted to come and pay my respects." He replied, "You have come in peace. Very few white men do." Then, searching for something that would be within the chief's ken and link our two so very different worlds, I continued, "The greetings I bring you from America are the good wishes of a wise and great leader, Dr. Martin Luther King." As this was translated, there was a flicker of recognition. He mumbled a phrase of thanks. I looked around the hut and was greatly saddened at the poverty I saw there. I was even more saddened by the obvious atmosphere of despair. I added, "Sir, I hope the next time we see each other will be a time of greater freedom for you and your people." The old man, half blind, looked up and said something which, as it was translated, brought a lump to my throat. He said: "When will that be? I am an old man and I'm about to die." He motioned for me to sit and partake of the food and drink. We sat in silence for a while, and then I caught my guide's eye. He nodded; I rose, the old man shook my hand in a feeble grip, and we left, going back to the meeting tent by the same route we had come. I rejoined Olga Levinson in her car and told her that the music had been terrific—which was no lie—and that I was grateful to her for giving me the opportunity to listen and record it. She never found out the real purpose of my visit.

A few years later, Clemens Kapuuo was murdered by some white radicals who wanted to prevent his leadership of the tribe.

Murder and mayhem, destruction and death. More than anyone else, the meek and peaceable, the preachers of nonviolence and coexistence, reaped a harvest tragically different from the seed they spread.

14

I Sing and I'll Keep Singing

Je chante si je chante
Pour qui veut m'écouter
Je chante, je m'invente
Une autre vérité
Elle semble utopique
Elle existe pourtant
Je la mets en musique
Pour la dire en chantant.

I sing and I'll keep singing
To all who'll listen to me
With words that are stinging
As all truth has to be
I'll make music a measure
To tell right from wrong
To give pain and give pleasure
And I'll do it in song.
I sing of the great promise
Which nobody will keep,
Of a wish for noble dreaming
When there's only dreamless sleep.
I sing of desperation
and I've never known despair
Of hope and expectation
When there's hardly any there.

—Georges Moustaki © 1975
English adaptation T. Bikel

In the beginning I was drawn to folk music because of its story-telling aspect, because this was the musical tradition I was brought up in, and maybe also because my musical aptitude did not extend to more involved and sophisticated styles. Had it not been for folk songs

I might soon have become a man out of his time and place. I stayed around for a long, long time in the midst of movements that mandated contacts not only with civil rights workers and labor, but with people many years younger than I. As a political liberal, I would have been involved with allies in the movement anyway, but because of the music I could do it without regard to any generation gap. Folk music made possible a fusion between the artist and activist in me.

Back in the sixties, there were several major songwriters who dealt specifically with political events. One was Tom Paxton, who still continues to be extraordinarily productive, albeit not exclusively in the broadside vein. Another was a young man named Phil Ochs. Phil's pain from what he read and saw resulted in a prolific flow of lyrics from his pen and of music from his guitar. He would come to my apartment and sing for me his latest songs. I was often struck by the thought that he could not possibly keep on with these raw feelings without psychologically coming to grief. Little did I know that he would come to even greater harm than that. Occasionally I would sing his songs to people who were not familiar with Phil Ochs and the songs made quite an impact. One time I was a guest in Senator Gaylord Nelson's house in Maryland when Hubert Humphrey came to visit. I decided to sing Phil's song "I Ain't Marchin' Anymore" and wondered how the guests would take it. They applauded heartily, but I also saw some disturbed looks in their eyes, as though I had broached a subject that might better have been avoided in polite society.

With time Phil Ochs became embittered. Perhaps one should have had an inkling of what was going through his mind when, sometime around 1964, with John Kennedy dead and buried, he said to Bob Dylan, "Politics, it's all bullshit, man. That's all it is. If somebody was to tell the truth, they're gonna be killed." Phil Ochs was a man who had dreams and a vision of a just society. Then he gave up on the dream and went and took his own life. He was right to have had the dream: How tragic that he lost it.

We all treat grief in different fashions. The day JFK was shot, I arrived in Boston after an overnight flight from California, preparing to do a concert that evening. Mike Scott, my road manager, called my room and told me to switch on the TV. I will not describe the horror; every single one of us who lived through those hours has his own recollection of them, if he has not blotted it out of his memory as I did for a long time. But we also had a decision to make. Manny Greenhill, the local promoter, called to consult with me on what to do about the concert. Should we cancel, and if we did, how could we notify patrons in such a short time? I told him to meet me at the hall an hour before the announced start and we would decide then. Around seven o'clock I went to the concert hall and saw that many of the people there were milling around restlessly. They all knew what had happened, but had come nonetheless, if for no other purpose than not to be alone. I made a decision. I told Manny that I would go through with the concert if he would agree to turn over all the proceeds to the civil rights movement, as I would do with my portion. For good measure, Bill Lee, my bass player, said that he would do the same with his fee. When the audience was in their seats, I spoke briefly of the tragedy and said that the reason we decided to perform was that we could all share something this evening. I told them that all the money would go to the cause of which our murdered president had been such a champion. Then I proceeded to sing songs not from my regular repertoire, many of which I had to dredge up from memory. It was my way, I told the audience, of saying kaddish.

THE NEWPORT FOLK FESTIVAL continued to grow through the early sixties. Although every performer was on an equal footing at the festival, there were undisputed stars. Joan Baez was the darling of the folk world: Wherever she went, crowds would follow. She did not behave like a star; in fact she often did very simple and disarmingly human things. For example, when she arrived at the festival with her parents, her sister and brother-in-law Mimi and Richard Fariña, and two other people, they all piled out of a hearse. The story was that Joan had called a friend to say that she did not know how she would get all these people down from Boston to Newport in one small automobile. The friend suggested that she rent a "Hertz." That she did arrive in a hearse is absolutely true; the explanation may be merely apocryphal, but it is too good not to be kept alive.

If Joan Baez was the queen of the Newport Festival, then Bob Dylan was—at least the first time they appeared together—the prince consort. It did not take long for him to carve out his own eminence; the reputation he had acquired in the Village and the acclaim of his early recordings guaranteed that.

Like the work of Tom Paxton and Phil Ochs, Bob Dylan's early work concerned itself with social issues. "Blowing in the Wind" and "The Times They Are A-changing" are two prime examples of Dylan's preoccupation with themes of injustice and the need for change. The metamorphosis he underwent later, when he "went electric," was heralded as the "real Dylan," somehow denigrating the earlier work as less valid. The truth, as I saw it, was that it was all the "real Dylan." Of course, he was no stranger to denials of former self; I do not recall any mention of Bob Zimmerman from Hibbing, Minnesota, in any of Dylan's public utterances. Worse yet, there was no hint of the world of Zimmerman in the work of Dylan. When talking to students about Jewish identity, I used to describe Dylan as a perfect example of a functional amnesiac. An actual amnesiac has no memory of any past, a functional one behaves as though, for all intents and purposes, there were no memory. In later years Dylan vacillated, sometimes acknowledging Jewish roots and then walking away from them. There is a published photo of Dylan donning a yarmulke at the Western Wall in Jerusalem. During that period, he was quoted as saying that Israel seemed to be "one of the few places left in the world where life has any meaning" (*Bob Dylan,* by Anthony Scaduto). He also toyed with Chassidism but later wrote and recorded a series of born-again Christian songs. He even received a Grammy Award for this album. My friend and former manager, Harold Leventhal, was present at the Grammy ceremony. After the award for the Christian album was presented to Bob Dylan, Harold walked over to Dylan's table, put out his hand, and said, "*Mazel tov!*"

Back in 1962, Dylan had been considered a promising young performer and songwriter. By the following year he was a full-fledged star, or as close to one as the folk world would permit. At the 1963 festival, the closing number was not the traditional "Good Night Irene" or "This Land Is Your Land"; at the finale we were all lined up onstage, as many performers as could fit, and, led by Pete Seeger, Joan Baez, Peter Paul and Mary, the Freedom Singers, and myself, we sang Dylan's "Blowin' in the Wind." Tellingly, in an interview Dylan had indicated that his work was now no longer influenced by Woody Guthrie, but by Bertolt Brecht. One could understand that; gurus and role models tend to change for all of us. What was less understandable were his general demeanor and his attire. He wore cowboy clothes and went about with an enormous bullwhip, which he cracked from time to time. If he ever explained why, then I missed the explanation.

By 1964 a further change had taken place in Dylan. Rather than protest songs, he wrote bitter love songs. The guru was no longer Brecht, the guru was himself. However, the really monumental change did not come until a year later, on July 25, 1965. Bob Dylan was scheduled to appear at that evening's concert. A day or so earlier he had gotten together with Paul Butterfield's Blues Band, who were scheduled to perform at another part of the festival, and had rehearsed a few songs with them. As usual, the board members took turns introducing the various acts. When Bob's turn came, Peter Yarrow made the introduction. A changed Dylan made his entrance. Gone were the jeans and the work shirt and in their place we saw a black leather jacket, black slacks, and pointed black boots. Instead of the acoustic guitar, there was a shiny electric model. He plugged in and, accompanied by the Butterfield band, he launched into "Maggie's Farm," very amplified. The audience was stunned; some booed, some yelled out for old favorites. It was only later that one realized that he was singing his declaration of independence. He wasn't going to work on Maggie's farm no more—nor on anyone else's for that matter. When he finished, there were both cheers and boos from the audience, more of the latter than the former.

Backstage there was no less consternation. This clearly was out of place at the folk festival. I was upset. Peter Yarrow tried without success to put a good spin on the situation, and Pete Seeger had tears in his eyes. I heard Pete say, "I feel like going out there and smashing that fucking guitar." Language quite out of character for Pete, who, despite being an ultraliberal, was not given to using words like this. After the boos, Dylan was visibly upset and left the stage earlier than he had intended, while the audience was still shouting pros and cons about the "new" Dylan. Peter Yarrow asked Bob if he would be prepared to go back onstage with the acoustic guitar. To his credit, Dylan agreed, much like a rider thrown from his horse for the first time and climbing back on, convinced that there was no other way of conquering fear. Yarrow went out to the microphone and asked the audience if they would like to hear more from Dylan and his old guitar. There was a roar of approval and Bob went out there to sing. But, although he played the acoustic guitar, this was not the old Dylan, either. For what he chose to sing was also a continuation of the rebellion against the past. "It's All Over Now, Baby Blue" was as much of a manifesto of a new personal direction as "Maggie's Farm" had been.

For the moment we were all upset about what seemed an intrusion by rock-and-roll into what we considered to be our pristine world of folk. At one point there was even a heated altercation, with actual fisticuffs, between Alan Lomax and Al Grossman, Dylan's manager. The festival had been open to much change in musical styles and content, and we had been ready to present all of them. We had used amplification for only one purpose: to make sure that the performers could be heard. Had the performers played and sung in a room to a handful of people, no microphones would have been needed, but the music would have been exactly the same. This was different; this music did not exist apart from the amplification. I remember saying to Pete that I was sure this kind of music had a place somewhere, but that the place was not here. I also remember thinking that Dylan had found a way out that allowed him to continue creating music, despite his disillusionment with politics. Looking back I am convinced that, assuming that Dylan's passion for righting the world's wrongs had been genuine in the past, this retreat into self-absorption was a kind of salvation for him. The music blared outward, but the texts had turned inward. With it Bob Dylan survived, something his equally disillusioned friend Phil Ochs was unable to do. For Phil there was no way of rechanneling or retooling words and music. His honesty had nowhere to go except for the ultimate act of protest.

Dylan continues to perform, but he seems more aloof than ever. In June 1993 I attended a Dylan concert in Israel with my older son, Rob. While the makeshift setup in the Haifa harbor was less than ideal for a concert, I guess it was nice to see Bob perform in Israel. Whether this was just another concert venue for him—part of an overseas tour—or whether the locale had any special meaning for him was hard to tell. Dylan is perhaps one of the most uncommunicative performers I have known. He does not reach out toward his audience by either word or gesture; they have to come to him all the way. There is absolutely no "It's good to be here again" in Bob's stage vocabulary. In fact, there is no vocabulary at all.

I DEEPLY REGRETTED missing the famous March on Washington in 1963, the event at which Martin Luther King Jr. made his famous "I have a dream" speech. My friend Rabbi Joachim Prinz also spoke at this mass rally; as a victim of persecution he spoke of the crime of silence. Joan Baez, Pete Seeger, and Peter, Paul & Mary all participated in this stirring program, of which I saw only glimpses on television in the wee hours of the morning. I was then on a concert tour of New Zealand, which had been booked much earlier and could not be rescheduled. It was ironic that I had a run-in with the head of the concert department of the New Zealand Broadcasting Corporation over the playing of the "Star-Spangled Banner," of all things. We were informed that the United States Ambassador would be attending the final concert of my tour in Wellington, New Zealand's capital. I, who normally would not be too concerned about protocol, wanted to make sure that the ambassador, a Kennedy appointee whom I had known during the campaign, would not be slighted in any way. According to custom all over the British Commonwealth, "God Save the Queen" was played at the beginning of all public functions. I told the NZBC promoters to make sure that in the presence of the U.S. ambassador the American national anthem would also be played. I was assured that it would be. Then, on the afternoon before the performance, I received a message that no recorded copy of the "Star-Spangled Banner" was available to be played. I requested that the director of the concert division, Mr. Glubb, meet with me to discuss the matter. It so happened that the name Glubb was not unfamiliar to me. In the 1948 Israeli War of Independence the one crack regiment that had given the Israelis more trouble than all the mostly disorganized Arab troops combined was called the Arab Legion. It had been organized on behalf of Jordan's King Hussein and was commanded by a British brigadier general named John Glubb. He was known under the title of Glubb Pasha. This was a first cousin of the New Zealand Glubb, whose accent was pure upper-class British, which in an argument sounds so snobbish as to set your teeth on edge.

Mr. Glubb informed me that no copy of "this American anthem" could be found. When I said that it would be easy to procure one from the U.S. embassy, he replied, "Oh no, we always have them in the record library of the Broadcasting Corporation." "But you don't seem to have this one, do you?" I asked, somewhat irritated. "Well, no, we don't," he replied. "Then get it from the Americans, if not from the embassy; then there is a splendid version of it the U.S. Air Force has. They have a large base here in New Zealand." "No, no, that wouldn't be right, we don't go outside the Corporation for recordings. We always have them." "You don't always have them," I began to shout, "because you don't have one now!" "No need to shout, old boy," he said. "Don't call me old boy; I am nobody's old boy, least of all yours," I said, and continued, "All right, I'll tell you what we'll do. If we can't play both anthems, we will play neither." That shocked him; he said in a tone that implied deep offense: "'The Queen' is always played." "Well, tough shit; she won't be played tonight. Or you can play 'The Queen' and then we'll all go home, because *I* won't play after you have insulted my country's ambassador." As he retreated out of my dressing room he mumbled something about having to make a few telephone calls. At the door he turned around and said, "I don't mind telling you that I find your attitude most annoying." *Might as well go for broke,* I thought, and said to him as he left: "You know what? I don't like you and I don't like your fucking cousin, either." Miraculously, by evening, we had copies of both anthems, and thankfully I never had to lay eyes on Mr. Glubb again.

In the spring of 1968, two men who had started to change the direction of America were murdered. Had they both lived to continue their tasks, America might have accepted a different norm and lived by a different code of behavior. During the first half of 1968 I was in Las Vegas, of all places, for the first of my many engagements of *Fiddler on the Roof.* I found the place debilitating and shallow to an insufferable degree, because all around me there was a total lack of concern with world and national events. My wife and I were shaken by Dr. Martin Luther King Jr.'s death; we watched television coverage every single minute I was offstage, and we called friends all around the country who shared our feeling of outrage and shame. In downtown Vegas, there was nothing—less than nothing; the casinos carried on, oblivious of the national tragedy, with a general "So what?" attitude from the few who had bothered to take note at all of what had happened. When a period of national mourning and a compulsory two-hour closure of all businesses was declared by the federal government, Las Vegas complied in a curious fashion: All shops and casinos were ordered closed from 4:00 to 6:00 A.M., the slowest time.

The black community of Las Vegas announced that on the following Sunday a memorial meeting for Dr. King would be held in the largest black church in Las Vegas, to be followed by a march downtown. On that day, the church was filled to overflowing with the largest crowd ever, many spilling over into the street. Among the thousands of people mourning the death of the great leader that day in Las Vegas, there were but four whites: the mayor of Las Vegas, ex officio; Hank Greenspun, the publisher of the *Las Vegas Sun* newspaper; and Rita and I. Of all the many thousands of whites in the area, only four—and three of them Jews. As we marched down the thoroughfare after the service and the speeches, I was deeply embarrassed for the entire community. If I had not been too fond of Las Vegas before, what I felt now was close to outrage.

I remember these events as vividly as though no time had passed. As I write this, it is twenty-five years to the day after the assassination of Martin Luther King, Jr. It is early morning. A few minutes ago I stood stock-still in my underwear in the middle of a hotel room in Scottsdale, Arizona, watching a replay of Martin Luther King's funeral cortege, his plain pine coffin on a "poor man's burial cart" drawn by mules. Tears streamed down my face. The memory has not gone away; I guess it never will. It never should.

Why would I assume that the glitzy show biz and gambling crowd was capable of sharing America's grief about Dr. King? And would the treatment meted out to the memory of his martyrdom remain just an isolated case of callousness? Far from it; there was still more to come. When Robert Kennedy was assassinated a couple of months later, the reaction of the Las Vegas community was again nothing short of scandalous. Since Bobby Kennedy as attorney general had gone after the mafiosi and their involvement in the casinos, this town (which by now had declared itself to be clean of these elements) not only did not mourn, it celebrated! There actually were parties going on, and there was no question but that the national mourning period would be as disrespectfully observed in Bobby's case as it had been in Dr. King's.

The Robert Kennedy assassination hit me hard for several reasons. For one, I knew Bobby, had been with him on a number of occasions, had helped him in his campaign for the Senate seat from New York, and had announced my support for his candidacy in the upcoming presidential elections. (I had been elected as a delegate pledged to Senator Eugene McCarthy before Bobby Kennedy announced his intention to run. Under the rules, at the Democratic Convention I would have to cast my vote for McCarthy on the first ballot only, after which I was free to switch my vote.) The other reason was my friendship for Paul Schrade, the head of the Western region of the United Auto Workers union (UAW). He had put his regular work aside for a few weeks in order to concentrate on delivering the California vote for Bobby. He was standing next to Kennedy when he made his victory speech in the ballroom of the Ambassador Hotel in Los Angeles, was walking next to him as he passed through the kitchen, and was hit by the bullets from the same gun that killed Bobby. The attack left Paul with a bullet wound in his head that would take a long time to heal. At the time it was uncertain whether he could recover at all from the damage inflicted by Sirhan Sirhan's gun.

Where were you when it happened? They keep asking this question when talk gets around to national or international catastrophes. When Bobby was shot, I was onstage at Caesars Palace doing my *Fiddler* chores. Rita was backstage in my dressing room and saw the report on television, as did other members of the cast who were off-stage at the time. Knowing what my reaction would be, she begged the cast not to let me know anything until the final curtain, when she could break the news to me, especially about what had happened to Paul Schrade. Naturally, some gossip slipped me the news anyway. I was devastated, and I do not remember how I finished playing the show; I must have been on automatic.

The next couple of weeks filled me with impatience. It did not feel right for me to be where I was, entertaining audiences as though everything were normal. I wanted to be in New York. I wanted to travel to Washington for Bobby's funeral. I also wanted to be in Los Angeles, where Paul lay severely wounded. But my sense of responsibility toward the job allowed me to do none of these things. I remained where I was. It might have been easier to bear had there been people around me to share my feelings. Aside from Rita, there were pitifully few.

After a few weeks I did get to see Paul Schrade. He came to Las Vegas at the invitation of Howard Hughes, of all people, who had offered Paul a chance to recuperate at his private ranch. (This ranch had at one time belonged to Vera Krupp, of the German arms manufacturing family.) On the face of it, one would think the reclusive superbillionaire and the labor union executive of the United Auto Workers would have had only a single thing in common: the adversarial, combative relationship between management and labor. But earlier that year a strange circumstance had brought these two representatives of totally disparate interests together to make joint cause. The U.S. government's Atomic Energy Commission announced that nuclear bomb tests would be conducted in Nevada, some seventy miles north of Las Vegas. Howard Hughes opposed the plan: Hughes Aircraft had extensive operations in Nevada as well as an airport, and he was convinced that the testing would do harm to both industry and tourism. In making his stand in opposition to the Atomic Energy Commission he was looking for allies, and found a very eloquent one in Paul Schrade.

Paul's opposition—and the UAW's—to the testing was rooted in ideological and environmental concerns. Although these were different from the pragmatic motives of the Hughes Corporation, the two organizations formed an alliance to pressure the U.S. government to call off the testing. I found out about this after Rita and I had independently sent wires to the White House urging that the nuclear testing be called off. We reminded President Johnson—who we hoped would get to read some of the protesting telegrams—that at a previous test in Utah, dozens of sheep had been exposed to radiation and had died as a result. This time, we argued, human beings would be put in harm's way. While we waited for a reply, we heard that Schrade and the UAW were also making representations to Washington to call off the testing. Neither we, nor they, nor Howard Hughes, had any success.

The test was scheduled for 5:00 A.M. The day before, Paul arrived in Las Vegas. Having exhausted all the last-ditch avenues of protest, he wanted to actually be present when the dreaded event occurred. I would have preferred to leave the state, but I was working onstage until 2:00 A.M. I suppose Rita and I could have chartered some form of transportation to get away from Las Vegas, but in the end we were shamed by Paul's courage. We were also curious. There was no point in going to bed; we stayed up with Paul in our suite at Caesars Palace and waited. We had the radio on, which had promised a direct broadcast of the countdown and the detonation. The media and the government spokespeople had made much of the fact that this was to be an underground test. We were hardly reassured; all the recent tests had been underground, including the one in Utah. We listened to the countdown: 8-7-6-5-4-3-2-1-0. We heard a rumble on the radio; apart from that nothing happened for about a minute. Then the chandelier in the suite started to sway. We looked out the window and it seemed that the hotel's parking lot was moving, an eerie sensation. We looked at each other with a "What now?" question in our eyes. It took a while for things to subside. When we went down to get some coffee, the slot machines were going and the gamblers were at the blackjack tables. I had read somewhere that the only living things liable to survive a nuclear holocaust would be cockroaches. Wrong, I thought. Gamblers also.

We did get a reply from the White House, albeit after the fact. In essence it said: "See? Nothing happened." We sent one more missive, wondering what kind of reply we might have gotten in the event that something catastrophic had happened. We got no reply, nor had we expected any.

It turned out that they were wrong about the absence of after-effects. In southern Nevada, an area that included Las Vegas, the number of miscarriages tripled during the months following the test, both in comparison to previous years and to the national statistical average.

Thus it was that after RFK was assassinated and Paul was shot, Hughes extended an invitation to Paul to recuperate at the Hughes ranch in style, with cook, chauffeur, and butler in attendance. Naturally, Paul's friends were welcome to come and cheer him up. Our mutual friend Vera Dunham, born Vera Grigorievna Sandomirskya in Russia, made the trek to Las Vegas from Detroit, even though her husband had been in a bad auto accident and she was torn by conflicting loyalties.

I had met Paul through Vera, who lived in Detroit and taught Soviet literature at Wayne State University. During the Cold War her expertise in interpreting what the Soviets published, what they said, and what they omitted to say had caused the Pentagon to enlist her help in second-guessing Soviet intentions. She had told me how amused she was at the suspicious looks she would get from officers who could not understand what a civilian woman with a strong Russian accent could be doing in the corridors of the Pentagon. This extraordinary woman was as effusive and emotional as her professor husband, Warren, was not. He was a noted sociologist and as Middle American as can be. Vera, by contrast, remained as thoroughly Russian in manner and speech as though she had not been living in America for decades. Yet she was totally involved in the American political scene and was a passionately vocal political liberal. For me, she was a mentor in things Russian and has remained a close friend through the years. Friendships to her are a sustaining force; she worries about the well-being of her friends even when there is no cause to worry, and far more so when there is. It was no wonder, then, that after Paul was shot she insisted on coming to hold his hand in Las Vegas. Paul Schrade eventually made a complete recovery, but with a bullet hole remaining in his skull as a permanent reminder of the ordeal.

The memory of Bobby Kennedy played an important role at the 1968 Democratic National Convention in Chicago. I was determined to attend the convention in August; fortunately the *Fiddler* run in Las Vegas was over by the end of June. Earlier I had been elected a full delegate to the convention, with the highest number of votes of any delegate in New York State. Some of my detractors ascribed this to the fact that I was known for other areas of endeavor; I maintained that it was due to my political acumen. The arts were represented at the convention by relatively few people. The only other actor from New York State was Robert Ryan, serving as an alternate. Also from New York was Jules Feiffer, the satirist, cartoonist, and playwright. Among the Connecticut delegates were Arthur Miller and Paul Newman. The recognizable show business names in the California delegation were Roosevelt Grier, Warren Beatty, and Shirley MacLaine. It was one of the rare occasions when artists were not relegated, as they usually are, to the sidelines of the political process, welcomed only as shills to attract crowds or as the beaters of drums and strewers of rose petals before the arrival of the ruler. This time we would actually be among the kingmakers.

The feeling of national malaise had taken its toll long before the convention was called to order. The nation had been dragged into a war half a world away. How that war served our "national security" was barely understood even by those who blindly tended to support any policies emanating from the White House. At the 1964 Democratic National Convention in Atlantic City, I had been on the outside and had demonstrated for a different cause, that of equal justice and civil rights for all citizens and all races. We were then secure in the knowledge that our allies could be found in the highest places within the power structure itself. I was a friend of senators and congressmen, gained access to the hall as a guest, and thus made the case for civil rights inside the hall as well as outside. Senator Frank Church of Idaho and his wife, Bethene, were good friends, as was Senator Gaylord Nelson of Wisconsin. Gaylord and his wife, Carrie Lee, had me stay at their house on a number of occasions, including the week of Lyndon Johnson's inauguration, which I attended as the senator's guest. LBJ himself had been very cordial to me at White House receptions, including one honoring folk music. With the rest of the liberal camp I had been grateful to this president, who in his Southern drawl had announced support for civil rights and had ended his address quoting the motto of the movement: "We shall overcome."

Hubert Humphrey and I had worked together many times in the past, and through Gaylord Nelson we also met socially and informally. The day after Humphrey's inauguration and swearing in as vice president in 1964, Senator Nelson and I attended a luncheon honoring Humphrey. Hubert stood up and gave a speech in his inimitable way, beginning with this story: "There once was a family with two sons. One ran away to sea, the other became vice president of the United States, and neither of them was ever heard from again!"

Once while I was staying with the Nelsons, they gave a party that Humphrey attended. Hubert had just seen *The Russians Are Coming, the Russians Are Coming*. There he was in the living room, the vice president of the United States, demonstrating how in the film Carl Reiner and Tessie O'Shea jump up and down to get to the telephone while tied up together. Then he took the Nelson children outside with him and pointed out Secret Service men in the bushes. "There's one! There's another one!" Humphrey was a great supporter of labor, a great supporter of Israel, and a great supporter of the arts, and we had been together many times as allies in the same causes.

But all that was in the past. Much that happened during Johnson's tenure had changed the nation's mood—and mine. We of the liberal left had very little affection in 1968 for the Johnson administration, and we were determined to make the peace plank a central focus of the 1968 convention. Opposing the Vietnam War was easier for me than coming out in opposition to Hubert Humphrey, who was an immensely likable man for whom I retained great affection. He had been a man of principle and courage, not at all the namby-pamby, smiling Hubert-doll as some chose to depict him. This was the man who, as early as 1948, incurred the wrath of Dixiecrats by forcing a convention to adopt a strong civil rights plank. This was the man who advocated Medicare fully fifteen years before it became law and proposed the Peace Corps about a year before it was established. Moreover, he had impeccable credentials as a supporter of labor and as an advocate of peace who pushed for adoption of the Limited Nuclear Test Ban Treaty. But now, in 1968, we were mad at Hubert. We were no longer nostalgically grateful for what he had been and done, but exasperated by his blind support for all of Lyndon Johnson's agenda, especially Vietnam. As we perceived his desire to please the man who had elevated him to the second-highest office in the nation, we got angrier yet. I shared the anger and the frustration, and in my anger I forgot how much I liked him. Mostly I thought of the hopes and aspirations of young Americans who in Hubert Humphrey would never have the kind of leader assassins' bullets had robbed the nation of twice, in 1963 and now again in 1968.

Regretfully, I realized that Eugene McCarthy would not be that kind of leader, either. He was a man who had embraced our principles; he seemed prepared to be offered the prize but less than eager to reach for it. At least we hoped that under Gene McCarthy's banner we would be able to force the nation to take note of what we believed in and what we rejected. It would not be easy; the "regulars," men like Richard Daley who had the entire Chicago delegation and the police in the street under his thumb, and Carl Albert, who wielded the chairman's gavel and the entire well-oiled machinery of the old-line Democrats, would make it very difficult for us to present our case.

Still, we went to Chicago, hoping for respectful political discourse, hoping against hope that ideological differences could be aired with civility and that, in the end, a partnership of sorts would emerge, so that the fall campaign against the Republicans led by Richard Nixon could be waged with the Democratic party intact. When, on the first day, we made the trip to the convention hall and I saw that the convention site was in the middle of the Chicago stockyards, I began to have an inkling that what we were in for was not a civilized process, but a slaughter. The full severity of it did not dawn on me until a couple of days later. Even from the beginning, the convention hall was an armed camp where entry and exit was a painful process for visitors and delegates alike. Every instinct in me rebelled against the treatment meted out to us at the various entry points. The security staff had to have been recruited from among off-duty prison guards.

Within the hall itself it was not much better; strong-arm tactics were employed that contravened every parliamentary protocol under which duly seated delegates should have rights of movement and access to fellow delegates. Clearly the staff had been told that being polite to the delegates was not part of their duties, and the supervisors were not inclined to interfere while the guards were taking uncivil liberties. Even the seating arrangements had been rigged beforehand. Since it was known that the New York and California delegations had large numbers of peace delegates in their midst, those two delegations were seated near the back of the hall away from the podium and, so the organizers hoped, far from media attention. Getting up and moving around was sometimes capriciously hindered. At one point, after a sergeant-at-arms had ordered a delegate back to his seat and the delegate refused, the convention police actually dragged the man from the floor. Paul O'Dwyer, one of the leaders of the New York peace group and a candidate for a Senate seat, clung to the delegate as he was being dragged away and was pulled from the hall with him. Suddenly there was a stench of oppression in the hall. The Daley people had the upper hand; they who usually operated out of back rooms had come out in the open for these few days of convention ritual, their faces permanently flushed by large daily doses of whiskey and beer and their teeth tobacco-stained from the cigars clamped in the corners of their mouths. They looked on passively at the spectacle that so outraged us.

On the second morning of the convention, as we entered the hall, the atmosphere was already heavy with tension. During our caucus back at the hotel, we had decided that we would protest any infraction of our rights. I was walking alongside a fellow delegate, a university professor from Rochester, New York, named Loren Baritz. He presented his credentials to the guard; we started to move into the hall when the man decided that he would like to inspect Loren again and more closely. He put a restraining hand on Loren's arm and Loren said firmly, "Take your hand off my arm." The man continued to grip him. Loren repeated, louder this time, "Take your hand off my arm." A supervisor or sergeant-at-arms who was nearby heard the commotion and rushed over to inquire what was happening. Loren said with indignation, "I want that man to take his hand off my arm." Since notice had been served to some staff to prevent infractions, the supervisor decided to restrain the guard. He grabbed the guard's arm to pull him away from the delegate, whereupon Loren Baritz called to him with indignation: "Take your hand off that man's arm!" Principled to the end.

The goings-on from the platform had started to wear us down from the second day on. The peace delegates caucused early at the hotel and then joined the full state caucus to battle the regulars, all this before we even got to the convention itself. As the proceedings wore on, we feared that some maneuvering would deprive us of the main purpose, which, win or lose on the presidential candidacy, we insisted on fulfilling: The debate and vote on the peace plank was the most important issue of the day. There had been interminable wranglings and roll calls on credentials, and it looked as if the establishment had contrived to delay both the presentations and the vote itself until the wee hours of the morning, when America would be asleep. There were shouts back and forth of "Let's have the debate" from some, and "Let's go home" from others. Finally, even Mayor Daley had had enough; he stood up and said that the galleries were trying to take over the meeting and that he was ordering his delegates to go home. That must have displeased the dais, but we would get our chance to debate and vote on the peace plank the next day, at an hour when the nation was watching and listening.

The next day, Wednesday, was busy. This was the day of nominations and now it was also the day of the peace debate. As it happened, the debate was not altogether satisfying; neither their big guns nor ours were in evidence. McCarthy stayed away because LBJ would not address the convention. It was left to Congressman Philip Burton of California to present the case for peace, and for Senator Ed Muskie, later Humphrey's running mate, to defend the administration. Other speakers followed on both sides; ours had Ted Sorensen, former aide to John Kennedy; Pierre Salinger, JFK's former press secretary; and the senior senator from Tennessee, Albert Gore. Counting noses we knew we were going to lose, but in the end it was respectably close: 1,560 of their votes to our 1,040. Earlier the caucus had determined that if we lost we would mount a protest on the floor, and I should be the one to lead it. What kind of protest would it be? Neither booing, shouting slogans, nor other jarring disruptions. For me there was only one logical kind: singing, of course. While the vote was being counted, a note was passed to me from Murray Kempton, the journalist, also one of "our" delegates. He suggested that we start by singing "The Eyes of Texas Are Upon You" as a mock tribute to Lyndon Johnson. I dismissed the idea. When the moment came and the vote was announced, I began to sing and was joined in short order by our delegation. Later Kempton wrote his account of this moment: "There rose from the left of me the music of 'We Shall Overcome' and I understood why the choice was Bikel's by right; the professionals do not play jokes."

We continued to sing and the peaceniks in the other delegations took up the chant. I led them in "Ain't Gonna Study War No More" and "We Shall Not Be Moved." We walked around the floor linking arms while the chairman banged his gavel in vain, calling for silence and the orders of the day. He motioned to the convention band, which began to play "Happy Days Are Here Again" in an effort to drown us out, but to no avail. The protest went on for quite a while. All the network and local TV cameras were focused on what we were doing and why. At one point NBC's John Chancellor came over to me. He himself was at one point ejected from the convention hall; so much for freedom of the press. He was working the floor as a reporter, and he looked like a Martian with antennae on either side of his head and a hands-free microphone in a holding contraption in front of his face. He covered the mike with his hand momentarily to cut out the sound and said to me: "We are not supposed to take sides but you are doing great work; keep it up." Finally we let the chanting subside so the convention could go on to the business of nominating a presidential candidate.

During the previous night the horror stories of what was happening in the streets of Chicago and in Grant Park at Daley's direction had reached us. We were horrified to hear of kids who had come to Chicago to demonstrate against the Vietnam War being clubbed into unconsciousness; of mass arrests, tear gas, mace, not only against protesting kids but against mere bystanders as well. A doctor in his white coat with a Red Cross armband was clubbed and kneed in the throat as he attempted to render medical help to a beaten protester who was bleeding profusely. These things could not go unremarked from the floor. The chance came during the nomination speeches. As expected, the speech by Mayor Alioto of San Francisco, who placed Hubert Humphrey's name in nomination, contained no reference to the turmoil in the streets and to the repressive tactics of the Chicago cops. Even Governor Harold Hughes of Iowa, nominating Eugene McCarthy, only referred to it obliquely by quoting JFK: "Those who would make peaceful revolution impossible make violent revolution inevitable."

It remained for Senator Abraham Ribicoff of Connecticut to say the words that needed to be said. He had never been a powerful orator, but as he began a nomination speech for George McGovern, his voice had a ring of indignation. He said that he had come prepared to make a nomination, but, he went on, "as I look at the confusion in this hall and watch on television the turmoil and violence that is competing with this great convention for the attention of the American people, there is something else in my heart tonight and not the speech that I was prepared to give." The delegates quieted down some, waiting for something out of the ordinary. At first the speech went along conventional lines, extolling the virtues of Senator McGovern and calling up the memory of JFK and Robert Kennedy. But then it came: "With George McGovern as President of the United States, we wouldn't have those Gestapo tactics in the streets of Chicago." After a couple of seconds the floor and the galleries erupted and we could barely hear Ribicoff say, "With George McGovern we wouldn't need a National Guard." I looked toward the front of the hall where the

Illinois delegation was seated, most of them now no longer sitting. Mayor Daley was standing there, red in the face and shaking his fist at Ribicoff. He was shouting something; since he was not on mike only those in his immediate vicinity could hear what he was saying. But national television showed a close-up of Daley and one did not need to be a hearing-impaired person to be able to read his lips: "Fuck you, Abe," he said, "Fuck you!" Ribicoff looked back at him and leaned close to the mike; we could all hear him say in a dignified voice: "How hard it is to accept the truth." Two longtime politicians facing each other across a demarcation line of morality. If this was Abe Ribicoff's finest moment it was also, at the same time, Richard Daley's shoddiest.

When the balloting finally took place it was almost anticlimactic, except that the polling process elicits cute remarks from the various delegations, each getting in a quick commercial for their respective states. We already knew what the count would turn out to be. When Pennsylvania announced 103¾ votes for Humphrey, that was the ball game. In the end Hubert had garnered 1,761 votes to McCarthy's 601 and McGovern's 146; some other declared and undeclared candidates received a few votes, including the Southern gadfly governor George Wallace, who received one half vote.

Throughout the convention but especially on this Wednesday, TV and radio reporters had a field day. The best sideshow was the debate between William F. Buckley and Gore Vidal. Both were extremely articulate, extremely intelligent, and extremely antagonistic toward each other. My wife, so recently a television producer of news specials, made the rounds of the various media rooms and temporary studios off the convention floor and happened upon a violent confrontation between the two men that threatened to erupt into fisticuffs. In the heat of the debate, no longer civil as befits two authors and members of prominent families, Buckley made a derogatory homophobic reference about Vidal, who retorted by calling Buckley a "cryptofascist."

By the time the convention recessed for the evening, we were all weary; it had been a long and arduous day. But we were not prepared to let matters rest until the next morning. We were too frustrated and too angry about the mangled political process inside the hall and the storm troopers beating up kids outside. We contacted the McCarthy, McGovern, and Kennedy people in the various delegations and made plans to organize a demonstration of solidarity with the war protesters who had been so brutally treated. It was decided that we would hold a midnight candlelight march to downtown Chicago, four miles away, and then down Michigan Avenue. Paul O'Dwyer was to lead the march, and I was once again put in charge of the singing. I argued that it would be all right to sing on the way out of the hall and through the stockyards, but once we got to the residential areas we should march in silence. No need to wake up a sleeping populace, and whoever was awake would be more impressed with a line of delegates carrying their lit tapers in silence. When we got to Michigan Avenue, that would be the time to start singing again. A few voices were raised, expressing fears that such a march through Daley's Chicago was not exactly a safe thing to do; we would be walking through the "black belt" and the very conservative Polish neighborhood whose Democratic constituents were fiercely loyal to Daley's machine. We argued back, saying that we had no right to mount a protest of principle only when doing so was perfectly safe. And so we went, some by bus as far as the Art Institute of Chicago, to link up with the rest of the marchers. We had been warned that the city of Chicago was likely to invoke all kinds of ordinances against marchers, peaceful or not, and that arrests might be made. One of the delegates joked about what to do after an arrest: "If they hand you a bar of soap and tell you that you are about to go into a shower, don't take it." Jittery as we were, people laughed at this. I still could not bring myself to enjoy this particular humor.

Our column was stopped both by police and the National Guard, which was out in force. We were informed that we could not go beyond Eighteenth and Michigan. We proceeded anyway, Paul O'Dwyer and I at the head of the column. I had been given a bullhorn earlier and started to sing, with the delegates joining in: "We shall not, we shall not be moved, Just like a tree that's standing by the water, We shall not be moved." Then I changed the lyrics: "Tell Richard Daley he shall be removed, Tell Richard Daley he shall be removed, Just like a pail of garbage in the alley, He shall be removed." It was a bit of a miracle that, after singing this verse, I was not immediately arrested. Others were, though—Dick Gregory, no stranger to arrests, among them. As we proceeded, the picture became downright sinister. We were walking through two rows of National Guardsmen who had their rifles, with bayonets fixed upon them, pointed at us. "Remember this," I spoke into the bullhorn, "remember it well and never forget it. Remember how free Americans who came to an American city to exercise an elected duty were made to face American soldiers pointing guns at them. Never forget it." They were so young, these guardsmen, some scared and some pained at what they had been made to do. One moving moment came when the tallest

man among us, Dr. Kenneth Galbraith, the eminent Harvard economics professor, walked past a young man in riot gear pointing his
rifle. The young man went white in the face as he said, "Forgive me,
Dr. Galbraith. I was your student at Harvard."

There was one more day of ritual to be gone through: choosing a
vice president, to be followed by the acceptance speeches. We had
already lost on the main nominee and some had decided to go home;
what was the point on having the establishment rub it in for one more
day of ordeal? However, most of us stayed, and as it turned out, we
were right to do so. There was yet another moment of glory in store.
At the beginning of the day's proceedings, a half-hour-long filmed
tribute entitled *Robert Kennedy Remembered* was shown. When the
movie came to an end and the lights were brought up, people were
crying. The delegates came to their feet and applauded the empty
screen. The peace delegates, at this moment, felt doubly bereft; having
lost the peace plank a day earlier, our tears were tears of the leaderless.
The notion of peace, our peace, would have been Bobby's to put into
reality. The filmed tribute had been previously announced, and some
hand-lettered signs saying "BOBBY, BE WITH US" were held up. Someone had even made an enormous sign which looked to be eight feet
high. It said "BOBBY, WE MISS YOU." The sight of it brought another
lump to my throat. Again I began to sing. "Mine eyes have seen the
glory" was the song that had accompanied Bobby's funeral cortege. As
I sang it, the New York delegation took up the song and it spread
around the hall like wildfire. "Glory, glory hallelujah" echoed from all
the corners of the vast arena. It went on and on. There were frantic
phone calls between the floor managers and convention chairman Carl
Albert on the podium, who had been banging his gavel for silence,
without success, as we sang and sang, determined that if we had to
lose our case at this convention, at least let the ghost of Bobby be the
winner and remain so forever. It occurred to me that here was a lesson
I had learned in drama school put into action. It is said that while
comedy is pessimistic in nature, forever having people laugh at missteps and misfortunes of others, tragedy is optimistic. The protagonist
invariably dies, but the idea he embodies lives and grows, often to
nobility and greatness, in the eyes of the spectator. Robert Kennedy
was our protagonist in this drama, no longer alive but very much in
evidence.

They finally managed to quiet us down—not by the seemingly
hundreds of hand-held signs reading "WE LOVE DALEY" and the posters
"CHICAGO LOVES MAYOR DALEY," which had obviously been printed
up overnight. These were held up and waved; this was supposed to be

a signal for a chorus of "WE LOVE DALEY" chanters to drown us out. Ironic, when you think of Daley, the old Kennedy man of the Midwest, trying to shut up a demonstration for Bobby Kennedy. Even more ironic that the same Daley had, only a couple of days earlier, tried to persuade Teddy Kennedy to allow his name to be put in nomination for vice president. They were well organized; what the posters could not do, a clever device accomplished. A roar went up, followed by momentary confusion and silence from everyone who thought that some incident had taken place. In the momentary lull, one of Daley's black delegates announced from the podium a minute of silence in memory of Martin Luther King, Jr. Naturally, we were obliged to be silent for a minute. As soon as it was up, the convention secretary proceeded to read some announcements—and that was that.

The remainder of the convention was, for me at least, anticlimactic. The human psyche cannot experience all drama with equal intensity. Senator Edmund Muskie of Maine was nominated for vice president after Julian Bond—another of "our" standard-bearers—had graciously withdrawn. Muskie gave a workmanlike speech, decent but uninspired. Hubert Humphrey finally came out of the cocoon of the Hilton Hotel to receive the ovation of the delegates. I listened to his speech also. It was a fair one, but I was too mad to give it many points at the time. I should not have been, nor should the others in the peace camp have been. Some were so petulant as to flirt with creating a third political party overnight. Some others announced that they would be sitting out the presidential election and even I was foolish enough to consider doing that. Such elections—ones that don't seem to offer voters genuine alternatives—are not a choice between Tweedledum and Tweedledee, either, as they are invariably characterized by people who shrug their shoulders and say: "What's the point of voting this year?" They are real contests, on the outcome of which hang important decisions affecting our very lives. Eventually I came around and worked to get Hubert Humphrey elected over Richard Nixon, who was, Lord knows, no Tweedle of any kind. He was neither dumb nor dee, but a formidable threat to all who harbored liberal thoughts. Most of the other liberals also started to work for the election of HHH, but we had made a fatal mistake. We took up the fight too late. Nixon won by a very small margin—and we would have made the difference. I have always blamed myself for the fact that Nixon was elected, and for his legacy, which survived on the Supreme Court and in other vital areas. It was an expensive lesson.

The 1968 Democratic National Convention in Chicago was an often squalid and debilitating experience, but with moments of personal and collective epiphany. I had had a vision of civilized, democratic, and respectful political discourse; that vision was almost shattered. The democratic process had not exactly been slaughtered in the stockyards of Chicago, as I had feared, but it had been deeply wounded. Only wise leadership would be able to repair the rifts. Beyond leadership we also needed a nation willing to listen to other points of view, to strive for respect, and to respect dissent. It did not happen then, and has not happened since. We have become more fragmented and confrontational as a society, and are getting more so by the minute. Chicago was a catharsis of some kind, but no lesson. When it was over, I was glad to go back to acting and singing songs.

15

versatility

FROM TIME TO TIME PEOPLE WOULD ASK ME, "How come you do everything so well?" My answer is invariably, "Simple. Whatever I don't do well, I don't do." The truth of the matter is that there are many things I don't do well at all. Some of them I am forced to do from time to time because of the demands of my profession. I am a clumsy and reluctant dancer but I do dance when the role asks for it. Get me to dance in social situations—forget it. I have spoiled the mood of quite a few dates and lost out on romantic postludes because of such refusals. Also, I have never been good at sports; the parting advice of the Austrian professor about staying away from football came to embrace all sports in my mind. I don't even watch sports other than the occasional tennis tournament. Once, when my boys were little, I took them to a baseball game at Yankee Stadium and disgraced myself by displaying my ignorance. I kept asking the boys what was happening on the field and why. As they answered, they kept looking around furtively to see if anyone had taken notice of what a stupid father they had. We have never gone to another game and I still don't know why people run when they run and stand still when they don't. They keep stealing bases without getting arrested for it; people applaud for no discernible reason and just as mysteriously yell, "You jerk!" When I die, if there should be a test to get into the place, I just hope it does not have any sports questions; I'll flunk it for sure.

Among my other shortcomings is a tendency to go for facile solutions. Because my ear was quicker than my eye, I never properly learned how to read music. I retained melody and harmony by listening to them and let it go at that. I tend to go for the end results by the shortest possible route, and there is a danger in this. Minutiae that could be uncovered only by painstaking work on detail can be overlooked to the detriment of the work. As an actor, other than in television where it is necessary to be both good and fast, one should not have too early a grasp of the full image of a role. Quick intelligence can be a detriment here. Thus, at times I have had to arrive at the detail only by retracing my steps. The more logical approach is not to be in too much of a hurry, to let things develop organically. For years I carried a slip of paper in my wallet that said: "*Quidquid agis prudenter agas et respice finem*" (Translated with an attempt to keep the hexameter: "Do what you do with prudence/with the goal kept firmly in mind"). I suppose I tend to pay more attention to the last part of the exhortation than to the first.

That slip of paper inscribed in Latin almost got me into trouble. When I first arrived in England in 1946, the immigration officer was meticulously looking through everything I carried. The right-wing Irgun, Menachem Begin's people, had blown up the British headquarters at the King David Hotel, and young Jews arriving in London from Palestine were automatically viewed with suspicion. The immigration authorities had no way of knowing that no one could have been further from the ideology and practices of the Irgun than I. They looked at the Latin legend and also at the next one, which read "*Anthropos politikon zo'on*"(Man is a societal creature), in Greek script no less. I had a hell of a time convincing them that I was not carrying coded messages.

I have an inclination to perceive the world not so much in terms of its physical motion but rather with my auditory senses. I am, for want of a better term, a word man. If this is a failing, then I guess it is one I have in common with my ancestors. You sit and study, you sit and discuss, you sit and eat. My people were known to sit a lot. No wonder Jews are more inclined toward hemorrhoids than other peoples.

To my delight, my sons have also shown a proclivity for words even at an early age. One time, when Danny was about four years old and Robbie not quite six, I heard the sounds of fighting from one of their rooms. Something fell and I heard both of them yell. I rushed into the room and saw that they were both red in the face but otherwise unharmed. "What on earth is going on?" I asked. "Tell him to stop breathing on me!" Robbie shouted. Danny said with the righteous indignation only a four-year-old can muster: "He *brothe* on me!"

I am less attached to places than I am to people. There have been places in my travels which I have found extraordinarily beautiful, but whenever I wander, it is the people and the music that move me to return. Movies were often filmed abroad, but television work mostly kept you in the country, either in New York or in Los Angeles. On rare occasions there would be a foreign location for a TV program. One such exception was the 1966 film *Who Has Seen the Wind?* a TV special partially sponsored by the United Nations Office for Refugees. The harrowing story, based on absolute fact, concerned displaced persons who had been made stateless by the redrawn map of Europe, with its new political configurations. Not only individuals but entire families found themselves stuck on cargo ships, never to be permitted ashore at any port. They were shuttling back and forth across the · oceans, working the lowliest menial jobs on the ships so as to feed their families. The children received only such schooling as the parents could provide, from whatever knowledge was stored in their own memories. That situation still existed in 1966, when we shot the film. In this docudrama I worked with Maria Schell, Stanley Baker, Gypsy Rose Lee, and the director George Sidney. The filming was not without danger. A storm at sea brought us perilously close to capsizing as we were being shuttled in a small tender. But the project was exhilarating all the same. We were in Mazatlán, Mexico, at that time off the beaten track, and out of season as well. In the evenings we were thrown on our own devices and became very close; perhaps the heat and the tequila contributed to it. Our Mexican staff also joined in the conviviality. At one point, the camera operator, with whom I had become quite friendly, said to me after I had made a remark that he considered to be profound (the tequila again!), "You know, Teodoro, you quite somethin'. They broke the mold and then they made you!"

I took part in a TV program entitled *Diamond Fever* with Peter Lorre; I believe it was the last time he appeared on the screen. This Viennese actor, who kept being cast in Oriental roles because of his face and eyes, was a very dear man and more than a little eccentric. He gave the most outrageously high tips wherever he went; it was not unusual for him to leave a hundred-dollar bill on the table after he had paid a thirty-dollar check for a meal. He seemed to prefer Oriental restaurants, possibly because their staffs treated him with special reverence. No doubt this was because he had portrayed the famous detective Mr. Moto. I was amused by the idiosyncratic differences in the pronunciation of his name: In Chinese restaurants, they called him "Mistah Lolly," while in Japanese establishments it came out "Mistah Rorry."

By the time we worked together Lorre was not terribly well, and also not quite able to retain his lines. Despite the fact that in TV one could do short scenes and then break, he would get confused and we had to repeat many scenes too many times. On the last day of taping we worked till late in the evening, and the producers were afraid that we would slide into a new day if we had to go past midnight. An expensive proposition. The scene we had to finish had Lorre's character shoot my brother and then whirl around and point his gun at me. We had rehearsed this teleplay for some two weeks, and now everyone was keeping their fingers crossed, hoping that Peter would come through. At ten minutes before midnight we were shooting this final scene. As rehearsed, Peter shot my brother, who crumpled to the ground. Then, for some unfathomable reason, he threw the gun down beside the body. But, remembering what had to come next, he whirled around and threatened me with a cocked finger! There was a roar of frustration from the control room. Luckily they had two cameras rolling and were able to edit around it.

After not seeing Sam Wanamaker for years, I ran into him at an Academy screening in Beverly Hills. He was about to direct a segment of the very popular show *Columbo*. They were just about to cast their guest star, and Sam suggested me for the role. My old friend Richard Alan Simmons, from the Dick Powell days, was the executive producer, and he accepted the idea readily. The setting was a Mensa-like society of superbrains, one of whom murders another in such an ingenious way that no ordinary mortal would be able to solve the murder, least of all a detective in a dirty raincoat who had not even gone to a decent college. I was to play the brilliant murderer. I had been a member of the real Mensa Society for a number of years. Thus, for this role, I did not have to pretend to be an intellectual; I only had to pretend to be a murderer. I let my membership in Mensa lapse, though. I had expected that a society of superbrains would contribute somehow to the betterment of mankind. What I found at the meetings I attended was that outside of playing three-dimensional chess, what they did was stand around with cheese and wine and chat up members of the opposite sex—things all ordinary mortals do.

Unlike other TV shows, the production of *Columbo* was very much under the control of the star of the series, Peter Falk. He was very gracious, told me not to be pressured into hurrying; we would do as many takes as necessary until I was satisfied that I had given my best performance. Most unusual, compared to the pressure-cooker atmosphere of most TV productions of the day.

Respect for performers is becoming a rare commodity in Hollywood, which subjects established actors to the demeaning process of having to audition and reintroduce themselves each time they apply for a role. A notable exception is the show *Murder, She Wrote*. From its star Angela Lansbury on down—most probably because of her—everyone treats the performers with care and polite respect. When they offer you the role, they do so because they consider you a person of talent who will prove himself in front of the camera without having to go through the cattle call of auditioning first. I did four enjoyable guest shots on the show, one of which was quite flamboyant—that of an Italian tenor. My wife was played by Carol Lawrence, who had an accident on the last day of shooting. It happened during night location filming on the back lot of Universal. My character has suffered a heart attack, and is being rushed on a stretcher into an ambulance. Carol, as my wife, insists that she be allowed to accompany me in the ambulance. The paramedic objects, but she overrules him and jumps into the back of the van. He shrugs, closes the door, and runs around the front to drive off in a hurry. As the cameras rolled, all went well—except that the back door was not properly closed. When the ambulance sped away, the door swung open and Carol tumbled out and landed on the ground. Everyone was horrified, the director yelled "Cut," and people rushed to see what shape Carol was in. She was bruised and shaken, and had to be taken to the infirmary to ascertain whether there had been hidden damage. It turned out that she would have to be bandaged for a few days, but was otherwise all right. The scene we had shot was actually the last one she was involved in. While we waited for the report from the infirmary, still all shaken up from the incident, I walked over to the director, Walter Graumann, to say how terrible it was that we were all so vulnerable. I too could have tumbled out; tied as I was to a gurney, who knows what might have happened? Walter was silent for a bit and then he said, "You know, basically all directors are shits." I asked why, and he said, "Do you know what my first thought was when the thing happened?" I had a flash of insight: "Yes. I know exactly what you were thinking. 'How much of the take can I use?' That's what you were thinking." "Right," he said.

The reputation I have of being a "serious actor" gave me trouble over the years. On occasions, too rare for my liking, they take a chance and cast me in roles that call for subtle or broad comedy. *All in the Family* was a case in point. I played a German butcher, a widower, who was in love with Edith Bunker. The fact that I got to play that role probably had more to do with my being able to do a better German accent than most than with any acknowledgment of my comedic potential. The segment, entitled "Love Comes to the Butcher," turned out to be so hilarious that they followed it up by writing me a second one a season later. Work on the show had an informality to it and the encouragement to improvise was such that one started out less with a script than a blueprint for things to be filled in later during the four rehearsal days. Everyone was permitted to contribute suggestions, and they were all taken seriously. It did not matter whether they came from the regular stars of the show, the guest stars, or the bit players. If the suggestion was good and funny, it was accepted. The story goes that a delivery man arrived once with coffee and Danish, stayed for a while to watch the rehearsal, and made a suggestion the director and cast liked. They used it.

One of my own best moments in the show came about as a result of an improvisation. I ask Edith to call me by my first name, Albrecht, which she has difficulty pronouncing. I shorten it to Al. Then she asks me to call her Edith. Germans have great difficulty with the "th" sound. I call her "Edit" and she corrects me, saying it's Edith. I make a long pause pondering this elocutionary obstacle, and then I said "Edit" but, as an afterthought, stuck my tongue out, adding a careful "th." In the second segment they wrote for me, I came to introduce a girlfriend to the Bunkers. Her name was Judit-"th." Afterward, Norman Lear said that this bit of comedy would be remembered long after I am gone. That pleased me. There are comedians who from time to time play serious roles; I am a serious actor who gets a lot of laughs.

Being cast in a recurring role in the megahit *Dynasty*—but one that did not go very far, for that particular story line in the series was aborted after a few segments—gave me a chance to renew some old acquaintances. I had known Joan Collins from my time in England; she was then a budding starlet some eighteen years old. She was at that time married to a hunk of man, a handsome but very bad actor named Maxwell Reed. He was so bad, in fact, that the studio hired me once to dub his entire dialogue in a film. "Let the voice have some color, at least," they said. The man was just as inarticulate off-screen as on. I remember being at a party with the two of them, during which they sat on a couch. She said little, obviously deferring to him, and he said nothing at all. After what seemed to be hours, he finally said in a cockney accent: "This is quite a nice party not sexy enough though"— all in a complete monotone with the only emphasis on "though." Little wonder, since he couldn't even read his own lines, that he had trouble with other people's. He was also intent on displaying manifest machismo. At one point Joan had evidently called him by a term of endearment, and I heard him raise his voice to her: "Sweetie? Sweetie?" he said irately, "Do me a fuckin' favor!" I thought then that, unless this beautiful young girl was an all-out masochist, this marriage was not long for this world. Now, some thirty-five years later, Joan Collins is a superelegant, supergroomed superstar, and Maxwell Reed unremembered by anybody except idiots with a head for trivia—like me. Good for her.

John Forsythe, the male star of *Dynasty* and the heartthrob of all middle-aged ladies, was clearly pleased to see me. Years earlier he had briefly served on the Equity Council when I was serving as the top officer of the union. As we sat in adjoining makeup chairs on my first day of shooting, he suddenly said to me, "I have to tell you something. I never think of Ronald Reagan as my president. I only think of *you* as my president."

The Final Days was the title of the three-hour ABC television special, filmed in 1990, that was based on the Woodward-Bernstein book about the inexorable process leading to the resignation of Richard Nixon from the presidency of the United States. This was a very ambitious undertaking from every point of view. The book had met with some criticism concerning the accuracy of its facts and the direct remarks attributed to some of the major players in the scenario, because they had been made within the earshot of no one. Then there were the partisan critics on the right for whom Nixon was still a revered leader. The actors attempting to portray the events were also vulnerable. The faces and mannerisms of the major characters were too well known. This was especially true of Nixon himself, Alexander Haig, and Henry Kissinger. I eagerly accepted the challenge of playing Henry the K. His vocal mannerisms, the German accent, and the low growling monotone were not difficult for me; in fact, the producer and director had hired me after they heard me "do" Kissinger in their office. The visual part was harder. I had to lose the beard, of course, and my natural hairline had to be altered. But all that was in the realm of the physical. How to crawl inside the man's mind was quite another matter.

I read everything I could lay my hands on, including Kissinger's memoirs and Nixon's account of the events. There were contradictions in the two descriptions that were not easily reconcilable. In particular, the encounter between Nixon and Kissinger in the Lincoln sitting room of the White House on the night before the resignation announcement gave me trouble. This was the scene we would have to reenact, and it needed to be as factually and emotionally accurate as possible. Although Woodward and Bernstein had reported it in their book, no one had been present apart from the two men, and any reported speech between them had to be conjecture. Nixon's account told of how he almost broke down and said to Henry words to the effect of "I am not a very observant Quaker and you are not a very Orthodox Jew but the time has come for us to pray." He then asked Kissinger to kneel down with him, and according to the President they did so and prayed. Kissinger's account fudged on this point. He says in his memoirs that he did not remember whether he knelt or not but remembers thinking of a piece of poetry instead of a prayer. *Come on, Henry,* I thought when I read this, you are a statesman, a diplomat, and a historian to boot. Whatever your failings may be, a lack of memory is not one of them. It was highly unlikely that he should not have remembered every minute detail of that emotionally charged encounter, which was so different in every respect from all the meetings he had had with Nixon through the years. If he said in his book that he did not remember kneeling, I would bet that he did kneel, and either chose not to remember or was embarrassed to say that he did. Lane Smith—who gave an extraordinary performance as Nixon—and I spent an entire day on this scene. It was one of the hardest tasks I ever had as an actor. I played the embarrassment, but at the same time I had to be reassuring to the man who was on the brink of despair, to be part nursemaid and part witness.

A very short time after *The Final Days* had aired, I was at a reception for Lech Walesa at the White House. Dr. Kissinger was one of the invited guests and I told him that I feared he might not want to speak to me because of the program. He said that he had seen it, and that he had no quarrels with my portrayal. He had some reservations about the scene, but they had more to do with the deportment of the Nixon character than with mine. Nixon had not beaten the carpet with his fists, he said. He had been very exercised and shaken, but not quite hysterical. I then broached the subject of the kneeling, essentially repeating what I had concluded after reading his account, saying that I was puzzled that he, of all people, should have had a faulty memory. He said that he really did not remember whether he knelt or not. I pressed further, asking if perhaps he chose to suppress the memory because kneeling was a particularly un-Jewish thing to do, and perhaps even more of an un-Kissinger thing? He gave me a lopsided smile and said in his guttural growl, "Well, that's a possible interpretation." Months later, while dining at Spago's restaurant in West Hollywood, I saw Kissinger sitting at a table with my friend Sherry Lansing. He looked across, nodded at me, and smiled. On his way out, he came over to my table and said, "So, are you going to do me again?" I guess I would, given the chance.

It's an eerie sensation to stand on the transporter pad of the Federation starship *Enterprise*. You know that these are just special effects—just as you know you aren't really traveling the galaxy in the twenty-fourth century. But you've been watching *Star Trek* since the sixties, and all the familiar aspects of the show are like old friends, even if you've never truly been a Trekker. So when they ask Transporter Chief O'Brien—actor Colm Meaney—to "energize," you almost believe that it can happen. Yet, despite the science fiction and the futuristic aspects making for both less and more than reality, my guest appearance on an episode of the TV series made me contemplate cultural parallels.

We were on a soundstage on the Paramount Pictures lot on Melrose Avenue, one of the oldest original studios, shooting an episode of *Star Trek: The Next Generation,* one of the most popular television series on the air. My character, Chief Rozhenko, a retired blustering Starfleet engineer, and his wife are being beamed aboard the *Enterprise* to visit their adopted son, the fearsome Klingon Lieutenant Worf, played by Michael Dorn. Like any father, I embarrass my son by telling the *Enterprise* crew stories of his growing up. Worf bristles about the psychological yoke of his human father's presence and his gloating over his son's accomplishments, not unlike a Jewish parent. Yet in the story my son is an alien-born warrior who must not only pass the tests of his Klingon heritage, but also accommodate himself to his father's humanness. Each could not be more different from the other.

The irony is that Rozhenko has raised his son to be a Klingon rather than an oversized human. In so doing, Rozhenko has preserved his son's ethnic identity, rather than forcing him to conform to his own and consigning him to a cultural melting pot. Even in the fictitious future world of a galactic twenty-fourth century, I had found another parallel to my thoughts on cultural conformism.

I could not possibly cover the entire range of roles my television career allowed me to portray. It was a veritable smorgasbord of characterizations. If it turned out that the roles were much different one from the other, I welcomed it.

I played a ruthless murderer in *Hawaii 5-0,* a kindly Armenian merchant in *Ironside,* a Polish professor in *Charlie's Angels,* an American university professor in *Paper Chase,* a South African policeman in *The Equalizer,* and an Italian opera star à la Pavarotti in *Murder, She Wrote.* I played fools, farmers, and traitors as well as superintellectuals, cops, lawyers, artists, and even critics.

The drawback was that not only was the audience confused by not being able to identify the real Theo Bikel, but the producers often were not able to do so, either. During the earlier days it was easier; they took more chances and were far more willing to cast not for type but for talent. Over the years that boldness has disappeared, and executives, casting directors, and even some directors who in the past were willing to bet on the performer's ability are looking to be safe. That means pressing talent into a mold and forcing known actors to audition for every role as though they were inexperienced neophytes. Even Shelley Winters, I am told, was asked to read for a role. She asked to come back on the following day for the audition. When she did, she sat down, opened a large purse, took out not one but two Oscar statuettes, put them on the table, and said, "Now, do you still want me to read?"

My case is not much different. Whenever a role comes up that is straight English or American, it's an uphill battle to remind everyone that my English is impeccable, that I was schooled at the Royal Academy of Dramatic Art, and that I was nominated for an Academy Award for playing a Southern sheriff. With idiotic persistence the myth continues to be cultivated that Bikel is too serious, too intellectual, too Russian, or too European (one wonders if that means "too Jewish"). Withal, I am thankful that, at least until the mid-eighties, I was rarely at the receiving end of such executive shortsightedness. It has become a different process in the eighties and nineties. Alas. So very few who are in the decisionmaking position of hiring and firing actors have the wisdom, grace, and sensitivity of some of their predecessors. There should be a sign in every office that reads TRUST TALENT!

OVER THE YEARS my musical career underwent some changes, not quite as drastic as those of the general music scene since Dylan's metamorphosis at the 1965 Newport Folk Festival. A whole new hybrid genre came into being, loosely termed "folk-rock." Some artists made a complete transition into that genre; others have straddled both the old and the new. Some have stayed within the customary mold of folk music that includes recently written material but delivered without electronic help. As listeners we have all come to accept the new techniques; as folk performers we use them sparingly, if at all. For myself, I have acquired a healthy respect for the high-tech methods of performing and recording, a respect recently reinforced by the fact that my younger son, Dan, makes very talented use of them. They allow him a much broader horizon than that which we older folks were stuck with. He is able to employ musical styles from just about any period or country, from baroque to Beatles, from bouzouki to banjo. It is a marvel what electronic sampling is able to achieve.

I still perform much material that is folk-based. Mixed in with it, however, are so-called "art" songs, such as material from the pen of Jacques Brel, Kurt Weill, Georges Moustaki, and Sting. In addition, my repertoire includes material from the musical theatre. Since the late seventies I have regularly performed with the backup of piano instead of the bass accompaniment of Bill Lee or Bill Takas. Elliot Finkel—also my musical director and arranger—is my regular accompanist; Jonathan Irving, the son of my late friend Ben Irving, pitches in when Elliot is unavailable. The programs I do with large orchestras are of the pops variety, containing some Broadway numbers but also a great deal of folk-based material. I have done this sort of program with symphony orchestras from the Israel Philharmonic under Zubin Mehta to the Los Angeles Philharmonic at the Hollywood Bowl and the Baltimore Symphony conducted by Sergiu Comissiona. My program is a real change of pace for full orchestras. After one performance Maurice Peress, then the conductor of the Kansas City Symphony, said to me, "I am not sure that I like what you do with an orchestra." When I inquired why, he replied, "Because you have a knack of turning an entire orchestra of one hundred pieces into one damn guitar!" A reviewer in the *Los Angeles Times* put it another way: "Theodore Bikel has a knack of turning the entire Hollywood Bowl with 18,000 people in attendance into a living room."

Over the years I had gotten to know and like Zubin Mehta; I always establish a quick rapport with multilingual persons. Once at an Indian restaurant in New York, he ordered dishes in several Indian dialects, and then carried on a conversation in several European languages, including broad Viennese with me. Another time in Los Angeles, after an evening at the Philharmonic, he invited about a dozen friends, myself included, to a late dinner at Spago. After dinner, which went on for so long that our party of twelve were the only customers left, Zubin asked me to bring my guitar in from the car and play. "One of these days," Zubin said, "we should do something together."

Purim, in late spring, is the one Jewish festival that permits, even encourages a carnival attitude. Children wear costumes, makeup, use noisemakers, all in celebration of the Jews having managed to avert the attempt of Haman, the Persian king Ahasverus's vizier, to put them all to death. In the spring of 1984, when at Mehta's urging the Israel Philharmonic Orchestra (IPO) asked me to appear at a Purim concert in Tel Aviv, I readily accepted, for two reasons: One, the IPO did not as a rule schedule Pops concerts, and two, Mehta was going to conduct this concert himself. During that concert at the Mann Auditorium when I introduced a Purim song with a few words about the holiday, Mehta and I traded impromptu barbs, including his quip that as a Farsi, he was in all likelihood a descendant of the notorious Haman.

Now he had a lifetime appointment as music director of a Jewish orchestra. At the end of the program we took the customary bows before leaving the stage. In the wings, with the crowd still applauding, Zubin motioned for me to return to the stage for our encore, saying that he would be right behind me. I made my entrance and was met by a big laugh from the audience. My first impulse was to check whether my pants were properly zipped up, but the crowd was not laughing at me. Looking around I saw the maestro mounting the conductor's podium wearing a bright blue wig!

At times Mehta communicates with the orchestra in Yiddish, and his command of it can come in handy at unexpected moments. When the Israel Philharmonic toured the United States in 1985, they played a concert in Tallahassee, Florida's capital. Governor Bob Graham of Florida was running for a seat in the U.S. Senate. Like all campaigning politicians, he was looking for as much exposure as he could get. Remembering that both the American and the Israeli anthems would be played at the start of the concert, he had a bright idea. He asked Mehta if he would let him conduct the orchestra in the "Star-Spangled Banner." Being an amiable and accommodating man, the maestro agreed, but invited the governor to come to his dressing room so he could give him a short conducting lesson. A few minutes into the lesson it became quite obvious that Bob Graham was incapable of conducting a streetcar, much less an orchestra.

But a promise is a promise. Both men mounted the podium, and Mehta told the audience that the governor had asked for the privilege of wielding the baton for the playing of the National Anthem. With a flourish he presented the conductor's baton to the governor, but then turned to the musicians and said loudly and in Yiddish, "*Farmakht di eygalakh!*" (Close your eyes!)

These forays into the larger world of symphony orchestras are still the exception in my musical career, as were my three engagements in opera. In any event, only one of these three was a singing engagement. In 1989 I played the peddler Isacco in Rossini's *La Gazza Ladra* (The Thieving Magpie) with the Philadelphia Opera Company. Shortly thereafter, when I attended an arts breakfast in New York, I was seated next to Beverly Sills, the former opera star and director of the New York City Opera. I told her of my experience and said that after years of working in musical theatre with a conductor in the pit, I was astonished at the difference between that and opera. In the theatre the conductor acts as an accompanist: He breathes with you, pauses with you, and adjusts the tempo to the way you happen to feel on a given night. In opera, by contrast, the conductor is the absolute authority. He does not follow you; you follow him. "You found that out, have you?" said Miss Sills with a twinkle in her eye.

My other two operatic engagements were with the Cleveland Opera and the Los Angeles Opera Company: Mozart's *The Abduction from the Seraglio,* in 1991, and Strauss's *Ariadne auf Naxos,* in 1992. Both were speaking roles, and both in German. I think I was the only participant in *Ariadne* who got a favorable review from the *Los Angeles Times* critic, who suggested that the rest of the ensemble should have taken lessons from me on the pronunciation of German! Thanks for the compliment, but impeccable German was not all that hard for me to manage.

With those few exceptions, I continue to perform folk songs. Much of the time the venues are under Jewish auspices, as expected. I am one of the few performers left who presents ethnic Jewish music with authenticity. Jewish organizations or events that engage the services of singing stars often complain when there is not even a nominal effort to include something in the program that might relate to the purpose and theme of the evening. I can, and do. Yet the fact that I am able to relate to Jewish audiences on a more intimate level has its drawbacks. Once again it means that I tend to be labeled a "Jewish" performer, with no indication that I am capable of covering a great deal of general music, ethnic and otherwise.

Where I was not labeled a "Jewish" performer in the music field, I was stuck with the same curse that follows me in most fields of my endeavor: I do too many things. Despite my having been a cofounder of the Newport Folk Festival, the folkies, too, wondered whether I was seriously involved or just dabbling.

People are mistrustful of general practitioners; they always seem to look for specialists. What is he, they ask, an actor, a folksinger, a political commentator, a lecturer? When I try to tell them that I am a human being with a variety of talents and the ability and desire to use them, I get raised eyebrows. It is written in no book, to my knowledge, that one cannot use more than one function and acquit oneself of the task in a professional manner. While I do not claim to be a specialist in all the fields, I do have more than a smattering of knowledge in everything I undertake. I have a healthy dose of intellectual curiosity, and I ask pertinent questions from time to time. Often also impertinent ones. Where folk music is concerned, I have followed its lure since an early age. Unlike a scholar in the field who is obliged to look at every text and listen to every note, I can play favorites. I can sing what I like and disregard what does not speak to me. Once I found out that I did not have to love all of it, I could choose what I wanted to love and love it fully. And I was privileged to meet others who loved it just as much.

I HAD SIMILAR good fortune in much of my work in film. I had the opportunity to work—however briefly—with two ladies named Hepburn. Both Katharine and Audrey were indeed ladies in every sense of the word. The chance to work with Audrey Hepburn came in 1964, when my agent sent me to meet with the legendary director George Cukor, who was casting the film version of *My Fair Lady*. He evidently liked me and cast me as Zoltan Karpathy, the language expert who is fooled in the ballroom scene into believing that Eliza Doolittle is of noble birth. Karpathy is a Hungarian; but, being a speech expert, he out-Britishes the British. Just up my alley. As the "hairy hound from Budapest" I would need to be flamboyant, insufferable—and hairy. They experimented with my hair; I have a lot of it, an inherited trait from my father, who at his death at age eighty had his entire shock of hair. They made curlicues and ringlets, partings and cross-combed streaks until I fit the alliterative description of "hairy hound" in the lyric. (I often wondered whether the character had been made Hungarian for the sole reason of rhyming "hairy hound from Budapest" with "Never have I ever known a ruder pest.") In addition to the hair, I had to be instructed in the art of smooth ballroom dancing. The character was supposed to cut in on Eliza, ask her to dance, and then pump her for information. This was to be done in mime, as it were; we were to be seen in medium and long shots, waltzing around the room while I animatedly talk to Eliza. Since, as I mentioned, I am no great shakes as a dancer, I asked for practice sessions. The feet should be able to do their work automatically and seemingly without effort, so that I might concentrate on what my face was doing without at the same time stepping on Audrey Hepburn's toes.

Once those things were out of the way, I was ready for my scenes. Short as they finally were on the screen, my part kept me on the set for fully two weeks. Before we shot my first entrance down the grand staircase to greet Professor Higgins, George Cukor called me over for a little conference. He wanted to know how I visualized my first encounter with Higgins. What would this Hungarian do, how would he behave when first meeting his former illustrious speech teacher? I said, "Mr. Cukor, when it comes to how a Hungarian would behave, it seems to me that between the two of us, *you* are the Hungarian while I am not." He said, "Yes, but you are the actor and they usually have better instincts." Admirable, I thought. "Well, since you are asking, this Hungarian would rush up and kiss Professor Higgins on both cheeks before saying anything." Cukor nodded and said: "Why don't you do that, then?" And so it came about that I was the only male actor in films ever to make an entrance, come up to Rex Harrison, and kiss him on the cheeks.

The two film projects that followed were entirely different in nature. The locations alone were far removed from the exteriors of Covent Garden and the interiors of a palace ballroom which Warner Brothers had re-created at the studio for *My Fair Lady. Sands of the Kalahari* took me to the Namibian desert in South-West Africa. The story concerned five travelers, strangers to each other, thrown together by fate. They are over the desert in a private plane that runs into a swarm of locusts and crashes. The film's plot is the story of their survival. I played an Indian, Dr. Bondarakai, who is psychologically less equipped to deal with the situation than some of the others. In the end I am forced by the bully of the group, played by Stuart Whitman, to walk away on my own carrying a small supply of water in two hollow ostrich eggs. I am finally rescued by a band of Bushmen, chattering away excitedly in their click-tongue. Stuart was the only other American in the movie; the others were British: Stanley Baker, who also produced, Harry Andrews, Nigel Davenport, and the lone female, Susannah York. The director was Cy Endfield, American-born but a longtime resident of England.

The strangeness of the location was enhanced by the fact that many of the local blacks had received their education in schools run by German missionaries who had set up shop in the territory when it was still German Southwest Africa. It was disconcerting, to say the least, to sit in the small dining room of our hotel in Swakopmund, and have a waiter ask, *"Alles zufriedenstellend?"* (Is everything satisfactory?) Issuing from the mouth of a taller-than-six-foot African black, that phrase seemed to me the height of incongruity. Most of the white population of Swakopmund was German, including the owner and manager of the hotel, Herr Rummel. Before we arrived, they had built a small annex to the hotel to accommodate the actors. It was quite comfortable, and even the new parts had an old-fashioned feel to them. The food was decidedly German, of the cabbage and sauerbraten variety. One might have thought oneself to be in Germany but for the climate and the various facilities bearing signs of BLANKES and NIE BLANKES ("Whites" and "Nonwhites.")

As far as the work itself was concerned, we never knew from one day to the next which location we might go to; the weather determined that. It was not unusual for the second assistant director to knock at my door at 5:00 A.M. and say, in an apologetic tone of voice, "I'm afraid it's the dunes today, sir." The local fauna that were used in the picture were sometimes quite unpleasant; the only docile creatures were an occasional impala or a wildebeest, both tranquilized. In one scene I had to lift a giant lizard by the tail to show what I had caught for our meal. The creature was almost four feet long, and to me it looked like a small crocodile. It hissed ferociously. The animal warden had warned me not to touch its mouth: Not to touch its mouth? If I'd had my druthers I would not have gone near the damn thing altogether. They had taped its mouth shut with transparent tape as a precaution, but the lizard's saliva kept loosening the tape. Finally they hit on a ruse: The warden put a bag of ice on each side of the lizard's head. Within minutes it was fooled into thinking that winter had arrived, went into hibernation mode, and slept long enough for us to get the scene shot.

The most annoying and sometimes dangerous animals we had to work with were the baboons. Among all the apes these are surely the most unpleasant ones; they are definitely not cute. They snarl and bite and, except when they hunt together, are quite unsociable even among themselves. Our story called for baboons as an important element; we lost time in the effort to film the baboons in the right places and the right positions. They had to be staked down with nylon ropes, which did not always work. Once a baboon escaped and we had a hell of a time trying to lure it back into the jeep, dangling pieces of melon as bait. When the creature finally hopped in, they tried to put a rope over its head; it was too quick and kept removing it. Finally, it jumped on the driver's lap. He was a strong black man but was clearly frightened. While the animal keepers attempted to lasso it once more, the baboon peed on him.

Whenever we had the baboons on the set, before the work could begin the assistant director had to go around and inquire of every woman on the set whether she had her period. Apparently when the baboons smell menstrual flow, they go crazy. One day, after having gotten negative replies from every woman, including some visitors on the set, we started work. All of a sudden, one of the baboons took a wild leap and attacked one of our visitors. She was a girl of about thirteen; our assistant director had thought of her as a child rather than as a woman, and had not asked. Luckily, two keepers quickly tackled the animal and got it off the frightened girl, who only sustained a few scratches.

As far as entertainment was concerned, we were left to our own devices. There was not even a movie house in the town. We made our own fun; some soccer (not me!), some dancing to taped music (also not me!), some chess, and a lot of Scrabble (definitely me). We had a Scrabble board going incessantly both during and after work. The waiting times while the crew made adjustments between rehearsal and shooting were heavy with debates over permissible words. We even carried a *Concise Oxford Dictionary* in the makeup truck. Cy Endfield played Scrabble the same way he played table tennis and everything else—with a fierce determination to win. I had never known anyone so unable to bear losing a game. The first time he lost to me at chess, he hovered over the board for a full ten minutes, trying to figure out what he might have done differently that would have turned the game in his favor. The same with Scrabble. Once when we had been playing on and off during the day and evening, again there were debates over allowable words, which were decided by recourse to the dictionary. That night I was awakened by my door being jerked open; none of us locked a door, there was no need. There stood Cy in his bathrobe, glowering at me; he looked as though he had not slept. I looked at my watch; it was 3:00 A.M. Thinking that we had some kind of emergency, I cried, "What's up, Cy?" He said quite angrily, "What the fuck do you mean 'vox' isn't a word?"

In addition to starring in *The Sands of the Kalahari*, Stanley Baker was also the film's producer. This robust, fun-loving Welshman was on his way to becoming something big and important. Not long after *Kalahari* was released, he received the highest recognition a British actor can get—a knighthood. Sir Stanley Baker died of cancer in his prime. He had not been a close friend—very few people who frequent pubs are close friends of mine—but I had liked him.

There was little question in anybody's mind as to whether I would be cast in *The Russians Are Coming, the Russians Are Coming,* due to start filming in the fall of 1965. When it turned out that the role of the submarine captain had no English dialogue but was to be entirely in Russian, there was even less doubt. I consider my Russian to be very poor, but my accent is impeccable—not just by American standards, but by Russian ones. Performing Russian songs for these many years and joking, singing, and making merry with Russians had given me an imprimatur of "all-purpose Eastern European" in the Hollywood colony. Such a handle would normally be a hindrance to one's career, since it narrows the scope, but in this instance it was useful. Norman Jewison gave me the role and promised me a good time. He made good on that promise, too; the good times happened and they made for one of the best location shoots anyone could wish for. The main action of the film takes place on a small island off the coast of New England, where a Russian submarine, with a captain curious to see the American coast, runs aground.

Norman Jewison picked a location in Northern California with a coastline and a landscape very similar to that of New England. We were some 120 miles north of San Francisco; the film unit was headquartered in Fort Bragg, California, a fishing harbor. Some of the cast, myself included, rented log cabins or small houses in the woods between Fort Bragg and Mendocino. For a stay of ten weeks it was worth it. At night I made a fire, cooked dinner, listened to music, read, and felt pretty terrific. Deer would come by and peer into the window, quite unafraid. At regular intervals you heard the sound of a foghorn, and the blinking beacon from the lighthouse was ever present. Not everyone was called to work every day; since most of us had rented cars, we explored the wine country. It was idyllic. The only things that were missing, Carl Reiner, Alan Arkin, and I agreed, were lox, bagels, corned beef, and pastrami. We found a solution for the lox; the fish-processing house in Fort Bragg had a setup for smoking fish. Hand them a salmon and they would smoke it for you. It was not quite Jewish deli, but a fair substitute. Jay Bernstein, who was then my public relations person, decided to fly up to the location for a visit. I gave him a shopping list over the phone; Nate 'n' Al's Delicatessen in Beverly Hills would make a parcel, which he would bring up: bagels, pastrami, corned beef, pickles, and salami. People kept moving away from him at the airport and changed seats on the plane because of the smell.

Lee Hays of the Weavers, who knew several people in the cast besides me, also came to visit. One, Alan Arkin, was a very close friend with whom he had recorded an album. He stayed for a couple of weeks, watched the shooting, and livened up the parties at which we frequently entertained ourselves in this remote part of the West Coast. When Lee arrived he had been fitted with a new pair of dentures that bothered him enormously—so much so that he gave up solid food in favor of a liquid diet. One night he came to Alan Arkin's party without his dentures. "Lee, what happened to your teeth?" I asked. "Ah hell," he said toothlessly. "They hurt so much, I finally took 'em out and left them on the bureau. Let the fuckin' things hurt by themselves."

The entire town of Fort Bragg, indeed the entire area, was drawn into the process of making the movie. Some were recruited as extras, and those who were not came almost every day to follow the progress of the filming. At the end of each workday a plane would fly the film to Los Angeles for processing. On the following day a copy of the processed film would arrive back at the location for the director to look at. Most directors have an aversion to people watching the "dailies"; actors are not often welcome to sit in and hear the technical staff's comments about the work. Norman had an entirely different attitude. The only place where the dailies could be screened was the local movie house, which we rented for an hour each evening. Not only were the actors invited to watch, the whole town was welcome to sit in. Each evening there would be a throng of people at the movie house. After a while there were regulars who had become amateur movie critics. Doing this achieved something wonderful; the whole town felt that they were partners in the enterprise and part of the movie, whether they were in it or not.

We organized something else to which all the townspeople were invited: an evening with the cast. After all, we had some wonderful performers among the actors, some of whom were in great demand as solo artists and others who came from the improvisational theatre. Between us we could put on an entertainment the combined fees of which no promoter would have been able to afford. It turned out to be a long and wonderful evening: Among the participants were Tessie O'Shea, Carl Reiner, Alan Arkin, Richard Schaal, Jonathan Winters, and Paul Ford. They were joined by two wives, performers in their own right, who had no roles in the film but who were along for the ride: Alan's wife, Barbara Dana, and Richard Schaal's then wife, Valerie Harper. This illustrious cast put on various pieces of comedy and improvisation. The musical portions were mostly left to me and Alex Hassilev, my Limeliter friend, who played one of the Russians in the film. We had accomplices, especially for the Russian music. Some of the actors who had smaller parts in the movie played instruments, and so did the film's Russian-language expert, Leon Belasco. Admission to this megaconcert in the town's high school auditorium was free; it was our gift to the town.

The Russians Are Coming was a huge success everywhere except in Russia, where it was not shown at all. Its message of conflict that resolves itself in laughter and, in the end, gives peace a chance was not palatable to the Soviets in the late sixties. Their top brass saw the film, both at the Soviet embassy in Washington and in Moscow, where Norman had taken it in an effort to persuade them that this was just the sort of gentle medicine needed to diffuse international tension. They laughed at its humor, and then decided against permitting it to be shown. When I attended my first meeting of the International Federation of Actors in 1973, my Soviet colleague, Gennadi Pyatakov, told me that he had seen the movie. He also told me that he and his colleagues had decided that I was an authentic ethnic Russian but that, to judge by his accent, Alan Arkin had to be from Soviet Georgia.

Bob Radnitz was a producer of motion pictures that were aimed at a family market: children's stories and award-winning novels with appeal to a youth audience. I played leading roles in three of his films. Two of them, *Dog of Flanders* and *The Little Ark,* were shot in Holland, and the third, *My Side of the Mountain,* in Canada. They were decent little films, not overly ambitious, and they achieved exactly what was intended. The making of each one included a certain amount of unavoidable roughing it. *Dog of Flanders* had yet another canine for us to contend with. He was a seasoned film actor, known elsewhere as Old Yeller, and his keeper, Frank Weatherwax, came from a dynasty of animal trainers for the movies. "Mah brother, Rudd Weatherwax, looks after Lassie," he would announce proudly and toothlessly. Then he would point to Old Yeller and proclaim, "This dog never have bit nobody."

My Side of the Mountain had to be filmed in two segments. The first and longer one needed summer; the last sequence called for deep winter. It was set in Eastern Quebec, and we shot the first part in the late summer months of 1967. Then we went home, and came back when the snow was on the ground some three months later. In the interim I had started to grow a beard, as I was to begin my *Fiddler on the Roof* engagements as soon as the movie was finished. Actually, the beard worked out fine; I played an itinerant folklorist who finds and befriends the young runaway who insists that he can survive alone. I teach him a few skills and then leave, returning months later to help bring the boy back to civilization. What was unusual about this production was that they asked me not only to sing and play, but to write the songs as well. With the exception of one French-Canadian tune, "*Un Canadien Errant,*" for which I only wrote the English lyrics, for all the others I wrote words and music.

During the summer of shooting Rita and I had a personal crisis. We were expecting our first child, and looking forward to it very much. One night she was seized by very painful cramps and we rushed her to a hospital in Montreal some sixty miles away. For the next few days I commuted to the hospital; the movie people were very understanding and rearranged some schedules. Despite the efforts of the doctors, Rita had a miscarriage. We felt the tragedy keenly, Rita especially; for me it was a psychological shock, while for her there was not only extreme anguish but physical pain as well. No man can possibly know the feeling of bereavement of a woman who sustains such a loss. To make matters worse, the nursing staff made a thoughtless mistake. A nurse, not checking that this particular patient had not given birth, showed up to ask whether Rita was ready to nurse her baby. If Rita could have thrown her out of the room bodily, she would have done so. I was horrified at this insensitivity and told them so, but the harm was done. Before having our first child, we would have to go through still another miscarriage the following year, our hopes dashed once more.

Finally, in 1969, our first son, Robert Simon, was born. He was named Robert after his maternal grandfather and Simon after his paternal great-grandfather, Reb Shimon. I was present at Rob's birth, having trained in the Lamaze method in preparation for the event. At the time the baby was due, I was working on a film, *Darker Than Amber,* which was being shot on location in Florida. I had my agents put a "paternity clause" into the contract. When I received word from our doctor in New York that the event was imminent, the movie would have to let me go for four days. Even if we hadn't been following the Lamaze training, according to which I was needed to help, I was not going to miss the birth of my child for anything in the world. To have your first child at age forty-five is leaving it pretty late, but I didn't care. Someone asked me after Robbie's birth what I intended to do about the PTA, seeing that all the other parents there could easily be my children. I replied that there were only two possibilities: Either I would not go or I would dominate the proceedings. In the end I did not go.

A couple of days after Rob was born, I called my friend Rabbi Joachim Prinz to ask him if he would officiate at my son's *bris,* the ritual circumcision to take place in the hospital on the eighth day. In his brusque Teutonic fashion, Joachim said, "Two conditions." When I asked what they were, Dr. Prinz replied, "First, I won't do the ceremony in the hospital; I can't stand the sight of blood. My son Jonathan [also an ordained rabbi] can do that one. I'll repeat the ceremony later in your house. That's the first condition." When I asked him what the second condition was, he said: "For the ceremony you must get me a bottle of superb French wine, because I don't drink this Israeli crap." That's my friend Joachim, I thought.

After our son was born, travel became more of a production. Baby carriage, collapsible crib, Pampers, and an additional person, the

English nanny Zena Waldron, to be known as Wawa. Add our Scotty dog Monty, and the simplicity of the days when I would just grab a guitar and a garment bag became just a nostalgic memory. After our second son, Danny, was born, the equipment portions of the trips doubled. It was all worth it, but it was no longer simple. At one of the foreign airports, Amsterdam I think, a customs agent had never seen Pampers and suspected contraband. He opened up several before he was finally convinced that we were not smuggling anything.

One day my old pal Herb Cohen, with whom I had opened the Unicorn in Hollywood, gave me a call. He had gone on to become a manager of rock groups; his star clients were Frank Zappa and the Mothers of Invention. Herb wanted to know if I would meet with Frank, who had a film project he wanted to discuss with me. Frank arrived at my hotel and proceeded to tell me the plot and outline of a film about the life of a rock group on the road. There was no script yet, he said, but he knew in detail what the action and the characters would be. The picture was to be called *200 Motels,* and my role was to be the manager of the rock group, a character to be called Rance Muhammitz. Frank Zappa was a very engaging man; his descriptions were vivid and also funny. Usually one does not accept a role without reading a script, but he was so persuasive that I agreed to do the film on the basis of his presentation alone. Later I asked myself whether this was a big mistake.

The filming was to be done at Pinewood Studios outside London, where I had done a number of pictures during my English period. We packed up the babies, the equipment, and Wawa, the nanny, and flew to London. The nanny would be in her element in England, where the rest of the populace was as devoted to the sacred ritual of afternoon tea as she. Come to think of it, I hardly remember her without a cup of tea at *any* time of the day or evening. Because of her we all got into the habit of drinking tea; she was even known to feed it to the dog. On this trip, despite his Scottish pedigree, Monty had to be left behind in New York because of the British insistence on six-month quarantines for animals.

I got several shocks when I started work on *200 Motels.* The set swarmed with groupies who were only too eager to do anything—and I mean anything—to please Frank and the band. A few of them had been cast in the movie as—what else?—groupies. The trouble was that a couple of them failed to pass the medical examination that every film company requires. The girls were emaciated to a dangerous degree; some had a drug habit or had otherwise plainly abused themselves in pursuit of whatever gratification. Despite the doctor's refusal to give them the required clearance, Frank used them anyway.

Also hanging around the movie set was a woman named Cynthia whose last name I never learned; she was known around rock music circles as Cynthia Plastercaster. Her specialty was casting rock stars' penises in metal, bronze, silver, whatever. I was told that Mick Jagger's wife had ordered a cast of Mick's dick in fourteen-karat gold to adorn the couple's mantel over the fireplace. Cynthia was not terribly attractive, but she had a very pretty assistant whose job it was to see that the subjects achieved and maintained full erectile glory until the plaster was applied. She was known as "the plater."

Another shock was the script. There were the expected songs, of course, but there was a proliferation of Zappas, too. Not only did Frank play himself, but Ringo Starr also played Frank, dressed exactly like Frank, and was given alter ego chores. For good measure, there was also an inanimate dummy dressed in the exact same costume, so that at times there were three Zappas to be seen at the same time. In addition to playing the role I had been hired for, Frank suggested that I also play a nun in drag. I balked at that, arguing that I was not sure whether I would be able to show my face among the Jews after the release of this movie; it was asking too much for me to spoil any chance I might have with Catholics as well. In the end the role of the nun was played by Keith Moon.

One of the sets built on the soundstage was a replica of a concentration camp; it was difficult to fathom why. Even more difficult to grasp was the notion that the entire London Symphony Orchestra, which had been hired to accompany the Mothers of Invention in several scenes, was to be dressed in striped prisoner's garb. The craziest thing about these scenes was that Herbie Cohen was made to wear a Nazi uniform and sit in the watchtower with a machine gun. One of the musicians did walk off the set, but not for that reason. When the harpist found out that one of the numbers the orchestra was supposed to play was entitled "Penis Dimension," she packed up her harp and left. I had participated in many films before this one and was used to the fact that often you find yourself in the midst of organized chaos. This was different; it was unorganized chaos. Despite it all, when the picture was released, it became a cult film. It even gave me a certain amount of recognition among rock audiences and flower children.

Some of the films I participated in during the eighties and nineties disappeared into the cracks somewhere. A movie written and directed by a Russian expatriate, Vladimir Rif, first entitled *The Communal Flat* and then retitled *Very Close Quarters,* hardly saw the light of day, or more appropriately the dark of a movie house. Despite the fact that the cast included some very good actors like Paul Sorvino, Dennis Boutsikaris, and Shelley Winters, it never made the grade. I never even saw it myself, perhaps all for the better. I recall a conversation I had with Paul Sorvino during the filming, which was done in a drafty warehouse in Queens. "How come you are doing this picture?" I asked Paul. "I'm doing it because you're doing it," he said. "Sonofabitch, I'm doing it because *you're* doing it," I said. "Well, at least between Shelley and you and me," said Paul, "each of us is getting five percent of the profits." I said, "So what? Five percent of nothing is nothing. And, what's more, ten percent would have been better."

The other film I was in that nobody ever saw had a location in Barcelona, at least. The film, *Dark Tower,* was a gothic tale of sinister forces and spiritualist carryings-on. Again there were good people in the cast: Jenny Agutter, Michael Moriarty, Carol Lynley, and Kevin McCarthy. But this film seems to have disappeared altogether from the face of the earth. The only thing I ever saw was a poster they sent me, which I have hung in my office to prove to my family that my trip to Spain was not for idle pleasure. To add to the mystery, the poster lists as director someone I have never met. To think that I could have been a bank clerk with an ordered and predictable life.

A whole genre of films went down the drain with the demise of the Soviet Union. All those lovely plots revolving around the rivalry between the U.S. and the USSR, all the spies in and out of the cold, the CIA trying to outwit the KGB—all these will be regarded in the future as cinematic museum pieces with little relevance to the world at hand. For a time, some of these stories will continue to be made, especially the sequels to earlier successes, but there is no doubt that the movies have lost a source of material which until 1992 seemed inexhaustible. In 1992 I was involved in the making of a film, *Crisis in the Kremlin,* whose subject matter had become irrelevant by the time the picture was ready for release. The story line concerned a plot to assassinate Mikhail Gorbachev. I played a former KGB agent who comes out of retirement to help the CIA foil the plot. The CIA is involved because they are afraid that Gorby's downfall might cause a backslide into the bad old days. When we shot the film Gorbachev was in office—we filmed it in Bulgaria instead of Russia, so as to avoid offending any Soviet citizens. None of it would have mattered anyway, because by the time the picture was edited, Gorbachev was gone. The film was hardly worth releasing; its topicality had vanished overnight.

Of greater interest was a radio program I did for National Public Radio, although its subject, too, had been overtaken by history. It was an adaptation of Gorbachev's own account of the August coup of

1991. I played Gorbachev; radio permits you to do with your voice things that would not work visually. I was very interested in this project, which was a dramatic reenactment incorporating the man's own words from his diary. It would be the historical record of an important event made accessible to English-speaking audiences. Such an account, on audiotape, had a chance to survive.

For quite some time past the world has been Hollywood's backlot. Where studios once built a replica of the Acropolis, a New York street, a London market, or a Cairo bazaar in their own backyards, film units have in recent years traveled everywhere for authentic locations, which often turn out to be cheaper than staying at home. Now that the Iron Curtain has lifted for good, the former Soviet Union and its satellites have opened up as well. After 1991 I worked in films that were shot on location in Yugoslavia, Bulgaria, and Russia. Although far less comfortable than location shoots in the West, they were interesting and, for me, a welcome way of listening to Eastern European music at the source. Never mind that instead of a dressing trailer I had a military armor-plated vehicle with a wood-burning stove in Bulgaria.

Over the years, my work in films has given me the chance to travel to places I might otherwise not have seen, or if so, then only as a tourist. I regret that I did not do more. But to my utter amazement I discovered that one cannot be in all places and do all things all at one time. Much as I hated to admit it, there were limitations.

MUCH OF MY work in musical plays after *The Sound of Music* was done outside of New York—Tevye being the role that went longer and took me farther than any other. On Broadway itself I did two more original musicals, *Café Crown* and *Pousse Café,* in 1964 and 1966. Neither of them was a success. In fact, they were dismal failures. Both of them had the word "café" in the title, and both of them ran for three performances, which made even an unsuperstitious person like myself vow never to do another play with "café" in the title. *Café Crown* was based on a straight play by Hy Kraft about Yiddish actors in their habitual hangout on the Lower East Side. It was a funny play and worth reviving, as a subsequent production in 1990 by Joe Papp's Public Theater showed. But the musical version we worked on in 1964 simply did not come together, despite some good songs by Albert Hague, some decent lyrics by Marty Brill, choreography by Ron Field, and the considerable talents of my costars Sam Levene and the opera singer Brenda Lewis. One of the supporting roles, that of the young man who arrives from out of town looking for his roots, was excellently played by Alan Alda. The director was the problem. He had described everything very well, first in parlor meetings and then in preliminary readings around the table, but when it came to putting the thing on its feet, it was a lead balloon. All of us felt we came off looking bad—even foolish for having lent our talents to such a weak piece of work.

Two years later I was persuaded to do the other *Café* musical. This one also had promise: a story based on the famous book and film *The Blue Angel*—and a score by Duke Ellington, no less. I was to play the role of the university professor who throws away his life because of his infatuation with the cabaret singer Lola. Emil Jannings had played this part in the early German movie that had made Marlene Dietrich famous. Years later Edward Dmytryk directed a Hollywood remake of the film, this time starring Curt Jurgens and Mai Britt. In that film version, I played the owner of the Blue Angel cabaret, a thoroughly despicable character. *Pousse Café* transposed the action from Germany to a New Orleans cabaret visited by students from a boys' school who are breaking the rules of curfew. In this stage musical I played the professor, and by rights it should have been an important milestone in my career. Why it did not turn out to be was, in some measure, my own fault. One must never think of playing an important role as though it were an important role. There was, however, enough blame to go around.

To start with, there was the fact that Duke Ellington was nowhere to be found either in the beginning or for any rehearsals. That was a money decision. He had written a number of songs, which were put into various parts of the script in an attempt to make them part of a whole, but that is no way to put a musical together. The songs have to be an integral and organic part of the process, and the composer needs to be present for it. They did not want to pay the Duke for being around, and so he stayed away, and all we had were the songs he had originally done. The book by Jerome Weidman (*I Can Get It for You Wholesale*) was fine, but it had to be acted right. And right there was our major stumbling block. Our leading lady was Lilo, the French cabaret star. Unfortunately, she just couldn't handle the demands of this role. The trouble was, she could not be fired, either; her husband was the producer. He was a French nobleman, the Marquis de la Passardière. These titles in countries that have ceased to be monarchies are just titles, but people cling to them. He had a habit of kissing women's hands and then letting his lips work their way up to their armpits. His was an oily sort of elegance, at best.

We knew that we were in trouble well before we hit New York.

In Detroit, there was a procession of directors; each arrived to take a look and decide whether he would be willing to be the doctor who would make this patient well. In the end, they hired José Quintero, the renowned director of American classics. He came in, ordered rewrites, shuffled scenes, and attempted to give some life to the show. But with Lilo's limitations that was a virtual impossibility. José, not known for sobriety at the best of times, drank especially heavily during this ordeal in a vain effort to get through it unscathed. He was particularly incensed about the Marquis's inability even to see the problem, let alone solve it. At one point José said to me in his heavy Panamanian accent: "He is a bastar'. Dossent he know the French Rebolution happened?"

We opened on Broadway on March 17, 1966. A disaster. The closing notice was up even before the opening night. This is one of the cute things producers can do to save themselves from having to run an extra week, in case the thing flops. As a result, you can open on a Friday, as we did, and close on Saturday night after three performances. We should have closed on Friday night or—like a play in England I read about—after the first act. The reviews were unkind—and totally justified. Mine were bad, too; not too easy to take after a long career in the theatre with good and quotable notices. For honesty's sake, here is what the *New York Times* reviewer, Stanley Kauffman, said about my role in *Pousse Café:* "Theodore Bikel gives a performance that begins at the mediocre and declines to the maudlin." I actually did not mind this review; it meant that I had to work to reestablish myself. Apart from that, I took away very little from this misguided venture. Only a few good memories of some pleasant relationships with colleagues, among them Charles Durning, who has since gone on to do great character work in all media.

As I divided my time between the various disciplines, I realized that the attraction I felt for America stemmed from its potential more than its reality. This was as true of my attitude toward the country as it was of my profession. The distances are vast, the audiences practically unlimited, and Broadway is only a small corner of it all. No sour grapes, it would take more than two flops to persuade a professional stage actor that an eventual return to the Great White Way was not desirable or possible. Apart from Broadway, there was theatre to be done in the provinces, in summer stock, in tents and hardtops, in dinner theatres, and in regional theatre. Off-Broadway in 1962 I did *Brecht on Brecht,* a compilation of pieces by the renowned anti-Nazi playwright that George Tabori had adapted as a theatrical presentation. We did it at the Theatre de Lys in the Village, and later at the

Playhouse in the Park in Philadelphia. I had always been partial to
Brecht, and it was a glorious opportunity to speak words I had known
in German, words that had been written by a non-Jewish German
who loathed the barbarism his nation had indulged in and who had
been driven from his own homeland just as if he, too, had been a Jew.

One of my favorite pieces by Brecht speaks most movingly of the
predicament of the refugee:

> I am sitting by the roadside watching the driver changing
>   wheels
> I do not like the place I am coming from
> I do not like the place I am going to
> So why am I watching the driver changing wheels
> With such impatience?

Viveca Lindfors, George Tabori's wife, was one of the participants
in *Brecht on Brecht*. This strange Swedish woman was at times quite
brilliant and at others totally and irrationally off the mark. You never
knew what the next performance might bring, or even what the next
ten minutes of the same performance might bring. I get rattled and
confused by brilliance that is not consistent. In Viveca's case, I did not
try to understand or define it, beyond an assumption that there must
be a Twilight Zone, a fourth dimension, and that she was in it.

Another nonplay I performed in on several occasions was *Jacques
Brel Is Alive and Well and Living in Paris*. The first time we performed it
was in summer stock at the North Shore Theatre in Beverly, Massachusetts, in 1974. This was the first time the piece had been done at
a theatre-in-the-round, actually an ideal space for this kind of show.
Our cast was also quite unique; apart from me there were the superb
actress, dancer, and singer Chita Rivera and Gil Price and Judy Gibson. Two women, two men—two whites and two blacks. It made for
a terrific mix of voices and attitudes. The material was well served.
Dobbs Franks, a lanky Westerner who later moved to Australia to
conduct operas and ballets, was our musical director. He taught me
the material. Dania Krupska was the director, her experience as a
choreographer very valuable as we used the stage circle. Working theatre-in-the-round is a technique which must be mastered; it is quite
unlike proscenium work. You must not only make sure to move often
enough so that people all over the house get a chance to see your face
but also suppress the instinct that moves you to face the people nearest
you in the audience. When you do that, only the smallest portion of
the house sees you properly. The thing to do is to face the audience

across the expanse of the stage, thus confronting the largest slice of the pie.

As for *Jacques Brel*, we were able to elicit from even the staid New England audiences the kind of response I had not thought possible. Despite sometimes coarse imagery, the lyrics captivated ladies in steel-rimmed glasses who would normally be shocked by a "damn." They never hissed, booed, or walked out, even the one time when "fuck" was uttered—by a woman, no less. At the end of the show we sang "If We Only Have Love," then I made a little curtain speech, telling the audience about Brel, his life and his death, and then invited them to stand, hold hands, or come up onstage while we all sang the song again with the audience joining in. We did this at the end of each show, not only then but at subsequent engagements as well—at East Windsor, Connecticut, and at Westbury, New York, with Julie Wilson and Lainie Kazan. It never failed; the audience was moved every time and so were we. Even though Jacques Brel is no longer living—in Paris or anywhere else—he *is* alive and well and will be for as long as his songs are sung.

I did some lesser and lighter plays around the country, most of which were fun, although they had to be put together in far too great a hurry. This can be especially cumbersome when you are doing a piece which you have not previously performed, in a company of players to whom the material is also new. We tried to mount *The Rothschilds,* for example, in one week. None of us had ever done the musical, and some of us had not even been to see it when it was on Broadway. Yet there we were trying to accomplish the impossible. On the Wednesday I called the cast together and made a little speech: "I do not know who decreed that this can be done in this short a time. Only God can make a world in a week—and he screwed it up." We opened all right, but the first three performances were not giving the patrons their money's worth. Playing Mayer Rothschild was also phys-ically taxing; he goes from being a young man in the Frankfurt ghetto to manhood and very old age in the play. Nor had it been an easy play to write. Sheldon Harnick and Jerry Bock, the creators of *The Roth-schilds* and *Fiddler on the Roof,* confided in me that writing a play about five rich Jews had been much harder than writing about one poor milkman.

I did the obligatory light fare in various theatres: *Marriage-Go-Round, "I Do! I Do!," Sunshine Boys,* and the like. But what was more memorable were the times when I got to play world literature on-stage. The Romanian director Liviu Ciulei had been confined to his homeland for years, and banned from directing plays there because of his unorthodox staging of certain plays that the regime considered counterrevolutionary. One of these plays was Gogol's *The Inspector General,* a spoof about bureaucracy and the foolish reactions of a frightened and corrupt populace. For years Liviu was forced to make a living as a stage designer, one of his other talents, but not the one his heart and soul were devoted to. When Liviu was finally permitted to leave Romania, he worked in various countries in the West with great success, finally arriving in the United States. In the fall of 1979 the Circle in the Square Theatre asked him to direct *Inspector General* again. He met with me and offered me the role of the Mayor, the chief target of a deception that starts with a mistaken identity, which is then exploited by the imposter. Liviu is an incredibly inventive director. For example, the Mayor has the first line of the play: "Gentlemen, we have a grave problem." There were a full six minutes of action in pantomime on stage before those words were spoken. Officials entering, preening themselves, jealously jockeying for position around the table, and harrumphing. Then there is a maid, Avdotya, who has no lines at all in the play. In Liviu's production, she talked incessantly in some incomprehensible gibberish, and in the context of her physical actions, what she said was totally clear.

Playing *Inspector General* was a fine experience. Unfortunately, when we opened, all the New York newspapers were on a prolonged strike and we had no reviews at all. There was also no newspaper advertising available. Shows that had opened prior to the strike had a chance to pass out leaflets with reprints of the critics' comments. We were entirely at the mercy of word-of-mouth publicity. Still, we did fairly well, and ran the number of weeks we had been scheduled. I had to take compassionate leave for three performances in the middle of the run. My father was dying of cancer and was in the hospital in Israel. I flew there the day before Yom Kippur to see him briefly, and then returned to the play. Afterward I only had one more chance to see him before he died a few months later.

The second time I had a chance to work with Liviu Ciulei was at the Guthrie Theatre in Minneapolis. Liviu had asked me to meet him because he had a proposition to make. By now he was the artistic director of the Guthrie with a commitment to direct a number of plays himself. The Guthrie had scheduled Brecht's *Threepenny Opera* in the Marc Blitzstein adaptation, and Liviu wanted me to go to Minneapolis for a three-month guest engagement. What role? I wanted to know, expecting to hear Mr. Peachum or the Police Chief. He surprised me by asking me to play Mack the Knife. I told him that I was flattered but that it sounded a little crazy for me to play Mackie, bumming around in whorehouses and also two-timing Polly and Lucy, the police chief's daughter. This was a Kevin Kline role, I said. Liviu said no; he saw Mackie as a businessman whose business was crime, an older man who likes young girls. So I accepted and went to Minneapolis.

This production too was innovative. The stage was hung with rags, and multicolored graffiti were scrawled on the walls. As the play opens, the floor of the stage is covered in brown wrapping paper. Somewhere in the middle of the eight-minute overture, an umbrella pierces the wrapping paper from below, and a very tall young woman, a hooker, rises up through the hole. Knives cut the paper and other characters appear: vendors, pickpockets, other hookers, who all proceed to go about their nefarious occupations. By the time the overture has ended, the stage is populated and teeming with life, the paper has been pushed into the orchestra pit—the orchestra playing elsewhere onstage—and the play begins.

I worked hard on Mack the Knife. The songs were the easiest part for me. The presentational style of the play presented greater difficulty—perhaps because I had been doing so much in the naturalistic school of acting in films and TV, which demand it, and also in stage plays that had been directed in a style different from the one Liviu employed. I also was still not quite convinced that I was right for the role. Although I got good reactions from the audience and from some—but not all—of the critics, I do not think that I did my best work in the play. Perhaps one should rely on one's gut reactions and follow self-critical impulses rather than give in to the praise of others. Still, I was glad to have the learning experience.

There is another way of learning, however, which is not in a public forum. Failure is costly in a free-market world, and therefore actors and other theatre professionals tend to play it safe. This essentially guarantees that no one attempts to widen his or her horizons. You do only what you do best and stay away from experimentation, from offbeat roles in offbeat plays, and also from the classics. For that reason, actors' workshops have sprung up and they fill a real need. They are to an actor what a gym is to an athlete, exercising creative muscles so they will not atrophy. They are also safe places to fail. I belong to two of these workshops, Theatre Artists Workshop of Westport, Connecticut, and Theatre East in Los Angeles. You perform scenes and monologues, you get to direct other actors, and you do it only for your peers, without any outsiders present. The critique that follows each piece can be very helpful. So can offering critique to others, as it hones your analytical senses.

Theatre is and has been the mainstay of my artistic and emotional equilibrium. Not only is it the granddaddy of the performing arts, it also nurtures the other outlets of an actor's work and gives solid grounding to his craft. Of course, it cannot be the only source one draws upon. An actor also has to have a level of general intellectual curiosity that seeks information from all sources. I have often stressed this to students, especially those training to be actors. We all make use of whatever tools we possess. An author writes, an architect designs, a minstrel finds expression in poetry and song. Most of us ply whatever trade or calling we have, using the specialized knowledge our training has given us. But we cannot be so intent on our specialty that we attempt it in a vacuum, unconnected to the world around us. A businessman who opens his morning paper to read only the business section, an engineer who neglects all but the science section, an artist who finds interest solely in the arts pages—these would, in the end, be poorly equipped to serve either themselves or the community around them. In the end, they would also be poor actors, scientists, or engineers.

In that spirit I addressed the students at the University of Hartford when I received an Honorary Doctorate of Fine Arts. I said, "The world can either be ignored or made to inform our process of thinking, of planning, and of working. Even in ancient Greece that seemed to be understood: '*Anthropos politikon zo'on*,' they declared, 'Man is a societal animal.' Your university education has given you the wherewithal both to specialize and to proliferate. My counsel to you is: Do both to the fullest extent. Be rounded human beings, informed about everything, curious about everything. Be a part of the world rather than remain apart from it."

I shall remain a theatre person to the end, although I have discouraged many young people from entering a profession which only the passionate can endure. Most of those who set out to have a life in the theatre are lucky if instead of a life it merely turns out to be a living. And all too often it isn't even that. To quote the late Moss Hart: "You can't make a living in the theatre. You can make a killing, but you can't make a living." But even had I known everything I know now, I would not have changed my choices and my direction. For I do have the passion. And I have been given the rare privilege—for which I shall always be grateful—of being permitted to escape from the absurd artificiality of everyday living into the reality of theatre.

Tevye

MELAMED (HEBREW TEACHER): *If I could only be Rothschild! You know, if I were Rothschild I would be richer than Rothschild.*
A BOY'S FATHER: *Why is that?*
MELAMED: *Because I could teach Hebrew school on the side.*

—JEWISH ANECDOTE

I_F THERE ARE SUCH THINGS AS PREORDAINED EVENTS, then I was surely destined to play Tevye the Milkman. Not only did I have the requisite talent and the voice for this musical role, I also had a personal background that put me much closer to it than many who would need a longer reach in order to make the part their own. The literature was something I grew up with; twenty-six volumes of the works of Sholem Aleichem in Yiddish sat on our bookshelves during my early youth in Vienna. The books were well used; my father would read short stories or plays aloud to us. The books were rescued from the Nazis by my maternal grandmother with some of our other belongings and followed us to Israel. I grew up with the world of Sholem Aleichem at my fingertips; I was a young Jew who had started his life in the diaspora and who, as a boy of thirteen, had played a thirteen-year-old in a Sholem Aleichem play. As a professional actor my first paid engagement was at the Habimah Theatre, playing the Constable in *Tevye the Milkman* in Hebrew. I was a natural for the part of Tevye when *Fiddler on the Roof* was first mounted in 1964; I was also unavailable. Not that they were clamoring for my services at the time; Zero Mostel had the part locked up. It would be some time before they got around to me.

The world of Anatevka, the mythical town in which *Fiddler on the Roof* is set, has been written about many times. Within the Russian empire, the Pale of Settlement, the carefully circumscribed area outside which Jews were not permitted to take up residence, contained small villages very much like Anatevka. This was the archetypal *shtetl* in which Eastern Europe's Jewish life unfolded, where the Yiddish language flowered and where richness of spirit stood in such contrast to the poverty of the inhabitants. (A diminutive of the Yiddish word *shtot* or "town," *shtetl* literally means "little town.") They were people guided by rules of behavior laid down by the *halachah,* a set of codes compiled over centuries by the rabbis. These codes governed not merely religious ritual, but all facets of life outside the house of prayer as well. They covered birth, circumcision, betrothal, marriage, cleanliness, and the behavior of one Jew toward another at all times. Sabbath and the festivals turned even the poorest of shtetl Jews into a wearer of a nobleman's mantle. There was danger and pain in this place of poverty, but there was also beauty and there was song. This world furnished endless material for Jewish writers, poets, and singers in Eastern Europe; translations into many of the world's languages followed. The works of Sholem Aleichem, I. L. Peretz, and Abraham Goldfaden were performed on stages wherever the Yiddish language was spoken: Poland, Argentina, Mexico, and the United States. It was only a matter of time before someone would decide that here was material for the Broadway theatre as well.

Nevertheless, this did not look to be a safe move. How much of an audience could there possibly be for a play set in a poor little Jewish village in Eastern Europe whose inhabitants wore shabby and threadbare clothes? How could such a play compete with the elegance of settings like the Ascot races in *My Fair Lady* or Captain von Trapp's château in *The Sound of Music?* Would such a play have an audience at all beyond Jewish theatergoers? It was a gamble but they decided to take it anyway. The creative ingredients were right: Jerome Robbins, the preeminent choreographer who proposed to direct as well; Harold Prince, an enterprising young producer; a book by Joe Stein based on Sholem Aleichem's Yiddish play; composer Jerry Bock and lyricist Sheldon Harnick, the creators of *Fiorelllo!* They did create a remarkable show and a sensation to boot. The predictions of the naysayers who maintained that this play would only have a narrow ethnic appeal were proved wrong. It had widespread appeal, and not only in America, where the rhythm and language of Eastern Europe's Jews had gained common currency because of a whole genre of literature and a host of New York performers. When the play was produced in Japan, local theatergoers inquired whether it was true that *Fiddler* had been a huge success in America. When they were told that indeed it had been, they shook their heads in bewilderment. "Strange," they said, "but it's so Japanese!"

I saw *Fiddler* twice in its original Broadway run, the first time quite early on and the second time some three months later. There was a pronounced change in Zero Mostel's performance the second time, one that probably stemmed from the fact that he tended to get bored rather quickly and needed the stimulus of inventing new stuff to keep going. When coupled with self-discipline, that can be all right. But self-discipline was not one of Zero's strong suits. He committed excesses on stage that delighted the audience because they were funny. Everything Zero did was funny, but not necessarily right. That second time around I saw Tevye's hand "accidentally" fall into a pail of milk, and for the next three minutes the play revolved around wringing milk out of a sleeve. He also managed a shake of his derriere that defied any notion of shtetl authenticity.

During subsequent productions of *Fiddler,* Zero managed more outrageous behavior. While playing the show at a theatre-in-the-round, he actually sat on a patron's lap in the audience. Another time he was singing the duet "Do You Love Me" with Golde, then played by Thelma Lee. The number finishes very sweetly with Tevye patting Golde's hand. But then Zero ran up the aisle in the dark and shouted from the back of the auditorium, "And that night Tevye had Golde!"

I had known Zero for some time. If one were to attempt a one-word definition of him, it would be "uncontainable." He was larger than any room he inhabited, larger than any stage he bestrode, larger than any character he portrayed, larger than anything that was permitted by any standards of stagecraft, indeed any standards of life. When he played *Rhinoceros* on Broadway, very few people in the audience retained any memory of the play beyond Zero himself. Someone said to Lee J. Cobb, "Lee, you must go see Zero in the play. It is uncanny. Before your very eyes, without the aid of makeup, the man turns into a rhinoceros!" And Lee replied, "I have yet to see him in a play when he doesn't."

I personally experienced the bellow of Zero's rhinoceros one time during the Passover holidays. I had invited him to my midnight seder and was disappointed when he did not show up. A few days later I was walking on Fifth Avenue when all of a sudden I heard a roar that came from the other side of the avenue. It was Zero, of course. "Theo," he yelled, "I couldn't come to your seder, I had matzo poisoning!" The line played very well with the passersby, especially the ones who had just come out of St. Patrick's Cathedral.

There was a serious side to Zero, of course, especially his painting, which saved his sanity during the long dark period of the blacklist. He was a good artist. Painting was also one area where he worked in solitude, with no one present. No jokes. But talking with him about that period could be disturbing. I remember mentioning to him someone whom neither of us knew terribly well. The guy had named names before HUAC and had been suicidal since, a destroyed human being. Zero was not a forgiving man; let the bastard die, he said, and he justified his anger by quoting the talmudic prohibition against informers. There is no disputing that he had every right to be angry at anyone who cooperated with the blacklist. Still, this was not a conversation I remember with much fondness; it was too acerbic for my liking.

Whenever you talked with anyone who had anything to do with Zero, the talk would invariably revolve around something outrageous he had said or done. He cultivated this image, even reveled in it. After I had seen him in Joyce's *Ulysses in Nighttown,* in which he gave a remarkable performance, I went backstage and told him that I had overheard a conversation in the foyer. This play was so outrageous, the man had said to his companion, that Mostel looked normal. Zero was actually pleased by that report. I did not have the heart to tell him that I had made it up.

Thelma Lee played my Golde more often than any other; once her sister Madeleine Gilford, Jack's wife, came to visit backstage. The Gilfords and the Mostels had been close friends for many years; Madeleine and Kate Mostel had even collaborated on a book. We started talking, once again telling stories about Zero's excesses on- and offstage. Zero had been dead for several years, and I said to Madeleine that I did not know where he was now; but wherever it was, I was sure they had already asked him to leave.

Two other Tevyes followed Zero in the role before I was asked to take the lead in the national company in 1967. Both came from families of Yiddish actors. Herschel Bernardi was proud of the fact that his father had tried unsuccessfully to be accepted by the Hebrew Actors Union, but had made a career in spite of it. Luther Adler came from one of the most illustrious of dynasties of the Yiddish stage; the father, Jacob Adler, was considered one of the finest actors of his day. Gentiles would come to the Yiddish theatre to watch a play in a language they did not understand, just to see him perform. Both Herschel and Luther were properly cast as Tevye, and each gave to the role something it needed, something Zero had been less than willing to give: seriousness. In a sense, Luther's was perhaps too serious. He treated the musical basically as a straight play. That is what one should ideally do, but not at the expense of the music, which must be an integral element of the presentation. Luther thought some of it an intrusion; he was the only Tevye who actually suggested that "If I Were a Rich Man" be cut.

My association with the play started in a curious manner. On one fall day in 1967 I received a long-distance call from Las Vegas and immediately recognized the perpetually hoarse voice. It was Harry Belafonte, who miraculously manages to sing beautifully despite the hoarseness, or possibly because of it. Harry told me that he had been talking to "the guys," the people who ran the hotel and casino at Caesars Palace. For a couple of years now this particular hotel had been presenting condensed ninety-minute versions of successful Broadway musicals in its main showroom. A recent one had been *Sweet Charity,* starring Juliet Prowse. At alternate times they continued to present big-name stars in cabaret-concert style. Harry Belafonte was their current attraction. Apparently they were planning to mount *Fiddler* as their next musical and "the guys" had asked Harry's advice as to who should headline their company. Belafonte suggested Theodore Bikel, and they jumped at the idea; my audience appeal at that time cut across several areas of performing and several lines of gender and ethnicity. They asked him to find out if I would have any interest in performing the role in Las Vegas. I told him that the idea appealed to me. In truth, I was less interested in performing in Las Vegas than I was in playing Tevye. But they had no need to know that. With my agreement in principle, they went to Hal Prince in New York and booked the presently touring company into Caesars, stipulating that I be the "headliner." The deal was for four months, with a possible extension of a further two.

Rehearsals would be needed, of course, not only so I could make the role my own, but also because the entire company would need to adapt themselves to the severe cuts necessitated by the Las Vegas format. Cutting the show to ninety minutes without losing essential elements of it seemed an impossibility, more so to the people who had been doing the full play than to me, who came fresh to the condensed, or "tab," version. In the end, Actors' Equity permitted one hundred minutes of show for artistic reasons. As it turned out, the tab version was much harder for me to play than the full one was subsequently. Most of the cuts concerned other characters, with the result that Tevye would be onstage most of the time with no respite. There was no intermission and, as is the Vegas custom, we were to do the play twice nightly, seven days a week, in a tiered showroom with patrons sitting at tables.

Luther Adler had headed the *Fiddler* company until a couple of weeks before I was brought in. The role was played in the interim by Paul Lipson, who regularly portrayed Lazar Wolf, the butcher, and who would continue doing that role with me for many years to follow. The national company had been on tour for many months and was, at that point, playing in Oklahoma City. I had been rehearsing the role in New York without the company, and basically without a director. The stage manager, Jim Bronson, and the assistant choreographer, Tom Abbott, aided by a rehearsal pianist, had been putting me through the paces on an empty stage, with the two men playing all the other roles from Golde on down. It was time for me to work with the actual people, a prospect I both looked forward to and dreaded. Only once before, in *Streetcar,* had I played a major role in a company that had been used to the tempo and dynamics of another actor before me. Growing into the role and the play is something that casts do together; that is the natural process. This way you had to take shortcuts of both the physical and mental kind. The former are the easier ones; the latter can be bruising. In the case of *Fiddler,* Tevye is pivotal and everything hinges on the proper concept and execution of this one role. I came into a company that had had months of getting set in another Tevye's ways. In this situation, you cannot easily impose your imprimatur on an ensemble that knows the show better than you do, especially since you have not quite perfected the imprimatur yourself. It would be a little while before we all managed to breathe together as one organism.

Now it was time for me to open in this play that would become part of my professional life for the next quarter of a century. The place was Las Vegas, and the year 1967. It was Christmas—what a fitting time to open a show with such a strong Jewish background! The locale was a gambling casino with a leitmotif of ancient Rome. Caesars Palace featured various classically named amenities such as the Atrium Restaurant and a twenty-four-hour coffee shop cutely named the Noshorium. The world of Anatevka—at least once removed from the glitter of Broadway—was surely totally alien to the glitz of the Las Vegas strip. How would the tale of these simple Eastern European Jews be received by people who had just taken a couple of hours off from heavy gambling at the tables or slot machines? Would they not just as soon go back to the good old days when the amusement was an hour of Tony Bennett and a chorus line of scantily clad beauties?

Lo and behold, the magic of *Fiddler* worked even here. The first test of this came a week after we opened, on New Year's Eve. Out of force of habit, the staff of the casino showroom had placed noisemakers on each of the tables. I did not find out about this until after the play had started, and it was too late to remove these objects with which one drunk could ruin the play. But—miracle of miracles—the audience was so wrapped up in the action that not one person picked up a noisemaker. Some might already have toasted the New Year with a few glasses of champagne, but they were with us all the way nonetheless. They laughed in all the right places, were still in others, and applauded exactly where more sober audiences had. I have sometimes called a good audience, one that follows you where you are leading them, a "good bull." I learned this metaphor in Spain, watching bullfights. A good bull is one that follows the cape, charging it, hooking right or left, exactly as the matador intends.

Still, Las Vegas itself was a debilitating experience. The hotel brass were very accommodating; the star usually gets everything on a silver platter. We had a three-room suite and were sent flowers and bottles of expensive liquor as welcoming gifts. Before we arrived, Rita had asked that a kitchen be installed in our suite; we were going to spend many months in the place, and she wanted to create an atmosphere of home away from the bustle. The management was a little offended at the request; after all, they argued, this was one of the finest hotels, with several restaurants on the premises. What would we want a kitchen for? But we insisted on our kitchen, which turned out to be a very smart move on our part. The public rooms were very public indeed; gawkers, autograph hounds, and plain boors abounded. Independent of the hotel restaurant for meals, we were able to keep to ourselves a good portion of the time. Unlike the usual stars who appeared at the casino-hotels, I spent no time at the tables, another source of puzzlement for the hotel owners. After a couple of weeks or so, we received a message: "We haven't seen you downstairs at the tables." Whether the idea was that my presence in the casino would add glamour to the place, give publicity to the show, or was simply a way of having me return part or all of my salary—I was not going to play. My understanding was, as I told them, that they owned me and my talent for two shows a night, each lasting one hundred minutes, and that during those times, I would give them the best damn performance I was capable of. But beyond that, nothing. The flowers and the brandy stopped coming, but I didn't care.

The audiences did not stop coming, either. In fact, *Fiddler* was a huge success even in its abridged format. To the delight of the management, the show attracted people who normally do not frequent casinos; thus they were getting a new clientele as well. The theory behind show attractions in these places is that the audiences gamble on the way in and on the way out. The more popular the show, the more traffic can be expected. The length of the show is calculated at one and a half hours for the same reason: It's enough to satisfy the crowd, but doesn't keep them out of the action too long. Not all of our special audiences were inclined to gamble, though. Our play was very popular with nuns, who sometimes came in groups, quickly rushed past the slot machines to get to the showroom, and dashed out just as quickly after the show. Within the first two weeks it was obvious that, whether I behaved like a Vegas star or not, they wanted to keep us around. They picked up the option for the additional two months, and the result was a full six-month run in Sin City.

I needed to keep my on- and offstage existences strictly separate for psychological reasons. They paid Theodore Bikel, the actor, a very large salary by current standards so he would portray a poor milkman—so much so that I had to be careful not to feel self-conscious when singing "If I Were a Rich Man." Also, the contrast between Las Vegas and Anatevka was enormous. In New York at least there is a Lower East Side with its echoes of the shtetl, and there are pockets of poverty in other places in America to provide some kind of parallel reference. Around the casinos, evidence of poverty is well hidden; the only poverty we saw was self-inflicted by reckless gambling. Like most people, I'll feed a few coins into slot machines from time to time. Unfortunately, one or two members of the cast were seriously addicted to gambling. Everyone would get paid on Thursday; by Saturday morning, a certain member of the *Fiddler* chorus would start borrowing money from anyone who was willing. He sent away to New York to cash in whatever reserves he had, and by the end of the Las Vegas engagement had to sign up for another year's worth of touring. It took him the better part of that year just to pay back what he owed his colleagues in the company.

I came across some very sad stories of lives ruined by the folly of gambling. A young woman working in the casino confided in my wife that she was stuck in Vegas with little prospect of getting out. Some years earlier, she had come on a short visit and had gambled and lost everything, including her return fare. A man offered to stake her to the ticket money if she would go to bed with him. As she saw no other way out, she did. The next thing she knew, one of the concierge bosses called and told her they were aware of what she was doing and would inform her mother of it (she had given a home address on checking in). When she begged and pleaded for them not to do that, the boss said fine, if she would stick around for a while and continue to turn some tricks under his supervision. "A while" turned into several years of servitude. When we first got to the hotel, we were intrigued by a voice page that frequently called for "Princess Fatimah" to contact the operator. After a couple of weeks we found out that no such royal personage existed; this was a code for the next available girl to report in.

Playing in our orchestra was a Brazilian cellist who had been a world-renowned concert musician. Years earlier he had visited Las Vegas, and it became his undoing. His sickness was gambling for high stakes. He lost everything and borrowed heavily to gamble more. He lost again, and then it was indentured servitude for him. This brilliant musician was stuck for life playing in a show band for the visiting acts. Sometimes I would leave the theatre at 2:00 A.M. and hear beautiful cello music. He was sitting alone in the dark orchestra pit, playing solos. It filled me with great sadness. But an hour or so later, when I would walk our little dog, Monty, I would pass the casino and see my cellist at the tables, gambling again. Then my sadness gave way to anger. I remembered a legend: When Sodom and Gomorrah were about to be destroyed for their evil ways, the angels pleaded with God to spare the two cities. God told them that he would withhold his wrath if they could find ten righteous men in these sinful places. As they could not, they pleaded for a lesser number, seven or five or three. God said that if they could find *one* righteous person he would spare the cities. They were unable to find even one. I sometimes got so angry that I thought to myself, if the same measuring stick were to be applied to Las Vegas, the city would have to be destroyed.

Some of it was amusing. Among the slot machine aficionados were my co-star, Dolores Wilson, who played my wife, Golde, and Baruch Lumet, who played the rabbi. Lumet, father of the movie director Sidney Lumet, was a dear old man, well versed in the Yiddish theatre and an acting teacher as well. He liked to go into the casino between shows and visit the one-armed bandits. One night, at the midnight show, as we started the wedding scene and the crowd sounded various wishes of "*Mazel tov*," as the play demanded, Lumet shook my hand and said in his Yiddish accent, "*Mazel tov*, twenty-fife dollars, a jeckpot!" The old man had very bad eyesight; he was waiting for his vision to deteriorate to the point when he would be ripe for a cataract operation. One night as I greeted him onstage, he walked toward me to shake my hand, missed it, and actually walked past me.

My first *Fiddler* cast gave me a taste of what I would experience many times over the years: actors who knew nothing of the background and history of Eastern European Jews, and yet who absorbed the ways of Anatevka as if by osmosis. You do not have to be Jewish to play in *Fiddler on the Roof,* you only have to be a good actor. Intelligence and well-rounded knowledge also help. By the same token you do not have to be black to play Othello or Asian to play *Miss Saigon.* From time to time one gets a little startled to see entire Jewish families on stage or screen portrayed by Gentiles. But it is annoying only when it is badly done.

In my first company we had some people who needed no special briefing about the background and history. Fyvush Finkel (Mordcha, the innkeeper), the aforementioned rabbi, and Maurice Brenner (the beggar), as well as some other Jewish actors, had some grounding by upbringing or education. But others, like Dolores Wilson, my Golde, whose background was Italian, lived the part so well that no one could question their authenticity. Perchik, played by Joe Masiell, also had ethnic Italian roots. He was wonderful as the rebellious student because he avoided the danger of playing the outsider as though Perchik were trying to be a Gentile. On the contrary, despite having moved toward secular enlightenment, Perchik was every inch a Jew. Even some Jewish actors who played Perchik did not manage to convey this as well as Joe did. Tragically, Joe died young, one of the earlier victims of AIDS.

One of the Jews in the cast playing the constable did not do so well precisely because his being Jewish made him self-conscious about doing these terrible things to the villagers of Anatevka. He looked perfect for the part, gruff and stocky, with a handlebar moustache. But he looked positively pained every night when he ordered his Russian hooligans to wreak their havoc and destruction. I asked him why he always looked so apologetic during those scenes, and he told me that he was afraid friends or acquaintances in the audience would see him in a bad light! But that was just the bad actor speaking, unable to divorce his life offstage from the stage persona. We first met him as he was walking his dog in front of the hotel. When our dog peed on his dog I should have gotten the idea right there and then that this guy was not going to work out too well. This man Clarence worked as a taxi driver in New York when he could not get any work as an actor. One afternoon early in the run I was sitting in the steam room with Joe Stein, who had written the book for *Fiddler.* We discussed the cast and Joe and I agreed that the constable was terrible. A little while later

Joe said pensively: "You know, it's a good thing that this guy is in this cast." I said, "Why? I thought we agreed a moment ago that he was terrible in the part." Joe said, "Yes, but while he is here in Las Vegas he is not killing anybody on the streets of New York!"

With the exception of a couple of the daughters and some younger chorus members, we were not a terribly smart-looking bunch. Quaint, yes, a little outlandish, even, but smart—definitely not. Maurice Brenner, who played the beggar, wore street clothes that looked worse than what he was wearing onstage. Bets were taken on whether he would try to persuade management to let him purchase his stage costume for personal use. Still, the town took to us. There was absolutely no question that we were a sensation in this jaded place: Perhaps this was due in part to the unusual look and feel of our motley troupe of players.

Among our more unusual followers was an oil millionaire with the improbable name of Smokey Ballou. He saw the show a number of times, each time bringing larger parties of friends with him. He would send gifts backstage, buckets of champagne for the cast, just as if he were courting some topless girls in a chorus line. He also treated me like a long-lost friend, coming backstage after each performance he attended to tender his congratulations yet again. One time I happened to have quite a number of friends and well-wishers in my dressing room. Among them were Paul Schrade and Gregory Peck. Smokey Ballou barged in, wearing his ten-gallon hat, parted the circle of people around me, and cried, "Hot damn, where's mah boy!"

After that night Gregory Peck never missed an opportunity to comment on my performance as Tevye. Some years later, I ran into him at a reception for Shirley MacLaine. I went to the men's room; there was a line waiting to use the facilities. Gregory Peck stood in the line before me. As we waited he said to me, "I probably told you this before, but I must tell you again. I have seen *Fiddler on the Roof* about five times with different Tevyes. Yours was far and away the best." Considering that we were in a men's room, I asked if I could get him to write it on the wall with a crayon.

On the one hand, for me and my colleagues *Fiddler* was another theatrical engagement and it seemed to furnish endless material for such theatre anecdotes as I have told here. On the other hand (as Tevye would say), there was a side to *Fiddler on the Roof* that was a constant reminder of how the world of Tevye related to me personally. Whatever sources other Tevyes may have drawn on, I was playing my own grandfather, Reb Shimon Bikel. I remember him quite well, even though I only met him a few times during my summer vacations before he died. In order to see him, we had to make a long train journey, some twenty-seven hours or so from Vienna. My grandfather still lived in Czernowitz, the provincial capital of Bukovina, the area in Eastern Europe where both my father and my mother were born. Bukovina, part of Romania when I visited there (now part of Ukraine), had been the easternmost province of the Austrian Empire prior to World War I; as the Russian troops advanced, my mother's family had fled to Vienna. After finishing his military service in the Austrian army, my father had also made his way to Vienna to enroll in the university. It was there that my parents met, courted, and married. It was natural and logical for Jews from Bukovina to gravitate toward Vienna; it had been the seat of a benign emperor, Franz Joseph, the one Catholic potentate whose proclamations to the Jewish enclaves under his rule began with the words "*An meine lieben Juden*" (To my beloved Jews). While this may have been no more than a formulaic greeting, it was nonetheless one which no other ruler before him had cared to use.

Reb Shimon Bikel was very much like Tevye, a mixture of piousness and irreverence. He also had a Tevyelike self-deprecating sense of humor. For example, he had a small reddish beard, among Jews a sign of tightfistedness and ill temper. My cousin Shlomo Bickel, a Yiddish writer of note and the family chronicler, reports that Reb Shimon was heard to say, "I am a very poor man. So everybody points his finger at me and says, 'There goes that red-bearded Jew.' Had I been rich, they would have said, 'What a lovely blond man!'" At one time Shlomo Bickel, having abandoned adherence to Jewish strictures, was strolling on the Sabbath along the town's promenade. He was nonchalantly smoking a cigarette, something not permitted on the Sabbath, as it involves lighting a match. Suddenly he saw my grandfather walking toward him. He quickly took the cigarette out of his mouth and hid it behind his back. As Reb Shimon passed him, he said, "Good Sabbath, Shloimele, I saw."

Reb Shimon himself had periods when, disgusted with the shabby treatment providence had meted out to him, he refused to pay obeisance to Jewish law and custom. For almost two years he would not go to the synagogue, although from force of habit the dietary laws continued to be observed in his house. One morning the family entered the living room to see my grandfather with his prayer shawl draped around his shoulders and the phylacteries tied to arm and forehead. He was moving back and forth rhythmically as Eastern European Jews are wont to do in prayer. When he saw the astonished looks on the faces of the family, he interrupted the flow of prayer for a minute and said with a shrug, still rocking back and forth, "Maybe this will help." You can't get more like Tevye than that.

I should explain the difference in the spellings of my family name. Its origin dates back to the time when all the Jews were ordered by the authorities to take family names. Prior to that time, they had been known among themselves either by their occupation, as in Lazar Wolf, the Butcher, or by patronymics, as in Chaim ben Moshe. Both the Russian czar and the Austrian emperor decreed at about the same time that everyone was to be registered by family name. The minor officials charged with the task often played cruel games with people who were unable to bribe them, and gave them horrible-sounding names. Those able to afford it picked nicer names full of euphemisms or wishful thinking: Goldberg (mountain of gold), or Himmelfarb (the color of the sky). A Yiddish story was told about the chicanery of name-giving that, rendered into English, goes like this: A Jew who had been in the name registry office came out beaming: "I've got my name. It cost me five hundred roubles but I've got my name!" "What name did they give you?" asked his friends. "Shnit," he replied. "Shnit? You paid five hundred roubles for 'Shnit'?" "No," said the man, "just for the 'n.'" Little wonder that many Jews did not wish to subject themselves to the pranks of officialdom and requested upfront that they be given names that related to their status within the Jewish religious hierarchy: Cohen for the priestly title passed for generations from fathers to sons, Levy for the hereditary title of priestly servants. Many permutations of these names exist, and all indicate Cohanim or Levites. Levine, Levin, Levinson, Lavin, Levene, Loew, Loewe—all these are stand-ins for Levy. Cohen also has many permutations: Cohn, Kohn, Kohner, Cahane, Kahane, Kagan, Kaganovich, and even Katz (the Hebrew acronym for *cohen tzedek,* a righteous priest).

My father went through the first twenty years of his life carrying one of those ridiculous names. His parents had been married in a religious Jewish ceremony, but had neglected to go through civil proceedings to confirm their union. As a consequence, my father bore his mother's name until he had it legally changed over to his father's. Had he not done so, I would have been stuck with the name of Hasenfratz. This translates as "loutish rabbit." Some of my cousins in Israel still carried that name until they changed it to an innocuous Hebrew one. While the mention of "Hasenfratz" was a source of amusement for me during my early youth, I shudder to think how it would have looked on a theatre marquee.

It turns out that Bikel is also a Hebrew acronym. I am a *cohen,* as were all my male ancestors. But when my great-grandfather was called upon to pick a family name for himself, he did not want to take the name Cohen, because there was another *cohen* in the village who had done so before him. He opened the old prayer book at random, placed his finger on the page, also at random; it landed on a phrase that said in four Hebrew words: "The Children of Israel are holy to God." The letters were bet, yud, kuf, and lamed. String them together and they spell B-Y-K-L. When the need arose to transcribe them into Latin characters, my grandfather, Reb Shimon, preferred Bikel; the other branch of the family used Bickel. My cousin Larry in Brooklyn inherited the "ck" in the name, but wanted the stress on the last syllable and so he uses the spelling Bickell.

My mother's family hailed from the same region as my father's, albeit some distance, a few hilltops, away. There was a greater distance in terms of attitude, language, and observance. Where, despite his occasionally stubborn rebelliousness, my grandfather Reb Shimon was an observant Jew, my maternal grandfather, Maier Riegler, only adhered to the customs in a perfunctory manner, being otherwise quite removed from custom and even language. (Jewish custom decrees that children may only be named after relatives who are deceased. This grandfather was no longer living when I was born; I was named Meir after him.) Yiddish was the language spoken in Reb Shimon's house. Not so in Maier Riegler's household; there the two languages were German and Ruthenian. (The local peasant population spoke Ruthenian, a close derivative of Ukrainian.) His occupation was also unusual for a Jewish man: He was a government official, the warden of the local jail in the village of Unter Stanestie. His photographs show him to be a robust man with a moustache twirled to a point at both ends, looking every inch like the Austrian gendarme he had been before his promotion to the prison job. My grandparents lived in a grace-and-favor apartment in the jail. My mother was born there; years later, as a boy, I would tease her about having been born in prison.

It was a small prison; most of the inmates were peasants arrested for drunkenness or some minor stealing offense. When my grandfather had to go out on an errand, he would leave my grandmother, Regina Riegler, in charge. If the prisoners thought that this would give them a chance to take liberties, they were quickly disabused of the notion. Once while she was in charge an inmate tried to escape. My grandmother took the jail keys, a bunch of old-fashioned mammoth keys, and threw them at the fleeing peasant, knocking him out cold. None of them ever tried to escape again. My grandmother was also charged with the task of cooking for the prisoners. Assimilated though my grandparents were, she kept to Jewish dietary laws, either from force of habit or because she had not learned to cook "goyishe" food. That furnished little cause for complaint; what she did know how to cook was very good. I can attest to that from personal experience. In truth, she was a much better cook than her daughter.

My mother had five brothers; she was the only girl in the family. At birth she was named Maria Gisela, not very Jewish names. Throughout her life, she was known as Gisa; only much later, in Israel, did she rename herself Miriam, the Hebrew for Maria. Whatever there was of Jewish life in her house during her early youth revolved around Friday nights and the major festivals, chiefly Rosh Hashanah, Yom Kippur, and Passover. I recall that during my childhood, Grandmother kept four sets of dishes: two sets for milk and meat for year-round use, and separate milk and meat dishes for Passover use only. Sabbath in the jail, I was told, was not much different from any other day. But on Friday nights, my grandmother would light the candles, say the blessing over them, my grandfather would recite the kiddush over the wine, and the family would be served a festive meal on a freshly starched white tablecloth. After the meal they did something that I would bet no other Jewish family had incorporated into its Sabbath ritual. My grandfather would take his six children into the living room. An almost life-sized portrait of the Emperor Franz Joseph was hung over the mantel. He would neatly line up the children in front of the picture in order of size and ask in Ruthenian: "*Kto to ye?*" (Who is this?) And the children would reply in unison: "*Nash Pan Tsissar, za zdrovu!*" (Our Emperor, may he be healthy!)

My mother's family had fled from the onslaught of the Russian troops during World War I. They were afraid of Russian excesses, and felt especially vulnerable because of my grandfather's position, although minor, as an Austrian civil servant. By the time the war ended, so had the Austro-Hungarian monarchy. When I was born, in 1924, Austria had been a republic for several years and its area covered only a fraction of its former territory. This causes some confusion at times when officials try to pin down the location and country of origin of one's parents. When I applied for a beer and wine license for my coffeehouse in Hollywood, I had to fill out application forms. One particular item on the questionnaire I felt was inappropriate, improper for them to ask and improper for me—or anybody—to answer. It requested information on "ethnic origin." Such an answer could be held for you or against you; my civil libertarian instincts told me to leave it blank. When I came to the desk sergeant in charge, he pointed out that I had neglected to answer all the questions. Feigning ignorance I said that I had not understood what was being asked. He said, "Where were you born?" I said, "No, sir, that question is further up on the page where it says 'birthplace.'" "Well, your folks, where are they from?" "No," I said, "I answered the questions under 'father's birthplace' and 'mother's birthplace.'" He looked at the names I had entered, "Sergie" and "Unter Stanestie," and asked: "What country is that in?" Patiently I explained that the area was named Bukovina, that in 1870 it had been Russia, that it then became Austria, that in 1919 at the Treaty of Versailles it was ceded to Romania but that in 1946 at the end of World War II it had become Russia again. "What would you like me to put down under 'ethnic origin'?" I asked. "Why don't you write 'Bukovinian'?" he suggested. "No, sir, I can't do that because the only logical answer to such a question in my case would be 'kike.'" He looked somewhat stricken. "Don't make trouble," he said "I'm only a sergeant." The question remained unanswered. Many people don't know the origin of the word "kike." When Jewish immigrants were processed through Ellis Island, those who could only write in Hebrew were asked to sign with a cross instead. Jews would refuse to make the sign of the cross and urged each other to draw a circle instead: "*Mach a kikle.*" The officials overheard and referred to Jews with the pejorative "kike."

After World War I there were elements in Austrian society who hankered after the good old days of the Austrian empire and its preeminent position in Central and Eastern Europe. Regardless of the fact that the vast holdings in Hungary, Bohemia, Slovakia, Slovenia, Galicia, and Bukovina were no longer under Austrian sovereignty and were respectively parts of Hungary, Czechoslovakia, Yugoslavia, Poland, and Romania, there was a group in Vienna known as *kaisertreu* (faithful to the emperor). The group was neither large nor influential; it was mostly viewed with amusement. Their candidate for the Austrian imperial throne, the Archduke Otto von Hapsburg, was living in exile and stood no chance at all of ever occupying his father's throne.

My mother with her childhood past of "our Emperor, may he be healthy" declared herself to be one of the faithful to the emperor, to the embarrassment of my father, a socialist who held no brief for kings and princes. Even the middle-of-the-road positions of the social-democratic Austrian government were too tame for him. I tended to rely on my father's views and judgments far more than on those of my mother, and therefore shared at least the amusement about her professed royalist inclinations. I recall dancing around her in the apartment and chanting a rhyme I had made up: "*Unser motto—Kaiser Otto*" (Our motto—Emperor Otto).

The contrast between my parents was not between assimilation and strict Jewish tradition, however. My father's commitment as a Jew had been channeled into new areas. Like Perchik, the student in *Fiddler*, my father was the politicized secularist Jew. After they were married, my father prevailed on my mother to learn how to speak Yiddish. She acceded to his wishes, but never really mastered the language. When well spoken, Yiddish has a timbre, rhythm, and sound all its own; in my mother's mouth it always somehow sounded like watered-down German.

Of my five maternal uncles I only knew one; all five died of tuberculosis at a very early age. One of them, Max, was stricken while serving in the Austrian army. He was buried in the portion of the Central Cemetery in Vienna reserved for servicemen who died while on active duty. *Heldenfriedhof* they call it, a burial place for heroes. Dying of TB did not exactly qualify as a heroic death, but the family and the doctors were convinced that exposure to the rough elements and the lack of any rest hastened his demise considerably. My uncle Heinrich, whom I do remember, died when I was very young, and was buried next to his father. A joint marker was erected over their graves. On a visit to Vienna in 1992, I set out to find the grave. It was a dismal task. The Jewish portion of the cemetery was overgrown with weeds, a jungle, in sharp contrast to the neat and carefully tended rows of the Christian parts on the other side of the walkway. Although I had the exact location of the grave, which I had gotten from the register of the Jewish community, it took two cemetery attendants a long session of hacking away at underbrush before they uncovered the mud-caked stone, which had tipped over. They wiped off enough of the earth and dust so the inscription could be seen, put it right side up, and left; my son Rob and I remained standing at the site while I recited the kaddish. I felt shame and disgust, thinking about the years of neglect before my eyes. They had tortured and helped murder the living, I thought, and they did not even respect dead Jews in their graves.

AT THE END of the six-month run in Las Vegas, management asked me to continue heading the company for the balance of its national tour, but I declined. I came away a little weary from having played this taxing role twice nightly, and went on to other things. It would be two years, 1969, before I would undertake the play again, this time in yet another unusual place: Honolulu, Hawaii.

If I thought that Las Vegas was as far from Anatevka as you could get, Honolulu—my first venue as Tevye in a full production of the play—was in some ways farther. Not only were the audiences not Jewish, a great number were not even Caucasian. They were of Chinese, Japanese, or native Hawaiian extraction, and I feared that the play would be too far a reach for them. But, just as the original *Fiddler* naysayers had been wrong, so too I had not reckoned with the extraordinarily universal appeal of the play. We received standing ovations, and there were crowds waiting for me at the stage door after each performance. Often, after matinees, I would chat with some autograph seekers and engage women with Oriental features in conversation. "What does this play mean to you? Eastern Europe, Jews, Russians, pogroms; what does all this mean to you?" As they would wipe away the mascara where the tears had smudged their faces, they would reply: "Tradition. We know what that means. We know what it means when children do not want to follow the tradition anymore." The Chinese women would add that they also knew about poverty, hard work, and persecution. Proof again that the human experience as expressed through art evokes a sympathetic response anywhere, and that good plays and good literature will find their audience.

IF I WAS the first American Tevye to play the role offshore, I was also the first to play it at theatres-in-the-round. This uniquely American institution, originally created to accommodate summer audiences and big crowds, lends itself surprisingly well to the presentation of some musicals. Despite the necessarily scanty stage sets and the fact that entrances and exits of furniture and actors are all effected down the various aisles, basically in full view of the public, the audience readily accepts the convention. Some plays do better in the round than others. Those that ordinarily require lavish sets are at a disadvantage; often they have to make up for it by the lavish costumes and require greater imagination on the part of the audience. *Fiddler on the Roof,* however, is an ideal piece to do in the round. Not only is the image of the small village with its poor inhabitants enhanced by the space limitations; there is even a philosophical advantage. In the proscenium production, Tevye frequently speaks to God, who is always up to the right just above the highest set of seats in the balcony. In the round, however, Tevye finds Him anywhere around the rim of the auditorium. Clearly, God is not in one place; He is everywhere.

Working in summer theatre carries certain risks, mostly connected with weather. Some of the places were not hardtops but tents. A rainstorm can play havoc with the performance. Such was the case in

Springfield, Massachusetts, one foul summer's night. It had been raining all day long, and there was no letup in the evening, either. The rule says that shows have to begin no later than one hour after the announced curtain time, and at least one full act must be played. Otherwise the audience's money has to be refunded or patrons will have to be accommodated free of charge on another night. Either way, this means a severe loss at the box office. That night in Springfield, we played the first act of *Fiddler* in stops and starts. When the rain got too heavy, the audience could not hear a thing. Although we were amplified with microphones hanging down from beams, the rain drumming on top of the tent was amplified more loudly than we were. We managed to get through the required first act, and management was home free without loss of revenue, but I was not going to have the audience sent home after half a show. I told the producers and the stage manager that we would go on and that they were to take their cues from me if it got terrible again. Sure enough, during the confrontation scene where Chava declares her intention to marry the gentile Fyedka, the heavens opened up again and not a word could be understood. I waved all the actors off the stage, went to the orchestra pit, and had one of the musicians hand me his microphone. With it held close to my mouth I could be heard. I proceeded to tell the audience the rest of the play, acting out snippets of the action and singing the songs, all by myself. The last few phrases of "Anatevka" I had to sing a cappella because the water was rising in the orchestra pit and the musicians had packed up and fled. I finished describing the end of the play, with Tevye and his family on their way to a train and a boat, which would take them to America. As I was miming the exit where I am pulling the cart with our meager belongings, the audience stood and applauded long and hard, much longer than other audiences had before. Not one person asked for his money back; for years I continued to receive letters from people who were present on that memorable evening.

Another time, in Indianapolis at the Starlight Theatre, where the thousands of seats as well as the stage are totally under open skies, we came dangerously close to being rained out on a completely sold-out Friday night. The published curtain time was 8:30 P.M. That came and went, as did 9:00. The audience had been asked to wait outside the gates and told there would be an announcement if and when the show could begin. There were literally thousands of umbrellas to be seen, with the people under them patiently waiting. At 9:15 it was still raining and we began to give up hope. But at 9:20 it let up. By 9:25 the apprentices were furiously mopping the stage, attempting to somehow get it dry. The audience had been allowed in and they were all wiping their seats with handkerchiefs, tissues, or paper towels, which the prudent patrons had thought to bring. I called the cast together and told them that it appeared we would be going on, but that no one was to do any of the involved steps in the inn scene; no one was to run the risk of twisting or breaking ankles. At 9:29 we were still not quite ready with the stage and the props, but under the rules the show had to start before 9:30. Thus, at 9:29 and 30 seconds, the orchestra started to play; overtures count as the start of the show. However, those who are familiar with the show will remember that *Fiddler on the Roof* does not have an overture. The orchestra simply played a medley of the tunes until they got a signal that we were ready to begin. The show did not end until close to 1:00 A.M. that night, but it was another memorable experience.

Most of the time one manages to ignore intrusions of the outside world while a play is in progress. The most annoying of these are sirens; the Russian village of Anatevka around the year 1905 can ill accommodate such sounds. When they occur, actors and audiences alike blot out the sound and are mostly successful in retaining their concentration on the play. I can recall one time when I decided on the spur of the moment to actually use an intrusion while staying true both to my character and to the play. It was the night of July 4, and we were doing *Fiddler* in a tent theatre at Valley Forge. Toward the end of the play, the Jews of Anatevka had been forced to leave by the anti-Semitic Russian authorities. We were in the middle of the scene when I am saying good-bye to Lazar Wolf, played by Paul Lipson, as usual. Just at that moment, the Fourth of July fireworks went off, loud as you please, in a series of sharp cracks. It could hardly be ignored; it was also too good to be ignored. I turned to Lazar Wolf and said in a voice that indicated yet another tribulation: "See? They are killing Jews!" The audience loved it.

PLAYING TEVYE IN *Fiddler on the Roof* forced me to think long and hard about the fate of the Jews in imperial Russia and their subsequent treatment. Many Jews were socialists like Perchik, the student in *Fiddler,* and they hoped to build a state where justice would reign and prejudice, including prejudice against Jews, would be eradicated. Later they became victims of the very regime they helped to nurture and build. The innate anti-Semitism of the Russians and the Ukrainians would not be stifled by officially benign proclamations or even by a statute—the only one in Europe—specifically declaring anti-Semitism a crime. The excesses against Jews were given legitimacy by the tyranny and persecution complex of Josef Stalin himself. He declared that a plot by Jewish doctors to murder him had been foiled; after he had the doctors summarily executed, open season on the Jews was the order of the day. Some tended to see the treatment of Jews under the Soviets as analogous to the Nazi persecution, but these were facile attempts to link dissimilar events. While suffering is suffering, Soviet anti-Semitism was, in policy and practice, discrimination by a regime that oppressed all its people but hit the Jewish targets harder and with greater brutality. Unlike the Nazis, the Soviets never had a plan to exterminate the entire Jewish people. Soviet Communism had held out a promise of freedom for Jews which was cruelly thwarted, and that betrayal was hard to bear. Jewish victims of Nazism experienced no such betrayal, because there had been no promises. Jews had never bolstered or supported Nazism, in theory or in practice. When excesses by the Bolshevik regime occurred, its Jewish adherents and supporters both inside and outside the USSR at first tended to excuse them with blind faith. One of the last of the American Jews to stop defending the Soviet regime was my old nemesis, Lillian Hellman. Like a number of others, she refused to believe for the longest time what had emerged as a painful truth.

As anticipated, in the Soviet Union *Fiddler on the Roof* was not produced during the many years of its successes elsewhere in the world. When a Jewish theatre group was finally permitted to mount the play, they were forced to make changes in the script. The pogrom by the Russians against the Jews was softened and the antagonism between the two groups was made to occupy a low priority within the action. Most disturbingly, the ending was radically changed. Tevye and his family could not be allowed to leave Russia for a free life in America. They were made to wander off into the sunset to find a new and freer life in the Soviet Union after the revolution, as part of a glorious society which they would help to build. Joe Stein, Jerry Bock, and Sheldon Harnick[1], the creative team of *Fiddler,* protested such radical surgery and attempted to withhold permission for performing the play with these changes, but the production was mounted over their objections. Especially in the light of how Soviet Jews had fared under the regime, this was a cruel hoax.

Toward the end of the sixties, the reports about the fate of the Jews under Soviet rule reached alarming proportions. Those of us who were exercised about it embarked on a campaign that eventually would have far-reaching effects and help bring about a modern-day exodus as well.

---

1. The Harnick family hailed from Bukovina, as did our family. According to my mother, they are distant cousins of ours.

One of my earliest efforts combined my activism with my abilities as an artist. A Canadian-born scientist, Ted Friedgut, had been in the Soviet Union on a scholarly trip in 1969 and made contact with Soviet Jews. Moved as he was by their plight, he attended meetings in apartments, back rooms, and cellars, and he took along his tape recorder. Invariably, songs were sung at these clandestine get-togethers, songs that spoke of the longing for freedom. The songs were mostly in Russian, as the younger generation was no longer fluent in Yiddish and Hebrew, which had not been permitted to be taught. Withal, there were secret teaching sessions and some of the teachers, when caught, actually went to jail for "anti-Soviet activities." Thus a few of the songs had Yiddish and Hebrew texts as well. On the tape there were snippets of conversations Friedgut had conducted with Jews in a mixture of Russian, Yiddish, English, and Hebrew. None of this was without danger: It took courage for Friedgut to smuggle the tapes out of the USSR. He came to see me in New York and let me listen to the material. He had also contacted Issachar Miron, the Israeli composer of the popular Israeli song "Tzena, Tzena, Tzena," who was living in New York. Issachar and I decided to make an album using the smuggled tapes as source material. We also decided to donate all the proceeds to benefit Soviet Jews in some fashion. We finally settled on creating a scholarship fund at the Hebrew University in Jerusalem, which would be used exclusively to enable young émigrés from the USSR to study at the university. Issachar wrote musical arrangements for the songs and we made the album. At my suggestion, we interspersed among the songs the spoken voices of the Jews Ted Friedgut had interviewed. We called the album *Silent No More*. It was widely sold and generated a decent amount of money, all of which went into the scholarship fund—one that remains operative to this day.

In the beginning, activism on behalf of Soviet Jews was focused on disseminating information so as to enlist the broadest possible support for the movement. Later we took to the streets, protesting in front of consulates and embassies, at stage doors as visiting Soviet artists arrived, and at diplomats' compounds. As a performing artist I was pained by some of the crude tactics employed by militant groups against visiting Soviet performers. Interrupting a ballet or an opera with rude shouts and noises made no converts to the cause among the audience; in fact, it achieved the opposite effect by antagonizing them. It also did nothing to bring closer any relief for Soviet Jews themselves.

The ultimate travesty was a bomb attack at Lincoln Center while a performance of the Moiseyev Ballet was in progress. Although it could have been much worse, it was a dastardly attack and there were some casualties. The Jewish Defense League at first claimed responsibility for the attack and then, when public outrage mounted, later denied it. A well-known tactic: Claim credit, then deny responsibility while at the same time "applauding" the act or calling the reasons for it "understandable." Cultural events are neither an ideal nor a proper forum for such protests. Unless there was reason to believe that the ballet company itself had been engaging in anti-Semitic acts, such an attack did little but make hostages of performers who, like it or not, were guests in our country. Had any of the performers been harmed, it would have created an international incident. As it turned out, all the victims were Americans and, by all appearances, many of them Jews.

Centuries of vilification, persecution, pogroms, and genocide have not succeeded in making us abandon our self-image as a cultured people with instincts far nobler than those of our enemies. That surely will continue to stand, despite the excesses of some Jewish fanatics. I never advocated a total avoidance of protests at cultural events, but I insisted that they be done with taste and designed to remind audiences and artists alike that Jews in the Soviet Union were hurting. At one of the Bolshoi Ballet performances I devised the following plan, which was executed to perfection by a number of young people. We bought tickets to the performance and, true to custom, brought flowers into the auditorium to be presented to the company at the curtain call. The flowers were blue and white and wound around triangle-shaped frames. Each one of us held a small triangle. At the appropriate moment as the dancers took their bow, we rushed forward and presented our flowers, handing them up to the stage. But at the last minute we combined the small triangles so that they formed a large blue and white Star of David. The message was not lost on anyone.

The opportunity to see for myself what I had been writing, speaking, and singing about presented itself in 1977, when the FIA had an Executive Committee meeting planned in Moscow. As a representative of Equity, I would be attending, and I was determined to make contact with Soviet Jews, some of whose names I had been given by the various organizations that dealt with Soviet Jewry matters. There was one man in particular whom I was very eager to meet. His name was Vladimir Slepak; he had spent time in jail for Jewish activism and had only recently been released. At one point I slipped away from the actors' conference and from the Soviet staff members assigned to hover solicitously over the delegates, particularly those from the West. I had been given both an address and a description. The address was 15 Gorky Street; the description sounded as though it had been lifted from a John Le Carré novel: "Take the elevator to the seventh floor, walk up one flight of stairs to the eighth, then look along the row of doors. When you come to the door that has the jimmy marks of forced entry on it, you'll know that you have found what you are looking for."

Not without fear I followed the directions exactly as I had been given them. My heart was hammering as I looked for the splintered doorjamb. When I found it, I knocked, and a slightly bearded man opened. This was Slepak, the man I had come to see. His wife, two sons, and daughter-in-law were also present. They greeted me like a long-lost friend; Slepak had heard of me and had even obtained a cassette copy of the *Silent No More* record. What was extraordinary was the sight of the room as I entered. There were more Jewish and Israeli memorabilia all over the walls and tables than I had believed to be in existence in Russia. Maps of Israel, flags, pictures, menorahs, Stars of David, even sports trophies from the Maccabiah Games, the international sports competition held every four years in Israel. We spent time talking, exchanging views about the situation, and figuring out ways to get help from abroad. I went back one more time during the week I was there. That time I took my guitar. Vladimir was by himself that day, and we both sat while I played Yiddish and Hebrew songs for him. Years later, when he was free and living in Israel, we met again in America, both of us still active in the cause of freeing Soviet Jews.

I was determined before leaving Moscow to make contact with other Jews as well. The best place to do this, I was told, was late morning on a Saturday in front of the synagogue on Archipova Street. My problem was this: We were seldom left alone to roam about. I had managed to slip away a couple of times to see Slepak and to peek into the synagogue on a weekday. But this would be Saturday, my last day in Moscow. With the conference over, our interpreters were assigned to take us sightseeing or shopping at our leisure. My interpreter was a young woman named Marina Elyan who had been doing her chores all week long, wrestling with the technical terms of theatre, film, and TV in both languages, and acquitting herself very well indeed. She also seemed to be a nice person. But I was about to do something the Soviet authorities would surely frown upon, something that would fit into no category of shopping or sightseeing. What to do? Give her the slip, dart into doorways, and do a James Bond routine?

I decided instead to tackle it head-on; what will be will be. Marina had asked me earlier what I wanted to do, and I said, let's go to the Kremlin. I had been there a couple of times before, but it was fairly close to the synagogue. As we walked around Red Square I asked her if she knew where Archipova Street was. She said that it was not too far away and why did I want to know? I told her that there was a synagogue on that street. She asked me if I was Jewish, and when I nodded, asked how I knew where the synagogue was. I told her that I had been there once before, earlier in the week. "In that case, why do you want to go again?" she asked. Here we go, I thought. I explained to her that Saturday was when most Jews come to the temple and that afterwards they tend to stand and chat outside for a while. I told her that she must surely be aware that Jews did not lead too easy an existence in the Soviet Union, and that they might welcome a friendly face and a friendly word from a fellow Jew. That seemed to satisfy her and we started walking toward Archipova Street.

I decided to go a step further and told her that I was afraid that the people would not want to talk to me if I arrived with her by my side. She asked me, "Why? Because I am a shiksa?" I was taken aback. "Where do you know this word from?" I asked. She told me that she had read it in a book entitled *Portnoy's Complaint*. That astonished me even more. "Where on earth did you find this book?" I asked. "In Cairo," she said. "Egypt?" I asked, even more flabbergasted. "I was stationed at the Soviet Embassy as an interpreter," she said. "I went out one day and browsed in a bookshop and found this book. I found it very interesting." I was sure that she had been able to learn more about Jews from Philip Roth than from any Soviet encyclopedia. Well, now that the mystery was cleared up, I felt it safe to proceed. "Your being a shiksa is probably as good a way of describing my difficulty as any. These Jews are fearful and will shy away from anyone with whom they will not feel secure. I would deem it a personal favor if you were to wait for me in this little park. Take my camera bag and wait for me, if you would; I don't propose to take any pictures anyway." She asked with some concern in her voice, "You are not going to start any kind of demonstration, are you?" I replied, "Come on, you have seen me now for a full week. I am a very responsible person who came here representing thirty thousand American actors. I am not going to blow it with silly demonstrations." She agreed to wait.

As it happens, I was more than a little apprehensive. A week or so earlier, the Moscow correspondent of the *Los Angeles Times* had been expelled from the USSR for accepting a package containing some scientific material from someone and agreeing to take it to America on his next trip home. Although the papers were totally nonsensitive in nature, he was thrown out of the country just the same. I was determined not to make similar mistakes. I would take nothing from anybody. What I had brought into the country by way of prayer books and other Jewish paraphernalia I had already given away at my earlier visit to the synagogue. When I got to the place, there were many Jews milling around in front of the temple. Recognized by my clothing as a visitor from abroad, I was approached by a number of people. I was quite aware of the KGB agents watching on the surrounding rooftops, presumably with high-powered binoculars. The Jews who spoke to me here were younger than the ones I had met in the synagogue earlier in the week, and I suspected that they had not even attended the service. Saturday afternoon in front of the synagogue was a focal point for activists to meet each other, and possibly to make contact with visitors from abroad.

The talks were lively and for me very informative; I would have plenty of ammunition to take back with me to be used in the continuing struggle. One man in his thirties did ask me if I would be prepared to take some messages out with me. True to my resolve, I declined to take anything from anyone's hand. I told the man that he could give me a couple of messages verbally, however. Since I was an actor, memorizing things was something I was used to. What he wanted me to do was give a message to someone in Ramat Gan, in Israel; he told me the man's name and number, which I memorized. The message itself struck me as very curious. He asked me to memorize a certain Moscow telephone number. The person in Israel was to call that number on the following Thursday at the appointed time. I told him that I was prepared to deliver the message, but I was curious to know several things. How could an Israeli call anyone in Moscow, as the two countries had no telephone service linking them? He explained that they had found a way: Calls from England could be placed to Moscow; the Israelis called a friendly Jewish firm in London. The firm's switchboard patched the calls through to the USSR. I was still curious. If they had arranged appointed times, how come they did not also know which number in Moscow to call? And were they not afraid that the KGB would be listening in? The answers to those two questions were linked. The KGB could not possibly monitor all the telephones; hence they rotated numbers to call. The new number was usually for a telephone in an empty apartment. When some Jewish family had finally managed to satisfy all the bureaucratic chicanery and had left, it would take the phone people weeks to come around to disconnect the service. The activists remaining behind had a key to the empty apartment, and waited there at the prearranged time to speak to the Israelis. As this was my last day, I was able to fulfill my promise within forty-eight hours.

When I returned to the little park where Marina waited, she had a quizzical look in her eyes. I said, "You see? Nothing happened." "You are a funny man," she said. "How do you know I am not KGB?" I told her that, while I had no way of knowing whether she was a KGB agent or not, the fact that she asked the question gave me a pretty good idea that she was all right. Besides, I pointed out that the KGB could not possibly have any interest in me. I had gone and talked to a few Jews after synagogue services. I did not give them anything and I was not handed anything. What could the KGB want with me? She said that I was right, and that she had nothing to do with the KGB; she was an interpreter, pure and simple, and as such she was in demand. "Besides," she said, "I am an Armenian. That's only half a step removed from being a Jew."

Back in the United States I continued to be active on behalf of Soviet Jewry. This took many forms, involving both overt and covert actions. It involved rallies, meetings, strategy sessions, and debriefing of Jews who had managed to emigrate to Israel, the United States, or Canada. I did not always see eye to eye with some of the other Soviet Jewry activists. For example, there were those who tried to make the Jewish issue a part of a general anti-Soviet campaign. I was not prepared to have this issue used as a stick in a general crusade, one that would also attract allies from the radical right with whom I personally would find it difficult to make common cause. The other sticky point was the desire of some Jewish organizations to help Soviet emigration only if the people liberated from the Soviet Union would make *aliyah* to Israel. (*Aliyah* literally means the act of ascending. As Jerusalem was situated in the hills, ascending the mount was synonymous with pilgrimage. Modern Hebrew uses *aliyah* as a term for immigration into Israel. Conversely, *yeridah,* or descending, is used disparagingly for emigration from Israel.) I found it almost contemptible to deny any Jew who wished to leave the Soviet Union help on any grounds. It seemed to denigrate their suffering. Those who chose for one reason or another to go to a place other than Israel had a right to do so, and we had no right to invalidate them as Jews.

I met on a number of occasions with people who had managed to overcome the obstacles and emigrate from the Soviet Union. It always impressed me how hard it was for them to get acclimated to freedom. Once I sat in a room at the King David Hotel with a group of Jewish émigrés, discussing various aspects of the campaign to further Jewish emigration from the USSR. Some of them had already been in Israel for over a year and one would have thought they would by now have overcome the fear that had been their constant companion throughout their lives. As we talked there was a knock at the door; Rita had come to bring me the key to our suite. At the sound of the knock all conversation ceased, just as though we had been conspirators in enemy territory. How hard it is to get rid of the legacies of oppression, I thought, and how long before these people will walk and talk as free men in a free country?

The effort to achieve freedom for oppressed peoples—including Soviet Jews—involved public exposure and led, at times, to clashes with the law. As a leader of the American Jewish Congress (AJC), an organization always on the cutting edge of social action, I was involved in several demonstrations, and in the short space of several months I was arrested twice. Both protests were in Washington and both at embassies. The first was a protest against apartheid at the South African embassy; Henry Siegman, AJC's executive director, Ted Mann, a former president of the organization, and I were among the first to join an action that saw daily arrests at the gates of the embassy. Why would Jews be in the forefront of such protests? Injustices committed against any people because of their race or ethnic identification are an affront against Jewish sensibilities. When we were delivered in handcuffs to the downtown police station, the sergeant, a big burly black man, inquired what we had been brought in for. "Protesting at the South African embassy," the arresting officer said. "Oh yeah?" said the sergeant. "Let's loosen their cuffs a bit."

The second arrest was at the Soviet embassy. This time there were eight of us from the leadership of AJC, seven men and one woman, Jacqueline Levine. We asked to be admitted to the embassy to talk with the ambassador or the chargé d'affaires, and were refused entry. We stood in front of the gates and demonstrated the only way one can in a peaceful manner: We sang. The D.C. police had been informed beforehand of what we intended to do, and they were there, ready with their paddy wagon. A few minutes into our protest, the sergeant came up and, pro forma, recited his piece—how it was against D.C. regulations to demonstrate within five hundred feet of an embassy. He asked us to leave, or he would have no recourse but to arrest us. I said very politely that we declined to stop. "In that case," he said, "you are now under arrest." As we continued to sing, they took us one by one to the van to be handcuffed. However, the sergeant came up to me and said with just the hint of a smile, "I'm leaving you for last; you've got the best voice."

They took us to the police station to be fingerprinted and arraigned. It was all quite polite and nonthreatening. Some time later our attorneys, who had been forewarned, posted bail and we were free until the following morning, when we had to appear before the judge.

He had a stern look about him but was quite ready to listen to our case, which was probably a welcome change after the various misdemeanor cases he had dealt with before ours. After we pleaded guilty, each one of us defendants asked to be allowed to make a statement about the reason for our actions. The attorneys among us said lawyerly things and the nonlawyers gave emotional underpinnings to what had moved such a respectable bunch of Jews to subject themselves to handcuffs, fingerprinting, and an appearance as defendants in court.

When my turn came, I said the following: "Your Honor, I do not break laws easily or lightly. If I have, in this case, knowingly violated a lawful ordinance, then I have done so only because this was the most forceful way to point to a great evil. If Jews in the Soviet Union were able—and daring enough—to engage in a peaceful demonstration such as ours, they could certainly not expect treatment as courteous as that which we received at the hands of the D.C. police. Nor would they be confronted by a judicial system as fair as the one which brings us to this courtroom, a system for which we are deeply thankful. Indeed, they would face callousness at best and brutality at worst.

"If Your Honor will permit me, I would like to recite the titles of the songs we sang as we were arrested at the gates of the Soviet embassy: 'We Shall Overcome,' which by now has become the anthem of all who are oppressed. '*Hine Ma Tov*,' 'How Good It Is for Brethren to Dwell Together in Peace and Unity,' a Hebrew song which expresses the most fervent wish of Soviet Jews, indeed of all Jews. '*Am Yisrael Chai*,' 'The People of Israel Lives,' a song which is so often sung in the Soviet Union in back rooms, in cellars, and in jails. We feel that, as the voices of our fellow Jews are being muzzled and suppressed, it is up to us to be their voice. Finally, Your Honor, I sang a song in Russian: '*Pharaonu, Otpusti Narod Moy*,' which translates as 'To You, Pharaoh, I Say: Let My People Go!'"

I thanked the judge and as I stepped down, I thought I detected a softening, a blink of emotion on his previously dour and forbidding Irish face. Moved or not, he found us guilty anyway, and fined each one of us fifty dollars. I thought the price was well worth it. The Soviet embassy had left it to the police to charge us with a violation. They never issued an official complaint in such cases, as they did not want to have to appear in court and engage in a colloquy about the issues. But we made our case anyway.

In the course of my four visits to the USSR I witnessed many changes that affected the lives of Jews in there. The years 1977 and 1984 were not very much different one from the other in terms of the oppressive atmosphere. There had been some emigration but the Ovir, the dreaded office that gave out exit permits, often capriciously with-holding them at the last minute for the flimsiest of reasons, was still operating in full swing. In 1988 things had changed for the better. I could announce that I wanted to go to the synagogue freely, would even be driven there by my hosts, who four years earlier would have pretended that such institutions no longer existed in the USSR. The day before I left, there was a bloodless coup: Mikhail Gorbachev ceased to be "chairman" and became president. Everything was so tranquil that Raisa Gorbachev even attended a musical event, an American-Soviet coproduction. She sat four rows ahead of me.

Two years later came the big upheaval, and the Soviet Union ceased to exist. If anyone thought that the Jews could breathe more freely, they were mistaken. With freedom of speech also came a return of the old freedom to hate. Anti-Semitism reared its head, in all its manifestations, its foul smell permeating Russia once more. A radical organization named *Pamyat* (Remembrance) urged a return to the "old values," which included Jew-baiting, but more brazenly and openly than during the Communist regime. As the Russian economy slid into chaos, Jews could be blamed again for any ills that befell Rus-sia. Graffiti appeared on the walls, including swastikas intertwined with stars of David. Slick anti-Semitic leaflets are distributed, and ral-lies attended by thousands of Russians feature speeches accusing the Jews of ruining Russia as the crowds cheer and jeer.

February 27, 1993. Once again I was in Moscow, for the first time since the breakup of the Soviet Union. I had been here last in 1988, the very week Gorbachev ceased to be chairman and became presi-dent. The official rate of exchange then was something like one ruble to $1.40. Now one dollar was equal to six hundred rubles at the offi-cial rate—higher at the unofficial one. Most basic items had become five or six times more expensive than before, and the cost of a few others had gone up by 12,000 percent! By now Gorbachev was also history; he no longer held any position of power but was relegated to private-citizen status.

Once again I paid a visit to the synagogue. It was much sadder than the previous times. During my earlier visits, the synagogue had been a place of old people, most of whom were resigned and fearful. The young ones were there, too, but outside, using the synagogue on Archipova Street as a rallying point rather than a place of worship. Yet there was an underlying spirit of hope and Jewish renewal. This time I saw no young faces at all and the old ones were more resigned than before. It was as if, in earlier times, they could say to themselves, "If only we could get rid of the bastards, there would be hope for us."

Well, now the bastards were gone and a different mood was holding sway in the land, a mood no more friendly to Jews than the Communist attitude had been—less so, in fact, because the language this new anti-Semitism speaks is somehow sanctioned by a misunderstood notion about what freedom of speech means. While the Russians are still struggling to find their own definition of democracy, they have already managed to thwart one of its basic tenets: Freedom is not absolute; it does not include the freedom to incite against others. Freedom in a democracy is predicated upon respect for the rights and safety of others. Simply put in folksy terms: Your freedom to swing your arms ends where the other fellow's nose starts.

There were more beggars, too, this time at the portals of the synagogue, and they broke my heart. To have gaunt men and women implore you in Yiddish to part with a dollar so that a whole family may have bread is not easy to bear. There are poor Jews in many parts of the world, even in affluent America. But they rarely have to actually beg like this, with an outstretched palm that is veined, wrinkled, and trembling from the cold and from old age. I wished I could take them all with me to Israel, to America, anywhere except here, where hope is just as scarce a commodity as food seems to be. How much better it would have been if all the Tevyes and their families had escaped from this land which was and is so inhospitable to its Jews.

Some evenings, as I made my exit at the end of *Fiddler on the Roof*, pulling the heavy cart, I would ask myself a question: What kind of life might Tevye and his family have fashioned for themselves in America in 1905? Would they, like so many other Jews, try to create a new life for themselves with a new outlook? Or would they simply escape from the oppression of the pogroms to a land that held out the promise that they would be free to replicate their old life in the new world? Would they continue the anachronism of ghetto existence when they were no longer forced by the surrounding world to do so? Would they incongruously dress like Russian Jews—in long, heavy black garb and fur hats—despite the warm climate? To this day, ultra-Orthodox Jews are seen in the streets of America for whom time seemingly has stood still, and the fact that they are in the United States seems to have made no difference at all, to judge from their mode of living. Even the Lubavitch sect of Chassidim has retained most of the trappings of dress and attitude that are from another time and another place; this despite the fact that they also use high-tech equipment, rent planes, drive automobiles, and produce CD recordings. They use these modern means merely as tools to convey an ancient message of unchanged tradition. They use flatbed trucks and RV vehicles, dub them "mitzvah tanks," and roam the streets of New York, seeking not to make converts among Gentiles but rather, to use their phrase, "to make Jews out of Jews." They build a mobile *sukkah,* a shelter of branches, on the flatbed and drive to the college campuses to enable students to experience the spirit of the harvest holiday called Sukkoth. I have seen them park a converted motor home in front of Grand Central Station; they stop passersby, inquiring, "Excuse me, are you Jewish?" If the answer is negative, they say, "Have a nice day." If positive, they invite the person inside the vehicle. Men are asked to put on *tefillin* (phylacteries), and women are given instruction on how to light Sabbath or holiday candles and say the blessing over them. Despite the RV vehicles and the global radio and television hookups, they are still not part of today, either as Jews or as Americans.

When my son Rob was about six years old, we would take him to Sunday school at the reform temple in Ridgefield, Connecticut. On the last day of school before summer vacation, I went to pick him up, and as I waited for him I caught a glimpse of a black-coated man with a dark beard inside the building, an unusual sight in those surroundings. Robbie emerged clutching a small candlestick. When I asked him where he had gotten it, he said, "A rabbi with a beard came and gave me this for my sister." Then he added, "I forgot to tell him that I don't have a sister." For the next few weeks we lit three candles on Friday night in honor of the nonexistent sister. Still, I was amazed that the arm of the Lubavitchers had reached out as far as southwestern Connecticut, and even into a reform temple, which other strictly Orthodox Jews shun as if it were a church. The Lubavitch sect also goes by the name Chabad, an acronym derived from *chochmah, binah, and da'at,* wisdom, understanding, and knowledge.

When the drive to free Soviet Jewry was proceeding at an intense pace, we decided to hold a rally at the foot of the Statue of Liberty. Its proclamation "Give me your tired, your poor, your huddled masses yearning to breathe free" seemed to make it a fitting place to hold such a rally. It was decided we would do this on a Sunday morning; we would take the ferry ride across, make a few short speeches, sing songs, and blow the *shofar* of freedom. On the appointed Sunday, so many people showed up that a second ferry had to be commandeered. I went over on the first one; there were many young people, some of them playing instruments and singing Hebrew songs, and there were dignitaries, including a couple of New York congressmen. On the way over, two black-coated figures approached me. They wore hats that were one size too small for their heads; obviously Chabadniks. Though fairly young, they already had the look of the old Jews they emulated. "You're Theodore Bikel, aren't you?" they asked. "Yes," I replied. "And you are Lubavitch Chassidim." Astonished, they asked: "How did you know?" I said: "That you are Chassidim is obvious from the way you are dressed. That you are Lubavitcher Chassidim is obvious to me also because if you were any other kind, you would not be mixing with goyim like us." Ignoring that last reference, they said, "It's true, we are from Chabad. We were wondering"—why did it sound like "wonderink" in the mouths of these young men who were born in America?—"we were wondering if you already put on tefillin today." I admitted that in truth not only I had not done so that morning, but had not done it for a very long time. They said that it was only midmorning and that it was permitted to don tefillin until the early afternoon. It would be such a great thing if all the young people present could see Theodore Bikel perform this mitzvah. (A mitzvah is the observance of a commandment of Jewish law or of a good deed.)

I said that I had no objection, that I had never refused to perform any Jewish ritual, but that I was bothered by one thing. Would they, as Orthodox Jews, not view this as hypocrisy on my part? After all, I said, I gave performances on Friday nights, traveled at times when it was not permitted to do so, ate all manner of cockamamie food; I was not a kosher Jew by their standards. Would it not be hypocritical if, for the sake of showing off, I were to publicly perform this religious ritual? They said no, the Rebbe, *shlit'a,* had evolved the theory of the partial mitzvah. (The spiritual leader of Chabad, Rabbi Menachem Mendel Shneerson, is known as the Rebbe. *Shlit'a,* another acronym, is a wish for a long and fruitful life.) I asked them what that theory might be, and they explained that putting on tefillin was only one of the 613 required mitzvoth. You say the blessing, tie one phylactery to the left arm, the other to the forehead, and merely recite the short *sh'ma* (Hear O Israel.) The full morning prayer should also be recited, but that was a different mitzvah. The Rebbe argued that if one were to put on tefillin regularly, one would also get into the habit of regular prayer. Eventually one might get around to as many of the other 611 mitzvoth as possible. It was a foot in the door, they said. I told them that I was intrigued by sophistry like that and I would do as they asked. I do not think they were sharp enough to know that sophistry meant unsound or misleading reasoning. Be that as it may, I rolled up my left sleeve, recited the blessing, and put on the tefillin. While I am at it, I thought, I might as well *daven,* recite, the morning prayer (see? this partial thing was already working), and so I did that also. As I removed the phylacteries, the young Lubavitchers shook my hand in gratitude for having permitted them to lead me to a good deed—and then came the unexpected American part. They handed me a large yellow campaign button that read: "I put on tefillin today, did you?"

IN AMERICA, Tevye would have remained an Orthodox Jew to the end. But I am convinced that he would also have looked, listened, and learned. He might not have done things his faith forbade him to do, but he would have been curious about his surroundings—more so than the Chassidim of Chabad—and wise enough to know that the next generation would surely lead a far more secular life than he. He would be tolerant. In short, he would turn out to be very much like Reb Shimon Bikel.

17

From Jerusalem
to Jerusalem

THE ROLE OF TEVYE CAME NATURALLY TO ME for a number of
reasons. The musical tradition I inherited from my family was
that of the shtetl and of the later emergence from it. These were the
songs of the Pale of Settlement, of *amcho,* the simple working people,
of things sacred and of things secular. The songs were the product of
two cultural processes, one simple and one complicated. The simple
one related to the cycle of days and months; of weekdays and of Sab-
baths; of the festivals; of births, betrothals, and marriage. Jewish life,
more than any other, was regulated and dominated by the calendar.
The complicated process had to do with the abandoning of the safe
cocoon of carefully ordered lives by halachic (talmudic) precepts while
retaining Jewish awareness and ethnic pride. Venturing beyond the
t'chum, the borders of the Jewish enclave, was at first a bold step. Jews
were warned by the elders and rabbis that looking beyond the shtetl
and the *shtibl* ("little room," or house of study) meant endangerment,
and touching what lay beyond meant contamination. Still, during the
years of *haskalah* (enlightenment), some Jews of Eastern Europe
insisted on looking and touching, at first because of intellectual curiosity, and later because of political awareness, socialist leanings, and Zionist longings. These were what had moved my father as he sang for me
his Jewish songs of labor and of longing.

In the diaspora, the melodies were often borrowed from the musical modes surrounding the Jews. I learned a Yiddish song from my father, the Labor-Zionist, which I assumed to be a Jewish original. The words certainly were, but I soon found out that the melody was purloined from the Russian tune "*Stenka Razin*":

Groyser Got mir zingen lider / Unzer hilf bistu aleyn / Nemt tsunoyf di snopes, brider / Biz di zun vet untergeyn (Great God we sing to you/Our help are you alone/Gather up the sheaves, my brothers/Till the setting sun is gone.

The early settlers in Palestine brought with them precious little baggage. But they brought poems, songs, and *niggunim*—wordless melodies. The early music of the *chalutzim* (pioneers) leaned heavily on a Russian idiom. Even though the language of the songs was Hebrew, the tunes were nothing if not derivative. The same held true for the later wave of immigrants, notably from Poland, Germany, and Austria. But then the borrowed melodies began to intermingle with what was already there, including the lilting tones of the Arab shepherd's flute from across the valley. Soon Israeli composers, even though they hailed from Eastern Europe, leaned heavily toward Middle Eastern modes. As must be evident even to the casual listener, today's song of Israel has its own texture and pattern. To be sure, there is from time to time a detectable whiff of antecedent melodies. But by and large there is a new body of music that draws its inspiration both from history and geography. Liturgy often furnishes the text. Even the most irreligious of Israelis—and there are more of them than of the other kind—are familiar with chapter and verse—not with prayer as prayer, but with prayer as poetry.

Jews arrived in America from the 1870s on, some seeking to find a new style and a new life, others to continue the old life in a new land that promised freedom—if not from discrimination then, at least, from persecution. It also promised streets paved with gold. Alas, for most of the immigrants *di goldene medine,* the golden land, did not live up to its promise of bounty, and many of the songs give evidence of the immigrants' disappointment. Morris Rosenfeld sang of the father in the sweatshop who never got to see his little son because he was still sleeping when Papa had to leave for work, and had long been in bed when Papa came home. But even in bitterness there was humor. *Di grine kuzine,* the greenhorn cousin, arrives in America, pretty and hopeful, with a laughing face and dancing feet. Not too much later she is seen, no longer pretty and vivacious but bone-weary. The question "How are you?" she answers only with a sigh. But her demeanor indicates that, for all she cares, Columbus's Promised Land could go to hell.

Jewish song in America today—wherever it still exists—is changing in form and shape. In normal times this would be a natural process. But these times are not normal; we live in a pressure cooker that does not permit the slow processes of acculturation and change. Not only is the Yiddish word disappearing with every gravestone in the Jewish cemetery, it is also not being supplanted by much else of folkloric value. To be sure, there are individuals and groups, such as Safam, which cultivate a new Jewish-oriented song; klezmer groups all over have rediscovered an instrumental genre of Jewish culture and audiences for this music are growing; there are temple youth groups that sing *adon olam* ("Master of the Universe") to the tune of the Beatles' "Yellow Submarine." And of course there are still the Chassidim and their followers. But by and large, our musical output in Jewish America is much thinner than our numbers merit. Maybe this has to do with the fact that we are success-oriented, forever looking for "hits" rather than for quality. Our surroundings and the seductive ease of blending instead of retaining distinctive cultural traits have taken their invidious toll. I have repeatedly admonished Jewish audiences by saying: "We fancy ourselves to be Jews, yet our lifestyle gives the lie to such a claim, for it is curiously un-Jewish. If we care about any of this at all, then we shall have to learn anew; to learn or relearn to live, think, move, talk—yes, and to sing—as Jews."

I am often brought up short by being defined by my birthplace. When I tell an American that I was born in Vienna, the response is often, "Ah, you are Austrian." I am nothing of the kind; I am an Austrian-born Jew. I refuse to let a country that so shamefully treated my people lay any claim to me, to my life, to my successes, to my failures, to my very identity. But even in a country such as Mexico, where there is little or no persecution of Jews, Jews are not called Mexicans. Though they may be third- or fourth-generation Mexican-born, neither they themselves nor their compatriots call them that. And when a real-life Tevye and his family finally arrived in America, would anyone have called them "Russians" and not be met with gales of laughter?

Much of what I am telling here might give the impression that I am forever looking backward and inward, that somehow I have never gotten rid of the yoke of the Jewish history of suffering and persecution. The truth of the matter is that, while the yoke without a doubt is present at all times, it sits lightly on my shoulders, for I am also intensely involved in the twentieth century. Living in America has removed much of the onus of Eurocentrism from me as well as any attitudes reminiscent of the Jewish ghetto. Withal, I have never been inclined to water down my commitment to the Jewish people in the name of some vague hankering for political ecumenism. I am still puzzled by the insistence on hyphens. Why does a restaurant that serves Chinese food advertise "Chinese-American" food? What is there about its Kung-Pao chicken that is American, except the self-consciousness of the owner? Why call food Mexican-American, why Jewish-American, when what is meant is Mexican or Jewish, period?

I have so often been disturbed by our American inability to make the distinction between nationality and peoplehood, citizenship and cultural identity. Throw religious identification into the pot and it muddles the issue even further. An Irishman manages to be as American as he wants to be, yet still has tears in his eyes when "The Rose of Tralee" is sung; his attachment to the Irish people, to Irish song, and even to the Irish soil hardly ever calls into question his American patriotism. He is seldom accused of dual loyalty. Jews almost invariably are, and I believe that as a reaction to the accusation we either cringe and seek to demonstrate that each one of us is more patriotic than "thou," or we engage in a defiant particularism. Neither attitude is healthy. My own mixture of ethnic awareness on the one hand, and of social and political involvement with the world around me on the other, often confuses people, even members of my own family. My sons and I had several animated discussions in the course of which they so much as charged me with not being a fully fledged American, forever having one foot elsewhere. I cannot blame them for this perception; even after all these years as an American resident and citizen, I probably exude an aura of homelessness, a particular Jewish affliction. Even my politically universalist passions are probably suspect and perceived as barely disguised rootlessness. The truth is that since the destruction of the Temple and the dispersion, our notion of belonging has not been tied to geography. Home is to be found not so much in space as in time.

Despite my being a completely secular human being, to many of my friends I remained the Jewish guru. Peter Yarrow was the Jewish member of the Peter, Paul & Mary trio. That is not to say that the others were not involved with Jewish affairs. Mary, especially, became very active on behalf of Soviet Jewry, and Paul (Noel) gave solo concerts and workshops in Israel. But Peter was the ethnic Jew. He used to come to my house for Jewish festivals, especially for Passover. He would bring his mother and they would *kvell*. Years later, when his mother was no longer alive, he got engaged to Mary Beth McCarthy, Senator Gene McCarthy's niece. He called me on the telephone and told me the news, adding that, because Mary Beth's family insisted upon it, they would be married in a Catholic church, but that the children would not have to be "signed over" before birth. He kept me on the phone for a very long time, explaining that the church marriage was a pro forma matter, and that he had a request to make of me. He wanted to be sure that his fiancée would experience his background and roots; it was important to him that she be aware of what made him tick. To that end he wanted me to promise that at Passover, I would invite them both to my seder, as I had invited him and his mother in the past. Finally, after I had assured him that he was invited, he hung up.

My wife wondered what the long conversation had been all about: "What did he want?" I answered: "Absolution."

For quite a while I maintained a loose association with Chabad. I had found them to be the most accessible of all the Orthodox Jews I had contact with. I was also friendly with some of the rabbis, particularly Shemtov in Philadelphia. At the time when I was doing my best to reach young Jews on the college campuses, arguing a mixture of ethnic pride, folklore, and political activism, Chabad were fairly successful in reaching them religiously. I gave them credit for that, although I had never been sanguine about single-channel adherence. When all was said and done, Lubavitch was still a religious sect, perhaps closer and more familiar to me because it was a Jewish sect, but nevertheless beset by a measure of fanaticism. Its followers' blind obedience to the pronouncements of one man—recently declared by some to be the Messiah—caused me some personal apprehension. On those occasions when I was taken into the Rebbe's presence, I found him to be a fascinating man and I could well understand the charisma. But just as I have grave reservations about an absolute and fatalistic belief in God because it exonerates all human agency, I am leery of unquestioned authority emanating from any rabbinical source, however benign.

There were other differences between my views and the attitude of the Rebbe and his followers, which over the years turned out to be unbridgeable. There was meddling in Israeli politics in a manner that exceeded the urging and advice-giving that all the rest of us do. Planeloads of Chassidim who held dual citizenship were dispatched to Israel for the purpose of voting in the Israeli elections and influencing the outcome in favor of the religious parties. I understood this to be one of the two taboos for American holders of dual citizenship, the other being service in another country's armed forces. On the domestic front, Chabad tried to erect menorahs on public lands, a practice not permitted under the separation of church and state. The American Jewish Congress had fought long and hard for many years to preserve that wall and to vigorously oppose any perceived breach in it. We objected to the use of public facilities for religious symbols of any kind; it was inconceivable that we should not fight the placing of menorahs just as vigorously as we had crosses and crèches. I was an officer of a Jewish organization that had to fight Chabad in court on this question of principle. Just as vigorously we defended their right not to be obstructed in their religious practices in any way that did not involve the public purse or the use of public land.

I had never liked the Jewish attempts to put Chanukkah on an equal footing with Christmas. I was well into my adult years before I made any connection with Christmas at all. Having grown up in an atmosphere where the non-Jewish side of the street represented threat and danger to us, its celebrations did not fill us with envy. Suspicion and fear, yes, but hardly envy. There were no little Jewish children to be found in Central Europe who would press their noses against a cold and wintry windowpane wishing they could be inside opening packages under a Christmas tree.

As I found out much later, it was somewhat different for Jewish children in America, where the dividing lines were neither as strict nor as forbidding. Jews even wrote Christmas songs. Isn't it strange that two of the most popular ones, "White Christmas" and "Chestnuts Roasting on an Open Fire," were written by Jews—Irving Berlin and Mel Tormé? Of course, in America Christmas grew to be less and less about Christ and more and more about merriment and gift-giving. Little Johnny and Mary got all these presents, and what about little Irving and little Ruthie? Something had to be done to rectify the imbalance. As a result, Chanukkah, a relatively minor holiday with mostly historic connotations, was promoted into a major one that would try to equal Christmas, at least as far as the volume of presents was concerned. I made my peace with Christmas, mostly because of the music. Yes, and the parties, too. I like to listen to the carols and sometimes even sneak into the back row of a church at Christmastime to hear the organist and the choir. But I won't have a Christmas tree in my house. I don't observe the holiday, I just observe.

Midnight Mass in Bethlehem. You can't get much closer to the Christmas holiday than this. The year was 1971, and the date January 8, a little late for Christmas, so one might have thought. Rita and I were in Jerusalem for a series of concert appearances. I got a call that day from Teddy Kollek, the mayor of Jerusalem, inviting us to accompany him to an interesting ceremony. The Armenians go by a later calender than other Christians, and it was their Christmas that evening. Teddy asked whether my wife and I would care to join him that night to attend midnight Mass at the Church of the Nativity in Bethlehem. We accepted eagerly.

We were picked up around 11:30 P.M. in the mayor's car and driven from Jerusalem to Bethlehem, a short ride of some twenty-five minutes. Manger Square was chock-full of Armenian worshipers; the interior of the cathedral was crowded with many more people standing shoulder to shoulder. There were also two big and unwieldy television cameras, marked ISRAELI TELEVISION, and their crews. We made our way down to the Grotto of the Nativity, a not-very-large underground hollow, lit by many candles. This place holy to Christians, the spot where, according to legend, the baby Jesus was born, was simply decorated and roped off. It was also jealously guarded by a monk whose face clearly showed that, while all Christians were permitted to worship there, he was in charge. Nor was he intimidated by the Armenian archbishop in his resplendent robes, who had taken his place at a slightly raised spot, ready to begin. The narrow grotto held as many worshipers as could reasonably fit in the place. In addition to the several dozen Armenians, there were only a few outsiders: my wife and I, the Jewish mayor of Jerusalem and his wife, the Arab Christian mayor of Bethlehem and his wife, two high-ranking Israeli police officials—and two more television cameras.

Mass was quite beautiful and somewhat exotic because of the language and the music. It was also quite tiring because we were all standing, either because of the lack of space or because the ritual demanded it—I do not know which. Curiously, at the end of the ceremony the archbishop gave a short sermon in English. Then we, along with other VIP guests, were invited to join the archbishop for a libation at his official residence in the Old City in Jerusalem. By now it was well after 2:00 A.M.

The archbishop of Jerusalem is the highest-ranking Armenian churchman in the world. The residence is, consequently, quite impressive. We were served strong coffee and very sweet cakes in the large reception room with the archbishop seated in a thronelike chair. He was a smallish, jovial man with a ready smile. His face and beard made him look somewhat like the late Maharishi Mahesh Yogi; his high-pitched voice was similar to the Maharishi's, too. We had a chance to chat and I said to him, "I would like to ask you something, Your Beatitude." (What an extraordinary title! but that is how he is addressed.) "Tonight was the highlight of your religious year, was it not?" "Indeed, Indeed," he replied. I asked, "Did you not find the presence of the television cameras intrusive?" "Intrusive?" he asked in his high singsong voice. "No, I insisted on them!" Seeing the astonished look on our faces, he went on. "I went to the authorities and said to them, 'You must televise my midnight service. You televised the Catholics and the Protestants, the Greek Orthodox and the Russian Orthodox, you must televise the Armenians. I have here in the Middle East many thousands of Armenians, they all listen and watch TV. Even the ones across the border, they may not admit it, but they watch. I have in the United States some two hundred thousand Armenians, they watch TV. (Aha! hence the sermon in English.) You must televise!'

"Then the Israeli authorities said to me, 'We cannot arrange it. We are new to this television business. This is—how you call it?—a remote, a remote broadcast; we cannot arrange a remote broadcast in four days!' So I said to them, 'You can win a war in six days—you can arrange a remote broadcast in four days!'" Another high-pitched giggle. Yes, I made my peace with Christmas.

My SONS AND I have had a running argument over the years that gave me—still gives me—a lot of grief. It has to do with an acknowledgment of your Jewishness beyond the mere fact of Jewish birth and attendance at seders. As a teenager, Danny wrote a paper entitled "Which One Doesn't Belong?" It was a very good paper, well reasoned and well phrased, but its conclusions troubled me. In the first instance, there was once again the underlying assumption that being a Jew had to do solely with religious practice. If that were so, then in the absence of an attachment to religion or belief in a Jewish God—any God, for that matter—one's Jewishness would become an irrelevancy.

Even the atheistic Jew went to the synagogue because he had no other forum in which to argue atheism. First he would *daven* along with the rest of the congregation; then, when the service was over, he would declare, "This is all nonsense; it's meaningless. I refuse to be confined by all this. I am an atheist, thank God!" In fact, both political and religious discourse found a setting in the synagogue. It was there that my father argued not just for Zionism, but for socialism as well.

To perceive Jewishness as solely a religious orientation is to ignore the fact of Jewish peoplehood, of an ethnic and cultural, indeed a familial, bond that ties us, horizontally and vertically, to a continuum of Jews. Horizontally—as brother, cousin, kin to all Jews living today, wherever they may be. Vertically—as descendant of all Jews who came before us, and as ancestor to all Jews who will come after us.

Group memory has to do not only with an intellectual awareness of history, but also with an atavistic and visceral reaction to the world that *is* in the light of recalling a world that *was*. There are two different biblical commandments relating to memory: *zachor,* remember, and *lo tishkach,* do not forget. The two are not synonymous. Both commandments do, however, assume a familial identification with the body politic of Jews. It is difficult to remember things one never knew or cared little to know.

Danny wrote at the end of his beautiful discourse: "I want to think and live unfettered, not in spite of my religion, but because of it. You see, with all this nonsense, I will defend my being a Jew to the teeth." Okay, here then is my problem: If defending against attacks is to be the hallmark of one's Jewishness, then a problem arises. Say the defense succeeds—there's a question about that, too: How much of the "success" is self-delusion or wishful thinking?—but say we are safe. Then safe to be what? to do what? to practice what? Do we secure rights to safeguard them for the few who wish to avail themselves of the freedom, but not for ourselves? If our commitment rests upon the premise that as long as others seek to harm or destroy us we will oppose them with vigor, does that not then allow the anti-Semites who roam the streets yelling for Jewish blood to define our Jewishness for us, to choose the times and places where we would assert it and how loudly and how proudly we would proclaim it? Do we ignore or neglect the Jewish continuum as soon as the attacks abate or stop? If that is all there is to it, then Judaism can live only as long as its enemies. An ignoble lesson to draw from four thousand years of endurance and survival.

I do not suggest that Jewish descent alone should determine my self-definition as a Jew. That would be an exercise in mindlessness. Being born Jewish just makes you Jewish; it doesn't make you a Jew. There are no shortcuts to being a Jew. Being called Schwartz or Goldberg doesn't suffice, nor does circumcision. I am talking about a Jewishness that, if not committed, is at least aware. It does not come to you by osmosis, it has to be worked at. In the first place it means a trip to the library. You have to go after the knowledge of what it means to be Jewish. It means books. In all this tactile world, we Jews are still a linear people. Books are central to our Jewishness and also to our ritual: We read from the Torah. So I counsel trips to the bookshelves and trips inside oneself, in preference to the societal aspects of Jewish living. Being Jewish has to be active, not merely reactive. Demographic Jewishness is only half a step removed from culinary Judaism. Eating gefilte fish or drinking Manischewitz wine doesn't make you into a Jew. Living in areas populated by Jews, playing cards or golf with Jews won't do it, either.

Years ago I had occasion to speak to the president of an all-Jewish fraternity at the University of Texas. A nice, polite, tall, and athletic-looking boy. I asked him about the Jewish activities of the fraternity. "What Jewish things do you do?" "Handball, basketball," he replied in a charming Texas drawl. "No, I mean what do you do that's specifically Jewish?" "Well, we're all Jews," he said. I got the idea. He had the same mistaken notion as his mom and his dad; they thought that playing bridge and golf was Jewish merely because all the participants were Jews.

What does make you a Jew is awareness. You can do it on several levels. You can do it on the ethnosociological level, you can do it on the folkloric level, you can do it on the linguistic level by cultivating Hebrew or Yiddish. You can do it on the religious level or you can do it on the political level. "I'm a Zionist, hence I'm a Jew" will work, even for those who never set foot in a synagogue. But what you can't do is do *none* of these and still call yourself a Jew in the strictest sense of the definition. I insist that being a Jew is as much a cultural statement as it is an ethnic or religious identification. Add Israel and you have a political statement as well.

The acknowledgment of the "familial bond" tying all Jews together, for which I have so often argued at home—with less success than I would have hoped—rests on active commitments made by modern and aware people; in other words, it assumes *consent.* This is not just true for Jews in America: It started with the *haskalah,* or enlightenment, in the Eastern European shtetl experience. In *Where Are We,* published in 1988, my friend Leonard Fein makes the point that *Fiddler* is perhaps an allegory for this: The eldest daughter, Tzeitel, rejects the arranged marriage and chooses her own mate—the beginning of discarding strict tradition, yet adhering to most of it through personal consent. The second daughter, Hodel, goes farther: She has a mind of her own and chooses to marry a revolutionary (perhaps a heretic), but still a Jew. Descent is still important. There is still some adherence to tradition through consent: "We will be married under a canopy." The third daughter, Chava, however, rejects both tradition and descent, and Tevye (who accepted change, however reluctantly, in the first two cases) cries out in anguish, "If you bend us that far, we will break!" There is for any cultural, ethnic, or religious community an obligation to accommodate itself to change; but there is also a breaking point.

The phoenix is a mythological bird who sprang out of the desert crying "Here I am," without parentage and memory. My regret is that so many of my contemporaries treat themselves to a phoenixlike existence, thinking that one can exist without respecting one's roots, without acknowledging yesterday or the value of memory. That casts into doubt one's ability to deal with today, one's ability even to survive tomorrow.

I am convinced that contemporary American thinking and Jewish memory do not need to do battle with each other, for these provinces of the mind are not mutually exclusive. Too many young Jews seem to think that they are. The failure is surely not theirs alone, but ours as well, for not having made this argument convincing—or for having failed to make it at all. I do not exempt myself; I, too, am to blame. I have not been able to give my sons an adequate underpinning of thought so that they could share my philosophy. Mea culpa. Nearly two hundred years ago, Charles Lamb said, "I am determined that my children should follow their father's religion—if they could find out what it is." When I think about the decades of successful involvment with Jewish youth, of the speeches and lectures I gave on campuses, the colloquies and debates with Jewish students, I regret my inability to achieve similar success at home. "They made me keeper of the vineyards," it says in the Song of Songs, "but mine own vineyard have I not kept." Like most parents of my generation, I know that no matter what paths our children take, we will not lose their love. But there's always the hope that they will be more than occasional visitors to our world.

I DEFINE MYSELF as a universalist within the context of all I have lived through. But in my case, that universalism works best as it emanates from a particularist stance. To be a Jew, to me, means a heightened awareness of the human condition, and the sad-sweet knowledge that where we stand someone has stood before. It means a mode of living and a method of survival. Spiritually and culturally, to be a Jew is to be on the road from Jerusalem to Jerusalem. I am an American; that is my home and my daily solace. Jerusalem, however, is my hope and inspiration.

18

Entebbe, Vanessa, and Other Thoughts

JEWISH HOSTAGE (Theo Bikel): [*After showing a tattooed number on his arm.*] Again. Germans pointing guns at Jews.
GERMAN TERRORIST (Helmut Berger): We have nothing in common with the Nazis. It's not the same.
JEWISH HOSTAGE: It's the same.

—FROM THE TELEPLAY *VICTORY AT ENTEBBE*

IN THE USUAL COMMERCIAL HASTE THAT MOTIVATES most studio executives, the heroic feat of the Entebbe raid in July 1976 spawned three—count 'em, three—movies; all of them were filmed within weeks of the incident. The funny thing is that all of them were good movies and were successful, even though they were in direct competition among themselves. For sheer international breadth of performance, *Operation Thunderbolt* was the best, I think. I know that the production company, Golan and Globus, thought theirs was the best because they'd produced it, and I must admit it was very good.

The one I was in, *Victory at Entebbe,* was not far behind; we had the legendary Helen Hayes, we had Richard Dreyfuss, a grown-up Duddy Kravitz with an Uzi; we even had Elizabeth Taylor in a cameo role and the Austrian actor Helmut Berger playing the German terrorist. Godfrey Cambridge was cast as Idi Amin. He had not been well for the past years, was grossly overweight, and, under doctor's orders, had lost close to sixty pounds. While standing by to make his entrance for his big scene, he keeled over with a massive coronary attack. We were all in shock as we watched the paramedics trying to revive him. They worked for close to an hour, but it was hopeless; he was dead. On the following day we shut down filming for a couple of hours so that everyone who wished could attend Godfrey's funeral. I was one of the pallbearers, a role that still is not easy for me. Through my youth I was told that a hereditary *cohen,* or priest, was not allowed to enter a cemetery for religious reasons. It was something I overcame only late in life.

Godfrey was replaced by Yaphet Kotto, also a very good actor, and the filming of *Victory at Entebbe* continued. (So did the race to have an earlier release date than the other Entebbe stories.) The thing that made Israeli military stories successful, at least before the tragic invasion of Lebanon, was that in them Israel was seen fighting for its very survival and prevailing against the odds; the issues seemed clear-cut, even if they weren't in real life.

One would like to say that the entire world held its breath during the standoff at Entebbe Airport on the shore of Lake Victoria in Uganda, when Palestinian and German terrorists held hostage the passengers and crew, Jewish and Gentile, of a hijacked Air France jet. One would like to say that there were real international outrage and thundering denunciations from the pulpits of the world's diplomatic community over that act of piracy and kidnapping. One would like to say that civilized nation after civilized nation sprang to the defense of the imprisoned passengers, travelers who had no part in any disputes, and rattled sabers at the Arab nations that had bought and paid for the hijacking as if they were hiring a crew of roofing contractors. One would like to say it, but one can't because it wouldn't be true. There were pro forma denunciations at the United Nations, and the United States flexed its muscles. But by and large the world watched impotently while a gang of Palestinian and German terrorists separated out the Jews from the rest of the passengers and threatened them with death. Idi Amin joined in the fun and, like any good despot, even asked the Jewish passengers to acknowledge him as their protector.

There were some who privately believed that Israel had brought it on herself because of her refusal to deal directly with the Palestinians. Nonsense. Whether or not you believed that the Israeli government could have been more flexible in its positions, hijacking international travelers and holding them hostage was an outrage. As at the Munich Olympics in 1972, Jews were again held at gunpoint on the world's stage. Only this time it would be different.

As the crisis lingered on day after day, people wondered whether Israel would finally cave in and accede to the Palestinian demands, the principal one being for the freeing of a number of Palestinian terrorists being held by the Israelis. Perhaps this time there were too many Jews held hostage. Perhaps this time they were too far away in a hostile country where no one could get them out. Not even the United States marines could stage such a rescue. This time, people might begin to think, maybe the hostage-taking was a good tactic because once Israel was forced to bend, the whole Middle East crisis might be resolved. Maybe, just maybe, an international crime like this would actually pay off. Maybe it would keep the Jews in their place for a while. And that's the kind of thinking that made us all the more worried.

For most of the world's Jews, Entebbe was a nightmare replaying itself on a world stage: not just Arabs alone but also the German Red Brigade holding machine guns on Jewish tourists and frightened old women; Palestinian guerrillas swaggering up and down the aisles of a jumbo jet rerouted to a hostile country and spitting their demands into the radio; and a fascist Third World dictator, already accused of genocidal crimes against his own people, naming himself the protector of the Jews and confining them "for their own protection." What human being could look at this and say that maybe it was part of a peace process? For me, who had once lived through a Nazi occupation, however briefly, there was only one response: no, not again, not this time!

What the world didn't know was that the Israelis had a plan. It was to go straight at the terrorists, land a strike force under the cover of darkness, roll a Mercedes limo out of the transport plane's cargo bays—a duplicate of Idi Amin's own—along with jeeps and crack troops. One group of soldiers would take the Entebbe air terminal by force while another group would take out the control tower and perimeter guards, kill or take prisoner the terrorists guarding the plane and extract the hostages, load them onto the transports, and fly out of Uganda while a rear guard blew up as many MIGs on the runways as they could—and get the whole task force back to Israel with as few losses as possible. It worked.

The morning following the raid on Entebbe the whole world learned what the Israelis had done. Those who were hoping Israel would give in to the terrorists were mistaken. People who thought privately that the Jews needed a little putting down had to bite their lips as they read of the success of the raid. Some nations complained that Israel hadn't used up all diplomatic solutions before—"flagrantly" was the word they used—violating the sovereignty of Uganda. Still other nations blamed Israel for an act of international terrorism, as if rescuing your own people while the world stood by to watch them suffer was an act of terrorism.

But Israel didn't pay heed to what the world thought about proper diplomatic solutions to terrorism and personal assault. And when the cargo bay doors opened and the former hostages walked onto the Tel Aviv airport tarmac, there was a genuine celebration through Israel and the rest of the world. In many ways, it was like another Exodus.

You could say that the Entebbe movies succeeded because everybody likes a winner, but you'd be less than half right. These particular movies, especially, were like modern morality plays: The criminals got what was coming to them, the innocent were rescued, the blustering dictator lost most of his air force, and everybody got the chance to feel better about a world in which justice prevails in the end. Personally, I think the real reason for the success of the movies that reenacted Entebbe was that they made all of us—Jews and Gentiles alike—feel a little more secure about the world. As for the Jews, Israel is vital to their sense of security in their respective countries around the world. It is essential to the preservation of their self-esteem because Israel has become the center of their emotional equilibrium.

Like most groups, Jews need emotional security in order to survive as a group. Israel as a physical presence represents that emotional security, and the battering she takes becomes emblematic of the battering most of us take in life. Even peacenik Jews have been known to line up Sunday mornings at Zabar's deli counter on New York City's Upper West Side to talk about the latest military action of the Israeli army—as if they were talking about the New York Giants football game the week before. They believe that whatever it takes for Israel to survive is okay. While I would draw the line at such a blanket endorsement of any and all official Israeli actions, I think something vital and irreplaceable would die were Israel to suffer a crippling defeat. Emotionally, I cannot conceive of such a horrible prospect. Intellectually, I know that if Israel were to suffer defeat, it would not be the end of the Jews, although we would for a time believe that it was. It would be a terrible blow, but, like the proverbial ants thrown off the top of the hill, we'd crawl up it yet again, and keep working until there was another Jerusalem.

As I see it, American Jews' sense of Israel is more powerful and real than the physical entity that is Israel, so that we tend to be less critical of Israeli policy than we would be of our own government's—even when that policy is wrong. For example, how many American Jews are as passionately opposed to the settlement policies on the West Bank as they would be about any other government's appropriation of land anywhere else? Ironically, a majority of the Jews in Israel believe that the settlement policies are more of an obstacle to real peace than a guarantee of security.

A major wrinkle was thrown into the peace process when it was proposed in 1989 that new arrivals from the Soviet Union be located in the territories. It caused great concern in the Soviet Union, and even greater concern in Washington. It also threw the peace movement in Israel into an emotional turmoil. All agreed that the needs of Soviet Jews for land and housing were as real as the needs of any new group of immigrants arriving in Israel. But it was unacceptable that they should be used as pawns in a political game of creating more "Jewish" land in the territories. The Likud government had created a conflict where morality appeared to be pitted against compassion. Everybody was put in a bind. Even Mikhail Gorbachev, who had allowed higher levels of Jewish emigration, was put into the odd position of appearing to be responsible for the establishment of new settlements in the territories. Arab governments who thrived on U.S.-Soviet rivalry in the region loved the new leverage they had over the already beleaguered head of the USSR. They argued with him that he could safely stop the flow of Jews out of the Soviet Union because of Israeli policy, not Soviet policy, and still save face with the U.S., which was already on record as opposing the new settlements.

In Jerusalem at a meeting of the Emergency World Jewish Leadership Conference, I argued that creating new settlements on the West Bank for the Jewish immigrants from the Soviet Union was a threat to the peace process that had begun with the Camp David accords. In my view and that of many others, putting Soviet Jews into the territories would permit the Israeli government to present these settlements as a *fait accompli*—once done, difficult to undo. This would remove an important chip from the bargaining table, making the "land-for-peace" formula—which had worked in the Camp David negotiations with respect to the Sinai peninsula—less likely to succeed in future negotiations.

As much as anything else, creating these settlements, I argued, was also an insidious way of tilting Israeli public opinion away from any notion of compromise, without which no peace process is feasible— and making hard-liners even of those who might be inclined to give peace a chance. If they previously had been prepared to entertain the thought of giving up territory in return for an acceptable settlement, they would be less likely to do so when relinquishing such territory meant having to expel and relocate Jews already there. This mental block was hardly productive, I said, as all of us saw when the much smaller issue of giving up just one established foothold at Taba caused great emotional turmoil.

The Likud government managed to put the Bush administration in a bind. Secretary of State James Baker was circulating new peace proposals and trying to set up some formula for face-to-face negotiations among all parties, including the Palestinians, in Washington. Time was on his side. As Gorbachev became weaker, he could no longer be seen as the counterweight to U.S. influence in the Middle East. Indeed, after the Russian coup and the breakup of the Soviet Union, the U.S. was the only world power capable of dealing in the region. The Gulf War proved that. It also meant that in the future, the U.S. would have to be more evenhanded, if only because it had to be seen now as an arbiter and not as an unqualified supporter of Israel— despite Israel's sacrifice when it took such a pounding from Saddam's Scud missiles without retaliating, so as not to upset the U.S.-Arab alliances. The Arabists in the State Department needed a pretext for pressuring the administration to be evenhanded. The Israeli government furnished it by refusing to give up its policy of new settlements in the territories.

For all of us who had toiled for years to effect freedom for our brothers and sisters in the Soviet Union, the Israeli policy was a slap in the face. They were willing to compromise the legitimate good feelings of the rest of the world toward the refugees by playing Monopoly with the entire peace process. The subsequent debates between the Bush administration and the Likud government over $10 billion in U.S. government loan guarantees for new settlements for Soviet Jewish immigrants further confused the issue. American Jews were torn between their desire to see a movement toward peace and their elation over the large numbers of Soviet Jews allowed to immigrate. It was only the defeat of Shamir and the Likud party in the general election that provided some thawing out of hardened positions on all sides of the issues, and made it possible to start the peace process up again. But the feelings that were stirred up among American Jews who did not want to compromise the emotional security they felt in Israel's safety, even when Israeli policy collided with their sense of right and wrong, demonstrated just how anxious American Jewry is over the meaning of Israel.

At the best of times, the chances of success at the negotiating table are not the brightest, given the number of obstacles in the way. But with the territory-for-peace formula hampered, the prospects are surely much dimmer. The battle at the bargaining table is a process where pitfalls abound and where the outcome depends as much upon agreement with some of one's allies as with one's adversaries. One thing is certain: No negotiation has ever been successfully concluded without a feeling of dissatisfaction on both sides. As a labor leader of many years' standing, I can state from experience that an agreement from which one or the other party walks away having won on all points is the kind that will be broken almost before the ink on the signatures is dry.

I was personally appalled by the Israeli invasion of Lebanon in 1982 and by what happened at the Sabra and Shatila camps. Arab Phalangists perpetrated a massacre upon the refugees in those camps, Arabs killing Arabs, a human tragedy, with no one calling a halt. There was considerable debate in Israel as to whether General Ariel Sharon, as commander of Israel's invasion force, should have foreseen such an event and taken steps to prevent it. Certainly, the general feeling was that once under way, the massacre should have been stopped by the Israeli forces who were within arm's length of the camps. Many American Jews were particularly disturbed by what they perceived as Sharon's apparent lack of concern over the fate of these hapless victims. Quite a number of us—myself included—were frankly outraged. In the Jewish community, as usual, there were two different reactions to this horrendous situation. The first was the habitual motto of Jews in America: "Israel can do no wrong." This time, however, there were many who were so disillusioned that they refused to give their usual support; the United Jewish Appeal (UJA) had a tough time getting out attendance at its meetings. Some came reluctantly and voiced bitter disappointment. Some left in anger, announcing that it would be a long time before they would find themselves able to give their support once more. I was asked by the UJA to travel around the country and speak at meetings to control the damage. I debated with myself long and hard whether I could and, if I did, what I could say that would express my own feelings honestly and without the hypocrisy that usually attends PR spins. After all, I was no less disgusted than the disillusioned Jews who were in the process of walking away from their commitment. I reminded myself, however, that my own commitment to

Israel's survival was not tied to any policy decisions by prime ministers, cabinets, or generals. Governments come and go, they can be right or they can be wrong, but *Netzach Yisrael lo yeshakér,* "The eternity of Israel shall not be betrayed." Even before Sabra and Shatila, I had considered Ariel Sharon to be a barbarian pig who single-handedly had raised vulgarity to an art form. I would not allow him to control the level of my support for Israel or cause me to withdraw it.

I confronted the issue squarely, telling other American Jews of my own anguish, but urging them to consider the consequences of leaving the fold rather than doing what true partners are supposed to do: Argue it out, use powers of persuasion, and even the power of the purse to deliver a strong message to the Begin government about moral and ethical conduct in wartime, as well as in peacetime. Walk away, I said, and you have lost any standing to make such an argument. I incurred some displeasure on the part of those present who would brook no criticism of Israel's conduct of any kind, those who maintained that we, as Americans, had no right to voice anything but wholehearted support. The Israeli emissaries were not enchanted, either. Some of them arrived with an attitude of "So maybe somebody made a mistake; so what?"[1] That might sit well with the no-matter-what supporters, but it was hardly designed to persuade those who had grave doubts. Even Yael Dayan, Moshe Dayan's daughter with whom I shared the podium on such occasions, was plainly annoyed at my frankness. Later, as a politician and as a member of the Knesset, she espoused views very similar to my own, but at that time she and the other Israelis were defiantly insouciant. It is fair to say that their attitude swayed few of the people who were on the point of withdrawing support and contributions from Israel. My hope was to prevent them from taking flight, and I was relieved that in many cases, I succeeded.

My argument has always been that there are familial bonds which tie all Jews to each other and to Israel. With that as a given, Israel is not just another country; all Jews have a stake in its survival and are entitled to be concerned about its conduct. The Israelis themselves constantly stress the theme of "partnership" when they refer to this mutual relationship. The trouble is that they are looking for yea-sayers and for funds tendered without any opinions or conditions attached to

---

1. A story: Four diplomats are standing in a group at the U.N.—a Russian, a Pole, an American, and an Israeli. A reporter approaches and says, "Excuse me, I'd like to get your personal opinion on the shortage of meat." The Pole says, "What's meat?" The Russian says, "What's a personal opinion?" The American says, "What's a shortage?" And the Israeli says, "What's 'excuse me'?"

them. That could only be likened to the kind of partnership that exists between a farmer and a milk cow. Both Israelis and American Jews are entitled to better than that. Frankness is called for, even when it causes some strain. How many mistakes and missteps in the world have been swept under the rug because of the slogan in "My Country Right or Wrong"? If American Jews believe in "My Israel Right or Wrong," perhaps they should be reminded of Senator Carl Schurz's reply when the phrase was coined in 1872: "When right, to be kept right; when wrong, to be put right!"

There is no way that either the Jewish or the Palestinian presence will be eradicated in the region. Coexistence is the only answer. Jewish Israel must educate itself to accept that fact. Israel and the Palestinians must work to dissipate the years of accumulated bitterness for which both must bear a great responsibility. For most Israelis, the Arabs have for years been an invisible people. Now, when Israel needs a moderate Arab constituency to move the peace process forward, they will have to establish new bridges and rebuild the bridges so carelessly burned. The Arabs, on the other hand, will need to rid themselves of the notion that all this is a passing phase of history, and that in time the Jewish presence will disappear. That attitude creates a mind-set that views all solutions and all peace arrangements as temporary measures, eventually to give way to a Palestinian Arab hegemony. This will not happen, and both Palestinians in the territories and Arabs within Israel need to acknowledge it, and not only at the leadership level of a Hanan Ashrawi or Faisal Husseini (members of the PLO National Council).

Whenever I think of the dire necessity of coexistence, the image of Sidney Poitier and Tony Curtis in the film *The Defiant Ones* comes to mind. A black man and a white one, hating each other's guts, yet tied together by a steel handcuff. Pulling apart from each other, all they can get are bloody wrists. In the end, to survive they must pull together in one direction. If this is paradigmatic for blacks and whites in America, it holds just as true for Jews and Arabs in Israel.

There are cultural components to this process. Israel's government will have to do much more by way of integrating Israel's Arabs into the nation's life while respecting the differences in culture and religion. Until someone thinks of better ways to achieve harmony in this tortured society, think of kindergarten as a first step. It would take much more than a few educational reforms to bring about peace, but such a move may help weaken the strong societal taboo against intermingling. I know only one Israeli who has an Arab friend (both are musicians), and know but very few who are even acquainted with an

Arab. That is worse than the situations in other places that have a culturally and ethnically divided populace. There is far more social intercourse between francophones and anglophones in Quebec, between the Flemish and the Walloons in Belgium, between blacks and whites in America, than between Jews and Arabs in Israel.

If this is criticism, let no one make the mistake of suggesting that it is offered from any motive but a passion for Israel's survival, with its heritage of moral rectitude intact. I have had to endure attacks from both the right and the left, neither of which I shied away from. Meir Kahane sparred with me on *The Dick Cavett Show.* He started out by saying to Cavett that he and I were supporters of the same cause, the Jewish people and Israel. That was before the conversation got more heated. I told the audience that I have no more stomach for Jewish fascists than I have for the Gentile kind. If Kahane and his Jewish Defense League (JDL) tried to pretend that they were on my side because we are all Jews and "defenders" of Jews, then they had no idea of what my side was. Being a Jew has no meaning at all to me unless one is governed by moral precepts. I was surprised, I said, that I had to tell this to a rabbi. But then, what kind of a rabbi is it who would advocate mass expulsions of Arabs from a country whose Jewish citizens have themselves been victims of ethnic cleansing? I was very sorry that Kahane was shot dead, and more sorry still that the murderer was an Arab; making him a martyr lent a spurious legitimacy to Kahane's abhorrent theories.

After my confrontation with Meir Kahane, the JDL declared me "an enemy of Israel" and missed few opportunities to yell insults and worse. During one of my concerts at the Hollywood Bowl in front of sixteen thousand people, the JDL disrupted the performance just as I began an Israeli song; they rushed down the aisles shouting, "Down with Bikel, the enemy of Israel." I paused briefly, telling the audience that I hoped one song of mine would speak more of the love of Israel than the shouts of a thousand hoodlums could drown. The audience applauded, the protesters were escorted out, and I started the Hebrew song again.

Note that I called them "hoodlums." I did not call them "Zionist hoodlums" because they lack any legitimacy that would permit them to be called Zionists. It was left to Vanessa Redgrave to come up with that infamous phrase during her acceptance speech after winning an Academy Award for Best Supporting Actress for *Julia* in 1978. I don't know what turned Vanessa into the villain she became. If she was appalled at conditions at Palestinian refugee camps, so was I. If she thought that Palestinians were entitled to civil rights, so did I. But she believed far more than that. She believed that Jewish blood must be shed to achieve those rights, that Israel must be defeated on a battlefield, that Israel must be made a pariah among nations. The difference between us was that I would never dance with an Uzi calling for the death of anyone, Arab or Jew, while she in her film *The Palestinian* had danced with a Kalashnikov to demonstrate solidarity with those who demanded the destruction of Israel.

We all knew that Vanessa Redgrave had an ax to grind from seeing her propaganda film. We also knew that she had had the chutzpah to ask Jewish producers she was working with to fund her Workers' Revolutionary Party, and when she was turned down, she took it rather badly. But nobody expected her to use the Academy Award podium as a pulpit for the Palestinians in such a way as she did that night. Not that other Oscar winners like Brando hadn't turned their awards into political gestures in previous years, but Redgrave's broadside at Zionism—in the process offending not only Israel but the United States and the Jewish people in general—split the pavilion like a bolt of summer lightning. You don't stand up to accept your award and talk about "Zionist hoodlums" in front of a mostly pro-Israel audience without realizing that people are going to take it gravely amiss.

It so happened that the producer Dan Melnick, the late Paddy Chayefsky, and I found ourselves in the men's room together a little while later. There we stood in front of our respective urinals, discussing her shocking display and wondering how it could be answered. I told Paddy and Dan that I would most certainly call the press in the morning and issue a statement expressing what so many of us felt when we heard the offending remark. But that would not suffice; what had been heard by millions of people on live TV could not be answered in the print media, where only a fraction of that number would see it. Then Paddy Chayevsky said, "Wait a minute, I'm scheduled to present an award later. I'll say something." When I got back to my seat, Alan King was onstage and made reference to what Redgrave had said, but it needed a stronger response. When Paddy Chayevsky got up to the podium, he made a strong statement about abusing the world forum to further one's own political agenda and finished by saying: "In accepting the award, a simple 'thank you' would have sufficed."

My feud with Vanessa went back some time. As president of American Actors' Equity, I had emphatically rejected her call for a cultural boycott of Israel, which she had made in an appeal to British Actors' Equity. I said that her attempt to ban the release of all taped and filmed material by British actors for TV showings in Israel and her call for a cancellation of all prospective and current British actors' contracts within Israel forced me to state on behalf of American Actors' Equity that we considered such a move destructive of the relationships within the international acting fraternity. As a result of my remarks, Ms. Redgrave campaigned to have me impeached as president of Equity on political grounds. She said that in that capacity, I had criticized her film *The Palestinian*. Nothing could have been further from the truth; I had always been meticulously careful to speak for the union only on union matters. The issue of her attempted boycott of actors' performances in Israel was such a matter; my criticism of her propaganda film was not. When the impeachment matter came up for debate in the Equity Council, I told them that they could save themselves some trouble. I had written a letter of resignation in which I stated that any time the Council felt that what I said or did as a private citizen or as a Jew came into conflict with my position as president of the union, they were free to use it. I informed them that I had placed the letter in the unlocked top drawer of my desk. The motion to impeach was unanimously defeated.

I had criticized her film *The Palestinian* as a private citizen. She had financed the film, produced it, and participated in it, including the dancing scene with the rifle. In an open letter I called her to account; I told her that in the film Yassir Arafat had reiterated his call for the elimination of the State of Israel without any disagreement or demurrer from her. I also cited to her the watchword of the Palestinian credo, as set forth in their own covenant in 1964 and again in 1968, that "the establishment of Israel is null and void." Even PLO "moderates" had publicly called for the destruction of Israel in stages: "The first phase is [return] to 1967 lines and the second to the 1948 lines . . . the third stage is the democratic state of Palestine." It was Arafat, I told her, who came to the U.N. wearing a gun and declaring that he was against Zionists, not against Jews—the very phraseology used by Vanessa herself. It was all right, it seemed, in the wake of the Holocaust, to be against Jews as long as you called them "Zionists." It would have surprised Redgrave to learn that many good Zionists, the kind that she and Arafat longed to hate, were, like myself, in favor of legitimate Palestinian rights and even of a separate Palestinian homeland. But, I wrote, she had made herself an ideological partner of the murderers of schoolchildren at Ma'alot, of pregnant women at Kiryat Shemona, of Olympic athletes at Munich, of those who murdered the Arab minister Wasfi Tal and who killed hundreds of Jews and Arabs in Jerusalem, Gaza, and Tel Aviv. I said that Redgrave had dishonored all of us as human beings by pretending that there was a difference between the Jew-haters who destroyed Jerusalem two thousand years ago and those who still seek to destroy it today.

Thus continued our running battle, as I attempted to reply to her mixture of old-fashioned and outmoded Marxist revolutionary rhetoric and sanctimonious moralizing. The irony of it all was that I owed much gratitude to her father, Michael Redgrave, for it was he who had helped launch my career when he first saw me perform in London and had recommended me to Olivier. I also became friends with her sister, Lynn, and Lynn's husband, John Clark, over the years. Lynn, the good one, and Vanessa, the Bad Witch of the WRP.

Redgrave's throwing the gauntlet down in front of everyone at the Academy Awards and the brouhaha that ensued somehow revived the notion that film was a "Jewish" profession. It is not that the films themselves are Jewish or bespeak Jewish themes—which they did not do until very recently—but that historically the heads of the studios and the major agencies were Jewish. Indeed, the world of Hollywood was a world created, in part, from the visions of studio heads L. B. Mayer, Sam Goldwyn, Nicholas Schenck, Irving Thalberg, Harry Cohn, and Jesse Lasky. Far from promoting Jewishness through the work, these founders of the industry seemed intent on removing any Jewish identification from it. Hollywood's Golden Age coincided with the greatest influx of Jewish immigrants from Eastern Europe this country had yet seen. In many ways that immigration had a lasting impact on American society in terms of its values and achievements, but despite the creative and managerial talents brought to Hollywood by the Jews, the early films from the silents through the thirties bore little witness to the Jewish presence in America and Jewish talent in show business—viz., George Burns, Jack Benny, Al Jolson, the Gershwins, Fanny Brice, the Marx Brothers, Milton Berle, and George Jessel, to name a few. In fact, through the forties, when the world's attention was turned toward World War II, Jewish filmmakers spent most of their time depicting a country-club, golf- and bridge-playing world of WASPs, with occasional portrayals of upwardly mobile Jews who had elevated themselves out of Lower East Side ghettos and into the suburbs.

We watched the Old Testament through a WASP prism in *The Ten Commandments* and *David and Bathsheba*. When anti-Semitism was finally tackled, we observed the problem from a safe distance in *Gentlemen's Agreement*. Then we saw sanitized WASP reinterpretations of Jewish biographies in *The Eddie Cantor Story* and *The Benny Goodman Story*. More genuinely Jewish films came later—Meyer Levin's *Compul-*

sion, Abraham Polonsky's script of the Jerome Weidman novel *I Can Get It for You Wholesale*, and Paddy Chayefsky's *Middle of the Night*.

When I first arrived in 1956, the attitude in Hollywood was still one of playing down ethnic identification, especially of the Jewish kind. People might begin to ask in a normal tone of voice—except for the last word which was dropped to almost a whisper—"TELL ME, IS JEFF CHANDLER jewish?"

The upsurge of interest in questions surrounding ethnicity in the 1960s was marked by films like *The Pawnbroker* and *Lisa* and Barbra Streisand's portrayal of Fanny Brice in *Funny Girl*. Much later Streisand would struggle to make a far more audaciously Jewish film when she took on Isaac Bashevis Singer's story *Yentl, the Yeshiva Boy* and turned it into a picture with music. Even Israel got some recognition and filmic treatment in the 1960s, in the films *Cast a Giant Shadow* with Kirk Douglas and the epic *Exodus* with Paul Newman.

Most important, the 1960s saw the beginning of Jewish self-examination, without nagging doubts as to whether it was proper to do so in front of the goyim. Philip Roth's *Goodbye Columbus*, directed by Larry Peerce, was the forerunner of films depicting Jews wrestling with their own identities, examining their foibles, trying to determine what the turbulence of the age had done to their Jewishness and whether it had any relevance at all to their lives, beyond a hankering for gefilte fish and kreplach. There had been hints of this in earlier works, and there had been comedy treatments with a wry complexion such as Neil Simon's *Come Blow Your Horn* and Carl Reiner's *Enter Laughing*. But *Goodbye Columbus* was, to my mind, a breakthrough of some magnitude. I believe this was the start of a genuine search, in artistic terms, for a three-dimensional, living expression of Jewish self-examination. Many Jews disliked *Goodbye Columbus* intensely; it cut too close to home.

Film had come a long way from the mid-twenties, when Jews were depicted, if at all, as outlandish buffoons, or greenhorns who spoke English badly (for example, the film *Cohen on the Telephone*), or cowards (*Fighting Is No Business*), or plainly unethical men bent on exploiting others. Those characters were all designed to be laughed at rather than with. Jewish filmmakers have by now learned to express in the American context something we have known for ages: how to laugh at ourselves and to make the world laugh with us. In great measure this is due to Neil Simon, Mel Brooks, Carl Reiner, Sidney Lumet, Paul Mazursky, Elaine May, and many others. But no one has made us laugh at the nebbish image more, nor portrayed it more truthfully, than Woody Allen. The work of these talented people spelled the end of the old extremes in Jewish images on film: bland assimilation at one end and rabid ethnocentricity at the other.

In 1963, I remember once running into the actor Lee J. Cobb at the studio (his real name was Lee Jacob). He had been cast as the father in the film version of *Come Blow Your Horn* and was preparing to give a nice funny Jewish performance as the father, in a role created on Broadway by Lou Jacobi. Some two weeks later I met him again and he told me that, inasmuch as Frank Sinatra had been cast as the elder son, the entire movie was now about Italian-Americans. One week after that I saw him again in the studio commissary and he said, "We're back to Jewish." I asked him, "Tell me, do you think you can make the adjustment?"

We have not seen the last of Sophie Portnoy, the stereotypical Jewish mother, yet. She has already reappeared in several metamorphoses: as Shelley Winters in *Enter Laughing,* as Barbara Barrie in *Private Benjamin,* and as Lainie Kazan in *My Favorite Year.* I am sure she will continue to exasperate and amuse us. In addition to Jewish mothers, we have seen Jewish daughters, working women or princesses, wise, glib, spoiled, or rebellious. We have seen Jews as winners and Jews as losers. We have seen Jews of moral rectitude as well as corrupt ones. We have seen them assimilated and hiding; we have also seen them fighting and proud. We have vicariously witnessed the cultural conflicts and the torment of losing the old without gaining the new. We have seen Jews as rabbis, as scholars, as scientists, as cops, as thieves, as psychiatrists, as prostitutes, as intellectuals, and as boors. We have seen them rejected by the world around them; we have also seen them hating themselves and rejecting their own. We have seen them secular and religious, and we have seen them gay and straight. We watched them on film chastised, victimized, praised, admired, adorned, or stripped of glitter. The question must be asked: By what standards shall we measure the image of the Jew in films?

The answer, I suspect, lies in how we measure not only ourselves as individuals and as a group, but also in our perception of art and imagery in general. If we assert, as many of us do, that in the words of Shakespeare the function of art is to "hold as t'were a mirror up to nature," then the answer is fairly clear. First, while film among all the performing arts is the epitome of naturalistic presentations, even total naturalism commands writers, directors, and performers to have in mind not only truth but also a point of view about what that truth means. In this spirit, we are obliged to accept some unpleasant mirror images of ourselves which, though unflattering, it would be dishonest to suppress. Thus, some films will find us up in arms because the image of the Jew in them is so distorted and untruthful. But more often we will be just as exercised because what we are seeing is so painfully true. Hence the Jewish objections to *Goodbye Columbus*. The question, however, must not be, "Is it good for the Jews?" but rather, "Does it serve to inform us about ourselves and others about us?" Not as we would wish to appear, but as we are.

That we can laugh at ourselves is surely our saving grace. We are capable of laughing through tears and we find a smile even in the midst of despair. This is a gift not innately granted to many people. It may very well be that when America counts the contribution made by Jews to this land, it will not be forgotten amidst the mention of doctors, scientists, scholars, and philosophers that we have taught America how to laugh. As Sholem Aleichem said, "You've got to survive, even if it kills you."

Even the survivors of the Holocaust knew how to laugh and how to sing. The liberators and the hostages of Entebbe, including the sick and the wounded, also sang on their way home. I doubt whether Vanessa, despite all her talent and intelligence, despite her valiant attempt at portraying Fania Fenelon, a member of the Auschwitz women's orchestra, in *Playing for Time*, has a visceral understanding of Jews as Israelis and of Israelis as human beings. Nor of Israel as a place of redemption.

19

zorba

The way his body and soul formed one harmonious whole, and all things—women, bread, water, meat, sleep—blended happily with his flesh and became Zorba. I had never seen such a friendly accord between man and the universe.

—NIKOS KAZANTZAKIS, *ZORBA THE GREEK*

*A*S A RULE, AN ACTOR BRINGS TO A ROLE whatever he can from the arsenal of knowledge and emotion he carries as his personal baggage. Whatever you don't have, you purloin from literature and from imagination. In lifting a role from the printed page you add those elements, in a sense subsuming parts of your own life for the enrichment of the character. Rarely does the character add elements to the actor. That is as it should be: Who needs to absorb into one's own life the shallowness of a fool, the villainy of an assassin, or the mannerism of nobility, merely because he has played a village idiot, a murderer, or a king on-stage?

In my career, the rare exception was the role of Zorba. Having played him in the stage musical caused a distinct change in my own character and outlook. My professional curiosity about the man gave way to envy, almost, to a longing somehow to become more like him. I envied his being so unencumbered by physical possessions—whatever he carried in his knapsack was already too much for him, convinced as he was that the things he owned would end up owning him instead. None of us living in this modern urban world could hope to emulate such freedom successfully, but the awareness of its existence alone can ennoble your life. It did mine.

What else makes Zorba so irrepressible? I think that it's his individualism in the face of the world's constant demand for conformity. Zorba tells us that it's okay not simply to express oneself, but to do so at precisely the moments when everyone expects you to sublimate that which is you. I've heard a lot of different explanations for Zorba's endearing—and enduring—nature. People have said that he is of an older generation, and thus more sure of what and who he is; others have said that he is an uncomplicated man of nature who's not constrained by the necessities of social convention. Still others have said that he is just plain simple and charming, the kind of guy who would point out to the assembled populace that the emperor's not wearing any clothes.

I have a different take on all of this. I believe that Zorba exists for Zorba, and in so doing, he makes a larger statement. We live in a world in which individualism is repressed as part of the process of getting business done. The world doesn't set out to repress anybody deliberately, just as there is no sentient malevolence behind the killer frost that literally explodes the last lingering tomatoes we've left on the vine at the end of October. But when you walk into your garden the next morning and see your hapless vegetables, you ask yourself, what monster could have done this?

Just so does the social pressure of the world grind down individualism. Zorba, however, refuses to be ground down. He becomes an irritant, a gadfly, a subversive almost, who undermines the political and moral fabric of society by the expression of his joie de vivre. That's why I like him so much. He, in his single-minded devotion to his own individualism, is certainly a braver person than I can claim to be. I merely tried to carry away from him at the end of the play the courage to be the individual with the resources I had to muster to play the role. And sometimes to use the force of Zorba's identity to convince other people to express their own individual identities in the face of the world's conventions.

In the sixties, the great fear was the alienation of the young from their parents' world, their roots and background. Instead of merely joining the chorus of those who moaned in dread of such alienation, I decided then to take to the campuses, look at the phenomenon, and initiate a dialogue. When I spoke before groups of Jewish students, I stressed identity. I did not concern myself with Jewish identity alone;

when I spoke to Americans of Greek or Italian or Hispanic origin, I would make an equally good case that they should keep their own heritage intact—make it contribute to their humanity in the first place, and to their Americanism in the second. For Americanism, too, is a misread and misunderstood notion; we keep thinking that what is required is conformity of some sort, cultural conformity. Unfortunately, this notion persists to this day, and I continue to argue against it, and not only in speeches. If I can put my artistry to use in making a point, then it is to glory in the ethnic diversity that exists in America. I am curious enough to learn my neighbors' mores, my neighbors' language, my neighbors' songs. I go into my neighbors' living rooms, showing them the courtesy of singing not only neutral WASP music, but songs of their own traditions, in as authentic a way as I can. And I hope, in return, to get the same courtesy from my neighbors, that they will try to understand me and learn my ways. We may be different at the outset, but rather than accept melting-pot conformity as the only response to cultural differences we have to seek out other routes.

I was fortunate enough to know Professor Horace Kallen, who taught at the New School for Social Research, and to enjoy his friendship. Professor Kallen coined the phrase "cultural pluralism" as a description of America at its best. The proponents of the melting-pot theory are sometimes tempted to decry cultural pluralism as nothing more than thinly disguised ethnocentricity. Not so. In fact, a "melting pot" is a notion as silly as it is dangerous; from it can come only cultural disaster. For it leads inexorably toward a no-shape, no-color, homogenized nonculture, where everything is reduced to the lowest common denominator. In cultural terms that turns out to be both low and common. I perceive the world, especially American society, as a kaleidoscope. In my view of things, the only logical alternative to the melting pot is the kaleidoscope where each particle is clearly delineated, each aware of its identity, aware of its circumference, aware of its temporality and its energy levels. We are not all the same, and we shouldn't behave as though we were. For example, it makes no sense for Jews to become what might be called WASH: White Anglo-Saxon Hebrews. Your cocktail hours become indistinguishable from your neighbors'; so do your mores, your way of life, your modes of behavior. Maintaining a cultural and individual identity is difficult, especially in suburbia, where we live in houses that all look the same and worship in houses that are indistinguishable one from the other. To be truthful, I dislike Frank Lloyd Wright synagogues because I see nothing in them that denotes a synagogue. I like a church to look like a church, a Shinto shrine to look like a Shinto shrine, and a Jewish house of worship—if it can't look and behave like a shul—at least to look like a synagogue. All of this uniformity drives me up the wall. Sometimes it's worse: a church and a synagogue standing side by side without anyone knowing which is which unless they read the signs. Worse still, neither one looks like either a church *or* a synagogue, because both were built by a Japanese architect. Why should I have to go into a synagogue with partitions like Japanese *shoji* screens and with a centerpiece that looks dangerously like a cremation oven? There is one like that somewhere near Chicago. It makes no sense.

My involvement in the civil rights movement was directly related to my active sense of being Jewish. Having lived under the Nazis in Austria, I was permanently influenced by the terror and violence of it all. When they dragged us into the streets to beat us up, there were some very nice well-meaning Gentiles who lived next door. I call them nice and well-meaning because they never joined the beatings, the haters, the slogan-chanters, the Nazi thugs who roamed the streets. But they also didn't open their doors or windows to cry "Halt!" Even today no one—least of all history itself—can absolve them of guilt or complicity, for silence at such a time is a statement, just as nonaction is an act. In this context, both are criminal. Consequently, when it came to somebody else's deprivation and the discrimination directed against another people, I could never claim that this was not my fight and that I was to be called upon only when Jews were the target. My civil rights activity was clearly a Jewish commitment. My motives were Jewish, but it was important that others perceive my actions as flowing from those motives. For instance, while I'm anything but an Orthodox Jew, when they put me in jail in Alabama for taking part in demonstrations, I insisted on kosher food. It was important for me to demonstrate that I was acting not only as an American citizen with a conscience, but as a Jew. I was only in jail for a day or so, and it took them almost a day to provide me with a kosher meal, but the point was made.

To be Jewish is to be particular and universal at the very same time. It is as if being a Jew exacerbates the human condition. Everything for me is in much sharper focus because I'm a Jewish human being. This is not to say that I'm in any way better, only that I can see things in a certain perspective because of my Jewish experience. It doesn't mean that my conditioning and reflexes are much different from someone else's who isn't a Jew, only that I perceive things in a hotter light. The highs are higher, the lows are lower. The pressure toward conformity exerted on everything and everybody in our present-day society has propelled me toward Jewish arts and music far more intensely than it might have done at a time when the ethnic enclaves were more intact. Again, I emphasize that what moves me is not ethnocentric pride or arrogance; I make no claim that the Jewish song is better than the song of my neighbor. But it is mine. And since it is the song of my people, it is up to me to cultivate it lest the blooms wither and the garden becomes bare and desolate.

With the advent of nuclear weapons, the world became attuned to the specter of possible annihilation. For the world this is new; we haven't been on that street for long. We have to face it now. Even without the threat of nuclear war, we look at the hole in the ozone layer over the South Pole getting larger every year. We look at the greenhouse effect gradually raising the world's temperatures, in part because of our excessive consumption of fossil fuel. We look at the rampaging destruction of the world's forests, lessening the earth's capacity to regenerate CO_2, and so creating the danger that the envelope of air around all of us may literally burn up. We look at the famines in Africa and hear that the fertile farm belt is shifting, changing entire economic patterns on the African continent, and we wonder if what we are looking at may be far more than just the erosion of our natural resources.

We're staring at our own death as a race, as a human race. This is a gruesome, terror-filled prospect. Our forebears always knew that they would survive, that there would be enough coal, enough food, enough of this and that to get them through. They never thought that they would be looking at the specter of their own extinction or that they would see it in their own lifetime. Yet it will be happening in our lifetime unless we can do something to stave it off. Jews have been on that street before; we've stared our own death in the face all along. Perhaps the world can learn something from us here, because we have developed the mechanisms to deal with the specter of annihilation. We have learned how to work, to pray, to sing, and to laugh, even in the face of death. We laughed faster and better because we knew the laughter might not have long to live. You may call such laughter the highest form of faith or the final manifestation of the madman. I profess it to be the former. We Jews are essentially a sane people and convinced that survival is not only possible, but inevitable.

They tell the following story. A couple of nuclear scientists were experimenting with a new thermonuclear device. To test it they picked an area out of harm's way, or so they thought. They went to the North Pole, as far away from human habitation as possible. They set up their instruments in a command post many miles away and proceeded to explode the device. All seemed to go well until an unanticipated chain reaction set in. The amounts of heat generated were so immense that the ice on the polar cap began to melt, and an inexorable process was set in motion. The levels of all the world's oceans began to rise, and a few simple calculations determined that within twenty-one days, the entire landmass of the globe would be submerged, and life would come to an end. Panic and pandemonium ensued. People drank or drugged themselves into forgetfulness, and end-of-the-world orgies became commonplace in cities soon destined to end up at the bottom of an endless ocean. However, the religious leaders of the world felt they had to lead their flocks to their inevitable death by keeping the moral precepts of their faiths. And so the pope celebrated a public Mass at the Vatican, carried by live hookup to all the corners of the earth. At the conclusion, he announced that confession would be taken by both priests and laymen, and extreme unction given so that all Catholics would able to meet their maker in twenty-one days, cleansed and pure. The Protestant leaders, not to be outdone, held services of their own and asked the listening and viewing congregants to forgive each other and lead a clean life, at least for the next twenty-one days, so that they, too, would be able to go to their watery graves as good Christians should. The Rebbe in Brooklyn also conducted a service carried over the airwaves. He davened *mincha,* the afternoon prayer, then took the microphone and addressed all the Jews thus: "Nu, we have twenty-one days to learn to live under water!"

There are scholars who say that the ultimate enlightenment is so blinding that you go mad. I'm not a Kabbalist, although I've attempted to read parts of the *Zohar,* the mystical thirteenth-century text that is one of Kabbalah's primary sources. I confess I couldn't get close to it or into it. I know enough about my own fears about mysticism to know that there are certain corners I don't go into. I do not want to go to a place where I am obliged to stare my own soul in the face; I don't believe I'm ready for that. To me, the process of living is mystery enough: having to look for underlying ways and causes is egregious. Ultimate truths are to me anathema. I don't want to know any ultimate truth. I don't think any human being is equipped to handle ultimate truth. In my view, the quest devoted to it alone may actually be harmful.

I understand that mine is possibly an old-fashioned view, especially as we approach the end of the millennium. For years now I have observed many young people, especially many young Jews, questing for their souls in what can only be described as incredible turmoil. In this drama, the growth of exotic religiosity is an act of ultimate denial of their own roots, astounding in its intensity. Thus many have become Eastern mystics and mantra-chanting eccentrics—in some cases still calling themselves Jews. I have frequently asked myself if the attraction to these cults among young Jews is a true step toward enlightenment, or simply an expression of their not having understood what was already there in the first place.

We all have an attic. Our grandfather's attic is full of wonderful heirlooms, most of them dusty and dull. A little dust on the old heirloom is not terrible. We can brush it off and make it shine again. It's very simple, a little metal polish and that's that. But some of us don't even know that there is an attic. The access has been bricked up. All that many young Jews see today is wall-to-wall carpeting, the kind of life-style that they don't like or particularly admire. They see hypocrisy in their parents, who at times say things that have a vaguely moral echo, overtones of something. At the same time they see the way their parents live and behave, and they don't see the morality there. The grown-ups don't do what they say or profess.

When these very adult children don't like what they see in their parents' lives, or in their own for that matter, they look elsewhere for truth. Sometimes that search takes them as far afield from their own roots as possible. But it does no good for a young Jewish kid to say, "Well, I don't care for the Jewish crap that I see." He thinks that he is walking away from Judaism, when in reality he is only walking away from certain Jews he knows, mainly his own family. He does this not because they're Jews, but because they are less than what Jews should be. And he often doesn't realize that his is an act of social and psychological separation, not an act of religious fervor born of moral enlightenment.

If in his eyes Judaism and his parents are synonymous, then he is not so different from the WASP kid across the street, a Presbyterian or an Anglican whose parents profess Christianity but behave as less than Christians. They have the same wall-to-wall carpeting, only in a whiter shade of pale. So he goes after the earth tones. He goes to the Eastern mystics, the Hare Krishnas, the Jews for Jesus, or the Moonies. He goes back as far as he can but he is not really culturally equipped to deal with Eastern mysticism. He sits on the floor and chants a mantra, if he can remember it. Beyond that he knows precious little, although he pretends to himself that he is an instant Hindu sage. He could have found the entrance to his grandfather's attic, if he had only looked. Bricked up as it may be, the journey there is shorter than all the translations and transmutations he must go through to reach the ecstatic heights of whatever belief system he has fastened onto.

There are too many synapses. It is like the old story where one person told a joke in one language and the listener then passed it along in another language. Someone tells you a joke in Bulgarian, you tell it to another person in English, she translates it into German for another person, who retells the story in French. You go through eight of these and then the joke is told back to you in English and you can't recognize it. The more translations you go through, the more you lose. In a way, this is what happened to the dropout youth as they went through numerous translations to get back to what they originally were taught. The search for truth and the search for religious ecstasy—or ecstasy of any kind, for that matter—would have been far easier and far more productive had these young people found their way back to grandfather's attic. The road of return is clearer and shorter.

Of course, the majority of this generation of young Jews does not drop out in any apparent way. On the contrary, most aim to submerge themselves even further in the mainstream of American mores and behavior than their parents did, striving to strip their existence of the last vestiges of ethnicity. If they retain anything at all, then it is the once-a-year pro forma attendance at temple, since they will have effectively finished their Jewish life with the advent of their Bar or Bat Mitzvah, a milestone that by rights was meant to signal not an end but a beginning. I don't know which of the two alternatives is worse: conforming to an alien cult or to the culture of suburbia.

In a backhanded way, Zorba gave me the impetus for these thoughts. Zorba is more possessed by the quest for individualism than by the simple assertion of it. This quest is the wellspring of energy that drives his character and gives it the resilience to stand against the conformity the world insists upon. The importance of the quest is that it in itself is a source of self-renewal and an expression of individualism. Nowhere is this quest for individuality more important than in the life of the artist. And, ironically, the place where individuality is most under attack is in the arts.

It is in the nature of those who feed the appetite of American audiences to impose a certain amount of conformity upon artists. Works, be they in literature or performance, demand a modicum of success before they can have a chance at an afterlife. If a new television series has a particular formula that works, you can bet that within weeks producers will be rushing to duplicate the formula to fill network time slots in the following season. They will change it around just enough to make it appear different and original, but the formula will be the same. Screenwriter and movie historian Garson Kanin told a famous story about how Louis B. Mayer picked the stories he wanted to make into pictures. If you pitched him a story, Mayer would dig into his top desk drawer for the listing of box office receipts or the latest issue of *Variety*. He'd match your story up with a similar story on the box office listings and check the receipts. If the receipts were to his liking, he'd make the movie. More often than not, though, L.B. would hold up the chart, shove it in a writer's face, and berate him for not writing stories that had already proved themselves successful. Conformity to success is conformity no matter how you describe it.

By consistently playing to the largest possible audience, the artistic mass market, promoters of these goods seek only the most acceptable version of a mirror of society. Whether or not such fare is a true reflection of society is secondary; what is important to them is whether it sells. As a player to the mass audience, I have helped feed this market because, like the next person, I had to pay a mortgage, get braces on the kids' teeth, and pay the garage mechanic for fixing the car. But I have a conscience about it. I will stand up in front of a commission on the arts or a congressional committee and argue that while the needs of the marketplace will have to be satisfied, there also needs to be proper support for the artist who refuses to conform.

There are two myths abroad in America concerning the performing arts. The first says that we in America are the greatest patrons of the arts the world has ever known. Figured on a per capita basis, the myth would have us believe that Americans attend more concerts, lectures, and other live performances than any other nation. And the second myth asserts, more or less crudely, that the arts are basically "sissy games" indulged in by and catering to a small New York elite of "nattering nabobs," to use a term coined by former Vice President Spiro Agnew. That these two myths contradict each other doesn't seem to bother people overly much, and that broad-based support for the arts and New York elitism are antithetical one to the other does not seem to faze those who voice these theories, sometimes simultaneously, at all.

As it happens, our national devotion to culture and the arts is not as deep as we would like to pretend. Nor is it true that Americans who are audiences for the arts are confined to the Eastern megalopolis. Of course, numbers are less meaningful when assessing cultural values than they are in evaluations of the stock market. It does little to boast with statistical glee that more books are bought in the United States than anywhere else, which happens to be true, when no statistics are available on what kinds of books and how many of them are read or finished or enjoyed or maybe just slightly understood. Quantities are misleading; it is the quality not of the artistic offering but of the spectator's appreciation that counts in the end. Somehow it is difficult to rid oneself of the suspicion that at a given point in time America was allowed to choose between culture and civilization, and that we ended up making the wrong choice.

A measure to be taken is our support of nonprofit theater, one of the more courageous expressions of individualistic artistic endeavor and one of the more daunting ventures to undertake. If box-office success is to be the only measuring stick, the only criterion that decrees life or death for these ventures, then surely the classics, for example, will be doomed. When only the vagaries of the marketplace are used to determine the survival of theatrical works, then the classics will be banished to the library shelf or confined to the do-it-yourself efforts of the high school drama group. Had it not been for the late Joseph Papp with his Shakespeare in the Park, or venues like Arvin Brown's Long Wharf in New Haven, Robert Brustein's American Repertory Theatre in Cambridge, Massachussetts, or the Guthrie in Minneapolis and a few other nonprofit enterprises, there would have been no professional American performances at all of the foremost classics of the English language in recent years. So much for Webster, Marlowe, Jonson, or Wycherly. As it is, a whole generation of Americans has grown to adulthood without having the opportunity to see the greatest dramatist of their language performed by the foremost artists of their own country.

Thankfully, that is changing. The National Endowment for the Arts, though under attack by the Reverend Donald Wildmon and others of the religious right, is making it possible for the nonprofit theater and for the opera and the ballet to survive. Other art forms, too, are beginning to flex their creative muscles, despite the constant demand from people like Senator Jesse Helms for cultural conformity. But what a modest budget we allot to all of them. Countries far less affluent than the United States support their arts far more than we do. And yet the strident voices on the right protest most vigorously even the measly sixty-five cents per capita per year that this country manages to scrape up for the arts. A country like Austria, quite a small country, gives a per capita contribution of a little more than $2 per annum to the arts. In Canada, no less beset by budget troubles than the U.S., it's $1.45. And in Britain, with a sorely taxed economy, it's still a relatively whopping $1.35. To repeat an apocryphal-sounding but, alas, true mantra: The entire allocation of the National Endowment for the Arts to music, opera, and theatre combined is smaller than what the Pentagon spends on military bands.

There once was a congressman who with idiotic consistency opposed all budgeting for the arts on the grounds that funds were used to support belly-dancing. One suspected the congressman of being incapable of distinguishing belly-dancing from ballet dancing. One also suspected him, not unreasonably, of being a boor. But then perhaps he represented a constituency that shared his views—and I don't mean the geographical constituency he represented, but a nationwide constituency of the boorish and the uncultured. This is no reflection on his state, for there were at least two congressmen in his immediate vicinity who could be counted among the most vociferous and eloquent defenders of the arts. I crossed swords with this gentleman on a number of occasions when testifying before House committees. Thank goodness he is no longer in government. Had he continued to run, I would have broken an old rule of mine not to be a carpetbagger, and would have gone to Iowa to campaign against him.

During a session of a House subcommittee of which this congressman, H. R. Gross, was a member, the question of the deployment of cultural attachés was being examined. I testified on behalf of the arts community. After my statement Gross moved in to attack. "Can you tell me," he asked in a dyspeptic tone, "Can you tell me, Mr. uh, uh"—he consulted his notepad—"Mr.—uh—Bikel, why the United States of America should need to have a cultural attaché in Belgrade, of all places? Can you tell me that?" "Congressman, I am going to give you two answers," I replied. "The first one will probably not mean much to you, but it is the one which I and the people I represent find eminently persuasive. The second answer will convince you, I think. The most valid argument for having a cultural attaché even in the remotest country in which we maintain an embassy is that a country as great as ours can ill afford not to show that we are a people of culture and not just profit-oriented, camera-toting 'ugly Americans,' as we are often depicted. We have military attachés and commercial attachés attesting to our might. How can we not keep the cultural flag flying as well, to show that we are a nation that values its arts, music, and literature? That's my first answer. The second answer, sir, is that the United States needs to have a cultural attaché in Belgrade because the Russians have two." He glowered at me and let it pass. Frankly, I had no idea how many attachés the Russians had, but the ruse carried the day.

It is really difficult to detail the anguish of the individual performing artist. It's a lonely business being an actor. How do you square the loneliness of the creator, which is ever present in any artist, with working in a medium that does not permit you to perform in a void? A sculptor can sculpt by herself; her audience will attend weeks later, twenty years later, or even centuries later when she has been relegated to the syllabus of Art Appreciation 101. Nothing will be lost except by those of the artist's own century who knew nothing of her. A painter can do likewise. A writer can write in the solitude of the study and will or won't be appreciated by a contemporary audience. To a lesser extent, a recording artist also plays to an empty room, although the need for road concerts to promote the release of new albums makes recording artists more and more like performing artists, too. For the stage actor, however, an immediate audience is an absolute necessity, for a live audience is the sole market for his or her creative wares. Whether that audience will demand that the actor confine himself to formulaic performances to reinforce expectations, or permit the actor to open new territories, is up to the venue, the sophistication of the audience, the quality of the script, and the will of the performer not to compromise. And how successfully that performer will be able to stand his ground depends as much on the track record of his past work as it does on the performance in question. It sounds crass, but that's why it's called show business. (I have never been comfortable with that term; I'm not in show business, I'm in the arts. The fellow who sits in the box office and sells tickets, *he's* in show business.)

Where there's more show and less business is in the nonprofit performing arts. I believe the arts are the outward expression of an aesthetic perception of life. Without them, life would be a mere exercise in survival. If the artist has any function, it is to be the chronicler of events as well as an entertainer capable of furnishing an ennobling experience and dispelling the fears and moods that beset us. Tragedy or comedy, both have a function. In one instance they heighten perception, and in the other they lift the spirit. The artist is called upon to be a visionary and a mountebank, both a soother and a ruffler of the spirit, creating clarion calls to awaken the populace to danger or to pacify them with a lullaby. It's a hell of a task. In the last analysis, no one—except for scholars—remembers which battle was won or lost, or by whom, unless there is a poem, a painting, a play, a film, or a song that tells the story. And that is how it should be. For we, the artists, are the nation's tears, the nation's laughter, and ultimately, the nation's memory.

For years now it has been my task to help convince the government that it has a vital supportive role to play in the arts, remembering always that no government institution creates art. We, the artists, do. But what government can do is create mechanisms that enable artists to perform their functions. Art is not self-sustaining. Artists in the past relied on their patrons for commissions, which often made the difference between mere survival and the freedom to create works that express the individuality and uniqueness of human beings. In Europe the patron was a king, an emperor, a duke, or some other aristocrat. Well, we don't have those anymore; we have government patronage instead. Government, however, must play its part in this not grudgingly—as if it is doling out charity to welfare recipients—but happily, because no society can be considered great unless it provides it heirs with a cultural and artistic legacy.

My direct association with the National Endowment for the Arts—apart from having argued in the sixties for its creation before Congress—goes back to the mid-seventies. In 1975 the director of the Endowment's theatre program, Ruth Mayleas, asked to meet with me the next time she was scheduled to come to New York. My name had been suggested for an appointment to the theatre panel. (The various panels sift through the applications for grants in their respective disciplines and then submit their comments to the National Council on the Arts and the chairman of the NEA for action.) I had invited Ruth to come to my office at Equity. I was surprised when the receptionist told me that there were two ladies on their way up to see me. When the two visitors were shown into my office, I was even more surprised to see that the other person was the formidable Nancy Hanks, the chairperson of the NEA herself. Ruth explained that Nancy had also made the trip up from Washington for various appointments and had expressed the desire to sit in on the meeting. Ruth asked me about my views regarding the Endowment, the state of the theatre, and various other topics relating to the relationship between the arts and government. I began to realize that Nancy Hanks's presence was not just due to idle curiosity; there was a purpose.

From the drift of the questions I detected a subtext. I was being scrutinized in order to allay some fears of the Washington establishment regarding the appointment of labor union people. Although there was an obligation in the statute for broad-based representation, including labor, when making appointments, the Nixon-Ford White House was not overly eager to have anyone comply too diligently with such directives. If it had to be done, then they might at least make sure that no rabble-rousing socialists would inadvertently get appointed. Obviously, neither Nancy Hanks nor Ruth Mayleas suspected me of being a crypto-revolutionary. But they did clearly want to know how much of me was the entrenched union official and how much was the artist. They must have been satisfied with what they found, because I was appointed to the theatre panel the following week.

In 1976 Jimmy Carter was elected president, and his election gave me a chance to play a larger role in the Endowment's decision making through a seat on the National Council of the Arts.

Before an appointment could come up for Senate confirmation, there had been the usual FBI check into one's background. I don't know what they were looking for or what they feared they might find, but I didn't make it all that easy for them, either. They came and quizzed me about myself, they asked neighbors and associates, and I wondered whether they also looked through the trash. The agents asked me for the names of two people they could talk to about me. One person whose name I gave them could be found in Florida. The other one lived on Maui. Damned if they didn't talk to both of them—in person, not by phone. Much to my disappointment, there were no black marks against me to be found. (I had always regretted that my arrival in America had been just a little too late for me to have been blacklisted like some of my friends. I was also offended that I had not been included in Nixon's "enemies" list—not that this would have barred me from serving in a Carter administration.) But I was clean, and my appointment sailed through.

At the first National Council of the Arts meeting I attended as a full member there was a swearing-in ceremony, and Livingston Biddle administered the oath of office to the newly appointed members. It was an impressive occasion, although I was a little thrown by the oath itself. It turned out that this was the identical formula recited by the president and vice president at inauguration ceremonies. I found it intriguing to swear an oath in which I pledged to defend the nation against all enemies foreign and domestic. The closest domestic enemy I could think of in the arts field was David Merrick; I strained hard and failed to come up with a candidate for foreign enemy. After the swearing-in I asked the chairman whether it would be appropriate for me to recite something; after all, we concerned ourselves with matters artistic—why not do something to demonstrate it? Liv Biddle said the Council would welcome the opportunity to hear me. The visual artists who were members, like Jamie Wyeth and Jacob Lawrence, could not whip up a painting or a sculpture on the spot. Theo Bikel would recite.

I decided to do Brecht's Parable of the Burning House. It seemed fitting to do a piece by an author, playwright, and poet who had been made a refugee by the Nazis, had fled through various countries, and had ended up in the United States, only to find himself grilled by the witch-hunters of the House Un-American Activities Committee. He had been made to leave here, too, during a dark period when noble instincts gave way to baseness. In the very town where Brecht had been humiliated, I recited his poetry, as a free American in an America that was on the mend at last. Here is a part of the poem:

The Buddha told the following parable:
Recently I saw a house; It was on fire
Flames were licking the roof.
I stepped closer and saw that there were still some people inside.
Some asked me while the flames were already licking the roof
What it was like outside
And how about the wind
And was there another house to live in
And questions like that.
Without replying I walked out on them, thinking
These people will have to burn
Before they stop asking questions.
Now really, my friends,
If the heat in the house is not hot enough
For them to be wanting to change to another kind of house,
If, in other words, they prefer to stay and burn,
Well, then I have nothing to say to them.

With this piece of poetry began my service on the National Council on the Arts. The next four and a half years were spent shuttling between professional engagements and Washington, not only for the full Council meetings, held five times a year, but for committee work in between as well. It was not unusual for me to finish filming at a studio in California on a Friday night, get on a redeye flight, and take my seat at the Council table in Washington at 10:00 A.M. on Saturday. After two days of deliberations and debate I would fly back to Los Angeles on Sunday night, ready to resume shooting on Monday morning. Sane people don't do things like that, but I have never been entirely sane and have certainly never led a sedentary existence. Had I wanted that, then I might have become a bank clerk. Service on the Council had its compensations; not monetary ones—the government paid for your flight and a modest per diem far lower than your actual expenses. The compensation I speak of was in terms of the quality of discussion and the caliber of the discussants. To look around the table and see among your colleagues Van Cliburn, Jerome Robbins, Billy Taylor, Hal Prince, I. M. Pei, Erich Leinsdorf, Robert Shaw, Toni Morrison, or James Rosenquist was in itself a heady feeling. Of course, not all the members were artists; some appointees were from the private sector, supporters or patrons of the arts or arts administrators.

The Council had been in existence for some fourteen years when I came on board in 1978. The day-to-day procedures under which it operated were pretty much in place, a little too entrenched already, as usually happens in any bureaucratic setup. What was not in place was a way to address growth in an orderly fashion, and this required the ability to look and plan ahead. The Endowment had grown from a fledgling agency with a mere $10 million budget to an enterprise with some $130 million to administer and disburse. While this was a piddling amount compared to other federal agencies, it was considerable to us, and we felt a burden of responsibility to dispose of the public's money wisely and circumspectly. Livingston Biddle, who had just taken over the chairmanship from Nancy Hanks a year earlier, was aware of the growing scope of the NEA's activities and of the consequent need to plan ahead. To that end he asked one of my colleagues on the Council, J.C. Dickinson, the head of the Florida State Museum, to chair a committee on policy and planning and appointed me cochairman; other members were Martin Friedman of Minneapolis's Walker Arts Center, the choreographer Jerome Robbins, State Arts Council director Bernie Lopez from New Mexico, the composer Gunther Schuller, and the country's foremost authority on jazz, Dr. Billy Taylor. Ours was a formidable task, at once philosophical and pragmatic. We fashioned the language outlining the Endowment's role within the artistic life of the nation. We also undertook a projection of where the various components of the NEA were headed several years hence. We enunciated the Endowment's policy, its raison d'être: the belief in a response to the world in terms of aesthetic awareness. We defined the cultivation of this awareness as a societal good, an appropriate concern of the people, and hence a proper concern of government. And we outlined policy—not national policy, but Endowment policy.

Quite rightly, our inclination in America is to be suspicious of any attempt to dictate arts policy from the top, whether by a czar or by a committee. It was not our intention to recommend to the Council that it define "art." The term had to be understood in its broadest sense. We had to think of the arts in America with full cognizance of their pluralistic nature, quite deliberately disclaim any endorsement of an "official" art, and insist on a full commitment to artistic freedom. The Endowment could not be much more than a support system for the arts, a source of seed money that would stimulate funding from other sources. To be sure, on occasion there were very probing and often exquisite colloquies at Council meetings regarding the general state of the arts in the country, but the level of those conversations had more to do with the stature of the people serving on the Council than with any attempt to make "national policy." When our committee delivered its voluminous report, it was received with acclamation and endorsed by the Council. Our conclusions were ambitious enough for us to know that even if they were but partially realized, it would mean a great improvement. I derived an additional bonus from the exercise: I came away with great admiration and affection for Josh Dickinson, who was a Southern gentleman of the old school and able to handle everybody with great tact.

Needless to say, not everyone on the Council was equally well versed in all of the disciplines the Endowment's work covered. Yet we had to vote with confidence on all of it, across the entire spectrum of the arts. It was as though each one of us was required to become an instant expert on everything. In reality we each came armed with a different expertise, and we leaned on those of our colleagues who had knowledge of topics we knew less about. That portion of architecture that came under the "arts" rubric was not familiar territory for me, but I could call on I. M. Pei for advice. Similarly, the visual arts grants sometimes gave me problems in assessing artistic excellence. But there was Martin Friedman who could be relied upon to analyze for me the quality of modern art, helping me to inform myself and to cast intelligent votes. Similarly, colleagues would come to me for advice in the fields of theatre and folk music. There were others who knew as much about the theatre as I, but nobody else was very knowledgeable about the folk field. Bess Lomax Hawes, Alan Lomax's sister and the director of the folk program, needed an ally on the Council, and in me she had one. This was a most remarkable woman, and I was proud to work with her and call her a friend.

Work on the Council was not always smooth sailing. I had strong views and never hid or softened my disagreement. Those differences of opinion ranged from form to substance. Rhoda Grauer, the director of the dance program, and I were friends. Nonetheless we exchanged sharp words in public over a matter of grants to an organization that was paying substandard remuneration to actors. I had opposed the grant. During a coffee break, in front of other Council members and staff, Rhoda accused me of conflict of interest. I bristled; neither I nor anyone I knew personally had anything to gain from the position I had taken. I had argued in principle on behalf of actors in the workplace whose identities were unknown. I demanded—and received—an apology. But this incident pointed up the constant suspicion I was under as a labor person, even from friends.

Still, the incident had repercussions. At the urging of some Council members who had always resented the presence of labor representation, Liv Biddle had to call a special hearing to determine a new NEA definition of "conflict of interest." I presented a strong argument at this hearing, insisting that "conflict of interest" was solely defined as support of something from which you, your family, or your business derive personal gain. While they admitted that no such situation existed in my case, they still voted to broaden the definition so as to exclude Council members from the vote on applications that might affect members of organizations (in my case, Equity) in which they held elective office. I lost on that issue. I still think their position is an untenable one.

Taking staff to task on matters of form and semantics was more fun. Each time a program drew up new guidelines for applicants, the format had to be approved by the Council. One time a set of guidelines was presented to us that had neat notations in the margins to orient applicants more quickly by pointing them to the various sections of the regulations. I read the following notations in the margin to the left of the text: "Who we fund," and later, "Who we do not fund." I took the director of the program aside and asked him whether he had ever played "Knock-knock." When he said that he had I suggested we play. I said, "Knock-knock." He answered, "Who's there?" I said, "Fuck," and when he asked, as the ritual demanded "Fuck who?" I said, pointing to the notation in the margin of his draft, *"Whom!!"*

Joan Mondale, Vice President Walter Mondale's wife, was always most supportive of all our efforts in the arts. She made herself available to us and sometimes hosted meetings in the vice president's official residence. For example, we had pushed for official presidential recognition of artists of merit by means of a medal of the arts, something that exists in most other civilized and even not so civilized countries. Several of us spent an entire morning at the residence hammering out the final details of the plan; we then submitted it to President Carter at the White House that afternoon. Also present, in addition to Jerry Robbins and myself, was Lew Wasserman, the head of Universal Studios, who had been a supporter and fund-raiser for the Democratic party in the last successful election. The president liked our idea and signed off on it. However, George Stevens, Jr., had a more ambitious plan, which took off at the same time. Called the Kennedy Center Honors, it would be an annual event honoring several individuals who had demonstrated a lifetime contribution to the arts, celebrated with great panache and showmanship with a White House reception and a show at the Kennedy Center. Presidential medals in the arts are still given each year, but the Kennedy Center Honors is a splashier affair and eclipses the other effort—justly perhaps, because it really is a superb tribute to the individual honorees as well as to the arts in general.

In the middle of my term at the Endowment, in 1980, Jimmy Carter was defeated for reelection and Ronald Reagan became president. One would have thought that a former actor would have some feeling and compassion for the artists in the nation, that the NEA might enjoy his support and patronage. Not so. But then, one also would have thought that a former president of a labor union—the Screen Actors Guild (1947–52 and 1959–60)—might have some compassion for working men and women. Again, not so. One of the early budget-cutting measures he proposed was a slash of fully 50 percent of the NEA's budget. This would have been a crippling blow. To examine the workings of the Endowment, a special task force was put together under the chairmanship of a troika: Charlton Heston, president Hanna Gray of the University of Chicago, and Daniel Terra, the newly appointed ambassador-at-large for cultural affairs. Underlying the task force's stated mission were two questions: Where are the mistakes? What can be eliminated? Since the creation of the task force coincided with the request to cut funds, an implication was clearly present that mistakes had to be found to justify cuts. I testified before a meeting of the task force, as did some of my colleagues. Our reception was cordial; Chuck Heston is a gracious chairman. The group wasn't composed solely of people hostile to the arts or the Endowment; among the people serving were two of the past NEA chairmen, Roger Stevens and Nancy Hanks. Nancy Mehta was as supportive as William Coors—how did the beer czar get in on this?—was not.

In the end, the task force, against all expectations of the White House, issued a report giving the NEA a clean bill of health and recommended that everything remain in place "as originally conceived." The 50 percent cut also did not materialize; the reduction in the final version of the bill was a mere 6 percent. If one man could be credited with this miraculous rescue of the Endowment from disaster, it was Representative Sidney Yates of Illinois, chairman of the congressional subcommittee overseeing the NEA; the arts could not ever hope to have a better friend in the Congress. The nonprofit arts would continue to be supported by federal funds, no thanks to President Reagan. Some of my international colleagues ventured an opinion that artists seemed to enjoy the esteem of the American people, seeing that they had elected an actor to be president. With some sadness I had to state that Ronald Reagan had not been elected because he was an actor, but in spite of it.

Not that the Republican administration under Reagan was necessarily opposed to the arts; they were only opposed to government support of it. That attitude became more evident when Liv Biddle, who
had been Carter's man, was replaced as chairman of the National
Endowment, and Frank Hodsoll was chosen by Reagan to be the new
chairman. Unlike Liv Biddle, a published author, Frank did not come
from an arts background. He had been working at the White House
under James Baker, and he arrived at the NEA with an attitude that
echoed the sentiments we had heard expressed by the new administration, namely, that the burden of supporting the arts in America should
be shifted to the private sector as much as possible. We knew from
experience that federal grants were essential in priming the pump; the
matching requirements, especially, had a stimulative effect on private
giving. The collective quality assessment of the panels and the Council
were important, but so were the grants. When Frank Hodsoll assumed
his post and chaired his first Council meeting he kept asking whether,
instead of money, we could not give letters to the applicants stating
that the Council—composed of luminaries in the arts—deemed the
artist or the arts organization in question to be one of quality and
deserving of support. With such a prestigious letter, Frank argued, the
artists could approach the private sector for grant support. I grew
more amused as the meeting went on, and finally asked to speak. I
said: "Mr. Chairman, I assure you that with a letter like that the artists
can go to the private sector and get it matched—letter for letter."
Everyone laughed, including the new chairman, who began to see the
improbability of the course he had advocated. At that first meeting I
also remarked, trusting it would not be taken amiss, that so far Mr.
Hodsoll seemed only to have a toe in the arts, while the rest of his
body was still in the White House. In due course I hoped that this
state would become the exact reverse. As time wore on, Hodsoll did
become a champion of the arts and became more knowledgeable
about the various art forms, just as the rest of us had had to do.

Whenever one speaks of government support of the arts, one is
describing a pie that is finite. It can be sliced up, but the larger the
slice you cut in one instance, the smaller the piece you leave for others
who may be less eloquent and less powerful in arguing for their discipline. Who is to get the largest slice? How does government determine which arts and which artistic groups are more "needy" than others? How do we address our legitimate fear that in the United States
some groups will be underrepresented and underfunded because of
race or cultural origin? Who decides?

All of these issues represent pitfalls in the interaction of government with the arts. When federal support of the arts, even on modest levels, is administered in a racially and culturally balanced way, there is always the danger that an "official" art is being unwittingly perpetrated—an amalgam of culturally conscious but politically correct projects that represent but do not offend. The more we develop into a pluralistic society, the greater the opportunities for offense and for artistic expression to engage the tripwires of political competition.

I used to fear that some kind of an official art might come about because we have a dominant culture and because homogeneity is built into governmental thinking processes. I feared it because the arts cannot, and should not, be forced into such a mold. Life is not homogeneous, nor is this nation homogeneous. I am more confident now that what I feared about cultural dominance will not come about. There are so many points of divergence among the different cultures that make up the artistic constituency that the danger of creating a homogenized political pudding is lessened. This is to be encouraged; the alternative would be to create a new melting pot out of which we yank a marbelized sludge and call it a national art—politically pure, guaranteed inoffensive, devoid of any clear cultural message. Do we want this?

That must fail because it is pernicious to try to force black artists into white molds, or Latino artists into black molds—all of which has been attempted. Nor it is meet and proper to neglect—merely by dint of the numbers involved—such growing but still relatively small artistic communities as Koreans, Vietnamese, Slavs, or Croats. What do we do about Portuguese poets and writers who choose—as a deliberately cultural, not political, act—to write in their own language? Although these find support from time to time, at other times they find it hard to get a literature grant from the government because nobody feels equipped to judge the quality of their work.

Do bureaucrats have any business judging the arts? From a strictly bureaucratic point of view, what are the funding criteria? Does the artistic project have to appeal to a broad enough audience to justify the expense? Does it have to be readily understandable so that the bureaucrats can report to other bureaucrats that after processing a good day's worth of applications they can summarize the artistic projects in single-sentence descriptions? Clearly, these people are concerned more with cutting up the pie into slices for everyone than with supporting the most worthy artistic projects. It is precisely for that reason that artists and others concerned with the arts were charged with making the decisions affecting the arts.

It didn't always work well. When I served on the National Coun-

cil I often had to argue with some who put more faith in actuarial figures than in the living and breathing processes of the arts and their
practitioners. A fellow Council member of mine, a San Francisco
banker by the name of James Robertson, a Nixon appointee, caused
me to go through the roof more than once. "If that's the only application from Iowa in that category, I guess then we'll have to fund it," he
would say. I remember exploding: "That's nuts! You haven't even
looked at the quality yet. If it's a lousy application then I'll be damned
if I'll vote for it. And if there are ten good applications from Iowa, I'll
argue for funding them all. This is about artistic excellence, for God's
sake, it is not a revenue-sharing process!"

In fact, too many people do want a piece of the pie. The guidelines as originally written cite professional excellence as the prime criterion for government grant-making in the arts. But since more
extensive funds have been available for a few years, people who are
neither professional nor work within accepted standards have wanted a
slice of the pie. With certain notable exceptions, that is not healthy.
The exceptions are in fields less amenable to measurement by usual
professional yardsticks. An example of this is the folk arts field, where
a person does not necessarily make his or her life's work in the art
form but works as a professional in another field—such as a blacksmith
who plays the fiddle, or a fisherman who paints. Another field that
allows some exceptions is what we loosely call "expansion arts." This
includes the art of the inner city and minority arts where the artists are
not striving to become part of the majority culture, but are creating
within the community and seek to remain there to continue to create.
There, the definition of professionalism can and should be relaxed.

Other than those exceptions, professionalism is the *sine qua non* in
considering a grant application. If we were to relax our standards and
allow anything and anybody who has some vague hankering toward
the arts to call on our limited resources, then we would dissipate what
is very precious and very pointedly focused. A yearly budget of $175
million is hopelessly inadequate to meet the needs of the arts in all
fields, and we shouldn't fool around with it. At the same time we must
encourage experimentation in uncharted waters. For example, National
Science Foundation grants are given to reputable scientists with a view
that whether they succeed or fail, the cause of knowledge will be
advanced. Failure in science is usually noble, and provides data for the
next experimenter. I maintain that in the arts, too, the government
should take risks and not shy away from the unusual, as long as the
endeavor meets a standard of professional excellence. If that is elitist,
then so be it. The search for excellence is, by definition, elitist. We

should not be in the business of making the mediocre palatable, but of identifying the best there is and then giving it the widest distribution to the most people. That is the populist part of the equation.

I do not assert that the process is perfect. No process is. Nor do I mean to suggest that when mistakes are made they should remain unacknowledged or be accepted without comment and criticism. And what of the argument, "Make your mistakes by all means, but not with the people's money"? This argument contains both a fallacy and a double standard. The U.S. government funds a great many things in a great many fields without demanding—or expecting—a success rate of 100 percent. Research in medicine, physics, space, and computer technology as well as in pure (as opposed to applied) sciences all receive heavy public funding. In those fields the unconventional, the experimental, the bold, and the innovative all demand the respect—often the awe—of the keepers of the public purse. Why should we acknowledge an expected failure rate in all other publicly funded enterprises that is sometimes as high as 90 percent, but in the arts insist on a 100 percent rate of success—otherwise the funding becomes endangered? Is it perhaps that in those other fields lawmakers fear to tread because there they freely acknowledge their lack of expertise, but in the arts have shamelessly decided that anybody is an expert? Will color-blind congressmen render judgment on paintings, will tone-deaf senators turn music critics?

Art, at its best, is an expression of individualism. That's why the Soviets both hated and were fascinated by it. They tried to create art in the image of the worker, but often looked upon art that reflected individual emotion as bourgeois and self-indulgent. Zhivago the doctor, ministering to the troops along the German front, was a hero of the people. Zhivago the poet, writing of his first meeting with Lara, was, in their eyes, an enemy of the people. Yet the Soviets, the champions of conformity, were the most protective of their art, because they, unlike us, respected it and truly understood its historical purpose.

I once wrote to the secretaries of defense and the interior on the question of measures to preserve this nation's art treasures in case of an unthinkable tragedy such as a nuclear attack. I learned that contingency measures had been developed with respect to evacuation of the population from urban centers, but no thought had been given to safeguarding our priceless art treasures. On a trip to the Hermitage Museum in Leningrad, on the other hand, I learned an extraordinary fact: Early in World War II, at the first sign of a conflict between Germany and the Soviet Union, all the art was shipped to a remote Eastern location and buried as deeply as possible under proper climatic conditions. There the artifacts remained, untouched and unharmed, while the Hermitage Museum itself suffered the bombing. I maintained that our country could do no less, and that emergency measures of this kind must be worked out by our government. Although it was not in my immediate area of expertise, I approached the government on this issue because I felt the matter to be within my mandate as a member of the National Council on the Arts. Indeed, the Council adopted my letter as its official position, and awaited the results. They were fairly long in coming. A few months down the pike, a minor-league government official from the Department of the Interior made an appearance before the Council. This affable, pipe-smoking, avuncular type rambled on about premises having been secured by the government in Omaha at the cost of one dollar a year to store the nation's priceless art treasures in case of a national emergency. They had given no thought to climatic conditions and made no plans at all toward transporting the works from the National Gallery to Nebraska. It was vague to the point of being ludicrous. At the end of the man's presentation, I suggested that the response was wholly inadequate, but that I was prepared to recommend him for a grant from the Folk Arts Program for excellence in storytelling.

The matter of the nation's art treasures concerned me because human beings are transitory, while art is not. Individual lives are perishable, art endures. In the end, art turns out to be the quintessence of human remembrance and the distillation of humankind's dreams. Through art, we have the means to assert our individualism for all time, even overcoming the grinding conformity of death itself.

That, too, is a Zorba thought.

20

Toward the Millennium

Zog nit keinmol az du geyst dem letsten veg
Khotsh himlen blayene farshteln bloye teg
Kumen vet nokh unzer oysgebenkte sho
S'vet a poyk ton unzer trot—mir zaynen do!

Never say that you are walking your last way
Though leaden skies above blot out the blue of day.
The hour for which we long will certainly appear,
Our steps shall thunder and proclaim: We are still here.

    —HIRSH GLIK 1922–44 (TRANSLATED BY E. PALEVSKY AND T. BIKEL)

*A*LL THAT IS LEFT FOR ME BEFORE CONCLUDING this narrative is to cast a last long look backward and a quick glance forward.

I consider 1993 and 1994 milestones, both in terms of world events that affected my life and in terms of personal history. The year 1993 was the sixtieth anniversary of Hitler's rise to power, an event that the world remembers as the beginning of state-sanctioned criminality, which left scars on Europe's face and consciousness that will not fade for many decades. In personal terms, 1993 marked twenty-five years since I first played Tevye the Milkman, the role that since then has been the mainstay of my stage career—I played my thousandth performance as Tevye in September 1990, two days after Rosh Hashanah, in Providence, Rhode Island. And 1994 is the fortieth anniversary of my arrival in America. I must also take note of the fact—not without a little shock—that May 2, 1994, marked my seventieth birthday. A chronological fact luckily backed by little evidence of physical or mental erosion.

The poem with which I started this chapter is the text of a song that has become the anthem of Holocaust survivors. It is always sung standing; each year after 1945 my father would sing it during the Passover seder as we all stood and recalled the memory of the martyrs. I have continued the custom. Among the more public and solemn occasions when I sang it together with thousands of survivors was the 1993 commemoration of the uprising in the Warsaw Ghetto. This marked the fiftieth anniversary of that tragic and yet heroic event in the modern history of Jews. With Madison Square Garden filled to overflowing, I acted as master of ceremonies. I introduced various dignitaries and speakers, including one of the few survivors who had fought in the Warsaw Ghetto, Vladka Meed. As I recited the poem "*In Varshaver Getto*" by Binem Heller in Yiddish and in English (in the translation by Max Rosenfeld) it was difficult for me to avoid being overcome by my own emotion, yet I had to—my job was to stir others to remembrance. If there were to be tears, they should be theirs, not mine. I read the final lines of the poem:

> But no more will Jews to the slaughter be led
> The truculent jibes of the Nazis are past.
> And the lintels and doorposts tonight will be red
> With the blood of free Jews who will fight to the last.

As I said these words, I glanced toward the audience and saw Elie Wiesel in the front row; it became much harder still for me to retain my composure. But none of us could. We had already been through a solemn and harrowing ritual. A seemingly endless procession of women had mounted the stage and lit hundreds of candles to commemorate the innocent victims as well as the heroes who went down as they fought and died. There was hardly a dry eye in the vast hall, including all of us on the dais, from Vice President Al Gore on down.

That week in April had more in store. On April 22, the Holocaust Museum in Washington, D.C., opened its doors with a dedication ceremony attended by the president, the vice president, President

Chaim Herzog of Israel, and other dignitaries from around the world. I attended the ceremony on that drizzly morning and would later in the evening greet the survivors at the end of their candlelight march with songs of the ghetto, ending the evening again by singing the survivors' anthem "*Zog Nit Keinmol*"—"Never say that this is your last road." But it was the morning ceremony that brought me, along with the thousands who had come to pay homage, to an emotional catharsis. Once again it was Elie Wiesel who stirred the conscience of all who were listening. His words were, as they so often are, an affirmation of human decency, which can triumph over evil and outlive it. As indeed it must, if we are to survive as a race. He also gives the lie to the notion that calling up the memory of the Holocaust must invariably cast Jews as victims. There is something ennobling and redemptive about this storyteller's words and demeanor; one hopes that, having come through a living hell with his soul intact, he may guide us to a place where we might save ours.

Some people had voiced doubts about the wisdom of creating a Holocaust museum, and some others had questioned its situation in Washington, where the visitor from rural America would receive his first, perhaps his only, view of Jews. If this should be the only showcase for Jewish history and Jewish existence, was it proper to have death as its only theme and focus? Jews, it was argued, surely had other faces than merely those of sacrificial lambs on the altar of racial supremacy. But when I went through the museum, painful as the experience was, I found it absolutely right and proper that the museum should exist, that it had been put in exactly the right place, and that it showed exactly what had to be shown. The designers took great care to shield the most gruesome sights from the eyes of small children by placing baffles in front of the most horrifying exhibits, too high for children to see over. The rest of us are spared nothing.

Just as the Nazi machine forced the Jews into mechanized and impersonal cruelty, so does the museum compel the visitor to look, to listen, to experience an unrelenting and unforgiving savagery. Quite unlike other museums, where the visitor enters and works his way up from the ground floor to the top, here we are taken up to the top floor in elevators that already evoke the feeling of boxcars. From there you begin what I can only describe as a descent into hell. Every turn is an assault on your senses and sensibilities; all the objects displayed are real, all the films are real also, from the archives of a mad nation that not only committed atrocities but arrogantly documented them in still pictures and movies. Even the model layouts of camps and crematoria bear witness to the clinical self-congratulatory conceit of Nazi planners who prided themselves on a meticulously planned and executed campaign of death. I must confess that I was seized by an irrational feeling of claustrophobia. Knowing that the perpetrators of the horror before me were gone, that I was in a museum in the year of 1993, did nothing to alleviate my pangs of anxiety, which were extreme. It is perhaps the sign of a brilliant architectural concept that such feelings are evoked in that space. Seemingly, the visitor has choices whether to take a left corridor or a right; it turns out to be no choice at all. Even in the camps the selection to one side meant death and to the other temporary survival. Here, whichever way you choose to go, there is only death. I asked myself: Why am I here? Every fiber in my body told me that I should not be here, must not be here. Equally loudly, everything in me said that I could not possibly be anywhere else.

The Holocaust Museum is not only a place of numbers, it is a place of individual pain. Cumulative deaths are unimaginable, while a single death is unbearable. One Anne Frank did more to rattle the world's conscience than the listing of actuarial figures of corpses. In treating both mass destruction and the suffering and dying of single human beings, the museum achieved for me a subtle balance that will surely be recognized as one of its greater assets. Yet the memory of the martyred millions of the Holocaust has not remained unmolested. Even while the dedication of the museum was going on, neo-Nazi hooligans outside the security cordons shouted slogans of "We don't buy the Holocaust lie." None of these can learn anything from the memorial, even were they to enter its doors. They will insist, in their single-minded stupor, that the story of the Holocaust was concocted by Jews who had nothing in mind except blackmailing the world into supporting Israel.

But the millions of Americans who knew little about the Holocaust or cared very little even if they had some vague knowledge of it, care very much—when these Americans visit the museum, it will have an impact not only by resurrecting history but by teaching them a lesson about the fragility of civilization. If they are able to draw the parallel, they will see that, though the Holocaust was a uniquely Jewish experience, its lesson must be a universal one. Memory, especially memory of horrors, which tends to be buried deep, is fragile and perishable. This museum's irrefutable evidence will be one of memory's few safeguards.

What a different experience this was from a visit to the Vietnam War Memorial! Some months earlier I had paid a visit to that shrine. I remember seeing my own reflection in the polished black stone as I walked from one end to the other. The stone wall gradually rises above you, looms above and engulfs you, dominates you with darkness and shadow as you proceed along the trench. But then gradually you rise to the surface again as the list of the dead grows smaller and you are exactly where you began. The ground at the end is as level as it was at the beginning, and the names of the dead are behind you. No matter one's views about the Vietnam War, the dead of that war died in a purposeful sacrifice for what they believed was the good of their country. As you remember them, you think little about those at whose hands they died. At the Holocaust Museum you never stop thinking about the monsters whose deeds obscured centuries of noble thought, and you come away ashamed of humanity with its thin veneer of civilization. When you emerge from the Holocaust Museum, nothing is the same as it was and the dead are not behind you, will perhaps never be behind you.

After the dedication and my journey through the museum, it was as if my life as a human being and as a Jew had come full circle. It had started with the bar mitzvah boy in Vienna who was immediately thrust into the maelstrom that marked the beginning of the age of turmoil. During my entire life I was never far away from that memory. I had escaped the Holocaust's deadly grip, but I could never evade the pall of my people's remembrance of it. This, as much as anything, moved me to say and sing as I had done for years. I would remind my own people of what they lost and what they must retain so as not to lose even more. I would also remind the enemy, the Jew-hater, and the Jew-baiter, saying and singing *Mir zaynen do!*—we are still here.

J ANUARY 1979 was not an easy month. I was on my way to an FIA conference in Geneva, having stopped off in London for one night on January 8. I felt quite ill during the night in my hotel room and even contemplated waking up my friend Arnold Kalina. He had been my doctor when I lived in England and had remained my close friend over the years. In the end I decided to tough it out until morning rather than trouble him in his professional capacity, but I felt really bad. It seemed as though my innards were turning inside out; most unusual for me, who is not given to bouts of illness. I still do not know what was wrong with me that night, and I decidedly do not believe in psychic phenomena, but in the morning my wife called me from Connecticut to tell me that my father had passed away in Tel Aviv in the early hours of the morning. I flew to Tel Aviv to bury this man who had had such an influence on my life, both positive and negative.

My father Joseph Bikel, né Hasenfratz, had a life not so much of missed opportunities as of missed chances. Poverty was what he had battled as a young man; it thwarted his academic ambitions and eventually forced him into making a living in ways that were always a step or two beneath his intellectual capacities. The need to make enough money for his family and to give me the opportunity to complete my education, which he himself had been unable to do, forced him into the ranks of the lower middle class. The fear of poverty haunted him all his life and prevented him from enjoying life fully, even when it became quite clear that he would never have to face poverty again. My parents became past masters at cutting corners; they would deny themselves little luxuries and would not even dream of big ones. I remind myself constantly that I must guard against any inherited traits of this nature. Another bad trait I seem to have inherited, and one that troubles me, is the inclination toward a violent temper. In my father's case it was not the kind of violence that draws blood or even smashes objects; it was yelling loudly in a torrent of verbal abuse. Quite early in my life, I discovered that I, too, had a temper. When in a fit I broke a school bench, it frightened me so much that I resolved to keep my temper in check, and for the most part I've been successful.

Another thing I learned from my father by negative example. When I was about eleven years old, they brought him home from the office where he had collapsed: nicotine poisoning. It shocked me so that I vowed there and then never to become a smoker. I never did. My father, however, continued to smoke for several more years, despite this episode. When he finally quit, both my mother and I were immensely relieved. His doctor said that it would take a long time before his lungs would cleanse themselves. It is ironic that thirty-five years after he quit smoking, my father died of lung cancer.

The good heirlooms I got from my father were not material in nature. They were like the proverbial kiddush cup handed down from generation to generation; in my case, a cup filled with stories and songs. I inherited from my father a love of languages, an aptitude for learning them, and a love of singing. In his good periods, he was a fine and intellectual human being, rightly much loved by his family and colleagues. I did not like some of his ways; his tendency to watch jealously to see whether anyone was slighting him in some way drove me up the wall. He was not a very tolerant man, and it caused an adverse reaction in me toward intolerance of any kind. But I also inherited from him a love of Jewish culture, and for that I shall be eternally grateful to him. He had quite a good life, especially during all the years he lived in Israel; more especially still, after he finally retired as an official of the health services department of the Histadrut, the Israeli labor organization, the equivalent of the AFL-CIO. I wish he himself had realized how good a life it really had been.

Toward the end of his days my father lost much of his hearing. The joke went that he turned deaf so as not to hear what my mother was saying to him. In the end it turned out that hers was the only voice he could hear. He was also too vain to use a hearing aid. I tried to persuade him to use one by getting him devices that were very small; he balked. Finally I got him one that was built into the temple of some eyeglasses, and even those he would rarely use. One time, when he again misheard what I had said to him, I got mad. "You know you can't hear," I said. "Why don't you wear your glasses?"

Thankfully, he had a relatively short bout with the cancer that took his life. At the funeral my mother walked after his coffin and ahead of the rest of us with the grim steps of a brave warrior. I let her walk alone; after fifty-eight years of marriage this was her right and this was her place.

That same month I had another trying experience which at one point could have become very dangerous. I found myself on a hijacked plane. Strangely, this was not an international flight going to exotic places, it was a 747, United Airlines Flight 8 from Los Angeles to JFK. It seemed an uneventful flight: cocktails, a meal and a movie, and all the other trappings. It turned strange when we got near the East Coast and the plane kept flying in circles. It could not have been the weather; there was an absolutely clear and untroubled sky. The captain was totally uncommunicative and so were the cabin crew. After a long delay we landed at JFK, taxied to a remote spot, and then simply sat. Beyond the instruction to fasten seatbelts and stow tray tables, there had been no word. We just sat. After a long while I went to talk to the chief flight attendant. I asked him what was happening and he hemmed and hawed, saying something vague about there being some trouble in the terminal that we would have to wait out. I told him that I was a seasoned traveler and that the explanation made no sense to me: If there was trouble in the United terminal, common courtesy would have prompted any other airline to permit us the use of their gates. Or we could have been let out by means of an exterior stairway and bused to a terminal. I promised him that I would not start any kind of panic, but that I would rather know what was wrong than not know. "Is someone holding a gun on the captain?" I wanted to know. He said no, the trouble was not in the cockpit. I said, "All right, now we know where it isn't. But where is it?" Finally he decided to trust my promise not to start a stampede and came clean.

It appears that there was a woman sitting in the coach portion of the plane in seat 44-J who, about ten minutes into the flight, had handed a note to a flight attendant to give to the captain. In the note she said that she had nitroglycerine in her handbag, and she would blow up the plane with it unless her demands were met. Clever, because nitroglycerine in a glass or plastic container could not be detected by devices screening for metal. The flight supervisor did not know exactly what her demands were, only that she insisted that Charlton Heston, Jack Lemmon, or Lindsay Wagner read over the air a note she had left in a locker at the L.A. airport. Later I learned that Chuck Heston, as always ready to be a good citizen, had been located, had interrupted a rehearsal, and had driven to the L.A. airport to stand by if needed.

I went back to my seat in the forward cabin, quite a ways from the hijacker, of whom I had caught a glimpse. She appeared to be a woman in her forties with a bandanna on her head. I did not stare because the last thing I wanted to do was rattle her. I began to feel a little queasy, somewhat claustrophobic, and just plain afraid. The passengers were getting restless, but true to my promise I did not let anyone know what I had found out. I wished I had, because then I could have shared the feeling and not been alone with my fears. We had now been on the ground for over an hour and still had not been told anything. In fact we were never told the truth of what was happening. The passengers did find out, but not from me. A couple of travelers had brought out their portable radios and had tuned in to the news. From the broadcast everyone learned that we were on a hijacked plane. To my chagrin I also heard my name mentioned as one of the passengers, along with the actors Sam Jaffe and his wife Bettye Ackerman, as well as Dean-Paul Martin, Dean's son. How stupid, I thought. The media had no way of knowing what kind of operation this hijacking was, how well organized, and whether there were any accomplices on the ground. If they had been Palestinian terrorists, broadcasting my name would have surely put my life in danger. By the time the broadcast was heard and repeated, the woman hijacker had demanded and received a telephone so she could communicate with the authorities. The technician who brought her the phone was actually an FBI agent, but she did not know that.

Some people had begun to get very nervous and upset. I myself felt that I could not just sit there and do nothing. I took my guitar case out of the coat closet, pulled out the instrument, and started to play. This is a stupid way for one's life to end, I thought, but if it has to, then at least I will end my life as I have lived it—playing songs. The first thing that came to mind for me to sing was Jim Croce's

"Time in a Bottle." The lyric was apt in light of our situation, and the choice, I later realized, was ironic, since Jim Croce had died in a plane crash. We sat captive on the aircraft for six and a half hours after a flight of five—eleven and a half hours in all. I played and sang for the last four of those stressed hours. I was told that my doing this had prevented a panic among the passengers. I know for sure that by singing and playing I had prevented my own.

In an unguarded moment when she was distracted, the FBI agent overpowered the hijacker and wrested the handbag from her. When the contents were later examined, there was nitroglycerine all right, but only in the form of pills for a heart condition. No explosives were found; still, no one could take the gamble of assuming that there would not be any. The woman was neither a Palestinian nor a terrorist. She was a disturbed human being who had a gripe against the Catholic church, and against an ex-husband whom she blamed for their failed marriage. This was a solo act. What was remarkable was that she never went to the bathroom during all those hours. The hidden message was never found and never needed and Charlton Heston returned to his rehearsal after spending some hours at the Los Angeles airport. Rita had rushed to the airport when she heard the news on the radio and had spent some anxious hours there before we were released and could drive home to Connecticut. A few days later, the chairman of United Airlines sent me a beautiful crystal bowl in recognition of my having "calmed the fears and anxieties" of my fellow passengers. In my reply I thanked him and said that I would not like to have to go to such lengths again to find an audience. (It also occurred to me that there had to be easier ways to get crystal bowls.)

WITH THE REST of the world Jewish community I have always shared the fear that the first war Israel loses will be its last. Israel never had the luxury its hostile Arab neighbors have—to lose, lick their wounds, and come back another day to fight again. The threat "to push the Israelis into the sea" was always a real one, and it made us tremble each time there was more than just a border skirmish or a terrorist infiltration. The wars of 1948 and 1956 saw Israel emerge unscathed and with an image of invincibility. I thought this to be dangerous, both in terms of how Israelis might see themselves and in how the world would relax its concern for the Jewish state. When the Yom Kippur War broke out in 1973, catching the Israelis by surprise, there was deep worry among Israel's supporters. For the first few days its military fortunes seemed to be on the wane, heavy losses were inflicted, and, as we heard it, morale was lower than it had been in the previous crises.

Rita and I agreed that I could not stay away; all the speeches I had given, all the rallies I had attended over the years in support of Israel would not count for much if, in its hour of isolation, I did not do what I could, as an American Jew and as an artist, to lend to the struggle whatever prestige and talent I had—in person. I contacted the Israelis, announcing my readiness to help, and was put on a planeload of young men returning to join their army units. Regular El Al flights had been suspended, and all the planes had been put to such use as the government and the military required.

Tel Aviv had a different face when I arrived. There were no tourists; in fact, the entire Tel Aviv Hilton, where I had been assigned a room, was full of war correspondents from all over the world, and was teeming with men and women in uniform doing liaison chores and conducting briefings.

I had not come as a journalist, or as an observer, or as a fighter. I did want to go to the trenches and I had brought the only weapon I have, my guitar. The army command assigned me a car and driver as well as a liaison officer, and at first I was taken to hospitals where the wounded had been brought from the battlefields. Having arrived from peaceful America, I found the sights shocking to the senses. But I had come to help, and I played and sang in large and small hospital rooms, first to men who were lightly wounded and could laugh and clap. But then I also played for the severely wounded who could barely acknowledge that they were able to hear. The nursing staff encouraged me to persevere; they had always found music to have a therapeutic effect, even on these patients. One of the most gratifying experiences I had was in one of the army hospitals where severe shell-shocked cases had been brought. One man had been in a catatonic state ever since they had brought him in. His tank had been blown up by a direct hit; he survived—miraculously—but the doctors had some doubts that he would come out of his severe mental trauma. He had been sitting open-eyed in one position for several days and had been artificially fed; he reacted to nothing. I played in his room for a long while, and suddenly there was a small foot movement keeping up with the beat of the music. The nurses hugged him and me and I had tears in my eyes.

Then I was taken to the very battle zones where the fight was raging. I played and sang in gun emplacements, in bunkers, and in improvised shelters where soldiers temporarily off duty were taking a breather. All the men wore a stubble of beard several days old, and they sang along with me as best they could. This was on the Golan Heights, with the guns booming from the Syrian side. Someone counted fourteen miniconcerts I gave in one day. Among other places, I played in Quneitra, a town then under Israeli control that was later ceded back to the Syrians. I sang in Hebrew, in Yiddish, and in Ladino; and I also sang in a dozen other languages. As I tell audiences from time to time, I do not only sing of Jewish hopes and dreams; I sing about hopes and dreams, period.

The song I sang most often was Jacques Brel's "If We Only Have Love." I had known it in French and English before; on this trip I learned the Hebrew words to it, and so I could sing it in three languages. When the peace process that began in 1977 with the famous trip to Jerusalem by Anwar Sadat was concluded by the signing of a treaty between Israel and Egypt in Washington in 1979, I was there. I was invited to attend a reception given at the house of Esther Coopersmith for Madame Jihan Sadat, whom I found to be a very gracious lady. When they asked me to perform, I decided to sing the Brel song. I explained that I had sung it at a time and in a place when bombs were exploding all around us and shrapnel was flying. I had sung then about the only road to peace, which was love and understanding, and I would sing of it again on this night. My recalling these events raised a few eyebrows, but I assured them that it was all right. If you are not willing to remember the bitter times, then you cannot savor the sweet taste of peace, either.

The Gulf War of 1991 presented another kind of threat. Israel was not a combatant in the war, and yet it was put in the direct line of fire by an irrational tyrant who tried to make points with his Arab adversaries by hitting targets in the territory of their common enemy. The tactic did not work, but it threw Israel into a solely defensive stance, bracing for hits without hitting back so as not to upset the alliance between the United States and its partners in the war against Iraq. We kept watching CNN to see the fireworks as the Scud missiles streaked over Israel and sometimes hit random targets. My mother, then ninety-three years old, sitting in her room at the senior citizens home in Ramat Chen, at first refused to don the obligatory gas mask during the raids. "At my age, what can they do to me?" she would say. Finally the staff at the home and I, via long distance telephone, prevailed on her to do as the Israeli government had directed. Whenever I saw a raid, I tried to get through to her; usually the phone lines were jammed. Once I had my phone in Los Angeles in the automatic redial mode while a Scud alert was happening and, after numerous tries, got through to my mother. She answered, speaking with difficulty through the gas mask she was wearing.

The next attack found its mark in Ramat Chen, a mere eight blocks from the home. There were casualties and there was great anger also, and not just because of the destruction. Israelis were not used to sitting actionless while being attacked. I felt that I had to go to Israel, be there, offer help, and do what I could. Once again I took my guitar and flew to Tel Aviv. On arrival at the Ben Gurion airport I was handed a gas mask and instructed in its use. That first evening I saw that the Tel Aviv I had known for so many years had vanished into thin air. Nothing moved at all except the occasional lone police car or ambulance. The town was one of the liveliest I had ever known: Even on the eve of Yom Kippur, the only day of the year when no vehicles would move, you saw pedestrians walking. Now the town was dead, nothing. It was eerie.

Zubin Mehta had been in Israel from the beginning of the crisis. When I arrived he asked me to come up to his suite at the Hilton and gave me some directions on how to get to the shelter in case of an attack. He had already been through several. Zubin has a close and intimate relationship with Israel: He is so committed that he will put himself into harm's way in national emergencies. As I sat there facing him, I started to laugh. Here was this man—not Jewish, an Indian-born, Vienna-trained artist with whom I sometimes speak German in a broad Viennese dialect—and here he was giving me instructions about gas masks like a veteran Israeli warrior. I remembered the joke about the man who comes home to find his wife in bed with his friend. The man starts to laugh as he says to the guy in the bed: "I *have* to—but you?" I gave Zubin a lot of credit. There were no evening concerts, but the orchestra would play some afternoons. The hall would be full of people holding cardboard boxes containing gas masks on their laps. The most courageous act was Isaac Stern's. The warning sirens went off in the middle of his afternoon concert. The entire audience donned the masks; everyone except Isaac, who continued playing without. It may have been part theatre, but if so, then it was the theatre of fortitude and defiance.

As I had done in 1973, I placed myself at the disposal of the Israeli army, which sent me to various places to entertain. Unlike that other time, when I got up early and was driven for several hours to the front lines, this time there was no front; the front was the entire country. Anywhere you were you slept in your clothes with the gas mask beside you, knowing that when the alarm sounded, you had less than three minutes to get to shelters that were sealed against penetrating gases. There may have been no front but there were casualties. I performed in hospitals and in places where troops stood by in readiness, should Israel decide to retaliate. I also performed in absorption centers where newly arrived immigrants from the Soviet Union had been put up. These were people who had been relieved to arrive in a place that held out the promise of freedom and safety; here they were, frightened and bewildered, fearing attacks that could come from the sky at any time of the day or night. Some of them, from the Asian part of the USSR, spoke Georgian and Russian and had not learned any Hebrew yet; they had no idea who I was, but I had come from America to soothe their spirits, and that was good enough for them.

The day before I left I entertained at a Patriot missile site. My audience consisted mostly of American military personnel and some Israeli soldiers who were being instructed in the use of the equipment. These were secret installations, and I was brought to them not quite blindfolded but in roundabout ways. Although a TV crew was permitted to film inside the tent, no exterior photographs were allowed. Since CNN could be seen by friend and enemy alike, security was making sure that the Iraqis would be unable to pinpoint the locations. Inside the large tent I entertained the off-duty personnel, Americans who were glad to see someone from home. They were a serious bunch, aware of their purpose. The captain of one battery, Lt. Colonel Harry Krimkowitz, happened to be Jewish; he was pleased both as an American and as a Jew to be stationed in this place during this particular war. Then I talked to Battalion Sergeant-Major Shepard, who was black, and asked him what his feelings were about being stationed here. He felt it was right for Americans to be defending Israel's soil. "This is the Holy Land," he said.

While in Israel I spent some time with a group of American Jewish leaders who had come to demonstrate solidarity with the embattled country. We had meetings with Prime Minister Shamir and attended a reception given by President Herzog. There was also a dinner in the middle of which the air raid sirens blasted their warning of an impending Iraqi missile attack. The warning had come just as Binyamin Netanyahu, then deputy prime minister, was about to speak. We all rushed into shelters and remained there until the all-clear sounded. This was a full-blown attack, and the strangest feeling was that in the shelter we were able to watch on a television screen a CNN live transmission from Atlanta, showing us what was happening outside! There were women and small children in the shelter and we all wore our gas masks. It was most disconcerting to watch a little child cry because she could not figure out why it was impossible for her to put a pacifier into her mouth through the mask. When the all-clear sounded we resumed the dinner, but before Netanyahu began his speech again, they asked me to calm the spirits of the assembled dignitaries. I sang a few songs, again finishing with Brel's "If We Only Have

Love" in Hebrew and in English. In his speech Bibi Netanyahu made reference to the song by saying that it would take much more than love to settle the conflicts that are plaguing the Middle East.

I am not a naïve person, and I know that it will take far more than love. But I doubt whether the medicine can be gotten from Dr. Netanyahu's prescription pad. His opposition to any formula of land-for-peace not only imposes psychological hurdles that prevent negotiators from being open to all possibilities, it also presents a greater danger in the long run. Suppose Israel were to incorporate the occupied territories into Greater Israel, which some have advocated—then what? Apart from the necessity of becoming permanent occupiers in hostile areas, do these advocates fail to see the demographic time bomb looming on the horizon? Given the different birthrates of Arabs and Jews, Greater Israel would have a population with an Arab majority in very short order. Then there will only be two choices, both equally impossible to accept. Israel can remain a Jewish state or a democratic state, but not both. If the former, then the Arabs will have to be relegated to second-class citizenship without the rights and privileges of Israeli Jews. In other words, the South African formula, which is disappearing even in South Africa and which has had simmering revolt as its constant companion. A never-ending *intifada*. If the latter scenario, Arabs will outnumber and outvote the Jews, and the political makeup of the state will be so radically altered as to make Israel disappear. Scratch *Hatikvah* and the Star of David.

I am worried about the preoccupation American Jews have with the defense of Israel and how little thought is given to the ideological underpinnings without which there could have been no Israel. The very notion of Zionism seems to have been relegated to history, and although today's friends of Israel care about its body, they seem to care as little about its soul as they do about their own. The American Jewish response to Israel is woefully monolithic; we who are so capable of intricate thought are almost boorishly insistent about viewing the complexities of Israeli society and political makeup through a one-channel, narrow prism. Our very reaction to statesmen and diplomats makes the point. American reaction to these Israelis varies according to how well they speak English. American Jews loved Abba Eban—but for the wrong reasons: He was right on the issues, but they did not care about that because they didn't understand what he said—just that he said it so beautifully. They also loved Netanyahu: He was wrong on the issues, but they didn't care about that, either—just that he spoke terrific American English.

I am not only worried about the Israel of the future. I am worried about the Israel at present, about its own sense of moral rectitude—or the lack of it. Occasionally I am reassured when government institutions, notably the courts, reaffirm the image of Israel as a country of laws. John Demjanjuk's case, although extremely painful for Holocaust survivors, was an occasion for such reassurance. I would have been quite content to see him deported from the U.S. on the grounds that he lied about his wartime activities on his visa application. But he had not been deported, he was extradited to Israel on one specific charge only, namely that he was the Nazi camp guard known as Ivan the Terrible. Once the court was unable to establish that he was that particular Ivan, questions about his serving as a guard in other camps became irrelevant to the legal process which had brought him to that court. The charge had been too specific, and unfortunately, fishing with a wider net after the fact was not permissible under any standards of jurisprudence. I say "unfortunately," because clearing him of the charge of having been Ivan the Terrible did not automatically anoint him Ivan the Innocent. They had to let him go, perhaps to face another day in another court in another country. It was a painful decision, but precisely because the court reached it after agonizing deliberations, it pointed to the kind of moral fiber not often found in the Western world and almost never in any other country of the Middle East.

Yet other questions of morality are contributing to a sense of unease about Israel. A friend's son, serving in the Israeli army, told his mother that the most harrowing part of his tour of duty involved battling stone-throwing children barely in their teens. He realized that the unrest had to be contained, but it caused a conflict of conscience. Fighting armed grown-ups and terrorist infiltrators he could cope with; taking the fight to women and children in villages and refugee camps was the hardest. After all the years of talk in which Gaza and the West Bank figured prominently and disturbingly, I had to see the center of unrest with my own eyes. On January 17, 1993, I joined a trip to Gaza and Dir al Ballah, a refugee camp in the strip, which had been organized by an Israeli human rights group. We were a couple of dozen Americans and Israelis; we were taken in buses which let us out at the entrance to the Gaza strip. From there Arab buses with church markings took us the rest of the way. Despite the neutral appearance of our transportation, as we drove through the streets of Gaza on our way in, a stone shattered the window of our bus and showered those sitting near it with glass. It was an immediate and shocking reminder that we were considered the enemy, regardless of who we were and of what had brought us to this place. Other American Jews might have turned around and gone back; I am glad we did not.

It turned out to be a harrowing day, seeing with my own eyes what Jews turned occupiers were capable of doing to another people. I hold no brief for Arab terrorists who kill and maim Jews; I am horrified by such deeds. Like all criminals, they must be hunted and brought to justice. But none of it could justify random violence by Jews in uniform against villagers, even those whose family members are suspected of terrorist acts or sympathies. I could no more sanction this than I would the blowing up of houses in the Bronx or in Miami because relatives of people living in them were suspected of crimes, even if they included murder. Yet in Gaza I saw wanton destruction of houses, leaving entire families enduring cold winter nights in temporary tents supplied by relief agencies. I talked to the family of a sixty-three-year old man who had been killed a week earlier because he had ignored an order to stand still—an order he could not hear because he was deaf. Can we who have been the victims of brutality for so many centuries allow ourselves to become even in the remotest way like our enemies? I was forcibly reminded of something Golda Meir once said: "I could possibly forgive the Arabs for killing our sons but I could not forgive them for turning our sons into killers." But that, too, removes the onus from us, the responsibility not to say and think, "So what? They had it coming." The responsibility to act instead with decency and proper regard for human rights is ours alone.

We had a very long session with Arab leaders at the Gaza Center for Rights and Law. These included Raji Sourani, a human rights lawyer who has argued hundreds of cases before Israeli courts (winning none of them), and Dr. Haider Abdel Shafi, one of the leaders of the Palestinian delegation to the Israel-Arab peace talks. Disappointingly, they suggested no solutions, no new resolve to break the stalemate. They offered little besides repeated assurances of the Palestinian leadership's commitment to peace. The group did offer moving recitals of desperate scenes. They pleaded for U.S. help in securing self-determination, but also insisted on the "indivisibility of the peace process," an assertion that all elements had to be negotiated in a bundle and that partial solutions toward a comprehensive peace were not acceptable. Disappointing to those of us who believe that gradual steps on the road to peace are preferable to no steps at all.

Afterward, when the question was asked whether our group should recommend that other American Jews visit Gaza as we had done, I counseled against it. It was useful for us to see and hear what we had, as it encouraged us to look for further avenues toward peace. If others had experienced the same trip, I argued, they would probably have remembered nothing beyond the shattered glass.

The visit and the talks with these leaders had not in one fell swoop turned them into friends of Israel in our minds, nor could we assume that they necessarily shared our vision and our version of peace. But if they were the enemy, then they are precisely the people—our enemies—with whom we must conclude a peace. Not with third parties nor with innocuous middlemen who speak for nobody, but with the very enemy with whom shots were exchanged only yesterday. That thought had been voiced for years by Abba Eban, the statesman and diplomat, former ambassador to the U.S. and the U.N., and former foreign minister of Israel. Eban, now out of office and out of the Parliament, had become the Adlai Stevenson of Israeli politics. Now his formula for negotiating with the enemy had been adopted by the prime minister of Israel himself. This formula led to clandestine talks between Israel and the PLO in Norway, talks that most certainly would have been impossible to conduct openly and under the glare of public scrutiny. In the end it led to a process which surfaced in September 1993 and which, within days, saw former archenemies shake hands in front of the White House.

On Friday, September 10, while in California, I received a call from the White House inviting me to the signing ceremony of the peace accord, which would be held three days later on the South Lawn. It seemed that I was getting to be an old hand at this; I had met President Clinton in April at the opening of the Holocaust Museum, and again at the White House only ten days earlier, at a pre–Labor Day reception. "You wear so many hats," the president had said to me then. (Even he recognized the problem . . .) This time, however, was going to be very special; the pundits had described an invitation to the signing ceremony as one of the "hottest tickets to get."

I arrived on the redeye from Los Angeles at 5:30 A.M., changed my shirt, and had a bite of breakfast before heading over to the White House. I ran into Ron Silver, my successor as Equity president, and shortly after 8:00 A.M. we walked some six blocks over to the East Gate, where a line had already started to form, even though the ceremony was scheduled for eleven o'clock. There was heavy security; Shoshana Cardin, the former head of the President's Conference of Major Jewish Organizations, was almost kept out because she had no picture ID. I had to vouch for her identity. No one minded the long wait; the excitement of the occasion carried us all. There were embraces between old friends and even old ideological adversaries; there were tentatively friendly contacts between Jewish and Arab guests; and there was much rubbernecking as various dignitaries arrived to take their seats. There were so many of them—civic leaders, senators, congressmen, ambassadors, and cabinet members. Until the loudspeaker announcements heralding the arrival of the First Lady and Mrs. Rabin, of the vice president, of former Presidents Carter and Bush, and finally of the president, accompanied by Prime Minister Rabin and Yassir Arafat, the dignitaries all arrived without fanfare. Only one unannounced entrance received applause from the assembled: Abba Eban. How well deserved, I thought.

I will not attempt to describe the scene as a journalist might; I am not a journalist and the moment needs to be recalled in more personal terms. It was not quite Camp David revisited; then the players had been equals, representatives of two sovereign nations both of whom were able to make good on a promise of peace. This time the partners to the agreement were unequal; a nation on the one hand and on the other an organization still outlawed but pledged to abandon terrorism. There were no flags. Still, there was a momentous feeling of hope. When President Clinton ended his remarks with the words "Shalom, salaam, and peace," I felt more than just the satisfaction of his having said the right words at a historic junction. And there was more to come.

To watch Shimon Peres and Yitzhak Rabin standing to Bill Clinton's right and Yassir Arafat in his traditional *keffiyeh* (but without the pistol strapped to his belt) to his left aroused feelings of uneasiness at first. How would this be played out? Would the right words be spoken in the right tone? Would they all be more intent on saving face than on saying words of grace, true words of peace? Would they abandon mundane purpose and rise to the nobility of the moment? As I looked at Rabin's stony expression, I was able to detect nothing that might foretell his actions during the next hour. I looked at Arafat's face, as always unshaven, but smiling today, and I thought of Golda Meir's first words to Anwar Sadat as he stepped off the plane at Ben Gurion airport in 1977: "What took you so long?"

"May He who maketh peace on high bring peace to all of us and all of Israel." When the ancient Hebrew words rang out over the loudspeakers on the South Lawn of the White House, they reached not only those of us who were physically present but many millions more all over the world who were watching their screens and listening to their radios. The prime minister of Israel, a former general and a man not usually given to emotional utterances, resorted to the poetry of the prayer book as he finished his remarks with the words Jews use daily at the conclusion of prayer. As I sat in the noonday sun not a hundred yards from the podium where history was being made, it was not lost on me that these words are also recited at the conclusion of the mourner's kaddish. How fitting, I thought, that the prime minister had carefully avoided the temptation of saying that what had happened in the past was now over and done with. Had he done so, he might have trivialized the suffering and the bloodshed, the turmoil and the agony of the past decades. On the contrary, he stressed that the wounds of the past could not easily heal, and that this peace had come too late for those who had died so that Israel may live. What he did express, however, was the hope and the conviction that, from this moment on, there could be a new start on the road to peace.

When Yitzhak Rabin said, "Enough. Enough of blood and tears," tears came to my eyes and to the eyes of most men and women around me, and those faces were not just the faces of Jews. When the handshake that shook the world happened, it brought all of us—Jews, Arabs, Christians, and Moslems—to our feet. Near me, a Jewish woman and an Arab woman had sat next to each other, strangers before that morning. They embraced each other and it was no empty gesture.

No one could fail to be moved by the spirit of the moment, by what it said to our generation who had never known peace in the region and who had thought it impossible even to take a first step toward it during our lifetime. While no one is naïve enough to assume that what happened on September 13, 1993, was anything more than the beginning of a journey fraught with dangers and pitfalls, it was nonetheless an occasion for joy and elation. It may have been symbolism, but our world is a world of images and symbols. Symbols can telegraph good or evil, love or hate, suspicion or trust, despair or hope. For a glorious moment, in front of the White House, there was hope. For that alone I murmured a heartfelt *Shehecheyanu,* a prayer of thanks that Providence had permitted us to come this far.

Still, there were troubling questions, relating not only to political pragmatism but to collective mind-set. Are we as human beings equipped to handle peace, to disengage from instincts that breed hatred of our fellow humans? Can we give up the temptation to cling to a rhetoric of mistrust and contempt for those outside our own circle? Can Arabs give up the inflammatory and warlike language directed at Israelis and Jews? Can Jews abandon the expressions of contempt and disdain when speaking not about specific terrorists but about Arabs in general? We keep quoting *Ve'ahavta Lere'acha Kamocha,* "Love thy neighbor as thyself," apparently ignoring the fact that the words refer not to "Jewish neighbor" but to "neighbor." Period. Can we apply this to Arabs, to "goyim" in general? I am always afraid that age-old attitudes of mistrust and fear of persecution have left some scars on the Jewish psyche of wounds that are not easily overcome. But we must overcome such attitudes, especially in Israel where Jews and Arabs live and work in such close proximity. They will either live together or die together. On September 13, 1993, former sworn enemies decided to choose life over death, healing over bloodshed, and peace over war. Would we deny them that chance and decry both the process and the aims? To be sure, Yassir Arafat had not turned overnight from an enemy into a friend, nor had Israel abandoned vigilance over its own security; both sides acted in their self-interest. But they may very well have, in the process, saved the region—perhaps our world—from an early conflagration.

Alas, as we made our way into the ceremony, there were protesters in front of the White House in Lafayette Park, already determined to say no. To my dismay, they did not wear only traditional Arab *keffiyehs*, but also prayer shawls and phylacteries. As I watched them sway in prayer, I asked myself what they thought they were praying for. Not peace, surely, but a continuation of the status quo, with its daily portion of sacrifice in human lives. I thought of Isaiah, *Shalom shalom ve'ein shalom*, "Peace, peace, they mouth, and yet there is no peace."

After the ceremony there was a lot of milling around; I talked with the First Lady and Tipper Gore; with Henry Kissinger, Jimmy Carter, and Coretta Scott King. Martin Luther King, Jr. would surely have been here had he lived, I thought—the apostle of nonviolence, of tolerance and peace, Jimmy Carter was here as a reminder that the architect of Camp David had a special reason to harbor a feeling of satisfaction. All agreed that, while there were many pitfalls in the road ahead, this was a day of great import. I talked to as many people as I could, and was especially interested in making contact with some of the Arab dignitaries. As we were filing out, I saw a few paces ahead of me one of the chief spokespeople for the Palestinians from the West Bank, the university professor Hanan Ashrawi. I wanted to get some idea from her about the shape of the immediate future she envisaged. Just as I started to introduce myself, there was a shout: "Hanan!" It was Jesse Jackson, who hugged her and led her away from me; the moment was gone.

I had been invited to a number of receptions scheduled during the afternoon and evening. Although the Israeli Embassy was the logical place to go, my first errand after leaving the White House was elsewhere. I still felt that making contact with Arabs, perhaps specifically with Palestinians, was something that needed to be done on this day. Earlier, I had already shared a hug with an old ally in the peace efforts, Casey Kasem, the well-known radio personality who is of Lebanese origin. Dr. James Zogby, the president of the Arab American Institute, had been introduced to me before the signing ceremony, and had invited me to pay a visit to their office, where a small celebration would be held. I decided that I should go, not merely as a courtesy call but to help initiate a process that was long overdue. I was received very courteously and given a taste not only of falafel, kibbeh, and baba ghanouj, but also of a new camaraderie. Next to me stood Andy Young, an old associate from the civil rights days, later United States Ambassador to the U.N. (during which time he did not endear himself to the Jewish community), and later still mayor of Atlanta. There were smiles all around; it seemed no one had stopped smiling from Bill Clinton's opening remarks on through the speeches of Peres, Rabin, and Arafat.

Afterward I went back to the White House for a briefing of Jewish and Arab leaders by Secretary of State Warren Christopher, Vice President Gore, and President Clinton. If the invitation to the morning ceremony had been a hot ticket, this was a hotter ticket yet. One hundred fifty people were admitted to this briefing, seventy-five Arabs and seventy-five Jews. Questions and comments from the floor were permitted and even encouraged. There were some sober voices who cautioned that feelings of euphoria had to be contained because peace was some way off, and the road to it could have mighty stumbling blocks impeding progress. But by and large, the glow of what we had witnessed in the morning permeated even this high-powered get-together.

An Arab-American, a physician originally from Gaza, spoke of the needs of his region in an eloquent plea. But it was heartening also to hear him say that on this historic morning he was prepared to greet all the assembled and especially the Jewish leadership with a sincere "Shalom." Symbolism again, perhaps, but his people had for so long been adversaries of a Jewish presence in the region that even a "Salaam" directed at Jews would have been highly unusual.

As I write this account, I am aware that history might well render the images of September 13, 1993, hollow and perhaps meaningless. The peace promised on that morning might have been too fragile to begin with and apt to be shattered by extremists on both sides. By now, the Middle East could well be plunged into yet another round of hostilities. But my memory of that glorious morning will not give way to any feeling that the exercise was futile and therefore dangerous. Only our peaceable instincts make us human. The snarling of hate and the brandishing of weapons is what diminishes us.

As we all sat that morning waiting for the ceremony to begin, I looked around me and realized that each of us had come to this point having walked different paths. Those assembled here had been moved by different ideologies, different agendas, different imperatives. They had come together on this day, some merely as witnesses and others as participants in the unfolding drama. Some had lived through events in the area as combatants, some others had rendered support and succor to one side or the other. I reminisced about my early years in Palestine, guarding fields on horseback and carrying a rifle that, fortunately, I never had to fire. I remembered the constant vigilance, the exercises in preparedness, the weapons smuggled under the noses of the British, weapons to defend the Jewish settlements against hostile neighbors. I remembered also the constant struggle within myself, one part of me taking pride in the fighting Jew who could at last stand up to any enemy, and the other part striving for peace, grieving for every victim and regretting all bloodshed—of friend and foe alike. In the end the man of peace always won out, and I am convinced that I emerged a better person. On that sunny morning in September I had a sense of personal fulfillment; my political agenda seemed to be several steps closer to realization. Yes, *Osseh shalom bimromav,* I said to myself—"He who maketh peace on high will bring peace to Israel." Yet I knew that such a peace could not just come from on high but would need much help and nurturing by human hands. It couldn't just be His peace, it would have to be our peace.

Epilogue

While I hope that it is far from over, it's been quite a journey. Through all the peregrinations and vicissitudes, I have learned a lot about art and about life—though, I am afraid, less about myself than I wanted to, and considerably less than I needed to. Throughout this book I have spoken at times as a union leader, at other times as a politician, a lecturer, a would-be scholar, a musician, a dialectician, or a Jewish activist. True, I am a little bit of all of these, sometimes more and sometimes less. But I am none of these as much as I am an actor. When I was a young boy I learned that on the Hanseatic building in Hamburg there was a Latin inscription, NAVI-GARE NECESSE EST, VIVERE NON EST NECESSE. It roughly translates as, "It is far more necessary to ply the sea in ships than it is to live." This mirrors my own attitude toward my profession. It is more important to act than to live—almost. I add the qualifier because I am a father and my sons' well-being is of paramount importance to me. But when I speak of everything else, I am first and last an actor. I honor my profession, whose practitioners society so often treats with derision or neglect.

In this book I have tried not to dwell much on could-have-been's and might-have-been's. Why should I? There is far too much in one's life that is positive. Even weaknesses can be turned into strengths and, even if not, can be propped up with laughter. We all make and break promises, to others and to ourselves. I am no exception. While I am happy that I managed to keep some of the important ones, I regret those I broke. Promises broken remain broken promises, despite the excuses you make to yourself. Many times, in terms of career and position, I was not where I wanted to be and was often not what I wanted to be—but I was always who I wanted to be. Have I changed much since my early days? I don't think so. People don't change; they just become more of what they were to begin with.

Having recalled here as much as I could, I do not know to what extent I was able to uncover any hidden demons and, if I did, whether I was able to exorcise them. Looking back at my years, I think about the roads traveled; about the times I tried to hide and the times I refused to hide; about the static and the moving; about what I loved and what I loathed. Then I ask myself: How much of it was truly my time and who, among all of them, were truly my people? The answer must be that, in a sense, all of it was really my time and all of them were my people. More than that, all of it was my song.

Zol zayn az ikh boy in der luft mayne shleser,
Zol zayn az mayn Got iz ingantsn nito,
In troym iz mir heler, in troym iz mir beser,
In troym iz der Himl gor bloyer vi blo.

Zol zayn az kh'vel keynmol tsum tsil nit derlangen,
Zol zayn az mayn shif vet nit kumen tsum breg,
mir geyt in deym ikh zol hobn dergangen,
Mir gety nor in gang oyf a zunikn veg.

Could be that my whole world is only confusion,
Could be what I thought was God's word isn't true,
Yet my dream is as bright as the brightest illusion,
And the sky in my dream is much bluer than blue.

Could be that I'll not see the fruit of my yearning,
Could be that I'll never be rid of my load,
What matters is not the end of the journey,
It's the journey itself on a bright sunlit road.

—I. PAPIERNIKOV (TRANSLATED BY T. BIKEL)

Postscript 2002

The events I described in the final pages of this book took place more than eight years ago. In the interim so much has changed the world and our perception of it that I feel the need to take stock once more. The events that brought together Yassir Arafat and Yitzhak Rabin at the White House and gave rise to so much hope, expectation, and promise, were also fraught with dangers and pitfalls that I recognized even then. Alas, we were not able to bask in the aura of this promise for very long. We have moved further and further away from the peace we all worked and prayed for and have become mired in a cycle of violence that has prompted even our most pacific instincts to be suppressed.

So much hope was placed in the Oslo agreement and in the peace process that was to follow. The handshake on the South Lawn was a symbolic mutual affirmation of two peoples, bitter enemies in the past, of a firm intention to take the first steps on the road to peace. But in order to make this a reality there had to be a genuine resolve on both sides, a promise to talk instead of shoot. No love fest was heralded, no suddenly discovered mutual affection; such naïve notions cannot be in the vocabulary of pragmatic national leaders. Leaders, moreover, who operate in the mercurial climate of the Middle East. There was a half-hearted smile that accompanied the handshake, a polite acknowledgment of solemn intentions; symbolism again. But symbolism can only go so far; reality must take over. As Amos Oz, the great Israeli writer and peace activist wrote: "The moment of poetry is over and now it is time for the prose."

Yet the prose of politics in the Middle East is a bitter one. Arafat is still on the scene, a leader of damaged reputation, a terrorist who failed to turn into a statesman, Arafat redux—neither peacemaker nor peacekeeper.

And Rabin is gone, his loss not Israel's alone. Murdered, and by whose hand? The myth that a Jew would not kill another Jew is no more than just that—a myth. Jews have killed Jews in the past. Within our own Zionist history, there have been such killings: the Altalena shot up by the Haganah in 1948, Chaim Arlosoroff murdered by right wing opponents in 1933. And there is the ancient history of the Jewish kingdom before the Diaspora, when Jews were fighting and killing each other even while under siege from outside. We are not quite as noble as we like to believe. For there is the constant contradiction in our claims of being *Am S'gulah* (a people of distinction) on the one hand, and *goy k'chol hagoyim* (a people like all others) on the other; claims often made in the same breath. It is time to wake up to a stark truth: we Jews also sometimes thrive on intolerance one toward the other. Murder is only the starkest, the most obscene outcropping of the rhetoric of hatred. It does not just stop with the yelling.

I must confess that, as an American Jew, I most strongly feel the burden of culpability that perforce rests on the shoulders of the American Jewish community. Baruch Goldstein, who massacred twenty-nine Arabs at prayer at a mosque in Hebron in 1994, was born and raised in America. His deed, a blot of shame on the pages of Jewish history, was perversely hailed by some in America and in Israel as the act of a redeemer— just a little short of blasphemy. The extremist hawks among American Jews are guilty not only of exporting their rabid ideologies, nurturing them in their Israeli confederates, but of financing them heavily to boot. Far too many of the intransigent elements in Israel and in the territories who carried slogans of "Death to Rabin" were bred in America or else were supported by big money raised in the U.S. Everyone professed to be shocked by the murder of Yitzhak Rabin; but even before the end of *shiva*, voices were heard justifying the murder and a media appeal was created to raise money for the assassin. *Plus ça change . . .*

After the assassination, the peace camp faced a heavy task. Predictions that the world and the Jewish community would be so shocked by the events as to be propelled to greater support for the peace process turned out to be wrong. Serious analysts warned then that one would have to continue not only to deal with former enemies but with new foes as well, foes of peace from within. That such foes could not all be contained— or detained—is obvious. One might try to draw them into the process, an uncertain task. The opponents of peace on the right, extremists claiming to be religious, would have to be reminded that long before you are permitted to reach for the voice of God, you must heed the voices of man. An argument they would be unwilling to accept from learned rabbis, much less from secular leftist sinners.

At this juncture, "Peace Now" has become a slogan that has all but lost its currency. "Maybe Later" is the most that many beleaguered Israelis would concede, if at all. The climate of constant threat, hostility and violence has created a national impatience in Israel, making it very hard to defuse anger or debunk stereotypes. The accusation hurled at the peace camp from within is plainly unjust with its implication of treasonous leanings. Regrettably, the term "loyal opposition" has lost its meaning since it seems that all opposition is deemed to be disloyal. The truth is that Peace Now, Meretz, and others of the peace camp, have never been pro-Palestinian; they are pro-peace. That assumes, of course, that one would have to sit down and talk to enemies directly, not with or through third parties. This one must do, not because one loves the enemy but because there is no other alternative—other than accepting a permanent state of belligerence or opting for out-and-out war. No people can or should have to live this way.

The situation in the Arab-Palestinian camp is far, far worse than what continues to be described in the short television sound bites the West is offered. There is an aura of hopelessness, of thwarted expectations, of mistrust in the corrupt Palestinian leadership. In any other society that disaffection would have been directed against its own leaders. Palestinians were instead offered a better target by Arafat and his colleagues, one that would deflect the anger from himself and toward the Jews across the green line.

The effect of Arafat's missteps was far-reaching and disastrous. By allowing, indeed encouraging, the *intifada* to take place he dealt a severe blow to the peace camp and its supporters not only in Israel and America but among his own people as well. He also, perhaps intentionally, made possible the election of not one but two right-wing prime ministers in Israel, first Bibi Netanyahu, and later Ariel Sharon. Arafat's doing; no one else's. This after having rejected the most far-reaching peace offer by Ehud Barak and thus dooming any immediate chance of realizing the Palestinians' dream of statehood and, in the process, putting an end to Barak's prospects for reelection as well.

Arafat's miscalculations about his enemies were pitifully naïve. He either thought that the terror would provoke so massive a reaction that the international community would intervene, or that it would break the resolve of the Jews, demoralize them so that they would make peace on almost any terms. Jewish history, had he bothered to learn it, might have taught him something about the Jewish psyche. Throughout the centuries we have accepted the fact that we would be beset by enemies against whom we were powerless. One might still acknowledge the historical fact that the world resorts to Jew-hating at any juncture, with or without provocation. Being hated and often destroyed might have been our fate in the past, but it is a destiny now no longer inevitable. Arafat should have noticed not only Israel's superior hardware but its resolve not be cowed by hatred, threats, stones, and guns. (As I write these words I add a mental caveat to myself: We must never assume that justice is on the side of the strong. All too often with strength comes arrogance.)

For us, there was the shocking realization that Arafat not only turned out to be no partner for peace but that he had never intended to be such a partner in the first place. Oslo and the handshake gave him the cachet of peacemaker; it also gave him half of a Nobel Peace Prize which, if he had any sense of shame, he would return. In truth, Oslo was for him nothing more than an opportunity to obfuscate and spin wheels. In all the summit meetings he appeared to be pacific, conciliatory, and seemingly accommodating, yet he withdrew as soon as real concessions were required. Because of his push-me-pull-you tactics, the pursuit of the peace process was fitful when it should have been steady and stagnant where it should have been propulsive. He never meant for the Oslo agreements to be implemented and his *intifada* made certain that Israeli leaders were put in place who were as opposed to Oslo as he and helped move the process further and further away from a resolution.

What went wrong and where did it go wrong? In the Oslo agreements both Israel and the Palestinians signed a mutual agreement that obligated the parties to two major undertakings: The Palestinians were to stop every act of violence and terror immediately; the Israelis, for their part, undertook to gradually dismantle the mechanisms of the occupation in the West Bank and the Gaza Strip. (One notes the difference between "immediately" and "gradually.") In reality, of course, neither side kept the bargain. But for brief lulls, acts of terror not only did not stop but increased and Israel not only did not dismantle settlements in the Territories, they expanded them.

Regrettably, Israel is making a colossal mistake by continuing to support the settlement enterprise. The settlements, perhaps the single most important obstacle to peace, undermine Israeli security and impede progress toward peace. If there are ultimately to be two separate and sovereign states, then the settlements make all but impossible the completion of Israel's separation from the Palestinians, something that is critical for Israel's future as a Jewish democratic state.

No one in the Israeli government is entertaining the notion that the settlements should stay in place and be subject to Palestinian sovereignty, either before or after a Palestinian state is established. They are meant to be permanent Israeli enclaves, facts in place under sole Israeli control and protection. To that end, an entire Palestinian population has in effect been sealed into restricted areas, confined by a network of roads meant for settler use only. The roads were very carefully planned; two hundred thousand Jews have freedom of movement while three million Palestinians are locked into discontiguous areas, Bantustans as it were. The frustration, while no excuse for violence, is understandable.

Why is Israel so intent on keeping the settlements in place, and upon whose insistence? The ultra-orthodox elements within Israel, very powerful, even though they are in the minority, are the single most vociferous defenders of keeping the settlements in place. No wonder, since many of the settlements are populated by ultra right wing *haredim* (ultra-orthodox Jews, literally God-fearers). In this area, as in so many others in Israeli society, the *haredim* are the obstacles to what the majority of Israelis desire: to live in a Jewish state, a secular democracy without coercion of anyone by anyone.

What happened to the Zionist dream, Theodore Herzl's dream of a democratic Jewish State, the vision he proclaimed at the First Zionist Congress in Basel in 1897? In August of 1997 the centennial of this congress was celebrated in the very same hall in Basel and I was present as part of the U.S. delegation. Many thoughts ran through my head during that memorial meeting and later that year at the Zionist Congress in Jerusalem that I also attended as a delegate. I felt that no examination of "whither the Zionist Movement" could be undertaken with any measure of honesty without an appraisal of the changes time had imposed upon Israel, on the world Jewish community, and on the relation between the two. It would be foolhardy to cling to structures and formulations dating back to the Balfour Declaration, or to the Zionism at the creation of the State of Israel. No movement can afford to be caught in a time warp and exist in a state of suspended animation. While all could agree that the Zionist ideal is alive and well, there is serious doubt whether the Zionist movement can be said to be an ongoing proposition, fragmented as its components are in ideology and in practice.

At the World Zionist Congress in Jerusalem there was a strong temptation by the delegates to emerge with a declaration of unity; I argued against giving in to such temptations. It was my assertion that our strength lies not in unity but in diversity. Historically in Jewish history, in one way or another, there has always been disunity, friction between scholars, strife between Pharisees and Sadducees, or between *Chassidim* and *Misnagdim*. What kept us alive was the sharp discussion, mind pitted against mind, and man wrestling with God.

Unity may be something to be desired, to be striven for, but it cannot be willed into being by mere declarations. For unity to come about there must be respect for differing viewpoints, different modes of living, differing strains of thought. As a human being, a Jew and a lifelong Zionist I deplore disharmony and its manifestations. But respect is a two-way street and only when given, one will return respect for respect, tolerance for tolerance, acceptance for acceptance. In the absence of a clear and honest resolve on everyone's part to respect one another's beliefs, one should not waste time with declarations that are hypocritical and a sham.

I firmly believe that Jewish life, indeed any communal life, can only be organized according to democratic principles. The very antithesis to democracy is autocracy, or worse—theocracy. Today the world Jewish community is on dangerous ground, with one faction seeking to dictate to all others and admitting of no definition but its own. It shames all those who have toiled in the service of the Jewish people and of the Zionist ideal, even laid down their lives for it, without the need for any declaration other than "I am a Jew."

It is no secret that throughout the Diaspora—possibly no less so than in Israel itself—there is a crisis of faith in the course the Zionist movement has taken. The movement is weakened and is being blamed—justly or unjustly—for any actions the government of Israel makes that raise doubts about its wisdom, its probity and its determination to build upon the gains of its predecessors. Whenever the stability of the area is threatened either by the actions of the government, or by its failure to act, there is a discernible flight from the ranks of those who but yesterday declared themselves as Zionist supporters.

That feeling of Zionist malaise is intensified by the perception that certain factions are pushing for a religious de-legitimization of otherwise clearly committed Jews. When this is done with governmental acquiescence, if not downright support, the split becomes intolerable. We are either partners or we are not. If indeed we are, then it must be a partnership between fully recognized Jews in fact as well as in law. Let no religious divisions keep Jews apart. And who is to say that totally secular, nonreligious Jews have less of an attachment to their identity than those who only define themselves religiously? What of the legitimacy of culture and language, Hebrew, Yiddish, Ladino, or whatever other language in which Jewish creativity can be expressed?

In my closing remarks to the Zionist Congress I made a plea on behalf of all those Jews who had turned their backs on Israel and Zionism in frustration and disenchantment. I said: "Listen to their voices, listen to them carefully; confront their anger, their resentment and their feeling of having to give up on the dream. They do not do so lightly; they grieve over it. Listen to them, if not for their sake then for ours.

"I believe the Zionist movement can be rescued but only if we are honest with ourselves. In our predicament only one exhortation makes sense, if we apply it to everything we do: TZEDEK, TZEDEK TIRDOF. Justice, justice shalt thou pursue."

Now the *haredim* are not only dictating to the rest of the Jewish community who should or should not be legitimized as a Jew but they are also playing territorial games. When the religious wield not only spiritual but also temporal power, then we are all endangered. (Remembering the history of Europe, one is ever mindful of the oppression that occurred when popes were heads of state as well as heads of the church.) The specter of rabbis controlling votes in the Knesset while other groups of rabbis are brandishing guns in the territories fills me with great apprehension

On the other hand, the obstacles put in the path of peace by the Arabs are no less daunting and their stance is demographically entirely indefensible. That obstacle is the "right of return" to Israel proper of pre-'48 Arab residents demanded by Arafat. He must be well aware that, if implemented, this would mean the end to Israel as a democratic state with a Jewish majority. Instead, Israel would become home to two peoples locked in perpetual conflict, with Israel being forced to decide either to grant full citizenship rights to a people that do not support a Zionist state or to create a two-tier, undemocratic apartheid system. Neither of these alternatives is an acceptable one.

Whichever way you look at it, the *intifada* finds its source among clerics and teachers. Where but in the teachings of the *imams,* the *mullahs* do we find the promise of rewards in paradise for boys who would strap explosives to their bodies and set out to kill dozens of innocent youngsters out for an evening or of women shopping in a mall? What of the schoolbooks that teach hatred of nonbelievers (read: Jews), what of the song young Arabs are taught *"Falasteen biladna wal yahood kilabna"* (Palestine is our land and the Jews are our dogs)? I know of no comparable lyrics sung about Arabs in Hebrew.

We keep insisting that our quarrel is not with Islam. Indeed, we are right; history tells us that Jews found a safe haven in Muslim countries when the Catholic Church persecuted them, forced them to abjure their faith and then burned them at the stake anyway. But with the establishment of the State of Israel there is no longer any comfortable existence for Jews in Arab lands. Jews are outcasts, pariahs, considered enemies by countries they and their ancestors have called home for centuries. Nowadays the Church has come to terms with Jews and with some of their history as it dealt with Jew-hatred. Perhaps now it is Islam's turn to direct its ire against the Jews. Arafat is an opportunist, not much of a Muslim himself, yet he is not loath to hitch his wagon to Islamic extremists. There are others also who have little, if any, religious motivation for their activism, like Edward Said or Hanan Ashrawi. Yet they, too, seem to have no compunction about supporting a religious holy war.

The world paid attention to Arafat's public pronouncements before and during summits because they appeared reasonable. But that was when he spoke in English; the press rarely took note of the speeches he made hours later in Arabic for home consumption. His insistence upon calling terrorists "martyrs," attending their funerals and praising their "heroism" instead of condemning their acts and seeking out accomplices, these were not the acts of a responsible leader. They were the incitements of a rogue, a rabble-rouser, a demagogue. What was one to make of a speech he gave in Ramallah calling for "millions of martyrs" to march on Jerusalem, saying, "Please God, give me the honor of being one of holy Jerusalem's martyrs"? No wonder that moderate Palestinians—and they do exist—never dared to come out of the woodwork.

Yet the answer—if there is an answer—must lie with the moderates, those few courageous voices who speak out publicly about the immorality of the course pursued by the *intifada* and all the other acts of terror committed in the name of an Islamic "holy war." More important, it must rest on those Muslim clerics who told us that the taking of innocent lives is against the teachings of the Koran and that the heavenly reward promised for mass murder is political trickery. Again, they say these things to us in English; that is not good enough. They must say it to their own people in Arabic. And the American government must bring all its influence to bear on the Palestinians' educational system to insist that hate teaching be outlawed and schoolbooks purged of literature that incites Arab children against their neighbors.

I know, there may be an outcry against these suggestions by some of my civil libertarian friends. To them I will argue that American standards of freedom of expression do not apply in lands that have not arrived at any minimal modes of democratic behavior. Even more civilized societies have been rethinking the notion that hate speech is covered by statutory freedoms. If Germany can outlaw all expressions of racism, anti-Semitism and Nazism, so can and should the Arab world.

And then came the horror of September 11, turning all our lives upside down. No matter where you were—I was in Los Angeles—the atrocity hit (you) squarely and surely just as the criminals had intended. To bear this alone was all but impossible; I had to reach out to friends. I went to services several times, not just the obligatory High Holiday attendance. That was helpful; it was possible to stand next to a friend at one side and a stranger on the other and be unafraid and unashamed to shed tears.

At services on Rosh Hashanah, Rabbi David Wolpe made some very poignant and moving points. He said that we should not stop the self-examination because of what happened. The magnitude of others' sins does not wipe out one's own. We did not deserve this cruelty; our sins are sins of imperfection, not of evil. What *they* did to us was evil. For centuries we were powerless but to be powerless is not moral, it is merely to be powerless. Now we no longer are, and power requires a great guarding of the soul. Indifference is the epitome of evil, as Elie Wiesel wrote. But in fighting what we despise we must not in return become what we despise. In fighting the monstrosity we must make sure that we guard against the temptation to think and act like our enemies. A hard task.

Being the targets of atrocity is not new for us Jews, we could teach a lesson in victimhood. Of course, today Israel is not only victim but also in a position to punish terrorism and its supporters. Now at last perhaps, one thought, journalists and diplomats will stop describing acts of terror and acts of punishing terror as morally equivalent. The Bush administration that had in the past criticized Israel was now taking precisely the same actions against terrorists—and talking the same talk—with the might of the United States behind it. Of course, power means moral choice every time.

In a tape at the Holocaust Memorial Museum in Washington, a survivor tells of a man who was praying in the camp. When he asked him why he was praying he said that he was thanking God. Then this survivor was stunned and asked him what there was to thank God for in this hell. And the man replied, "I am thanking God that he did not make me like them."

The question is: "What is owed to the victims?" Subsumed under that question are two more issues: "What we owe to the dead" and "What we owe to the living." A friend once told me that one should not mistake pain for virtue. I keep thinking of that each time the pain threatens to overwhelm and push aside attempts at overcoming, enduring, continuing. There are people who seem to want everything to stop at the point of pain, possibly think it blasphemous to find song once again, joy once again. To them I have to say that we are obligated, even commanded, to resume our lives. Not as though nothing had happened, but precisely because of what happened. To do otherwise would give the barbarians yet another victory.

At services I decided to read a poem from the bimah, a poem W. H. Auden wrote in response to Germany's invasion of Poland. Entitled "September 1, 1939," it seemed uncannily prescient. Thinking of the horrendous images of the World Trade Center coming down, how strange it was to read lines like "Where blind skyscrapers use / Their full height to proclaim / The strength of Collective Man," and "Into the ethical life / The dense commuters come." The poem, which is set in Manhattan, speaks symbolically of "The unmentionable odour of death / Offend[ing] the September night." It even closes with a candlelight vigil—so much like the vigils we went on following the catastrophe—and reads "May I . . . / Beleaguered by the same / Negation and despair, / Show an affirming flame." What comfort there is in poetry!

But we have moved much beyond poetry since that fateful day in September 2001. There is a full-scale war on terror, a war prosecuted by a new administration and a new president. Bill Clinton is gone. He was a fine president, effective, articulate, eloquent—a leader capable of rising to great heights. He may have been a flawed husband; in any other society but ours with its hypocritical pretensions that would have been his wife's concern, not the nation's. President Bush, his successor, put in the White House after an election of dubious legitimacy would, but for the war, be much discredited in the eyes of most Americans. It is not only that George W. Bush, when making unscripted remarks, drives those of us who love the English language to a frenzy of despair. That may be a minor matter compared to his ability to pursue unchecked a domestic and fiscal agenda incredibly skewed toward big business, specifically oil interests. To be able to mortgage Social Security and Medicare for older Americans is no small matter. But a wartime leader has carte blanche and seems free to get away with measures that would be anathema to the people at any other time.

Much has been written about the pursuit of the war on terrorism. I will only add to it by reiterating a theme I raised earlier with respect to the Palestinians. This is not only a military struggle; it is wrestling for the minds of millions of Muslims around the globe. We feebly counter their immense superstitions and their belief in the "holy war" against the unbelievers. First it was mainly directed against the Jews; now it is all of the Western world, chiefly America. We say that our fight is not against Islam and we may believe it. But it is not the same the other way around. Even "moderates" in the Muslim world have come to believe that it is indeed Islam against America and the West. For months after the attack, whole communities still did not believe that the assault of September 11 was the work of Arab terrorists but insisted that it was engineered by Israelis. Entire high schools in Pakistan and elsewhere asserted the firm belief, when questioned, that four thousand Jews were advised not to show up for work in the World Trade Center on September 11. Do we counter this by editorials in the *New York Times*? We are supremely arrogant by assuming that we can make our case on the airwaves and in print in English and the Muslim world will listen. What Arafat, Osama, and radical Muslim clerics say to the Islamic world is what incites them against us. When will we, in turn, start making our case in Arabic, in Farsi, in Urdu, and in the other languages spoken in Muslim countries? More important, when will the Muslim clerics who spoke *bism'illah*—in the name of Allah—at the memorial meetings mourning the murderous assault do so to their own people in their own language?

Our world, our way of life in America, will no longer be what it was. Our assumption that we are invulnerable, protected by two oceans and by modern technology, has been shattered. We were wrong to have been complacent and for caring little about the turmoil elsewhere. Then it hit us where we lived and we experience the fear others have always known. We were wrong to be complacent but we did not deserve this. I count on the resilience of the American people but I wonder if we will be able to develop the mechanism to deal with our new fears. The people of Anatevka in *Fiddler on the Roof* knew how to survive; they had their faith and their structured lives were informed by their traditions. But most of us in America do not live by tradition. Finding a way to live in the post-9/11 world is not a matter of pop psychology, sound bites, quick fixes, and short monosyllabic bursts. Sentient and intelligent human beings need to do better than quick fixes.

We will find a way because we must. We may never get back the world we had before September 11, but, in the words of the song, we will "try to remember the kind of September when life was slow and oh so mellow." To suffer the loss of innocence is something we may have to bear; to lose the memory of it would be far worse still.

Index

Abbott, Tom, 326
Abduction from the Seraglio, The (opera), 301
Ackerman, Bettye, 413
Actor Prepares, The, 25
Adler, Jacob, 324
Adler, Larry, 62, 84, 85
Adler, Luther, 324, 326
African Queen, The (film), 102, 104, 105, 114, 115, 123
Agnew, Spiro, 390
Agutter, Jenny, 312
Albert, Carl, 280, 286
Alda, Alan, 314
Aleichem, Sholem, 26, 116, 321, 322
Alexander of Yugoslavia, Prince, 108
All Quiet on the Western Front (film), 121
Allen, Woody, 178, 379
Amfiteatrof, Daniele, 200
Amin, Idi, 367
Anderson, Jean, 128
Andrews, Harry, 303
Angeli, Pier, 147
Angelou, Maya, 163
Angry Hills, The (film), 194, 195
Anouilh, Jean, 41, 42, 141
Anthony, Joe, 141, 143
Antigone (play), 41, 42
Antony and Cleopatra (play), 58
Arafat, Yassir, 423, 425
Ardèle (play), 41
Ariadne auf Naxos (opera), 301
Arkin, Alan, 165, 306, 307, 308
Arnaud, Yvonne, 131
Asch, Moses, 164
Asherson, Renee, 57
Ashrawi, Hanan, 425
Atkinson, Brooks, 139, 146
Attenborough, Richard, 120

Audley, Maxine, 63
Auntie Mame (film), 199

Bacall, Lauren, 114
Baez, Joan, 166, 180, 181, 269, 270, 272
Baker, Ella, 254
Baker, James, 371, 401
Baker, Stanley, 194, 262, 291, 303, 305
Bakstansky, Levy, 98
Ballou, Smokey, 331
Baritz, Loren, 281
Barnes, Sir Kenneth, 37-38, 40, 42
Barrault, Jean-Louis, 82
Barrie, Barbara, 380
Barry, Margaret, 89, 168
Barry, Marion, 254
Beatles, 357
Beatty, Warren, 278
Becker, Bruce, 132
Begin, Menachem, 290
Belafonte, Harry, 166, 178, 325
Belasco, Leon, 307
Bellamy, Ralph, 223
Ben Gurion, David, 47, 48, 417, 423
Ben Hur (film), 201
Bennahum, Midge, 79
Bennahum, Theo, 79
Benny Goodman Story, The (film), 378
Benny, Jack, 114, 378
Benois, Alexandre, 97
Benois, Nadia, 97
Ben-Yossef, Avraham, 30, 31
Berger, Helmut, 367
Berle, Milton, 378
Berlin, Irving, 360
Bernardi, Herschel, 324
Bernstein, Felicia, 143
Bernstein, Jay, 306

Bernstein, Leonard, 136, 141, 143, 253
Bernstein, Shirley, 150
Beryozka Ballet (folk troupe), 175
Betrayed (film), 117
Bettauer, Hugo, 4
Bibb, Leon, 154, 179
Bickel, Shlomo, 332
Bickell, Larry, 334
Biddle, Livingston, 229, 395, 397, 399, 401
Big Country, The (film), 199
Big Knife, The (play), 85
Biggest Thief in Town, The (play), 86
Bikel, Danny, 290, 298, 310, 362
Bikel, Davide, 77, 78, 80
Bikel, Joseph, 410
Bikel, Ofra, 131, 144, 150
Bikel, Reb Shimon, 331, 332, 334, 354
Bikel, Rita, 230, 231, 308-309, 327, 414
Bikel, Robert Simon, 290, 309
Blondell, Joan, 145, 146
Bloomgarden, Kermit, 141
Blue Angel, The (film), 200, 314
Bock, Jerry, 317, 322, 341
Bogarde, Dirk, 123
Bogart, Humphrey, 102-103, 104, 105, 113, 114
Boguslav, Ray, 154
Bond, Gordon, 121
Bond, Julian, 255
Boucher, Pierre, 245
Boutsikaris, Dennis, 312
Boyd, Stephen, 201
Boyer, Charles, 186, 189, 190
Brademas, John, 228
Braden, Bernard, 57, 59, 65
Brand, Oscar, 108, 154, 155, 158, 166, 171, 180
Brando, Marlon, 64
Brassens, Georges, 82
Braun, Otto, 10, 54
Brecht, Bertolt, 270
Brecht on Brecht (play), 315, 316
Brel, Jacques, 299, 416
Brenner, Maurice, 330, 331
Brice, Fanny, 378
Brickman, Marshall, 166
Bridge of San Luis Rey, The (TV movie), 185
Brill, Marty, 313
Britt, Mai, 200, 201, 314
Bromberg, Conrad, 87-88
Bromberg, J. Edward, 85, 86-88
Bronson, Jim, 326
Brook, Peter, 71
Brooks, Mel, 379
Brown, Arvin, 391

Bruce, Lenny, 163
Brustein, Robert, 391
Brynner, Yul, 91
Buckley, William F., 284
Bujold, Genevieve, 185
Bullock, Beattie, 63, 64
Burns, George, 378
Burton, Philip, 282

Cabaret (play), 208
Caesar and Cleopatra (play), 58
Café Crown (play), 313
Call, Rita. *See* Bikel, Rita
Cambridge, Godfrey, 367
Cameron, Isla, 107, 170
Campanella, Joe, 139
Čapek, Karel, 34, 35
Captain's Paradise (film), 131
Carawan, Guy, 258
Cardin, Shoshana, 422
Carey, Bob, 166
Carmichael, Stokely, 259, 262
Carney, Art, 145
Caron, Leslie, 145
Carson, Johnny, 117
Carter, Jimmy, 228, 394, 400, 425
Casals, Pablo, 55, 235
Caspi (wardrobe master), 26
Cast a Giant Shadow (film), 379
Cat on a Hot Tin Roof (film), 199
Cathay, Irving, 210
Chance Meeting (film), 119
Chancellor, John, 282
Chayefsky, Paddy, 376, 379
Chekhov, Anton, 94
Chin Yu, 88, 89
Christopher, Warren, 426
Church, Bethene, 278
Church, Frank, 278
Citizen of the World (play), 50
Ciulei, Liviu, 317, 318
Clancy Brothers, 154, 155
Clark, John, 378
Cleve, Edie van, 140
Cliburn, Van, 396
Clifton, Bill, 180
Clinton, Bill, 422, 423, 426
Cobb, Lee J., 323, 380
Cohan, George M., 223-224
Cohen, Herb, 161, 310, 311
Cohen on the Telephone (film), 379
Cohen, William, 251
Cohn, Harry, 378
Cohn, Roy, 83
Colditz Story, The (film), 120
Colleano, Bonar, 57, 64
Collins, Jackie, 194

Collins, Joan, 294, 295
Collins, Judy, 178, 179, 183
Come Blow Your Horn (film), 379, 380
Communal Flat, The (film), 311
Compulsion (film), 378-379
Conklin, Alice, 180, 254
Connor, "Bull," 255
Conrad, Michael, 144
Cook, Eddie, 132, 135
Cooper, Clarence, 166, 180
Coopersmith, Esther, 416
Coors, William, 400
Coriolanus (play), 71
Cornell, Katharine, 186
Corri, Adrienne, 128
Crisis in the Kremlin (film), 312
Crisp, Donald, 204
Croce, Jim, 413, 414
Cry the Beloved Country (film), 88
Cukor, George, 302, 303
Curtis, Tony, 197, 198, 199, 375

Dajou, Rico, 126, 127
Daley, Richard, 280, 282, 283, 284, 285,
    287
Dana, Barbara, 307
Dark Tower (film), 312
Darker Than Amber (film), 309
Darling, Eric, 180
Dashiel, Bud, 163
Davenport, Nigel, 303
David and Bathsheba (film), 378
Davies, Brian, 215
Davis, Betty Ann, 65
Day to Remember, A (film), 125
Dayan, Yael, 373
Dear Charles (play), 131, 132
Decroux, Étienne, 82
Defiant Ones, The (film), 197, 218, 374
de Koven, Roger, 144
Delahalle, France, 247
del Pozzo, Teresa, 254
Demjanjuk, John, 420
DeSapio, Carmine, 250
Desperate Moment (film), 123
Diary of Anne Frank, The, 13
Dickinson, J. C., 397, 398
Dietrich, Marlene, 200, 201, 314
Dimitrievich, Sonia, 90
Dimitrievich, Valya, 91
Directions '61 (TV show), 172, 173
Divided Heart, The (film), 120, 125, 126
d'Lugoff, Art, 175
Dmytryk, Edward, 169, 200, 314
Dog of Flanders, The (film), 204, 308
Donahue, Vincent, 209
Dorn, Michael, 297

Douglas, Kirk, 379
Douglas, Nathan. *See* Young, Nedrick
Draper, Ruth, 94
Dreyfuss, Richard, 367
Dullea, Keir, 188
Dunham, Vera, 277
Durning, Charles, 315
Dybbuk, The (TV movie), 185
Dylan, Bob, 178, 180, 258, 268, 269, 272

Eagle, S. P. *See* Spiegel, Sam
Eban, Abba, 120, 419, 422
Eddie Cantor Story, The (film), 378
Edmondson, Travis, 163
Eisenpreis, Alfred, 6
Elizabeth, Queen of England, 111, 112
Ellington, Duke, 314
Elliott, Jack, 157
Elyan, Marina, 344
Emerson, Faye, 210
Emrich, Duncan (doctor), 167
Endfield, Cy, 303, 305
Enemy Below, The (film), 192
Ennis, Seamus, 107, 182
Enter Laughing (film), 379, 380
Equalizer, The (TV series), 41
Evans, Edith, 72
Evans, Maurice, 185
Evita (play), 208
Exodus (film), 379

Falk, Peter, 189
Fariña, Mimi, 183, 269
Fariña, Richard, 183, 269
Feiffer, Jules, 278
Fein, Leonard, 364
Felious, Odetta, 160, 161, 171
Ferrer, Joe, 117
Ferrer, Mel, 147, 199
Fiddler on the Roof (play), 169, 215, 231,
    273-274, 308, 317, 322-331, 338-
    341, 351
Field, Ron, 313
Fighting Is No Business (film), 379
Finkel, Elliot, 299
Finkel, Fyvush, 330
Finkelstein, Louis (doctor), 172, 173
Fiorello! (play), 322
Fleta, Ignacio, 148
Ford, Paul, 307
Foreman, James, 254, 259
Forester, C. S., 103, 104
Forsythe, John, 295
Franciosa, Anthony, 149
Frank, Anne, 409
Franks, Dobbs, 316
Fräulein (film), 199

Freedom Singers (musical group), 270
Friedgut, Ted, 342
Friedland, Tsvi, 23
Friedman, Martin, 397
Front Page, The (film), 121
Funny Girl (film), 379

Gable, Clark, 117, 118, 186, 216
Gabor, Zsa Zsa, 117
Galbraith, Kenneth, 286
Galitzine, Emmanuel, 74, 76, 77, 90, 108
Galitzine, George, 74, 75, 76, 119, 148
Galitzine, Nicholas, 74
Gandhi, Mahatma, 253
Gardner, Ava, 216
Gelles, Aharon, 145
Gentlemen's Agreement (film), 378
George VI, King of England, 37, 40
Giaimo, Robert, 228
Gibson, Bob, 183
Gibson, Judy, 316
Gielgud, Sir John, 71
Gierasch, Stefan, 208
Gigi (film), 199
Gihon, Israel. See Braun, Otto
Gilbert, Ronnie, 164, 180
Gilford, Madeleine, 324
Gill, Geula, 158
Gish, Lillian, 223
Glubb, John, 273
Glücksmann, Klaus, 33
Goldfaden, Abraham, 322
Goldner, Charles, 131
Goldoni, Carlo, 31
Goldstein, Kenneth (doctor), 168
Goldwyn, Sam, 378
Golmann, Stephane, 81
Goodbye Columbus (film), 379, 381
Gooding, Cynthia, 154, 158
Goodman, Andy, 261
Gorbachev, Mikhail, 312, 350, 370, 371
Gorbachev, Raisa, 350
Gorby, Sarah, 90
Gordon, Colin, 95
Gore, Al, 282, 407, 426
Gore, Tipper, 425
Gorrin, Michael, 137, 208
Gottlieb, Lou, 163
Goulesco, Lida, 90
Graham, Bob, 300
Grant, Gary, 197
Granville, Freddie, 61, 135
Grauer, Rhoda, 398
Graumann, Walter, 293
Gray, Hanna, 400
Greco, Juliette, 82
Greenblatt, Aliza, 158

Greenhill, Manny, 268
Greenspun, Hank, 274
Gregory, Dick, 285
Grier, Roosevelt, 278
Griffiths, Corinne, 189
Grimes, Tammy, 143
Grody, Don, 237
Gross, H. R., 391
Grossman, Albert, 160, 176, 258, 271
Grunbaum, Tuvia (Herbert), 34
Guinness, Alec, 51, 131
Guthrie, Arlo, 158, 183
Guthrie, Woody, 157, 167, 270
Guttman, Karl, 35

Hague, Albert, 313
Haig, Alexander, 295
Hall, Peter, 145
Halliday, Richard, 212, 213
Hamilton, Gloria, 209
Hamlet (play), 51
Hammerstein, Oscar, 205, 209, 210
Hanks, Nancy, 394, 397
Hapsburg, Otto von, 336
Harnick, Sheldon, 317, 322, 341
Harper, Valerie, 307
Harris, Julie, 141, 144
Hart, Moss, 56, 320
Harvey, Bill, 154
Harvey, Ken, 217
Hassilev, Alex, 163, 174, 307
Hathaway, Henry, 201
Hawes, Bess Lomax, 398
Hayden, Jeff, 147
Hayes, Helen, 367
Hays, Lee, 164, 173, 174, 306
Hayward, Leland, 205, 213, 217
Hayward, Susan, 201
Helfman, Max, 146, 147
Heller, Binem, 407
Hellerman, Fred, 164, 174
Hellman, Lillian, 141, 142, 143, 144, 341
Helms, Jesse, 228, 391
Henske, Judy, 179
Hepburn, Audrey, 147, 302
Hepburn, Katharine, 102-103, 104, 113, 114, 115, 302
Herzl, Theodor, 14
Herzog, Chaim, 408
Hester, Carolyn, 183
Heston, Charlton, 201, 400, 413, 414
Hillel and Aviva (Israeli duo), 62
Hitler, Adolf, 68
Hodsoll, Frank, 401
Holzman, Jac, 154, 163, 164, 178, 230
Home, William Douglas, 122
Hooker, John Lee, 179

Hopkin, Mary, 175
Hopper, Hedda, 79
House, Sam, 210
Huber, Gusti, 187
Hughes, Harold (governor of Iowa), 283
Hughes, Howard, 276, 277
Humphrey, Hubert, 195, 229, 263, 268, 279, 283, 284, 287
Hunted (teleplay), 191
Hurt, John, 183
Hussein, King of Jordan, 273
Huston, John, 102, 104, 105, 116, 117
Hyde-White, Wilfred, 58
Hyland, Frances, 65

I Can Get It for You Wholesale (film), 379
Ichilov, Ofra. *See* Bikel, Ofra
I Do! I Do! (play), 317
I Want to Live! (film), 201
Insect Play, The (play), 34, 35
Inspector General, The (play), 318
Irving, Ben, 213, 214, 299
Irving, Henry, 240
Irving, Jonathan, 299
It's Hard to Be a Jew (play), 116
Ivanov, George, 90
Ives, Burl, 170, 171, 199

Jacobi, Lou, 380
Jacobowsky and the Colonel (play), 35
Jacques Brel Is Alive and Well and Living in Paris (play), 316
Jaffe, Sam, 413
Jagger, Mick, 311
Jannings, Emil, 314
Javits, Jacob, 229, 230, 251
Jessel, George, 378
Jewison, Norman, 306
Johns, Glynis, 85
Johnson, Arte, 114
Johnson, Lyndon B., 227, 228, 276, 279, 282
Jolson, Al, 378
Jourdan, Louis, 135, 138
Julia (film), 375
Julius Caesar (TV movie), 185
Jurgens, Curt, 192, 193, 200, 314
Justin, John, 122

Kagan, Michael, 159
Kahane, Meir, 375
Kalina, Arnold, 61, 144, 410
Kallen, Horace, 384
Kallis, Stan, 189
Kanin, Garson, 222, 389
Kapuuo, Clemens, 264, 265, 266
Karlin, Miriam, 99

Karloff, Boris, 141, 144
Kasem, Casey, 425
Kassal, Bentley, 251
Kasznar, Kurt, 208
Katselas, Milton, 144
Kauffman, Stanley, 315
Kaufman, George, 56
Käutner, Helmut, 194
Kazan, Elia, 169
Kazan, Lainie, 317, 380
Kempton, Murray, 282
Kennedy, Edward (Ted), 229, 287
Kennedy, John F., 213, 227, 228, 230, 235, 250, 268
Kennedy, Robert, 274-275, 277, 278, 287
Kent, Duchess of, 52, 109, 111
Kerr, John, 147
Kerr, Walter, 144, 211
Kessel, Joseph, 91
Khan, Sadruddin Aga (Prince), 143
Kidnappers, The (film), 128, 129
King, Alan, 376
King, Coretta Scott, 425
King, Martin Luther, Jr., 253, 255, 262, 272, 274-275, 287, 425
King of Lampedusa, The (play), 28
Kingston Trio, 166, 178
Kirkland, Lane, 229
Kiss of the Spider Woman (play), 208
Kissinger, Henry, 295, 296, 425
Klein, Gerschon, 34
Klemperer, Werner, 235
Kline, Kevin, 319
Knüpfer, Felix, 69, 70
Koch, Edward I., 250
Koenig, Martin, 159
Kollek, Teddy, 360
Korda, Sir Alexander, 88
Koster, Henry, 200
Kotto, Yaphet, 367
Kraft, Hy, 313
Kramer, Stanley, 197, 198
Krents, Milton, 172
Krimkowitz, Harry, 417
Krupp, Vera, 276
Krupska, Dania, 316
Kutako, Hosea, 264, 265
Kvaran, Aivar, 133

La Belle Hélène (opera), 31
La Gazza Ladra (opera), 300
La Guardia, Fiorello, 156
L.A. Law (TV show), 1-2, 25
Ladd, David, 204
Lamb, Charles, 365
Lampell, Millard, 89, 170
Lancet, Batya, 30, 31

Lansbury, Angela, 293
Lansing, Sherry, 296
Lark, The (play), 141, 143, 144, 145
Lasky, Jesse, 378
Lawrence, Carol, 293
Lawrence, Jacob, 395
Layton, Joe, 209
Leacock, Philip, 128
Leadbelly (performer), 167, 171
Le Carré, John, 344
Lee, Bill, 257, 269, 299
Lee, Gypsy Rose, 291
Lee, Thelma, 323, 324
Leigh, Vivien, 57, 58, 59-61, 63, 64, 65, 71, 86, 221
Leinsdorf, Erich, 396
Lemmon, Jack, 413
Les Enfants du Paradis (play), 82
Les Miserables (play), 208
Lessing, Gotthold Ephraim, 44
Lester, Julius, 262
Levene, Sam, 313
Leventhal, Harold, 160, 165, 174, 270
Levin, Meyer, 378
Levine, Jacqueline, 348
Levinson, Olga, 264, 265, 266
Levinson, Sam, 173
Lewis, Brenda, 313
Lewis, John, 254, 259
Lichtenstein, Rosa, 30, 33
Lindfors, Viveca, 188, 316
Lindsay, John, 251, 252
Lipson, Paul, 326, 340
Lisa (film), 379
Little Ark, The (film), 308
Little Kidnappers, The (film), 128
Loesser, Frank, 205
Lom, Herbert, 69
Lomax, Alan, 89, 155, 180, 183, 271
Lomax, John, 89
Lonesome Train, The (musical cavalcade), 88
Lopez, Bernie, 397
Lorca, Federico Garcia, 34
Loren, Sophia, 197
Lorre, Peter, 291-292
Lortel, Lucille, 177
Love Lottery, The (film), 120
Love of Four Colonels, The (play), 86, 94, 96, 101, 102
Lowenstein, Allard K., 263, 265
Lumet, Baruch, 329
Lumet, Sidney, 185, 329, 379
Lupino, Ida, 189
Lynley, Carol, 312

McCarthy, Eugene, 275, 280, 282, 283, 284, 338

McCarthy, Joe, 83, 85, 172
McCarthy, Kevin, 312
McCarthy, Mary, 142
McCarthy, Mary Beth, 358
MacCready, George, 188
McCurdy, Ed, 154, 168
McDew, Chuck, 254, 259
McGhee, Brownie, 153
McGovern, George, 283
McKenna, Siobhán, 145
MacLaine, Shirley, 278, 331
MacRae, Duncan, 128
Mahoney, William, 254
Makarios, Archbishop, 195, 196
Makem, Tommy, 154, 155
Mangwani Mpulele (Zulu song), 88
Mann, Danny, 65
Mann, Ted, 348
Mapes, Jo, 154, 159
Marceau, Marcel, 82
Margaret, Princess, 110, 111
Marina, Princess of Yugoslavia, 109
Marriage-Go-Round (play), 317
Martin, Dean-Paul, 413
Martin, Mary, 204, 205, 207, 209, 211, 212, 215, 217, 221
Marx Brothers, 378
Mary, Queen Mother of England, 49, 110, 111
Masefield, Sir John, 111
Masiell, Joe, 330
Massey, Raymond, 174, 185
Mature, Victor, 118
May, Elaine, 379
Mayer, Louis B., 378, 389-390
Mayleas, Ruth, 394
Mazursky, Paul, 379
Meaney, Colm, 297
Medford, Don, 190
Meed, Vladka, 407
Mehta, Nancy, 400
Mehta, Zubin, 299, 300, 417
Meir, Golda, 421, 423
Melba (film), 79, 121, 122
Melnick, Dan, 376
Menjou, Adolphe, 189
Meron, Chana, 34
Merrick, David, 221-222, 226, 395
Messina Brothers, 64
Mészöly, Tibor, 246
Meyer, Henri, 77
Meyerhold, Vsevelod, 23
Middle of the Night (film), 379
Migden, Chester, 246, 248
Mikes, George, 44
Milestone, Kendall, 79
Milestone, Lewis, 79, 121

Miller, Arthur, 278
Miller, Martin, 69
Miller, Robert Ellis, 132
Mills, John, 120
Miron, Issachar, 342
Miss Saigon (play), 330
Mitchell, Chad, 171
Mitchum, Robert, 192, 194, 195
Mograbi, Avraham, 32
Mograbi, Rakhel, 32
Mograbi, Shlomo, 32
Mograbi, Tewfik, 32
Mograbi, Yaacov, 32
Mondale, Joan, 238, 399
Montand, Yves, 82
Montealegre, Felicia, 136, 139
Moon, Keith, 311
Morgan, Michele, 147
Moriarty, Michael, 312
Morrison, Toni, 396
Moses, Robert, 259
Mostel, Zero, 169, 216, 322, 323-325
Moulin Rouge (film), 116, 117
Moustaki, Georges, 299
Munk, Kai, 49
Munsel, Patrice, 121
Muskie, Edmund, 282, 287
Mussolini, Benito, 10
My Fair Lady (film), 302
My Favorite Year (film), 380
My Side of the Mountain (film), 308

Negulesco, Jean, 79
Nelson, Carrie Lee, 278
Nelson, Gaylord, 268, 278, 279
Netanyahu, Binyamin, 120, 418-419
Never Let Me Go (film), 117, 118, 119
Neville, John, 40
New Lost City Ramblers (musical group),
    157, 166, 183
Newland, John, 210
Newman, Paul, 237, 278, 379
Ngakane, Lionel, 88
Niven, David, 120, 189
Nixon, Richard, 280, 287, 295, 296
Norton, Eleanor Holmes, 214

O'Bradovich, Bob, 186
O'Casey, Ronan, 86
Ochs, Phil, 268, 269, 272
O'Connor, Carroll, 190
Odetta. *See* Felious, Odetta
Odets, Clifford, 85
O'Dwyer, Paul, 281, 285
Of Mice and Men (film), 121
Olivier, Sir Laurence, 56, 57, 58, 59, 70,
    72, 186

O'Neal, Frederick, 223, 226
O'Neill, Tip, 229
Operation Thunderbolt (film), 366
O'Shea, Tessie, 279, 307
Oussoff, Dima, 90
Oxenberg, Catherine, 109

Paar, Jack, 173, 212
Pacovsky, Josef, 29, 30, 32
Pacovsky, Yemima, 30, 33
Palestinian, The (film), 376, 377
Palmer, Lilli, 69
Papp, Joseph, 313, 391
Pappas, Irene, 195
Pawnbroker, The (film), 379
Paxton, Tom, 171, 183, 268, 269
Peck, Gregory, 331
Peckinpah, Sam, 190
Peerce, Larry, 379
Pei, I. M., 396, 398
Pell, Claiborne, 229
Pepo. *See* Pacovsky, Josef
Peres, Shimon, 423
Peretz, I. L., 322
Perez, Yvonne, 148
Perlman, Itzhak, 235
Perlmut, Abraham, 47
Persoff, Nehemiah, 191
Peter, King of Yugoslavia, 109
Peter, Paul & Mary (trio), 179, 270, 272,
    358
Petrie, Daniel, 185
Philip, Prince, 111, 112
Piaf, Edith, 82
Pickow, George, 108
Playing for Time (film), 381
Plummer, Christopher, 141, 143, 217
Poitier, Sidney, 197, 198, 199, 375
Poliakova, Nastya, 90
Polonsky, Abraham, 379
Polyakoff, Volodya, 91
Portman, Eric, 120, 129
Pousse Café (play), 313, 314, 315
Powell, Dick, 146, 189, 192, 193
Price, Gil, 316
Pride and the Passion, The (film), 197
Prince, Hal, 208, 215, 231, 232, 322, 325,
    396
Prinz, Joachim (Rabbi), 309
Private Benjamin (film), 380
Profitt, Frank, 168
Prowse, Juliet, 325
Pyatakov, Gennadi, 246, 247, 308

Quintero, José, 315
Quo Vadis (film), 101

Rabin, Yitzhak, 423, 424
Rabinowitz, Victor, 254
Radiguet, Jean, 81
Radnitz, Bob, 204, 308
Raim, Ethel, 159
Randolph, John, 208
Raskin, Eugene, 175
Raskin, Francesca, 174
Ray, Edward, 45, 46
Reagan, Ronald, 295, 400
Redgrave, Lynn, 378
Redgrave, Michael, 378
Redgrave, Vanessa, 374, 376, 377
Reed, Maxwell, 294, 295
Reiner, Carl, 279, 306, 307, 379
Reinhardt, Gottfried, 117
Reinhardt, Max, 117
Renaud, Madeleine, 82
Rhinoceros (play), 323
Ribicoff, Abraham, 283, 284
Richman, Stella, 50, 144
Riddleberger, James, 195
Riegler, Maier, 334
Riegler, Regina, 9, 334
Rif, Vladimir, 311
Rinzler, Ralph, 180
Ripley, Leonard, 154
Ritchie, Jean, 107, 108, 154, 180
Rivera, Chita, 316
Roach, Hal, 149
Robbins, Jerome, 169, 322, 396, 397, 399
Robert Kennedy Remembered (film), 286
Roberts, Pernell, 139
Robertson, James, 403
Robinson, Earl, 170
Rodgers, Richard, 205, 207, 209, 210
Rohrabacher, Dana, 228
Rollins, Avon, 254
Roosevelt, Eleanor, 213
Rope Dancers, The (play), 145
Rosenfeld, Max, 407
Rosenfeld, Morris, 356
Rosenquist, James, 396
Ross, Bill, 143
Roth, Philip, 345, 379
Rothschilds, The (play), 317
Rovina, Chana, 27
Rummel, Herr, 303
Russians Are Coming, the Russians Are Coming, The (film), 279, 305
Rustin, Bayard, 262
Ryan, Robert, 278
Ryder, Alfred, 185

Sadat, Anwar, 416
Sadat, Jihan, 416
Saint, Eva Marie, 147

Saint Joan (play), 53
Saint Joan (TV movie), 185
Sainte-Marie, Buffy, 158
Salinger, Pierre, 282
Sandomirskya, Vera Grigorievna. *See* Dunham, Vera
Sands of the Kalahari, The (film), 121, 303, 305
Sartre, Jean-Paul, 81
Scaduto, Anthony, 270
Schaal, Richard, 307
Schaefer, George, 185, 186
Schary, Dore, 149
Schell, Maria, 291
Schenck, Nicholas, 378
Schiff, Dorothy, 216
Schine, David, 83
Schlamme, Martha, 174
Schlesinger, Arthur, 228
Schmerler, Kurt, 61
Schneider, Alan, 138
Schoenkopf, Sarah, 254
Schrade, Paul, 275, 276, 277-278, 331
Schrift, Ben, 62
Schrift, Shirley. *See* Winters, Shelley
Schuller, Gunther, 397
Schurz, Carl, 374
Schuschnigg, Kurt von, 4
Schweitzer, Lou, 177
Schwerner, Mickey, 261
Scott, Mike, 268
Scourby, Alexander, 136
Scruggs, Earl, 168
Seeger, Charles, 165
Seeger, Pete, 89, 152, 157, 164, 165, 166, 167, 169, 170, 171, 172, 174, 180, 258, 270, 271, 272
Seeger, Toshi, 180
Seldes, Marian, 222
Seltzer, Dov, 159
Selznick, Irene Mayer, 57
Serling, Rod, 188-189
Servant of Two Masters, A (play), 31, 34
Settle, Mike, 158
Shafi, Haider Abdel, 421
Sharon, Ariel, 372, 373
Shaw, George Bernard, 185
Shaw, Robert, 396
Sheridan, Ann, 191
Shmulikl. *See* Spiegel, Sam
Shneerson, Menachem Mendel (Rabbi), 353
Shrike, The (play), 85
Shumlin, Herman, 132, 135, 136, 137, 138
Sidney, George, 291
Siegman, Henry, 348

Silent No More (album), 342
Silver, Ron, 422
Simmons, Richard Alan, 189, 292
Simon, John, 254
Simon, Neil, 379
Sinatra, Frank, 380
Sinden, Donald, 125
Singer, Isaac Bashevis, 379
Sirhan Sirhan, 275
Sitwell, Edith, 111
Skinner, Cornelia Otis, 94
Slepak, Vladimir, 343
Smith, Ruby Doris, 254
Snowman, Emmanuel (doctor), 101
Solomon, Maynard, 164
Solomon, Seymour, 164
Sorvino, Paul, 312
Sound of Music, The (play), 138, 156, 207-
    208, 212, 216, 218, 219, 223, 313
Sourani, Raji, 421
South Pacific (play), 88, 209
Spiegel, Sam, 79, 103, 104, 105, 121, 122
Sprung, Roger, 157
Stalin, Josef Vissarionovich, 83, 340
Standard, Michael, 254
Stanislavsky, Konstantin Sergeyevich, 23,
    24-25, 26, 43, 65
Starer, Robert, 10
Starr, Ringo, 311
Stein, Joe, 322, 330, 341
Stern, Isaac, 235
Stevens, George, Jr., 399
Stevens, Roger, 400
Stevenson, Adlai, 422
Stookey, Noel, 176
Streetcar Named Desire, A (play), 56-57, 64-
    65, 66
Streisand, Barbra, 237, 379
Streng, Walter, 9-10
Sunshine Boys (play), 317
Sweet Charity (musical), 325
Sweet, Sheila, 65
Sylvester, Bill, 65

Tabori, George, 315
Takas, Bill, 299
Tal, Ada, 28, 206, 207
Tana, Dan, 193
Tarriers (musical group), 157, 166, 173,
    178
Taylor, Billy, 396, 397
Taylor, Elizabeth, 367
Taylor, Paul, 84
Ten Commandments, The (film), 378
Terra, Daniel, 400
Terry, Sonny, 153, 166
Tevye the Milkman (play), 26, 321

Thalberg, Irving, 378
There Shall Be No Night (TV movie), 186
Thistle and the Rose, The (play), 122
Thomas, Brandon, 34
Thompson, Frank, 228, 229
Thorndike, Sybil, 50
Threepenny Opera (play), 318
Tibbet, Lawrence, 174
Titus Andronicus (play), 71
Tonight in Samarkand (play), 132, 135, 140
Torem, Charles, 79
Torme, Mel, 360
Torn, Rip, 235
Townsend, Peter, 110
Travers, Mary, 160, 176
Treasure of the Sierra Madre, The (film), 104
Trenet, Charles, 82
Treves, Luisa, 35
Trumbo, Dalton, 86, 171
Turner, Clifford, 40, 41, 45
Tutin, Dorothy, 40
Twelfth Night (play), 71
200 Motels (film), 310
Tynan, Kenneth, 50, 51, 71, 106

Ulysses in Nighttown (play), 324
Underwood, Blair, 2
Ustinov, Peter, 93, 94-97, 101, 109, 117

Vakhtangov, Yevgeny, 23, 65
Valk, Frederick, 69
Vanbrugh, Irene, 38
Vass, Imre, 246
Vassilchikov, George, 76
Versois, Odile, 125
Very Close Quarters (film), 311
Victory at Entebbe (film), 367
Vidal, Gore, 284
Vintage, The (film), 147, 148
Voight, Jon, 216

Wagner, Lindsay, 413
Waldron, Zena, 310
Walesa, Lech, 296
Walk in the Sun, A (film), 121
Walker, Wyatt Tee, 255
Wallace, George, 284
Wanamaker, Sam, 85, 292
Wasserman, Lew, 399
Watson, Doc, 166
Watts, Richard, 144
Wayne, John, 186-187
Weatherwax, Frank, 308
Weatherwax, Rudd, 308
Weavers (musical group), 164, 165, 169,
    172, 173, 174, 178
Webber, C. E., 50

Weicker, Lowell, 251
Weidman, Jerome, 314
Weill, Kurt, 299
Wein, George, 179, 180
Weintraub, Fred, 179
Weissberg, Eric, 166, 168, 171
Wendhausen, Friedrich von, 68
Werfel, Franz, 35
Weston, Eddie, 222, 223, 226
White, Josh, 169, 170
White, Josh, Jr., 171
Whiteley, Jon, 128
Whitfield, Robert, 254
Whitman, Stuart, 303
Who Has Seen the Wind? (TV film), 291
Wiesel, Elie, 12, 408
Wilczek, Taddeusz, 130, 144
Wildmon, Donald, 391
Williams, Cara, 199
Williams, Tennessee, 56, 106
Wilson, Dolores, 329, 330
Wilson, Julie, 317
Winters, Jonathan, 307
Winters, Shelley, 62, 298, 312, 380
Winter's Tale, A (play), 209
Winter, Vincent, 128
Wiseman, Joe, 141, 143
Wise, Robert, 202, 217, 218
Wishengrad, Mort, 145, 146, 147, 186, 191
Woman Obsessed, A (film), 201

Wood, Mary Laura, 86
Woodward, Edward, 41
Woolf Brothers, 105
Wright, Frank Lloyd, 384
Wright, Maudie, 39
Wyeth, Jamie, 395
Wynter, Dana, 199, 200

Yadin, Yigael, 34, 123
Yadin, Yossi, 34, 123
Yarbrough, Glenn, 154, 163
Yarrow, Peter, 176, 180, 270, 271, 358
Yates, Sid, 228, 400
Yentl, the Yeshiva Boy (film), 379
Yepes, Narciso, 148
Yogi, Maharishi Mahesh, 361
York, Susannah, 303
You Can't Take It with You (play), 56
Young, Andrew, 255, 426
Young, Gig, 199
Young, Israel, 156
Young Man and a Maid, A (record album), 159
Young, Nedrick, 198
Youngstein, Max, 259

Zagby, James (doctor), 426
Zangwill, Israel, 100
Zanuck, Darryl, 105
Zappa, Frank, 310, 311
Zetterling, Mai, 123